GOD'S
self-confident
DAUGHTERS

W9-CHP-403

GOD'S
self-confident
DAUGHTERS

EARLY CHRISTIANITY AND THE LIBERATION OF WOMEN

ANNE JENSEN

TRANSLATED BY O. C. DEAN, JR.

Westminster John Knox Press
Louisville, Kentucky

Translated, and slightly abridged, from the German of *Gottes selbstbewusste Töchter: Frauenemanzipation im frühen Christentum?* © Verlag Herder Freiburg im Breisgau 1992

English translation © 1996 Westminster John Knox Press

All rights reserved. No part of this book may be reproduced or transmitted in any form or by any means, electronic or mechanical, including photocopying, recording, or by any information storage or retrieval system, without permission in writing from the publisher. For information, address Westminster John Knox Press, 100 Witherspoon Street, Louisville, Kentucky 40202-1396.

Unless otherwise noted, scripture quotations are from the New Revised Standard Version of the Bible, copyright © 1989 by the Division of Christian Education of the National Council of the Churches of Christ in the U.S.A., and are used by permission.

Book design by Jennifer K. Cox
Cover design by Kim Wohlenhaus
Cover illustration: Three Marys at the Tomb, *Adolphe William Bouguereau, 1825–1905. French. Courtesy of SuperStock*

First edition

Published by Westminster John Knox Press
Louisville, Kentucky

This book is printed on acid-free paper that meets the American National Standards Institute Z39.48 standard. ⊗

PRINTED IN THE UNITED STATES OF AMERICA

96 97 98 99 00 01 02 03 04 05 — 10 9 8 7 6 5 4 3 2 1

Library of Congress Cataloging-in-Publication Data

Jensen, Anne, date.
    [Gottes selbstbewusste Töchter. English]
    God's self-confident daughters : early Christianity and the liberation of women / Anne Jensen ; translated by O. C. Dean, Jr.
      p.   cm.
    Includes bibliographical references and index.
    ISBN 0-664-25672-4 (alk. paper)
    1. Women in Christianity—History—Early church, ca. 30–600.   I. Title.
BR195.W6J4613   1996
270.1'082—dc20   96-19385

CONTENTS

PREFACE

On Research into the History of Women

In the subtitle of this study, "Early Christianity and the Liberation of Women," two very different subjects are joined together with the catchword *liberation:* the abstract conceptual category *Christianity* and real people of the feminine gender, that is, *women.* The phrase can be understood differently, depending on which of these subjects one takes as a starting point. The research project "Woman and Christianity"[1]—which was initiated by Hans Küng, together with Elisabeth Moltmann-Wendel and Bernadette Brooten, and supported financially by the Volkswagen Foundation—was at first given the following guiding question: To what extent has Christianity promoted the liberation of the woman, and to what extent hindered it? At the time hardly anyone objected to the fact that the abstract subject *Christianity* was juxtaposed with the likewise abstract subject *woman.* (Today we would prefer "Women in Christianity.") The historical question, Has Christianity promoted the liberation of the woman? can be (mis)understood in an apologetic sense, for even in the negative question, Has Christianity hindered the liberation of the woman? Christianity remains the subject, and the woman the "object" to be liberated. Now, the apologetic question for me as a Christian theologian is by no means a matter of indifference, for I must take a position in regard to the challenge of a radical feminism that regards the Christian religion as hopelessly "patriarchal": a church of men in service to a male God, which women can only flee, if they do not want to continue to live in alienation from themselves.[2]

Yet the "to what extent" of the guiding question already indicates that this question about women's liberation cannot be answered with a clear "Christianity has promoted it" or "Christianity has hindered it." One hypothesis has already been tacitly dropped in the way the question is asked, namely, that Christianity could have helped and indeed even invented women's liberation in antiquity. All too clearly and irrefutably, the feminist critique has made us aware that within Christianity an increasingly misogynistic ideology was able to develop and later reach its sad climax in the macabre theory and horrible practice of the persecution of witches. As Christian women and men we cannot avoid dealing with tendencies in our own religion that are misogynistic.

Yet if we begin with women and not Christianity as subject, the question of liberation has a different accent: What role have Christian women played in history in general, in church history, and in the history of women? Have they made a specific contribution to the matter of liberation? Have women in Christianity lived or been able to live autonomously? Answering these questions was from the beginning an express aim of the research project: the reality of feminine life was to be reconstructed and women made visible as subjects of historical activity. In her own concept Bernadette Brooten[3] was able here to build on the first insights and results of research into the history of women, which in the meantime have become more profound and more precise.[4]

"On the question of women in history it was never only a matter of filling in gaps in research and placing new material in the usual historiographic categories; it was rather a question of a new look at 'history in general.' . . . Women have remained invisible primarily because they, their experiences, activities, and spheres did not seem worthy of historical interest. The new view, therefore, had to turn upside down the hierarchies between historically important and unimportant, and there has been a reexamination and reevaluation of what women want to do, are supposed to do, and have done."[5] So writes Gisela Bock, an eminent representative of this direction in research, and in so doing she appeals to the formulation of the American historian Joan Kelly, who postulates two aims: "to restore women to history" and "to restore history to women."[6]

This addresses a dimension that calls into question an alleged value-neutral "objectivity" in the writing of history. When the contributions of women to the history of humankind and of the church were suppressed, the interests of men came to the fore. This enabled history, or the silencing of history, to become an instrument of suppression. Helping the disadvantaged half of humankind regain its own history is a necessary act of restitution. In this sense women's research is partial but not biased, for it reveals its own subjectivity and its specific interest. The traditional norms of objective scholarly methodology are, of course, respected and applied.

In 1985, after the departure of Bernadette Brooten,[7] I took over the part of the project dealing with the early period of Christianity and continued this initiative in the study of the history of women. The aim of the work was, on the one hand, to give back to women their roots and thus their self-confidence and, on the other, to change both the image of women and the image of history and the world, as well as the concomitant hierarchy of values. Thus, as a woman the author is not a neutral but rather a critically involved observer. Yet research into women's history is not the exclusive domain of the female sex. The conscious change of perspective, which after centuries of one-sidedness now puts women in the center and interrogates them as the subjects of history, can—and should— also be carried out by male researchers if a more complete perception of historical processes is to be achieved. Yet on the basis of their subjective involvement, it may be easier at first for women themselves to discover and recover their forgotten and suppressed history.

Since the emphasis in this study is on the quest for women, their accomplishments, and their self-understanding, a new one-sidedness is consciously accepted.

The previous "androcentric" perception is opposed by an intentionally "gyno-centric"[8] perspective, for "it is still too early to rewrite history as the history of both sexes."[9] It is first a question of filling in the blank areas on the map. The way to an often-postulated "humanist" theology necessarily leads through an explicitly "feminist" one, for only thus can the previous implicitly "virist"[10] one be corrected: a direct path from the thesis to the synthesis while omitting the antithesis is not known to exist in the dialectic of history. Nevertheless, the (ultimate) goal remains to gain a new "objectivity of subjectivity" in the dialogue of the sexes.

Another point must be stressed: subjectivity and partiality do not mean that present-day conceptions of discrimination and liberation should serve as norms for other historical epochs. What Doris Kaufmann made a principle in the context of the project "Woman and Christianity" for her work on the Protestant women's movement in the first half of the twentieth century is valid all the more for research into Christian late antiquity: "Instead of . . . seeking mere identification models for the present, it seems to me that at the moment it is still the task of women's history to investigate each epoch as, so to speak, 'immediate to God' (Leopold von Ranke). No universal categories such as patriarchy or patriarchal oppression should block a differentiated perception of the relationship between the sexes and the 'varieties' of women's experiences and possibilities of action."[11] The dialogue with women of other centuries (as well as the intercultural dialogue) presupposes a readiness to deal with otherness and to examine one's own understanding of liberation. The dialogue with Christian women of late antiquity must now be conducted in that spirit.

But first a note on the problem of "sexist" language. In "inclusive" language usage the masculine form has traditionally also stood for members of the female sex: when we speak of "Christians," for example, we automatically include "women Christians."[12] In fact, however, this way of speaking has a tendency to be "exclusive," for it often leads us to forget that of each species there are not only male but also female examples. The exegete Elisabeth Schüssler Fiorenza has pointed out an instructive example of one such reading that excludes women on the basis of the different treatment of masculine terms in the New Testament. With *disciples* one naturally assumes that women are also meant, but if the topic is *apostles,* one presumes that it is exclusively a question of men.[13]

The effort to include women in linguistic formulations is a thoroughly justified concern, but how is the problem to be solved within a particular language and culture? The occasional mockery over contortions with double-sexed formulations by means of numerous parentheses, hyphens, and slashes is understandable. What may be sensible in job announcements proves to be hardly practicable in a text with a certain literary claim. Also, many new recommended linguistic formations are useful food for thought, but in an article such unpronounceable abbreviations become stumbling blocks. Abstraction from the particular gender (*they* instead of *he or she*) is likewise unsatisfactory, especially since the attempt runs aground when the singular is required. This leaves the consistent parallel usage of masculine and feminine forms, yet constant repetition is tiresome for the reader.

Thus I have decided upon a compromise between current language usage and the feminist concern for making women visible. I use the masculine form inclusively in the traditional way when the topic is the functions themselves and the sex of the bearer does not matter, for example, in general comments on prophecy, martyrdom, or ministry; but to remind us that the language usage is to be understood as really inclusive—that is, it also means women—I will also from time to time speak emphatically of prophetesses and prophets, women and men martyrs, and so forth.

Technical Notes

In the present investigation I have adhered to all the usual standards of scholarly research, but I have at the same time made an effort to find a style that permits the results to be communicated beyond a small circle of experts. Naturally, this required compromises. For example, the knowledgeable will find more information in the notes than they need, while the less knowledgeable will find things missing.

Since the study of women's history is still in its infancy, this book is intended to stimulate others to further work and make help available. In this regard, special effort was applied to the list of sources in Section I of the bibliography. Since today, even in academic circles, only a few have mastery of ancient languages and thus access to many of the texts important for women's research, I have not only given the edition of the original but also referred to translations and commentaries in easily accessible European languages. I have forgone the practical Latin abbreviations that have become common for the Greek writings and in their place used modern titles that reproduce the original title as faithfully as possible. The original Latin titles are given; the Greek as a rule are not. In transliterating the Greek, η is rendered as ē, and ω as ō.

Section II of the bibliography contains works on early Christianity and late antiquity in general and on women in early Christianity and late antiquity, as well as miscellaneous relevant studies. Completeness was not the aim, but important works have been entered even if they are not cited directly. Studies of the New Testament[14] were included only in special cases. In the notes, at the beginning of each thematic unit the most important literature is listed by author or editor and title; subsequent references are usually by author and brief title.

The dates of birth and death and the like are taken from either special investigations or Bertold Altaner and Alfred Stuiber's *Patrologie*. The quotations from early Christian literature were either translated by me or adopted from available translations, often in slightly revised form.

TRANSLATOR'S PREFACE

In German there are feminine forms of many of the terms used to describe Christian roles: for example, apostle, Christian, confessor, disciple, proclaimer, teacher. Only rarely are there corresponding terms in English, such as deaconess, martyress, empress, and prophetess. Rather than slowing the reader down with extra verbiage, I have followed the author's example and let the one form cover both sexes, except where phrases such as "woman disciple" and "male and female teachers" are required for clarity or to remind us that women were also active in a particular role.

For the most part, I have translated the German of the author's quotations from ancient and modern sources. Some (especially lengthier) quotations, however, are taken—sometimes in slightly modified or corrected form—from available translations, for example, in Ancient Christian Writers, The Nicene and Post-Nicene Fathers, and Musurillo's *Acts of the Christian Martyrs*. Quotations originally in English are usually given in their original wording.

ACKNOWLEDGMENTS

Research that focuses on feminist issues is controversial terrain. Thus I am grateful to the Catholic Theological School of the University of Tübingen, which accepted the present study as *Habilitationsschrift* on 17 January 1992. Special thanks go to the experts there, whose careful reading of the manuscript made it possible to correct many details before printing, as well as to the dean, Prof. Michael Theobald, for his help in the carrying out of the process.

In looking back at the long path to the *Habilitation*, I see I am also indebted to many other helpers. The first is the Volkswagen Foundation, which for four years generously supported the project "Frau und Christentum" as "unconventional research" and thus sent an encouraging signal. The greatest debt of gratitude is owed to Prof. Hans Küng, who made possible the carrying out of such a project at the Institute for Ecumenical Research in Tübingen and who, despite numerous conflicts and opposition, brought it to a successful conclusion. He followed this study with patience, constructive criticism, and encouraging solidarity over long years, and in the end he defended it as a highly involved expert.

My thanks go to him, however, not only as the supervisor of this work but also as the director of the Institute for Ecumenical Research: the atmosphere of unreserved openness and an untiring willingness to dialogue made it far more than a place to work: it is a spiritual home. Here my thanks are likewise owed to my colleagues Dr. Urs Baumann and Dr. Karl-Josef Kuschel, with whom I am connected by more than a decade of cooperative work in collegial friendship and from whom I have received much support.

For numerous stimuli in the realm of feminist theology and the historical study of women, I am indebted to Dr. Elisabeth Moltmann-Wendel, the co-initiator and advisor of the research project, as well as to my colleague Dr. Doris Kaufmann, who worked on the subproject on Christian women in the twentieth century. My coworkers, the Evangelical theologian Gerlinde Keppler and the philologist Ulrike Rüpke, helped to carry out the initial phase of arduous search in a new area of study with great involvement and much creativity. In the final editing the help of Gerhard Jockers as "private secretary" was indispensable; he also prepared the index. Two scholarly coworkers and computer experts then had a final hand in the project: with great care Matthias Schnell gave the manuscript the perfect layout, and Stephan Schlensog, as an inventive designer, translated my ideas into tables and overviews. Finally, I would especially like to thank Annegret Dinkel, the longtime secretary of the Institute, who in her (alleged) retirement has looked after my physical well-being.

It is impossible to list here all the women and men to whom I am indebted for scholarly ideas, yet I must at least mention representatively Prof. Luise Abramowski and Dr. Hildegard Cancik-Lindemaier in Tübingen, as well as Prof. Willy Rordorf, Prof. Kari Elisabeth Børresen, and Prof. Elisabeth Gössmann, who have supported my work in special measure with much advice and encouragement. My thanks also go to Dr. Karin Walter of Verlag Herder, who guided the book project with loving and persistent patience. Very special thanks are owed finally to many female and some male students: to those whom I know because they have enriched my own thought in seminars, but also to those not known to me personally, who through their involvement in women's politics at various universities carry forth the feminist-oriented academic discussion. I would be very pleased if this book were to encourage them!

Anne Jensen

Tübingen, March 1992

ABBREVIATIONS

I. Abbreviations for Journals and Standard Works

AAS	*Acta Apostolicae Sedis*
ACW	Ancient Christian Writers
AnBoll	Analecta Bollandiana
ANF	The Ante-Nicene Fathers
ANRW	*Aufstieg und Niedergang der römischen Welt*
ATR	*Anglican Theological Review*
AuC	*Antike und Christentum*
Aug	*Augustinianum*
BEP	Bibliotheke Ellenōn Paterōn kai Ekklesiastikōn syggrapheōn (library of Greek fathers and church writers)
BHG	Bibliotheca hagiographica graeca
BKP	Beiträge zur klassischen Philologie
BKV	Bibliothek der Kirchenväter
ByZ	*Byzantinische Zeitschrift*
BzA	Beiträge zur Altertumskunde
CCSA	Corpus Christianorum. Series Apocryphorum
CCSG	Corpus Christianorum. Series Graeca
CCSL	Corpus Christianorum. Series Latina
CH	*Church History*
COD	Conciliorum Oecumenicorum Decreta
Conc	*Concilium*
CrossCur	*Cross Currents*
CSCO	Corpus Scriptorum Christianorum Orientalium
CSEL	Corpus Scriptorum Ecclesiasticorum Latinorum
DACL	*Dictionnaire d'Archéologie Chrétienne et de Liturgie*
DS	*Enchiridion Symbolorum* (ed. Heinrich Denzinger and Adolf Schönmetzer)
EKKNT	Evangelisch-katholischer Kommentar zum Neuen Testament
EvK	Evangelische Kommentare
EvT	*Evangelische Theologie*
FaCh	The Fathers of the Church
FCh	Fontes Christiani

FRLANT	Forschungen zur Religion und Literatur des Alten und Neuen Testaments
FSt	Feminist Studies
GCS	Die griechischen christlichen Schriftsteller der ersten drei Jahrhunderte
GOTR	Greek Orthodox Theological Review
Hist	Historia: Zeitschrift für alte Geschichte
HR	History of Religions
HTR	Harvard Theological Review
IJWSt	International Journal of Women's Studies
IKZ	Internationale Kirchliche Zeitschrift
JAAR	Journal of the American Academy of Religion
JAC	Jahrbuch für Antike und Christentum
JEH	Journal of Ecclesiastical History
JES	Journal of Ecumenical Studies
JFSR	Journal of Feminist Studies in Religion
JTS	Journal of Theological Studies
JÖB	Jahrbuch der österreichischen Byzantinistik
LR	Lutherische Rundschau
LTK	Lexikon für Theologie und Kirche
Mansi	Sacrorum conciliorum nova et amplissima collectio, ed. Johannes Dominicus Mansi et al.
NPNF	The Nicene and Post-Nicene Fathers
NTD	Neues Testament Deutsch
NTS	New Testament Studies
OC	Orientalia Christiana
OCA	Orientalia Christiana Analecta
OCP	Orientalia Christiana periodica
OS	Ostkirchliche Studien
PG	Patrologiae Graeca, ed. Jacques-Paul Migne
PL	Patrologiae Latina, ed. Jacques-Paul Migne
PTS	Patristische Texte und Studien
QD	Quaestiones disputatae
RAC	Reallexikon für Antike und Christentum
RassTeol	Rassegna di teologia
RBén	Revue Bénédictine de critique, d'histoire et de littérature religieuses
RelS	Religious Studies
RHE	Revue d'histoire ecclésiastique
RHPR	Revue d'histoire et de philosophie religieuses
RNT	Regensburger Neues Testament
RQ	Römische Quartalschrift für die christliche Altertumskunde
RTL	Revue Théologique de Louvain
SC	Sources Chrétiennes
SIFC	Studi Italiani di Filologia Classica
SpicSol	Spicilegium Solesmense

StMed	*Studi medievali*
TD	*Theology Digest*
TeD	Textes et documents pour l'étude historique du christianisme
TLZ	*Theologische Literaturzeitung*
TQ	*Theologische Quartalschrift*
TRE	*Theologische Realenzyklopädie*
TRev	*Theologische Revue*
TS	*Theological Studies*
TU	Texte und Untersuchungen zur Geschichte der altchristlichen Literatur
TWNT	*Theologisches Wörterbuch zum Neuen Testament*
TZ	*Theologische Zeitschrift*
US	*Una Sancta*
USQR	*Union Seminary Quarterly Review*
WdF	Wege der Forschung
ZKG	*Zeitschrift für Kirchengeschichte*
ZNW	*Zeitschrift für die neutestamentliche Wissenschaft*
ZTK	*Zeitschrift für Theologie und Kirche*

II. Other Abbreviations

1. Frequently Cited Sources

Epiph. *Pan.*	Epiphanius, *Panarion*
Euseb. *Ch.Hist.*	Eusebius, *Church History*
Iren. *AH*	Irenaeus, *Against Heresies*
Pall. *Hist.Laus.*	Palladius, *Historia Lausiaca*
Ruf. *Ch.Hist.*	Rufinus, *Church History*
Soc. *Ch.Hist.*	Socrates, *Church History*
Soz. *Ch.Hist.*	Sozomen, *Church History*
Theod. *Ch.Hist.*	Theodoret, *Church History*

AC	*Apostolic Constitutions*
AH	*Against Heresies* (various authors)
ACM	*The Acts of the Christian Martyrs* (see Bibl. I: Martyrs)
AP	*Acts of Paul*
ATh	*Acts of Thecla*
MP	*Martyrs in Palestine* (Eusebius)
NA	*Neutestamentliche Apokryphen* (ed. Schneemelcher, see Bibliography I: *Apokrypha*)
RH	*Religious History* (Theodoret)

2. Frequently Cited Literature
(see Bibliography II)

MA	May, "Apelles"

HM	Harnack, *Marcion*
LC	De Labriolle, *La crise*
LS	De Labriolle, *Les sources*
MM	May, "Marcion"
MOT	*The Montanist Oracles and Testimonia,* ed. Heine

3. General

anon.	anonymous (male)
Arm.	Armenian
bibl.	bibliography
cent.	century
Copt.	Coptic
Eng.	English
Eth.	Ethiopic
Fr.	French
FS	Festschrift
Ger.	German
Gk.	Greek
Lat.	Latin
masc.	masculine
n.s.	new series
neut.	neuter
NT	New Testament
OT	Old Testament
repr.	reprint
rev.	review
Syr.	Syriac
trans.	translation, translated, translator

INTRODUCTION

1. Late Antiquity and Young Christendom

In the textbooks and handbooks of traditional theological study the early church is usually treated as if the first Christian women and men lived in isolation. Among philologists and historians of that period there is a similar tendency toward a "division of labor": Christianity is often left out or regarded as what came after antiquity, not as an integral part of the late period. The emphasis is on contrasts, not on similarities. Little has been adopted from studies interested in religious-historical comparison, such as those presented by Franz Josef Dölger[1] in the journal *Antike und Christentum (AuC)* in the 1930s.

Happily, some things have changed in this regard in the research landscape if not in the textbooks. In Dölger's spirit, the *Reallexikon für Antike und Christentum (RAC)* was started, and the Jahrbuch für Antike und Christentum began publication in 1958. Recent times have also seen an increase in studies and anthologies on late antiquity, in which Hellenism, Judaism, and Christianity are no longer regarded in isolation but in their mutual involvement against the background of a culture and mentality common to them all.[2] Women's studies make this perspective especially necessary methodologically, because playing off Greek, Roman, Jewish, and Christian women against each other apologetically would contradict their intentions.[3]

Many Religions

In late antiquity quite varied forms of worshiping God were proclaimed and practiced, yet they had in common a basic kind of religious mood and expectation. Thus, in the old religions of the Greeks and Romans, which were oriented toward this world, a transformation begins to take place: the beyond becomes important, and there is a striving to break away from the earthly world. In the Hellenistic world, young Christianity, with its message of resurrection, is perceived from the beginning as a religion of redemption. In the course of this study we will encounter many other commonalities in the religions of late antiquity. If one visits in succession the National Archaeological Museum and the Museum of Byzantine Art in Athens, one is surprised to note that the continuity in architecture and symbolism in the transition from classical to Christian antiquity is more striking than the break between the old and the new religion. It is true that the different forms of faith competed with each other, but they were also in dialogue with one another. The Jews had a special status in the Roman Empire that enabled them to preserve their own customs.[4] The new eastern cults,[5] which included young Christianity, were also tolerated as long as they were organized in private associations and did not threaten the official state cult.

In the following we will avoid the designation *pagan* for those who worshiped the divine in a multiplicity of goddesses and gods. We are inclined not to take the ancient forms of piety very seriously, yet Walter F. Otto has pointed out that there are no grounds for believing that the religion of an advanced culture like that of the Greeks was primitive.[6] The cultic practices of folk piety are always to some extent antithetical to elevated theological reflection, but they are not to be simply dismissed as "superstition" and "idolatry." The words *pagan* and *heathen* are often used today as shorthand for "neither Christian nor Jewish"—thereby sparing the effort of differentiating among the other religions. Yet in antiquity the terms were used differently. Where we read "Gentiles" today, in the Bible we often find, without negative connotation, "the nations"[7] as the counterpart of Israel, the special chosen people of God. Only against the "worship of images" in the form of gods and goddesses do we find strong polemics. In some passages in the New Testament, as in many early church texts, the word translated "Gentiles" really means "Greeks." Even if the term was often used disparagingly, it was, nonetheless, not negative in itself and could be used neutrally or positively in other contexts.

Yet to find a substitute for the category *paganism* is not easy. It is important to understand the word *Hellene* in late antiquity not in the sense of a nationality but as a designation of a *cultural identity* in which religion and philosophy belong together. *Rome*, by contrast, is a *political entity*, the name of a world empire of which one was a citizen. In this sense the Greeks were "Romans" and the Romans "Greeks." Thus if women and men converted to another religion, they still remained Roman citizens who were rooted in Hellenistic education and culture. Only in a later phase was the church pervaded by a mentality that identified philosophy and paganism, though even early on there were individual representatives of such a mental attitude. In any case, it is better in the translations to let the value-neutral word *Greek* stand, even when "non-Christian" is intended, instead of rendering it with the derogatory word *pagan;* I will use that word only when a disparaging term is found in the original.[8]

Within the framework of this study it is not possible to compare the religious practices of Christian women with the female adherents of other religions; this can be accomplished only with interdisciplinary cooperation.[9] Here we must expressly point out the danger of a latent anti-Judaism, which is also frequently found in feminist theology.[10] Yet if the only topic here will be Christian women, we must not forget that they themselves often previously knew another religion from within—over which, it is true, they preferred Christianity, but from which they also carried many things over into their new faith. We must remember that women participated in many cults as priestesses.

In this plurality of offerings Christianity had to find its place. In so doing it went through various stages: from Jewish sect and "dropout" religion it gradually became a kind of "civil religion" of the Roman Empire, until finally, as a new state cult decreed by the emperor, it took the place of the old religion of goddesses and gods, whose adherents it finally vehemently fought, along with the Jews and dissidents in its own ranks. We will see what role women played in the various phases.

Many Confessions

The new religion that sought to gain a foothold in a religiously diverse society was also diverse itself, for it was not yet the "early church" but early Christianity. There was no firmly established organization with clearly defined doctrine but an open movement with many streams and directions, which in part were later discredited as "heretical and schismatic." Here too women's studies make us sensitive to conceptual clichés and compel a revision of usual categories. For in the search for early Christian female personalities we make contradictory discoveries. One of the most venerated saints of Christian antiquity was Thecla, yet her story is recounted in a writing that was first banned from the canon and later classified as heretical.[11] Other well-known female figures of the early period were revered by some as prophetesses and decried by others as heretics. How then is one to judge the relationship between "heresy" and "orthodoxy"?

What is regarded in Christianity as "orthodoxy," as authentic doctrine, was ultimately determined by those who carried the day in early church disagreements. If one does not want simply to adopt their view as the norm, it is again difficult to find an appropriate vocabulary, for all the usual terms imply value judgments. The most neutral in German is the *Grosskirche* ("great church, church at large"); in English we can speak of *mainstream Christianity* or the *mainstream church* (the usual translation here). Yet in the end these terms are deceptive, since they convey the impression that "heretics" were mainly insignificant fringe groups. As a matter of fact, however, the so-called orthodox who were finally able to prevail were by no means always in the majority.

For the period after Constantine the designation *imperial church* can be meaningfully used for that part of Christendom that placed itself under the special protection of the now Christian emperor—yet he was not always "orthodox." Imperial church is the counterpart of the geographically limited "heresies," Christian groups who defended their own local tradition against supraregional standardization or for national reasons wanted to be monopolized neither by the Roman Empire nor by the church of the emperor. More judgmental is *catholic*, the self-designation of the orthodox: they called themselves the "universal" church in order to distance themselves from those who in their view were sectarians—that is, heretics.

The Greek word *hairesis* comes from a verb meaning "to separate" and denotes first a particular group. The translation as *sect* is therefore more accurate than *heresy*; better yet would be the less disparaging word *party*. Later the term served more and more often to designate not a particular group but their specific doctrinal opinion. The word *heresy* renders only this meaning. Yet an actual break by no means always meant a deviation in questions of faith but was often based purely on church politics. Over the course of this study we will see how differently one must judge the individual "heretical" movements that developed into separate churches and confessions.

The division of Christendom into the "orthodox" and "heretics" represents the view of the victors, which we today must not simply adopt uncritically if we want to get a picture of the early centuries that is to some degree realistic.[12] In the beginning Christendom was diverse; that means that a great deal could have turned out differently than it in fact did. Yet it is hardly still possible to reverse this view of the victors and perceive the past in the open, future-oriented perspective of our time, since the only sources available to us are the ones whose traditions were promoted or at least tolerated by the victors. Much has been definitively lost. What was and is read, copied, and studied is above all Greek and Latin texts, that is, writings in the languages of the Roman Empire. The traditions of the churches who did not want to join Rome or Constantinople are known only to a few specialists. For women's studies they are no doubt important for getting a comprehensive picture of early Christendom in its totality.[13] The present study has as its object only the churches in the Hellenistic world.

2. Christian Women of Late Antiquity

If it is difficult today even to find a trace of the self-understanding of the Christians who did not belong to the victors' party, then it is much more difficult in the case of women. They are at a disadvantage in their entirety, for even the "orthodox" ones barely appear in the extant sources of mainstream Christianity. We still have only four writings that were written by women (which we will examine below). As a result, one can almost say that the self-understanding of women and their real life can be inferred only indirectly through the testimonies of men. Up to this point relatively little consideration has been given to inscriptions, papyri, and visual representations, the only testimonies of antiquity that could not be falsified through the glosses and interpolations of later copyists.[14] Yet a remark that was made in reference to the Middle Ages also applies to Christian late antiquity: "The 'long-serving' traditional source materials are absolutely fertile"[15]—if only they are approached with the right questions. But the work of reconstruction is extremely arduous. All the available material must be examined with regard to whether it contains explicit or implicit information about women. If we want to interpret it correctly, we must in each case consider the intention of the author and the context in which the information is found. For the most part a reading "against the grain" is necessary: polemical texts must be examined for the facts that are hidden in their distorted presentations; laws

and norms, for the practices they regulate or fight against and to which they indirectly testify.[16]

The State of Research

The study of women's history arising at the end of the 1960s—which no
longer asks about the ideals and norms for the female sex that are defined by men
but instead seeks the self-understanding of women—is new in its specific approach and in the methods developed from that approach. Yet there are certainly
precursors. In the broadest sense this includes the "querelle des femmes" ("quarrel about women") of the early modern period, the argument about the educa-
bility of women, which was thoroughly investigated and documented by Elisabeth Gössmann.[17] Appearing in the polemical writings of this early epoch are
many names of early church women that in the meantime have been almost entirely forgotten.

Yet since the middle of the last century the so-called first women's movement
in particular has given rise to consideration of the role of women in the history
of Christianity. Liberal theology, committed to historical-critical research, has
achieved the most important results here. Adolf von Harnack, in his *Mission und
Ausbreitung des Christentums in den ersten drei Jahrhunderten* (1902), pointed
to the significance of women in the early period.[18] Appearing that same year was
Leopold Zscharnack's *Dienst der Frau in den ersten christlichen Jahrhunderten*,
which may be the most thorough collection yet of source material that was already read against the grain of traditional church doctrine of subordination.
Zscharnack—at this point very Protestant—made the rise of monasticism responsible for the suppression of women. We will see that from the women's perspective the ascetic tradition had definitely liberating dimensions and that it was
precisely in the cloister that an egalitarian ethos[19] was maintained for a relatively
long time. In this respect Zscharnack's still very helpful work needs revision.

Now, we will not mention all the recent investigations of the position of
women in early Christianity. They have in common that they no longer have any
interest in legitimating the subordination of women but rather emphasize the
liberating aspects in early Christian, early church traditions, not least of all with
the good intention of bringing about equality in the present-day church. Yet this
hasty effort to present the philogynous side of Christianity ultimately hinders a
radical critique of our own tradition—that is, a critique that goes to the root of
the evil.[20]

Klaus Thraede broke with this apologetic tendency when he found in early
Christianity "a general retreat from the phenomenon of 'the liberated' woman
and a relapse into developmental stages that had already been almost overcome
in pre-Christian life and thought."[21] To his great merit he cleared Christian
heads of the still firmly entrenched prejudice that holds that Christianity at first
brought to the oppressed women of antiquity a minimum of liberation but then
finally succumbed to the pressure of the patriarchal environment. Nevertheless,
Thraede is still guided by the question of the position of women as defined by

men. It is true that he does well at juxtaposing theories about the female sex with testimonies about women who really existed, yet the self-understanding of Christian women and their specific accomplishments hardly come into the picture. Even his selection of names is quite arbitrary. For example, he names Chrysophora, Flora, and Tatiana, about whom we know only that early Christian theologians devoted a writing to them, but he does not mention Perpetua, Proba, Egeria, and Eudocia, who themselves wrote important works. Nonetheless, his presentation of early Christianity against the background of women's liberation in antiquity remains a milestone for further research.

In the 1960s and 1970s the question of the ordination of women was in the forefront of theological discussion. The most important investigation of the official functions of women in early Christianity is the uncommitted but very thorough and precise study by Roger Gryson, *The Ministry of Women in the Early Church,* yet its focus is more on the ministries than on the ministers. The history of the denial of ordination to women in the Roman Catholic Church has been investigated by Ida Raming.[22] While in the Protestant churches the barriers were gradually set aside and the Episcopal Church in America for the first time even ordained women deacons as priests, in 1976 the Vatican Congregation for the Doctrine of the Faith responded to similar strivings in the Roman Catholic Church with a decisive no.[23] Since the traditional reasons (female subordination, cultic impurity) are no longer advanced by the ecclesiastical teaching office, we find here a new argument, which was later also adopted in modified form by the Eastern church:[24] a woman cannot act "in persona Christi," cannot "represent" Christ, and in particular cannot "represent" the male Jesus in the celebration of the Eucharist. We will see in the chapter on women martyrs that this argument contradicts early Christian traditions.[25]

The image of women, teachings about women, the position of women—these perspectives dominate many publications by women theologians who have turned to women's studies. Published in 1968 was Kari Elisabeth Børresen's study *Subordination et équivalence,* on woman as the image of God (*imago dei*) in Augustine and Thomas of Aquinas. Here the quintessence of classical church doctrine is stated precisely: subordination in spite of equality. In the meantime this author has carried out a research project in Norway on the *imago dei* debate especially in early Christianity, in which many women scholars took part; the results were recently published.[26] We are also indebted to her for a very detailed report on the literature in theological women's studies.[27]

Jean Laporte is less interested in the image of women than in their concrete possibilities in the early church; her work, published in the United States in 1982 under the title *The Role of Women in Early Christianity,* is an annotated collection of sources. In the meantime, literature of this kind, in which early church texts that speak of women are presented without a thorough theological analysis, is available in many languages, from both male and female writers,[28] and these works are very helpful for an initial orientation.

The 1970s, especially in the United States, have seen the appearance of works by Rosemary Radford Ruether, Elizabeth Clark, Ross Kraemer, Jo Ann McNamara, and Elizabeth Castelli, which point to the connection between sexual continence and liberation, which initially seems paradoxical: hostility to sex does not necessarily have to be coupled with hostility to women.[29] The already mentioned patristic scholar Elizabeth Clark has arranged for the English translation and publication of sources in which this ascetic-egalitarian direction is represented, in particular in several tractates of John Chrysostom.[30] Stevan L. Davies has also emphasized the aspect of rejection of marriage in his study of the apocryphal *Acts of the Apostles*, called *The Revolt of the Widows* (1980);[31] Virginia Burrus takes up this motif again in *Chastity as Autonomy* (1987).[32] The only monograph in German so far on women of early Christianity[33] also has the ascetic movement as its object: Ruth Albrecht, in *Das Leben der heiligen Makrina auf dem Hintergrund der Thekla-Traditionen* (1986), examines the portrait that Gregory of Nyssa paints of his older sister and at the same time offers a comprehensive presentation of ascetically oriented women and their self-understanding.[34]

Another emphasis of feminist research in the United States lies in the realm of Gnosticism, stimulated primarily by the work of Elaine Pagels, who points to the positive use of feminine metaphors in this movement and emphasizes other philogynous elements.[35] This evaluation has evoked vehement criticism by Susanne Heine.[36] Yet in her book *Frauen der frühen Christenheit* (1986) Heine has not offered a comprehensive study but merely reacted to some directions of feminist theology that she accuses of methodological murder and wishful thinking. On many issues the criticism is justified, but unfortunately the author also makes wholesale condemnations of some women theologians without acknowledging their positive accomplishments. This is especially true of Elisabeth Moltmann-Wendel, who to a special degree deserves credit for having communicated the central concerns of feminist theology in broad ecclesiastical circles.[37]

Finally, we are indebted to American scholars, both women and men, for making easily accessible in one volume the few manuscripts of early Christianity written by women. In 1981 *A Lost Tradition: Women Writers in the Early Church* appeared. It includes (1) the martyrdom of Perpetua and Felicity (part of the report was written in prison by Perpetua herself),[38] (2) Proba's epic of salvation from Virgilian verses (called *Cento*),[39] (3) the report on a pilgrimage to the Holy Land by Egeria,[40] and (4) the deeds of St. Cyprian and St. Justina by Empress Eudocia.[41] In each case there is an English translation of the source, as well as an introduction and commentary, by various experts. In the same year Elizabeth Clark and Diane Hatch published a larger English edition of Proba's epic of salvation with the Latin text and a detailed commentary: *The Golden Bough, the Oaken Cross*. This made the theologically most interesting work of a Christian woman author of late antiquity available for research for the first time to those beyond the circle of specialists.[42]

The Search for Traces

Thus I was able to build on the named works in the area of historical-theological women's studies when in 1985, after the departure of Bernadette Brooten, I took over the first part of the project "Woman and Christianity," which had the working title: "Sexuality, Marriage, and Alternatives to Marriage in the First Four Centuries." In addition, a book by the German New Testament scholar living in America, Elisabeth Schüssler Fiorenza, was published in 1983: *In Memory of Her: A Feminist Theological Reconstruction of Christian Origins*. In it the author had worked out important hermeneutical principles as to how androcentric sources could be used for the reconstruction of women's history,[43] and she was able to demonstrate that in the early Jesus movement women were more active than the reports in the New Testament on first glance would lead one to believe. Even if with regard to the "discipleship of equals," which Schüssler Fiorenza postulates for the beginning, a certain skepticism may be advisable,[44] one still cannot doubt that the beginnings were at the least far more philogynous than later epochs of Christianity. Yet can this be attributed solely to the still influential message of Jesus? The first women followers of the Nazarene were Jewish, Greek, and Roman women before they became Christian women. Hence the question must be asked: Was it not they, above all, who brought emancipatory consciousness into Christianity?

This was the starting point from which I myself now set out on the search for traces of women in early Christianity who really existed. But where was I to begin? Since the question of the self-understanding of Christian women stood in the foreground, it would have been obvious for me now to begin with the four writings that were extant. Yet how were they to fit into the overall picture that we can paint of the real life of women in the church of the first centuries? Four writings, which are also extremely different in form and content, cannot be representative of "women."[45] Only if the general background is illuminated can the special significance of these particular works be established. Thus it seemed urgent to go in search of other Christian women about whom we know even less.

Also conceivable would have been an approach through the investigation of early church descriptions of lives, although their exclusive concern is women who have devoted themselves to asceticism.[46] However, this particular aspect had often been studied by previous scholars.[47] But what about the many other Christian women? In which writings could one hope to learn something about them?

I finally hit upon the idea of turning first to the *ancient church histories*. In the oldest and best known of these, that of *Eusebius*, the first three centuries are described; three later authors, *Socrates, Sozomen*, and *Theodoret*, continue the account into the middle of the fifth century. The comparison makes one thing quite clear: substantially more women were actively involved in church life in early centuries than in later ones. Now a further question had to be asked of the church histories: Were their accounts objective or tendentious in regard to Christian women? In order to answer this question it proved necessary to compare the official historiography with the testimony of other sources from the same period: church decrees, theological tractates, and epistolary literature.

After this general panorama was established (chap. I of the present work), it seemed reasonable to study the group of women about whom we could learn the most: *martyresses*. In some cases we still have transcriptlike records of the trials, as well as reports that were written immediately after the events, that is, sources that have been revised relatively little as literature. Moreover, through *Perpetua's* notes in prison before her execution, we have the precious self-testimony of a woman who died for her Christian conviction. The examination of this material forms chapter II of this book.

Finally, in the church history of Eusebius a large role is played by the dispute over a *prophetic movement* in Phrygia that is connected with the names *Prisca, Maximilla,* and *Montanus.* Why was this movement so vigorously opposed in the second century and later? Apparently not because of the female sex of the two famous prophetesses, since their opponents assert that they recognize the prophecy of women in principle. Here the reconstruction work was substantially more difficult than with the martyrs, since Prisca's and Maximilla's writings, as well as the testimonies of their contemporary followers, were destroyed. We can get a picture of them only through the polemic of their opponents. It is true that *Tertullian,* the great African theologian, defended them and joined their movement, yet he did not know the prophetesses personally. In chapter III, I have attempted to place the personalities Prisca and Maximilla in the context of early Christian prophecy.

In the field of feminine prophecy I found the name of a woman who is totally unknown today but in second-century Rome headed a *Gnostically oriented* school and rivaled no less a figure than *Marcion,* namely, *Philomena.* The source situation here was even more difficult, since only the testimonies of her opponents have been passed down. Nevertheless, from fragments we not only can demonstrate the significance of Philomena in her time but also can reconstruct the basic concerns of her theology, which involves an excursus into the early history of dogma. Chapter IV is dedicated to this teacher and prophetess.

Here the investigation ends, but this is more the beginning of the work than the end. At the moment the reconstruction of the early Christian history of women is at a stage in which we must collect the individual mosaic stones from which the overall picture is to result. Yet the mosaic has some gaps and in places is irregular. Even if clear outlines are already indicated, many years of patient research and the cooperative efforts of scholars in various disciplines will be necessary to complete the picture.

I. WOMEN IN THE CHURCH HISTORIES

Development into the Church of Men

> Before we begin the fifth book of our history, we must beg those who may peruse this treatise, not to censure us too hastily because having set out to write a church history we still intermingle with ecclesiastical matters, such an account of wars which took place during the period under consideration, as could be duly authenticated. For this we have done for several reasons: first, in order to lay before our readers an exact statement of facts; but secondly, in order that the minds of the readers might not become satiated with the repetition of the contentious disputes of bishops, and their insidious designs against one another; but more especially that it might be made apparent, that whenever the affairs of the state were disturbed, those of the Church, as if by some vital sympathy, become disordered also. (Socrates, *Church History*)

Quarrels of the bishops and bloody battles of the emperors: when we read the church history of Socrates, we get the impression that these things more than anything else shaped the life of the church in his time.[1] If we had no other sources for reconstructing the history of early Christian women, we would have to be satisfied with rather meager results. In exoneration of Socrates, a historiographer of the fourth to fifth centuries, we can say that the viewpoint he shared also shaped the general writing of history well into our era; the attempt to write a "women's history," and through it to grasp "history" in general in terms of its content and values, still remains in its infancy, as we have seen. Nonetheless, Socrates also makes a critical comment on the connection between bishops' quarrels and emperors' wars. Thus before we can begin to bring together the meager information about women, which is available as a by-product despite the fixation of traditional historiography on these rulers of church and state, the sources force us first to take a look at the men to whom we owe these meager bits of information.

1. Four Different Authors

From the first centuries of Christianity four larger histories of the church have been preserved.[2] Eusebius, the bishop of Caesarea (d. 339), was the first to conceive a plan of Christian historiography.[3] He understood the first three centuries up to the "Constantinian turning point," through which Christianity was finally able to become the state religion, as a last attempt of Satan to prevent the victory God had wrought in the resurrection. The devil, he says, devised two means to this end: the "sowing" of false doctrines and the cruel persecution of Christians. This church history ends with the description of Constantine's military victory (323); for Eusebius this was God's great deed of salvation that brought peace to Christians: now the world stood under the sign of the kingdom of Jesus.

Even if from our perspective this decidedly salvation-historical view is more the interpretation than the writing of history, one of the special services of the bishop of Caesarea was to excerpt numerous original documents from the earlier period. We are indebted to him for the preservation of at least a few fragments from many early Christian writers—unfortunately none of them women! It is true that in his selection he presumably did not proceed according to objective criteria, but since he left the most varied documents standing side by side without making an effort to reconcile any possible contradictions or to discover which of the sources were more credible, we hear in many cases, at least fragmentarily, an *ipsissima vox* from witnesses of the second and third centuries. The learned bishop of Caesarea remains the only one who has informed us systematically about the first three centuries of Christianity. Although he had numerous successors in the fourth and fifth centuries, none of them reworked the earlier period, and thus for that era we remain dependent on the church history of Eusebius.

For the next century and a half the situation is different. For this period we are informed by the comprehensive reports of three quite different writers, who were in part dependent on each other: Socrates (d. after 439), Sozomen (d. ca. 450), and Theodoret (d. ca. 466).[4] We will look briefly at these authors and their work. The church history of Socrates[5] (the "Mark," as it were, among these three "synoptists") is the most comprehensive in terms of time; it comprises the period from 306 (Constantine's ascension to the throne) to 439 (reign of Theodosius II). Sozomen[6] reports on the period from 323 to 423 (his church history breaks off without a conclusion). Finally, Theodoret's account[7] spans the years from 324 to 429. Even before them, the theologian Rufinus (d. 410), who belonged to ascetic circles, had translated the church history of Eusebius into Latin and in the process lengthened it by two chapters (to the reign of Theodosius I).[8] These chapters are included here when there are parallel traditions.

Socrates and Theodoret both announce at the beginning of their church histories their express intention to continue the work of the bishop of Caesarea, and Socrates expands somewhat the last part of Eusebius. Continuation is also the concern of Sozomen, yet he begins first with a general reflection: often he has wondered why the Greeks converted to Christianity more willingly than the Jews, although the latter stood in the historical succession of divine revelation. In order to examine this question he at first wanted to write a church history from the beginning, but since the writings of Clement, Hegesippus, Africanus, and above all Eusebius were available, he satisfied himself with a short summary of this period in two books.[9] He then explains how he has dealt or wants to deal with his sources, excuses himself somewhat for the large space that is required for the quarrels of church people with each other, announces that he wants to include also the churches outside the imperial boundaries and—his special concern—create a monument to the fathers of monasticism.

Bernard Grillet, coeditor of the still-unfinished French edition in the Sources Chrétiennes, believes that Sozomen's claim of continuing the work of Eusebius is unjustified: as a layperson he observed church history from the outside and was therefore more oriented toward the emperors than the bishops.[10] This is a curiously clerical understanding of church history! If Grillet were correct, all this would also apply to Socrates. Yet the reason for the difference in historiography lies in the new situation in the fourth century: church and state now form a union.[11] But this new perspective, which is common to all three church histories, is not in contrast with Eusebius but rather was anticipated by his vision of a Christian Roman Empire under a Christian emperor.[12]

It is strange that neither Theodoret nor Sozomen names the work of Socrates as one of his sources, although it is certain that each knew and used it; with Sozomen in particular the direct dependence is unmistakable—it must be assumed that with his reworking of the material he hoped to suppress and replace the church history of Socrates.[13] Socrates, on the other hand, names Rufinus as his immediate source, yet only after he discovered discrepancies that necessitated a new edition of the first two books of his church history.[14]

The dependence of Sozomen on Socrates is undisputed, yet the opinions on the historiographical qualities of the two authors are divided. The Sozomen commentator Guy Sabbah tends to enhance the later author: he succeeded in a more convincing synthesis of Christianity and Hellenism, whereas the work of Socrates soon proved to be "hopelessly anachronistic."[15] Yet that is doubtful. The judgment of the Sozomen translator at the end of the previous century is quite different: Socrates had the sharper mind; as a historian he was superior in every respect.[16] Also Glenn F. Chesnut believes him to be "perhaps [the] greatest successor" of Eusebius.[17]

Unfortunately, we have no other sources for Socrates than his own work, and the same is true for Sozomen. The two were not clerics but lawyers who had contacts with the court in Constantinople. Nevertheless, Sozomen was profoundly shaped by an intellectually rather narrow monastic education, while Socrates had an outspokenly open mental attitude. According to the judgment of his translator, A. C. Zenos, "of all the Christian writers of his day he is the fairest towards those who differed from the creed of his church."[18] Out of a pacifist basic attitude he criticized both the wars of the emperors and the church's intramural theological quarrels.[19] In one chapter he expressly defends the study of Greek philosophy, since the Holy Scripture promotes piety and a proper lifestyle but does not teach the art of argumentation (3.16). Socrates was a loyal representative of the mainstream church, but that did not keep him from depicting such fanatical leaders as Cyril of Alexandria and John Chrysostom in a critical or negative manner. In spite of many errors in his church history, he among his contemporaries best meets the (present-day) expectations of a historiographer. Through his work he presents himself both as a convinced, broad-minded Christian and as a citizen and heir of the Roman Empire and its Hellenistic culture.

Sozomen offers us a different picture. Though he too was shaped by ancient education, he is less open, more churchly and pious. His church history is permeated by sometimes quite bizarre miracle stories. His editors are at pains to interpret away this belief in miracles: Guy Sabbah explains it with the general enthusiasm for miracles in late antiquity;[20] Chester D. Hartranft with the "Christian consciousness of the age."[21] The latter's assertion that Sozomen was no more believing in miracles than Socrates (and other contemporaries) is not supported by the wording of the two church histories. Certainly Socrates is also familiar with miracles, but with him they are substantially less frequent and far less fabulous.

The second characteristic feature of Sozomen's work has already been mentioned: it is the broad glorification of monasticism and the ascetic way of life. We will become acquainted with examples of this later. At this very point lies the significance of Sozomen's church history beside the higher quality work of Socrates: through it we are confronted with the complexity of that period, which cannot be reduced to a unified "Christian consciousness." The comparison of the two church histories is so interesting precisely because Sozomen does not represent a liberal, "bourgeois" direction like Socrates but a more strongly dogmatic, apologetically and ascetically oriented counterdirection.

In contrast to the "laymen" Socrates and Sozomen, but similar to his great predecessor Eusebius, Theodoret pursued a classical church career. After years as a monk he became bishop of Cyrrhus (near Antioch). As a theologian he is known through many exegetical writings as well as through his participation in the christological disputes over Nestorius and Cyril, which were decided in favor of the latter by the Council of Ephesus in 431. According to present-day scholarship, Nestorius "need not have been condemned."[22] In the turmoil following this dispute about the two natures in the one person of the incarnate Son of God, Theodoret became, more than a hundred years later, the victim of posthumous condemnation as one of the *tria capitula* (the three alleged fathers of Nestorianism). In his basic intellectual position he is closer to Sozomen's enthusiasm for miracles and asceticism than to the objectivity of Socrates, which naturally comes out even more clearly in his work on the ascetic way of life. According to his editor Léon Parmentier, his church history is less historiography in the real sense than "a defense of the orthodox church against the Arians."[23]

Christianity was split for centuries by the doctrine of Arius (d. 336), a priest from Alexandria, who, while not questioning the church doctrine of the divine sonship of Jesus, wanted to distinguish the divine nature of the Father from that of the Son. The emperor finally convened the imperial Council of Nicaea (325)— familiar to us today as the first "ecumenical" council. It condemned Arius and accepted into the confession of faith the formula that Jesus Christ, the Son of God, was "consubstantial" (*homoousios*) with the Father, but this still brought no unity. Since the emperors sometimes supported one, sometimes the other party, there were violent disagreements over these issues.

Throughout this church history of Theodoret written against the Arians there are scattered anecdotal reports without much chronological order or recognizable intention by the author. That is where we will find the few elements of interest for women's studies—mostly doublets of the stories of Socrates and Sozomen (and Rufinus). At the end of this first part there is a comparison of these doubly transmitted but quite differently recounted traditions, but first we must compare the general picture of women passed on by Eusebius with the corresponding balance of the later period: with the overall picture that Socrates, Sozomen, and Theodoret together have drawn, even if each did so in his own way.

2. Statistical Matters

When we now begin to examine these four church histories with regard to their reporting on women, we will be aided first by a statistical overview (Appendixes II and III, pp. 240–55), which is to be consulted while reading the following explanations. These tables indicate the functions in which women appear in the investigated church histories. The members of imperial families are given first; since they have a special position, they are only listed here as a group; in this study they will, with few exceptions, be excluded from the investigation.[24] In the other tables the order has a certain significance; that is, it follows one (not "the"!) rank order of early Christianity, which is to be demonstrated in detail in the course of the investigation.

With Eusebius we would expect to find the women apostles of early Christianity in first place. One might let it pass that the authors of the later church histories report on women missionaries without giving them the honorary title of "apostle" that was commonly used in the patristic period. But the fact that the first Christian historiographer, who devotes great attention to the male disciples of Jesus (and indeed by no means only "the twelve"!), mentions neither Mary Magdalene nor Salome nor Mary and Martha of Bethany nor any of the other women around Jesus—who, we know from early church traditions, played a definite role—is, to say the least, striking. The only one mentioned is Prisca, the wife of Aquila, yet not in her role as apostle but as victim of the first persecutions under Claudius.[25] In the church history we do not even find Junia, the only woman expressly designated as an apostle, and indeed as a "prominent" one (Rom. 16:7).[26] In the liturgy of the Eastern church she is still celebrated today as an apostle.[27] [English translations remain divided on the name, often giving alternate readings[28]—Trans.]

In the early period prophetesses and after them martyresses were considered persons who had been chosen in a special way by the Holy Spirit. Understanding themselves as the successors of these two groups were the ascetics, who renounced life in the world.

Already in Paul voluntary celibacy was called a *charisma*, a special gift of the Spirit (1 Cor. 7:7). In the following centuries an ideal of abstinence developed and, alongside anchorite and communal lifestyles, also led to the so-called spiritual marriage in two forms. Either an already married couple forswore sexual relations with some kind of vow, or a woman and man who had both committed themselves to abstinence lived together without marrying; the latter form was soon criticized, and women were labeled with the derogatory term *syneisaktai* ("brought in together").

The first organized group of people attested to forgo marriage voluntarily was the widows. In the beginning young women who did not want to marry were counted with the widows, but since their number grew constantly, virgins finally became the common designation for the ecclesiastically recognized order of unmarried women who lived a voluntarily continent life. Although for us today the word is loaded with many negative associations and sounds antiquated, the designation is retained here, given the lack of a viable equivalent. What qualifies the ecclesiastical virgin, however, is not an unspoiled body but the renunciation of the status of wife and mother. Hence it is *not a biological but a social category.*

After long conflicts in the fourth and fifth centuries, deaconesses—that is, the ordained officeholders on the bottom edge of the hierarchy—largely replaced the widows and virgins who were not ordained but initially performed similar functions in the church. The latter group, the virgins, led—or were forced to lead—an increasingly withdrawn life in convents.

Thus under the key terms *martyress, prophetess, ascetic* the table comprises first the charismatic female personages of the early period; then under the categories widow, virgin, deaconess come the women who belonged to one of the ecclesiastically recognized female orders. Under the latter rubrics the questions asked of the authors of the church histories are whether for them the education of women mattered and whether slaves played a role in their description of Christianity. Finally, we have the category of heterodoxy, in order to document adherence to a confession that deviates from the mainstream.

One will correctly note that two key words are missing in the tables: wives and mothers. It is true that with several of the named women a husband or children are occasionally mentioned—this is made clear in the table with the symbols Wf (wife) and Wf+C (wife with child[ren])—and sometimes the topic is "men, women, and children" or "families" in general. Yet nowhere is a married couple presented in a positive and exemplary way, nor is a woman valued as an ideal wife and mother. Only in a very few places do we get a glimpse of the real life of these "normal women" and the quality of their family relationships.

The individually named persons were counted for statistical purposes; they appear in the Overview (Appendix II) and Tables (Appendix III) in bold print. If they appear in several categories, secondary entries are placed in angle brackets: < >. To their names or the ersatz name *Anonyma* are added the symbols of their functions. The Tables also contain brief descriptions and corresponding source references.

The Language of Numbers

Even at first glance the Overview (Appendix II) makes clear that Eusebius offers by far the most colorful picture in regard to women—in terms of both the number of names and the variety of functions. In Eusebius most of the names of women are found in the category of martyresses; in Socrates, Sozemen, and Theodoret, under the rubric of empresses. That can be explained initially by the different epochs: the time before Constantine, with its various persecutions of Christians, explains the high number of martyrs in Eusebius; the conversion of the court to Christianity explains the high number of empresses in the other accounts. Certainly it would be wrong to suppose that Eusebius was less concerned with the imperial court than were his successors in the writing of church history. For him the explanation of different epochs is quite accurate: if more empresses had been interested in Christianity earlier, the bishop of Caesarea would certainly have mentioned them! Yet for the martyresses the explanation is more complex: their large number in Eusebius points to a high number of women who during the time of persecution were active in the churches in exposed positions. Thus one would expect that just as many women would appear in Socrates, Sozomen, and Theodoret, but now no longer as martyresses. Finally, there is less talk of martyrs but not less of men. Thus, when the number of women mentioned in the later church histories decreases, one must presume that the actual influence of women was suppressed, that they received less attention in general, and that they were indeed perhaps even deliberately left unmentioned.[29]

Let us do a little arithmetic and create yet another small overview. First, the number of women in the imperial residence is compared with that of the other women named. Then the others are divided into the number of women mentioned by name and the number of anonymous women (omitting those in the imperial court). When a person is mentioned in more than one church history, she is counted only once in the overall total (S/S/T).

Mention of Women in the Church Histories			
	Court	Others	Named	Anonymous
EUS	7	55	26	29
S/S/T	22	43	13	30
SOC	19	14	4	10
SOZ	14	33	10	23
THE	7[30]	15	3	12

The result of this exercise: *In his church history Eusebius mentions more women than the other three church historians combined!* The ratio is 55:43; even if the court is considered, the result is almost equal: 62:65. In what follows, the numbers given do not include members of the imperial families. We must also make clear the striking imbalance in the naming of women and men even in the most philogynous of the authors: among some 700 *masculine* first names found in the index of Eusebius, there are only 30 *feminine* names![31] Beyond this imbalance, however, an obvious decline can be seen from EUS to S/S/T: *the number of women clearly decreases.*[32]

Anonymization

Not only are fewer women named; there is also *a pronounced tendency toward anonymization*. This can be observed already in the New Testament when the people ask of Jesus: ". . . are not his brothers James and Joseph and Simon and Judas? And are not all his sisters with us?" (Matt. 13:55–56). The ratio of the named to the anonymously mentioned women is 26:29 in EUS, 13:30 in S/S/T; individually the ratios are SOC 4:10, SOZ 10:23, THE 3:12. At first glance the result for Sozomen seems more positive, but the appearance is deceptive: 13 of the women mentioned (all anonymous) fall under "other"—5 of them are merely the "object" of a miracle, and 5 are involved in sex stories. Of the 10 mentioned by name, 6 are deaconesses and 2 virgins—that is, unmarried women with an ecclesiastical status. In Theodoret also, one of the three mentioned by name is a deaconess. Hence women's deprivation of office may have contributed considerably to making them invisible to history!

The anonymization of women is all the more striking in light of the fact that it is also to be observed in important pieces of tradition that are reported in all three church histories, for example, in the report on the incident in Edessa in which a massacre was prevented through the brave action of a Christian woman, and in the story of the conversion of "Iberia" (Georgia), which is the work of a Christian woman prisoner of war.[33] What male missionary of an entire land has remained anonymous in church history? In the course of this study it has become very clear to me how difficult it is to talk about people who have no name. In order to mitigate this evil, a little trick will be practiced in what follows: for the many nameless women the common substitute term *Anonyma* will occasionally be treated like a feminine first name (as will *Anonymus* for unknown males).

From our authors we do not learn a great deal about women. Again, some 700 men's names are found in the church history of Eusebius, as compared with about 30 names of women (including those in the court). Nonetheless, these few are worth investigating—and that is about to happen. As already indicated, because of their special position the female members of the imperial house will not be included, apart from a few exceptions. Yet most of the women who are mentioned belong to the upper stratum. To examine the entire corpus from the perspective of social history[34] would be a task in itself and cannot be accomplished in an initial examination.

Because of the paucity of sources, one must naturally raise the question regarding each event: Was it representative of current living conditions for women, or was it an exception? Often it can be answered only hypothetically or must remain unanswered. Here we will first gather what has been reported about women. It must be emphasized once again that in what follows it is a matter of a *reading "against the grain."* That is, the topic here is not Eusebius, Socrates, Sozomen, and Theodoret; it is neither the theological interests they represent nor their understanding of church history. It was not the intention of these authors to report on women; this is only an incidental by-product of their activity. We will ask of the texts no unjustified questions, but our questions are different from those the authors themselves were trying to answer in their day. Since we have only a very few sources written by women, we must attempt to derive from the testimonies left by men what is relevant for a reconstruction of the real life of women.

3. Women as a Qualified Minority

The Church History of Eusebius

In the following section we cannot examine in detail all the listed reports on women. Since the next two chapters are devoted to prophetesses and martyresses, they are treated only in summary fashion in this first round. By contrast, the relationship between women in the mainstream church and women from other confessions will be treated more fully. The ascetic traditions will be examined more closely; from a feminist perspective they are especially interesting, since they represent a break with the woman's traditional role of wife and mother. It must be expressly noted that here we will present only the reality of the time as reflected in the perception of each author. Yet we will occasionally draw on other sources in order to make clear the limited nature of these perceptions.

a. Women from All Classes

As the Overview (Appendix II) indicates, martyresses are the largest group of Christian women mentioned in Eusebius: out of a total of 55 women whom the bishop mentions in his church history, 29 risked their lives for their conviction; 16 names are still known to us. We have already pointed out that this relatively large number indicates a remarkably active presence of women in the churches during the time of persecution. The second chapter of this book is devoted to martyresses; here they will be considered only in regard to the participation of women in the life of the church. It should be noted that according to the early Christian understanding, "martyrdom" (literally, "witness") is determined not by the fact of violent death but by confession before a court in the face of death.[35]

It is interesting that these martyresses represent *all social classes:* from Flavia Domitilla, the relative of a Roman consul (3.18.4), to the slave Blandina (5.1.17ff.). There are women *of all ages:* with the virgin Apollonia and with Mercuria, their advanced age is emphasized (6.41.7, 18); Theodosia was not yet eighteen (*MP* 7.1–2). Ten martyresses are said to be virgins, at least three were mothers, and the remaining were presumably married or widows, yet this cannot be determined with certainty. Also, with these reports one cannot always determine with certainty whether virgin or widow here means ecclesiastical status or whether it is merely a question of the family status of "not yet married" or "widowed." Regarding Potamiaina and two nameless virgins, their beauty is mentioned (later a general cliché in martyrdom reports); wealth is emphasized twice, and noble birth five times. Also a "heretic," a Marcionite, is singled out among the martyresses (7.12). Especially striking in the report on the massacre of Christians in Lyon (5.1) is the fact that the slave Blandina plays a leading role, whereas her mistress is only mentioned in passing and remains nameless.[36] According to another source, Potamiaina is also supposed to have been a slave.[37]

An Anonyma should also be mentioned here, although she appears as an antimartyr: the mother of Origen. Her husband was already in prison, and the son, in his youthful enthusiasm, wanted to emulate his father as a witness for Christ. Only the prudence of Anonyma held him back: when words were of no avail, the resolute woman finally hid all his clothes. According to Eusebius, Origen came very close to forfeiting his life, if the divine, heavenly providence had not—for the benefit of many—thwarted his zeal through his mother (6.2.2–6). The behavior of Anonyma is in clear contrast to the later tendency, already perceptible in Eusebius, to present the persecution of Christians in the light of a romanticized enthusiasm for martyrdom.

b. Women in All Movements

With martyresses we were concerned almost exclusively with women from the mainstream church. Yet the persecutors hardly asked which Christian confession the accused belonged to. Thus we must now look at the Christian women who are traditionally called "heretics." In Eusebius the heterodox are the second largest group of individually named women, along with the prophetesses—and three names appear under both rubrics. Church schisms often had mainly political reasons. Walter Bauer has instructively demonstrated that in contrast to frequent clichéd presentations, the unified doctrine of the church was not the point of departure from which the "heretics" deviated; rather, in the beginning there were legitimate differences of opinion. With the later tendency to unify the original pluralism, some authentic early church theologies were later declared heresy, and those who remained true to them were finally excommunicated.[38]

Of the women Eusebius mentions by name or at least individually, five belong to movements outside the mainstream church, four of them in influential positions: Helena, the partner of Simon of Samaria, a legendary pair who were connected with the beginnings of Gnosticism (2.13.4);[39] Prisca[40] and Maximilla, the inspirers of the New Prophecy, alias Montanism (5.14, 16–19);[41] and finally the Gnostic teacher and virgin Philomena, who was followed by the Marcion student Apelles (5.13).[42] The fifth, one Anonyma, is presented positively as a martyress, although she was a Marcionite (7.12). Moreover, women are especially mentioned in the circle of Paul of Samosata, who had to justify himself because of his Christology (7.30.10ff.).

Eusebius used a not inconsiderable part of his church history to report on groups outside the mainstream church and their leaders. We will mention here only a few names and movements: Simon and Menander, the Ebionites, the Gnostics of Cerinthus, the Nicolaitans (part 3); Valentinus, Cerdo, Marcion, Musanus, Tatian (4); Montanus with Priscilla and Maximilla, Blastus, Artemon (5); Beryll, Hekesaites, Novatian, Sabellius, Nepos, Paul of Samosata, Mani (6 and 7). In addition there are anonymous heresiarchs and regional heresies. The New Prophecy and the controversies over Paul of Samosata are described in particular detail.

Nevertheless, the number of individually mentioned "women heretics" in Eusebius is not greater than in Socrates-Sozomen-Theodoret: there are in each case a total of five Christian women who do not belong to the mainstream church, or did not belong but then changed confession. Thus there is no confirmation here of the widespread prejudice that women are especially "susceptible" to heresy.[43] It proves to be the typical argument of malicious polemics: just as many Greeks and Romans who rejected Christianity denigrated the new cult as "women's religion,"[44] so now fanatical pugnacious types also do the same against differently minded comrades in the Christian faith. Yet in Eusebius it is neither asserted that there are more women in the separated groups than in the mainstream church, nor can one infer this indirectly from his presentation. The bishop takes no offense against the female sex of women heresiarchs: the critique is applied to the teaching or to the living praxis of the movements. There is no lack of polemical distortions, but the polemic is never aimed at the activity of women as such.

As earlier with martyresses, Eusebius also reflects the conditions of the early period with regard to Christian women outside the mainstream: the "heretical" scene in the not yet imperial church was considerably more colorful and had more open boundaries than in the post-Constantinian church. In Sozomen's later history we find an echo of this situation:

> During the reign of preceding emperors, all who worshiped Christ, however they might have differed from each other in opinion, received the same treatment from the pagans and were persecuted with equal cruelty. These common calamities, to which they were all equally liable, prevented them from prosecuting any close inquiries as to the differences of opinion which existed among themselves; it was therefore easy for the members of each party to hold church by themselves, and by continually conferring with one another, however few they might have been in number, they were not disrupted. (2.32; NPNF, 2nd series, 2:281)

Even if the various movements separated to some extent and refused each other eucharistic communion, a relatively peaceful coexistence of the confessions and churches was still possible despite all the verbal polemics of the theologians.[45]

The tension between theoretical rejection and practical recognition—and occasionally even personal admiration—of those with different opinions becomes especially clear in two passages in Eusebius, which at the same time also mention significant women. Thus, on the one hand the criticizer of sects describes the Jewish Christian movement of the Ebionites ("the poor"[46]) as heretics who have a "poor" doctrine of Christ, because they do not recognize the doctrine of the virgin birth (3.27); on the other hand he mentions, without critical reservation, a certain Juliana, who is apparently acquainted with both the strictly orthodox Alexandrian teacher Origen and the Ebionite Bible translator Symmachus: to the former she forwarded a work of the latter, which she had received from the author himself (6.17). Moreover, Palladius, the author of a history of asceticism, reports that she was a well-educated and trustworthy virgin, with whom Origen stayed hidden for two months.[47]

We find Juliana's openness duplicated with Anonyma, the foster mother of Origen, for she not only took this young man into her home but "also admired a famous man among the heretics who lived at that time in Alexandria: he was born in Antioch, and this woman treated him as an adopted son, for whom she was completely responsible" (6.2.13). Origen in no way shares Anonyma's friendly attitude toward the dissident named Paul: he offends him through his refusal of common prayer. Yet the majority of mainstream Christians seem to have had no fear of contact, for they gather as a matter of course with the "heretics" to hear the learned Paul (6.2.14). The atmosphere that may have reigned here is aptly described by Walter Bauer:

> If we set aside the conviction of the later churchman Eusebius that heresy and orthodoxy must always be clearly juxtaposed, we have the picture of a Christendom that finds nothing wrong with the fact that so worthy a member as the seventeen-year-old Origen, already generally known because of his rich gifts, is entrusted at such a sensitive age to a woman whose house is the center of a far-reaching movement that one may most certainly not call orthodox. Then we have before us a fellowship whose most intellectually demanding members without second thought meet their need with the Antiochene-Alexandrian heretic. A few pages later Eusebius reports something very similar of Origen. . . . Innumerable heretics (6.18), as well as orthodox, gather around him . . .[48]

In spite of mutual denunciation, in the pre-Constantinian church, as described by Eusebius, there is still a lively interaction and communication between congregations of the mainstream church and various movements and currents, as shown by the example of an open and unpolemical discussion in Arsinoe, presented as exemplary by Eusebius (7.24.6ff.)—the topic there is the thousand-year kingdom of Revelation. Women are present in both the mainstream and in the groups that deviate from it. Yet they hardly appear in as exposed a position within the mainstream church as outside. Does this correspond to reality, or is the reporting tendentious? We must come back to this question after examining the later church histories.

Finally, concerning the "women heretics" in Eusebius, we must briefly sketch two instructive reports: the episode of Anonyma, wife of Nicolaus, and the information on women in the circle of Paul of Samosata. In the discussion on the Nicolaitans,[49] who were rumored to be involved in wife-swapping in sexual activity,[50] Eusebius adopts the presentation of Clement of Alexandria (d. 215): Nicolas, the leader of the group and one of the seven "deacons"—that is, an officeholder of the Gentile Christians in Jerusalem (Acts 6:5)—was accused of jealousy by the apostles; in order to clear himself of this accusation, he then offered to sell his wife for marriage in the community; his followers then carried on shameless prostitution. Clement apparently considers the story an authentic tradition about the New Testament Nicolaus and excuses him: he only wanted to free himself from passion (3.29.2ff.). The feelings and reactions of the wife are not reported. The polemic here is apparently against the real or alleged heresy in which one "despises the flesh"—not in the sense of strict asceticism but in unbridled sexuality. Clement—and the Eusebius who quotes him—opposes this with the properly understood continence of Nicolas, whose children renounce marriage. The dignity of women is preserved neither in the allegedly partner-swapping Nicolaitans nor in the pious student of the apostle, as Clement describes him: in both cases they are treated like will-less objects. We learn nothing about real women in the movement named for Nicolas, for it includes neither Anonyma nor her daughters who live in voluntary celibacy.

By contrast, some of the women among the followers of the controversial bishop of Antioch, Paul of Samosata, who was deposed by a synod in 268, may have continued afterward to stand by him. Here Eusebius quotes in detail the synodal letter in which the verdict is substantiated (7.30.2ff.). Yet in so doing he simply omits the passages that relate to the essential indictment—christological heresy[51]—and reports only the complaints about Paul's conduct (incidentally, a general tendency in the reporting of Eusebius). There are two important points here: the love of the accused bishop for opulence, luxury, and the worldly holding of court, as well as his promotion of the so-called *syneisaktai*, that is, sexually continent women who lived together with an ascetic or cleric. The degree to which the condemnation of Paul of Samosata by the synod because of theological errors was justified must remain open here—based on the extant fragments of his statements, today he is considered "largely exonerated."[52] In any case, it should be noted that the free forms of interaction with the opposite sex were condemned by the Synod of Antioch, but not the actual object of the "heresy." In the criticized incidents it was not a question of the exceptional practices of a fringe group but of phenomena at the heart of the mainstream church, in one of its most important centers: Antioch. We do not know how many of the incriminated *syneisaktai* became "Paulianists" after the condemnation of their bishop. In any case, they were by no means necessarily "heretics." Thus they will not be treated under this rubric but in the section on women ascetics.

Other women, nonetheless, are brought more directly into the context of christological heresy. The *Synodal Letter against Paul of Samosata* (7.30.2ff.) names as its audience "men and women" who, in the opinion of Paul's opponents, cheer the bishop on in unseemly fashion. The indictment also indicates that on Easter Sunday women sang hymns in the main church in Antioch. Whether this women's choir was the rule or an exception cannot be determined from the text. A literal translation of the sentence in the synodal letter in which the female choral singing is mentioned reads as follows:

> He no longer has hymns [*psalmous*] sung to our Lord Jesus Christ, because they are written more recently and by younger men, but in the middle of the church at the high Easter festival he has women sing [*psalmōdein*] to him, which is dreadful for the listener. (7.30.10)

According to the overall tenor of the writing we may assume that the mention of women here has a disparaging undertone in the sense of "women's religion." Yet in the synodal letter, allowing women to sing in the church is in no way forbidden. The objection is rather to the songs that are sung—and at this point the bishop seems to have been conservative: he rejects new hymns to Christ. It is known that in the discussion on the correct doctrine of the Trinity and the nature of the incarnate Son of God, hymns played a large role. They were a popular medium for spreading dogmatic opinions—even today in the Eastern church liturgical hymns are shaped by this debate over Trinitarian and christological orthodoxy.

It is extremely unlikely that a bishop would have hymns sung "to him" instead of to Christ—this may be a polemical distortion of the facts. The real point of contention was doubtless the content of the songs: Paul apparently objected to the latest tendencies in the development of mainstream Christology. In order to discredit liturgical regulation in Antioch, the synodal letter, in an unspecific way, brings into play the question of the sexes, although it has nothing to do with the real quarrel, since it was permissible for both men and women to write hymns and to sing in church.[53] It is apparently a question of making the bishop look ridiculous with his "female supporters."

We mention here the interpretation of this passage by Gustave Bardy in his study of Paul of Samosata, for it typifies the fact that the viewpoint of a "modern" commentator can be more misogynistic than that of the ancient author. In the singing of the women in the church, namely, he sees an offense against the idea of "mulieres in ecclesia taceant" ("women are to be quiet in church") and even criticizes an article with that title by Pierre de Labriolle for not having mentioned this incident.[54]

Conversely, it is noteworthy that the translation of Philipp Haeuser, appearing a short time later, softens the misogynistic cutting edge of the text in order to make the real quarrel clearer: ". . . in the middle of the church on the great day of Easter he has women singing hymns. Hearing these hymns one would like to be appalled."[55]

The women's choir mentioned by Eusebius has an interesting parallel in a report of the Jewish theologian Philo (d. ca. A.D. 50), who says of an ascetic community near Alexandria: a double choir of men and women appeared there on Pentecost. Since the bishop of Caesarea—and in his day certainly not he alone—took Philo's report to be the description of a Christian ascetically oriented community, the mention of a women's choir apparently did not shock him and his contemporaries.[56] The New Testament "commandment of silence" no doubt does not refer to singing in congregational gatherings, for it was not generally recognized even as a prohibition of teaching for women in early Christendom.[57]

c. Women as Proclaimers

In the New Prophetesses Prisca and Maximilla, who were mentioned at the beginning of the previous section, we have already met two women who were recognized by many of their contemporaries as Spirit-gifted proclaimers of the Christian message. Also the virgin and teacher Philomena, characterized by Eusebius as "possessed," is distinguished in other sources with the title *prophetess*.[58] In Ammia of Philadelphia we meet a prophetess recognized in the mainstream church. Other women distinguished with this charisma are not mentioned in church history, apart from the daughters of Philip known from the canonical Acts of the Apostles.

Now, prophecy was by no means a phenomenon that existed only in the Jewish Christian tradition. In other ancient religions there were numerous forms of prophecy. The neat distinction between "pagan seers" (or even "fortune tellers") and "Christian prophets" is modern; in antiquity the designations were interchangeable.[59] The idea that God can and does speak through people was familiar in late antiquity. An old definition of prophetic oracle reads: "Nempe voluntas divina hominis ore nuntiata" ("when the divine will is proclaimed through the mouth of a human being").[60] It is interesting that in this source a saying of Cato, a teacher of morality, is being compared with an *oraculum* and he himself with a priest chosen by the gods.

The similarities of Christian and non-Christian prophecy in the ancient world have been worked out in an exemplary study by David Aune: *Prophecy in Early Christianity and the Ancient Mediterranean World*.[61] According to this work, mantic forms of religiosity were characteristic of the entire Greco-Roman period, and a growing preference for ecstatic forms is seen in the mystery cults (47–48). Oracle traditions were widespread: the believers queried the divinity and received an answer, which often first had to be deciphered (49). Nevertheless, "unbidden" revelations were also frequent and were mostly conveyed through dreams (66).[62] Christian prophecy developed no specific forms (231); only the beatitude is to be found above all in the Jewish and Christian context (64). Regarding the men and women who had the charisma, there were two fundamental conceptions: all are prophetically gifted, and only individuals are prophetically gifted. The principle of the prophecy of all was advocated mainly in theory; in fact, it was mostly individual personalities who distinguished themselves as prophetesses and prophets (201). Collecting prophetic oracles was common. Since they often expressed an anti-Roman attitude, the burning of such collections was ordered under Augustus, and their private possession forbidden (77ff.).

In the New Testament only the four daughters of Philip are named as bearers of the prophetic charisma (Acts 21:9), but the comments of the apostle Paul on worship services in Corinth[63] leave no doubt that women there with prophetic speech participated in the proclamation at the community gathering, for he gives notice that "any woman who prays or prophesies" is to wear a veil (1 Cor. 11:5). In Revelation Jezebel in Thyatira is mentioned, "who calls herself a prophet" (2:20), yet the writer polemicizes against her. Individual male prophets are more frequently mentioned. In Antioch Barnabas and Paul, and Simeon, Lucius, and Manaen belong to the group of "prophets and teachers" (Acts 13:1). Also designated as prophets are Judas and Silas, who are to make the decisions of the Apostolic Council known in Antioch (15:32). Agabus is an itinerant prophet who with the prophecy of a famine initiates a collection for those affected (11:27ff.) and who later in Philip's house announces Paul's arrest in Jerusalem (21:10–11)—the only description of a concrete prophecy in the context of a community meeting that we have in the New Testament. Apostles, prophets, and teachers, according to Paul, hold the top positions in the church[64]—even if all charismata of ministry are surpassed and relativized by love as the most important gift of the Spirit. "Pursue love and strive for the spiritual gifts, and especially that you may prophesy" is Paul's express advice (1 Cor. 14:1).

The Daughters of Philip

In chapters III and IV of this work we will look in more detail at the later discussions about prophecy in the church. Here we will examine the statements about the daughters of Philip,[65] who are regarded in Eusebius as the standard for "genuine" prophecy, as opposed to the "false" kind encountered in the "heretics." This writer of church history mentions these Anonymae once himself (3.37.1) and also quotes several other sources about them in quite varied contexts.[66] Just from the frequent references one may conclude that these women enjoyed especially high esteem in the early church.

In the reporting of Eusebius there is one notable feature: the *charisma of prophecy* is not coupled with the *charisma of celibacy,* although this is suggested by the text of Acts: Philip "had four unmarried daughters who had the gift of prophecy"[67] (21:9). The renowned Bible translator and very ascetically minded church father Jerome (d. 420) later makes the connection, for in his hymn of praise to the virgin Demetrias he writes: "She wished to belong to the choir of the four daughters of Philip and like one of them to acquire the gift of prophecy through virginal chastity."[68]

Interestingly, Eusebius offers by contrast various, in part contradictory, statements regarding the virginity of the prophetesses. Clement asserts that Philip gave his daughters in marriage (3.30.1);[69] Polycrates reports that two of the daughters preserved their virginity into advanced age and are buried in Hierapolis—in Ephesus rests a third, famous on account of her "walk in the Holy Spirit" (3.31.3). Proclus mentions only the prophetic activity, not the virginity of these women—all four are buried in Hierapolis (3.31.4). An Anonymus mentions Quadratus, who "like the daughters of Philip possessed the prophetic charisma" (3.37.1). Papias reports a resurrection of the dead through the daughters of Philip (3.39.9).[70] Likewise, another Anonymus, who refers to Miltiades, does not mention the virginity of the daughters of Philip in his listing of authentic men and women prophets (5.17.3).

One thing stands out in all clarity from these contradictory sources: all the authors recognized the prophetic authority of these women and by referring to them sought to legitimate their own particular interests. Like the apostles they are considered guarantors of ecclesiastical tradition. This makes the disunity regarding family status all the more surprising. In view of this contradiction it is improbable that at this point genuine historical memories have been preserved, especially since the prophetesses have been transformed from daughters of the "deacon" and evangelist Philip into daughters of the apostle Philip.[71] In the cited references the women are obviously used for apologetic purposes in the quarrel over the value of celibacy. The same quarrel is also attested by the polemic against the New Prophets: their opponent Apollonius accused them of having taught the dissolution of marriages, and he asserts that the "prophetesses of Montanus" were the first to leave their husbands "after they were filled with the Spirit" (5.18.3). This is apparently supposed to nullify the prophetic claim of the women by attributing to them an unchurchly doctrine and praxis with regard to marriage. Discrediting with this argument makes sense only in a time when the higher value of celibacy was still in dispute.

The foregoing reporting on the daughters of Philip demonstrates two divergent tendencies of the period: one follows the marriage ideology of the pastoral letters, whose author mistrusted ascetic ways of life; the other honors Paul's preference for virginity, which will lead to a moderate integration of the continence ideal in the mainstream church.

In Clement of Alexandria (d. 215), for whom the marriage of Philip's daughters is especially important, these two traditions cross. Whereas the later church fathers recommended celibacy as the actual higher ideal life that is appropriate to the time after Christ,[72] Clement still regards marriage as the normal Christian lifestyle and has serious reservations about fundamental, lifelong *enkrateia* ("continence"). In this spirit he fights the heresy of the so-called Encratites, who—really or allegedly—rejected marriage for baptized Christians;[73] he emphasizes the married status of all apostles and even turns Paul into a husband: in Philippi, namely, he asked his wife to help the discordant, apostolically active women Euodia and Syntyche.[74] Yet in his own way the teacher from Alexandria is himself an Encratite, since he believes continence to be worth striving for and allows sexual activity exclusively for the purpose of begetting children[75]—a view that many non-Christian contemporaries also shared. Eusebius himself seemed to have no particular interest in this question. This is also evident in his reporting on women living ascetically, as we shall see.

First, however, a general comment on the New Testament women whose name or presence is incorporated into Eusebius's church history. Here we would naturally expect Mary, the mother of Jesus, and we find her. Yet the early church historian is not interested in her person but only in the virgin birth, a doctrine about which the Jewish Christians wanted to know nothing.[76] He does not mention the later doctrine of the continuing virginity of Mary. Besides Prisca and the daughters of Philip, whom we have already mentioned, he also names Mary the wife of Clopas (John 19:25), but only in order to identify her son Simeon as an eyewitness of the Lord—he is supposed to have been the second bishop in Jerusalem (3.32.4). The "wife of Matthan" (Matt. 1:15) from the genealogy of Jesus is called Estha in Eusebius (1.7.8). An interesting tradition is handed down about the Anonyma suffering from hemorrhages whom Jesus heals (Mark 5:25–34). We will speak more of her later.[77]

Thus we must confirm a large deficit in the first writer of a church history: *he is silent about women apostles.* Whether this is a conscious or unconscious strategy cannot be determined—in the actual consequences it makes no great difference.

Yet in view of this negative balance, another fact has even more weight: *women are used to substantiate a doctrine or lifestyle as "apostolic."* When this password for authentic Christianity is used later, one thinks only of "the twelve."[78] This narrowing of the apostle concept was not adopted by Eusebius; when the need arose, the authors cited by him appealed even to known women figures of the apostolic period in order to legitimate their own standpoint. Here the prophetic daughters of Philip seem to have carried special weight as witnesses.

There is one final notable feature in the traditions about these women: the localization of their graves in Hierapolis and Ephesus. These are two cities in which female divinities had important centers of worship: Cybele, the great mother, and Artemis, the divine virgin and warrior. In both cases continence rules are attested for the priests and priestesses.[79] Tertullian (d. after 220), the first great Latin theologian from the cosmopolitan city of Carthage, expressly states that it is "hard" for Christian widows "for nothing," as it were, to practice continence for their God (*Dei causa*), while pagan virgins and widows could be priestesses of "their Satan."[80] The connection between old cultic places with male and female priesthoods and the newly arising Christian women's traditions, which at first developed around the real or alleged grave sites of well-known women preachers and martyresses, is very complicated. In later centuries the veneration of highly varied holy women was replaced by a unified cult of Mary, in which church ideology and old folk piety were mixed. All this needs thorough investigation with interdisciplinary collaboration. Here this suggestion must suffice.[81]

Ammia of Philadelphia

Were there any women at all in the postapostolic period who were active as prophetesses in the communities that later belonged to the mainstream church, that is, prophetesses who were recognized by catholic orthodoxy? One might doubt it if Eusebius had not left us a clear testimony. When in the second century in Phrygia there arose the movement that called itself the New Prophecy and whose leading personalities included two women, the mainstream church saw itself suddenly challenged: Where was the prophetic charisma still alive in its own ranks?

Eusebius passes on to us fragments of the contemporary debate. Anonymus, a confirmed opponent of the Phrygian movement, criticizes the inclination toward ecstasy: this kind of possession by the Spirit of God is not known in the Bible; therefore, the New Prophets cannot "appeal to Agabus or Judas or Silas or the daughters of Philip or Ammia in Philadelphia or Quadratus or anyone else, for they have nothing to do with these."[82] Yet at the same time the writer is testifying that the adherents of the Phrygian movement very probably regarded Prisca, Maximilla, and Montanus as legitimate successors of Ammia and Quadratus.[83]

Unfortunately, we learn nothing about the lives and teachings of these two personalities, since only two formal criteria are given for distinguishing the spirits: (1) a "prophecy appropriate to the New Testament"[84] may not be linked with ecstasy; (2) prophetesses and prophets must be in an ongoing succession. Neither is true of the New Prophecy, since no more charismatics appeared after the death of Maximilla.[85] The assertion of Anonymus that biblical prophecy was free from ecstatic phenomena is quite obviously wrong; hence this statement allows us no conclusions regarding Ammia's proclamation. The idea of a prophetic succession likewise says little about her person; it merely points to the rivalry with officeholders who appeal to apostolic succession and underlines the high estimation of charismatic authority in the second century. We will return to both questions in chapter III.

The few statements quoted by Eusebius are the only witness to this doubtless significant female figure in the early period. The addition "in Philadelphia" points to her locus of activity as one of the seven churches in Asia Minor to which the seer John directed his Revelation, the New Testament apocalypse.[86] Today we can learn no more about her. Nonetheless, it is certain that the name Ammia of Philadelphia was connected with the memory of a prophetess of highest regard, since both "orthodox" and "heretics" attempted to legitimate themselves with her authority.

d. Women in New Ways of Life
Continence as a Philosophy

As noted above, at the beginning of his church history Eusebius adopts the Jewish theologian Philo's descriptions of a cloister-like community of his religion in the vicinity of Alexandria[87] as a report on "our ascetics" (2.17). What is more, in the presence of women in the group, Eusebius sees proof that the so-called *therapeutae*[88] must have been Christians. After he describes their lifestyle, he concludes:

> We believe that these words of Philo are clearly and unambiguously related to our own. Let those who still persist in their objections renounce their disbelief and allow themselves to be convinced by clear proofs that are not to be found outside the gospel-based Christian religion. For women are also to be found among those about whom we speak. "Most of them are old women who have remained virgins and who have preserved their purity not by necessity, like some of the priestesses among the Greeks, but through free choice out of a zealous striving and longing for wisdom. Since they desired to orient their lives toward it, they were not concerned with the joys of the flesh, for they wanted not mortal but immortal offspring, which only the God-loved soul can bring forth from itself."[89]

Celibate and ascetically organized women as the trademark of Christianity? Apparently this is how Eusebius understood it, or preferred to understand it, for he confirms precisely through his disparaging remarks that continence was also practiced by certain groups in Greek and Roman religion. Likewise, Philo's writing shows that in late antiquity ascetic lifestyles were popular already in pre-Christian times both in Judaism and in Hellenism and were designated as *philosophy*—as they also were later by the church fathers. Thus asceticism was "love of wisdom," not in the sense of abstract speculation but as the practical, frugal art of living.

It also becomes clear that in these continence-practicing circles women could appear to have more or less equal status with men. Yet Eusebius omits from his report what Philo conveyed in concrete details about the life of women therapeutae in the middle of the male community:[90] they take part in worship in a separate area, where they can hear everything well; they participate in the great celebration of fifty days (Pentecost)—a feast day that is placed in a mystical relationship with virginity:

> At first they gathered every seven times seven days, since they admired not only the simple number seven but also its square, for they know that it is pure and always virginal. But this is the preliminary festival before the highest festival, which is reached with the number fifty. It is the holiest number and the one most in tune with nature, since it is formed from the power of the right triangle, which is the beginning of the origin of the universe.[91]

The evening worship on this feast day includes men's and women's choirs. The two choir directors represent Moses and Miriam; toward the end of the service the two choirs mingle in song and dance in remembrance of the mingling waters after the crossing of the Red Sea. This is what we learn from Philo's report on the therapeutae.

Love without Sexuality

In the time described by Eusebius there were still no organized Christian cloisters with both sexes; this great development of monasticism began in the fourth century. In this tradition, women and men pledged themselves to sexual abstinence but by no means to a strict separation of the sexes; on the contrary, they founded common communities.[92] This Christian tradition, which was both practiced and contested into the Middle Ages, had its beginnings no doubt with the *syneisaktai* and *syneisaktoi* and their practice of free and unabashed living together as women and men ascetics.[93] This epithet meaning "brought in together," which was applied one-sidedly to women living in "Spiritual marriage," seems to have arisen in Antioch—at least it is attested here by the already cited synodal letter against Paul of Samosata. (I will avoid the term in the following.) In agreement with their self-understanding, these women are called "Spiritual" marriage partners. Today it is still usual in Germany to speak of pastors and priests as *Geistliche*, "spirituals" (comparable to *spiritual leaders* in America). Underlying this familiar expression for clergy is the old idea that they can fulfill their duties only if they have a particular "charisma," a special gift of the Holy Spirit. The "Spiritual" leaders of early Christianity were *pneumatikoi*,[94] people seized by and filled with the Spirit. Since our term *spiritual* has become rather trite, the word is capitalized here in order to remind us of the intended pneumatic dimension. In Spiritual marriage—that is, in the pairing of a man and a women who both believe they have received the charisma of continence—it is ideally a question of the total "Spiritualization" of their love, a transcendence into the realm of the divine. In actuality there were also far more pragmatic motivations for such pairings.[95]

At the beginning of our century, when Hans Achelis, in his still important and highly interesting study *Virgines subintroductae*,[96] demonstrated an initial forbearance and leniency of the church toward this form of communal living, he let himself in for some criticism,[97] although he himself shared the moralizing skepticism of his contemporaries concerning this free association of the sexes and regarded the phenomenon as an early church naïveté. When this institution is discussed today, the first reaction is usually incredulity regarding the real sexual abstinence of these ascetic pairs. On this point, however, the ancient sources are quite clear, in spite of all their polemics: in general, the renunciation of sexual activity was really maintained. In the prohibitions we frequently find the suggestion that one had to anticipate moral insinuations on the part of "pagans," even if the continence of the ascetic women and men was beyond doubt. An early testimony in which this kind of communal living is described in a rather detailed way is the fourth letter of Cyprian, the famous martyr-bishop (d. 258); he attests for Carthage the same attitude and practice of which the clergy of Antioch were accused in the cited synodal letter against Paul of Samosata. Excerpts from Cyprian's letter are included in Appendix I of the present work.

From Cyprian we learn that women who wanted to live in Spiritual partnership were prepared to undergo an examination by midwives in order to prove their sexual purity. The bishop of Carthage expressly makes the positive result of such an examination the prerequisite for receiving excommunicated virgins back into the communion of the church. One hundred fifty years later, Ambrose, the bishop of Milan (d. 397)—to his great credit—fundamentally rejected this humiliating treatment of ecclesiastically recognized virgins.[98] But apparently some women wanted to take this upon themselves in order to be able to live undisturbed in a "Spiritual marriage." This early church practice was increasingly resisted when it involved an unmarried couple. Yet if the vow of continence was made and practiced by a husband and wife in mutual agreement, the married couple could count on unlimited ecclesiastical praise; in Socrates, Sozomen, and Theodoret we will learn of such cases and also go into the spiritual background of this free association of the sexes.

Neither Wife nor Mother

Yet these unconventional representatives of Spiritual marriage as a new Christian ideal were not the only source of conflict in early Christianity. From the strong polemic of the pastoral epistles against certain widows,[99] we can clearly see that certain conservative ecclesiastical circles fought against women who wanted to follow the advice of the apostle Paul and remain unmarried.[100] The "younger widows," who according to 1 Tim. 5:11 are not to be put on the list with the "real widows," include in all probability not only those widowed young but also single women who did not want to marry, for in Greek language usage *chēra* ("widow") is also used for divorced or single women.[101] Ignatius of Antioch, in his letter to the church at Smyrna, greets "the virgins who are called widows" (13.1). Belonging to the ecclesiastical order first and foremost were "real" widows who, following the Roman ideal, did not want to enter a second marriage,[102] then increasingly also young women who did not want to marry at all. Tertullian mentions a young girl who sits in church among the widows.[103] Thus widows and virgins form the first ecclesiastical "order" for which voluntary celibacy is attested.[104] We know very little about concrete organizational forms. The women apparently lived either alone, with their families, or in small, family-like associations.[105] These "virgins and widows" are regarded by many American feminist theologians as a kind of early women's movement—a value judgment clearly expressed in titles such as "Chastity as Autonomy."[106] The emphasis on the emancipatory aspect of continence is certainly correct and important, but through one-sided emphasis one runs the risk of reproducing on the feminist level the classical superiority of the virgin over the wife.

The Widow—Minister or Poor Woman?

Ecclesiastical widows are not to be confused with the "widows and orphans" who needed the support of the church and the bishop in a special way. Rather, they were women who were active in the churches. Yet in conflicts there is an attempt to classify them together with alms recipients. Even when many widows finally, under church pressure, led a withdrawn life of prayer, this was also a "rendering of service" according to early Christian understanding. The "honor" given to "real"—that is, ecclesiastically recognized—widows means an "honorarium" (1 Tim. 5:3). Family members should care for the other widows where possible, so that the money in the church will suffice for the "real" widows (5:16). The elders (presbyters) receive double amounts (5:17). In spite of the clear language of the following sentences—"You shall not muzzle an ox while it is treading grain" and "The laborer deserves to be paid" (5:18)—most modern translations veil the concrete sense of these directives.

The statements of the church histories about widows and virgins should be read against this background. Eusebius speaks of eighteen women who were virgins, and most of these cases may have involved members of the ecclesiastical order. We learn hardly anything from him about concrete lifestyles. He does not name widows as a separate order, but the context of his remark that in Rome "over 1,500 widows and needy were fed by the grace and goodness of the Lord" (6.43.11) raises the question whether it is really a matter here of only "poor widows" or whether ministers, and thus salaried women, are also involved. For in this passage the clergy of Rome under Cornelius (251–53) are precisely enumerated: 1 bishop, 46 presbyters, 7 deacons, 7 subdeacons, 42 acolytes, 52 exorcists, lectors, and doorkeepers; then come the "widows and needy." The term *clergy* actually means "share of the inheritance" and goes back to the biblical narrative of the division of land among the twelve tribes of Israel; the sons of Levi (that is, the lineage of the priests) received no land but lived from the tithe, since "the Lord is their inheritance" (Deut. 18:2). Thus, according to early church usage, *clergy* included all who received money from the church.[107] Not until much later did only bishop, presbyter, and deacon count as "clergy" and stand over against the mass of the "laity."[108] The early church, by contrast, was characterized by a multiplicity of different orders.[109]

Thus with Eusebius, or even with Cornelius, the widows are placed here between members of the clergy and the "poor." It made no difference to the treasury whether the church widows were "paid" or "supported," but it did to the self-understanding of these women! In many of the early church disciplines we find a sharp polemic of the kind in the pastoral epistles against this order of unmarried women. In the Syriac *Didascalia,* a kind of pastoral handbook from the third century,[110] they are nonetheless granted a regular wage, despite all kinds of restrictions:[111] from the gifts to the clergy a portion goes to the widows, twice as much to presbyters and deacons,[112] and four times as much to the bishop.[113] Thus the parallelization of widows and the needy in Eusebius (or Cornelius) could conceal the tendency to downplay the significance of these women in the ecclesiastical hierarchy.

This suspicion is confirmed when we look at another document, whose author wanted to establish a certain tendency in Rome toward "conservative" church discipline a few decades before Cornelius: the *Apostolic Tradition*[114] of Hippolytus (d. 235). It begins with instruction as to how the bishop, who is elected by all, is to be ordained and how he is supposed to celebrate the Eucharist (1–6).[115] Then the ecclesiastical orders are precisely described and defined. The presbyters receive ordination through the laying on of hands by the bishop and all presbyters present; they have a part in the guiding ministry of the bishop, that is, a seat and a vote in the presbyterium (7). The deacon, however, receives only the laying on of the bishop's hand, since he is consecrated not to the "priesthood" but to the "service" of the bishop (not the church!) (8).[116] In the following comments it is again stressed that he has no part in the guiding ministry but is only the recipient of directives. Thus the text clearly reveals a rivalry between presbyters and deacons, which Hippolytus wants to decide in favor of the presbyters. In fourth place for Eusebius are the confessors, that is, witnesses to the faith who have survived martyrdom: they do not need any ordination but already possess, through their confession, the rank of presbyters (9).[117] Now Hippolytus comes to the widows and thus to speaking for the first time about women in church ministry, for he does not mention deaconesses. The text is rather long and, as we shall soon see, even more polemical in tone than the restrictive rules for the bishop's servant. Then comes the short instruction for the lector: "His appointment is accomplished by the bishop's handing over the book to him, but he is not to be ordained" (11). The directive for the virgin reads: "A virgin is not to be ordained; rather, the intention itself makes her a virgin" (12). The subject is then subdeacons (13) and those who claim to possess the gift of healing—both are likewise not to be ordained

(14). The description of church ministries is then followed by instructions for the reception of candidates for baptism.

Now we come to the *directives for widows:*

> When a widow is *appointed,* she is *not to be ordained* but elected by name. She is to be appointed only when her husband has already been dead a long time; if her husband has not been dead long, she is not to be trusted. But even if she is already old, she is to be tested for a period of time. For even the passions can grow old when one gives them free rein. Thus a widow is supposed to be *appointed only with words;*[118] then she is to join the rest of the [group]. She is *not to be ordained, since she does not offer the gift and has no liturgical ministry.* The ordination of clergy takes place in respect to the liturgy. The widow is *appointed for prayer,* but this is "the duty" of all. (19; emphasis added)[119]

Several things are striking about this text—not least of all, of course, the vicious insinuations in matters of sexuality, which do not appear in connection with any other church minister, since no other is expected to be celebate. As for the bishop, he is expected merely to be "blameless"—and not even this minimal demand is found in all manuscripts. For presbyter and deacon no conditions for ordination are listed. Hippolytus names confessors after deacons, although he grants them the rank of presbyters—a clear restriction.[120] Then he puts the deacons in their place. With the widows he becomes downright abusive.

Interestingly, the widows are named here before the lector, and their appointment is discussed in detail, whereas all the following instructions consist of only one sentence. In some manuscripts the order of instructions is changed, so that widows and virgins appear one after the other following the lector. In the judgment of the specialists, an "original order" cannot be reconstructed from the manuscripts,[121] yet there can be no mistaking that a shift means a demotion. The order is not unimportant, since it corresponds to seating in worship and rank in the church hierarchy.

Thus, if we overlook the confessors, who will be discussed in the section on martyresses, here the widows have their place after or beside the deacons. For the latter the act of induction into ministry involves the terms *appointment* and *ordination:* thus a legal and a liturgical term are used in parallel. The laying on of hands with a prayer as a gesture of blessing accompanies many worship activities, in particular induction into church ministries. Ordination with the laying on of hands (*cheirotonia*) is now reserved for the "higher clergy," which Hippolytus again divides into "priest" (that is, bishop and presbyter) and "servant" (deacon).[122] Concerning the position of widows, it is crucial that in the ecclesiastical orders there is a difference not only between clergy and laity but also between ordained and nonordained male and female clergy. But where is the second cut to be made? For the author of the *Apostolic Tradition* the answer is clear: after the deacons; ordination is denied to the remaining servants of the church.

It is also clear, however, that Hippolytus is not describing reality: he wants to establish a norm. We know that he met with resistance in the Roman church as well as with the Roman bishop—thus the praxis was without doubt more liberal. It is apparent that in fact the widows performed the functions of deaconesses, but there was reluctance to grant them the corresponding ecclesiastical rank. It was the Roman custom to receive widows into this collegium of clerics with a solemn ceremony, a custom that even Hippolytus did not dare to question. The promise of celibacy, which is naturally presupposed, does not seem to be prominent here (as it was with the virgins!), but rather the transference of duty. Hippolytus reduces and reinterprets the ritual: the widow no longer receives the laying on of hands, but is instead "appointed for prayer." But since prayer is the duty of everyone, as the author emphasizes, a special appointment loses all meaning.

Thus in the *Apostolic Tradition*, as well as in the *Didascalia*, we are confronted with the same phenomenon: the activities of women in teaching and liturgy are to be suppressed as much as possible. Yet this resistance attests the contrary praxis at least indirectly. Precisely the strong emphasis of Hippolytus that the aim of the appointment of widows is not liturgical service suggests that they may very well have participated in worship activities. It is true that in the *Didascalia* the "ministry" of widows is likewise reduced to prayer, but unlike them, a deaconess, as servant of the bishop, is at least allowed to participate in the catechesis and in the baptism of women.[123] Even if Eusebius does not mention deaconesses at all and characterizes widows as recipients of alms, we may presume that he has a similar interest. Thus in the third century, when the structure of ecclesiastical institutions was developing, there was intense debate on the relationship between presbyters and deacons and on whether women could perform ministries that presupposed an ordination reserved for "higher" clergy. In I.4 we will see how the dispute was settled.

Celibacy and Asceticism

One point should be noted especially: while all ascetic women lived a sexually continent life, by no means did all women who practiced sexual abstinence want to live ascetically. Consequently, "virgins and widows" are not to be regarded automatically as nuns. Rather, from the frequently encountered polemic against "rich virgins" one should infer that they declined marriage in order to take part in public life. Such a conflict in second-century Carthage between self-conscious virgins and some churchmen intent on subordination and seclusion is described by Tertullian (who as a theologian belongs to the latter group!): he wanted to establish the veiling of ecclesiastical virgins but does not seem to have been successful.[124]

The great independence of virgins and widows is explainable through the almost complete dissolution of the old *patria potestas* ("patriarchal power") in the imperial period.[125] After the death of the father, both married and unmarried women could exercise control over their income and increasingly could handle legal matters without the mediation of a guardian. Roman women were also emancipated from the *manus* ("hand," that is, the power) of the husband, for the norm was the so-called power-free marriage, which rested on the free consent of the partners, was entered without great formality, and could also be dissolved again relatively easily.[126] Thus the women who turned to the ecclesiastical order of widows and virgins were already emancipated. Here, in a socially recognized status and in clearly regulated economic circumstances, they had the possibility of assuming a different function from that of wife and mother. Thus in their renunciation of sexual activity, marriage, and family, these women were not necessarily ascetically motivated; not all of them, by any means, wanted to renounce life "in the world."

Those women living autonomously in the deserts of Egypt and Palestine, on the other hand, understood themselves expressly as ascetics and in this way contributed to the development of Christian monasticism in the third and fourth centuries.[127] Famous personages received the honorary title of "father" (*abba*) or "mother" (*amma*). Later their more or less lengthy sayings (sometimes even anecdotes) were collected under the designation *Apophthegmata*.[128] The almost one hundred fifty names include three women:[129] Amma Theodora, Amma Sarrha, and Amma Synkletike, who is described in an early church biography.[130] In the already-mentioned work of Palladius on asceticism, an Amma Talis is attested, whom inattentive editors and translators have allowed to become "Amatalis."[131] Also of significance is the "exclusive" (that is, excluding women) tradition of translation: the gender-neutral designation "sayings of the ancients" (in Greek a participle in the genitive plural that does not reveal whether it refers to men or women) becomes in many modern languages "sayings of the fathers"—a practice begun by the Latin *Apophthegmata Patrum*.

We learn nothing from Eusebius about these developments of ascetic life in the desert. Thus the (supposedly) Christian women ascetics serve the bishop of Caesarea mainly as an apologetic element—he seems not to have granted them an important role in real church life. Virgins were valued as the most beautiful decoration of the church, but only as decoration!

e. Women with Education

We have already encountered some examples of female education.[132] The women's choir in the bishop's church of Antioch under Paul of Samosata (7.30.2ff.) presupposes a musical culture. Anonyma, the foster mother of Origen,[133] is presented as "a woman very rich in the goods of this life and also otherwise very remarkable" (6.2.13). Regarding the already-mentioned virgin Juliana, education is not expressly emphasized, but her contact with Symmachus, whose works she possesses, suggests this assumption; Palladius speaks specifically of her "great erudition."[134] Education is also to be presupposed for the "believing sister Chrysophora"; Dionysius, bishop of Corinth, dedicated a doctrinal work to her (4.23.13).

Besides these witnesses two further passages are worthy of mention. In Origen's secretariat more than seven stenographers reportedly took turns there with his dictation; in addition a like number of copyists were busy, as well as "girls practiced in calligraphy" (6.23.2). Thus Origen's work was passed on by feminine hands—as are so many typescripts of male authors today! Finally, Eusebius tells about an Anonyma, a "very prominent and well-known Christian" from Alexandria, who dared to oppose the sexual advances of Maximin and as a result had to accept exile and the confiscation of her property; she was "famous on account of her wealth, her origins, and her education" (8.14.15).

Such a statement echoes the old Roman ideal for women of the upper class: beautiful, rich, prominent, educated—a "worldly" ideal that the ascetic circles of Christianity oppose. Tatian, the second-century apologist, addresses the Greeks quite disparagingly regarding the numerous educated but allegedly unbridled women of antiquity, "so that you will no longer mock our women because they occupy themselves with philosophy."[135] The passage gives notice that there were also many educated Christian women. Tatian accuses the Greeks of a "cult of women" because they let themselves be taught by female lips—and he thereby provides the counterpart of the Roman criticism of the "religion of women." He is silent about the fact that Christian women also taught in his time and prefers to let them sing hymns at the distaff. Yet he responds to the Hellenes with a certain pride: "But you do not want to concede that there are also intelligent women among us!"[136] We already see here an ambivalent attitude toward educating women: men boast of the intelligence of Christian women but would like to forbid their public instruction. Opponents are discredited with female stupidity, but female education adds luster to one's own side. Thus here too "educated women" serve as an instrument of apologetics—in reality they are feared.

Women of the Lower Class

Education is a privilege of the upper class. What was life like for lower-class women? As already stated, we cannot undertake a social-historical investigation here. Yet one thing can be ascertained without special effort: seeing a "discipleship of equals"[137] realized is not a concern of the bishop of Caesarea. He does not reflect on the slavery question.[138]

In the nineteenth century Franz Overbeck pointed out that the widespread opinion that Christianity effected the abolition of slavery rests on completely uninformed apologetics.[139] The restructuring of the old Roman social order was based primarily on economics. Moreover, our ideas of the oppression of slaves in late antiquity are often exaggerated. There is no doubt that slaves were second-class citizens, but they at least enjoyed a certain protection of the law and could even hold important positions, especially if they attained the status of the "emancipated." The extent to which all this was also true for female slaves requires its own investigation.[140]

In early Christianity the slavery question resulted in conflicts similar to those on the question of women. Initially equality was practiced widely in the churches; then a growing antiempancipatory attitude developed, which insisted on subordination. The timid argument, "Subject yourselves voluntarily so that the Greeks will take no offense," finally turned into the ideology that "The master/husband represents Christ or God." This intensification of the theological argument occurred within the so-called household rules of the New Testament and was continued by the apostolic fathers.[141] The martyr-bishop Ignatius of Antioch (d. ca. 110) gives clear instructions:

Let male and female slaves not behave arrogantly! They also should not puff themselves up but continue to be slaves to the glory of God, so that they may attain a better freedom from God. They should not long to be free at the expense of the church, so that they will not become slaves of desire.[142]

The quotation testifies indirectly that there were Christian men and women who thought differently and above all acted differently, namely, by releasing slaves and even purchasing their freedom. At that time the idea of abolishing the institution occurred to very few—not even to the slaves themselves. In the known insurrections they were fighting merely for an improvement in their situation. We find almost the same humanitarian ethos in non-Christians and Christians; the apostle Paul and the Roman philosopher Seneca—both victims of the emperor Nero—represent similar standpoints: slaves deserve the same human dignity as free people, and this must express itself in the concrete behavior of the free toward slaves. Yet the abolition of slavery is not demanded.[143]

In the privately organized cult associations of the Roman Empire, as also in Christianity, slaves and women were in part accepted as full-fledged members. The position of Christian missionary women at the head of house churches seems to have corresponded to the position of the *patrona* in the collegia:[144] basically, this function could also have been exercised by slave women. In Eusebius we find the name of a woman who could have been a *patrona* in Smyrna: Alke. Yet she belongs to the upper class. Ignatius greets "the name dear to me" in two letters.[145] In the martyrdom of Polycarp, which Eusebius cites, her brother Niketes, who does not belong to the church, is identified through her; he intervenes with the Roman administrator to keep the body of Polycarp from being turned over to the Christians.[146]

In the church history of Eusebius only one passage gives some hint of the ideals of the early period. The slave Blandina plays a central role in the report on the massacre of Christians in Lyon (177). We will meet her again in the chapter on martyresses. An early non-Christian testimony indicates that Blandina was not an isolated case: in the sporadic persecutions under Trajan (98–117) the well-known official Pliny (the younger) had intentionally tortured two *ancillae ministrae*—that is, women slaves who had a ministry in the Christian church—because he hoped to gain information about the worship of Christians.[147] Philo reports that the therapeutae fundamentally rejected slavery. As we saw, Eusebius claims this Jewish source as Christian, yet in his rather detailed description of the ascetic community he says nothing about the practice of equality in regard to slaves.[148] In Philo, by contrast, we read:

> They do not let themselves be served by slaves, since they regard the possession of slaves as completely contrary to nature. For nature brought everyone forth as free, yet the unrighteousness and greed of a few who strive for inequality, the source of all evil, brought people under their yoke and gave to the stronger ones power over the weaker ones. (§ 70)

We have no Christian source that speaks with such unambiguous language.[149] Yet at least in the monasteries the early ethos of the equality of slave and free was really practiced. By contrast, while the equality of men and women was advocated theoretically for the cloisters—the *Codex Justinianus* still speaks in the sixth century of equal laws for the two sexes[150]—the actual development, especially in the West, finally placed women in strictest confinement.[151]

f. Veneration of Women

To close this section we will look at traces of a special veneration of the women disciples immediately around Jesus. But first there are some miscellany that do not fit under the previous rubrics. Eusebius (citing the Jewish writer Josephus) tells of an act of desperation by a prominent woman named Maria, daughter of Eleazar, who in the famine of the Jewish war killed her own son (3.6.21ff.). From Justin's *Apology* he adopts the report of an Anonyma converted to Christianity, who tried in vain to keep her husband from leading a dissolute life and finally sought a divorce, whereupon the husband took her and her Christian catechist to court. This led to the martyrdom of the teacher and others. The woman herself received an initial delay in the trial, and the outcome is not reported (4.17.2ff.).[152] Also mentioned are some prostitutes who under threat of torture are forced to make false statements about perverse practices of Christians (9.5.2). Finally, there is a significant omission: Eusebius reports a debate on preaching by the laity (the topic here is Origen), and examples are offered to justify this practice (6.19.16ff.). The question whether women can preach is not even discussed here, although it was still controversial during the time of the famous Alexandrian teacher—Origen was against it, though a layperson himself.[153] Thus for him women were already "second-class laypeople." Naturally, this is even more true of Eusebius.

Two reports of Eusebius contain traces of venerated women disciples of Jesus. A story from the *Gospel of the Hebrews,* passed on by Papias, concerns an Anonyma who "was accused before the Lord of many sins"[154] (3.39.17). Regrettably we learn nothing about the content of this story, but the report at least attests to the memory of women who belonged to the circle around Jesus and passed on his message in the early church.

Much clearer is the tradition of the Anonyma who suffered from hemorrhages and was healed by Jesus (Matt. 9:20–22). In Caesarea Philippi her house and various other monuments were shown. Eusebius describes very exactly a devotional image in front of this building, which he himself saw:

> On a tall stone base at the gates of her house stood a bronze statue of a woman, resting on one knee and resembling a suppliant with arms outstretched. Facing this was another of the same material, an upright figure of a man with a double cloak neatly draped over his shoulders and his hand stretched out to the woman. Near his feet on the stone slab grew an exotic plant, which climbed up to the hem of the bronze cloak and served as a remedy for illnesses of every kind. The statue, which was said to resemble the features of Jesus . . . (7.18; Williamson, 302)

In Eusebius's opinion the work was created by Roman contemporaries of Jesus in gratitude for his miracles. Presumably it was originally a devotional image of

Aesculapius, the ancient god of healing, who is often represented with a plant[155]—a thoroughly worthy counterpart of the salvation-bringing Son of God of Christianity, as can be seen from the traditions of the famous ancient shrine in Epidaurus. Greek theology can build on ancient concepts of redemption when it interprets the Christian *sotēria* ("salvation") with the metaphor of healing and describes the "Savior" as a physician.[156]

The shrine of the woman with hemorrhages must have had great significance, for when the Roman emperor Julian (361–63) wanted to help the old religion regain its rightful place, he went to the trouble of destroying the stone.[157] If we may anticipate Sozomen here, it is significant how he changes the report of Eusebius. The latter told the story in order to show that even the Hellenes venerated Jesus and erected a memorial to him, which portrayed him true to life. The local cult's memory of a female New Testament figure still shines through clearly. Sozomen, by contrast, reports on the statue as an example of an anti-Christian iconoclasm, which was punished by a miracle:

> After Julian heard that in Caesarea Philippi [in Phoenician Paneas] there was a famous statue of Christ that was erected by the woman healed from hemorrhages, he had it torn down and a statue of himself erected. Yet fire fell from heaven . . . [Christians were ultimately able to save the fragments of the destroyed stone]. (5.21.1ff.)

Sozomen then refers expressly to Eusebius's story and adopts from it the description of the healing plant, yet he does not mention the healed woman. The memory of Anonyma's shrine is erased—only a memorial to a votive image remains.

Did such changes in historical tradition take place unconsciously or intentionally? We can no longer ask the author. In any case, we have here a typical example of how women's traditions were suppressed in the consciousness of Christendom. We will meet many more similar cases.

4. The Marginalization of Women

Socrates, Sozomen, and Theodoret

In our first statistical comparison of the church histories we established that our fifth-century writers mention *far fewer women* than Eusebius and that those named *often remain anonymous*. Now we want to investigate in detail the material available in Socrates, Sozomen, and Theodoret, using the same framework as that used with the church history of Eusebius.

a. Suppression after the Time of Persecution

As might be expected, in the later church histories the martyr traditions do not have as great a significance as in Eusebius. After Constantine's edict of tolerance (313), acts of violence against Christians occur primarily outside or on the edge of the empire. Only Sozomen, in his reports on the persecutions in Persia under Sapor II (309–78),[158] still mentions names and individual fates (2.8–15). At the end of his description he expressly emphasizes that women were among the victims (2.14). He also reports on the persecution of the Arian Goths, who were converted by the Bible translator Ulfilas (or Wulfila; d. 383),[159] and mentions "women who held small children by the hand or an infant at the breast"; they were burned up together with the men in a tent church (6.37). Yet caution is advised regarding the historicity of the details described in these various reports, since we are dealing here with a developed genre of martyrdom literature in which the cruelty of the persecutors is painted in the harshest colors. The mention of women also serves this purpose.

In particular we learn from Sozomen about the virgin Anonyma, the daughter of a presbyter (2.11): she was executed with her father (Ananias), another presbyter (Abedechalaas), and the Persian bishop (Simeon) of Seleucia-Ktesiphon. The same author describes in more detail the martyrdom of the sister of this bishop. The virgin Tarbula[160] lived with her slave Anonyma and her sister, also Anonyma, an ecclesiastical widow, in a kind of ascetic house community. Jews supposedly held that the women were sorceresses and were responsible for the illness of the queen; also Tarbula renounces the freedom offered to her and her companions at the price of sexual intercourse with one of the judges (2.12).[161] The especially cruel martyrdom of a group of virgins in Heliopolis is interpreted by Sozomen as the revenge of the populace for the fact that Emperor Constantine forbade the prostitution of young girls[162] and destroyed the temple of Venus (5.10). The church historian values, as an example of heroic chastity, the voluntary death of the Christian woman Nonnichia, which she took upon herself not for her faith but in order to escape violation by the Vandals (9.13).[163] Finally, the martyr tradition includes Sozomen's story about Zeno, the later bishop of Gaza, who successfully fled; one Anonyma (in an involved miracle story typical of Sozomen) delivers the bones of the murdered victims, which she hid at night (5.9).

Theodoret reports a new outbreak of persecution under Emperor Julian (361–63), who sought one last time to prevent the victory of Christianity. In Gaza and Askalon priests and virgins are named as victims (3.7). As already seen in Sozomen, it is notable that ecclesiastical virgins are perceived by the authorities as a special group within the top Christian leadership. They are apparently counted among the "officeholders" of whom, in accordance with imperial persecution policy, an example is to be made.[164]

The persecution by Roman officials comes to an end, but then come the first bloody acts of violence by Christians against Christians. Both Socrates and Theodoret report how in Alexandria orthodox are brought down by Arians in the most cruel way. Both cite Athanasius (d. 373), the bishop of this city and best-known defender of the Nicene Creed, who had to go into exile more than once. According to his report, even "orphans and widows" were not spared; not only men but once again virgins were especially mistreated: they were stripped and some were whipped to death. The few survivors ended up in exile.[165] Theodoret reports again on brutal violence against virgins in Alexandria at the hands of officials under Lucius the Arian, who is made indirectly responsible

(4.22). Also Socrates, referring to an eyewitness, tells once more about brutalities against women that are carried out by followers of the Arian bishop Macedonius (342–60) in Constantinople and vicinity (2.38).[166] Socrates is honest
enough also to report an especially gruesome murder committed by Christians
almost a century later in Alexandria; the victim was the Neoplatonist philosopher
Hypatia (7.15)—she and her tragic end will be discussed in the context of educated women. Thus we find sexual sadism toward women even among Christians—no less deplorable than that of the Romans against the martyresses who
are the topic of the next chapter.

Anonyma of Edessa

All three church histories report, finally, the courageous action of an
Anonyma, who through her readiness for martyrdom prevented a massacre
among Christians.[167] The incident, which happened under the Arian Valens
(375–78), had already been reported by Rufinus (2.5). In Edessa the emperor
gives his prefect the order to use force to prevent the gathering of the orthodox
on the square in front of the church of St. Thomas, which is in Arian hands.
Though a pagan, the prefect warns them, but they gather anyway. When the attack is supposed to begin, a woman steps forward, only scantily clad and with a
child in her arms, in order—as she says upon inquiry—to participate in the martyrdom. Now the prefect refuses to carry out the order—whereupon the emperor
finally desists from his madness, according to Rufinus. Whether Anonyma hoped
with her brave deed to be able to prevent the massacre or whether she actually
longed for martyrdom cannot be clearly determined from the story.

In the presentation of this incident, Socrates essentially follows Rufinus, yet
he moves the gathering into the church and does not mention that the prefect
was a pagan and risked his own life, nor does he say anything about the woman's
meager clothing.

Sozomen expands the story. He gives the prefect the name Modestus and
makes him an Arian. The clothing "improper for women" becomes the means of
getting the attention of the soldiers (in Rufinus Anonyma has no time to dress
properly). In a somewhat longer dialogue the prefect convinces the emperor not
to carry out the plan of killing. The story ends: "So the city of Edessa committed itself publicly to the peaceful settlement of issues of faith."

Theodoret goes even further in his elaboration of the story, yet he says nothing about the religion of the prefect Modestus and is silent about his rescue attempt; he also does not mention the scanty clothing. The prefect finally steers
the emperor away from the deadly order with the argument: "We will harvest
only shame from such a process, and we will not break their courage," but he
must instead gather priests and deacons, who must either divert the people away
from the catholic faith or go into exile. The story continues with the report on
the fate of these priests.

Here we will not undertake a detailed exegesis of this "synoptic" piece nor
propose a theory on the basis of this individual example, yet four features should

be emphasized in the elaboration of the story. (1) The later tradition gives the prefect a name but *leaves the woman in anonymity,* although she is the real heroine of the story. (2) *The apologetic function of the story is changed.* In Rufinus the inhumanity of the persecutor (N.B.: a Christian emperor!) is juxtaposed with the humanity of the unbelieving Roman and the bravery of the believing Christian woman: both want to prevent murderous madness. Socrates and especially Sozomen, on the other hand, shine a dimmer light on the prefect's deed, and Theodoret turns him completely into a pragmatist. (3) In Theodoret's reworking of the story *the female figure is depersonalized:* she is the model of the "soul who, inflamed with divine zeal, no longer knows human fear." (4) Finally, he *romanticizes martyrdom:* for such a soul "this terror is pure play," and death is "desired." What effect could such a reading of tradition have on the concrete living conditions of women? This question will be posed again later after the investigation of further examples.

b. Hierarchization of the Churches

When we now turn again to groups outside the mainstream church, we discover that in Socrates, Sozomen, and Theodoret, as in Eusebius, there are under the rubric "women heretics" only a few individual female personalities mentioned either by name or anonymously. The special susceptibility of the female sex to heresy finds no confirmation whatever. Norbert Brox has correctly stated that remarks on alleged successes with women served merely to discredit the heretics.[168] Yet, far more than heretics, such statements discredit women, and not as individuals but fundamentally and generally. Although the overwhelming majority of heretic leaders were males, it is curious that the conclusion was never drawn that men are extremely susceptible to heresy and therefore should be excluded from teaching.

Nevertheless, as we have said, the early historiographers do not establish a connection between female gender and false doctrine; they are exactly as little (or as much) interested in women heretics as in women followers of the catholic church—they devote special attention to neither. Only in Theodoret can we detect in the polemic against Arians a mild tendency to involve women. Thus he reports on trials against advocates of orthodoxy in which Arian women play a role (1.4), accuses young women in this confession of bringing Christianity into disrepute through their "unbridledness" (ibid.), and compares the pro-Arian influence of the empress Domnica with the seductive abilities of Eve; more precisely, he equates her consort Valens with Adam, who likewise let himself be seduced by his wife (4.12). Finally, an orthodox bishop is murdered by a stone thrown by an Arian Anonyma (5.4). Thus these representatives of Arianism are characterized by Theodoret in a completely negative way, yet the bishop of Cyrrhus does not develop his anti-Arian polemic into a basic theory for the disparagement of the female sex.

Through Theodoret we even meet a group of positively described women in the mainstream church in Rome, who resist the pro-Arian policy of the emperor.

The bishop there, Liberius, had been sent into exile by Constantius in the year 355. When the emperor came again to the western capital two years later, some prominent Roman women went to their highly placed husbands and threatened to leave them and follow the bishop into exile if the husbands did not effect his return through the emperor. They replied to their wives: "For us men he knows no pardon, yet for you he will be considerate: either he will fulfill your petition or turn you down without punishing you." The wives let themselves be persuaded, went to the emperor, and were actually able to have their wish fulfilled.[169] Thus here we have an example of women especially unsusceptible to heresy!

But let us turn again to women in other confessions. Actually, we learn very little about them. What Theodoret reports about Arian women has already been related. Otherwise, only women from the imperial family are named as supporters of this teaching; the sister of Constantine was sympathetic to it and before her death took one of the Arian followers under her wing;[170] with the advent of the doctrinal controversies around Arius, these questions were expressly laid before the members of the court and their wives for discussion;[171] later the empresses Domnica and Justina were convinced and contentious Arians.[172]

Manichaean women are the topic in two different contexts. Both Socrates and Sozomen mention an Anonyma who causes difficulties for one bishop: he is reproached for having admitted her to Communion without prior renunciation of her false doctrine (6.9/7.12). Considerably more interesting is what we learn from Socrates about another Anonyma, who is supposed to have played an important role in the tradition of this esoteric teaching even before Mani (d. 277). Eusebius writes this name *ho maneis* and derives it without scruple from the Greek *mania*, "insanity" (7.31). Yet for Socrates this is too superficial, and he undertakes a careful investigation of the origins of this Persian sect, which was close to Gnosticism (and later developed into an autonomous religion),[173] but he uses sources that are questionable by today's research standards (1.22).[174] He calls the movement a "hellenizing Christianity," which he traces back to a mixture of Empedocles, Pythagoras, and Egyptian wisdom. The connection is explained by the marriage of a prisoner of war (Anonyma) from Thebes to a Saracen (Skythianos), who followed her into her homeland. The teaching was finally preserved in several books by a student (Terebinthus). After his death they fell into the hands of an Anonyma with whom he had lived. She acquired the seven-year-old Mani as a slave, gave him his freedom, enabled him to be educated, and ultimately turned over to him the crucial writings of this Greek-Egyptian Christian teaching. The historical value of the source cannot be discussed here, but it is, in any case, noteworthy that the religious tradition is traced back not simply to the name-giver but to the long chain of tradition in which at least one, if not two, educated women played a key role.[175] These female figures in Socrates are not used to place the teachings of Manichaeanism in a questionable light.

In Socrates, as in Sozomen, we meet Macedonian women, that is, followers of the already-mentioned Pneumatomachian Macedonius. Socrates mentions only the founding of monasteries and convents by a former deacon of this heterodox bishop (2.38), whereas Sozomen passes on three stories about women of this confession. The first, an Anonyma, is forced by her husband to convert but remains secretly true to the sect. Her slave helps her in a host-switching maneuver during Communion, whereupon the bread changes into a stone (which can be seen, complete with the impression of the teeth, among the cathedral treasures in Constantinople!). Naturally, the scare leads to "genuine" conversion (8.5).

The second Macedonian woman mentioned is a deaconess Eusebia, who has preserved the bones of forty martyrs of Sebaste in her house. Before her death she asks the orthodox monks to bury her there and put the relics in her coffin, without informing anyone about it, and the monks comply. And this in turn made it possible for the empress Pulcheria to discover the bones of the martyrs by means of a vision and to make them accessible for general veneration (9.2–3).

In the context of the veneration of relics, we meet through Sozomen another Macedonian deaconess:[176] Matrona (7.21). This time it is the head of John the Baptist that gives rich nourishment to the church historian's belief in miracles and delight in making up stories. The Arian emperor Valens had already tried to transport to Constantinople this relic that was found in Cilicia, but the execution of his plan was thwarted while in progress by an incident regarded as God's judgment: the donkey pulling the cart refused to go any farther. The head remained at the place of the miracle, and a local cult had apparently developed, for when the orthodox emperor Theodosius made a renewed attempt to bring the relic to Constantinople, it was in the custody of an ecclesiastical[177] virgin and deaconess named Matrona and a presbyter Vincent—both of the Macedonian confession. The latter converted to the faith of the emperor, but Matrona energetically resisted the ruler. After tedious negotiations she gave up the relic, but she could not be moved to change her religious conviction, although Theodosius himself urged her to do so. In spite of her stubborn adherence to the "heresy," Sozomen writes, full of obvious admiration: "She remained in this place as the head[178] of ecclesiastical virgins, famous for her piety and wisdom. Many who were shaped by Matrona's instruction are still distinguished by their honorable character" (7.21).

Otherwise Sozomen mentions heterodox women only once more: the female followers of Apollinarius (d. ca. 390) sing at the loom songs that popularize their doctrinal opinion[179]—the men do likewise in their places of work (6.25). We have already encountered the singing of hymns as a means of spreading heresy or orthodoxy in connection with Paul of Samosata. Sozomen reports in detail how John Chrysostom in Constantinople successfully imitated the Arian singing processions and in this way finally surpassed his opponents (8.8). A similar competition occurs between the cultic events of the other religions and those of Christianity[180]—instead of the long-practiced tolerance in the Roman Empire, we now have the intentional persecution of Judaism and Hellenism. In 391 Christianity is declared the state religion, and other cults are now prohibited; the old temples and religious institutions are violently destroyed. Here we can only mention this sad chapter in Christian history.

Regarding women in other confessions we must state that just as in catholicism, they became marginal figures. The old movements in which women played an important role either shrank or developed in parallel to the mainstream church and had similar hierarchical structures. Women are no longer found in positions of leadership in either. Yet inside and outside mainstream Christianity what is new vis-à-vis Eusebius is the attestation of a special church ministry for women: concerning deaconesses Sozomen recalls numerous names and sometimes lengthy stories. We have already met two of them because they belonged to a church regarded as heretical—we will talk later about their orthodox sisters.[181] Indirectly we may conclude from the stories of Matrona and Eusebia how close to each other orthodox and heterodox in fact often were. It is especially clear with Eusebia: she had herself buried by orthodox monks beside the bones of orthodox martyrs, which were finally rediscovered by an orthodox empress! Whatever one thinks of the elaborate miracle story of the rediscovery of the bones of the forty martyrs, the fame of the burial place of Eusebia leads us to infer that she herself must have been an influential woman who was even esteemed by followers of the mainstream church. The same is without doubt true of Matrona.

c. The Dying Out of Prophecy

If the later church histories speak of one group, the deaconesses, that Eusebius does not mention, another category has completely disappeared: the prophetesses. Even male prophets no longer elicit interest. Rufinus had characterized Bishop Spyridon—father of the virgin Irene,[182] who worked miracles posthumously—as "a man from the order of prophets";[183] both Socrates and Sozomen omit this information (1.12/1.11). Socrates mentions the names Maximilla and Montanus, but only in a vague allusion and without dealing with the question of the prophetic charisma (2.37).[184] It is true that Sozomen occasionally gives reports of prophesying (6.40; 7.5, 22, 29), yet these are "miracles," not "prophecy." He applies this to the daughters of Philip, because they, like the apostle Peter and the evangelist John, raised someone from the dead (7.27); they have no meaning for him as prophetesses or virgins.

Yet even if the church historians no longer name real prophets and prophetesses, they still testify indirectly to two things: (1) in their time prophecy still enjoyed the highest reputation both inside and outside Christianity; (2) in both places it was dying out or had already died out. A graphic example of this is the story about the Apollo temple in Daphne near Antioch,[185] which through the Castilian source is connected with the famous shrine in Delphi: in Daphne the "demon" could no longer speak, because the Christian martyr Babylas was buried in the immediate vicinity. The priests of Apollo also make the grave of Babylas responsible for the silence of their oracle; therefore the emperor Julian orders its removal. The Christians must acquiesce, but they transform the moving process into a popular demonstration against the old "idols." In another story Theodoret has a pagan girl proclaim confession to Christ through a demon, "as did the maid in Philippi possessed by the pythonic spirit"[186] (4.21)—here too non-Christian prophecy stands in the background and is appropriated for Christian purposes through miracle stories.

Yet it is not always presumed that a demon is behind the ancient oracles. Many Christians accorded them authority and saw in many of their prophecies a fore-telling of the future salvation through the coming of Jesus.[187] Sozomen begins his church history with the indication that not only Hebrew but also Greek prophets—namely, "the Sibyl and other oracles"—foretold future events (1.1).[188] In the story of the discovery of the cross by the empress Helena, the Sibyl is even quoted: "O blessed wood on which God hung"[189] (2.1). Socrates reports something similar: in Egypt Christians saw crosslike hieroglyphs in the Serapis temple as an announcement of the passion of Christ (5.17). Thus in the fifth century we still find a widespread high estimation of men and women seers.

When the Phrygian movement around Prisca, Maximilla, and Montanus re-proached the mainstream church, saying that in it the prophetic charisma had died out, this may have largely corresponded to the factual situation. Even the testimonies from the second century cited by Eusebius name no contemporaries as charismatic proclaimers on their side, but rather predecessors from the early postapostolic generation: the daughters of Philip, Ammia, and Quadratus. Nev-ertheless, when Eusebius wrote his church history at the beginning of the fourth century, the memory of the prophetic charisma was still so alive that catholicism felt compelled to legitimate itself. Therefore Eusebius refers to Justin (d. ca. 165) and Irenaeus (bishop of Lyon in 177), who had witnessed the continuation of prophecy.[190] A century later, however, prophets and prophetesses are no longer mentioned. The connection between the disappearance of prophecy and the sup-pression of women will be examined in the third chapter of this book.[191]

d. The Domestication of the Unmarried

In his report on the therapeutae Eusebius said of these "philosophizers" that they "practiced the glowing faith of the *prophetic lifestyle*"[192] (2.17.5), which he derived from the commonality of goods in the early Jerusalem church (Acts 2:45).[193] Do we find this idea also in Socrates, Sozomen, and Theodoret? A certain contradiction is already ascertainable in Eusebius. On the one hand, he saw in the women adher-ents of the "philosophy" renouncing marriage and life in the world a *specificum christianum;* on the other hand, except for the testimony of Philo we find in him no report about individual women ascetics or groups of women ascetics.

Silence about Autonomous Women Ascetics

We can again discern a similar paradox: it is precisely in Sozomen, who expressly wants to erect a memorial to the monks—and does so[194]—that we find hardly a mention of female ascetic lifestyles. In the evaluation of Philo's report he is more cautious and precise than Eusebius, but he also holds that the therapeutae are Jews who have converted to Christianity and retain their Jewish practices (1.12). From his predecessor he adopts the Philo quotation in which virgins are mentioned.[195] In his work a positive witness to Christian convents occurs only indirectly through an opponent of Christianity: he reports that the emperor Julian, in order to limit the success of the new religion, sought to imitate its institutions within the old. In this context Sozomen writes: "He decided to found cloisters for men and women who want to devote themselves to philosophy, as well as shelters for foreigners and the poor and for other philanthropic purposes" (5.16). Independent women ascetics are mentioned only as objects of ecclesiastical-imperial legislation, which resists feminine strivings for autonomy.[196]

The silence regarding women ascetics is all the more astonishing because Sozomen apparently used a work of Palladius[197] to which we owe much information about women ascetics. Socrates, who writes comparatively little about monasticism,[198] refers expressly to this book and emphasizes that its author "also mentions several women who have adopted the same lifestyle as the men" (4.23). Theodoret names in his church history only a few monks who were directly involved in the Arian controversies (4.26–28), but in regard to their lifestyles he refers to his earlier writing *Historia Religiosa*. We will speak of this shortly.

For comparison purposes, let us first take a look at the book of Palladius (d. before 431), which was known to all three authors and is entitled *Paradise*. This author lived in Egypt as a monk for two years, before he became the bishop of Helenopolis in Bithynia. He was also a close friend and follower of John Chrysostom. Socrates and Sozomen used his book as a source for their accounts; using the same model, Theodoret created a companion piece focused on Syria. Tradition has given this work of Palladius the formal designation *Historia Lausiaca*[199] after the name of Lausus, who commissioned it. In addition, we also find the title *The Life of the Fathers*, although it was the express intention of the writer also to describe the life of the *mothers*, as we will soon see. The actual title, *Paradise*, which is based on the content, is seldom used, although it says precisely what the author had in mind: life in asceticism makes possible a return to the original paradisiacal state, as well as an anticipation of the final paradisiacal state; it is the *bios angelikos*, the angelic life beyond human sexuality.[200]

First, the statistical information in *Paradise* is amazing: according to the titles of the seventy-one chapters or stories, twenty deal explicitly with one or two outstanding women ascetics. Chapter 33 describes the cloister of nuns in Tabennisi, the female counterpart of the community of men founded there by Pachomius. In chapter 41 Palladius lists by name twelve more women ascetics, in addition to numerous others who are mentioned in the remaining stories. By contrast, in his *Pious History or Ascetic Way of Life* [201] Theodoret used only the last two in order to mention in an appendix, as it were, the existence of ascetic women. Socrates refers, as we said, expressly to Palladius, whereas Sozomen adopts the material but is silent about the source. The latter reports exclusively on male ascetics.

A second feature is striking in comparing the two works on organized asceticism: from the beginning *Paradise* is *conceived on the basis of equality*. The prologue begins with the following words:[202]

> In this book is recorded the wonderfully virtuous and ascetic life of *the holy fathers,* monks, and anchorites in the desert. It is written for the emulation and imitation of those who wish to succeed in the heavenly way of life and to take the journey which leads to the kingdom of heaven. It is written also to commemorate women far advanced in years and *illustrious God-inspired mothers* who have performed feats of virtuous asceticism in strong and perfect intention, as exemplars and models for those women who wish to wear the crown of self-abnegation and chastity. (ACW 34:17; emphasis added)

The author probably did not have in mind a distinctive, sex-specific modeling function, since the ideal of asceticism, after all, is the attainment of "sexlessness," so that one no longer has to distinguish between man and woman. At the end of the introduction, the addressee Lausus is even expressly challenged to seek contact with holy men *and* women.

In the short pages of the prologue the "fathers" are hardly ever named alone; we find an explicit parallel in five instances: men like women are fighters, bearers of God, and athletes—athletes of Christ. The metaphor of the athlete for Christ and the Christians who follow him was adopted from martyrdom theology.[203] In the translations there is a noticeable tendency to avoid pugnacious vocabulary for women, which might equate them with men and thus with Christ.[204] For Palladius ascetic women and men belong to the same heavenly living order and living fellowship, the *ouranios politeia.* Yet they also have the same weaknesses: men like women come to ruin through ascetic pride. At the beginning and the end of the introduction we find the same stressed parallelization of the two sexes; the topic is—literally!—"male and female fathers."

A similarly programmatic text introduces the already-mentioned chapter 41 with the title "Saintly Women." At the same time, a harsh critique of Jerome is voiced there, because he did not respect equality in practice (Jerome fell into the cross fire of criticism in Rome because of his extremely ascetic preaching and finally withdrew to the Holy Land with the prominent widow Paula and her daughter Eustochium[205]):

> I must also commemorate in this book the courageous [Gk. "manly"[206]] women to whom God granted struggles equal to those of men, so that no one could plead as an excuse that women are too weak to practice virtue successfully. Now I have seen a good many of them and I have associated with refined[207] women among virgins and widows. Among these was the Roman matron Paula, who was mother of Toxotius, a woman highly distinguished in the spiritual life. A certain Jerome from Dalmatia stood in her way, for she was well able to surpass everyone else, being a genius of a woman. He thwarted her with his jealousy and prevailed upon her to work to his own end and purpose. (ACW 34:117–18)

In a way similar to the beginning of the foregoing quotation, the prologue had already said at one point that women ascetics are "more like men in their nature" (ACW 34:19)—without doubt a questionable characterization. Here is a mixture of two different traditions of the early Christian ascetic understanding of equality in Christ. The one conceptual model of the relationship of the sexes (continence always being presupposed) is strictly egalitarian; I call it the *transcendence model:* women like men overcome their natural disposition as sexual beings; through continence they anticipate the asexuality of heaven, in which all differences are suspended. The other conceptual model is androcentric and in fact an *assimilation model:* through asceticism the woman becomes a man, as it were; here, apparently, only she has to overcome her natural disposition as a sexual being. In fact, the second model also leads to equality within the ascetic way of life, but the man is the model and norm of human existence to which the woman must assimilate. In the assimilation model, the stage is set for the increasingly favored parallel woman-man/body-spirit, which will lead to the *subordination model.* This is carried out in an exemplary way in Augustine (d. 430), who sets up the chain Christ/church, man/woman, spirit/flesh:

> In each case the first "member" looks after the second, while the second serves the first; all, however, are good: the beauty of the order is preserved in them in that the ones exercise leadership in an excellent way, while the others remain in appropriate submission.[208]

It is true that in the stories Palladius recounts about women and men ascetics we occasionally also find elements denigrating women, yet on the whole the transcendence model dominates with him: sexual continence leads both to the equality of men and women and to a very natural interaction of the sexes. Among the personalities who are described in *Paradise* we also find a married couple who with a daughter have chosen this way of life (chap. 41)—and this case is certainly not unique.[209]

Theodoret proceeds entirely differently in his *Pious History,* whose title could be freely translated as "history of friendship with God":[210] neither in his preface nor in his long epilogue on divine and holy love does he mention women ascetics. Not until the beginning of his chapter 29 do they become the topic:

> After describing the lives of the most excellent men, I think it is appropriate also to consider the women who have fought not less but perhaps even more. They deserve even greater praise, since they, with a weaker nature, showed the same courage as the men and cleanse the race of the primeval shame. (29.1)[211]

At the end of chapter 30 Theodoret mentions as a group other women whose lives "deserve notice," in order then to express this general reflection:

> Since Christ the Lord, born of a virgin, honored virginity, the pastures of virginity thrive and offer to their Creator these fragrant, unwilting flowers, to him who does not distinguish between male and female virtue and does not split philosophy in two. There is a difference in the bodies but not in the souls. For according to the holy apostle, "In Christ Jesus there is neither male nor female"; men and women are granted one faith. (30.5)

Yet the whole state of affairs in the book does not match these programmatic as-
surances: whereas Palladius, in addition to the chapters expressly devoted to
women, also mentions further women ascetics, in Theodoret we find information on three particular personalities only in the mentioned final chapters, although at the end he stresses again that among the "wrestlers" there were many
women (30.6). Thus with him we find traces of the transcendence model only
rarely; in fact, assimilation dominates: "manly women" are the ideal, but at the
same time they are the exception to the rule.

One feature should be emphasized: in both works on the ascetic way of life
there is virtually no phobic fear of the opposite sex. The woman as the epitome
of temptation for the monk—a widespread topos in ascetic literature—does not
occur in these stories. In Palladius free and natural togetherness is very vividly
presented. It is true that Theodoret states that Marana and Kyra received only
women visitors, but for him, the bishop, they often made a willing exception;
moreover, they traveled to both Jerusalem and the Thecla shrine in Seleucia (29).
Regarding Domnina, it is reported from the beginning that she lived with her
family, attended community worship services, and cared for the poor (30).

Against the background of these two contemporary works—especially that of
Palladius, which Socrates and Sozomen used as a source—the almost total silence
of our church histories on individual Spiritual mothers is surprising. Was there a
conscious strategy here? At the same time, both authors report in great detail the
ecclesiastical measures against the strivings of free women ascetics for autonomy.

These reports are about the Synod of Gangra, which condemned Eustathius,
the bishop of Sebaste, because of ascetic "heresies," probably in the year 340.[212]
Socrates summarizes the accusations without comment—hence, we must assume
that he held them to be correct and justified. Here is his summary:

> Eustathius [had] done many things repugnant to the ecclesiastical canons. For he
> had *"forbidden marriage,"* and maintained that meats were to be abstained from:
> *he even separated many from their wives,* and persuaded those who disliked to
> assemble in the churches to commune at home. Under the pretext of piety, he also
> *seduced servants from their masters.* He himself wore the *habit of a philosopher,*
> and induced his followers to adopt a new and extraordinary garb, directing that
> the hair of women should be cropped.[213] He permitted the prescribed fasts to be
> neglected, but recommended fasting on Sundays. In short, he forbade prayers to
> be offered in the houses of married persons, and declared that both the benedic-
> tion and the communion of a presbyter who continued to live with a wife whom
> he might have lawfully married, while still a layman, ought to be shunned as an
> abomination. For doing and teaching these things and many others of a similar na-
> ture, a Synod convened . . . at Gangra in Paphlagonia deposed him, and anathe-
> matized his opinions. (2.43; NPNF, 2nd series, 2:72–73; emphasis added)

According to today's scholarship, these accusations concern not the actual
teachings and practices of the bishop of Sebaste but at most those of some extreme followers.[214] The great Cappadocian theologian Basil of Caesarea[215] was

a student and friend of Eustathius—their break came later, not because of the ascetic questions but because of pneumatology.[216]

Sozomen is also among the defenders of the ascetically oriented bishop (3.14). His report on Eustathius appears in a group of stories about holy monks and monastery founders—Socrates' report, by contrast, was inserted in a series of condemned heretics. Sozomen talks first about the founding of a large community of monks in Armenia; Eustathius may even be the true author of the ascetic writings attributed to Basil, according to Sozomen. He says that Eustathius is alleged to have violated the rules of the church, but that in the judgment of many these accusations are unjustified. Rather:

> Many persons, however, justify him from this accusation, and throw the blame upon some of his disciples, who condemned marriage, refused to pray to God in the houses of married persons, despised married presbyters, fasted on Lord's days, held their assemblies in private houses, denounced the rich as altogether without part in the kingdom of God, contemned those who partook of animal food. They did not retain the customary tunics and stoles for their dress, but used a strange and unwonted garb, and made many other innovations. *Many women were deluded by them, and left their husbands; but not being able to practice continence, they fell into adultery. Other women, under the pretext of religion, cut off their hair, and behaved otherwise than is fitting to a woman, by arraying themselves in men's apparel.* (3.14.33–34; NPNF, 2nd series, 2:293; emphasis added)

After the condemnation of these practices by the Synod of Gangra, Sozomen continues, Eustathius forwent conspicuous clothing; he was no great orator but nonetheless usually knew how to convince. Sozomen then gives examples that all have to do with sexual abstinence.

The obvious contrasts in the reports of Socrates and Sozomen make clear the conflict between the "bourgeois" and "ascetic" camps among Christians. It is notable here that women do not fare well with the representative of the ascetic orientation: they are not capable of living a continent life. Let us now look at the way the two authors deal with the wording of the synodal letter:

> Since they [the followers of Eustathius] forbid marriage and assert that none who are married can set their hope on God, many married women deceived by them have left their husbands, and husbands their wives. Since these women[217] could not remain continent, they became adulteresses and were therefore covered with shame. (introd.)

Socrates adopts the (alleged) prohibition of marriage and says in a neutral formulation that Eustathius "separated many married people from their marriage partners"; Sozomen, however, mentions only the wives who leave their husbands and is silent on the opposite phenomenon. He adopts from the synodal letter the defamatory assertion that women were incapable of continence.

On the haircuts and clothing of women ascetics, the synod also expresses itself in more detail than the later historians:

Against custom, women wear the clothes of men, since they think they can achieve holiness in this way; under the pretext of piety some have even had their natural hair cut off. (introd.)

When under the pretext of asceticism a woman cuts off the hair that God gave her in order to remind her of her dependence, and she thereby abolishes, as it were, the commandment of obedience, she is excommunicated. (canon 17)

When under the pretext of asceticism a woman changes her clothing and puts on men's clothes instead of the usual women's clothes, she is excommunicated. (canon 13)

The synodal letter gives us almost unintentionally two important bits of information on the motivations of the women, which are found neither in Socrates nor in Sozomen. (1) The women who wear ascetic clothing "think they can achieve holiness in this way"—a morally noble motive! (2) For the renouncing of long hair the women give ascetic reasons (presumably renouncing "worldly" beauty and ornamentation). According to Socrates the short hair was prescribed by Eustathius. The interpretation as "male" coiffure is determined by the synod; they see it as a symbol of the claim of women to be equal to men and thus a symbol of the end of subordination and the duty of obedience. It is very doubtful whether the women themselves understood their choice of short hair in this way, that is, whether they for their part admitted the status of subordination in marriage. The interpretation of female hair growth as a "natural symbol" of the hierarchy of the sexes established by God comes, no doubt, from men, who did not want to recognize the equal birth of women.

The motif of the short hair and male clothing is already found in the *Acts of Thecla* [218]—there it is a means of protecting this woman apostle from molestation while traveling. Emperor Theodosius passed a law that threatened women who had their head shorn with excommunication and bishops who tolerated such a thing with deposition—Sozomen reports on this.[219] In the text from Gangra tonsure and clothing appear as outward signs of equality with men. How are we to judge the synod's polemical presentation on this point? Everything supports the idea that in the circle around Eustathius the praxis was actually egalitarian. This is also suggested by the allusion to "slaves who despise their masters" (introd., canon 3). It is not as clear that women regarded ascetic clothing as male clothing. It was perhaps more likely a question of *gender-neutral clothing*— a visible expression of the conviction that "in Christ" the transcendence of gender has become possible. Thus we do not have to assume that women regarded themselves as males. Yet the frequent shift from sex-neutral to male, which we also find as a positive evaluation of women especially on the lips of men, doubtless conceals within it the danger of alienation. When the topos *like a man* occurs, we must investigate exactly how it is meant.[220]

Interestingly, it comes at one point directly from the mouth of a famous Spiritual mother. Amma Sarrha says to doubtful ascetics, who want to humiliate her because of her sex: "By nature (*physei*) I am a woman, but not in thinking (*logismō*)!"[221] Her self-consciousness of being born equal to men is clearly expressed here. The remark can be misunderstood in an androcentric way: it is possible even for a woman to overcome her feminine nature and through the spirit become equal to men—she would then be the exception to the rule. The sense of Sarrha's statement, however, is much more likely that through the body every human being is a sexual being, yet the spirit is independent of gender—here women and men are not different.[222]

One problem remains: the ascetically understood equality in Christ overcomes the old hierarchy of the sexes, but at the same time it sets up a new hierarchy of married and unmarried. The polemic against the Eustathian circles may have been exaggerated at this point, but such attitudes may well have given real reasons for conflicts. Yet the deposing of married Christian men and women by no means occurred only in so-called heretical circles; special privileges for the celibate class are also found in the theology and practice of the mainstream church. In both places, nonetheless, the original equality of the sexes was increasingly lost, even in the ascetic environment. This may have led to women actually trying to live dressed as men in monasteries—a widespread topos in Byzantine hagiography.[223] This is not attested in the fourth century.

Spiritual Partners

In ascetic circles, nonetheless, there arose a new ideal of marital life that is defined quite apart from sexuality. Socrates and Sozomen refer at least indirectly to one woman ascetic as a partner in such a marriage: Anonyma, the wife of Ammon. He was one of the most famous figures in Egyptian monasticism. The tradition that both Socrates and Sozomen recount in their own ways is already found in Palladius (chap. 8). Thus, let us look first at this older version.

Ammon was forced into marriage by his uncle. On his wedding night he recommends continence to his wife and—by means of words "from the Apostle, from the Saviour Himself"—is able to convince her: she agrees to the renunciation of sexual activity but does not want to separate from him. They live eighteen years in the same house, without sleeping in the same bed. During the day he works in the garden; in the evening they devote themselves to prayer together and have a common meal. Finally she recommends separation: his virtue should no longer remain hidden in domesticity. Ammon turns the common dwelling over to her[224] and builds himself a hermitage in the mountains. During his remaining twenty years he visits his wife twice a year. Thus ends the story in Palladius.

Sozomen follows the text of Palladius very precisely, paraphrasing the dialogues between Ammon and his wife. Only the regular evening prayer and common meal are not mentioned (1.14). Socrates, on the other hand, is considerably freer with Palladius's story: he changes some of the facts and expands the arguments for virginity substantially. Instead of paraphrasing, I will quote the text from Socrates:

In his youth this person had an aversion to matrimony; but when some of his relatives urged him not to contemn marriage, but to take a wife to himself, he was prevailed upon and was married. On leading the bride with the customary ceremonies from the banquet-room to the nuptial couch, after their mutual friends had withdrawn, he took a book containing the epistles of the apostles and read to his wife Paul's Epistle to the Corinthians, explaining to her the apostle's admonitions to married persons [1 Corinthians 7]. Adducing many external considerations besides, he descanted on the inconveniences and discomforts attending matrimonial intercourse, the pangs of child-bearing, and the trouble and anxiety connected with rearing a family. He contrasted with all this the advantages of chastity; described the liberty, and immaculate purity of a life of continence; and affirmed that virginity places persons in the nearest relation to the Deity. By these and other arguments of a similar kind, he persuaded his virgin bride to renounce with him a secular life, prior to their having any conjugal knowledge of each other. Having taken this resolution, they retired together to the mountain of Nitria, and in a hut there inhabited for a short time one common ascetic apartment, without regarding their difference of sex, being according to the apostles, "one in Christ." But not long after, the recent and unpolluted bride thus addressed Ammoun: "It is unsuitable," said she, "for you who practice chastity, to look upon a woman in so confined a dwelling; let us therefore, if it is agreeable to you, perform our exercise apart." This agreement again was satisfactory to both, and so they separated, and spent the rest of their lives in abstinence from wine and oil, eating dry bread alone, sometimes passing over one day, at others fasting two, and sometimes more. (4.23; NPNF, 2nd series, 2:106)

Thus Socrates presents on the one hand a brief summary of current tractates on virginity with their very realistic arguments against marriage[225] and on the other hand veils the offensive eighteen-year close communal life of an ascetic man and an ascetic woman. Nevertheless, he passes on the reasoning used by this pair to justify their living together: they appeal to the early Christian confession handed down by Paul: "There is no longer . . . male and female; for all of you are one[226] in Christ Jesus" (Gal. 3:28). Yet Socrates moves the common life of Anonyma and Ammon into an appropriate context for asceticism, the mountain of Nitria, and replaces the report of twice-yearly visits with the description of a strict observance of fasting. Thus everything remains within the framework of conventional propriety.

From Theodoret we learn nothing about this ascetic couple, but he reports on the Spiritual marriage of a highly placed ecclesiastical officeholder with a different Anonyma:

Pelagius [bishop of Laodicea] had taken on him the yoke of wedlock when a very young man, and in the very bridal chamber, on the first day of his nuptials, he persuaded his bride to prefer chastity to conjugal intercourse, and taught her to accept fraternal affection in the place of marriage union. Thus he gave all honour to temperance. (4.13; 4.12 in NPNF, 2nd series, 3:115)

Further details about communal life in the bishop's house are not given. It is notable that here, as in the previously cited descriptions of sexual abstinence in marriage, the normally expected word *continence* (*enkrateia*) is carefully avoided, and in its place the more general terms *chastity* and *purity* occur. The idea, no doubt, was to obscure the apparent similarities of mainstream Christian teaching with the Encratite "heresy" in the valuation of sexual abstinence.

We can see that as long as Spiritual partnership preserved the legal form of marriage, it was granted the highest praise by ecclesiastical authorities. Yet many women and men committed to sexual continence also lived freely together without entering a formal marriage. This practice met with resistance—we have already seen testimonies from the third century for both Antioch and Carthage. How widespread the institution of Spiritual marriage still was even at the end of the fourth century is shown by the fact that John Chrysostom, the later bishop of the Eastern metropolis and imperial city of Constantinople, while still a deacon in Antioch, wrote two tractates against this form of communal life, one addressed to clerics and one addressed to virgins. Socrates mentions the writings in his church history (6.3)—and at the same time reports a concrete example that may have attracted considerable attention in his time: the relationship between the virgin Eustolium and the presbyter Leontius.

The background for the reports on their Spiritual marriage is the Arian controversy. Athanasius, the previously mentioned champion of the faith of Nicaea, had avoided the clutches of Emperor Constantius II through flight, which offended the ecclesiastical opponents of the bishop of Alexandria, who were not themselves necessarily "Arians" in their theological position. One of them was the already mentioned presbyter Leontius, who in the meantime had become the bishop of Antioch. Socrates gives the following report:

> When a presbyter, [Leontius] had been divested of his rank, because in order to remove all suspicion of illicit intercourse with a woman named Eustolium, with whom he spent a considerable portion of his time, he had castrated himself, and thenceforward lived more unreservedly with her, on the ground that there could be no longer any ground for evil surmises. Afterwards however, at the earnest desire of the Emperor Constantius, he was created bishop of the church at Antioch . . . (2.26; NPNF, 2nd series, 2:54)

The gesture of self-castration, which shocks us today, was not so unusual at the time, for in late antiquity there was little squeamishness in dealing with the male sex organs.[227] Many followers of asceticism held that Jesus' saying should be taken literally: "There are eunuchs who have made themselves eunuchs for the sake of the kingdom of heaven. Let anyone accept this who can" (Matt. 19:12). Modern translations have usually softened the crude language of the original. Luther's translation says: "There are castrated ones who have castrated themselves." The ecclesiastical synods, to be sure, forbade this practice: the first great council at Nicaea (325) made self-castration an impediment to ordination but admitted to church ministries men who had become unmanned for medical reasons or "by their masters or the barbarians" (that is, as slaves or prisoners of war) (canon 1). The so-called *Apostolic Canons* (c. 400) decreed that laymen who castrated themselves were excluded from Communion for three years (canon 24).[228]

Leontius, who performed this act upon himself, is described by both Sozomen and Theodoret. He is shown in a rather friendly light by the Sozomen. According to him Athanasius regarded his opponent as a heretic and preferred to celebrate the Eucharist with the Eustathians in a private house instead of in one of Leontius's churches, yet the bishop of Antioch even tolerated hymns that spread the doctrine of Nicaea.

For nontheologians, however, the distinction was hard to grasp. The Trinitarian doxologies had become the trademarks of each side. The old "Glory be to the Father *through* the Son *in* the Holy Spirit" was now considered Arian, because it emphasized the equality of the divine persons less than the new formula, "Glory be to the Father *and* the Son *and* the Holy Spirit." It is thus attested by Theodoret, who paints Leontius's portrait in the darkest colors (2.24). He adopts the story of the self-castration in the polemical version that Athanasius had put into circulation (see below); among his priests and deacons Leontius promoted "licentiousness" (presumably an allusion to the practice of Spiritual marriage among the clergy of Antioch[229]). The efforts of the bishop to mediate between the followers of Nicaea and the Arians are interpreted by Theodoret as a conscious veiling of his own heretical position. Theodoret is naturally the loyal echo of Athanasius himself, who defames Leontius according to all the rules of antiheretical polemic:

> They [the aforementioned Arians] omit no evil! As their life is, so is their thinking and their drivel. No one can even recount without blushing the numerous shameful deeds that they constantly commit. Leontius was thus accused because of a young woman named Eustolium. When he was forbidden to live with her, he castrated himself for her sake, in order to be able to continue their association. Yet he was not able thereby to allay suspicions; rather, he was for this reason deposed as a presbyter. Yet the heretic Constantius used his power to have him appointed bishop. (*Apology* 26)

> . . . the castrated Leontius could not have been admitted to Communion even as a layman, since he castrated himself in order to be able to sleep with a certain Eustolium, whom he made his wife, even though she was allegedly a virgin. (*History of the Arians* 28.1)

Again we learn almost nothing about the female partner: she was still young and seems to have belonged to the order of ecclesiastical virgins. If Leontius was prepared to take upon himself such mutilation for her sake, what qualities might she have had? The idea that the bishop of Antioch, only because he did not belong to the party of Athanasius, is supposed to have led a less respectable life with Eustolium than the bishop of Laodicea with his untouched wife Anonyma cannot be proved by any kind of fact: the basis for the deposition was, in accordance with the canons, the act of self-castration—neither he nor Eustolium was accused by the ecclesiastical court of impermissible sexual activity. The subtle twisting of the story by Athanasius, who apparently is trying to defame his opponent with sex scandals, is all the more tasteless, since the belligerent bishop of Alexandria also had to defend himself against similar calumnies.[230] Accusations before the court because of alleged rapes, in which women were paid as false witnesses, and other horror tales are often found in Theodoret.[231]

It is also interesting that in absolutely anti-Arian circles it was told that during the time of persecution Athanasius hid for six years with a very young and extraordinarily beautiful virgin.[232] The historicity of this tradition may remain undecided here, but it is doubtful, since the bishop of Alexandria mentions nothing of the sort in the report on his flight and exile experiences. In any case, it is notable that Palladius and Sozomen were apparently not afraid of compromising their "hero" with such a story. Yet they base the concealment with the virgin on divine revelation and add explanations—even if rather different ones!—for this unusual behavior.

According to Palladius Athanasius justified himself with the following words vis-à-vis his trusted friends, who would gladly have hidden him themselves:

> I did not flee to you, in order that you might be able to swear that you did not know of my whereabouts. It was the same in regard to the search for me. Now I took flight to one who would be the last to be suspected [of hiding me], she being so pretty and young. I paid court to her on two counts, really: her salvation—for it did help her—as well as my own good name. (63.4; ACW 34:145)

In agreement with Palladius, Sozomen reports that the youthful Anonyma was so beautiful that respectable men had to stay away from her in order not to be talked about. Yet in this unusual attractiveness he saw not nature at work but the virtues of a noble soul: therefore it was not offensive for the priest to have concealed himself with this so strikingly beautiful virgin. Sozomen, who would hardly have approved of the living together of unmarried continent couples, nonetheless attests indirectly through the recounting of this story that many of his male and female contemporaries took no offence at ascetic togetherness.[233]

Virgins and Virginity

In the church histories of the first centuries we do not learn very much about women who chose sexual abstinence and thereby traveled new ways that were controversial both in the church and in society. By contrast, we hear somewhat more from Socrates, Sozomen, and Theodoret than from Eusebius about the order of virgins as well as about particular representatives of this order. The story of the virgin Irene, which Socrates and Sozomen adopted, goes back to Rufinus.[234] The fact that a name appears here is an indication of the age of the tradition rather than the significance the authors attach to this female personage. In

Rufinus the virgin, who has already died, is mentioned in order to highlight the miraculous activity of her father Spyridon, who is both a prophet and a bishop. The miracle occurs after her death: someone gave Irene a deposit to hold and now wants it back; since the father cannot find it, he calls to his daughter for help, and from the grave she provides the needed information—a highly practical miracle!

Her life is briefly summarized by Rufinus: "After she had served him well, the virgin died." What is meant by this "service": a church ministry or household management? From the text alone the question can hardly be decided, but there are notable aspects in the adoption of the tradition by Socrates and Sozomen. First, both omit Rufinus's comment that Spyridon belonged to the "order of prophets."[235] Socrates reformulates Irene's "good service" or "good execution of ministry": she shared "in the piety of the father." Sozomen omits this sentence entirely but in its place adds at the end an additional edifying story in which the still living Irene is asked to go into the kitchen for a guest. He also believes he must excuse the bishop's marriage, which was blessed with children: "He did not on this account neglect the service of God." Since the virgin Irene, apparently without the knowledge of her father, was entrusted with a considerable sum of money, one could at least presume that she was active in the church as a deaconess and prophetess. In any case, the traditional name indicates that the daughter of Spyridon originally had more independence than our texts reveal.

A similar omission can be ascertained in the report on the feast for the ecclesiastical virgins in Jerusalem, which was sponsored by Helena, the famous mother of Emperor Constantine, who herself took over the serving.[236] Although the three later authors for the most part embellish the spare tales of Rufinus, here they delete a brief sentence that characterizes the behavior of the empress: "The Queen of the Earth and Mother of the Empire made herself the handmaid of the handmaids of Christ." This formulation (*famula famularum Christi*) recalls the designation that was later given to the Roman bishops: *servus servorum Dei*—servant of the servants of God.[237] This symbolic gesture, which, by suspending the secular rank order, honors the virgins here as an especially important group in the church, reminds us of Jesus and his disciples—and thus places the virgins close to the apostles. In later versions this impression is clearly diminished.

As in Jerusalem, so also in Alexandria,[238] as well as in Ascalon and Gaza,[239] "the virgins" are named as a clearly defined church group: like the clergy, they suffered especially under the persecutions. In Antioch, Publia heads a "choir of virgins, who had pledged lifelong virginity."[240] Since we do not find in Socrates and Theodoret any additional information beyond Sozomen, his report will serve as the foundation for the summary report.

Sozomen cites as one of the great deeds of Constantine the imperial "Legislation for the Facilitation of a Celibate Life": he abolished the privileges of the married that earlier emperors had decreed for promoting increased birth rate.[241] Moreover, Constantine allowed the unmarried to draw up a will before reaching adulthood, for he held that "those who choose virginity do not err in their judgment" (1.9.4). Here Constantine is following the example of the ancient Romans, who granted this right to the vestal virgins from the age of six.[242] For Sozomen these privileges of virginity are "the greatest proof of the emperor's concern for religion" (1.9.7). Yet the historian reports elsewhere that the introduction of mandatory celibacy for (male) clergy was prevented (1.23).[243] He reproduces the decree of Jovian that marriage with an ecclesiastical virgin was to be regarded as a capital crime, as was even the intention to abduct (6.3).

From Sozomen's church history we also learn something about the various situations and organizations of virgins. The already-mentioned virgin Irene, daughter of Bishop Spyridon, apparently lived with her father. The Macedonian deaconess Eusebia seems to have lived alone and independently in her house in Constantinople. The virgin Anonyma with whom Athanasius is supposed to have concealed himself in Alexandria is also presented as independent and living alone.

We discover in Sozomen's report on the martyrdom of Tarbula a kind of ascetic household: "Around the same time . . . Tarbula, the sister of Bishop Symeon, a holy virgin, was arrested together with her servant, who shared with her the same way of life, and her sister, who after the death of her husband had forsworn marriage and shared the same way of life" (2.12). No details are given about this emphasized "way of life" (bios).

Yet two aspects of this report are notable: (1) it names Tarbula's sister after her servant (because Sozomen valued virginity more than widowhood?); (2) it speaks of a common life of the mistress and the servant. The abolishing of class distinctions in the transition from the familial household (in the sense of the ancient oikos) to the ascetic community is also reported in The Life of St. Macrina.[244] A letter of Theodoret illustrates very clearly that equality of mistress and slave was by no means the general practice among Christians. He asks a bishop for help in liberating a noblewoman Maria, who together with her servant had fallen into slavery—Theodoret praises the fact that even in this situation the servant woman continues to perform her service as a slave to her mistress. Then he speaks only of the liberation of the noblewoman (letter 70). When we consult only the church histories, we learn almost nothing about the equality that was practiced in the churches in the beginning, at least in individual cases. Yet there are visible hints of this change in attitude. In Eusebius we learn the name of the slave Blandina; her mistress remained anonymous (6.1.17–18); in Sozomen, however, the slave of the virgin Tarbula remains nameless in spite of the ascetic equality; in Theodoret's letter regarding the anonymous slave of the enslaved mistress Maria, there is no effort at all to abolish the rank order, but instead the opposite.

Outside of the ascetic household, we find in the three church histories almost no larger communities of virgins, although at this time there were already significant communities of women. The deaconess Olympias mentioned by Sozomen founded and headed a cloister in Constantinople,[245] yet the historian says nothing about this. As for the virgins, whose leadership a certain Nicarete[246] did not want to assume, it could have been a matter of either a convent or an organization of independent women living a celibate life, yet we learn nothing more. An actual community is seen most clearly in Theodoret behind the "choir of virgins" in Publia's house,[247] since regular worship services take place there. It is true that in the report on the feast in Jerusalem, at which the imperial mother Helena waited upon the virgins, we read of "consecrated virgins" (Rufinus 1.8), "virgins entered in the canon" (Socrates 1.17), "holy virgins" (Sozomen 2.2), and "all [women] who had vowed eternal virginity" (Theodoret 1.18), yet with no reference to a particular community.

As in Eusebius, so also in Sozomen and Theodoret, "widows and virgins" are mentioned in direct connection with clergy.[248] The historians report on the contributions of Constantine, which are suspended by Julian and then renewed by Jovian. As in the Eusebian report on the church in Rome, here too we can ascertain an ambivalence between pay and alms, for in Sozomen we first read: "He [Julian] forced even the virgins and widows, who *on account of their poverty* were counted among the clergy, to pay back the contributions they had received from public means" (5.5.2; emphasis added). Yet in the reversal of the action this limitation does not appear: "He [Jovian] gave the religious privileges and contributions back to the churches and clerics, the widows and virgins" (6.3.4). It is not entirely clear here whether the poor are being supported or whether the ecclesiastical order of widows and virgins as such also receives financial means beyond the undoubted "religious privileges." Theodoret clearly describes Constantine's action as a fundamental and generous support of the clerical orders: "He decreed to the provincial governors that ecclesiastical virgins and widows, as well as persons consecrated to the service of God, were to be given yearly deliveries of grain; in determining the amount he followed his generosity, not the need. After the godless Julian revoked everything, his successor granted the same thing once again. A third of this is maintained today, for a famine led to reductions" (1.11). A comparison of the texts gives the impression that the clause on need is an interpretation by Sozomen.

Regarding ecclesiastical virgins Sozomen tells, finally, about a strengthening of the legislation concerning female celibacy that had entered the *Codex Theodosianus* (438). A marriage with a female cleric who is solemnly pledged to continence is penalized by death—allegedly the followers of the emperor Julian were especially committed to decimating the order of Christian virgins by means of marriage.[249]

With that we come to the end of the treatment of those Christian women who broke with the traditional role of wife and mother. The selective perception and reporting is very clear: asceticism in the desert is largely presented as a "male" lifestyle; it is assumed that women lead a withdrawn life in convents. It is true that the order of virgins enjoys high regard, yet their significance for the life of the church is not indicated.

How is such different reporting on men and women ascetics to be evaluated? Do we have a bourgeois, philogynous Socrates facing an ascetic, misogynistic Sozomen, with a moderate Theodoret in the middle? The analysis of the texts prevents such a simple classification. The sources are considerably more complicated. Socrates, who does not seem to be overly interested in either ascetics or women, tells nonetheless about women ascetics and Spiritual partners, as well as their spiritual motivation; hence, he is our most objective reporter. By contrast, Sozomen, who mentions more women than Socrates and Theodoret together and espoused the glorification of asceticism, is stubbornly silent about women ascetics and Spiritual partners—which can hardly be a coincidence. Theodoret is to be judged not only according to his church history, in which virgins are mentioned only as a group, but also according to his monastic history, where he is at least aware of women ascetics.

On the question of female asceticism Sozomen advocates most clearly (if not expressly) an ideological position: celibacy is worth more than marriage, men are more important than women, and virgins are to live a withdrawn life. We find a similar position in Theodoret, even if traces of a more open praxis are found in his monastic history. In Socrates, on the other hand, a certain reserve can be observed vis-à-vis the ascetic movement. Is he thereby muffling the claims to autonomy of women ascetics who have broken with the old role models? Apparently not, since he gives a thoroughly positive evaluation of such behavior in the non-Christian philosopher Hypatia.[250]

We find no express demand for female subordination in marriage in any of the authors—but no postulate of fundamental equality either. All three historians have in common with their predecessor Eusebius *an astonishing lack of interest in female asceticism,* if we compare it with the high regard for this lifestyle for the male sex: free women living unchecked was a disturbing and threatening phenomenon that one had better conceal or even fight.

Fortunately, however, there were also at the time men and male authors like Palladius who thought differently, and thus we know more about women ascetics than the authors of the church histories reveal.

e. Charity
instead of Education

We learn extremely little from Socrates, Sozomen, and Theodoret about female erudition. In their time, however, there was a real scandal in education, which concerned not the women's issue but Christians in general. In 362, upon ascending the throne, Emperor Julian announced his rejection of Christianity.[251] A few months later he promulgated a law that excluded "the Galileans" from every pedagogical office.[252] A storm of indignation arose and "caused more unrest than if the emperor had demanded blood and torture."[253] Hence, in church history writings Julian was increasingly condemned as "apostate," as deserter and turncoat: Sozomen paints him as being darker than does Socrates, and Theodoret turns him completely into a monster.[254] This hostile picture is in urgent need of correction, for the emperor was by no means a fanatical persecutor of Christians like some of his predecessors, but rather a reformer convinced of the humanity of the old religion.[255] Since he was in power only nineteen months, calm soon returned. Nevertheless, the indignation of Christians shows how much classical education meant to them at that time. We are still far from the rejection of "pagan" philosophy that was to lead finally to the closing of the academy in Athens a century and a half later (529).

In Rome at around the same time a work was written by a theological author who is to be numbered among the most gifted and brilliant of her contemporaries: Faltonia Betitia Proba (d. 370). Using Virgilian verse she fashioned a Christian epic of salvation that is considered one of the best creations of the so-called cento genre.[256] Yet she not only adopted the language of the poet but also interpreted the heroic figure of Aeneas as the *typos* ('model') of Christ and thus created her own kind of synthesis between the old Roman and the new Christian *pietas*.[257] The emperor Arcadius (395–408) had a personal copy made of this "Virgil improved in the divine sense."[258] Jerome (d. 420), on the other hand, made fun of men who let themselves be taught by women, as well as Bible scholars who must improve the scripture with "pagan" poetic art and even claim to discern a prophet in the Roman national poet. He no doubt had in mind the circle around Proba, but he does not give her name—she may have been held in too high a regard in Rome for him to mention her.[259]

Two centuries later Isidore of Seville (d. 636) considers her the "only woman among the men of the church"[260] and esteems her work in his lexicon-like *Etymologies*.[261] As long as educated Christians spoke Latin, her work was read with enthusiasm and used as a school text. Then it fell into oblivion—modern patristic scholars could not classify it either literarily or theologically. Its rediscovery and gradual rehabilitation began around the turn of the century. Yet it was only within the context of feminist theological studies in the United States that the work became available even to nonspecialists through its translation into English.[262] Thus the reception of this unusual work is just beginning. Since this Roman "prophetess"[263] and "incomparable wife"[264] was not considered worthy of mention by the historiographers of the fifth century, a reference to this omission will have to suffice at this point.

The omission is especially astonishing in Socrates, since he speaks of similar attempts by male authors and ardently supports the reading and study of Greek writers and philosophers even for Christians (3.16). Moreover, he also reports on the unusual education and the epic work of the empress Eudocia (d. 460), the daughter of the sophist Leontius of Athens, who before her baptism bore the name *Athenaïs*. He mentions the heroic poem with which in 422 she praised the victory of her husband Theodosius II over the Persians. Perhaps the historian died before Eudocia became an imitator of Proba: she created a *Cento on Christ* in Greek, using the verses of Homer. Nor does he mention the other works of this literarily very active empress: a poetic paraphrase of the first eight books of the Bible and the history of St. Cyprian and St. Justina—the latter is in large part extant.[265]

Apart from the philosopher Hypatia, of whom we shall speak below, Socrates does not expressly mention female education anywhere. Yet of the few women outside the imperial household that he names at all, most presumably belong to the upper class. Thus one can say that he was interested almost exclusively in educated women. This matches his interest in the court. He—and also Theodoret—never mentions a slave woman. In Sozomen, nonetheless, we find at one point the equal ranking of a slave woman and her mistress in the ascetic milieu;[266] concerning the slave woman of an apparently noble Macedonian woman, who quarrels with her orthodox husband, we do not even learn to which confession the slave herself belonged.[267] We cannot even determine whether the help of the slave is due to obedience or to solidarity between women—a theme that should be investigated independently by means of other sources.

Regarding the Christian women they mention, neither Sozomen nor Theodoret emphasizes intelligence or erudition as a particular virtue or laudable trait. Yet there can be no doubt that many of those mentioned were in fact highly educated. That is certainly true for seven of the eight mentioned deaconesses; we learn too little about the eighth to make a judgment.[268] In all probability the prisoner of war, Anonyma, who became a missionary to the "Iberians" (that is, the Georgians), was also highly educated. There are four different versions of her apostolic activity; their comparison forms the conclusion of this first part.[269]

Now let us turn to the report about a woman who in education may have exceeded all others named thus far, but who was not a Christian: the Neoplatonic philosopher Hypatia.[270] The description of her murder is one of the saddest chapters in the church history of Socrates and in church history in general. Hypatia, the head of the academy in Alexandria, was a friend of the Roman prefect Orestes, who was trying to preserve peace between embattled Jews and Christians in that Hellenistic metropolis in the Nile delta. Thus the philosopher and natural scientist became a target for the followers of Cyril, the extremely pugnacious bishop of Alexandria,[271] and in March 415 was murdered by the Christian rabble. Cyril is considered the father of orthodox Christology, since at the Council of Ephesus in 431 he was the chief opponent of the verbally no less pugnacious bishop of Constantinople, Nestorius. We know that in this disagreement he proceeded extremely fanatically, using uneducated, belligerent groups of monks and other very questionable means.[272] His guilt (as an accessory) in the murder is disputed.

One of Hypatia's students, Synesius of Cyrene, later became a Christian and even a bishop.[273] In a letter to a fellow student he enthusiastically recalls the lectures in Alexandria: "We saw with our eyes and heard with our ears the teacher who rightly holds the chair over the mysteries of philosophy!" (137). And to her herself, his "mother, sister, teacher, and above all benefactress" (16), he writes after bitter personal losses: "Yet the greatest loss for me is no longer to be in the presence of your divine spirit" (10). In a long writing he informs her about two books that he has already written; her judgment will determine whether he will publish them (154). Here is Socrates' short chapter on this "star of the humanities":[274]

There was a woman at Alexandria named Hypatia, daughter of the philosopher Theon, who made such attainments in literature and science, as to far surpass all the philosophers of her own time. Having succeeded to the school of Plato and Plotinus, she explained the principles of philosophy to her auditors, many of whom came from a distance to receive her instructions. On account of the self-

possession and ease of manner, which she acquired in consequence of the culti-
vation of her mind, she not unfrequently appeared in public in presence of the
magistrates. Neither did she feel abashed in coming to an assembly of men. For
all men on account of her extraordinary dignity and virtue admired her the more.
Yet even she fell a victim to the political jealousy which at that time prevailed.
For as she had frequent interviews with Orestes, it was calumniously reported
among the Christian populace, that it was she who prevented Orestes from being reconciled to the bishop. Some of them therefore, hurried away by a fierce
and bigoted zeal, whose ringleader was a reader named Peter, waylaid her re-
turning home, and dragging her from her carriage, they took her to the church
called *Caesareum*, where they completely stripped her, and then murdered her
with tiles. After tearing her body in pieces, they took her mangled limbs to a place
called Cinaron, and there burnt them. This affair brought [considerable] oppro-
brium, not only upon Cyril, but also upon the whole Alexandrian church. And
surely nothing can be farther from the spirit of Christianity than the allowance of
massacres, fights, and transactions of that sort. This happened in the month of
March during Lent, in the fourth year of Cyril's episcopate, under the tenth con-
sulate of Honorius, and the sixth of Theodosius. (7.15; NPNF, 2nd series, 2:160)

Not much can be added to Socrates' commentary. Though a real historical figure, the philosopher Hypatia appears as an almost timeless symbol of intellectual
superiority and moral integrity against brutal force: an unusually gifted woman,
still young and very beautiful, unmarried like so many of her Christian contemporaries,[275] falls victim to the basest instincts and bestial cruelty—a pattern that
is repeated in horrible stereotypicality in many reports of martyrdom.

It is sad and regrettable to see in the church histories of Socrates, Sozomen,
and Theodoret the beginnings of a development that will ultimately deny women
access to education. Intelligence and intellectual accomplishments of Christian
women are no longer mentioned: education is suppressed as a feminine ideal.

The Ideal of Service

Certainly the magnitude of the social commitment that led prominent and
rich women to undertake service to the poor is beyond question: in our church
histories we find the ideal typified in the figures of some empresses. Helena, the
mother of Constantine, was reputed to be concerned about the poor—the few
sentences on this topic in Rufinus and Socrates[276] are further developed by Sozomen (2.2). Socrates knows no gender-specific embodiment of service; he says
of the emperor Theodosius himself: "He rendered his palace little different from
a monastery" (7.22).

By contrast, in his portrait of the empress Flacilla, Theodoret clearly paints a
picture of the woman sovereign who serves others:[277]

In no way exalted by her imperial rank . . . she bestowed every kind of attention on the maimed and mutilated, declining all aid from her household and her

guards, herself visiting the houses where the sufferers lodged, and providing every one with what he required. She also went about the guest chambers of the churches and ministered to the wants of the sick, herself handling pots and pans, and tasting broth, now bringing in a dish and breaking bread and offering morsels, and washing out a cup and going through all the other duties which are supposed to be proper to servants and maids. (5.19; 5.18 in NPNF, 2nd series, 3:145)

Similar features are found in Sozomen in his portrait of Pulcheria, yet he emphasizes monastic withdrawal far more (9.1–3). For him the empress appears first as regent and guardian of her younger brother Theodosius. Here the historian praises her great education, her courtly protocol, her care for priests and monks, and her battle against heresies. Solemnly and publicly she pledged herself to virginity: the ceremony is described in detail (9.1).[278] This is followed by the elaborate, already-mentioned miracle story of the rediscovery of the bones of the forty martyrs (9.2). Then Sozomen presents Pulcheria and her sisters again according to the monastic model:

They all pursue the same mode of life; they are sedulous about the priests and the houses of prayer, and are munificent to needy strangers and the poor. These sisters generally take their meals and walks together, and pass their days and their nights in company, singing the praises of God. As is the custom with exemplary women, they employ themselves in weaving and in similar occupations. Although princesses, born and educated in palaces, they avoid levity and idleness, which they think unworthy of any who profess virginity, so they put such indolence far from their own life. (9.3; NPNF, 2nd series, 2:421)[279]

A new ideal that prefers piety and care of the poor to elitist education? That was the tendency, and not only for women. Social commitment is rightly regarded as a credit to Christianity, but does this justify the increasing disdain for reason and enlightenment? More and more in the later centuries the early Christian "philosopher," who united asceticism and education, is suppressed by the monk, who subordinates education to piety, if he does not replace education with piety altogether. The tendency is already very clear in Sozomen's description of asceticism (1.12), but far less so with Socrates in his corresponding chapter, although he also relativizes philosophical knowledge in a critical way (4.23).

This devaluation of education, which we can observe in Christianity, becomes evident especially in the development of a new ideal for women. In Eusebius it was still men who gained respect through their devoted care of the ill in Alexandria (7.22). Such tasks are now more and more turned over to women, and thus service is subtly *changed from a general Christian ideal into a specifically feminine virtue.* The result is an *extreme fixation of role:* women are finally excluded from education and teaching and obligated to charitable activities. Later even these activities were forbidden to women's orders, and they were banished into strict seclusion.[280] All of this is certainly only suggested in the three church histories: many of the Christian women were in fact highly educated, yet they were praised—if at all—for other qualities.

f. The Honor of the Men

In Socrates, Sozomen, and Theodoret, there are also many miscellaneous items about women that will not be presented here individually.[281] We will let one episode represent the entire collection of anecdotal material: it concerns a confession and its consequences.[282]

After the disagreements over the reception of the lapsed from the times of persecution,[283] the mainstream church, against the resistance of the Novatians, institutionalized (public) penance for serious sins. The aforementioned confession of a woman became the reason why in Constantinople, under Nectarius (381–97), the institution of penance was transferred into the private realm.[284] This is what happened: The confession of an Anonyma brought to light the fact that a deacon had slept with her. According to Socrates the woman accused herself of sinful sexual intercourse; according to Sozomen, the servant of the church raped the woman during the carrying out of penance after a preceding confession. However it happened, the deacon was deposed. Yet there was a desire to prevent similar scandals in the future, and therefore public penance was quickly abolished.

Both authors disapprove of this decision. For Socrates, Christians thereby took away the opportunity to name sins as such in the church. Sozomen ascribes to public penance the power of a healthy deterrent, the loss of which he regrets. He comments that Emperor Theodosius promulgated two laws precisely as a deterrent, namely, that women not be admitted to the diaconate until the age of sixty, and that women with short hair (and their bishops) be excommunicated. We should note that these are the only examples that occur to Sozomen for the catchword *deterrent*. Here his misogynist stance becomes quite clear: although in his variation the Anonyma was raped and hence actually innocent, from his perspective she is made responsible for the transgression of the deacon. It is apparently the fault of the woman if she becomes the man's impermissible object of desire—a mechanism that also reappears in the rape trials of our century. Protection is required, not for women against the assaults of male violence, but for men against the female art of seduction. And, above all, men's honesty cannot be called into question publicly. This conclusion, to be sure, was drawn at that time neither by Socrates nor by Sozomen, but by the ecclesiastical authorities in Constantinople: with the abolishing of the institution of penance, a certain legal protection for women was also lost.

At work here in Christianity was the old Roman ethos, which in questions of sexual morality clearly set out a double standard for men and women. This unequal application is established in the marriage law of the Eastern church: according to the canons a man *must* dismiss his wife if she commits adultery; a woman, on the other hand, *shall not* separate from him in the reverse case. Basil confirms this as the prevailing law of the church, although he himself comments: "The decision of the Lord applies equally to men and women: a marriage may be terminated only because of adultery. Yet the custom is different . . ."[285] The bishop then justifies the church's practice, which is contradictory to the gospel and which the *Codex Justinianus* later establishes for the Christian Roman Empire.[286] By contrast, in the West—despite contrary secular law—the church maintains a strict prohibition of divorce that applies to men and women equally.[287] Here the controversial formulation concerning divorce after adultery (Matt. 5:31) is interpreted differently: even unchastity (*porneia*) is no ground for separation.[288]

The problem of divorce cannot be examined here, but we can point out the fundamentally different view in the East. There the old Roman practice of marriage termination is tolerated as separation by mutual consent, but any second marriage, even after the death of the partner, is an offense against Christian morality, requires penance, and is an obstacle to ordination. On this issue the women's ideal of *univira* ("a woman married only once") also applies to men.[289]

In another respect, however, many church fathers at first adopt the old Roman tradition according to which chastity is a specifically female virtue and women are made responsible for the unchastity of men. This includes an overestimation of bodily integrity: women are praised when they escape a threatened rape through suicide.[290] Here a higher value is placed on the wife's "honor," which also represents the honor of her husband, than on her life. In Christianity, however, a spiritualization of the traditional Roman concept of chastity prevailed and made the physical aspect relative.

5. Innovations:
Progress or Regress?

If we look at the women named in the church histories, we have to conclude that the tendency in the later centuries was regressive. Yet there seem to be two exceptions:

1. In Eusebius the gospel was carried to the various peoples only by male apostles, but according to Socrates, Sozomen, and Theodoret, two lands owe their acquaintance with Christianity to the efforts of a woman. In Mavia, missionary to an Arabian people, we meet a widowed queen, a woman who had political power. Georgia, on the other hand, was evangelized by Anonyma, a powerless prisoner of war. Both traditions are doubtless based on historical fact, but in a comparison of the four versions at the end of this chapter, we will see how differently the facts are presented in the church histories.

2. In Eusebius no deaconesses are mentioned, and we learn nothing from Socrates about these ministers of the church. In Sozomen and Theodoret, however, we meet a total of seven women who are given this title—an eighth seems to have refused the position offered to her. Six of these eight are mentioned by name; we learn a good bit about most of them; two of them did not belong to the catholic church. We have here, quite obviously, a recognized order in the church for which there are clear laws. It seems natural to the authors that women

are deaconesses. How do we explain the survival of this controversial ministry, about which the first church historian is silent?

We will now turn to this question. First we will seek to clarify the legal development with help from the early church disciplines, in order then to compare it with the practice.

a. A Ministry for Women:
The Diaconate

The Theory

As we saw in the presentation (or rather *non*presentation) of the order of widows in Eusebius, in the third century both the status of diaconal ministry and the ordination of women for church ministries were vigorously debated. The solution in the local churches varied. The author of the *Apostolic Tradition* categorically rejects the ordination of widows for the church in Rome, but the author of the Syriac *Didascalia Apostolorum* ("teaching of the apostles") expressly demands the ordination of deaconesses, primarily—but not exclusively—for the catechesis and baptism of women. Both authors claim apostolic authority in order to substantiate their church disciplines—the usual early form of legitimation for ecclesiastical norms. Later it is replaced by appeal to synodal decisions.

A similar collection of "apostolic" canons from Egypt gives us a lively impression of early church strife over ministries for women.[291] Here the arguments are placed directly on the lips of male and female disciples of Jesus:

> Andrew said: "It would be useful, my brethren, to establish a ministry for women." Peter said: "We have already made arrangements. But we must still make a clear pronouncement concerning the oblation of the body and blood." John said: "You have forgotten, my brethren, that our teacher,[292] when he asked for the bread and the cup and blessed them, saying, 'This is my body and my blood,' did not permit these [women] to stand with us." Martha said: "It was because of Mary, because he saw her smiling." Mary said: "But I did not really laugh. For earlier, when he taught us, he said: 'The weak shall be saved by the strong.'" Cephas said: "You can doubtless remember that it is not fitting for women to pray standing, but seated on the ground." James said: "How then can we organize a ministry for women, except perhaps a ministry that would consist in supporting women who are in want?"[293]

It is obvious that the text is full of hostility against women: they do not have the necessary seriousness at the Lord's Supper, they are the weak sex, and they are not even permitted to pray standing up like the men. And it is precisely Mary and Martha who advance the arguments against women's ministry. Nevertheless, indirectly the text contains positive information. First, women are involved here in the debate of the apostles in making decisions about church discipline; hence, they count as "apostolic" authorities. Moreover, the discussion reveals that the involvement of women in the offering of bread and wine was still unclear and thus open to discussion. In *theory* the editor of the *Canons of the Holy Apostles* comes to the conclusion that a women's ministry could involve only charitable activities, but the *practice* in Egypt may have been different.

In the scope of this study, in which the primary interest is the rediscovery of real women, the institution of the female diaconate and its development are not presented, especially since both older and more recent studies are available.[294] Here we will merely lift up some important aspects.

In the letter to the Romans we meet Phoebe with the title of "deacon" (16:1–2; NRSV: "minister"). In Greek the masculine form *diakonos* can be either masculine or feminine, but it would be an anachronism to speak here of a "deaconess" in the later sense.[295] The same is true of the already-mentioned *ancillae ministrae* of whom Pliny spoke: these slave women were apparently perceived as persons who belonged to the leadership of the Christian "association," but the actual institution of the diaconate had not yet developed. In the third century, when the church ministries had been formed, the bishop was assisted by two official bodies, the presbyteriate and the diaconate. In addition there were numerous other functionaries, as well as groups or "orders" such as virgins and widows, who all received an ecclesiastical blessing and had fixed places in the worship service. At first the ministries of the presbyteriate and the diaconate were independent of each other; only in the course of increasing hierarchization did they become ranked, so that finally, in a developed theology of ministries, the diaconate was regarded as the lowest level of the priesthood, while the episcopacy was considered the highest.

Ecclesiastical deaconesses of the kind found in Sozomen and Theodoret are first attested in the *Didascalia*. In this old church discipline the bishop is instructed to take on deacons as helpers: ". . . a man for the administration of the many necessary concerns and a woman for service to the women" (16). It was the duty of the deaconesses to instruct the female catechumens and to perform a large part of the baptismal ritual with them: they undressed them and anointed their naked bodies with oil like the Roman gladiators, in order to prepare them symbolically for the battle with Satan that they had to survive in baptism in the understanding of the early church. Then they led the women to the pool, submerged them, and clothed them finally with the white garment of the newly baptized. Only the pronouncing of the baptismal formula and the final anointing of the forehead was reserved for the bishop. Deaconesses also visited the sick, brought them Communion, and laid on hands in prayer.[296]

The *Didascalia*—which is extant only in translations but was originally written in Greek[297]—also seems to have used the masculine form *diakonos* with the feminine article to designate the deaconess.[298] Beginning in the fourth century we occasionally find the feminized form *diakonissa*,[299] which was brought into Latin as *diaconissa*. It is doubtful that the linguistic differentiation initially meant a demarcation or reduction in status; in general the terms are interchangeable. In church documents we find side by side with equal status (1) deacon with the feminine article, (2) female deacon, (3) woman deacon, (4) deaconess.[300]

A better term for *deaconess* in the sense used here is *diaconal minister,* since the former brings to mind the modern role of a deaconess in Protestantism rather than the early church ministry; the latter makes clear the ministerial character of the diaconal role. It also overcomes the differences of gender and function that come to mind with the terms *deacon* and *deaconess;* these designations tend to divide between the sexes the openness and richness of the diaconate, which can mean both ministry and service.[301] In early Christianity the two were inseparably joined; both deacons and deaconesses had charitable, catechetical, and liturgical duties.

The contemporary Orthodox theologian Evangelos Theodorou has demonstrated that in terms of liturgical history, the traditional ordination formula for deaconess in the Eastern church has all the characteristics of a "higher ordination"; hence, the deaconess belonged to the ordained clergy, even if in the lowest rank.[302] The question of whether through diaconal ordination she shared in the "priestly service" or whether she exercised a "lay ministry" is a complicated dogmatic question whose answer depends on a prior judgment as to whether there could have been an early Christian ordination of women to the priesthood; it will not be discussed here.[303]

The church histories of Socrates, Sozomen, and Theodoret do not report on the great ecumenical Council of Chalcedon (451), which entered history as the fourth ecumenical council, but at least Theodoret experienced it firsthand. First and foremost, the classical doctrine of the two natures was defined there: Jesus Christ is "truly God and truly man" (*vere Deus, vere homo*). At the same time this council also clarified controversial questions of church law. Regarding deaconesses it stated:

> Only a woman who is over forty may be ordained a deaconess, and then only after thorough examination. If, however, she marries after ordination (*cheirotonia*) and a long period of ministry, she has scorned the grace of God and shall be excommunicated,[304] along with her partner." (canon 15)

Yet the first ecumenical council, the Council of Nicaea (325) under Constantine, had decided differently. Canon 19 sets the conditions for the reacceptance of the followers of Paul of Samosata: they are to be rebaptized; the clergy among them are to be reordained by the catholic bishop, provided that there are no hindrances in their individual lives. Then come the following statements:

> Deaconesses and in general all those who are in the canonical register are to be processed the same way. In regard to deaconesses who hold this position, we are mindful that they have no ordination (*cheirothesia*) of any kind but are to be counted among the laity in every respect.

At the time of the Council of Nicaea the terms *cheirotonia* and *cheirothesia* were still interchangeable (both meant the laying on of hands); later a distinction was made between *ordination* and *blessing.*[305] Attempts have been made to resolve the manifest contradiction between these ecumenical councils by saying that the statement about deaconesses refers only to the Paulianists. Theodorou writes that the Paulianists had no ordination like the catholics. He argues a posteriori: the ordination of deaconesses could not have been established later if the Council of Nicaea had rejected it.[306]

Based on the wording, the Nicaean statement is clearly to be understood generally: although deaconesses belong to the clergy—that is, they have a special ecclesiastical status and are presumably supported financially—they are not "ordained." "All those who are in the canonical register" also includes virgins and widows; in the understanding of the council fathers they are all "laity"; that is, they do not share in the priestly ministry. Thus, compared with the *Apostolic Tradition*, we have only a linguistic difference: women are granted the title *deaconess*, yet they are "not ordained clergy."

In the century and a quarter between these two great ecumenical councils the powers in favor of the ordination of deaconesses were able to prevail—they may well have included not least of all the affected women themselves. Basically the decision of the Council of Chalcedon was valid also for the western half of the imperial church. Why, nevertheless, no female diaconate developed in the West cannot be investigated here.[307] It should not be forgotten that the western empire was suffering under the confusion of tribal migrations and was extremely weak politically, whereas in the East the now Christian Roman Empire was experiencing a cultural golden age. Not until the ninth century was the West—in the form of the kingdom of the Franks under Charlemagne—able to compete with Byzantium, and this led ultimately to the splitting of Christendom.

In the East deaconesses remained a numerically significant group in the clergy, though they were subject to greater restrictions than their male colleagues. The institution of the female diaconate profited first from the general development of splendor and power in the churches, which now stood entirely within the radiance of the imperial court. The head church of the New Rome,[308] as Constantinople called itself after 451, became the model for the development of Byzantine liturgy and hierarchy. Justinian I (527–65), the great compiler of Roman law under the banner of Christianity, felt compelled to take steps against excessively luxuriant furnishings in the churches. He ordered a freeze on employment in order to reduce the clergy of St. Sophia to a healthy number: there were to be no more than 60 presbyters, 100 male and 40 female deacons, 90 subdeacons, 110 lectors, and 25 psalmists, in addition to 100 ostiaries (doorkeepers).[309] This means that twenty percent of the higher clergy were women.

In 691 the so-called synod "in Trullo"—named for the round building in which it met—expressly reconfirmed for the eastern half of the empire the legislation of Chalcedon. The synod is also called the *quinisextum*, because the emperor commissioned it to expand the fifth and sixth ecumenical councils through canons; hence, in Orthodox churches it is regarded as ecumenical and the ninety-eight canons decreed there are part of the basic law of the Eastern church. The synod also found an explanation for why the council fathers at Chalcedon had reduced the minimum age of deaconesses from sixty to forty years: the church of God had in the meantime been strengthened by God's grace and had made progress (canons 14 and 40). The minimum age for deacons, incidentally, was twenty-five years (canon 14). Theoretically these stipulations are still in effect in the Eastern church, and thus only psychological—not canonical—obstacles block the way to a revival of the old praxis. Let us turn again, however, to the situation at the beginning of the fourth century, before we attempt to strike a final balance in the development of the controversial female diaconate.

The Practice

The period on which Socrates, Sozomen, and Theodoret report lies between the two contradictory decrees of Nicaea and Chalcedon. Sozomen expressly mentions the restrictive legislation of Emperor Theodosius I, who placed the minimum age for deaconesses at sixty years, in conscious analogy with the widows of the pastoral epistles (1 Tim. 5:9).[310] Sozomen died before the ecumenical council of 451 made a different decision on the age question, yet he himself reports without comment an ordination at a young age, as we shall see. Hence the deaconesses that we meet in the church histories had in fact already acquired the status that the Council of Chalcedon sanctioned.

In all, Sozomen mentions six deaconesses, each by name. We reported above (section 4b) the little that we know about the two Macedonians Eusebia (9.2) and Matrona (7.21), who were also held in high regard in the mainstream church. All that we learn about one Nectaria is that her elevation to the diaconate was contested: she was excommunicated because of perjury (4:24).

The three other women mentioned by Sozomen belong to the ascetic groups around John Chrysostom: Pentadia, Olympias, and Nicarete. Thus their names do not appear for their own sakes; they are illustrations in the biography of this famous preacher, who in 398—at first against his will—was made bishop of Constantinople but soon became entangled in the web of church politics and was forced in 404 to go into exile, where he died three years later.

Thus in the presentation these women remain more or less on the fringe. This marginalization is clearest with Pentadia: Although as a deaconess she played an important role in the church of Constantinople, her ministry is not mentioned; in Sozomen she appears only as the asylum-seeking wife of the banished consul Timasius (8.7). There are three extant letters to her from John Chrysostom,[311] who also mentions her in one of his letters to Olympias.[312]

One of the most important Byzantine deaconesses, Olympias, was a true friend of the unfortunate bishop, who in exile addressed seventeen letters to her, in which very personal communications are mixed with lengthy, generally edifying discussions about patience in trial.[313] Her biography was written anonymously, and Palladius memorialized her in his *Historia Lausiaca* (56): based on her steadfastness in persecution she was numbered among the "confessors" in Constantinople.[314] In his description of John Chrysostom's life he also reports a great deal about the well-known deaconess.[315]

Sozomen mentions Olympias three times. He reports that the young widow, who "devoted herself to philosophy in the context of the institutional church," was ordained a deaconess by Nectarius in spite of her youthful age. Since she shared her riches all too generously, John Chrysostom urged caution (8.9). With these riches the banished bishop himself was later able to diminish the pain of exile and also buy the freedom of prisoners (8.27).

We learn more about her personality through the reporting of a court case. After fire broke out in a church in Constantinople, Olympias and other followers of John Chrysostom were accused of arson. She replied that in this case she was above suspicion, having invested a considerable part of her wealth in the construction of churches. Since no guilt on her part could be demonstrated, the judge wanted to sentence her on account of a lesser crime, and her codefendants, for fear of something worse, were ready to submit to this "settlement"; she, however, demanded a proper completion of the procedure, and the case was then postponed. Later she was sentenced to a large fine, because she was not prepared to recognize the successor to John Chrysostom as the legal bishop of Constantinople. Nevertheless, she accepted the loss of her property and finally followed her friend willingly into exile (8.24).

Other followers of the exiled bishop in the capital city withdrew completely from public view and no longer dared to visit "the forums and the baths" (8.23.4). These included Nicarete (8.23.5ff.), whom John Chrysostom would gladly have ordained deaconess and put in charge of ecclesiastical virgins, but she apparently refused.[316] She came from a very prominent family and was without doubt well educated. Like Olympias she calmly accepted the blows of fate and the loss of a large part of her vast wealth. Yet in spite of her age she was very clever at managing what little she had left, so that she and her household were able to continue living without want and even to support others. Moreover, she must have had extraordinary medical knowledge, for Sozomen mentions her therapeutic successes (not miracles!) in the care of sick people whom the doctors had sought in vain to help. She made her own medicines. Yet the church historian praises this physician of the poor above all for her persistent rejection of the ministries offered her, and he never tires of emphasizing the hiddenness of her life and her unusual talents.

Now, we read, however, on the one hand that Nicarete was "famous because of her continued virginity," and on the other hand that during the uproar around John Chrysostom she withdrew from public life and afterward apparently headed her own household. Thus she seems not to have joined a convent or community of virgins. One might ask: Did she really reject the ministries out of humility, or did she perhaps want to preserve her independence? Since we have no other sources, the question must remain unanswered.

Theodoret, from whom we normally learn very little about women, reports in detail twice on deaconesses whose education is likewise without doubt. In contrast to the women mentioned by Sozomen, they are more prominent as independent subjects, although one of them remains nameless. The story of the deaconess Anonyma takes place in Antioch against the background of the conflicts under Julian over the old and new religions. The presentation is fictionally embellished, yet it reflects real historical conditions:

A young man who was a priest's son, and brought up in impiety, about this time went over to the true religion. For a lady remarkable for her devotion and admitted to the order of deaconesses[317] was an intimate friend of his mother. When he came to visit her with his mother, while yet a tiny lad, she used to welcome him with affection and urge him to the true religion. On the death of his mother the young man used to visit her and enjoyed the advantage of her wonted teaching. Deeply impressed by her counsels, he enquired of his teacher by what means he might both escape the superstition of his father and have part and lot in the truth which she preached. She replied that he must flee from his father, and honour rather the Creator[318] both of his father and himself; that he must seek some other city wherein he might lie hid and escape the violence of the impious emperor; and she promised to manage this for him. Then, said the young man, "henceforward I shall come and commit my soul to you." (3.14; 3.10 in NPNF, 2nd series, 3:100)

The narrative then describes how the young man flees to her in Antioch, where at first she puts him up with Meletius, a "man of God." He is traced there, however, by the angry father, who tortures him and locks him up at home. As an old man he describes his rescue in the following words:

"Even as I thus spoke," he told me, "out fell the bolts and open flew the doors, and back I ran to my instructress. She dressed me up in women's garments and took me with her in her covered carriage back to the divine Meletius. He handed me over to the bishop of Jerusalem, at that time Cyril, and we started by night for Palestine." (ibid.)

After the death of Julian, the son is supposed to have led the father to the "knowledge of God."[319] The story is clearly written for the purpose of denouncing the alleged godlessness of the emperor and his followers and also of glorifying the Christians' courage as martyrs. Julian in no way staged a bloody persecution, as is asserted in Theodoret's church history. But priests whose family members refused to worship the gods were indeed supposed to be relieved of their ministry[320]—a mixed-marriage prohibition similar to that sometimes applied today to ministers of Christian churches. Thus the background of the story is completely realistic.

Notable here is the way the deaconess is presented. There is no mention of a community of virgins or clergywomen in which she lives. Apparently she gives instruction in her house to catechumens—people who want to become Christians. According to the *Apostolic Tradition* written two hundred years earlier, applicants for baptism were examined by catechists[321] before being entered in the register of catechumens and then had to "hear the word" for three years; that is, they had to be introduced to the study of Holy Scripture (15 and 17). We now find deaconesses in Antioch fulfilling exactly this function, teaching by no means only women, as the *Didascalia* would have it, but also men. Whether the story of the adventurous flight in women's clothing is true is not important for us; in any case we have here the picture of a resolute and independent woman, who had at her disposal financial means and important connections.

Theodoret's history of Publia, who was "well known and famous because of her virtuous achievements" (3.19), is also told against the background of the conflicts under Julian. We may have here one of the rare cases of the addition (instead of suppression) of a title by the translation, and not in the modern period but already by the copyists of the early church who spread Theodoret's work. The chapter title, which does not come from the author, reads: "On Publia, the deaconess, and her godly bold behavior."[322] Yet in the story itself we find no express reference to her diaconal ministry. In the modern period, however, the title *didaskalos* ("teacher") was translated away, as we shall see. Nevertheless, I will treat Publia here as "perhaps a deaconess," since the ancient copyists apparently felt it was logical to see her as an ordained clergywoman.

In any case, she was a widow, which Theodoret expresses in this way: "For a short time she wore the yoke of marriage, and had offered its most goodly fruit to God." That fruit was John, who headed the presbyteriate in Antioch but rejected episcopal office. Thus the mother is first defined in terms of her son but praised as a "marvelous foundation." Earlier Theodoret had announced apologetically "that he now wants also to report on a marvelous and wonderful woman, for the woman had, in divine zeal, also offered resistance to [Julian's] rage" (3.18). Publia is then described as the head of a monastic community:

> She maintained a company [*choros*] of virgins vowed to virginity for life, and spent her time in praising God who had made and saved her. One day the emperor was passing by, and as they esteemed the Destroyer an object of contempt and derision, they struck up all the louder music, chiefly chanting those psalms which mock the helplessness of idols, and saying in the words of David, "The idols of the nations are of silver and gold, the work of men's hands," and after describing their insensibility,[323] they added "like them be they that make them and all those that trust in them." Julian heard them, and was very angry, and told them to hold their peace while he was passing by. She did not however pay the least attention to his orders, but put still greater energy into their chaunt, and when the emperor passed by again told them to strike up "Let God arise and let his enemies be scattered." On this Julian in wrath ordered the choir mistress [*didaskalos*, "teacher"] to be brought before him; and, though he saw that respect was due to her old age, he neither compassionated her gray hairs, nor respected her high character, but told some of his escort to box both her ears, and by their violence to make her cheeks red. She however took the outrage for honour, and returned home, where, as was her wont, she kept up her attack upon him with her spiritual songs, just as the composer and teacher of the song laid the wicked spirit that vexed Saul. (3.19; 3.14 in NPNF, 2nd series, 3:102–3)

Here again we have problems with misleading translations. Since songs play a major role in the story of Publia, one is tempted to translate *choros* literally, although it certainly does not mean a women's church choir but a monastic community; in the previous narrative about Anonyma the community of Christians is similarly called a "choir of the pious."[324] When we get off on the wrong track, the phrase *choir mistress* naturally becomes a problem: we think of a choir director, and the title *didaskalos,* which implies charismatic teaching ability, is eliminated. Then we also fail to notice a carefully constructed juxtaposition: the parallel between the *didaskalos* Publia, the teacher of virgins, who with her songs defeats the emperor possessed by evil, and the *didaskalos* David, the psalmist, who with his music drives the evil spirit out of King Saul. David, however, is the archetype who prefigures Christ, the victor par excellence over Satan. We shall see that this identification with Christ, the warrior, the "athlete," has its roots in the symbolism of the baptismal rites.[325] Publia appears here so to speak as the performer of the exorcism, the ritual banishment of evil that prepares catechumens for actual baptism.

One may reject the bedevilment of Julian and find outlandish the loud singing of hymns instead of an intelligent dialogue between religions, but that is no reason to overlook the real message of the text. If Publia is made a choir director, we are left with only the courageous provocation of an emperor. Even then the story is still impressive, for boldness is not usually among the virtues for which virgins are praised! But we are left totally in the dark regarding the fact that the community was a place where women were educated.

Thus Anonyma and Publia both perform the function of a *didaskalos.* In Sozomen's church history we have already met in Matrona a similarly impressive personality, who was a teacher of Macedonian virgins. Eusebia, Olympias, and Nicarete are not expressly characterized as teachers, but we may easily surmise that they were highly educated and actively helped to shape life in their communities.

There are only a few snapshots in these two church histories that allow us to catch glimpses of the real life of deaconesses in the fourth and fifth centuries. In addition there are two letters from Theodoret to deaconesses. He writes a letter of condolence to Casiana after the death of her son,[326] and he writes to Celarina on account of christological errors of which he is accused and asks her for wholehearted support of "the teachings of the gospel and the peace of the churches"[327]—hence, her voice must have carried weight in theological questions.

The list of deaconesses still known to us today can be easily lengthened. Roger Gryson includes thirty-five names in his study (Anonymae are omitted from his index); eighteen of these were found on inscriptions.[328] Although Sozomen's report, as we saw, betrays something of the public influence of deaconesses, we also see there a clear tendency that will determine the further development of the institution: removal from public life and into the cloister. In Theodoret, by contrast, we have in Anonyma an example of the autonomous church deaconess and catechist, who taught in her own home. Later, convent heads in particular were ordained deaconess for the needs of their own communities. The emphasis on the teaching role with Publia and Matrona, as well as the efforts of the bishop of

Constantinople to acquire the highly educated Nicarete for such a ministry, shows that convents were places where the education of women was promoted. It is true that deaconesses like Olympias lived a withdrawn life in a cloister, but not in strict separation: they played an active role in church life. The public activity of women as teachers, catechists, and theologians requires a thorough investigation.[329] The cited material already indicates without doubt that many of them were appreciated and recognized as teachers even by men. Hence a large part of Christendom at that time must not have regarded the New Testament prohibition of teaching as a binding norm.

Today we are scarcely still aware that *teacher* is one of the oldest titles for Christ to be transferred to women and men who also teach. The Greek *didaskalos* is the translation of the New Testament title *rabbi*. The familiar translation *master* (KJV), in combination with *disciple* instead of *student* (NIV), makes the word close to *Lord* and evokes the idea of discipleship and obedience. For the Jews *learning*[330] is the epitome of the study of the Torah; for the Greeks the transmission of knowledge is more important. The Christian *didaskaloi* were theologians and catechists, both women and men, after the model of Christ, the "pedagogue"—this title was coined by Clement of Alexandria, the founder of the first great Christian learning center in Egypt's Hellenistic metropolis: the *Paedagogus* is the title of one of his works, in which God's salvific activity is described as "pedagogy" of the human race. The proclamation of the gospel in this specific form of teaching does not presuppose ordination.[331] Thus in the early church women could be theologians and catechists independent of the diaconate; as deaconesses, however, they taught with the authority of a ministerial function.

Progress or Regress?

In retrospect the picture of the deaconess in the middle of the fifth century is impressive. But was this acme in the development of the female diaconate also a high point in the recognition of female participation in church life? The answer is clearly no. Nevertheless, if we consider the dispute over the position of widows, the "conquest" of this rank in the hierarchy must be seen first as a victory for women—and for those men who were supporters of equality as partners. A policy of fundamentally excluding all members of the female sex from any official ministry in the church had proved to be unfeasible. Women finally had to be granted at least ordination as deaconess.

Like other ecclesiastical functions, the female diaconate is the result of an ongoing process of institutionalization within Christianity. Out of the multiplicity of charismata—the special gifts and tasks in service of the church ranging from proclamation to care of the poor and sick—gradually came the official ministries that presupposed ordination. This was a normal process, for an expanding movement must create for itself institutions that match its size. Yet this process encompassed men only—women fell by the wayside. In the beginning we find both sexes on all levels of Christian church life; later it was determined that women are by nature "laity."[332] Nevertheless, in the East there were ordained clergywomen for a thousand years. They were not at first to be excluded completely from the hierarchy.

Yet this initial victory of women was a Pyrrhic one. If a minimal concession was made at first, it was soon evaded, and ultimately deaconesses were hardly more than liturgical decoration. This was not entirely the result of evil intention. When the Roman Empire was Christianized, women played an important role, not because of a desire to promote freedom and equality for women, but for the simple reason that men did not have the same easy access to women's living quarters. Deaconesses likewise performed important functions in the solemn rite of baptism, for the ritual actions of male ministers with unclothed women were increasingly felt to be improper—although probably less than we would think today, since in antiquity mixed baths and naked bathers were the norm. If no deaconesses were available, the anointings were undertaken by male clergy. With the development of the popular church and the dwindling of adult baptism, clergywomen lost their importance as catechists and liturgists. Thus many conflicts over women resolved themselves in favor of official church policy. With the intentional transition from the old practice of charismatic widowhood to the institution of the female diaconate, a far better ecclesiastical control over the activities of women became possible. It is true that some representatives of the female sex gained access to the lowest rank of the hierarchy, but in return they lost their independence. And a great many women who had previously won recognition as servants of the church now became honorary helpers in works of compassion.

There is, however, a fifth-century document, from a church that had separated from Constantinople, which through its opposite choices makes clear how much the decision in catholicism *for* the ordination of deaconesses was at the same time a decision *against* the activity of the widows: the *Testament of Our Lord,* another "apostolic" church discipline.[333] The authorities named there include—in addition to five male disciples, Peter, John, Thomas, Matthew, and Andrew (15.1)—three women disciples, Martha, Mary, and Salome (16.1). Yet they are not included in the "we" of the apostles making decisions.

After the councils of Ephesus (431) and especially Chalcedon (451) large parts of the old patriarchates of Antioch and Alexandria separated from the imperial church protected by the emperor—splits that we now know had political rather than theological causes.[334] The so-called Monophysite[335] Christians provided in their church discipline for the ordination of widows and allotted to them important tasks in catechesis, pastoral care, and worship.[336] There were no age boundaries nor a clause regarding previous marriage, and widows, like bishops, presbyters, and deacons, were elected by the people (1.40). In the celebration of the Eucharist we already find a curtain between altar and people—a first step toward the iconostasis of the Eastern church. Behind it and immediately next to the bishop were the widows, in front of the presbyters and deacons (1.197).[337] In the prayer of intercession the widow is even designated with the female equivalent of *presbyter* (1.35.5).[338] Six times the "widows who have priority" are mentioned, and naturally this does not mean "respect for age."[339] When various members of the clergy are listed, the widows do not always appear in the same place; in the Ethiopic version they are once mentioned parallel to the subdeacons according to their number: "twelve presbyters, seven deacons, fourteen subdeacons and fourteen widows with priority" (32).[340] In ordination and in the description of their pastoral care duties, however, the widow is clearly ranked parallel to the deacon (1.40–43). Deaconesses are also mentioned in the *Testament*, but they have merely the rank of helpers and do not receive ordination—they are, so to speak, "subwidows"; subdeacons and lectors are in fact only appointed, but the vocabulary in the *Testament* varies between appointment and ordination. The demarcation between ordained and nonordained clergy is not as prominent as in Hippolytus.

The presence of widows in the altar area during the eucharistic celebration is all the more astonishing in view of the fact that in church discipline the *Testament* has already adopted a taboo: during their menstrual period women are to stay away from the altar; that is, they may not commune. The same rule applies to men after the involuntary ejaculation of semen. In both cases it is expressly emphasized that the individual is not therefore unclean; it is merely a matter of showing reverence for the holiness of the altar (1.23.13). Thus the taboo does not lead here to a general prohibition of women from the sanctuary.

With regard to official deaconesses, however, there is a positive statement that they can take Communion to the sick, and thus in this case they may touch the consecrated gifts. Presence at the altar during the eucharistic celebration is not demonstrable, yet initially it should be assumed rather than ruled out. According to church rules, the actual presentation of bread and wine was reserved for members of the presbyteriate—whether this was always observed is another question.[341] As we saw, this restriction also applied at first to male deacons; later, however, they were given liturgical functions in the eucharistic celebration, whereas women were banned completely from the altar area. Now we have the emergence of the already-mentioned taboo, which is not encountered in the early period: menstruation as cultic impurity. The *Didascalia* rejects such an understanding of the monthly period as "Jewish superstition" (26). Later these archaic proscriptions are carried over to the worship service and in particular to the celebration of the Eucharist—without direct continuity with the religious praxis of Judaism—in a specifically Christian reading of the Old Testament purity laws.[342] Thus we must guard against making "Jewish" misogyny responsible for Christian practice. Here we can only point to the beginning of this taboo tradition. It is connected with a second stage in the development of church ministries, which can be called "cultifying" and sacralizing or even sacerdotalization,[343] that is, "priestification."

The first stage was the transition from freely exercised charismatic activities to the ecclesiastical orders and ordained ministries.[344] These orders found outward expression in a certain seating arrangement during worship services, but they were not defined by liturgical function. Here, as we saw, women could still find a place. In the second stage congregational worship became increasingly sacralized, and the importance of a ministry was measured by its relationship to the Eucharist, now increasingly understood as "sacrifice." In the New Testament the word *hi-*

ereus (Lat. *sacerdos*), "priest," is not used for Christian ministers; now it gains entrance into the church vocabulary. Bishops and presbyters became "priests" in analogy to the Jewish and Hellenistic temple cult; the remaining offices lost their independence. If they were not eliminated entirely from the hierarchical structure, they were integrated into the cultically oriented priesthood as preparatory stages. In this phase of the sacerdotalization of the clergy, women were definitively excluded. Naturally, not only is their elimination to be lamented here, but also the clericalization and sacralization of the old ministries and proclamation functions is problematic as such. Yet these issues cannot be discussed here.

Compulsory Celibacy
for Women Clergy

While the questions of cultic impurity through menstruation and hence the definition of a woman as a "sexual being" in regard to ordination to church ministries were not employed as arguments during the period under investigation here, celibacy, nonetheless, played a role very early—at first without being expressly stipulated. Although in the Gospel of Matthew (19:12) the call to voluntary celibacy "for the sake of the kingdom of heaven" is androcentrically formulated (as a call to castration), it was apparently followed more often by women than by men. In any case, the refusal of widows to remarry was a particular aggravation in the young churches. A strong reaction against the celibate tendencies favored by Paul is found in the marriage ideology of the pastoral epistles: ministers of the church are to be reliable fathers of families; widows are to be motivated toward remarriage. They are not to be recognized as "ecclesiastical" widows until age sixty. As we saw, this strategy was unsuccessful. The widespread tendency toward rejection of marriage in late antiquity also gained broad currency in early Christianity. The voluntary choice of many women for a single life now proved to a certain extent to be a boomerang: it became compulsory. As a married couple, Prisca and Aquila had still been able without question to place their lives into the service of the gospel. Later, however, celibacy became the tacit prerequisite to any involvement of women in church ministries. Even for the ecclesiastically recognized widow of the pastoral epistles, the idea of remarriage is called "lusting against Christ" (Luther) and "following Satan" (1 Tim. 5:11, 15).

The point at which the explicit demand for the celibacy of clergywomen came into being has not, to my knowledge, been investigated. In traditional studies of the history of ecclesiastical celibacy one looks in vain for laws that concern women.[345] Since widows are unmarried by definition, one had only to turn de facto celibacy into a permanent ministerial obligation. And since deaconesses seem to have replaced widows, it is easy to assume that they too were unmarried, but the early sources are silent on this point: neither the *Didascalia* (third century) nor canon 19 of Nicaea (325) expressly states that they may not be married. Yet in canon 15 of Chalcedon (451) this seems to be presupposed, since it stipulates that a deaconess who marries after her ordination is to be excommunicated.[346]

Not until the so-called *Apostolic Constitutions,* a fifth-century rewriting of the *Didascalia,* do we find an express stipulation that only a virgin or widow may be ordained deaconess (6.17.4).[347] Justinian (sixth century) even punishes the violation of the vow of virginity with the death penalty for both partners, in an express analogy to the regulations for vestal virgins (*Novellae* 6.6). Fortunately, there is no known case in which the law was applied! According to Theodorou, Theodosia, the wife of Gregory of Nyssa, was ordained deaconess when he ascended the throne, yet this information is extremely doubtful.[348] Canon 48 of the Trullan Synod (691) provides for such an ordination only if, after voluntary separation, the female partner has entered a convent. The extant source material from the early Christian period does not substantiate a deaconess being ordained while a "practicing wife."

Thus in questions of ecclesiastical celibacy there was clearly a double standard for men and women. Celibacy was automatically required of deaconesses at a time when for all male clergy marriage was still more the rule than the exception. Even the lover of asceticism Sozomen reports with approval that the Council of Nicaea protected the marriage of church ministers; the council had debated whether to prohibit the sexual activity of clergy after ordination. After the energetic plea of a celibate confessor and bishop in favor of marital relations, it was nonetheless decided to leave the choice to the individual (1.23). Socrates also reports this decision (1.11) and elsewhere presents in detail the various practices in regard to clerical marriage (5.22). Around three hundred years later the Trullan Synod in the East (691) expressly distanced itself from the Roman tendency to see a fundamental incongruity between sexual activity and service at the altar. The East held to chastity before the Sunday celebration of the Eucharist but rejected the demand that clergy who were married before ordination must fundamentally renounce sexual activity (canon 13).[349] Thus in the fifth century bishops, presbyters, and deacons could still be married and carry on normal marital relations, but they could also obligate themselves to voluntary celibacy. None of these freedoms applied to deaconesses.

Result: Patronization

Thus, judging by its results, the establishment of the female diaconate in the church was a restrictive and patronizing measure, even if many women used the opportunity thereby offered them in a thoroughly liberating way. Yet through their very ministry, which was linked with celibacy, deaconesses ran the risk of contributing to the clericalization of the churches and to the demotion of wives. The progressive reduction of the deaconess's functions, especially of her teaching activity, attests again in its own way to the fact that women were increasingly kept from having a real influence on the life of the church.

With respect to the examined church histories, however, one thing still stands out: it was apparently this ultimately very modest ministry that enabled at least some women to enter history *by name.* With the diminution of the female diaconate, a further repression of women was preprogrammed—and today the denial of ministries to women still remains a sure way to keep the female sex invisible in the church.

b. Rewriting Traditions:
A Missionary through Prayer

Among the most detailed reports on women that we find in the church histories of Socrates, Sozomen, and Theodoret are the chapters on the Christianization of the Saracens, an Arabian people, and the "Iberians," that is, the Georgians. We find both traditions in Rufinus. In this case we are interested less for the historical processes than for the manner in which the four authors deal with a female figure whose appearance does not correspond to the stereotypes of femininity.

The Field Commander Mavia

As the queen of the Arabian people called the Saracens,[350] Mavia does not appear in our texts as a missionary who preaches, yet she played the crucial role in the evangelization of her land. She forced a church leader of her choice on the Arian emperor Valens: around 374 the episcopal see of Pharan on the Sinai peninsula was given to Moses, a famous monk.[351] The peaceful ascetic refused to be ordained by Lucius of Alexandria, since the latter had been involved in the bloody policy of persecution against non-Arians. Because of her military successes against Roman troops, Mavia was able, with the emperor's approval, to have Moses ordained by bishops whom Valens himself had sent into exile.

Let us now read the four versions of the church historians. We will look only at the part of the report that concerns Mavia, not the disagreement between Moses and Lucius, which follows each excerpt.

As we would expect, Rufinus presents the events in a terse but clear fashion:

> Mavia, the queen of the Saracens, had begun to convulse the villages and towns on the border of Palestine and Arabia with a violent war and to ravage the neighboring provinces. After she had worn down the Roman army in several battles, had felled a great many, and had put the remainder to flight, she was asked to make peace, which she did on the condition already declared: that a certain monk Moses be ordained bishop for her people. (2.6)

Now let us read how Socrates describes the same happenings. His main interest is in the making of peace, for he ends the chapter with these words: "And so scrupulously did Mavia observe the peace thus entered into with the Romans that she gave her daughter in marriage to Victor the commander-in-chief of the Roman army" (4.36; NPNF, 2nd series, 2:116). He describes the main story as follows:

> No sooner had the emperor departed from Antioch, than the Saracens, who had before been in alliance with the Romans, revolted from them, being led by Mavia their queen, whose husband was then dead. All the regions of the East therefore

were at that time ravaged by the Saracens: but a certain divine Providence repressed their fury in the manner I am about to describe. A person named Moses, a Saracen by birth, who led a monastic life in the desert, became exceedingly eminent for his piety, faith, and miracles. Mavia the queen of the Saracens was therefore desirous that this person should be constituted bishop over her nation, and promised on this condition to terminate the war. The Roman generals considering that a peace founded on such terms would be extremely advantageous, gave immediate directions for its ratification. (ibid.)

Sozomen expands the chapter on Mavia by including the prior history of the Saracens and also explaining their name: the Ishmaelites, who were descended from the son of Abraham's concubine, did not want to be regarded as sons of Hagar and thus as slaves; therefore they named themselves after Sarah, Abraham's legal wife (cf. Genesis 16 and 21). This church history contains the most detailed description of the Roman's unsuccessful war against Mavia (whom Sozomen calls "Mania"):

> About this period the king of the Saracens died, and the peace which had previously existed between that nation and the Romans was dissolved. Mania, the widow of the late monarch, led her troops into Phoenicia and Palestine. . . . This war was by no means a contemptible one, although conducted by a woman. The Romans, it is said, considered it so arduous and so perilous, that the general of the Phoenician troops applied for assistance to the general of the entire cavalry and infantry of the East. This latter ridiculed the summons, and undertook to give battle alone. He accordingly attacked Mania, who commanded her own troops in person; and he was rescued with difficulty by the general of the troops of Palestine and Phoenicia. . . .
>
> As the war was still pursued with vigor, the Romans found it necessary to send an embassy to Mania to solicit peace. It is said that she refused to comply with the request of the embassy, unless consent were given for the ordination of a certain man named Moses, who practiced philosophy in a neighboring desert, as bishop over her subjects. This Moses was a man of virtuous life, and noted for performing the divine and miraculous signs. (6.38; NPNF, 2nd series, 2:374)

According to the three versions examined thus far, there is no doubt that in the battle against the Romans, Mavia was the victor and dictated her conditions. But Theodoret deals quite differently with the story: with a few strokes of the pen he turns a military victory into an edifying conversion story:

> At this time the Ishmaelites were devastating the country in the neighbourhood of the Roman frontier. They were led by Mavia, a princess who regarded not the sex which nature had given her, and displayed the spirit and courage of a man. After many engagements she made a truce, and, on receiving the light of divine knowledge, begged that to the dignity of high priest of her tribe might be advanced one, Moses by name, who dwelt on the confines of Egypt and Palestine. (4.23; 4.20 in NPNF, 2nd series, 3:126)

In short, two of the four early church historians, Rufinus and Socrates, report the facts objectively, without commenting positively or negatively on the sex of the queen: they want to show how, through Mavia and the monk Moses made bishop by her, peace was established between the hostile peoples. Why Sozomen goes so far into the difficulties of the Romans in battle with the Saracen queen cannot be divined from his presentation—was it perhaps because she imposed an orthodox ascetic bishop against the stiff resistance of the Arians? Both he and Theodoret feel called upon to mention the contradiction between their conception of women and the reality experienced in Mavia. After the military victory they emphasize the role of the monk now appointed bishop in the work of reconciliation between the Romans and the Saracens—the queen no longer plays any role. Theodoret cannot ignore the fact of a female field commander, but he does not give her the victory, and he has her, as one now recently converted, "beg" for a bishop (this translation is an interpretation, for the Greek verb can also be rendered "demand").

Thus Theodoret succeeds, without gross falsification, in showing Mavia's personality and her part in the Christianizing of the Saracens in a light that makes her a supporting figure who conforms to the traditional image of women. And it is Theodoret's version of history that has subsequently prevailed.[352]

A Woman Ascetic as Apostle

We can make very similar observations if we compare the four reports on the Anonyma,[353] who as a prisoner of war evangelized the kingdom of "Iberia" in the south of the Caucasus.[354] The Georgia tradition, linking Rufinus's report with other legends, has given her the name *Nino*, which, however, probably means simply "nun."[355] Here, in agreement with the sources, I use *Iberia* as the designation of the land that accepted Christianity around 330.[356] The rather long story has five acts, as it were; we will again start with Rufinus.

1. *The presentation of Anonyma.* The prisoner of war is notable because she leads "a faithful, modest, and chaste life" with long prayers day and night. Asked about this, she simply replies that this is the way she worships her God Christ. The women are especially interested in this new piety and wonder whether it leads to anything.

2. *The healing of a child.* It is the custom of the land to bring a sick child to all the women so that the one most knowledgeable in healing may treat it. Thus a sick boy comes to the prisoner. She confesses that she has no medical knowledge, yet the God Christ, whom she worships, can heal even when there is no longer any human hope. Through her prayer the child recovers, and the event makes the nameless one known.

3. *The healing of the queen.* The queen, who is seriously ill, also hears about it and wants Anonyma to come. The latter declines; she wants to do nothing that "is not allowed for her sex."[357] Then the queen asks to be taken to Anonyma and is likewise healed through prayer. The prisoner "teaches that Christ, who gives her health, is God, the Son of the highest God, and she admonishes: the one

whom she now knows as the author of her health and her life is the one on whom she must call, for he is the one who grants the kings dominion and the dying life." When the king learns of the healing, he wants to reward Anonyma, but the queen says no: the prisoner disdains riches. Only one thing can be a reward for her: to call on her God Christ.

4. *The conversion of the king.* The king hesitates, but one day during a hunt the sky darkens, and the king loses his way in the forest. Then the idea comes to him: if the God Christ would free him, he would want to worship him. The miracle occurs. The prisoner is fetched to explain how one worships her God (*colendi ritum*). She teaches that "Christ is God" and explains the forms of the worship service "as much as a woman has the right to."

5. *The erection of a church.* Anonyma initiates the construction of a church according to her plans. The king gathers the people and reports what the prisoner "has done for him and the queen and what faith she teaches." So he becomes, "not yet baptized,[358] the apostle of his people." "The men believe through the king; the women through the queen," and the construction of the church begins immediately with the agreement of all. Yet there is an obstacle: the third column cannot be erected. The builders give up in despair, but Anonyma passes the night praying in the half-finished church. In the morning the column hovers over its base and finally settles into position before the eyes of all. After the completion of construction the king, at the urging of the prisoner, forwards to the emperor Constantine the request to send priests "who will complete the work of God already begun."

Rufinus's unusual story is repeated in detail by all three later authors. In each case the essential structure and essential statements are reproduced, but the rather theological formulations of Anonyma's preaching of Christ are found only in Rufinus; in the three later versions they are omitted entirely or reduced to very general formulas. Each treatment has its own particular features.

Compared to Rufinus, Socrates makes no great changes in the course of the story. For him, however, the child becomes the prince in a redactionally inept way, since the statement that "the queen also hears about it" now sounds strange. In apostolic activity, Anonyma moves more into the shadow of the king: she is the "reason why he becomes a proclaimer of Christ." In Socrates the initiative for church construction and the legation to the emperor come not from the prisoner but from the king.

Not so with Sozomen: he emphasizes Anonyma's active role even more than Rufinus. In the very first sentence he says: "A Christian woman, who had been taken prisoner, caused the Iberians to abandon the religion of their fathers." Otherwise he stays close to the tradition of Rufinus. Here too her instruction of the ruler is accompanied by the cautious restriction that "she explained to him only as much as a woman is allowed to say and do," without our learning anything about the particular content. In the instruction of the people it is again the king who teaches the men, and the queen, together with Anonyma, instructs the women.

Theodoret did a more literary reworking of his source. He omits the column miracle at the end, but he clearly focuses attention on Anonyma. Her strict asceticism is rewarded "with gifts like those of the apostles"—thus the prisoner is ranked with biblical figures. In another place also he reworks the story following the model of the New Testament: the king does not go astray in the fog but like Saul is suddenly struck blind. The building of the church acquires a completely different, tangential function: the queen erects a chapel in gratitude for her healing. Also, the king is no longer taught by the woman but asks her to prepare for him the design for the church building, for which—following a biblical model—she is inspired like the artist Bezalel, to whom the Spirit of God gave the plans for the furnishing of the tent of meeting that Moses erected in the wilderness (Ex. 31:2ff.).

At first glance the story seems to intensify the role of the woman, from the first version to the last (after a setback with Socrates), and it also increases in length. It is surprising to find the proviso "as much as women are allowed" in Rufinus but not in Theodoret. Yet we must not let ourselves be deceived by such verbal augmentations: a movement into the legendary is also a step into the unreal and the exceptional. Then the story loses all character as a model for women who really exist, for a unique miracle is not automatically repeatable and thus is not "risky." Rufinus was closer to women who claimed an active ministry in the church. After the exclusion of the female sex from priestly functions was implemented in church law, the fantastic elaboration of a woman's active role in missions seemed less disturbing. Moreover, if we read the texts more closely, the first impression proves false; in reality there is a decline from Rufinus to Theodoret.

Let us look more closely at the "proviso." In Rufinus it is not used with regard to teaching, which for him obviously needs no legitimation, but in reference to worship: we find the word *rite* three times. Regarding Anonyma's prayers we read that she "worships her God Christ with this rite" (*Christum se Deum hoc ritu colere*). When the king converts, he asks the prisoner to come so that she may pass on to him the "rite for the worship service" (*colendi ritum*). Anonyma then in fact teaches him the "rite of prayer and the form for the worship [of God]" (*supplicandi ritum venerandique modum*). Obviously the foreign prisoner not only taught but also held worship services. This is not mentioned in the later texts. In Sozomen she is asked only to teach "how one worships Christ." The verb used here (*thrēskeuein*) includes cultic activity, and one might ask whether the double formulation of the proviso in Sozomen, "what a woman is allowed to *say* and *do*," does not also point to worship activity. Socrates and Theodoret do not need the proviso because they do not present Anonyma in a teaching role at all.

Two more features of Rufinus's report are noteworthy. The first is a somewhat derogatory remark about the female sex: "As is usually the case, that time spent [in prayer] evoked a certain curiosity among the women; [they wondered] whether such great piety had a useful purpose." Thus it was the women who first gave attention to Anonyma and her religion. The first healing miracle also took place in the presence of women. This suggests that the Christianization of Iberia began from below, not from above, as indicated by the official report.

Then comes perhaps the most surprising fact in the whole story: the role of Anonyma in the construction of the church. Rufinus says plainly: "She ordered a church to be built and described its form" (*fabricari tamen ecclesiam monet, formamque describit*). Did she know something about architecture? The whole report on the column miracle, which has no proper function, makes more sense if the prisoner of war also was involved in carrying out the construction. Yet since we have no other sources, this question cannot even be developed into a hypothesis.

Let us again compare the presentation of Anonyma in the earliest and latest versions. In Rufinus we have a woman who first attracts attention through her unusual lifestyle and then gradually assumes the role of a missionary. In the process she proves to be capable of giving theologically based introductions to the Christian faith, leading worship, and even building a church. Only then does she ask the emperor for reinforcement.

Now, what does Theodoret make of this woman who is in every respect unusual? He turns her into a pious ascetic who as a reward for her hard life has received the ability to effect miracles through her prayers. She opens her mouth to teach only once, for the queen: "As well as she could, she presented the divine teachings and admonished her to erect a church for Christ, who had healed her." Thanks to her miraculous gift, she also succeeds in drawing a plan for the church. But since one cannot do much in a church without a priest, she suggests that the king ask the emperor to send "teachers of religion."

In Theodoret's version we have a perfect example of the reworking of an old tradition to serve an ecclesiastical ideology. One fact is clear: the gospel was proclaimed to the Iberians by a Christian woman who was a prisoner of war. But the norm of the church forbids women to preach and teach in public. At best, only the catechesis of women by women is allowed. Thus the story must be told in such a way that the norm is not called into question. Even in Rufinus we find in regard to teaching a neat separation of the sexes: the king teaches the men; the queen, the women. The instruction of the king—which, of course, only Anonyma could give, so that we have here without doubt a woman teaching a man—is placed in a nonpublic context. It was apparently less scandalous to bestow the title of apostle on the unbaptized king than on the Anonyma who was the actual herald of the gospel. As earlier in the case of Mavia, we have here the same subsequent history: Theodoret's version is the one that prevailed.[359]

Result:
The Normative Power of the Imagined

Even if we cannot say in particular cases whether an author consciously modified narrative traditions in order to forestall possible claims by women who wanted to participate actively in worship, preaching, and teaching, or whether authors unconsciously propagated a certain image of women, the result remains the same: women were unconsciously excluded from certain areas on the level of the imagination. Women apostles were described in such a way that their preaching and teaching activities were no longer visible. Later generations drew the conclusion that in Christian antiquity there were no apostolically active women and indeed could not have been. For the texts of the New Testament that try to limit the right of women to speak and teach publicly were no longer regarded as what they are: documents of a conflict over the lived gospel that are to be compared with the dispute between Peter and Paul over Christian freedom vis-à-vis the Mosaic law (Gal. 2:11–21). These late texts were no longer read in the light of earlier ones that testify to the equality of women in theory and practice (esp. Gal. 3:28 and Rom. 16:1ff.), but the other way around. Thus the deviation from the original equality of all the disciples of Jesus could become the law of the church.

Yet "early" or "late" is not the real criterion. The crucial point is that a misogynistic norm was sanctioned that contradicted both the progressive ethos of late antiquity and the message of the gospel. The fact that we find misogynistic texts even in the "Holy" Scripture is not the real problem, for in the formulation of Susanne Heine, "the history that is comprised in the canon of the New Testament is not only a history of successful praxis; in it both claim to and betrayal of the New Testament are equally represented."[360] The problem lies rather in the fact that these texts were declared the revelation of divine will and used for centuries to legitimate the suppression of certain groups of people as part of the created order. Let it be well noted that here it is not only a question of discrimination on the basis of sex. The undermining of the egalitarian ethos likewise affects slaves and ultimately even the male laity. The latter groups, however, could change their status; women could not.

Yet even in the fifth century the commandments of subordination and silence in the pastoral epistles were by no means regarded by all Christians as binding doctrine; rather, the conflict over equal status in the church continued. The revision of tradition was a subtle means of preparing the way for an increasing discrimination against women in the church. It is clear that by means of prescriptive and descriptive texts—that is, through legal measures and edifying stories—the conception of certain men of the church was supposed to be made the norm. If it was a question in the first case of a clear attempt to exercise direct and indirect power over women, then in the second case the process is much more unobtrusive: here an ideal is suggested that seems to elevate women but in reality takes their autonomy and commits them to inwardness. A withdrawn, prayerful existence is declared to be the basic content of their lives, and there is no alternative.

With one outstanding female figure of Christian late antiquity, the transformation from active woman apostle to withdrawn woman ascetic took place in grand style: Thecla of Iconium. We will not deal with her here, but she must be mentioned.[361] Who was she? In the oldest source, the *Acts of Paul*,[362] her picture is already fancifully drawn, and thus it is hardly possible to expose the historical core, but even in literary stylization, her figure goes beyond usual bounds. This writing focused on Paul is extant only in fragments; together with four other apostle stories it belongs to the early Christian literature that long enjoyed quasi-canonical esteem but was then increasingly contested. According to the pattern of romantic continence stories, which are found in all extracanonical acts of apostles,[363] Thecla leaves her fiancé and is persecuted because of this decision. Yet at two points her story is clearly different from the others. (1) It is not the apostle who is the focus but Thecla: she is condemned to death, not Paul. (2) Other female characters appear only as converts; Thecla, however, is determined to proclaim the gospel herself, and she does. What is more, she is commissioned by Paul himself: "Go forth and teach the word of God" (41). The short narrative ends with the words: "Afterward . . . she went to Seleucia; after she enlightened many through the word of God, she died a peaceful death" (43).

In the fifth century we find in the mountains near this port in Asia Minor an impressive shrine with many churches and cloisters under the patronage of this woman;[364] her story is written again, and the author succeeds in giving a misogynistic doctrine to the stubborn old tale in which Thecla travels and preaches in men's clothing.[365] The transformation of this woman apostle into a quasi-goddess, who is now praised simply as *the* virgin, has been thoroughly studied by Ruth Albrecht.[366] Yet even the "domesticated" woman apostle apparently represented a "dangerous memory,"[367] for her cult was gradually replaced by the veneration of the *theotokos* (mother of God) promoted by the church: the virginal mother replaced the apostolic celibate as the ideal female type. In Western Christianity the memory of Thecla was so thoroughly suppressed that after the Second Vatican Council the Roman Catholic church removed this early Christian figure from the calendar—a particular *damnatio memoriae!*

Yet between the suppressed woman apostle and the idealized virgin there was another tradition in the Christianity of late antiquity: Thecla was venerated above all as a martyress. The memory of a persecuted witness to the faith may be the historical core of the fancifully elaborated story. In the early church no one enjoyed higher regard than those women and men who confessed their allegiance to Christ at the risk their lives. They are the topic of our next chapter.

II. WOMEN IN MARTYRDOM

Courageous Confessors

1. Historical Background

a. The Sources

We are familiar with the designation *protomartyr* (that is, first martyr) for Stephen, whose stoning is reported in the canonical Acts of the Apostles (chap. 7). Early Christian tradition also bestowed this title on Thecla, and in the Eastern church she is still celebrated as first martyress and isapostolic one ["equal to or contemporaneous with the apostles"]. The separate tradition of the *Acts of Thecla* under the title *Martyrdom* or *Passio* shows that the ancient narrative was read not as part of a history of the apostles but as one of the *acts of the martyrs,* a separate literary genre, which we will discuss below. In the titles of the extant Greek manuscripts, *Acts [praxeis] of Paul and Thecla* occurs only once, but there are ten occurrences of *Martyrdom . . . of the First Martyress* (often in connection with the term for woman apostle), without mentioning Paul; the Latin manuscripts speak of the passion of the "virgin and martyress."[1] Only a few fragments of the Paul story are extant, but the entire Thecla story and the account of the apostle's death have come down to us; this shows the importance attached to martyrdom accounts.

Eusebius included the *Acts of Paul* among the books that are not to be counted as Holy Scripture,[2] but this attests to the fact that there was still no unity on the canon: he also classified the Revelation to John as "unauthentic," but today it is part of the New Testament. The naming of the *Acts of Paul* first leads one to infer especially high esteem. In any case, the gradual devaluation of the extracanonical writing did not put an end to the veneration of Thecla, for in one place Eusebius calls an eponymous Palestinian martyress the "Thecla of our time,"[3] which presupposes that everyone knew the one to whom he was alluding. For the church fathers, Thecla had the rank of a biblical figure. Even Tertullian—who attacks the *Acts of Paul* because in it the apostle commissions a woman to teach the word of God—does not call the martyress into question.[4]

The idea of assuming behind the Thecla story a historically authentic martyrdom account is not new: in 1893 William Ramsay made an attempt to reconstruct a written source that could have been available to the author of the *Acts of Paul.*[5] In 1903 Henri Leclercq published some unauthentic acts of martyrs together with the authentic,[6] since he believed that here "bits of highest [historical] value were mixed in the context of a freely invented plot, like grains of genuine metal in a thick sticky paste."[7] This judgment applied especially to the *Acts of Thecla*, which comes first in Leclercq. Ramsay's attempt could not convince scholars that the written source postulated by him existed. Prior oral traditions, however, are a different matter. Jean-Daniel Kaestli has pointed out that a unified theory cannot do justice to the highly varied acts of apostles and the ancient traditions they contain: each piece of tradition must be examined individually.[8]

It is impossible within the framework of this study to clarify the question of the historical elements in the Thecla story. But reference to the "first martyress" should remind us that the later (de)valuation of extracanonical literature must not be transferred into the early period. At that time the *Acts of Paul* was read with the same enthusiasm as the canonical Acts of the Apostle ascribed to Luke. Only the latter is still known to us today, yet both belong to the same literary genre, in which the "acts" (*praxeis*) of the apostles are described. Because of attestation in these "apostolic" writings, Stephen and Thecla were considered by the early church to be the first martyr and the first martyress, representing, as it were, men and women. This parity of the sexes was important to early Christendom: it expressed the awareness that both had in like manner received the gift of bearing witness to Christ.

Of the five extracanonical acts of the apostles, four also contain acts of the martyrs, for in each case they end with the account of the violent death of Paul, Peter, Andrew, or Thomas; we have no other sources on how the lives of these apostles came to an end. Yet in the context of the criminal prosecution of Christians, the term *praxeis* refers initially not to the glorification of heroic deeds but to documentation of the trial. Yet it was seldom a matter of the pure form of a trial record: the literal transcription of the proceeding was expanded with accounts by eyewitnesses and with commentaries, and thus the acts of the martyrs that are regarded as authentic today reveal varying degrees of literary revision.[9]

In what follows we will examine these sources for testimonies about women. In most reports we find brief mentions, and from these we will first assemble an overall picture of the historical facts. In Perpetua's dream visions, the experienced reality of the trial, the arrest, and the expectation of death are intertwined in a special way with the symbolic world of the baptismal ritual. This valuable self-testimony of a woman even provides a certain insight into an unconscious coming to terms with the imminent life-and-death battle in the arena. Hence, it will be analyzed in detail. Yet the other writings also contain theological models of interpretation. For the early church, martyrs had a special status, since through their witness the event of Jesus' death and resurrection remained present in the congregations. Therefore, the idea of the representation of Christ—which plays a role not least of all in the understanding of church ministries—is a central focus of this investigation.

Thus the documents must be examined twice: *for facts passed on* and *for theological interpretations.* In order not to confuse these perspectives, I shall first proceed in a narrative fashion: the shorter testimonies will be presented and then the longer reports on Blandina, Perpetua, and Felicity. In a second pass the dream visions of Perpetua will be analyzed, and then we will ask generally about the self-understanding of women martyrs and their position in the churches.[10]

One point is not to be forgotten in this chapter: the courageous confessors of both sexes were an elite that is not representative of the whole of Christianity in the second and third centuries. Also, Christians of that time were not simply "the church of the martyrs," as they are often idealized in retrospect. In the inflamed emotional climate of the persecutions, there were also pathological tendencies and intolerant fanaticism. For many, death for the faith seemed to be something desirable—the well-known letters of Ignatius of Antioch are a document of such a longing for martyrdom. Yet this attitude was less widespread than the exalted literary praise of martyrdom would lead one to believe. "Christians also 'liked to live,'" writes Dorothea Wendebourg with reference to the acts of the martyrs: "The spirit that governed the actual behavior of Christians in times of persecution was different from the one that pervades most of the writings *about* martyrdom."[11]

Most of those threatened were not striving for martyrdom; they were trying to avoid it through flight, for they plainly understood the saying in Matt. 10:23, "When they persecute you in one town, flee to the next," as a "commandment" in their situation.[12] They consented to martyrdom when there was no other way out. Then, however, it was regarded as fate willed by God and indeed as special election. To consent voluntarily to martyrdom, even to seek it intentionally, was seen by many as reprehensible arrogance: God alone determines the hour of final witness and death.

b. The Phases of the Persecution

We shall first look briefly at the history of the trials and pogroms of Christians in the Roman Empire. The persecutions began after the burning of Rome under Nero in 64.[13] Today there is still disagreement on whether the emperor ordered the persecution by edict, but this is likely, for, as Willy Rordorf remarks, "The later Roman legislation . . . is understandable only under the presupposition that Nero issued a mandate at least for the city of Rome that ordered the persecution of Christians."[14]

The description by Tacitus, who distances himself equally from both the Christians and the brutality of the emperor, is well known:[15]

> But neither human resources, nor imperial munificence, nor appeasement of the gods, eliminated sinister suspicions that the fire had been instigated. To suppress this rumour, Nero fabricated scapegoats—and punished with every refinement the notoriously depraved Christians (as they were popularly called).[16] Their originator, Christ, had been executed in Tiberius' reign by the governor of Judaea, Pontius Pilate. But in spite of this temporary setback the deadly superstition had broken out afresh, not only in Judaea (where the mischief had started) but even in Rome. All degraded and shameful practices collect and flourish in the capital.

First, Nero had self-acknowledged Christians arrested. Then, on their information, large numbers of others were condemned—not so much for incendiarism
as for their anti-social tendencies.[17] Their deaths were made farcical. Dressed in
wild animals' skins, they were torn to pieces by dogs, or crucified, or made into
torches to be ignited after dark as substitutes for daylight. Nero provided his Gar-
dens for the spectacle, and exhibited displays in the Circus, at which he mingled
with the crowd—or stood in a chariot, dressed as a charioteer. Despite their guilt
as Christians, and the ruthless punishment it deserved, the victims were pitied.
For it was felt that they were being sacrificed to one man's brutality rather than
to the national interest.

At this point Christianity was an officially prohibited religion regarded as a danger
to the state. We must not overlook the fact that the apocalyptic basic attitude of
many first-century Christians, with their disdain for the world and the state, contributed something to their being unpopular.[18] An echo of this attitude is found
in the Scillitan acts of the martyrs (180 in Africa) in the confession of Speratus: "I
do not recognize the empire [*imperium*] of this world."[19] This attitude was very
clearly expressed in the account of Paul's martyrdom in Rome (in the *Acts of Paul*).
    In the court proceedings merely being a Christian was sufficient to convict and
execute the accused, since the crime of religion was considered lèse-majesté. Not
only did this automatically bring the death penalty, but it also stripped the accused of all civil rights, since through the deed itself they had placed themselves
outside civil society—according to the legal construct.[20] When a conviction is reported solely on the basis of confessing Christ, we are probably dealing with a
very old tradition.[21]
    Although in 112 Trajan gave the directive that Christians were not to be
sought out but only condemned when they were accused,[22] there were numerous persecutions in the course of the second century. In the third century the
dominant tendency was to select and execute certain individual Christians in order to set an example. On the form and extent of the persecution under Severus,
which presumably began around 201 or 202, there are various opinions;
nonetheless, it seems to have affected catechumens and the newly baptized in
particular.[23] After Valerian's edict (257), which indirectly reflected the recognition of the church as an "association,"[24] persecution was directed mainly at ministers: bishops, presbyters, and deacons. In 250 under Decius there was a short
general persecution in which Christians were forced to sacrifice to the gods and
received a certificate attesting to this fact. The practice was then taken up again
in 303 under Diocletian in a wild rage of persecution, until in 313 the Edict of
Milan finally granted Christians the right to exist.

2. Deliverance into Prostitution:
The Double Martyrdom

    Thecla asks to be allowed to remain chaste before her martyrdom (*Acts of The-
cla* 27). It is not ascetic romanticism that lies behind this request, but brutal re-

ality: "Women who refuse to sacrifice are put into a brothel";[25] this is the threat against the slave Sabina in the proceedings against her and Pionius (second half of the third century). In his study Leclercq believes he must overlook this point out of shame,[26] but Friedrich Augar, at the instigation of his teacher Harnack, has investigated it thoroughly and soberly under the neutral title, *Die Frau im römischen Christenprozess.* Being turned over to a brothel—as happened in 304 to a woman named Irene in Thessalonica in execution of a judicial verdict—was not a romantic elaboration in the acts of martyrs for the purpose of contrasting the chastity of women with the evil of the "idolaters" persecuting them.[27] Rather, this measure lay in the range of the judge's legitimate discretion: it could be either a form of pressure to force the accused to give up her resistance or an increase in punishment.[28] The concrete motivation of the judge could be "leniency" (the desire to avoid the automatic death penalty) or pure sadism. The latter is portrayed tendentiously in later Christian accounts, but to assume that such things did not happen among the Romans with their consciousness of the law would be wishful thinking.

The assumption that, in Augar's view, "placement for the time being in a brothel was by far the lesser evil"[29] hardly corresponds to Roman sensitivity: bodily purity was so highly valued that women preferred suicide to defilement.[30] More apt is his observation that many judges sent Christian virgins into brothels "with extreme malice precisely to inflict the most acute punishment through their prostitution."[31] Since this double martyrdom of women receives little notice, it will be presented here in somewhat greater detail. We should note, however, that sexual sadism was also practiced on men: Eusebius gives one account of castrations.[32]

Outside of Christianity, only a single case of the public rape of a virgin before her execution is known: in a case of lèse-majesté in A.D. 31, not only was the guilty man—a certain Seian—executed but also his immature children. Tacitus writes: "Contemporary writers report that, because capital punishment of a virgin was unprecedented, [the girl] was violated by the executioner, with the noose beside her."[33] What implicit cynicism lies in such reverence for the patriarchal customs!

Augar documents a total of thirteen cases in which the accounts of judicial threat of rape, execution of rape, or deliverance to a brothel in trials against Christian women are demonstrated to be historically reliable.

a. The Legal Situation

There was no law that provided for deflowering before execution or that expressly forbade the execution of a virgin. Condemnation to a brothel as punishment for women is not attested by Roman law. Yet condemnation to lifelong punishment involved the loss of freedom. The following formulation from Justinian's collection of laws can be regarded as a summary of classical Roman law: "Those who are condemned to work in the mines or are thrown to the animals become penal slaves."[34] Hildegard Cancik-Lindemaier concludes from this: "Christian women who were sentenced in the persecutions—especially *ad bestias*—were

most certainly *servae poenae* (penal slaves) and as such to be used at will; bor-
dellos were found especially in the vicinity of the amphitheater and the circus."[35]

This legal situation came about not after conviction but with the accusation,
for the already-mentioned equation of the religious offense of which Christians
were accused with lèse-majesté meant the loss of civil rights protection. Yet this
seems to have been handled in different ways; the privilege of a Roman citizen
to be executed by the sword was usually respected in the trials. The use of torture, deliverance to a brothel, and the imposition of degrading death penalties
lay within the discretion of the judge. Outside of Christian persecutions such judicial proceedings against women are not attested—according to Augar.

b. Testimonies

The oldest historically reliable source for sentencing to prostitution is Tertullian's *Apologeticum,* in which he reproaches the Romans for summarily deliver-
ing a Christian woman to a pimp (*leno*) instead of a lion (*leo*), knowing that
Christians regarded this as a more horrible punishment than death.[36] In a similar generalization Hippolytus denounces the fact that in trials against Christians,
virgins and other women are subjected to "public rape and shameful mockery."[37]
Finally, Cyprian calls the dead martyresses fortunate because they can no longer
be threatened by the Antichrist "with rapes and brothels."[38] In the acts of the
Martyrs, however, it is not a question of general reproaches but of concrete individual cases; these will now be briefly described.

Among those accused with the presbyter Pionius[39] is the confessor Sabina.
Why a specialist like Herbert Musurillo in his *Acts of the Martyrs* renders the title *homologētria,* which in the text is clearly parallel to Pionius's presbyter title,
as "holy woman" remains his secret; here we have a further example of the "trans-
lating away" of female ministerial titles. Those who suffered persecution but survived were also called confessors and martyrs; they were held in high regard in
the churches.[40] In fact, the acts do not speak of Sabina's execution. The account
of the martyrdom of Pionius and his companions[41] is developed as literature, but
it contains authentic judicial records. It recounts how Sabina had been a slave
and hid herself with Pionius out of fear of her mistress, and thus was arrested with
him. Because of her faith this mistress had earlier abandoned her in the mountains, where she was secretly fed by the brothers and was finally liberated.[42]

The following hearing is typical of authentic acts of martyrs: brief, stereotypical interrogation on the part of the judge, calm irony on the part of the accused,
who occasionally answer with confessional formulas that are incomprehensible to
the Romans. Francine Cardman has correctly pointed out that the speeches before the court for the defense of men are substantially more detailed than those
of the women[43]—which did not necessarily correspond to reality. The dialogue
with Sabina reads: "Are you a Christian?" "Yes, I am." "What is your church?"
"The Catholic Church." "Whom do you worship?" "Almighty God, who made
the heaven and the earth and all of us, and who has been made known to us
through his Word, Jesus Christ."[44] In the preceding hearing for Pionius, how-

ever, Sabina had already been mentioned. When in response to the threat of being burned alive he replies: "It is far worse to burn after death," Sabina smiles
and is shouted at by the executioner and his people: "You laugh?" "If God so
wills," she said, "I do. You see, we are Christians. Those who believe in Christ
will laugh unhesitatingly in everlasting joy." Then she receives the already-cited
threat: "You are going to suffer something you do not like. Women who refuse
to sacrifice are put into a brothel." Still she replies calmly: "The God who is all
holy," she said, "will take care of this."[45] In this case, it presumably remained
only a threat.

Things were different, however, in Thessalonica in 304.[46] Seven women, all
mentioned by name, flee from persecution into the mountains but are arrested
in their hiding place. They are accused because they refuse to eat meat offered to
the gods. After the first hearing two of them are condemned to death by fire; the
other five are initially sent back to prison "because of their youth." Because of
the concealment of Christian books, Irene is then interrogated separately and
questioned in detail about the stay in the mountains. Apparently it was hoped
that she would betray the names of accomplices, but she answered cleverly. Finally comes the prefect's sentence:

> Your sisters, in accordance with my commands in their regard, have received
> their sentence. Now you were already guilty because you ran away and you con-
> cealed these writings and parchments, and hence I do not wish you to die im-
> mediately in the same way. Instead I sentence you to be placed naked in the
> brothel with the help of the public notaries of this city and of Zosimus the ex-
> ecutioner; and you will receive merely one loaf of bread from our residence, and
> the notaries will not allow you to leave.[47]

The order is carried out, but in the brothel none of the men dares to approach
her or even to humiliate her verbally. Then she is brought into court again. "Do
you still persist in the same folly?" "It is not folly, but piety."[48] Irene is subsequently burned to death. The fate of the other four women remains unknown.

In his church history Eusebius passes on an account of the martyrdom of
Potamiaina in Alexandria a hundred years earlier,[49] but the report contains no authentic trial record; rather, it exhibits fanciful clichés that praise the martyress's
love of virginity. Nevertheless, the sober core of the story can be regarded as historical. The judge first has Potamiaina tortured and then threatens her with rape
by "gladiators"—so the Greek text reports. The Armenian and Latin versions,
however, have "pimp" here, which may be the original reading that was toned
down out of special consideration for the women among the readers.[50] Her answer—whose content is not passed on—must have been provocative, since the
death sentence was immediately carried out. Her body is covered from top to bottom with burning tar. Eusebius reports that two other women could not bear the
"threat of rape" and therefore challenge the judge: they are executed with especially gruesome torture.[51]

Eusebius also reports on terrible martyrdoms in Thebais and on gruesome acts
of violence against women, some of which he himself experienced as an eyewitness:

But words cannot describe the outrageous agonies endured by the martyrs in Thebais. They were torn to bits from head to foot with potsherds like claws till death released them. Women were tied by one foot and hoisted high into the air, head downwards, their bodies completely naked without a morsel 'of clothing, presenting thus the most shameful, brutal, and inhuman of all spectacles to everyone watching. Others again were tied to trees and stumps and died horribly; for with the aid of machinery they drew together the very stoutest boughs, fastened one of the martyr's legs to each, and let the boughs fly back to their normal position; thus they managed to tear apart the limbs of their victims in a moment.[52]

Another group of stories reports on women who escaped impending rape through suicide—Eusebius praises this as the highest virtue. He tells of the following incident in Antioch. When a mother with two virgin daughters is captured while fleeing from soldiers, she impresses upon her daughters what they must now do: all three jump together into a nearby river and drown.[53] Eusebius reports the following from Rome: a Christian woman and senator's wife whom the tyrant Maxentius wanted to abuse was to be picked up from her house—the husband had agreed, out of fear of arrest.[54] When she heard the men in the house, she stabbed herself with a sword, in order to leave her rapist with only a corpse.[55]

Sozomen also reports a similar case, which, however, is not the result of the persecution of Christians but of political intrigue. When soldiers break into the house of the field commander Gerontius, he forgoes escape through flight because of his wife. He kills his companion Alanus, following his wish, and then also his Christian wife, at her request, in order to save her from rape. Finally he kills himself. Sozomen praises the behavior of Nonnichia as the highest Christian virtue.[56]

In these texts the basic events have already been greatly reworked to make them more like a Christian apologia. The motif of suicide for the preservation of chastity is even further developed literarily in the history of the virgin Pelagia, which is recounted by both John Chrysostom and Ambrose.[57] When soldiers enter the house during the persecution, she adorns herself like a bride and jumps from the roof. In Ambrose, Pelagia's mother and two sisters come back into the house afterward and then jump into the nearby river.[58] He expressly justifies this action and compares the water of the stream with the waters of baptism.[59]

These last texts show how in the later preaching of virginity, martyrdom traditions were linked with motifs of ascetic continence. The sober brothel accounts are similar: the preservation of virginity—perhaps in the acts of Irene to be explained psychologically by the situation—becomes the central theme and is exaggerated into the miraculous. In the acts of the saints Didymus and Theodora,[60] which are perhaps at least partly genuine, the usual sentencing of the virgin to a brothel occurs. She is then saved by a Christian brother, who goes into the bordello in soldier's clothing, enabling her to escape in these clothes, and for this is executed.

Palladius has a similar story. In Corinth a virgin is sentenced to a brothel and is supposed to bring in three gold pieces daily. She escapes through deception: at the moment, she says, she has a horribly evil-smelling abscess, but in a few days she will be available to all free of charge. In the meantime she asks God to save her. Here too a young man finally sacrifices himself for her, and she escapes in his clothing; as punishment he is thrown to the animals.[61]

Ambrose, who did not know the age of persecution from personal experience, broadly portrays this story (or a similar one) in his edification text *Concerning Virgins*[62] and in the process lets the narrative slip into the grotesque. After he first presents Mary of Nazareth and Thecla of Iconium as models of virginity, he wants to offer another example from the immediate past. Here too a virgin is saved by an unknown soldier in whose clothes she flees. Yet afterward she does not want to accept the sacrifice of the stranger but instead competes with him for the martyr's crown, which both finally attain. The brothel scene is portrayed in burlesque fashion: the second cheated customer calls out: "I had heard, but not believed, that Christ changed water into wine; now he is also beginning to change the sexes. Let us run away while we are still what we were!" The brutal reality of the time of persecution has become a miraculous and fanciful motif for edification, while the original gruesome seriousness and the suffering of raped women are threatened with oblivion! Yet on the positive side we note that Ambrose relativizes physical intactness; he has the virgin who must accept rape with martyrdom say to herself: "Better the virginity of the spirit than that of the flesh. Both are good, if possible; if not, may we at least be chaste before God, if not before human beings" (2.24).[63]

After the sad facts of this chapter of the Roman persecution of Christians has been reported, let it also be recalled again that a little later Christians also engaged in the persecution of dissenters with sexual sadism against women. Socrates reports on Arian methods of torture "unknown even among the heathen."[64] Since he otherwise holds the Arians in high regard and also refers to an eyewitness, we cannot presume any antiheretical polemic behind this report. According to Socrates the Arians "laid hold of women and children [of the catholic and Novatian churches], and compelled them to be initiated [by baptism]; and if any one resisted or otherwise spoke against it, stripes immediately followed, and after the stripes, bonds and imprisonment, and other violent measures. . . . They first pressed in a box, and then sawed off, the breasts of such women as were unwilling to [commune] with them. The same body parts of the persons of other women they burnt partly with iron, and partly with eggs heated intensely in the fire."[65] It is also Socrates who reports the murder of the Neoplatonic philosopher Hypatia carried out in 415 in Alexandria by a Christian mob under Bishop Cyril.[66]

Up to this point we have examined the acts of martyrs in regard to the special aspect of sexual sadism against women, which is found in many but by no means all martyrdoms of women. In the following sections we will examine the reports of the two theologically most important martyrdoms, which are connected with the names Blandina, Perpetua, and Felicity. First, however, we will mention the martyresses whom we know from the oldest documents. At the same time we must recall the accounts of Eusebius, Socrates, Sozomen, and Theodoret.[67]

In 160 *Agathonike* was burned to death in Pergamum together with Karpos and Papylos. There are two contradictory accounts of her martyrdom: it is possible that she offered herself voluntarily,[68] although she still had a son to care for. *Chariton* was the only woman among six martyrs arrested with the apologist Justin. They were publicly flogged and beheaded in Rome in 165. When it was suggested at her hearing that she was "deceived" by the talk of the others and had a bad reputation, she replied: "I am not deceived . . . rather, I have become God's servant and a Christian, and by his power I have kept myself pure and unstained by the taints of the flesh."[69] We have here possibly the echo of a slandering before the court; false statements against Christians are also attested elsewhere. Among the twelve martyrs who in 180 died by the sword in Africa are five women, but the report, a summary transcript, contains hardly any information beyond their names.[70] *Marcella*, the mother of Potamiaina, was burned to death with her daughter in Alexandria in 205.[71] In 304 in Tagora (Africa), in a carefully recorded judicial procedure, *Crispina* was threatened with the disfigurement of her beauty. Also mentioned is the execution of her women companions, which had already occurred. She herself was beheaded.[72] Finally, we learn about *Quartillosa*, who is reported to have soon followed the path of her own family: her husband and her son had already died as martyrs. She visited the martyrs in prison and had a prophetic vision, but she herself was probably not executed.[73] These are the few names found in the tradition, but they represent many others.

3. Blandina—a Slave
as Mother of the Church

The figure of Blandina comes to us in one of the oldest and theologically most important documents of the time of persecution: it is the report of the massacre of the Christians in Lyon and Vienne in 177, which was written by contemporaries immediately after the events.[74] From this account, which the persecuted Gallic Christians addressed to the churches in "Asia and Phrygia," we have only the detailed excerpts in book five of Eusebius's church history. He writes there in his introduction that he has published the full text in a "collection of martyrdoms," but this document has been lost. The letter, says Eusebius, has two parts: the communication of the facts and an instructive presentation.[75]

The persecutions of Christians in Lyon and Vienne apparently began with spontaneous acts of violence, which then led to regular trials and finally to intentional, systematic persecution of all Christians in these churches (8, 15). The account originally contained an exact list with the numbers and names of victims and also of those who survived the persecution, but it is no longer extant.[76] Still, some of the names are given in the course of the narration.[77]

An initial hearing before the city magistrate leads to the detention of Christians. The actual trial is conducted by the prefect—the court proceedings and public tortures extend over a long time. At the first proceeding about ten Christians are moved to apostatize (11). A prominent man, Vettius Epagathus, who was probably present at first as a spectator, cannot bear the senseless charges and becomes the advocate, the "paraclete,"[78] of the Christians. Here we have a play on words and an allusion to the Holy Spirit. Vettius has already been said to be "fervent in spirit" (9); now he is called the "Christians' advocate, but he had in himself the advocate" (10). The judge merely asks him whether he is a Christian. Through his confession "he, too, was admitted to the clergy[79] of the martyrs" (10). Thus, in the language of this letter, a martyr is someone who confesses Christ in court, apart from any eventual fatal outcome.[80]

The number of arrests climbs and also includes non-Christian slaves who gain their release by means of false statements, which then turn the masses against the Christians—earlier they tended to sympathize with the Christians based in part on personal contacts. These assertions involve the usual horror stories that are found elsewhere in the polemic against Christians: incest, orgies of blood, and the like. Many younger detainees, who are not prepared psychically and physically for persecution, die in prison (29–30). The ninety-year-old bishop Pothinus succumbs after two days to the effects of his public torture. The hatred of the masses, however, is directed especially toward four people (17): *Sanctus,* "the deacon from Vienne," *Maturus,* very recently baptized but a marvelous athlete,[81] *Attalus,* "who had always been a pillar and support of the church in his native Pergamum," and finally *Blandina,* who is presented in great detail:

> Through [Blandina] Christ proved that things which men regard as mean, unlovely, and contemptible are by God deemed worthy of great glory, because of her love for Him shown in power and not vaunted in appearance. When we were all afraid, and her earthly mistress[82] (who was herself facing the ordeal of martyrdom) was in agony lest she should be unable even to make a bold confession of Christ because of bodily weakness, Blandina was filled with such power that those who took it in turns to subject her to every kind of torture from morning to night were exhausted by their efforts and confessed themselves beaten—they could think of nothing else to do to her. They were amazed that she was still breathing, for her whole body was mangled and her wounds gaped; they declared that torment of any one kind was enough to part soul and body, let alone a succession of torments of such extreme severity. But the blessed woman, wrestling magnificently, grew in strength as she proclaimed her faith, and found refreshment, rest, and insensibility to her sufferings in uttering the words: "I am a Christian: we do nothing to be ashamed of." (17–19)

It is notable that the name of Blandina's mistress is not given. Apparently the slave woman had a far more important function in the church than her mistress.

Reported next is the hearing for Sanctus, who answers all questions with "I am a Christian." He is tortured on two successive days, yet without dying. Then he and Maturus are both thrown to the animals; since the two also survive this, they are finally strangled. Blandina and Attalus are likewise to be subjected to this battle with the beasts. The latter is led around the amphitheater with a placard reading, "This is Attalus the Christian," but then withdrawn when it is learned that he is a Roman citizen (44). Later he is tortured to death (50–51) together with a Phrygian doctor, Alexander, who "had a large measure of the apostolic gift" (49).[83]

Blandina's battle with the beasts is described as follows:

> Blandina was hung on a post and exposed as food for the wild beasts let loose in the arena. She looked as if she was hanging in the form of a cross, and through her ardent prayers she stimulated great enthusiasm in those undergoing their ordeal, who in their agony saw with their outward eyes in the person of their sister the One who was crucified for them, thus convincing those who believe in Him that any man who has suffered for the glory of Christ has fellowship for ever with the living God.[84] As none of the beasts had yet touched her she was taken down from the post and returned to the gaol, to be kept for a second ordeal, that by victory in further contests she might make irrevocable the sentence passed on the crooked serpent, and spur on her brother Christians—a small, weak, despised woman who had put on Christ, the great invincible champion, and in bout after bout had defeated her adversary and through conflict had won the crown of immortality. (41–42)

Those who had apostatized at the first hearing were also caught up in the intensified persecutions. They were accused of other capital crimes and put to death, burdened with the shame of their previous denial. This led the still hesitant now to confess their Christian identity bravely, and even some who had earlier apostatized made a confession of faith. Already at an earlier time Biblis had found herself again while under torture: like Vettius before her, through her confession, she "joined the [clergy] of the martyrs" (25–26). Recognition of the former apostates as witnesses of faith perhaps presupposes a kind of official reconciliation among the Christians in prison, for we read: "Martyrs were bestowing grace on those who had failed to be martyrs" (46).[85]

The fact that the former apostates now become martyrs increases the rage of the crowd once again. Finally, Blandina becomes the last to die:

> To crown all this, on the last day of the sports Blandina was again brought in, and with her Ponticus, a lad of about fifteen. Day after day they had been taken in to watch the rest being punished, and attempts were made to make them swear by the heathen idols. When they stood firm and treated these efforts with contempt, the mob was infuriated with them, so that the boy's tender age called forth no pity and the woman no respect. They subjected them to every horror and inflicted every punishment in turn, attempting again and again to make them swear, but to no purpose. Ponticus was encouraged by his sister in Christ, so that the heathen saw that she was urging him on and stiffening his resistance, and he bravely endured every punishment till he gave back his spirit to God. Last of all, like a noble mother who had encouraged her children and sent them before her in triumph to the King,[86] blessed Blandina herself passed through all the ordeals of her children and hastened to rejoin them, rejoicing and exulting at her departure as if invited to a wedding supper, not thrown to the beasts. After the whips, after the

beasts, after the griddle, she was finally dropped into a basket and thrown to a bull. Time after time the animal tossed her, but she was indifferent now to all that happened to her, because of her communing with Christ. Then she, too, was sacrificed, while the heathen themselves admitted that never yet had they known a woman suffer so much or so long. (53–56)

After the death of Blandina outrages against the bodies are reported, which remained unburied at the will of the masses. Finally, the dead were burned and their ashes scattered in the Rhône; in this way they believed they could annihilate the Christians' hope of resurrection.

This ends the martyrdom account itself. In the second chapter of book five Eusebius goes into various theological portions of the letter. We will come back to that later.

4. Perpetua and Felicity—Mothers and Martyrs

Like the account of the massacre of Christians in Gaul, the report on the execution of two female and four male martyrs in Carthage—the aspiring Roman metropolis in Africa[87]—has at its center the unusual personality of a woman who, like Blandina, is the last to die:

> Perpetua, however, had yet to taste more pain. She screamed as she was struck on the bone; then she took the trembling hand of the young gladiator and guided it to her throat. It was as though so great a woman, feared as she was by the unclean spirit, could not be dispatched unless she herself were willing. (21/R)[88]

Albert Ehrhard has rightly said: "This document is indisputably the most gripping of the whole persecution period."[89] Therefore it is among the most studied early Christian texts.[90] Nevertheless, there are two stubborn legends even in this specialized field of study. First, because prophetic authority and Spirit-effected visions play an important role in this martyrdom account, the writing is held to be "Montanist."[91] This was not the judgment of contemporaries, which moved Herbert Musurillo to remark that "the Montanist aspect of the work seems to have escaped the notice of Augustine and many of the early Fathers . . ."[92] The opposite conclusion seems more obvious: If the fathers saw no specific Montanist features there, but instead their own tradition, they were probably correct; we have no reason to be more patristic than the church fathers![93] The second legend has even less support in reality: Tertullian is the supposed author or at least the redactor. Recent scholars have dropped this thesis; it has been shown that the texts come from three different authors, as the narrative itself suggests.[94]

The story has come down to us under the title *The Passion of Saints Perpetua and Felicity,* although in Carthage in the year 203[95] four men and two women suffered martyrdom, including Saturus, the teacher of the small group. After a short introduction by an anonymous redactor (1–2), Perpetua's autobiographical account begins; in it she records not only her experience but also four dream visions (3–10). Next comes another vision that Saturus had and likewise recorded himself (11–13). Then the redactor completes the narration (14–21). Both the reported facts and the whole writing are regarded as historically authentic. The Latin text is considered the original, yet it is possible that Saturus's vision was originally written in Greek. A Greek translation appeared very early.[96]

Since Perpetua's account is *the oldest extant self-testimony of a woman* in the early church, it was examined early on by feminist scholars. In a brief study in 1976 Mary Lefkowitz inquired about the possible motivations of the martyresses—with a clear tendency to read modern interests into the text.[97] Adriana Valerio stayed closer to the early Christian self-understanding when in a 1981 article she investigated both the report on Agathonike, Blandina, and Biblis and that on Perpetua and Felicity; somewhat irritating there is the interest in differentiating the Christian martyrdoms from the Jewish and Stoic.[98] In the same year Rosemary Rader made the passion available in English translation and provided a detailed and reliable introduction.[99]

From women who do not work expressly from a feminist perspective there are two psychoanalytical interpretations of the visions in the martyrdom account. From the viewpoint of depth psychology they both confirm the authenticity of the dreams. The study of Marie-Louise von Franz, which also works through a great deal of religious-historical and theological material, sees in the visions a paradigmatic document of the crisis of transition from the old Roman to the new Christian religion.[100] Jacqueline Amat, by contrast, attempts to characterize the personalities of Perpetua and Saturus in terms of their differences.[101]

a. The Persons
and the Facts

The external course of events. The situation is different from that in Lyon. Under Septimius Severus there is no general persecution of Christians in Carthage; instead, five young catechumens are arrested: Revocatus and Felicity, Saturnus, Secundulus, and finally Vibia Perpetua, who is the only one presented in detail:

> [Married as a matron,[102] Perpetua was a] woman of good family and upbring
> ing. Her mother and father were still alive and one of her two brothers was a
> catechumen like herself. She was about twenty-two years old and had an infant
> son at the breast. (2/R)

Saturus, the teacher of these five catechumens, who was not present at the arrest, voluntarily presented himself later and suffered martyrdom with his students (4/P). In the days after the first hearing the catechumens received baptism;[103] then they were imprisoned: "I was terrified, as I had never before been in such a dark hole. What a difficult time it was! With the crowd the heat was stifling; then there was the extortion of the soldiers; and to crown all, I was tortured with worry for my baby there" (3/P). Yet two deacons, Tertius and Pomponius, succeed in moderating imprisonment through bribery. The actual trial takes place before the procurator Hilarianus: the accused are sentenced to battle with beasts, which is scheduled for the emperor's birthday[104] (6/P); Secundulus, however, dies beforehand in prison (14/R).

Perpetua always appears with the bearing of a Roman matron. She barks at the military tribune who shortened the food rations of the martyrs: "Why can you not even allow us to refresh ourselves properly? For we are the most distinguished of the condemned prisoners, seeing that we belong to the emperor; we are to fight on his very birthday. Would it not be to your credit if we were brought forth on the day in a healthier condition?" (16/R). The tribune is confused, blushes, and gives in. The earlier stringency is explained by the rumor that the prisoners could be liberated from prison through magic. When the Christian martyrs are asked to battle the animals in the clothing of priests and priestesses of Saturn or Ceres, Perpetua rejects this decisively: "We came to this of our own free will, that our freedom should not be violated. We agreed to pledge our lives provided that we would do no such thing. You agreed with us to do this" (18/R). Again the military tribune gives in. Even during the battle with the animals Perpetua is concerned with keeping her clothes and hair in order.

Saturnus, Revocatus, and Saturus have to fight with leopards and bears; Perpetua and Felicity are subjected to a wild cow: "For the young women, however, the Devil had prepared a mad heifer. This was an unusual animal, but it was chosen that their sex might be matched with that of the beast" (20/R). Since the battle with the beasts is not fatal, the five ultimately die under the sword, with Perpetua last, as we have seen.

The "fellow slave" Felicity. The information on Felicity comes not from Perpetua but from the redactor (15/R).[105] From the beginning of the account he calls Felicity the *conserva* ("fellow slave") of Revocatus, and thus it has usually been inferred that both were slaves. Yet this has been correctly questioned by Georg Schöllgen, since the word *conserva* had also found currency as the designation of a wife as "fellow Christian." Hence, Felicity and Revocatus could have been a married couple who were not slaves. The question must remain open. We may certainly assume, however, that Felicity was not a slave in the house of the patrician Perpetua, for the redactor does not connect the two women, and Perpetua does not mention Felicity in her personal memoirs. Thus it is probable that these two confessors were hardly acquainted before their imprisonment.

Felicity is in her eighth month of pregnancy and is greatly afraid of being held back and later having to face her martyrdom alone. They all pray for a premature birth, which then happens. When Felicity is moaning with the labor pains, a guard makes fun of her: "You suffer so much now—what will you do when you are tossed to the beasts?" She replied, "What I am suffering now . . . I suffer myself. But then another will be inside me who will suffer for me, just as I shall be suffering for him." She gives birth to a girl, who becomes the adopted daughter of a "sister," that is, a fellow Christian.

Perpetua's family. It is striking that while Perpetua's marriage is mentioned, her husband is not. With Felicity, too, we learn nothing certain about the father of the child. Many women interpreters claim to see an ascetic or women's liberation element here.[106] Yet the report as a whole offers no support for this. The question must remain open. Apparently in Perpetua's family only the father is not a Christian, for the martyress comments at one point: "I was sorry for my father's sake, because he

alone of all my kin would be unhappy to see me suffer" (5/P). Her mother and
brother visit her in prison regularly and partly assume the care of her baby.

The role of the father. The efforts of the father to save his beloved daughter
from martyrdom are described in detail by Perpetua herself. In his first attempt
to keep her from confessing as a Christian, he erupts in anger—the only time in
the whole story—but he gets hold of himself again. After his "diabolical arguments" Perpetua is relieved not to see him for a while (3/P). During the second
visit he reminds her that she is his favorite and begs her to have mercy on herself
and the whole family, upon which she is now bringing shame. Finally he falls
down before her in tears, kisses her hand, and calls her mistress (*domina*)—Perpetua tries to comfort him as well as she can (5/P). Then comes the trial: the father appears with the baby in his arms and cries: "Perform the sacrifice—have pity
on your baby!" When he continues to intervene, he is finally struck by the bailiff,
much to Perpetua's distress: "I felt sorry for father, just as if I myself had been
beaten. I felt sorry for his pathetic old age" (6/P). His despairing gestures on his
last visit in prison again stir Perpetua's profound pity (9/P).[107]

Perpetua and her child. When prison conditions improved after the first detention, Perpetua is finally able to suckle her half-starved baby, but it still remains
in the family's care. Finally she is allowed to have it with her in prison: "These
were the trials I had to endure for many days. Then I got permission for my baby
to stay with me in prison. At once I recovered my health, relieved as I was of my
worry and anxiety over the child. My prison had suddenly become a palace, so
that I wanted to be there rather than anywhere else" (3/P). During the trial her
father kept the baby; after her condemnation to death, when she asked the deacon Pomponius to fetch the child, the father refused to give it up. "But as God
willed, the baby had no further desire for the breast, nor did I suffer any inflam-
mation; and so I was relieved of any anxiety for my child and of any discomfort
in my breasts," comments Perpetua (6/P).

It is inappropriate to see the behavior of the two martyresses vis-à-vis their
children as a fundamental break with their role as mother,[108] for both find their
inner peace only when they know that their babies are cared for. Thus this is not
a rejection of motherhood but its relativization and transcendence! Also, there is
no reason to find a connection between the pregnancy of the martyresses and the
symbolic figure of the pregnant woman in Revelation, as Musurillo does.[109]
These characteristics of what is human and authentic need no "interpretation,"
but they do deserve to be emphasized.

b. The Visions

The autobiographical portions of the account contain detailed descriptions of
the dream visions of Perpetua and Saturus in prison. We have already encountered prophecy in the worship service in the church in Corinth, accompanied
there by an ecstatic form of prayer: speaking in tongues, or glossolalia (1
Corinthians 14). Paul expressly recommends striving for prophecy as a gift of the
Spirit, a "charisma."[110] In the introduction to the account of the events in

Carthage (1/R) the redactor connects the witness of the martyrs with their capability of prophetic vision: both are eschatological gifts bestowed by the Holy
Spirit. The concern of the author is to avoid nostalgia for the "good old days."
The new visions and new prophecies are greater miracles than the old: they are
the beginning of the fulfillment of God's promise. This double grace of the
church is to be proclaimed here and now through martyrs and visions "as a witness to the non-believing and a blessing to the faithful," so that "honour might
be rendered to God and comfort to [humankind]." The idea that unites
prophecy and martyrdom is "witness."[111] The dream visions reported here are to
be understood from this perspective.[112]

Perpetua's first vision (4/P) is suggested after the detention by her brother:
"Dear sister, you are greatly privileged; surely you might ask for a vision to discover whether you are to be condemned or freed" ("Domina soror, iam in magna
dignatione es, tanta ut postules visionem et ostendatur tibi an passio sit an com-
meatus"). Here the brother uses the honorific form of address *domina* ("mistress"), as does the father (5/P). The word *dignatio*[113] contains both a "pardon"
and an "empowerment": the brother is obviously of the opinion that Perpetua's
status as martyr gives her a claim to prophetic revelation—an opinion that Perpetua makes her own, since she does indeed ask for a vision and it is then granted.
The word *passio* evokes the identification of martyrs and martyresses with the crucified One. This is Perpetua's description of her vision:

> I saw a ladder of tremendous height made of bronze, reaching all the way to the
> heavens, but it was so narrow that only one person could climb up at a time. To
> the sides of the ladder were attached all sorts of metal weapons: there were
> swords, spears, hooks, daggers, and spikes; so that if anyone tried to climb up
> carelessly or without paying attention, he would be mangled and his flesh would
> adhere to the weapons.
>
> At the foot of the ladder lay a dragon of enormous size, and it would attack
> those who tried to climb up and try to terrify them from doing so. And Saturus
> was the first to go up, he who was later to give himself up of his own accord.
> He had been the builder of our strength, although he was not present when we
> were arrested. And he arrived at the top of the staircase and he looked back and
> said to me: "Perpetua, I am waiting for you. But take care; do not let the dragon
> bite you."
>
> "He will not harm me," I said, "in the name of Christ Jesus."
>
> Slowly, as though he were afraid of me, the dragon stuck his head out from
> underneath the ladder. Then using it as my first step, I trod on his head and went
> up.
>
> Then I saw an immense garden, and in it a grey-haired man sat in shepherd's
> garb; tall he was, and milking sheep. And standing around him were many thou-
> sands of people clad in white garments. He raised his head, looked at me, and
> said: "I am glad you have come, my child."
>
> He called me over to him and gave me, as it were, a mouthful of the milk he
> was drawing; and I took it into my cupped hands and consumed it. And all those

who stood around said: "Amen!" At the sound of this word I came to, with the taste of something sweet still in my mouth. I at once told this to my brother, and we realized that we would have to suffer, and that from now on we would no longer have any hope in this life.

Notable in this vision is how close the dream images are to the symbols and symbolic interpretations of the baptismal liturgy. This is also true in the second and third visions, but especially in the fourth. This reciprocal relationship between baptism and martyrdom, which is expressed in the visions, will be examined after the presentation of the visions.

The second and third visions (7–8/P). During a prayer gathering of martyrs in prison, Perpetua suddenly says the name *Dinocrates*, without being able to explain why. Dinocrates was her little brother who died at age seven from facial cancer. "At once I realized that I was privileged to pray for him" (7/P). She sees how the child Dinocrates, marked by the horrible wound, comes out of a dark cave and stands by a pool of water but cannot reach its surface for a drink. "Then I woke up, realizing that my brother was suffering. But I was confident that I could help him in his trouble."[114] Perpetua now makes intercession daily. Toward the end of her stay in prison she sees Dinocrates again in a dream; he is healthy: the old wound has healed into a scar; the edge of the pool is lower, and Dinocrates is drinking from a golden cup, whose water does not run dry. Finally, he begins to play happily like a child. "Then I awoke, and I realized that he had been delivered from his suffering"[115] (8/P).

Franz Josef Dölger has demonstrated that this dream is not based on a developed, specifically Christian doctrine of the world beyond, but rather is dominated by general ancient ideas and images of the underworld: in this worldview the reason for Dinocrates' suffering is his premature death.[116] Yet it is noteworthy that later church fathers discussed this vision of Perpetua's. They argued, however, not about the ideas of the world beyond but about whether Dinocrates was baptized or not. For those who were divided on this point, nonetheless, there was no doubt that Dinocrates was actually saved by Perpetua's prayer.[117] Crucial for our context is the fact that this power of intercession was apparently not granted to all believers but only to the martyrs.[118]

Perpetua's fourth vision (10/P) occurs immediately before the battle with the beasts and, in spite of its length, is reproduced here in full:

> Pomponius the deacon came to the prison gates and began to knock violently. I went out and opened the gate for him. He was dressed in an unbelted white tunic, wearing elaborate sandals. And he said to me: "Perpetua, come; we are waiting for you."
>
> Then he took my hand and we began to walk through rough and broken country. At last we came to the amphitheatre out of breath, and he led me into the center of the arena.
>
> Then he told me: "Do not be afraid. I am here, struggling with you."[119] Then he left.

I looked at the enormous crowd who watched in astonishment. I was surprised that no beasts were let loose on me; for I knew that I was condemned to die by the beasts. Then out came an Egyptian against me, of vicious appearance, together with his seconds, to fight with me. There also came up to me some handsome young men to be my seconds and assistants.

My clothes were stripped off, and suddenly I was a man. My seconds began to rub me down with oil (as they are wont to do before a contest). Then I saw the Egyptian on the other side rolling in the dust. Next there came forth a man of marvellous stature, such that he rose above the top of the amphitheatre. He was clad in a beltless purple tunic with two stripes (one on either side) running down the middle of his chest. He wore sandals that were wondrously made of gold and silver, and he carried a wand like an athletic trainer and a green branch on which there were golden apples.

And he asked for silence and said: "If this Egyptian defeats her, he will slay her with the sword. But if she defeats him, she will receive this branch." Then he withdrew.

We drew close to one another and began to let our fists fly. My opponent tried to get hold of my feet, but I kept striking him in the face with the heels of my feet. Then I was raised up into the air and I began to pummel him without as it were touching the ground. Then when I noticed there was a lull, I put my two hands together linking the fingers of one hand with those of the other and thus I got hold of his head. He fell flat on his face and I stepped on his head.

The crowd began to shout and my assistants started to sing psalms. Then I walked up to the trainer and took the branch. He kissed me and said to me: "Peace be with you, my daughter!" I began to walk in triumph toward the Gate of Life.[120] Then I awoke. I realized that it was not with wild animals that I would fight but with the Devil, but I knew that I would win the victory. So much for what I did up until the eve of the contest. About what happened at the contest itself, let him write of it who will.

Perpetua's account ends with these words. The redactor follows it with the vision of Saturus (11–13/S), which the latter likewise recorded himself. It begins after the death of the martyrs: four angels carry them up into heaven. Saturus says to Perpetua, who is next to him: "This is what the Lord promised us. We have received his promise" (11/S). They meet other martyrs, who lead them, together with the angels, to the throne of the Lord, around which, as in the throne scene in Revelation 4, the elders stand, while "Hagios, hagios, hagios" ("holy, holy, holy"[121]) is sung. After they have prayed to the "old man with white hair and a youthful face," they are told: "Go and play." Then Saturus says to Perpetua: "Your wish is granted." She replies: "Thanks be to God that I am happier here now than I was in the flesh" (12/S). Now follows a surprising scene:

Then we went out and before the gates we saw the bishop Optatus on the right and Aspasius the presbyter and teacher on the left, each of them far apart and in sorrow. They threw themselves at our feet and said: "Make peace between us. For you have gone away and left us thus."

And we said to them: "Are you not our bishop, and are you not our presbyter? How can you fall at our feet?"

We were very moved and embraced them. Perpetua then began to speak with them in Greek, and we drew them apart into the garden under a rose arbour.

While we were talking with them, the angels said to them: "Allow them to rest. Settle whatever quarrels you have among yourselves." And they were put to confusion.

Then they said to Optatus: "You must scold your flock. They approach you as though they had come from the games, quarrelling about the different teams."

And it seemed as though they wanted to close the gates. And there we began to recognize many of our brethren, martyrs among them. All of us were sustained by a most delicious odour that seemed to satisfy us. And then I woke up happy. (13/S)

5. Martyrdom and Baptism: A Theological Analysis of Perpetua's Visions

a. Interaction of the Images

As already pointed out, in Perpetua's dream visions there are repeated images and symbols that come from the liturgy of baptism—more precisely, from the rites of early Christian initiation in which the sacraments of baptism, confirmation, and Eucharist appear as a single celebration, though later they were distinguished liturgically and theologically.[122] After a multiyear instruction in Christian teaching and conduct, the immediate preparation for receiving baptism begins in a time of fasting and prayer, a time of especially intense struggle with the forces of evil, which takes the form of repeated exorcisms.[123] This battle reaches its climax in symbolic death in the waters of baptism, in which the baptismal candidate dies with Christ and like Christ, in order to be resurrected in a new life. This new life is expressed symbolically in the climb out of the water, in the anointment as a sign of the reception of the Holy Spirit, in acceptance into the new fellowship through the bishop's laying on of hands and kiss of peace, and finally through the anticipation of the heavenly wedding banquet in the celebration of the Eucharist. The death and resurrection of Christ, in which Christians participate in baptism, is seen as the New Testament fulfillment of the Exodus event: the Egyptians, the enemies of Israel, are defeated in the water, so that after liberation from slavery the people of God can move into the promised land, "a land flowing with milk and honey."[124]

This early church baptismal theology is broadly developed later in the catechetical homilies of the fathers, but the essential elements are already clearly attested in the *Apostolic Tradition* of Hippolytus (composed around 250 for the church in Rome).[125] It is true that Tertullian, a contemporary of Perpetua and Felicity, in his polemical tractate *On Baptism* is less interested in describing these images of struggle than in emphasizing, vis-à-vis contrary thinkers in Carthage, the necessity of water baptism for the forgiveness of sins.[126] Nevertheless, the metaphors are also found here: "What image could be more clearly contained in the sacrament of baptism than this? Through water the pagans are liberated from the dominion of the world and leave their earlier master, the devil, to drown in the water."[127] In another writing the same symbolism is attested in shorter form in the baptismal rites.[128] Thus we may assume that the liturgy in Carthage was similar to that in Rome.

In Perpetua's dreams we encounter an unusual interaction of images of these recently experienced initiation rites with images of the martyrdom that is both feared and definitely expected. Through this interaction *martyrdom appears as the fulfillment of baptism,* and at the same time *baptism is the interpretation of martyrdom.* For it is the close of the eucharistic celebration with the amen of the participants that convinces Perpetua that she must face death and will really undergo what the initiation symbolically anticipated.

The equating of baptism and martyrdom is found in many early Christian texts. Tertullian writes: "There is for us also a second baptism, which, however, is not different; I mean baptism in blood. . . . This is the baptism that replaces the real bath, if it was not received, and bestows anew what was lost."[129] The *Apostolic Tradition* says: "If a catechumen is arrested because of the name of his Lord, he must not waver in regard to his witness. For if violence is done to him and he is killed before the forgiveness of his sins, he will be justified, for he has received baptism through his own blood" (19).

Since Perpetua and Saturus are already baptized, the idea of martyrdom as a substitute for the initiation sacrament plays no role for them, but the identification of water baptism performed in ritual with blood baptism suffered in reality is also found in martyrdom accounts outside the dream visions. When Saturus's blood streams out after a leopard's bite, the crowd calls out the usual ancient bath wish in sadistic irony, in view of his "second baptism": "Salvum lotum" (freely, "well washed"),[130] on which the redactor comments: "Well washed indeed was one who had been bathed in this manner" (21/R). In Felicity's case the idea of blood baptism is linked with the idea of second birth: she was "glad that she had safely given birth so that now she could fight the beasts, going from one blood bath to another, from the midwife to the gladiator, ready to wash after childbirth in a second baptism" (18/R).

In the double vision about Dinocrates, Perpetua herself does not appear as subject, but in one sense the dream must be interpreted as a symbolic anticipation of her own fate.[131] Again, typical initiation images appear: the pool of water and the golden bowl. Even with all the differences, the first and second visions have important common elements: (1) the existence of an obstacle (ladder and dragon—the unreachable height of the bowl) and the attainment of a higher stage in its being overcome; (2) Communion gestures (eating milky cheese—drinking water); (3) symbols of rebirth (milk as children's food—childlike games).[132]

In the last vision, which Perpetua has the night before her battle with the beasts, the interaction of the initiation symbols with the images of the imminent real life-and-death battle is intensified again. Von Franz adopts the Jungian concept of *synchronicity* in her interpretation: "The images of the vision cannot be termed the cause of the external events, nor can the latter explain the particular nature of the dream symbols. It is, rather, a question of a *symptōma*, a coincidence of internal and external. . . ." "It is a matter of a noncausal, meaningful connection between temporally coinciding phenomena, especially internal and external events."[133]

It is noteworthy that on the one hand the dream symbols can clearly be called elements of Christian initiation on the basis of the connection with real life—Perpetua's baptism and martyrdom—but that on the other hand there is almost a total lack of explicit Christianity, for example, reference to the cross, the name of Jesus, or the Trinity. Apparently the Trinitarian confession, which is found in the baptismal rite after the rejection of Satan, does not have the same existential weight as the symbolic engagement in battle against evil. In the vision symbols and symbolic figures of the old and new religions are mixed. This is especially clear in the figure of the referee, in whom the real persons of a competition trainer and a Christian bishop (or priest) are melded into a kind of vision of Christ, and indeed into a vision of a Christ figure whose majesty is expressed in the clothing of a priest of Saturn. Von Franz correctly emphasizes, "How extremely similar the images and texts of developing Christianity were to the Gnostic and pagan mysteries it so ardently fought."[134] She comes to this conclusion:

> Thus, the law of the enantiodromy[135] of all archetypal opposites fulfills in the martyrs until the end those opposites whose breaking open created the gradient upon which the Christian culture of the following centuries was to build. The unconscious itself, however, sustained the martyrs through images promising new life and thereby gave them the inner ability to stand by their decision. . . . The visions of the *passio* of Perpetua reveal in their peculiarly complete form the whole unconscious situation of contemporary humanity, pagan and Christian. . . . The martyrdom itself had no other significance than the demonstration of this complete release and absolute hope in the beyond vis-à-vis the pagan world.[136]

Above and beyond von Franz one must emphasize that *this existential basic attitude was embodied not only in Perpetua's dreams but in the rites of baptism themselves*, as they were developed by early Christianity. Through the autobiographical account, however, it is possible for us to investigate how these Christian rites and convictions were concretely experienced and assimilated by a woman.

b. Rites of Initiation in Dream and Reality

The echo of the familiar liturgy in Perpetua's dreams is clearly expressed in the emergence of *ritual formulas* and the appearance of *liturgical mediator figures*, who are mentioned by name. In the first vision it is the catechist Saturus who leads the way on the ladder that symbolizes the harsh road to martyrdom (later he actually dies first). Clearly reflected here is the role of the catechist[137] as described in the *Apostolic Tradition* of Hippolytus:

> Those who are newly led to the faith . . . are first to be brought to the teachers (15). As soon as the teachers stop teaching, the catechumens are to pray on their

own, apart from the believers (18). . . . When the teacher lays on the hand after
the prayer, he is to pray and release them. Thus he should do it whether he is a
clergyman or layman (19). . . . But from the time they are separated [the time of
imminent baptismal preparation], the hand may be laid[138] on them daily when
they are exorcised. Now, when the day approaches on which they are to be baptized, the bishop shall exorcise each one of them, so that he may know whether
they are pure . . . for it is impossible for the stranger [that is, the devil] ever to
hide (20).

In Saturus's call and especially in Perpetua's answer in the dream, the liturgical
dialogue in exorcism can still be clearly recognized: "Perpetua, I am waiting
for you.[139] But take care; do not let the dragon bite you." "He will not harm me
. . . in the name of Christ."

The fourth vision begins quite similarly, yet this time it is not the catechist Saturus but the deacon Pomponius who fetches Perpetua in a white gown, as in baptism. He uses a formula of greeting almost identical to that of Saturus: "Perpetua,
come, we are waiting for you." Since Pomponius was already mentioned earlier
in the account by name when he intervened for the prisoners (3/P), we may assume that he actually exercised his liturgical function at the baptism of Perpetua.

According to the *Apostolic Tradition* two deacons stand beside the bishop or
priest with the oils for anointing the baptismal candidate, and then they lead him
or her down into the water. Since the candidate is fully naked at this moment,
the rite was performed in many churches by deaconesses when a woman was involved; in Perpetua's particular case, however, the functions of catechist and deacon were apparently exercised by men. Whether it was the bishop Optatus himself, who is mentioned later in the vision of Saturus, or a presbyter from Carthage
who baptized the catechumens before their martyrdom, we do not know. In any
case, the presiding figure seems to be embodied in the shepherd of the first vision: "And standing around him were many thousands of people in white garments" (4/P). He also greets Perpetua with a liturgical formula, "Bene venisti,
teknon" ("welcome, child"),[140] and hands her a bite of milky cheese, which she
receives with a Communion gesture, while those standing around say, "Amen";
Perpetua mentions the sweet taste in her mouth. For this vision we again have
the exact counterpart in the *Apostolic Tradition*:

> The deacons are to bring the sacrifice to the bishop, and he gives thanks over a
> loaf of bread, because that is the form of the flesh of Christ, and over a cup of
> wine, for that is the blood of Christ that is shed for all who believe in him, and
> over milk and honey mixed, to fulfill the promises given to the fathers, for he
> said, "I will give you a land flowing with milk and honey." This is the flesh of
> Christ, which he gave to us, so that those who believe in him may eat of it like
> children. He will dissolve the bitterness of the heart through the sweetness of the
> word. (21)

Hippolytus then mentions another cup: one with water (it is drunk as a sign that
the outward bath also affects the inner person).[141] Apparently an intensification

of the rite is intended here. Tertullian also mentions the drinking of milk and honey immediately after baptism and before the reception of bread and wine.[142] In the vision of *Quartillosa* a "young man of lofty stature" brings into the prison cups of milk that do not get empty.[143]

c. The Battle with Satan

All four of Perpetua's dreams end with a kind of closing formula: "I awoke and realized . . ."[144] After the first vision the realization consists in the certainty that she must offer her life in discipleship of Christ. Seeing the suffering Dinocrates in the second vision, she becomes aware of the power she has as a martyr: through her prayer she can save others, and thus the powerlessness of her concrete situation has a higher meaning. This interpretation of her suffering as giving meaning and salvation is confirmed in the third dream. The insight of the fourth dream reads: "I realized that it was not with wild animals that I would fight but with the devil, but I knew that I would win the victory" (10/P).

This interpretation that Perpetua herself gives to her experience and her struggle should warn us against the hasty conclusion of seeing in her readiness for death "a political deed against the world around her" and the concrete struggle against a patriarchal social order embodied in the figure of the father and the power of the state.[145] The lack of a vision of political resistance in early Christianity may be regrettable, but it helps very little to project one into the text retroactively. A look into the pagan acts of martyrdom,[146] which unfortunately are extant only in fragments, is enough to make the difference clear: there one meets death with uplifted head in the battle against proud Rome. The persecution of Christians by the Roman state, by contrast, is regarded by them as an immense misunderstanding: the emperors are persecuting their best and most morally upstanding citizens, because Satan blinds them to the coming of the kingdom of Christ. He must be conquered in death, following Jesus' example, and this will convert his blinded henchmen.[147] Eusebius sees the time of persecution as an extension of the passion of Christ, and the recognition of Christianity and its establishment as state religion by Constantine are regarded as the long-awaited victory won by God.[148] Also in the account of the massacre of Lyon, Satan is repeatedly named as the real subject of persecution.[149]

Yet one point is indisputable: among the values for which Perpetua is ready to die is the vision of a fellowship in which masters and slaves, men and women are brothers and sisters with equal rights. The powers of evil that must be fought certainly include, in modern terms, all "patriarchal" mechanisms of suppression, but "father," "state," and "society" do not in themselves appear as incarnations of evil; rather, they are seen as instruments in the hands of the devil, which block the victory of Christ.

Thus Perpetua survives this battle with evil in her last vision. The deacon Pomponius, who led her at baptism to the water that she then had to pass through herself, now brings her into the middle of the arena and releases her with a formula that seems to be less the words of the deacon than words of Christ: "Do not be afraid. I am here, struggling with you." Yet it is not the expected wild beasts who approach Perpetua; rather, her opponent, as in the symbolism of baptism, is a fighter, an Egyptian—and thus a representative of the enemies of the persecuted people of God, enemies who in passing through the Red Sea were conquered by miraculous divine power.[150] As with an athlete, by Perpetua's side are two assistants who anoint her after she is disrobed, as was usual at baptism and in gladiatorial competition. The rite is described in the *Apostolic Tradition:*

> One deacon brings the oil of exorcism and stands on the Priest's left, while another deacon takes the oil of thanksgiving[151] and stands on the priest's right. And when the priest takes hold of the candidates, he shall command them to swear with the following words: "I renounce you, Satan, your whole service, and all your works." And when they have all sworn that oath, he shall anoint them with the oil of exorcism and say: "May every spirit depart from you." And they shall turn themselves over naked to the bishop or the priest, who stands at the water and baptizes." (21)

Here it is the presbyter who undertakes the first anointing, while afterward the deacon leads the candidates into the water and with them says the Trinitarian formula of faith. In later texts the deacon usually anoints, and the baptismal formula and second anointing are reserved for the presbyter or bishop. We do not know who performed the initiation rites for Perpetua. As earlier in the dream the catechist Saturus and the deacon Pomponius had already spoken with the voice of Christ, as it were, so now the priestly appearance of the baptizer is transformed into a supernatural figure. After victory this heavenly referee, with clear allusion to the liturgy, receives the woman athlete with the kiss of peace and the greeting: "Peace be with you, my daughter" ("Filia, pax tecum"; 10/P). Yet at first he promises the victor only the paradisiacal symbol of life, a green branch with golden apples[152] (10/P).

Perpetua, who at the moment of her being undressed becomes a man, now begins the actual battle. Louis Robert has rightly pointed out that here we are not to think of the gruesome Roman gladiatorial battle, which the Greeks despised, but a contest without weapons.[153] It is described highly realistically—only one thing indicates that Perpetua is not fighting this battle alone: she is lifted into the air and strikes her opponent as if not touching the earth.[154] Then she can force him to the ground and put her foot on his head as a sign of victory.

Perpetua herself could not know how her dream would come true. The correspondences perceived in advance are impressive: the undressing is found again in the presentation of the naked women in nets, as well as in the tearing of the clothes that they are allowed to wear after the protest of the crowd; the being lifted up is recalled by the numbed condition that no longer lets Perpetua perceive the action; the singing of psalms in the arena actually occurs; the defeat of the opponent corresponds to the failed attack of the wild cow, as well as the unsure hand of the executioner, which misses its target. If in the dream Perpetua left as the victor through the "Gate of Life," in reality she enters the arena, already like a victor, as "wife of Christ," as "beloved of God" ("ut matrona Christi, ut Dei delicata"),[155] before whom all bowed their heads. The martyrs say their farewells with a final kiss of peace. In the presentation of her first dream vision Perpetua reports that the dragon seemed to be afraid of her (4/P). At the end of her martyrdom she guides the executioner's hand—for the redactor she becomes the symbol of "so great a woman," who was feared by the evil one (21/R).

In fact, in the image of the woman who puts her foot on the head of the dragon lies another important key to the interpretation of Perpetua's dreams.[156] We do not know whether in second-century Carthage the passages on the temptation of Eve and Adam by the snake in paradise and the temptation of Christ by the devil in the wilderness were read at the beginning of the time of fasting—that is, the actual time of preparation of the catechumens for their baptism at the Easter celebration—as is the case in the later liturgy. In any case, these two scriptural texts were brought together in the catechesis. In the Genesis story the punishment for the snake says: "I will put enmity between you and the woman, and between your offspring and hers; he will strike your head, and you will strike his heel."[157] In the church fathers' typological understanding of scripture, this so-called protogospel—God's first promise of salvation after the Fall—is not interpreted with regard to humanity in general; rather, Jesus Christ is seen as the "woman's seed," as the promised offspring, who will relieve humankind of the burdensome curse. Through the Vulgate's incorrect translation, "Ipsa conteret caput tuum" ("she will tread on your head"), the verse was later related to Mary in the Western tradition.

This image of treading on the snake is present in both of Perpetua's great battle visions. In the first vision it is the dragon that "would attack those who tried to climb up and try to terrify them from doing so," and Saturus warns Perpetua about its bite. Yet for Perpetua he slowly stuck his head out, as though afraid of her, and she uses it as the first step: "I trod on his head and went up" ("calcavi caput eius et ascendi"; 4/P). In the vision of the fight with the Egyptian, the allusion is even clearer: he "tried to get hold of my feet . . . I got hold of his head. He fell flat on his face and I stepped on his head" ("mihi pedes adprendere volebat . . . apprehendi illi caput; et cecidit in faciem et calcavi illi caput") (10/P). It is quite clear that Perpetua sees the fulfillment of the old promise in her own struggle. Firmly anchored in her is the certainty of being stronger than "the evil one."

Later Augustine, in his sermons on Perpetua and Felicity, will identify the martyresses with the female sex and make plays on words: their weakness can prove itself strong in battle; while Perpetua is weak in body, she is a man in spirit; the devil, who brought the man down by means of a woman, is now brought down by a woman.[158] Here we see already a contradiction between Perpetua's sex and her bravery.

In the acts of the martyrs, however, the image of the battle with Satan is natural for both women and men,[159] as the baptismal rite suggests. According to the early Christian understanding, the history of salvation is not realized statically and uniquely in the example of Christ (and Mary); rather, the salvation event continues to be written dynamically in the witness of the martyrs and martyresses. The focus is not on the idea of a metaphysical redemption of human nature through the incarnation, but on the communication of Jesus' message to all people through the witnesses. There is no sex-specific attribution of functions to the woman and her seed in the order of salvation; instead, both sexes identify with Jesus, who withstood Satan and thus trod on the snake's head. The symbol remains open: men and women are equally involved in the battle and can win the victory.

One feature in Perpetua's certainty of victory must still be noted: the idea of the annihilation of the opponent—though identified as the devil—is not involved in the victory. As we saw, in the first vision the head of the dragon becomes the lowest step of the ladder; in the last vision the enemy is conquered but not killed. Moreover, from the beginning there is no parity in the referee's victory promise, for he says, "If this Egyptian defeats her, he will slay her with the sword. But if she defeats him, she will receive this branch" (10/P). The nonviolence practiced by the martyrs in their resistance, the renunciation of revenge, and the unconditional readiness to forgive appear here as the content of the Christian message that is so deeply internalized by Perpetua that she does not annihilate her opponent even in her dreams.

d. Transformation
into a Man

One important question remains: How is Perpetua's becoming a man in her dream to be interpreted and evaluated?[160] Rosemary Rader is certainly right when she argues in her commentary against the idea that we have here the notion that a woman must become a man in order to reach salvation,[161] for Perpetua is a man only during the contest; as victor she is greeted by the referee as "daughter." Yet does Rader do justice to the problem raised here when she speaks simply of the "androgynous character" of the account? It is certainly correct that the martyrs understood themselves first of all as "Christians" and then as "martyrs" and "witnesses," without giving attention to sex roles. It is also correct that Perpetua is described in both male and female images, as bride and as warrior. She has the personality of a tender mother and also that of an energetic leader. But is Perpetua's becoming a man simply a sign of a Christendom that understands itself androgynously, a symbol of the "universal Christian" for whom gender no longer counts? Is Rader correct in saying that for Perpetua "the male/female attributes are so intrinsic to her character that the sexual imagery can be interchanged without loss of essential significance" (11)?

Von Franz sees the androgynous elements as not entirely positive. It is true that she also begins with an integration of the masculine[162] in Perpetua's personality and sees in the dream moment of the transformation the "unveiling of her masculine nature," but she evaluates this quite differently: there is no androgyny in the sense of psychic wholeness.

> Perpetua, as a twenty-two-year-old young woman with a small son, would hardly have had to suffer this fate if she had not assumed the masculine, aggressive attitude of a confessor and actively involved herself in the battle of the spirits. . . . In any case, the dream shows that in the conflict that is now breaking

out, she assumes a masculine, belligerent attitude and identifies completely with the Christian animus figures that in the preceding dreams appeared only as unconscious partial personalities. She now becomes a "miles Christi" ["soldier of Christ"] . . .[163]

In Perpetua's case, however, there is no actual uniting of opposites but a direct conversion, *which corresponds to a complete extinction of the previous self-consciousness,* in whose place another "spiritual" consciousness enters during the ecstasy. She becomes identical with the animus. But this circumstance must not be seen in this way from the modern standpoint and evaluated purely negatively, for it must be noted that the Christian doctrine of the Trinity corresponds to a patriarchal social order. A woman for whom the intellectual processes of her time gained any meaning at all could therefore almost not escape the danger of tolerating this process of transformation into the masculine. *This occurs here in the form of an almost total annihilation of the self*—in this case, one could really even speak of a violation by the self, through which, however, the self also appears in unique clarity, and in which the self experiences a sense of happening.[164]

Did things really have to be this way in Christianity around the year 203? Von Franz herself points to two counterexamples. Hermas, the apologist of ecclesiastical penance, is introduced to Christian doctrine by a woman.[165] The strongest counterexample to Perpetua's vision is doubtless the dream of the prophetess Prisca, in which Christ appears to her in feminine form.[166] "How needed this was is shown in a certain sense precisely by Perpetua's tragic fate," writes von Franz.[167]

e. Feminine Identification Figures?

We have seen that Perpetua's dream images and thus her unconscious identification figures are greatly determined by her becoming a Christian through catechesis and initiation. Apparently, in this regard she was thinking only of men. We may ask: How would Perpetua have dreamed if she had had women catechists and deaconesses, women presbyters and bishops? The question is not unrealistic, at least in regard to women catechists and deaconesses.

Perpetua's account does not reveal whether she herself knew women teachers and liturgists. Yet her contemporary Tertullian mentions women who derive their claim to proclamation from Thecla's example, and he expresses the fear that they might likewise claim for themselves the right to baptize.[168] Indeed, he even attests that "the women of these heretics" (whom he does not identify further) have been known to exercise the functions of catechist and exorcist and "maybe even to baptize."[169] It is true that he concedes priority to bishops, presbyters, and deacons in the celebration of baptism, but he is of the opinion that in principle it could also be dispensed by "all." Yet he then expressly excludes women from "all."[170]

Nevertheless, we have another document from the early period that expressly attests to, and even requires, the involvement of women (specifically, deaconesses) in catechesis and baptism, namely, the *Didascalia,* which we have already mentioned several times. This "teaching of the apostles"—a mixture of religious tract and church discipline—was written in Greek in the first half of the third century in Syria. The original is lost, but it survives in a very early Syriac version and in extensive Latin fragments from the end of the fourth century. In addition, at the end of the fourth century the *Didascalia* was adopted in a reworked form into the *Apostolic Constitutions,* in which several older church disciplines are compiled. Where the Greek text of the *Constitutions* agrees with the translations of the *Didascalia,* we can presume to have the original Greek version.[171]

In the description of the baptismal celebration in the *Didascalia* we find not two deacons in addition to the bishop, as in the *Apostolic Tradition,* but one deacon and one deaconess. At the same time this liturgical scenario is interpreted in a Trinitarian fashion: "The Bishop presides in place of God; the deacon takes the place of Christ and should be loved by you; the deaconess, however, is to be honored by you in place of the Holy Spirit." The priests, who surround the bishop during the worship service, stand "in place of the apostles," according to the *Didascalia;* finally, "widows and orphans" are mentioned and represent the altar.[172]

Here all those who in the liturgy are not simply among the people are given a certain "representative" function.[173] The testimony to the function of the deaconess in baptism carries special weight, since the *Didascalia* shows by no means a philogynous tendency but clearly endeavors especially to restrict the activity of widows—the noted comparison with the altar is used in another place[174] to bind the widow to the house: the altar does not run around either![175] As we saw, the Roman administrator Pliny had two *ancillae ministrae* tortured, hoping to learn more details about the Christian worship service—apparently without success.[176] The *Didascalia* is the oldest and only source that describes in detail the ministerial activities of women in the church.[177] Also the association of the female diaconate with the Holy Spirit, which gives special weight to the deaconesses through the connection with the doctrine of the Trinity, is not found again later. In Syriac the word for the (Holy) Spirit is feminine (like the Heb. *ruach*). Since the *Didascalia* was originally written in Greek, this relationship cannot be derived immediately from the wording. Yet how strong the concept of the femininity of the Holy Spirit was in the Syriac area is shown by the fact that it was adduced by Christian opponents of the virgin birth: a woman cannot have conceived from a woman.[178]

The corresponding passage in the *Apostolic Constitutions* has been given a restrictive addition that subordinates the deaconess to the deacon: even the Paraclete speaks and acts only according to the will of Christ! In the *Didascalia,* however, both deacon and deaconess receive their instructions in like manner from the bishop. Since men often cannot enter the houses of women, the deaconess is accorded the function of catechist—but only for women!—with express reference to the women disciples among Jesus' followers: mentioned are Mary Magdalene, Mary the daughter[179] of James, the mother of Joseph, the mother of the sons of Zebedee, "and others" (with reference to the same women disciples, the preceding chapter forbids women, especially widows, to teach in public!). In approving diaconal functions in baptism—which were almost insisted upon on grounds of propriety!—the *Didascalia* at the same time sets a clear boundary: the "calling of the names" (that is, the Trinitarian baptismal formula) shall take place "by a man" (not necessarily a presbyter or bishop!).[180]

Apparently the author of the *Didascalia* had in mind cases where baptism would not be performed in the normal liturgical procedure with all ministers of the church. In such cases deacons were conceded the right to baptize (in the full sense); deaconesses were granted only the preparatory anointing and the immersion in water. Nevertheless, baptism by a woman is not formally prohibited, only "advised against":

> . . . for that is a trespass of the commandment and very dangerous for her who baptizes and him [male pronoun!] who is baptized. For, if it were allowed to be baptized by a woman, our Lord and Master would have been baptized by his mother Mary; but he was baptized by John, like other people. So, do not bring danger to yourselves, brothers and sisters, by acting like those who stand outside the law of the gospel.[181]

Thus the writer of the *Didascalia* attests against his will, as it were, that women ministers in the church did far more than he wanted to concede to them.

On the issue of baptism and ministry, the African Tertullian clearly represents an even more conservative standpoint. Yet his opinions also do not reflect the actual conditions in Carthage, for otherwise his sharp polemic against teaching and baptizing women would be superfluous. With him and even more in the *Didascalia* we can recognize behind the restrictive rules an earlier more liberal practice, which granted women the right to teach and baptize—and not only women but also men![182]

Perpetua seems not to have had this experience. But the question of female identification figures does not focus primarily on Perpetua. In her case the experienced solidarity of sisters and brothers in prison and presumably beyond in the church of Carthage was apparently able to balance the deficit in women ministers, for she shows no psychopathic traits in her readiness for martyrdom. She did not "seek" suffering, as some commentaries assert; rather, it was forced upon her.[183] According to von Franz, the "battle with the snake," about which Perpetua so urgently dreams, is an expression of her will to live, an indication that her "unconscious did not drive her to martyrdom," "a vital reaction of the unconscious to the fate threatening from the outside." This inner conflict shows "that she was not an unnaturally fanatical woman but a normal person who, however, met an extraordinary fate."[184] Yet her dreams point to the danger of a psychic alienation through only male identification figures, which is still real for women today.

Behind Perpetua's dream is not the conscious or unconscious wish to be a man; the transformation into a warrior is pregiven in the symbolism of the baptismal rite. It is not the male sex that is important, but identification with Christ.[185] Yet we must still note that the metaphor of the athlete is in itself primarily a "masculine" symbol. The New Testament also has for baptism the "feminine" symbol of birth. In the homilies of the church fathers this metaphor is also occasionally used. In the rite, however, the battle metaphor is very one-sidedly developed. From there it is only a step to the image of the soldier to describe the Christian life.[186] The question of how Christianity could have developed if the focus had instead been on the symbol of birth is all too hypothetical and speculative to answer.[187] Yet we cannot doubt that the one-sided dominance of the battle metaphor had negative consequences.

6. Martyrdom and Representation of Christ

a. Martyrs and Confessors

Whoever is condemned for the sake of the name of God the Lord shall be regarded by you as a holy martyr, as an angel of God or God on earth, one who is clothed in the spiritual sense with the Holy Spirit of God. Through him you see the Lord our Redeemer, for he has become worthy of the everlasting crown and has renewed the martyrdom of suffering.[188]

When the confessor is put in chains because of the name of the Lord, no one shall lay hands on him for the ministry of deacon or that of presbyter, for he already has the status of a priest on account of his confession. But if he is to be appointed bishop, then hands shall be laid on him.[189]

These two texts from the first half of the third century both bear witness in their own way to the high esteem enjoyed by martyrs and confessors in the early church. And yet both texts are restrictive: the martyrs are not given what they themselves and many fellow Christians regarded as their special privilege: granting forgiveness to sinners—especially to those who had not held up during persecution. The authors of the *Didascalia* and the *Apostolic Tradition* wanted, rather, to strengthen the authority of the bishop.

First, however, let us clarify the two titles *martyr* (*martys*) and *confessor* (*homologētēs*), whose similarity and difference has been the subject of much disagreement.[190] Peter Corssen has expressed the relationship precisely:

It is true that the martyr and the confessor were distinguished from each other, but as long as time brought forth both, the distinction was frequently overlooked in practice and sometimes not maintained even in theory. Not until after the time of the persecutions did the term *martyr* become so fixed that it covered only those who earned the title through death and thus were now recognized as saints. It is a vain endeavor to distinguish temporal stages in the development of the relationship of the two concepts to each other. Rather, the fluctuation has been the same during the whole period and has its basis in the fact that the distinction between confessor and martyr was felt to be one of degree, not essence.[191]

The texts quoted above from the church disciplines no doubt speak of persons who did not have to seal their confession with death. Only once in the old documents do we find an express refusal to use the title *martyr* for a still living *confessor:* on the lips of the gruesomely tortured Christians of Lyon, as reported by Eusebius:

> So eager were they to imitate Christ, who though He was in the form of God did not count it a prize to be on an equality with God, that though they had won such glory and had borne a martyr's witness not once or twice but again and again, and had been brought back from the wild beasts and were covered with burns, bruises, and wounds, they neither proclaimed themselves martyrs nor allowed us to address them by this name: if any one of us by letter or word ever addressed them as martyrs he was sternly rebuked. For they gladly conceded the title of martyr to Christ, the faithful and true Martyr-witness and Firstborn of the dead and Prince of the life of God; and they reminded us of the martyrs already departed: "They indeed are martyrs, whom Christ judged worthy to be taken up as soon as they had confessed Him, sealing their martyrdom by their departure: we are nothing but humble confessors." (5.2.2–3)

This view, however, was in no way shared by the writer of the report but was instead deemed an expression of extreme humility and modesty; he himself did not follow this use of language. The no longer extant list of martyrs also included the names of the survivors (5.4.3).

We find the same open, almost interchangeable treatment of the terms in Cyprian of Carthage, who became bishop of this African metropolis in 248. During the Decian persecution (250) he fled the city; he suffered martyrdom in 258 under Valerian. He died by sword in the middle of his congregation, in accordance with a wish expressed in his last letter: "It befits a bishop to confess his faith in that city where he has been placed in charge over the Lord's flock, it is proper that the appointed leader in the Church should bring glory upon all his people by making his confession in their midst" (letter 81; ACW 47:105). Through Cyprian's correspondence we learn many details of the time of persecution, especially about the problems resulting from the martyrs' practice of granting forgiveness: by means of so-called peace letters they readmitted to Communion Christians who had fallen away during the persecution. The majority of the earlier letters (5–68) deal with these conflicts. The later ones are also connected with the problem, for they concern the Novatians, who refused to readmit the *lapsi* to the church.

Thus Cyprian could have tried to stop this practice of reconciliation through the distinction between dead martyrs and surviving confessors, but apparently the idea did not occur to him. Let us look at how he dealt with the conflict. The wording of one of the peace letters is extant in his collected correspondence:

> *All the confessors send greetings to pope Cyprian.*
> This is to inform you that all of us have together granted peace to those whose conduct since their fault you shall find, upon examination, to be satisfactory. It

is our wish that you should make this resolution known to other bishops also, and it is our desire that you should be at peace with the holy martyrs. Written by Lucianus, in the presence of an exorcist and a lector from the clergy. (23; ACW 43:108)

It is true that Cyprian complains about this behavior of Lucianus and the confessors in general,[192] yet not so much based on principle—only the bishop can grant readmission of the apostates!—but because he holds the hasty reconciliation to be premature: the apostates must first prove the sincerity of their regret through an appropriate penance. Hence he also did not call the undertaken reconciliations fundamentally into question—the confessors had no authority for this!—but left the decision to a future assembly. "Then, when, through God's mercy, we have come to you and the bishops have been called together, a large number of us will be able to examine the letter of the blessed martyrs and their requests," he wrote to his church in Carthage from his hiding place during the persecution (17; ACW 43:97).[193] Yet when death threatens, communion is to be given on the recommendation of the confessors (letters 18–20).

More than once he informs the church that he has entrusted certain confessors with clergy functions[194] (including Aurelius, who is also supposed to have issued peace letters,[195] and Celerinus, who had asked Lucianus to issue a peace letter[196]), while circumventing the usual procedure: "Dearest brethren, it is our custom when we make appointments to clerical office to consult you beforehand, and in council together with you to weigh the character and qualities of each candidate. But there is no need to wait for evidence from men when already God has cast His vote" (38.1; ACW 44:52). Even clearer: "Celerinus . . . has been joined to our clergy not by the election of man [humana suffragatione] but by the favour of God [divina dignatione]" (39.1; ACW 44:54). In contrast to what the *Apostolic Tradition* of Hippolytus foresaw, Cyprian ordained these men in spite of the martyrdom they suffered; he makes no distinction here between "confessors" and "martyrs": "For [the Lord] has deigned to glorify and honour His church in our day. For He has granted reprieve to His noble confessors and glorious martyrs, His purpose being that they who have made their confession of Christ so heroically, should subsequently bring lustre to the clergy of Christ in the service of ecclesiastical office" (ibid.). By contrast, a presbyter and a deacon who were not confessors but likewise admitted apostates to communion were excommunicated (34).

In Cyprian the term *confessor* is found more often than *martyr,* but what distinguishes them is not death resulting from confession but the degree of suffering tolerated. Johannes Ernst has examined the many passages in which one of the two terms or even both are found in parallel and offers the following result:

1. For Cyprian, complete martyrs, martyrs *kat' exochēn,* are those Christians who as a result of their confession of faith were executed or succumbed to the

torments of torture and other mistreatment, or who without such violent causes of death died in prison or in exile.

2. The title of honor of a martyr, however, also correctly (not in deviation from a "principle") belongs to those who for their open confession of Christ have suffered the torments of torture and other bodily mistreatment but as a result of the suspension of persecution escaped violent death and remain alive.

3. Those Christians who have confessed their faith and for this have been put in prison or driven into exile, without dying in exile or in prison or only being subjected to torture and other bodily mistreatment, have, according to Cyprian, a claim only to the title of *confessor*.

4. In several passages Cyprian takes *confessor* as a generic term that also comprises martyrs in the broad sense, who for their faith have suffered ordeals but not death.[197]

In terms of content, the two terms *confession* (*homologia, confessio*) and *witness* (*martyrion, martyrium*) are complementary, but a shift has occurred as compared to the language of the New Testament.[198] There the term *witness* always has a judicial connotation. Now, however, Christians stand before the court as the accused, not as witnesses: their statement is "confession" first in the sense of *admission* and as such also *profession*. Yet through this confession with the commitment of their lives, the message of the resurrection is, so to speak, guaranteed. "In this struggle of conviction, the martyr saw himself . . . as a witness and was regarded as such by the believers, since he seemed to prove not only the power of his own faith but also the objective truth of the content of this faith, and the church believed this as well."[199] The martyrs and martyresses were above all "witnesses to the resurrection"—this quality put them close to the "first witnesses," those women and men around Jesus who experienced his death and then met the resurrected One. The martyrs were considered successors of the apostles—and in this quality they stood in competition with the bishop.

b. Women Martyrs and Confessors

In the texts on the martyrs' and confessors' special position of honor that we have examined thus far, martyresses were nowhere expressly mentioned. That is true of both the sources and studies on the topic. But since there were without doubt women among the martyrs—and in great number—we must ask whether they had the same privileges as the men. I know of only one place where a woman's name is directly linked with the title *woman confessor* (*homologētria*):[200] Sabina bears it at the beginning of the *Martyrdom of Pionius* in the introduction of the people arrested (2). The translators have obviously had a problem with this. Musurillo, without giving any reasons in his Greek-English version, renders *homologētria* as "holy woman,"[201] and we find "pieuse femme" ("pious woman") in Hamman's collection.[202] Rauschen alleges that he holds to the early Latin translation, which in this passage lists only names: "Characteristic additions of the

Greek text are put in parentheses."[203] By Pionius we indeed find "(Presbyter)," but nothing by Sabina! Why such evasion in regard to a woman confessor? We learn only a little about Sabina's actual church activities, and this has already been reported in section 2b above. In any case, we have here again a slave who, like Blandina and Felicity, apparently played an important role in the church; she knew how to appear before the court in a sovereign fashion.

"Blessed, too, are the women who are there with you as partners in your glorious confession [gloria confessionis]," writes Bishop Cyprian from his hiding place to the Christians of his church in prison (6.3; ACW 43:65). Beyond this general praise the Cyprian correspondence contains a concrete, if also indirect, testimony about women who were recognized as martyrs and acted as such. From Rome, Celerinus writes to Lucianus in prison in Carthage on account of two women, Numeria and Candida, one of whom offered the sacrifice herself, while the other saved herself from sacrifice through bribery. In the meantime both regretted their behavior and rendered great service especially with the refugees from Carthage: they had taken all of them in and cared for them for sixty-five days. Lucianus is certain: "Christ will now pardon them if you, His martyrs, ask Him." He reports further: "Their case has already been heard and our Church leaders have bidden that they continue as they are for the time being until a bishop is appointed.[204] But we do beg that to your utmost through your holy prayers and entreaties in which we put our trust, for you are not only the friends but witnesses of Christ, we beg that you pardon them completely" (21; ACW 43:105).

In his answer (letter 22) Lucianus complies with the request of his friend. First he recalls the last wish of the martyr Paulus, who before his death said: "Lucianus, before Christ I say to you that should anyone seek peace from you after I have been called away, grant it in my name." And Lucianus continues: "And moreover all of us whom the Lord has deigned to call away in this time of great tribulation, we have all together issued a joint letter granting peace to everyone together. . . . And so, my very dear brother, send our greetings to Numeria and Candida. [We grant them peace] in accordance with the command of Paulus and of the other martyrs whose names I add: Bassus (died in the mines), Mappalicus (under interrogation), Fortunio (in prison), Paulus (after interrogation), *Fortunata,* Victorinus, Victor, Herennius, *Credula, Hereda,* Donatus, Firmus, Venustus, Fructus, *Julia,* Martialis, and Ariston—all by God's will starved to death in prison" (ACW 43:107, emphasis added). Thus the peace letters were cosigned by women! Also the closing "greetings to the confessors of the Lord" include the names of eight women (ibid., p. 108).

The testimonies are rather spare, but they are, nonetheless, unambiguous: many Christians accorded martyresses the same rank as male martyrs. The latter felt justified in granting ecclesiastical forgiveness, and there were men who recognized such acts by women. This information, which we can derive only with considerable effort from the testimonies of a time in which there was already conflict because of the martyrs' practice of forgiveness, is fully confirmed by the earlier sources. Thus let us turn once again to the martyrdom accounts from Lyon and Carthage.

c. The Service
of Reconciliation

The formulations used in the letter that the Gallic Christians sent to the churches in Asia and Phrygia indicate that for its writer all the persecuted people of Lyon, whether they died or not, had the status of martyrs, even if they in their modesty did not want to claim this title for themselves. They were counted as martyrs from the moment they confessed "I am a Christian" before the court. At this point there was no difference between men and women. This is demonstrated by three concrete incidents, which all end with the almost stereotypical formula: "He/she confessed and was counted among the clergy of the martyrs." We find this formula right at the beginning of the account when Vettius Epagathus gets involved in the court proceedings and thereby becomes a defendant himself: "In the clearest possible tones Vettius replied: 'I am.' And he, too, was admitted to the clergy of the martyrs" (1.10).[205]

It appears a second time in the report on Biblis, who at first failed, but when they tried torturing her in order to extract statements against Christians, she woke up, as it were, and rejected the slander about Christians: " 'How could children be eaten by people who are not even allowed to eat the blood of brute beasts?'[206] From then on she insisted that she was a Christian, and so she joined the clergy of the martyrs" (1.26).

In the third occurrence the formula is used for the entire group that initially apostatized. In spite of their denial of Christianity they were held in prison under accusations of the normal penal code (1.33–35). During the tedious time of detention for questioning a surprising turnabout occurred: the majority of the detainees revoked their rejection of Christianity. At a new hearing they—despite all the pressure that was exerted on them—remained constant in their confession, "and so joined the [clergy] of the martyrs" (1.48).

This talk of the *clergy of the martyrs* has its counterpart in the account of Perpetua, Felicity, and the other martyrs of Carthage in the term *dignatio*, the "gracious empowerment" that we have already discussed in section 4b above. It is used in the introduction to show that the church can and must prove itself through its Spirit-filled "martyrs and prophets." The *dignatio* of Perpetua as a martyr empowers her for prophetic vision and effective intercession (cf. 1, 4, 7).

From Cyprian's correspondence we have learned that the martyrs' readiness to forgive assumed a very concrete form: the production of peace letters. On this point the account of the martyrs of Lyon is not nearly as clear. As we have seen, the letter reports on two concrete cases of the readmission of apostates: first of Biblis and then of a whole group. With Biblis we find no indication of a mediation by other martyrs: it is the confession itself that restores her communion with the other prisoners. This corresponds completely with the view we have already come to know of martyrdom as a second baptism that replaces or reestablishes the first one. Yet in the account of the conversion of the remaining apostates there are images and expressions that suggest a kind of formal celebration of reconciliation, without this being explicitly stated. This part of the letter, however, exists only in fragments. The event is described as "a great dispensation [*oikonomia*] of God and the infinite mercy of Jesus revealed to a degree rarely known in the brotherhood of Christians, but not beyond the skill [*technē*] of Christ" (1.32). Beyond some "sons of perdition[207] . . . the rest were all added to the Church" (1.49). The behavior of the men and women who, in contrast to the apostates, were resolute from the beginning is described as follows:

> Their time of respite was not idle or unfruitful: through their endurance the infinite mercy of Christ was revealed; for through the living the dead were being brought back to life, and martyrs were bestowing grace on those who had failed to be martyrs, and there was great joy in the heart of the Virgin Mother, who was receiving her stillborn children back alive; for by their means most of those who had denied their Master travelled once more the same road, conceived and quickened a second time, and learnt to confess Christ. Alive now and braced up, their ordeal sweetened by God, who does not desire the death of the sinner but is gracious towards repentance, they advanced to the tribunal to be again interrogated by the governor. (1.45)

At the end of the account of the massacre in Lyon, Eusebius again quotes passages on the reconciliation activity of martyrs who themselves did not want to be called martyrs: "They defended all and accused none; they loosed all and bound none" (2.5). Here is a clear allusion to the Gospel saying: "Truly I tell you, whatever you bind on earth will be bound in heaven, and whatever you loose on earth will be loosed in heaven" (Matt. 18:18),[208] which is the basis of the traditional practice of ecclesiastical penance. Thus a specific celebration of reconciliation is suggested when we read:

> They did not crow over the fallen, but the things they themselves had in abundance they bestowed with motherly affection on those who lacked them. Shedding many tears on their behalf in supplication to the Father, they asked for life and He gave it to them. This they shared with their neighbours when triumphantly victorious they departed to God. Peace they had ever loved; peace they commended to our care; and with peace they went to God, leaving no sorrow to their Mother, no strife or warfare to their brothers, but joy, peace, concord, and love. (2.6–7)

Here there are doubtless allusions to the church's practice of reconciliation, but the expressions remain too vague to infer with certainty a concrete act of forgiveness on the part of men and women martyrs with regard to the initially apostate Christians that would correspond to the peace letters in Cyprian's Carthage. This is due not last of all to the historical situation that in regard to both intrachurch structures and Rome's anti-Christian policy was different in Lyon from that during the Decian persecution a good seventy years later. We do not know what role the survivors played after the massacre. The readmission of the apostates took place in prison during the trial, and those reconciled with the church suffered martyrdom themselves immediately afterward. There could be no conflict between the martyrs and the bishop, like that under Cyprian in Carthage, since Pothinus had already died.

Eusebius, who selected the passages from the account according to his interests, was not concerned with stressing the authority of the martyrs in the church but their charity: "The affection of those blessed ones for their brothers who had fallen from grace" is consciously set over against the rigorism of others "who later behaved so harshly towards the members of Christ's body" (2.8). Perhaps the writer of the letter wanted to forestall possible rivalries when he so clearly emphasized that the men and women confessors of Lyon did not claim for themselves the title of martyr. It was above all a question of whether apostates could be readmitted at all; next to this, the question of who performed the readmission was secondary. But even if there was no concrete celebration of forgiveness, one point still remains certain: the conversion of the apostates is regarded as a fruit of the confession and intercession of the martyrs and martyresses.

Similarly, while under arrest Perpetua exercised this intercessory power on behalf of her dead brother, and in the dream vision of Saturus (11–13/S) we have a kind of counterpart to the images of reconciliation from Lyon, which is less edifying and idyllic but perhaps reproduces the persecution situation more realistically: the church in Carthage in 203 appears to be not full of peace but full of strife. In the dream the angel rebukes the bishop because the Christians are not united; Bishop Optatus himself and the priest Aspasius ask the martyrs to bring peace between them, since they have gone forth without first having reconciled them ("sic nos reliquistis"; 13/S).

Naturally we cannot simply draw conclusions about concrete reality on the basis of a dream, but we also have a text by Tertullian that attests to both the tensions among the prisoners and the practice of giving letters of peace. In his exhortation *To the Martyrs*—Tertullian also addresses the persecuted naturally with the martyr's title!—we read: "It is the custom of certain people who do not have this peace with the church to beg it from the martyrs in prison. And therefore you must have it, love it, and keep it among yourselves, so that you will be able, if need be, to bestow it on others."[209] Here the theologian seems to have no objections to the practice of the martyrs "bestowing peace."[210] Earlier he characterized prison as a "dwelling of the devil," who tempts Christians there with "common hatreds, sluggishness, or mutual fallings out": psychologically a very understandable temptation during lengthy imprisonment in a confined space! Against this background Saturus's dream seems quite consistent with reality. Reconciliation between the martyrs (it remains unclear whether this means only Perpetua and Saturus or also others who died earlier), Bishop Optatus, and the presbyter Aspasius is indicated by an embrace. Interestingly, the angels criticize the fact that the latter two are seeking the mediation of the martyrs: "Allow them to rest. Settle whatever quarrels you have among yourselves" (13/S).

In the dream Perpetua—a woman—appears naturally as the mediator of reconciliation: a bishop and a presbyter make a request of her, a martyress, which evokes her astonishment. Be it well noted that it is not Perpetua herself who dreams this—one should not see here an unconscious striving for power—but Saturus. The vision of a woman before whom a bishop kneels to beg forgiveness and receives it from her is the vision of a man. Thus in this group of martyrs there is no contradiction between the self-understanding of the woman confessor and the recognition of her *dignatio* by her fellow Christians.

Conclusion. In all the documents of the early period we find the same conviction: (1) martyresses and martyrs have a special position in the church; (2) one becomes a martyr(ess) by making a confession before the court; (3) martyresses and martyrs are in a special way granted the right to reconcile with the church those who fell away during persecution, that is, to readmit them to Communion.

What gave the women and men confessors so much esteem and authority in the eyes of the early church was no doubt the identification of their fate with the fate of Jesus. It is no accident that the second word with which the Latin language designates martyrdom is the same as that used for the Passion story of the Gospels: *passio.* Out of the consciousness of this identity grew a double certainty: (1) it was Christ himself who suffered in the martyr and the martyress and thereby granted the power of victory; (2) the result of the suffering of the martyr and martyress was the same as the suffering of Christ: to them was ascribed a special capability of vicarious intercession.

d. The Dispute over Representation of Christ

As we saw, this veneration resulted in certain privileges, which were accorded the survivors. Through their confession, these most highly regarded members of the church acquired a charismatic moral authority, yet this very authority led to competition with the bishops. Who stood higher in the hierarchy of the church, the men and women martyrs, who through their witness had proved that the Spirit of Christ, the Holy Spirit, was alive in them, or the bishops elected by the church and properly ordained? As we have seen, on this question Cyprian made no clear decision; he did not want to resolve the issue of the apostates until after the end of the persecutions. For Rome a similar procedure is attested; there they wanted to follow his advice "that we must wait first, until the Church has peace, and then, after bishops, presbyters, deacons, confessors and the laity who have remained steadfast have exchanged views in conference together, we can deal with the question of the lapsed" (30.5; ACW 44:30).

Yet the two documents quoted at the beginning of this chapter, the Syriac *Didascalia* and the *Apostolic Tradition* of Hippolytus firmly establish the special place of honor of the martyrs as clergy, though they are clearly subordinated to the bishop—martyresses are not mentioned. According to Hippolytus confessors are granted at most the status of a presbyter—women confessors are not mentioned. The author of the *Didascalia* avoids addressing the potential conflict directly: in the many chapters in which the bishop is mentioned, confessors are not; conversely, in the chapter on confessors their relationship to the bishop is not discussed.[211] Yet in the language of the *Didascalia* martyr and bishop have one thing in common: *both represent God.*

Yet this is expressly said of the confessor *only once:* "He shall be regarded by you as a holy martyr, as an angel of God or God on earth, one who is clothed in the spiritual sense with the Holy Spirit of God. For because he has become worthy of the everlasting crown and renewed the martyrdom of suffering, through him you see the Lord, the Redeemer."[212] Nevertheless, concrete authority is not derived from this representation. The bishop, however, is said *innumerable times* and with the strongest language to represent God on earth: "The bishop is the servant of the word and mediator, but for you the teacher and, next to God, your father who brought you into being through the water. He is your head and leader and for you the mighty king; he rules in place of the Almighty and indeed is to be honored by you like God."[213] In this context his authority is at the same time raised above that of other ministers.[214]

Moreover, this representation of the bishop is precisely defined: he represents God in his specific function as judge over sinners; more precisely, he represents the God who is gracious and merciful to sinners and grants them forgiveness: "O bishop, . . . know that your position is that of Almighty God and that you have received the power to forgive sins."[215] Thus the Syriac church discipline represents a fundamentally more moderate standpoint. Here, however, only the bishop is recognized in the function in which the martyresses and martyrs also wanted to and were supposed to represent God, the gracious and merciful God, when they claimed for themselves the right to readmit apostates into the communion of the church!

The "representation" that the author of the *Didascalia* gives to women and men confessors is of a completely different sort: it is the presence of the suffering Christ, who needs someone to care for the believers. Thus the title of chapter 19 reads: "That it is our duty to care for those who for the sake of Christ's name must suffer as martyrs." Here much is demanded: "If you are rich, you must help them according to your wealth or even give all your possessions and free them from their bonds." Christians are to visit martyrs in prison, even if they risk becoming martyrs themselves. The idea of presence is understood here entirely in the sense of Matt. 25:40: "Just as you did it to one of the least of these who are members of my family, you did it to me"—this sentence from the Gospel is expressly quoted. It is true that in these formulations the idea of the martyr as a privileged witness of the resurrection is maintained; indeed, all of chapter 20, with the title "On the Resurrection of the Dead," deals almost exclusively with martyrdom. Yet the words, "He shall be regarded by you as a holy martyr, as an angel of God or God on earth," which are almost identical to the description of the bishop, are interpreted here completely differently.[216] There is a *revision of the idea of representation* like that already seen regarding widows: the vocabulary is retained, yet now it is not supposed to legitimate a function in the church but to provoke charity: bearers of authority become recipients of alms! This language is completely different from that of the martyrdom accounts.

The analysis of Perpetua's dream vision, with its interweaving of the experienced rites of baptism and the imminent suffering in the arena, has already shown that this was regarded as a battle with the devil and a repetition and continuation of the battle fought by Jesus Christ himself. The same idea also dominates the account of the martyrdom in Lyon: the Roman authorities recede into the background, and Satan repeatedly appears as the real subject of the action.

This enemy is not faced by martyr and martyress alone; Christ fights with them and in them. The same conviction with which Felicity confronted the prison guard who was making fun of her wailing in the pangs of childbirth: "What I am suffering now . . . I suffer by myself. But then *another will be inside me who will suffer for me*, just as I shall be suffering for him" (15/S), is expressed in the description of the torments of Sanctus: "But his poor body was a witness to what he had suffered—it was all one wound and bruise, bent up and robbed of outward human shape, but, *suffering in that body, Christ accomplished most glorious things*" (1.23). We read that the old bishop Pothinus was strengthened by the Spirit for martyrdom; in spite of the extreme bodily weakness of the ninety year old, his life was preserved in him, *"that thereby Christ might triumph"* (1.29).

In this battle Christ and the martyr are so closely united that they are interchangeable as subjects: Christ suffers in the martyr; the martyr renews the victory of Christ. This *identification with the crucified One* applies to men and women alike: they all fight the same fight. This is expressed most emphatically in the three scenes in which the martyrdom of Blandina is described.[217]

As a slave she could be easily sentenced to every imaginable torture. In body she was fragile and probably already older. Adriana Valerio has rightly pointed out that the beloved cliché in the hagiography of a beautiful young girl has no support in the text.[218] Blandina finds strength in her conviction of faith, which with all the torments allows her a peaceful end: "She was indifferent now to all that happened to her, because of her hope . . . and of her communing with Christ. Then she, too, was sacrificed" (1.56). Her figure stands at the end of the account, where she appears, so to speak, as the mother of the community of Christians: those who died before her are "her children" (*tekna*), whom she sent "before her in triumph to the King," as a field marshal sends his soldiers into war. Then "Blandina herself passed through all the ordeals of her children [*paides*] and hastened to rejoin them, rejoicing and exulting at her departure[219] as if invited to a wedding supper" (1.55; Williamson, 202).

We should note that Blandina, in spite of her female sex, is not described here as the "bride of Christ" but, like all martyrs, as a guest at the heavenly wedding banquet, in agreement with the New Testament texts. The bride-bridegroom motif is never found there as a metaphor for a person's individual relationship with Christ—to say nothing of metaphor specific to women—but is found only collectively for the church in a revival of the Old Testament image of God's covenant with his people. The wedding is the metaphor for the happiness of the *eschaton,* the kingdom of God.[220] The image has its liturgical counterpart in the Eucharist, which is interpreted as an anticipation of the heavenly wedding banquet. Not until the ascetic literature does the wedding motif become the bride motif and which is then applied primarily to virgins.[221] In the martyrdom accounts, however, it is found for men and women, for married and unmarried: all martyrs in Lyon are compared with an adorned bride (1.35).

At first glance things seem to be different with Perpetua. On her entrance into the arena she is called *matrona Christi* ("wife of Christ") and *Dei delicata* ("beloved of God"), which recalls the initial description of the young martyress as *matronaliter nupta* ("married as a matron") and suggests that the relationship with God/Christ may be thought of here as a substitute for earthly marriage. Still, the idea of a heavenly "wife of Christ" is attested nowhere else. The designation of Perpetua as "matron" at the end as well as at the beginning of the account is intended to emphasize her high status even in the humiliation of martyrdom: in the arena the spectators are forced by her gaze to bow their heads. Here too the real contrast is the terrifying earthly torment of death and the expected supernatural happiness, as the preceding sentence describing the entrance of the martyrs shows: "Gaudio pavente non timore" ("they trembled with joy, not with fear"). In this group the two women are especially emphasized, and their earthly experience is transformed into the spiritual: Perpetua's noble wedding becomes the metaphor of heavenly happiness, and Felicity's happy delivery becomes the symbol of rebirth to eternal life. Thus marriage and motherhood are not in opposition here to the heavenly wedding as in the ascetic preaching on virginity; rather, the heavenly wedding appears as the fulfillment and augmentation of the human experience of happiness on earth.

Like Perpetua, Blandina is described with male and female metaphors: as warrior and as mother. Conversely, female metaphors are used to describe male martyrs. For Alexander we find the image of someone giving birth: with gestures that to bystanders look like "birth pangs," he exhorts the former apostates to confession (1.49). All the martyrs together shine like "a bride adorned" (1.35), and they all forgive the apostates "with motherly affection" (2.6).

In the first martyrdom scene Blandina had already been called a great athlete (1.19). This image is taken up again in the second scene: ". . . by victory in further contests she might make irrevocable the sentence passed on the crooked serpent, and spur on her brother Christians—a small, weak, despised woman who had put on Christ, the great invincible champion, and in bout after bout had defeated her adversary and through conflict had won the crown of immortality" (1.42).

This is astonishing: what is said in the description of the martyr Sanctus about *Christ* "defeating the adversary" (1.23) is said here about the martyress *Blandina:* "in bout after bout [*she*] defeated her adversary." The same strong identification with Christ is already found at the beginning of this scene, when Blandina is hung on a post in the arena and exposed to the wild beasts: "She looked as if she was hanging in the form of a cross, and through her ardent prayers she stimulated great enthusiasm in those undergoing their ordeal, who in their agony saw with their outward eyes in the person of their sister the One who was crucified for them, that [she] might convince those who believe in Him that any man who has suffered for the glory of Christ has fellowship for ever with the living God" (1.41).

Yet at this point the translations differ. Who is the subject of the phrase that literally means "in order to give certainty to those who believe . . ."—Christ or Blandina? In the already-mentioned parallel passage from the martyrdom of Sanctus we have an almost identical formulation: "Suffering in [Sanctus's] body, Christ accomplished most glorious things, utterly defeating the adversary and proving as an example to the rest that where the Father's love is nothing can frighten us, where Christ's glory is nothing can hurt us" (1.23). Here Christ is clearly the subject: the main verb, "accomplished," has three dependent participles. The passage sounds as if a confessional formula is being quoted, which perhaps explains why Christ here is subject and also object, as it were (Christ promising Christ's glory).

In the report on Blandina, however, the martyress is clearly the subject of the main clause: "She stimulated great enthusiasm in those undergoing their ordeal"; then follows an inserted, substantiating genitive absolute, saying that with their outward eyes they could see the crucified One through their sister. Then comes a *that* clause: "that she/he might convince the believers . . ." (*hina peisē*). According to the normal rules of grammar, the dependent clause is dependent on the main clause: accordingly, it is Blandina who conveys the certainty of the resurrection to her brothers. The text is understood in this sense—correctly in my view—by Henri Leclerq, Philipp Haeuser and Arnim Gärtner, and Oda Hagemeyer. Nonetheless, Gustave Bardy and Herbert Musurillo, the editors of the newest editions of the text, relate the *that* clause to the crucified One: it is he who conveys certainty to the believers. Adalbert Hamman and Hugo Rahner also render the passage in this sense. It may be presumed that the reasons that led to this translation were theological rather than grammatical: the identification of a martyress with Christ seems hard to comprehend! This becomes quite clear in the translation by Rahner, who gives an interpretive paraphrase of "through[222] their sister" as "the outward eyes looked at the sister, but through her they saw Him." Hamman speaks of "the crucified virgin," which from the standpoint of the text is an invention. Is the ascetic idea of the sexlessness or even "masculinity" of the virgin still at work here, perhaps making it easier to accept the identification of a woman with Christ?

Be that as it may, even if one relates the dependent clause not to Blandina but to Christ, the fact remains that in their sister and through their sister, the small, weak slave Blandina, the brothers saw the crucified One and through her found the courage for their own martyrdom. Blandina, like all who sacrificed their lives for the faith, "represented" for them Jesus in his victory over death. Through her "Christ proved that things which men regard as mean, unlovely, and contemptible are by God deemed worthy of great glory, because of her love for Him shown in power and not vaunted in appearance" (1.17)—this the how the writer began his report on Blandina: it is the quintessence of Paul's great sermon on the cross in 1 Corinthians 1!

7. Conclusion

The picture that these two martyrdom accounts convey is the picture of a church in which neither internal nor external ecclesiastical status counts. In Lyon the slave Blandina is the main figure in a martyrdom in which her mistress, although herself a martyress, remains anonymous. It is not the "father" of the church, the undeniably arresting figure of the old bishop Pothinus, who is the focus, but the small, weak Blandina, the "mother" of the church. In Carthage the patrician Perpetua is the leading personality in the group of martyrs, yet also at her side stood perhaps a slave, or at least a woman of lower social status. Nothing is more telling than the scene in the arena when Perpetua, after the first attack of the wild cow, gets up again and sees that Felicity is lying on the ground: "She went over to her, gave her her hand, and lifted her up. Then the two stood side by side" (20/R). If we add the other acts of martyrs, the picture becomes complete. Slaves stand beside free, women beside men, personalities without ecclesiastical office beside bishops, presbyters, and deacons, wives and mothers beside women ascetics, fathers of families beside monks—in one great fellowship. For all of them only one thing counts: "I am a Christian."

Nevertheless, let us not be deceived by this picture: it is not *the* picture of *the* church in the second and third centuries. Not all martyresses and martyrs were the heroes and saints that the later hagiography presents. The "confessor arrogance" reproached by the bishops was certainly not merely an invention to strengthen their own ministerial authority. For a short time, however, in the exceptional situation, the early Christian ideal became reality. Yet other powers had long been at work and were later to prove historically overpowering. Nevertheless, the fact remains that the highest "representatives" of Christ at that time were not the priests and bishops but the martyresses and martyrs. It was not the eucharistic celebration that was the holiest place of the "real presence" but the arena in which the witness of faith was sealed in a life-and-death struggle. If the Roman Catholic Congregation of the Faith today bases the exclusion of women from the priesthood on the idea that only a man can represent the male Jesus,[223] it really cannot substantiate this argumentation by appealing to early church tradition!

III. WOMEN IN PROCLAMATION

Charismatic Prophetesses

1. Prophecy and Christian Existence

For the redactor of the passion stories of Perpetua, Felicity, and their companions there were two clear criteria for the presence of the Holy Spirit in Christendom: the courage of confession before the court when faced with the threat of the death penalty and the capability of prophetic vision. For him both charismata were united in an exemplary way in Perpetua: as a martyress she was at the same time a prophetess. Yet whereas the constancy of the martyrs was considered a gracious gift of the Spirit in the exceptional situation of persecution, the gift of prophecy was part of the everyday life of the church from the beginning of Christian proclamation.[1]

Speaking in Tongues and Prophecy

This gift is attested in detail in one of the oldest writings of the New Testament, Paul's first letter to the church he founded in Corinth.[2] His thoughts are briefly reviewed here, since they play an important role in early church disagreements. In this large Greek harbor town ecstatic expression in the worship service was apparently more the rule than the exception; Paul does not criticize this and even emphasizes that for his part: "I speak in tongues more than all of you" (1 Cor. 14:18). In the same breath, however, he relativizes this gift: "Nevertheless, in church [*ekklēsia*] I would rather speak five words with my mind [*nous*], in order to instruct [*katēchēsō*] others also, than ten thousand words in a tongue [*glōssē*]" (14:19). The ecstatic phenomenon mentioned here, "speaking in tongues" (glossolalia),[3] is characterized by the apostle as prayer: "For those who speak in a tongue do not speak to other people but to God" (14:2). He also talks of speaking "in the Spirit" (14:2) and praying "with the Spirit" (14:15–16). Prophecy, by contrast, is something quite different: "For those who prophesy speak to other people for their upbuilding [*oikodomē*] and encouragement [*paraklēsis*] and consolation [*paramythia*]" (14:3). Thus prophecy is a specific form of proclamation, a kind of short sermon. This capacity to "upbuild" people is the highest of the spiritual gifts (*pneumatika*) and is to be sought more than any other (14:1).

Thus for Paul the hierarchy of values is absolutely clear: "Now I would like all of you to speak in tongues, but even more to prophesy. One who prophesies is greater [*meizōn*] than one who speaks in tongues" (14:5), for speaking in tongues requires interpretation. Paul names four possible forms of interpretation: revelation (*apokalypsis*), knowledge (*gnōsis*), prophecy (*prophēteia*), and teaching (*didachē*), without specifying more precisely how these forms differ from each other (14:6). Yet they do have one thing in common: each involves rational speech for the upbuilding of the church. Although the apostle gives priority to prophecy, he refuses to see the ecstatic consciousness "with the Spirit" (*tō pneumati*) as basically antithetical to rational thinking "with the mind" (*tō noï*): "I will pray with the spirit, but I will pray with the mind also" (14:15). Beyond this Paul gives highly practical instructions: two or three people can speak in tongues, and then someone is to interpret (*diermēneuein*) (14:27). Likewise two or three can prophesy, and the others can judge (*diakrinein*) what is said (14:29). In any case, both charismata are to be promoted: "Be eager to prophesy, and do not forbid speaking in tongues" (14:39).

The whole fourteenth chapter is formulated in androcentric inclusive language (the masculine forms cover both sexes) and also contains an insertion according to which women are to be silent in church (14:34–35).[4] If Corinthian men and women had not quarreled over whether women have to wear a veil in worship,[5] we could not demonstrate with certainty that they were active participants in worship services. In 1 Corinthians 11, however, Paul takes a general position on order in worship and also speaks about the prophecy of women. The apostle emphatically insists on the veil, for he believes that "any woman who prays or prophesies with her head unveiled disgraces her head[6]—it is one and the same thing as having her head shaved" (11:5). We do not even know whether Paul and his "old-fashioned" view prevailed in Corinth. In any case, the prophetic speech of the women was in no way fundamentally controversial—only the form of their appearance. Thus the prohibition of speaking introduced later certainly cannot refer to prophecy. It is recommended to all members of the church.

The apostle does not distinguish the Christian prophets and prophetesses from those of the "old covenant," yet the new "life in the Spirit" is for him clearly connected with being "in Christ."[7] He includes the charisma of prophecy in the religious manifestations that belong to this world. In 1 Corinthians 13 he characterizes speaking in tongues, knowledge, and prophecy as gifts of the Spirit that will come to an end, in contrast to the three that remain eternal: faith, hope, and love, with the last being given highest status: "Love never ends. But as for prophecies, they will come to an end; as for tongues, they will cease; as for knowledge, it will come to an end. For we know only in part, and we prophesy only in part; but when the complete comes, the partial will come to an end" (13:8–10). This experience described by Paul, together with the Pentecost account of Acts and the texts on the work of the Paraclete in the Gospel of John, forms the background for the early Christian dispute over ecstasy, New Prophecy, and Gnosticism, to which we now turn. Even from these terms we can see that the various directions could with a certain justification draw support from the apostle.

"Your Sons and Your Daughters
Shall Prophesy"

For the apologist Justin (d. 165) the awakening of prophecy in young Christendom was proof that God's old gift to Israel had now been passed on to the
church.[8] Later Eusebius appealed to him to demonstrate the existence of orthodox prophets in the mainstream church of the second century: "He [Justin] also
tells us that right up to his own time prophetic gifts were a conspicuous feature
of the Church."[9] From the Jewish Bible the Christians adopted the promise of
Joel 2:28–29 (3:1–2 in Heb.):

> In the last days it will be, God declares,
>   that I will pour out my Spirit upon all flesh,
>   and your sons and your daughters shall prophesy,
>   and your young men[10] shall see visions,
>   and your old men shall dream dreams.
> Even upon my slaves, both men and women,
>   in those days I will pour out my Spirit;
>   and they shall prophesy.
>
>   (Acts 2:17–18)

The early Christians were convinced that this promise, which Peter quotes in his
Pentecost speech, was fulfilled in the descent of the Spirit, and that now the gift
of prophecy in the church must never be extinguished if the church wants to remain the church. Moreover, the prophetic charisma, as a sign of the end time,
was a gift to men *and* women; that is, the activity of the prophetesses was considered living proof that the church was truly gathered "in the Spirit." Irenaeus,
as bishop of Lyon around the end of the second century, proclaimed this conviction in all clarity,[11] but he does not name particular individuals, male or female, who were distinguished by this charisma. Nevertheless, in his church history Eusebius makes Irenaeus the star witness to the fact that in the time of the
Phrygian movement prophets were also active in the mainstream church. In reality his witness remains rather vague: "We hear of many members of the Church
who have prophetic gifts and by the Spirit speak with all kinds of tongues, and
bring men's secret thoughts to light for their own good, and expound the mysteries of God."[12] Furthermore, in the quotations cited by Eusebius apologetic
interests are clearly prominent: Irenaeus wants to distinguish miracle-working
church charismatics from powerless heretical imitators.[13] There is never an express reference to sisters with prophetic gifts.

We must ascertain a similar silence about prophetesses in two even older sources
on early Christian prophecy: the *Didache* and the *Shepherd of Hermas.* But since
they do not explicitly reject the charismatic proclamation of women, the question
must at least remain open as to whether their statements also apply to members of
the female sex.[14] Both writings come from the beginning of the second century.
The author of the *Shepherd of Hermas* lived in Rome; for the *Didache,* in which

even older traditions were compiled, the author question does not have a clear answer.[15] We will turn to the latter first.

No writing of the postapostolic period gives greater significance to the prophets than the *Teaching of the Apostles,* usually called simply the *Didache.* It is written in the style of an edifying sermon and was conceived and formulated entirely androcentrically, even if the frequently used form of address "child" (*teknon*) and the often employed imperative "You shall" are sexually neutral. Women are not explicitly named in any passage, nor are they at any point excluded from certain tasks in the church or admonished to subordination. The latter is notable, since in the *Didache* slaves are expressly asked to obey their master "with respect and reverence as an image of God" (4.11). Thus for slave and free the egalitarian ethos is already abandoned; for women and men, apparently not yet.

The first part of the *Didache* consists of short general instructions for Christian conduct; in the second part are elements of a church discipline for congregations whose life is shaped by the visits of itinerant apostles and prophets.[16] These are first mentioned together:

> In regard to apostles and prophets, proceed according to the commandment of the Gospel. Every apostle who comes to you shall stay only one day, or two when necessary. But if he stays three days, he is a false prophet. If the apostle is on his way, he shall receive nothing except bread until he stays overnight. But if he takes money, he is a false prophet." (11.3–6)

After this apostles are not mentioned. And other ministers? They hardly play a role. Mentioned at one point is a "genuine teacher": he is to be rewarded in the same way as a genuine prophet (13.2). Only in an appendix presumably added later do we read: "Elect[17] bishops and deacons worthy of the Lord, meek men— not greedy—upstanding and proven. They perform for you the service of both prophets and teachers. So pay careful attention. For they are the honorably distinguished among you, together with the prophets and teachers" (15.1–2). Thus we have here a charismatic church structure[18] that is clearly different from the episcopal church order that will prevail later. The most important personalities were clearly the prophets, to whom three long sections are devoted (11.7–13.7), which follow the instruction quoted above for dealing with itinerant apostles. First we read:

> And you are neither to test nor judge every prophet who speaks in the Spirit. For every sin will be forgiven, but this sin will not be forgiven. Not everyone who speaks in the Spirit is a prophet, but only those whose way of life is oriented toward the Lord. Thus by the way of life shall you recognize whether one is a genuine prophet. (11.7–8)

Thus the congregations are by no means uncritical and gullible in regard to prophets—in what follows instructions for dealing with charlatans are given in all clarity. The criterion for judgment is agreement of life and teaching,[19] not "speaking in the Spirit," that is, the specific, more or less ecstatic form of proclamation that can also be found in "false prophets." Greed in charismatics makes them suspect. Nevertheless, those who have proved to be "genuine" are to receive their support from the church. The "church tax" is regulated according to the model of the Jewish laws for the priesthood: "You are to give the first fruits to the prophets. For they are your high priests. But if you have no prophet, give them to the poor" (13.3–4). Then come detailed directions for the various first fruits.

Also in the worship service the special position of the prophet is stressed. At the beginning of this church discipline are rules for baptism, fast days, and the daily praying of the Lord's Prayer three times. Then we read: "Concerning the Eucharist, give thanks in the following way" (9.1), and then follow prayers of blessing over the cup and bread, as well as a long closing prayer of thanksgiving. Then comes the directive: "But allow the prophets to give thanks as much as they want" (10.7). There is no mention of a special function for other ministers in the Eucharist: "On every Lord's day gather, break the bread, and give thanks" (14.1).[20]

Is this early Christian prayer and church discipline, in which the Jewish heritage can still clearly be seen, the product of a charismatic fringe group? It was not, in any case, judged thus by the later mainstream church, for at the end of the fourth century the entire *Didache* was incorporated into a collection of older church disciplines, the *Apostolic Constitutions,* yet with appropriate updating: in most cases *prophet* was stricken and replaced by *bishop, priest,* or *deacon.*[21] As already indicated, we learn nothing about charismatically proclaiming women from this Magna Carta of early Christian prophecy: the existence of prophetesses is neither denied nor confirmed.

The results are similar for the second-mentioned writing from the prophetic tradition, the *Shepherd of Hermas.*[22] Its author Hermas supports the establishment in Rome of an ecclesiastical institution of penance and refers to the visions he has had on this question, which he describes in detail. For him charismatic proclaimers seem to have no preeminence but share equal status with members of the collegium of presbyters.[23] Since nothing can be learned from this book about the particular activities of prophets and prophetesses in the Roman church, it will not be examined further here. Yet it is noteworthy that in the described visions the figure of the *ekklēsia,* from whom Hermas receives his revelations, has the features of a very old woman seer, so that at first he takes her to be the Sibyl whose oracles are held in high esteem not only among the Romans but also among Jews and Christians.[24]

It is also notable that at the end this female figure commissions the author to send one copy of the book with the recorded visions to Clement and one to Grapte, two apparently well-known real people from the Roman church leadership:[25] "Clement is to send it to the cities outside, for that is his duty. Grapte is to convey it to the widows and orphans."[26] Finally, Hermas himself is to read the book aloud "in the city [Rome] in the presence of the presbyters who head the church."[27] The assignment of Grapte to the "widows and orphans" suggests a diaconal ministry, which in the early period may well have included teaching activity and prophetic proclamation. Thus the assumption that this woman could have had the role of a church prophetess is not improbable, but it remains an unprovable hypothesis.

Ordination of Prophetesses?

The high estimation of the prophetic gift is indirectly attested by the practices of a Gnostic teacher of the second century, whom Irenaeus gives the disparaging nickname "the magician": his name was Marcus, and he "bestowed" the desired charisma apparently by means of a kind of ordination, particularly on women.[28] Since the bishop of Lyon was an opponent of Gnosticism but absolutely affirmed authentic prophecy, his vigorous polemic against this group cannot simply be dismissed as malicious distortion, although a great deal of his presentation may be exaggerated. In his view Marcus was a charlatan who had duped many women—whether so harsh a reproach was justified cannot be decided here.[29] Irenaeus's account is often exploited as an example of the gullibility of women, although in the second part the critical ability of women is emphasized. It says there, namely, that many Christian women saw through the dubious charismatic and energetically resisted him:

> Yet other women, who were profound believers and reverent toward God, proved to be unenticeable. He attempted, of course, to lead them astray like the others and ordered them to prophesy, but they breathed on him as in an exorcism and withdrew from such an assembly, probably aware that prophetic speech is not bestowed on people by the magician Marcus. Rather, those who have the gift of prophecy, upon whom God has sent his grace from above, speak when God wills it, not when Marcus orders it. (*AH* 1.13.4)

This does not say that the critical women themselves were prophetesses; the theologian is merely confirming that they have the proper conception of prophetic charisma: this gift is bestowed directly by God; it requires no human mediation—not even through other charismatics or ministers of the church; indeed, they could not bestow it even if they wanted to.

We have already encountered the idea of *prophetic succession* in connection with the daughters of Philip and Ammia of Philadelphia. Now we have an attempt at a *prophetic ordination*. Does the idea of an ordination of prophets suggest a competition between prophets and ministers? Probably not. It is a question rather of a transition phase from freely exercised charismatic authority to the linking of exercised authority with prior ordination.[30] At first charisma and ministry do not seem to be antithetical: with ordination the special charisma bestowed on a person by God is recognized through an act of the church. In this sense all clergy are also "charismatics." What is rejected by Irenaeus and the women he names is an understanding of ordination by magic ritual.

By emphasizing that prophetesses and prophets are not to be ordained, the special status of the prophetic charisma is stressed: the recipients of this charisma belong, without ordination, to the highest level of the clergy, like the later martyresses and martyrs. They have been distinguished by God himself in a special way and therefore need no act of recognition by the church. Later the hierarchy is reversed: the nonordained charismatics should at least be subordinated to the bishops. The idea of a *prophetic succession* sank into oblivion, while the appeal to *apostolic succession* gained importance. This increasingly becomes understood less in the sense of a spiritual continuity than in a "material" one, as the unbroken chain of layings on of hands that goes back to the apostles.[31] Clergywomen are now tolerated only in subaltern positions. Prophetesses and prophets become increasingly rare in the clergy.[32]

As a result, from the material cited here we can see once again that women are interesting for ecclesiastical authors only when they can be used apologetically. Because prophecy by women is regarded as a Spirit-effected eschatological gift, the fact that there are prophetesses in the church is emphasized. Yet when there are concrete reports of prophetic activity in the church or prophetic ministry is to be regulated, we find neither individual women nor women as a group. This contradiction raises questions: Did charismatic women in the prophetically oriented circles of Christianity really have an equal position beside men, as the theory would require? Were they numerous, or were there only a few?

Since we can hardly find factual material from the sources of the second century, the answer to these questions is extremely difficult. It would be premature to infer from the silence of the sources that prophetesses did not exist; it is much more likely that they actually existed but the authors did not perceive them at all, considered them second-class, or even intentionally ignored them.[33]

A Way to Certainty

The hypothesis that the silence of the sources is to be interpreted as intentional silence finds some confirmation in the extracanonical *Acts of Paul*,[34] for there we see proclaiming women. Even if the stories in this early Christian novel of edification are mostly fictional, they offer, nonetheless, a lively insight into the mentality and ways of life of the second century. In particular, the milieu of the nomadic apostles, which we met in the *Didache*, is presented here in a concrete and graphic way. In two places the extant fragments describe the activity of prophetesses in Corinth; thus it is entirely conceivable that poetry draws upon historical reminiscences.

The first mention of such a prophecy is found in an exchange of letters between the church of Corinth and the apostle, a bit of tradition that in all probability was not inserted into the *Acts of Paul* until later.[35] Although the Corinthians know that Paul is approaching martyrdom, they still write to him about controversial issues in the church. They mention the statement of a prophetess: "We believe, namely—as was revealed to Theonoe—that the Lord has freed you from the hand of the lawless one."[36]

The second report is detailed. Paul himself is now in Corinth, where he preaches for a while. Then the final departure is imminent—the church prays and fasts with great sadness.

Cleobius, however, was filled with the Spirit and spoke to them: "Brothers, now Paul must fulfill the whole plan of salvation and go up to [the city] of death [. . . ?] in great instruction and knowledge and sowing of the word, and envied he must depart this world." But when the brothers and Paul heard this, they raised their voice and said: "God, Father of Christ, help Paul your servant, so that he may remain with us for the sake of our weakness." . . . [gap in the traditional text] But the Spirit came over Myrte, so that she said: "Brothers, why [are you frightened at seeing this sign?] Paul, the servant of the Lord, will save many in Rome, and he will nourish so many with the word, that there is no number to count them; and he will reveal himself more than all believers,[37] and great glory will [come] over him, so that there will be great grace in Rome." And as soon as the Spirit in Myrte had calmed down, each one took bread and ate with relish according to custom [. . .] with the singing of the psalms of David and of songs, and Paul also rejoiced. On the next day, after they had spent the whole night in accordance with the will of God, Paul said: "Brothers, on the day of preparation I will depart and travel to Rome, so that I may not postpone what has been commissioned and imposed on me; for that is my destiny."[38]

We need not be concerned about the poor condition of the extant text, since here it is solely a question of grasping the specific function of prophetic proclamation in the life of the church. It is completely different in these two examples. In the "revelation" ascribed to Theonoe, the church learns about a state of affairs of which it was previously ignorant but which could be communicated to it through natural means: Paul is still alive. Thus we have here an extremely questionable form of "prophecy." The "how" of the revelation is not described—hence, an ecstatic milieu cannot be excluded, but it can by no means be absolutely presupposed. In any case, nothing of the kind is mentioned.

In the second example the situation is entirely different. Here it is a matter of making a decision in view of the impending martyrdom. Expressed in the language of faith, the church attempts to learn the "will of God" in this specific situation, in order to be able to act in agreement with it. The words of the prophet Cleobius and even more clearly those of the prophetess Myrte bring certainty: Paul must face martyrdom. At the same time, the utterances of both convey strength and confidence to the church to face a difficult decision: the sacrificial death of the apostle will not be in vain. The prophecies of Cleobius and Myrte take place in the context of a prayer meeting of the church—afterward the Eucharist is celebrated in the usual manner. During her proclamation Myrte seems to be seized by ecstasy, since the Spirit in her must "calm down."

Thus we have here two completely different examples of early Christian prophecy. The comparison makes clear the whole *ambivalence* of the *phenomenon*. Like any other form of religious expression, it can be misused—from faith to superstition is but a step. Yet phenomena like trance and ecstasy, which are rather suspect for us today, are not necessarily a sign that the proclamation connected with them was less authentic than one free of them.

The *problem of false prophecy* is indissolubly connected with charismatically based authority. Already in the New Testament there are warnings about "wolves in sheep's clothing" and the advice: "You will know them by their fruits" (Matt. 7:15–16). Also according to Paul, prophecies are to be "tested," as we saw. And Justin admitted to his Jewish dialogue partner that things were not going any better now for Christians than they once did for the Jews: they had to grapple with "false prophets."[39] We find the problem in the *Didache* and again in the *Shepherd of Hermas*.[40] The criterion for judgment[41] in these early writings, as in the New Testament, remains the credibility of the charismatically gifted personalities, that is, their moral integrity: "Spirits and prophets are known by their works."[42]

Seen in terms of content, authentic early Christian prophecy, in correspondence with Jewish biblical tradition, is *praxis oriented:*[43] How was the gospel of Jesus to be concretely realized in ever new life situations? What was to be done? Prophetesses and prophets were considered especially gifted interpreters of the will of God.[44] The supernatural phenomena that accompanied prophecies were secondary to the message. Their forms matched the religious mentality of their time and doubtless also the temperament of the particular person.

2. The New Prophecy: Prisca and Maximilla

Against this background, how are we to judge the movement that appeared in the second century as the New Prophecy and claimed to be the continuation of the old, original prophecy? For a long time Montanism—in addition to Gnosticism—was considered the epitome of early Christian aberrations. Its abuses were often used to explain the fact that in the church prophets became suspect. A vague memory of Prisca[45] and Maximilla is awakened, combined with the idea of "crazy women" who in a mixture of hysteria and heresy are supposed to have given prophecy a bad name.

Previous Emphases in Research

In the meantime, modern research[46] has cleared the movement named after Montanus of the accusation of heresy, at least for the early period. Yet there has still been astonishingly little research on the two women at the center. In 1913 Pierre de Labriolle published a collection of all sources (*Les sources de l'histoire du montanisme*)[47] and in the same year presented in *La crise montaniste* the most comprehensive study of the movement and its history, but he devotes to these women only a few pages and explains their place "in the forefront beside the founder of the movement" with the general capacity of women for the kind of religious enthusiasm found in sects, which was especially strong in Prisca and Maximilla.[48] For the church it was very important to put them in their place; the author had already expressed this opinion two years earlier in an article whose title matched his conviction: "Ut mulieres in ecclesia taceant" ("women should be silent in church").

Nevertheless, even in a more recent dissertation by Frederick Klawiter ("The New Prophecy in Early Christianity," 1975 [see note 49]) prophetesses are mentioned only occasionally, although the author certainly no longer shares this view. He supports the thesis that the New Prophecy was distinguished by an extreme, apocalyptically influenced enthusiasm for martyrdom, coupled with political resistance against Rome, and was therefore rejected by the church, which wanted to come to an arrangement with the emperors. Yet his analysis of the sources is not very convincing. Above all, he loses sight of the real problem: the role of prophetesses and prophets in the church. Since Prisca and Maximilla were not martyrs, they hardly play a role in his study.[49]

In between the two there is only Wilhelm Schepelern's study (*Der Montanismus und die phrygischen Kulte*, 1929), which focuses on the Phrygian environment with its specific cults, in particular the veneration of the *Magna Mater* Cybele. Yet the parallels he constructs are hardly convincing, and thus Pierre de Labriolle's judgment about similar earlier efforts is reconfirmed: "I believe that in regard to Montanism the significance of its land of origin has been excessively emphasized."[50] In any case, Schepelern certainly does not do away with all the old clichés about the "women ecstatics" and the prophetic movement in general.

Unfortunately, this is also largely true of a new study on Montanist Phrygia by August Strobel (*Das heilige Land der Montanisten*, 1980). We can agree with him when he characterizes Montanism "as basically a deeply Christian movement, which *from the beginning* was embedded both in the Phrygian population and in its religious background, without completely committing itself in a syncretistic way"[51] (the emphatic "from the beginning" is directed against Schepelern, who advocates a gradual "Phrygianization"). I cannot judge Strobel's "religious-geographical" results concerning the later developments in Phrygia; his work with the sources regarding the origin of the movement, however, must be termed extremely uncritical: he accepts as "facts" all the statements of anti-Montanist polemic. Although he emphasizes the "preponderance of the matriarchal-feminine element" in the Phrygian popular tradition,[52] Prisca and Maximilla interest him only regarding the origin of their names,[53] and three pages are enough for him to deal with the affirmed "prominent role of the feminine element."[54]

Without doubt, the possible connections between the ancient Cybele cult and the high esteem of Christian prophetesses in Phrygia, to which the traditions about the daughters of Philip in Hierapolis point,[55] should be further clarified by interdisciplinary feminist scholarship. Yet should the explanation for Prisca and Maximilla's influence not be sought first in their personalities and their preaching? This will be our guide in what follows. In addition to the monographs on the origin, development, and battling of this movement, the background for my examination is formed by various articles or individual chapters, especially by Leopold Zscharnack, Walter Bauer, Heinz Kraft, and Kurt Aland.[56] Nevertheless, to track down these prophetesses and their proclamation, we must reexamine above all the ancient witnesses—and now we will get to the heart of the matter.

The Prophetesses and Their Advocate

The designation of the New Prophecy as Montanism after the name of the sect's founder and head is familiar to us today and seems to require no justification. Yet was Montanus really its founder? Did this "sect" have a head? In early Christian literature, at any rate, we do not find the term *montanoi* for the prophetic movement in Phrygia until around 350;[57] in the imperial legislation of the fifth and sixth centuries *montanistai* appears as one name among many for the embattled church (cf. 2e below). Otherwise we find in the writings of the opponents "the sect named after the Phrygians"[58] or simply "the Phrygians." The geographical name has a derogatory connotation: the group was supposed to appear to be local, so that it could be deprived of its "catholicity."[59] The movement itself called itself "Prophecy" or "New Prophecy." This expression of its self-understanding will be preferred here,[60] along with "Phrygian church" for the late period.

The fixation on the male member of the trio of Prisca, Maximilla, and Montanus is already found, however, in the writing of a contemporary opponent who—like many after him—sees the origin of the heresy in the preaching of Montanus.[61] Exactly when the movement began can no longer be said with certainty, since the sources are contradictory: presumably around the year 170.[62] Maximilla, the last of the trio, died in 179;[63] her death marked the end of the first phase of the New Prophecy, which later developed into a church,[64] especially in Phrygia, a mountainous highland in central Asia Minor; but it also exerted an early influence outside its traditional territory, as testimonies from Lyon, Rome, Carthage, and Alexandria show.

Now, if we want in what follows to attempt a closer look at the two prophetesses Prisca and Maximilla, we face the problem that their own writings, as well as those of other New Prophets and Prophetesses, were destroyed. Yet the voice of *one* early follower remains available: Tertullian's works from his "Montanist" phase. The theologian from Carthage, however, was not an eyewitness, and he presumably strongly influenced the development of the New Prophecy in Africa himself; thus his writings must also be read critically. We shall first attempt to examine the early testimonies on the Phrygian movement regarding the facts they pass on and supplement them with what is historically probable from the later sources. Then against this general background the few traditional oracles will be examined, especially the sayings of Prisca and Maximilla. The term *oracle* today has a pagan connotation, although it is completely appropriate for certain forms of Christian prophecy.[65] In the following we will speak synonymously of *oracle, saying,* and *logion* in the sense of *a statement considered inspired.*[66]

The reconstruction is complicated not only by the polemical character of most of the sources but also by the fragmentary nature of the early tradition: from the writings of eyewitnesses we have only the quotations that Eusebius included in his church history. He himself introduces the "heresy" as follows:

> Filled with hatred of good and love of evil the enemy of God's Church left no
> trick untried in his machinations against mankind, and did his best to make a

fresh crop of heretical sects spring up to injure the Church. Some members of these crawled like poisonous reptiles over Asia and Phrygia, boasting of Montanus "the Paraclete" and his female adherents Priscilla and Maximilla, alleged to have been his prophetesses. Others flourished in Rome . . . (5.14–15)[67]

This passage in Eusebius already contains a manipulation: Priscilla and Maximilla appear dependent on the "Paraclete" Montanus and subordinated to him. But according to the witness of earlier sources, as we shall see, there was no hierarchical relationship between Montanus and the women: all (New) prophets and prophetesses spoke in the name of the Holy Spirit, the "Paraclete." Since this term (variously rendered as *Comforter, Counselor, Advocate*) is used for the Spirit of God in the Gospel of John (cf. 14:16, 26; 15:26; 16:7), its use with Montanus seems offensive to us today, but it was not a problem for contemporaries: we have already encountered it for one martyr.[68] Eusebius does not criticize it either, and even later church fathers like Epiphanius and Theodoret, in spite of their criticism, confirm the orthodoxy of the "heresy" in regard to doctrine of the Trinity.[69] Others, however, have (mis)understood Eusebius's sentence in the sense of a blasphemous identification. Also among followers the equation of the two occurs later, as a Numidian inscription shows: "In the name of the Father and of the Son and of the Lord Montanus . . ."[70]

a. Witnesses to the Spirit?
The Judgment of Early Sympathizers

The witness of some contemporaries who were close to the New Prophecy is found in the account of the massacre of Christians in Lyon, yet it cannot be easily recognized. Eusebius, who has passed on this letter to the "brothers in Asia and Phrygia"—that is, to the churches in the movement's land of origin—was interested in presenting the martyrdom, but he has also eliminated any hint of sympathy for the New Prophecy.[71] Nonetheless, we learn the following from him:

> It was at that very time, in Phrygia, that Montanus, Alcibiades, Theodotus, and their followers began to acquire a widespread reputation for prophecy; for numerous other manifestations of the miraculous gift of God, still occurring in various churches, led many to believe that these men too were prophets. When there was a difference of opinion about them, the Gallic Christians again submitted their own careful and most orthodox conclusions on the question, attaching various letters from the martyrs fulfilled in their midst—letters penned while they were still in prison to their brothers in Asia and Phrygia, and also to Eleutherus, then Bishop of Rome, in an effort to ensure peace in the churches. (5.3.4)

Obviously many of the Christians persecuted in Lyon wanted to prevent a condemnation of the new prophets in Phrygia. Eusebius quotes no critical statements of any kind by the martyrs concerning the group regarded by him as heretical; he merely hastens to assure that their position was "pious and fully orthodox." We should also note that Montanus is not characterized as the leader of the group. We know nothing more about Alcibiades; in another place, however, one of Eusebius's informants ironically calls Theodotus "that marvelous first administrator of the so-called prophecy";[72] the same anonymous author also speaks of "the sect named after Miltiades."[73]

The affinity of the martyresses and martyrs in Lyon for the prophetic movement in Phrygia is also clear at another point. Vettius Epagathus, described as both an exemplary Christian and a "man of influence," became the "advocate" (paraclete) of the Christians when he intervened for them in court: he was "fervent in spirit" and "had in himself the Advocate [Paraclete]" (5.1.9–10). Similarly, at the hearing of the previously apostatizing Christians a certain Alexander of Phrygia is described, who stands beside the judge's chair, a doctor known for his "boldness of speech" and his "apostolic gifts." Since he encouraged the accused with gestures, he himself becomes a martyr, like Vettius before him. Here both the content and the language indicate a closeness to the Phrygian movement.

Finally Eusebius adds to his account of the massacre another story from the letter of the martyrs, which initially sounds like a pious anecdote:

> Among them was a certain Alcibiades,[74] who made a practice of extreme austerity. Hitherto he had refused everything, partaking only of bread and water, and he tried to go on like this even in gaol. But after his first ordeal in the amphitheatre it was revealed to Attalus that Alcibiades was not doing well in rejecting what God had created and setting others a misleading example. Alcibiades saw the danger, and began to accept everything freely and to give God thanks. For they were richly blest by the grace of God, and the Holy Spirit was their counsellor. (5.3)

Why is this story in the martyrs' letter to the churches in Phrygia? Since Eusebius has obviously removed it from its context, the question is hard to answer. He was presumably interested in emphasizing the martyrs' moderate stance on asceticism. The original author probably also wanted to highlight the authority of the martyr Attalus, who became a prophet. As with Perpetua, martyrdom here seems to be a kind of "empowerment" for prophecy.

Thus in this long edifying letter to the "brothers in Asia and Phrygia," the charismatically oriented movement is not portrayed as heretical; on the contrary, we find a great many similarities in thought. Is it possible that those who presume "Montanism" here are correct? Yet one would then have to include the presbyter Irenaeus, who himself came from Asia Minor and after the massacre became bishop of Lyon, for it was these very "Montanist" martyrs who sent him to Rome with warm recommendations.[75] This important theologian of the early period wrote a comprehensive antiheretical work with the title *Adversus haereses* (Against Heresies), which was directed primarily against the Gnostic schools. Should he then be the very one to overlook the endangerment of the church by the movement in Phrygia? No demarcation from it is to be found in his work.

Rather, he develops a grand theological outline of the work of the Spirit[76] and expressly distances himself from antiprophetic extremists:

> Others [previously the topic was Marcion] want to nullify the gift of the Spirit, which in recent times was poured out over the human race at the pleasure of the Father;[77] therefore they do not allow the Gospel form according to John, in which the Lord promises that he will send the Advocate [Paraclete], but rather reject both the Gospel and the prophetic Spirit. The unfortunate ones: they want no false prophets[78] and therefore reject the prophetic gift in the church. They behave like those who out of fear of hypocrites even forgo fellowship with brothers. Naturally, they also nullify the apostle Paul, since in the letter to the Corinthians he speaks in detail on the prophetic charismata and knows men and women who prophesy in the church. All this leads them to sin against the Holy Spirit, and they succumb thereby to the unforgivable sin.[79]

In this fundamental text of Irenaeus three points already mentioned at the beginning[80] are to be especially emphasized: (1) prophecy is regarded as a sign and gift of the end time; (2) by nature it is bestowed on men and women; (3) the opponents of prophecy are sharply criticized as adversaries of the Holy Spirit. Thus in the catch phrase "false prophets" we find no condemnation of the Phrygian movement; rather, the bishop of Lyon advocates a theology that is akin to it, as we shall see in more detail. Thus the convictions of the New Prophecy were shared in the second century by many Christians who without doubt did not belong to a sectarian fringe group.

b. A Fraudulent Organization?
The Voices of Early Opponents

What then do we learn from the early polemic of the opponents, which Eusebius quotes? First, Claudius Apollinaris, the bishop of Hierapolis in Phrygia, as well as "many learned men of the day" composed writings against the New Prophecy (5.16.1). Two of these authors—an Anonymus[81] (who for his part quotes one Miltiades[82]) and Apollonius[83]—are quoted in detail in Eusebius; nothing of the bishop's writing, however, has survived. Yet we learn from the church historian that Serapion of Antioch (190–210) sent it to Karikos and Pontios, two otherwise unknown personalities, with the comment: "In order that you may know this, that the working of the so-called New Prophecy of this fraudulent organization is held in detestation by the whole brotherhood throughout the world . . ." (5.19.2).[84]

Serapion's cover letter is not cosigned by "the whole brotherhood throughout the world,"[85] but according to Eusebius the letter is followed by "the signatures of various bishops" (5.16.3). He cites only two signers by name: "I, Aurelius Quirinius, a martyr, pray for your welfare." Was this confessor, who did not express himself on the issue, a bishop at all? The second calls himself, "Aelius Publius Julius, from Develtum, a colony in Thrace, bishop," and uses the opportunity expressly to take a position against the New Prophecy: "As God in heaven lives, blessed Sotas of Anchialus [Thrace] wished to drive out Priscilla's demon, and the hypocrites would not permit him" (ibid.). We will examine this incident more closely. Here we must first note with Walter Bauer, who has precisely analyzed the opposing voices passed on by Eusebius: "Basically the cited witnesses refute the proposed assertion through their small number and the inadequacy of their statements, even if we limit ourselves to the time of Apollinaris and 'the world' of Asia Minor and Thrace, leaving out Gaul, Rome, and North Africa."[86]

Nevertheless, we learn an important fact from the polemical letter: a bishop tried in vain to silence a woman leader in the movement. A similar failure of ecclesiastical measures is confirmed by the two reports on, or diatribes against, the New Prophecy that Eusebius quotes. Thus Apollonius mentions "that while Maximilla was pretending to prophesy in Pepuza, Zoticus . . . planted himself in front of her and tried to silence the spirit at work in her, but was prevented by her partisans" (5.18.13). Anonymus reports the incident in more detail and mentions another bishop. Both "were then present in order to test and converse with the spirit as it chattered." Yet this did not happen: they "were muzzled by Themiso and his henchmen, who would not allow them to silence the lying spirit which was leading the people astray" (5.16.16–17). This Themiso appeared with the authority of a martyr, as we learn later (5.18.5). The presentations leave open whether refutation was prevented by better arguments, or whether confrontation between Maximilla and the officials was avoided altogether. Do the reported measures against Prisca and Maximilla involve the same incident? Bauer assumes a wandering legend,[87] yet then not only the names of the prophetesses but also those of the bishops would be exchanged. It is certainly possible that such confrontations occurred more than once.

At any rate, it is notable that in each case a prophetess appears as the antagonist of the bishops and is defended by her followers. Later authors change this statement and make Montanus the opponent who is primarily (and successfully!) opposed. Thus there is, for example, mention of a "refutation of Montanus," which also applies to Prisca and Maximilla;[88] we read that a "bishop of Thrace called on Montanus and refuted the demon that spoke out of Montanus and Maximilla";[89] and even: Bishop Sotas, with twelve other bishops, refuted "Theodotus, as well as Montanus and Maximilla, who himself boasted of being the Holy Spirit."[90] In these later documents refutation and condemnation were apparently confused!

From the quoted texts of Anonymus,[91] who identifies himself as an opponent of the New Prophets in public discussions and then sets out his arguments in a three-volume refutation, we learn nothing about the content of the alleged heresy (which may be due to Eusebius's selection). Yet the rumor (called this by the author!) is spread that Maximilla and Montanus hanged themselves "like the betrayer Judas." Bauer comments: "One can hardly use the principle of *semper aliquid haeret* more cynically than this ecclesiastical champion does, who himself does not believe in the truth of the rumors he passes on."[92]

The information on the background of Montanus is perhaps historical. He is said to come from the village of Arbadau[93] in Mysia and have been a new convert at the time of his prophetic activity (5.16.7). Together with "two other

women" (their names are not given!) he gathered a small following around him
(5.16.9). Yet how does one then explain the numerous gatherings that are supposed to have taken place in Asia and the many refutative writings that were composed against the group? It is also possible that the characterization "new convert" was intended as disparagement, since at the same time Montanus is said to
have a craving for prominent places. Later he will even be made a former "priest
to idols,"[94] and Jerome calls him a "castrated, half man."[95] Although the two
statements are independent of each other, it has been inferred from them that
Montanus was a priest of Cybele, since such priests emasculated themselves in
honor of the goddess.[96] The discovery of the *Discussion of a Montanist and an
Orthodox,* an intriguing polemical treatise from the second half of the fourth century,[97] cast doubt on this view, since in it Montanus is likewise called a "priest to
idols" but also a "priest of Apollo."[98] Thus the ancient source does not place
him—in spite of his origins in Phrygia—close to the extreme ecstatic form of the
Cybele cult but compares the New Prophecy with the highly regarded Delphic
oracle, where the priests of Apollo "translate" the oracle of Pythia. The information hardly has a historical basis; it is apparently supposed to insinuate that
Montanus brought a "pagan" element into Christianity.

At another point Anonymus, in his efforts to incriminate his opponents, becomes entangled in even more contradictory argumentation. In the second book
of his work he poses an ironic question:

> Is there one person, my good sirs, among those from Montanus and the women
> onwards who started the chatter, who was persecuted by the Jews or killed by
> the wicked? Not one. Or was any one of them seized and crucified for the
> Name? No indeed. Very well then: was one of the women ever whipped in Jew-
> ish synagogues or stoned? Never anywhere. It was by a different death that Mon-
> tanus and Maximilla are believed to have died. (5.16.12–13)

This is followed by rumors of the shameful demise of Montanus, Maximilla, and
Theodotus, but the author does not want to vouch for them. Thus according to
the second book of Anonymus there were no martyresses and martyrs in the
Phrygian movement. Yet in his third book he contradicts himself, for there he
reports the following about the New Prophets:

> When all their arguments have been disposed of and they have nothing to say,
> they try to take refuge in the martyrs, alleging that they have a great number and
> that this is a convincing proof of the power of what in their circles is called the
> prophetic spirit. But this seems to be as false as false can be, for some of the other
> heretical sects have immense numbers of martyrs, but this is surely no reason why
> we should approve of them or acknowledge that they have the truth.
> (5.16.20–21)

Hence there were, after all, martyresses and martyrs in the Phrygian movement!
Anonymus confirms this yet again when he reports a concrete case in which confessors of the mainstream church distance themselves from Phrygian confessors

before they all suffer a common death as Christians (5.16.21).[99] Thus here he is arguing completely differently: since the New Prophets are "false" prophets, their martyrs are "false" martyrs. Externally they cannot be distinguished, but their courage in the face of death comes not from the Holy Spirit but from the devil. Thus even the polemicist attests indirectly to the authority of confessors in the churches. We will also find in the other testimonies controversy over the standing of their respective martyrs.

Does any argument of Anonymus prove to be tenable? One concrete reproach against the New Prophets remains to be examined: ecstatic speech. For this accusation the author of the refutative work quotes a polemical writing of Miltiades, yet he does so secondhand—that is, from a Montanist response. The cited mainstream postulate reads: "A prophet ought not to speak in a state of ecstasy" (5.17.1). Earlier Anonymus described the unintelligible stammering of Montanus and the two women in downright rapturous terms (5.16.7ff.). Yet even on this point he had to admit reluctantly that occasionally credible speech also came forth from the mouths of the New Prophets (5.16.9). Miltiades, whom he quotes, perhaps discussed the problem of prophetic ecstasy in more precise terms—we will learn more from Tertullian on this point of controversy.

Is Apollonius, the bishop of Caesarea's second informant (about whom nothing else is known),[100] an objective witness? Unfortunately, he is not! Bauer has aptly characterized his methods: "Something is rejected and portrayed with ugly distortion but is worthy of highest praise as soon as it occurs on the side of orthodoxy."[101] Eusebius first reports the polemicist's verdict on Montanus:

> This is the man who taught the dissolution of marriages, who laid down the law on fasting, who renamed Pepuza and Tymion, insignificant towns in Phrygia, as Jerusalem, in the hope of persuading people in every district to gather there; who appointed agents to collect money, who contrived to make the gifts roll in under the name of "offerings," and who has subsidized those who preach his message, in order that gluttony may provide an incentive for teaching it. (5.18.2)

What are we to make of these accusations? "Dissolution of marriages": as we will see, the New Prophets rejected only a second marriage. The "law on fasting": there is nothing offensive here, but it conflicts with the reproach of gluttony, which was made at the same time! "Pepuza and Tymion": the center of the movement[102] received the symbolic name *Jerusalem;* later interpreters believe that this is an expression of apocalyptic expectation, but this is not indicated by anything in Apollonius.[103] The collection of money and payment of preachers: these are so commonly practiced that this reproach vanishes entirely in later polemics; not even a general criticism of wealth is found later.[104] One thing is striking in the presentation: there is no reference whatever to ecstatic stammering; even in the description of prophetesses nothing of the sort is mentioned. Hence only one thing can be gained with certainty from the characterization of Montanus: he organized the Phrygian movement around a spiritual center, following an ecclesiastical model.

In a second passage Eusebius quotes Apollonius's statements about Prisca and
Maximilla:

> It is thus evident that these prophetesses, from the time they were filled with the
> spirit, were the very first to leave their husbands. How then could they lie so
> blatantly as to call Priscilla a virgin? (5.18.3)

Did Prisca belong to the order of virgins? Did Maximilla forswear marriage? Were
both strongly ascetically oriented? We know nothing certain about this, since they
are alternately or even simultaneously accused of asceticism and good living.
"Proof" is sought in vain in the cited passages. Voluntary celibacy was generally
considered praiseworthy; the polemicist expressly criticizes only the term *virgin*
for a formerly married woman—obviously a far-fetched charge made in order to
be able to accuse the movement of lying! Furthermore, Apollonius asserts that
Prisca gave herself to feasting with a martyr (5.18.6) and indicts prophetesses in
general for loving makeup, jewelry, and money (5.18.11). Nonetheless, he does
not dare to extend the polemic "from the table to the bed";[105] in this regard the
prophetesses' conduct of life was apparently impeccable.[106]

Since the persons of Prisca and Maximilla offered few points of attack, Apollonius seizes the issue of martyrdom in order to discredit the New Prophecy,
but here he chooses a different strategy from that of Anonymus: two prominent confessors of the Phrygian movement are morally disqualified. A certain Themiso—we have already met him as Maximilla's defender—based on his
martyr title, felt himself equal to composing a "catholic letter";[107] yet he did
not earn this title, for he bought his way out of prison, according to Apollonius. Alexander, with whom the prophetess is supposed to have "feasted,"
is even more fiercely attacked: he was in fact convicted as a robber after he
had already denied his faith, and this is supposedly to be found in court documents. We find here a notable parallel to the trial in Lyon, where it is said
that the apostates by no means got off scot-free after they apostatized, but
rather were charged with other crimes. Similar processes may have been at
work in Alexander's case: calumnies that entered the record as statements of
witnesses.

What have we learned from the examination of opposing voices? The answer
is summed up in Bauer's words:

> On the whole, the two books we have come to know are hardly more than slan-
> der. That of Apollonius earns this description even more than that of Anony-
> mus. The judgments that are found here, even if they are dressed in the cloak of
> historical presentation, must be rejected as biased, and we must let the facts speak
> for themselves. What is left in such a process, which is often an unintentional
> admission? First of all, that the prophetic movement, especially in Phrygia, was
> a great success, that people and means flowed into it, and that the seriousness of
> its dominant conception of life led many to become martyrs, whose blood
> proved to be a further attraction. The magnitude of its success corresponded to
> and was proven by the strength of ecclesiastical opposition.[108]

Obviously the New Prophetesses and Prophets did not advocate an erroneous teaching. The testimony of the opponents basically confirms the testimony of the sympathizers: the way of life practiced in the Phrygian movement corresponds in its essential features to the norms of the mainstream church. How then does one explain the violent conflicts? That question must be answered, but first we will attempt to complete the picture of the early New Prophecy with the help of a witness who, though he did not personally experience the proclamation of Prisca, Maximilla, and Montanus, stood completely behind them: the North African lawyer and theologian Tertullian.

c. Disputed Questions:
The Testimony of a Follower

"The most prominent of the Latinists[109] adopted the teaching of Montanus in the middle of his life, because he was driven to do so by the envy and slander of the clergy of the Roman church"[110]—thus writes Jerome about two hundred years after Tertullian's death. Speaking here, perhaps, is the sympathy of an ascetically oriented theologian for one of like mind, for Tertullian's sharp anti-Roman edge is perhaps best explained by the biography of Jerome, who had to leave the capital because of his ascetic preaching. Tertullian himself was not a priest, as Jerome believes,[111] and he reports no personal conflict with Rome, but we are indebted to him for important information on disagreements over the New Prophecy. Moreover, in his writings he passes on five authentic oracles, and he took positions on all the points of criticism that were advanced against the movement.

Let us begin with the facts of ecclesiastical politics. We learn from a polemical theological writing by the African that the reconciliation for which the martyrs of Lyon had so greatly striven almost came about: the Roman bishop was ready to acknowledge the authenticity of the New Prophecy and had indeed already composed and dispatched the appropriate written documents. Unfortunately, the mentioned events cannot be dated exactly, since the name of the bishop does not appear.[112] From Asia Minor a certain Praxeas came to Rome; he advocated a teaching according to which the Father is said to have suffered on the cross, and he was an opponent of the New Prophecy. To refute him Tertullian wrote a treatise in which he says:

> The first one to bring that distortion [patripassianism] onto Roman soil was this Praxeas, a disturbing [person], inflated by pride over martyrdom, although he had suffered only a simple and brief imprisonment. Yet even if he had surrendered his body for burning, it would have done him no good, since he did not possess the love of God and now also fought against God's charismata [cf. 1 Corinthians 13]. For when the Roman bishop had already recognized the prophecies of Montanus, Prisca, and Maximilla and on the basis of this recognition granted peace to the churches of Asia and Phrygia, this man forced him— through false witness about the prophets and their churches, as well as through emphasis on the authority of his predecessors[113]—to recall the already dispatched letter of peace and draw back from his intention to accept the charismata. In this

way Praxeas performed two services of the devil for Rome: he drove out prophecy and introduced heresy; he chased away the Paraclete and crucified the Father.[114]

From this passage we can see how insignificant the oppositions between mainstream church and New Prophecy were at first. Even in terms of church politics unification seemed within grasp. Theologically Tertullian and Irenaeus held the same fundamental position: resistance against authentic prophecy is resistance against the Holy Spirit. Let us now look at how the African follower of the Phrygian movement presented and defended its positions. A certain systematization here is no doubt his personal theological contribution. Did he in this process remain true to the original concerns of the New Prophecy, or did he use its message for his own interests? That question must be asked regarding each of the following points of criticism.

The Revelations of the Paraclete

The quarrel over the Paraclete forms the background of the disagreement over the New Prophecy. Today we wonder: Why was there a preference for this particular designation of God's Spirit, which we know only from the Gospel of John? The answer is simple: because certain statements about the work of the Holy Spirit are made there. In his farewell speech Jesus promised "another Advocate," the "spirit of truth," who will "teach you everything" and "guide you into all the truth."[115] All believed that this promise was fulfilled through the prophetesses and prophets, for through them the Spirit continued to speak. Yet did this mean that divine revelation continued? On this question opinions diverged.[116] Tertullian expressed himself clearly on the issue.

First, an equation of the Paraclete with the person of Montanus—even if only in the use of the term, as we saw in Eusebius—is nowhere to be found in the African theologian. Rather, the Paraclete is always the Holy Spirit, who speaks through the prophetesses and prophets—and indeed through all of them, not only through Prisca, Maximilla, and Montanus. Only two of the five sayings reported by Tertullian are from Prisca; the originators of the other three remain anonymous. The teaching of the Paraclete is developed in detail in two ascetic writings: *On the Veiling of Virgins* and *On Monogamy*. Now the dating of Tertullian's works is disputed, as well as the characterization of many writings as still catholic or already Montanist, if they do not contain a clear reference to the New Prophecy—this is another indication of the triviality of the differences! In the treatise on monogamy the author has clearly made the break with the mainstream church; in the polemic on the question of veiling, probably not yet. Yet in each case the teaching on the Paraclete is the same. It is most clearly developed in the introduction to *On the Veiling of Virgins*.[117]

In order to answer the question of new revelations of the Spirit, the astute theologian introduces a fundamental distinction: he differentiates between the teaching of faith (*regula fidei*), which is immutable, and the ecclesiastical regulation of the conduct of life (*disciplina*), which under the influence of God's grace experiences progressive improvement. "Our Lord sent the Paraclete so that the discipline within the church, through the representative of the Lord, the Holy Spirit, would gradually receive a direction and be put in order and led to perfection, since the people in their finitude cannot comprehend everything at once" (1.4). The epochs of salvation history are compared with the stages of maturation in human life: "With the help of the law and the prophets righteousness reached its childhood; then through the gospel it grew into strong youth, and now it is led by the Paraclete into maturity" (1.6). The concern of this distinction is clear: it enables one to make demands on the conduct of life that go beyond what is attested in the Gospels.

In this perspective of a growing moral perfection Tertullian's presentation may have come close to the concern of the New Prophets; in a quite similar way the highly orthodox authors of treatises on virginity also justify their praise of the single way of life.[118] But later this view of progressive revelation is presented in abbreviated form in the polemical critique of the prophetic church of Phrygia; thus we find, for example, in Isidore of Seville (d. 636) the formulation: "Montanus, Prisca, and Maximilla assert that the Holy Spirit came not in the apostles but in them."[119] Despite the distortion, the short text shows that the Spanish scholar read the polemical sources before him critically: Montanus is not presented as the head of the movement, and there is no discrediting of the three leading personalities. With a small correction the formula would also be correct: "The Holy Spirit came not *only* in the apostles but *also* in them." For the New Prophets by no means contested the Pentecost event, but for them it was the beginning of a process that continued in them and through them, not the sealing and thus the end of all revelation.

Regarding Tertullian's presentation we must ask whether the first representatives of the Phrygian movement distinguished between doctrine of faith and conduct of life as clearly as he did. Since prophetic preaching was practice oriented, the distinction hardly played a role. Yet for the theologian it offered the possibility of representing a very rigid position in questions of dogma (Tertullian wrote a wealth of antiheretical texts!) but allowed, nevertheless, innovations in moral questions—yet only in the direction of an increasing asceticism! His concern was to legitimate rigorous strictness, not to understand revelation as an open, ongoing process. Thus there are doubts as to whether he does justice to the basic concern of charismatic authority as the New Prophecy understood it. We will return to this question at the end of the chapter.[120]

Let us now turn to a concrete example that will show us how we must imagine prophetic proclamation in a worship service in Tertullian's Carthage. The following report is found in his anti-Gnostic writing *On the Soul:*

> Because we recognize the spiritual gifts of grace, we deserve, also according to John [the Baptist],[121] to attain prophecy. Thus there lives with us today a sister who has been given the grace to receive revelations, which she experiences in church during the celebration to the glory of the Lord through ecstasy in the Spirit: she speaks

with the angels—sometimes also with the Lord—sees and hears mysteries, looks through the hearts of various people, and receives instructions for the healing of those who need it. Now when scriptural passages are read, psalms sung, sermons given, or prayers spoken, for her they become the objects of her visions. It happened that we had just talked about the soul when that sister was in the Spirit. When the congregation was dismissed after the completion of worship, she said, in accordance with her custom of reporting to us what she saw (this is, you see, also very carefully described so that it can also be tested): "Among other things, the soul was shown to me in bodily form. It appeared to me like a breath, but not in an empty, hollow composition, but rather so that it even promised to let one hold fast to it, tenderly luminous, the color of air, with a form that was human in every respect. That is the vision." God is the witness and the apostle, who is the sufficient guarantor of the future presence of the gifts of grace in the church.[122]

Tertullian's description clearly shows how the ecstatic element was linked with the framework of the usual ritual forms of community worship and also how problematic the appeal to revelations of that kind is. In another passage Tertullian again reports briefly on the vision of a woman fellow Christian.[123] Yet in both cases it is apparently a matter of revelations "made to order," since the prophetesses are shown exactly what Tertullian would like to prove: in one case the "corporeality" of the soul, in the other the duty of veiling—even the exact length of the veil is "revealed"! Apparently Tertullian reserved for himself the "testing" of the prophecies. By what authority he derives this right for himself remains unclear. But one thing is clear: here he himself crosses the boundary he has drawn between church discipline and teachings of faith when he requires the vision of a prophetess to resolve a controversial theological opinion. Once again we get the impression that the theologian and the early movement in Phrygia had different ways of proceeding.

Prohibition of Marriage?

This second point of contention can be quickly clarified. Here too Tertullian's statements are clear: the New Prophecy knows no general rejection of marriage. He himself makes this criticism of other, unspecified heretics: "The heretics abolish marriage; the physicals multiply it."[124] *Physicals*—freely translated: "animal-like, earthy people"—is the name the polemical theologian calls the representatives of the mainstream church, because they tolerate a second marriage.[125] The New Prophets, however, advocate the middle way: "But for us, who, based on the recognition of spiritual gifts, are properly called spirituals, continence is godly (*continentia religiosa*),[126] just as permitted [marriage] is chaste (*licentia verecunda*). . . . We know only one marriage and only one God."[127] As we have already seen, the ideal of one single marriage was widespread, especially in the Christian East. Probably in the circles of the New Prophecy, greater pains were taken to hold to this ideal. Yet the practice of the mainstream church was hardly different, for there too a second marriage was not permitted, but had a penance imposed upon it.[128]

Rules of Fasting

In regard to the third point of contention, the rules of fasting, one can again ascertain no serious difference in practice. In the early polemic against the New prophecy it is not a question of strict asceticism at all, but rather of "feasting." Montanus was criticized not because of fasting but because he made rules for it— yet these appeared in all the churches around this time. The incriminating regulations were very probably connected with the organization of the pre-Easter time of fasting that was gradually becoming accepted. In Asia Minor there was no agreement on the date of the Easter feast.[129] Irenaeus succeeded at that time in convincing the Roman bishop Victor and other church officials that different customs on this question could be tolerated without endangering the unity of the church. In his statement the bishop of Lyon says expressly: "The dispute is not only about the day, but also about the actual character of the fast."[130] Thus in the polemic against Montanus it was in fact a matter of local Phrygian traditions.[131] Ascetic tendencies may have intensified within the New Prophecy, as they did in their environment,[132] and Tertullian was not the man to call for moderation here. On the contrary, he gave free reign to his mocking polemic against the "physicals": "They argue against the Paraclete and therefore reject the New Prophecy. Not, say, because Montanus, Priscilla, and Maximilla preached another God or canceled [faith in] Jesus Christ or called into question some other point in the rule of faith and hope, but only because they teach one to fast more often than to marry!"[133] Sarcastically he recommends that his opponents honor the Paraclete in Apicius, the author of a cookbook, since they do not want to recognize him in Montanus.[134] Thus the theologian from Carthage again claims the authority of the New Prophecy for a strictness that it certainly did not advocate with such rigor.

Voluntary Martyrdom?

The fourth point of contention, the attitude toward martyrdom, is harder to clarify. We have already seen that the opponents of the movement followed various strategies: (1) they denied that it had any confessors; (2) they rejected heretical confessors as "false" confessors; (3) they called their conduct into question. Only one reproach had not been made: that the followers of the Phrygian movement, in presumptuous self-confidence, had encouraged voluntary martyrdom. In later polemic the martyrdom question no longer appears at all as a point of contention. In light of this finding, it is curious that in the literature on Montanism the New Prophetesses and Prophets are so persistently said to have a "compulsion toward martyrdom."[135] Did the theologian from Carthage express himself on this topic?

Tertullian deals with controversial questions on martyrdom in three writings.[136] The first, *Scorpiace, or Medicine against the Bite of the Scorpion,* contains no allusion to the Paraclete or the New Prophecy; the writing is directed against the Gnostics, who generally reject the giving of one's own life in martyrdom. Their argument: "God is no murderer!" Tertullian, by contrast, stresses the unconditional obligation to confession.

Another writing, *From the Wreath of the Soldiers,* concerns a Roman custom and first relates a concrete incident: a soldier had refused to crown himself with the usual wreath and simply held it in his hand. The incident was investigated; the accused confessed as a Christian and was now waiting in prison to be "sacrificed for Christ." Yet in the church this behavior was criticized and characterized as "fanatical, rash, and death-obsessed." Tertullian's response: "Of all the brothers among the soldiers, he alone acted like a Christian." Indeed, he commented about the incident: "The only thing really left is for them to reject the martyrdoms also, after they have already disparaged the prophecies of the same Spirit!" After further mocking comments against Christians of the mainstream church and their shepherds, who in persecution took flight, he breaks off the discussion in order to come to the real theme—the crowning with the wreath. At the same time he announces a detailed treatise.[137]

On Flight in Persecution is the announced writing. If the Spirit of God on the one hand requires the testimony (martyrdom), then, says the author, he will on the other hand also bestow the strength for it: "Therefore the Paraclete is necessary, who teaches all truths and urges the endurance of everything. Those who have received him can neither take flight nor buy their freedom."[138] In the same treatise Tertullian passes on two prophecies in which the Spirit speaks:

> You are publicly exposed [*publicaris*]; that is good for you. For whoever is not publicly exposed before people will be publicly exposed before God. Do not be ashamed; righteousness leads you into the middle. Why are you ashamed? You will receive praise. Something powerful will occur while people look at you.
>
> Do not wish to die in bed, in miscarriage, or with debilitating fever, but in martyrdom, in order to glorify the one who suffered for you.[139]

How are these texts to be evaluated? We do not know when they were written—in all probability during the persecutions in Carthage. They certainly do not come from Prisca, Maximilla, or Montanus, for Tertullian surely would not have remained silent about their authorship. Do these prophetic texts contain a challenge to offer oneself voluntarily for martyrdom?

Without doubt they contain a certain exalted tone of martyrdom enthusiasm. Yet the Sitz im Leben one assumes for the oracles is important for the evaluation. Are these general instructions for behavior? Or were these words spoken in a prison, in a worship service for condemned people who faced imminent and inevitable martyrdom? The latter is much more likely. Such a situation, which we find many times in the authentic acts of the martyrs, makes the emotional transfiguration of suffering understandable: it was a help in enduring the difficult hours. The first text has quite clearly the character of such a comforting word. In the second, martyrdom is praised as the desirable death for Christians—but can we infer from this one logion an extreme enthusiasm for martyrdom in the entire New Prophecy? That seems very bold. A far stronger enthusiasm for martyrdom pervades the letters of the mainstream confessor-bishop Ignatius of Antioch.

Moreover, the facts speak a different language: no concrete case of self-denunciation out of enthusiasm for death in the arena can be demonstrated in the New Prophecy. Even if one tries to make Montanists of Vettius Epagathus and Alexander, who provoked their condemnation in Lyon, and the catechete Saturus in Carthage, who voluntarily follows his students into prison, we cannot speak of fanatical enthusiasm for martyrdom here: in all three cases it is a question of well-considered steps by prudent men who did not fanatically seek death. It is true that in the *Martyrdom of Polycarp* one Quintus from Phrygia is mentioned as a warning because he at first volunteered himself and then could not endure the torture, but it does not state that he belonged to the New Prophecy;[140] perhaps the episode involves an interpolation with which someone wanted to discredit the movement.[141] Also, Tertullian does not characterize the soldier who refused the crowning as a follower of the prophetic movement.

Hence we see that the thesis of enthusiasm for martyrdom in the New Prophecy has no real foundation at all. Not even the rigorous theologian from Carthage demands or recommends self-denunciation in his writings; yet he categorically rejects flight or buying one's freedom. Nor do the oracles quoted by him advise self-sacrifice; in fact they do not even contain a prohibition of flight, even if Tertullian interprets their statement in his sense. Here he himself has to place a treacherous limitation on the many prophetically inspired sayings, of which he merely quotes two: "*Almost* all urge martyrdom, not flight."[142] Thus we have no grounds for assuming that the position of the Phrygian movement was basically different from the position of the other Christians: enthusiasts and rigorists remained the exception. Nevertheless, a great readiness for martyrdom on the part of the New Prophets and Prophetesses is probable, and it earned them high regard—it was not for nothing that the opponents sought to discredit the followers of the movement honored as martyrs!

The Question of Repentance

With this fifth point of contention we encounter a new question that is not mentioned in the sources examined thus far. In early Christianity the possibility of forgiveness of sins after baptism was controversial, since the Letter to the Hebrews seemed to exclude it: "For it is impossible to restore again to repentance those who have once been enlightened . . . and then have fallen away" (Heb. 6:4, 6). Yet in the mainstream church the reacceptance of those who had fallen away, as well as the possibility of ecclesiastical penance for other serious offenses, gradually prevailed, whereas other Christian communities—in particular the Novatians, as we saw—held fast to the old strictness. Now on this question Tertullian not only took a clear position but again quoted an oracle in which the Paraclete is supposed to have spoken through the New Prophets: "The church can forgive sins, but I do not want it to, so that they will not commit other sins."[143] The context? In his writing *On Honesty* the rigorist once more crusades thoroughly against the "physicals." Presumably he was taking aim at the bishop of Carthage, who practiced ecclesiastical forgiveness after appropriate penance.[144] The primary sins involved here are adultery and unchastity, to which second marriage is also equated: Christians who have been guilty of this offense may not—according to Tertullian—be readmitted to Communion but must do penance the rest of their lives.

Yet this is not all. In addition the theologian basically denies the right of ecclesiastical reconciliation to bishops who only hold office without also possessing the charisma of an apostle or prophet: only upon the "spirituals" is the authority to bind and loose bestowed; therefore only the "spirit-church through a spiritual person" (*ecclesia spiritus per spiritalem hominem*) can forgive, not the "church-number of the bishops" (*ecclesia numerus episcoporum*).[145]

This time the theologian is waging a war on two fronts, as it were, for with the oracle he in his way is answering two different questions that we have already encountered in the context of martyrdom: (1) Can baptized people who have committed serious offenses be received again into the church? And if the answer is affirmative: (2) Who in the church can grant forgiveness? In theory Tertullian's sophisticated answer to the first question is yes, but in fact it is no. Thus the second question is actually superfluous, but the theologian answers it anyway: the right to forgive belongs to those who have the Spirit, not to ordained ministers. With this he confirms the charismatic authority of the prophets in order to be able to use them in the spirit of his rigorous morality.

Does this hair-splitting argumentation correspond to the ideas of the early New Prophecy? We do not have a direct statement on the repentance question, but we do know one thing: in contrast to the Novatians,[146] its adherents are not criticized by opponents for the irreconcilability of the "lapsi." Furthermore, Apollonius's mocking remark about Prisca's contact with the martyr Alexander (the thief, according to Apollonius) gives us something to consider: "Who pardons whose sins? Does the prophet [masculine!] forgive the martyr's robberies, or the martyr the prophet's covetousness?"[147] Here even the words of the opponent recognize the authority of the "Spirit-bearers," which is validated by Tertullian. In the Phrygian movement martyrs and prophets of both sexes were broadly accorded the right to grant forgiveness to the guilty and, indeed, apparently actually did so.

Once again, the rigorism that is expressed in Tertullian's argumentation and the logion he quotes is neither original nor typical of the New Prophecy. In all the points of criticism we have examined thus far, the African theologian considerably intensified in the spirit of rigorous asceticism an ethical seriousness that was doubtless already present. Thus the assumption that he finally left the Montanist church and gathered around him even stricter "Tertullianists" is at the very least not improbable.[148] Two final questions that are not of an ethical nature must still be examined: imminent expectation and ecstasy.

Imminent Expectation?

The opponents criticized the term *Jerusalem* for Pepuza, the center of the New Prophecy in the Phrygian highlands. As we saw already, the early witness Apollonius merely said that Montanus "renamed Pepuza and Tymion, insignificant towns in Phrygia, as Jerusalem, in the hope of persuading people in every district to gather there."[149] The idea that in Pepuza "Jerusalem will descend from heaven" is first attested by Epiphanius, the great heresiologist of the fourth century, yet as a vision of Prisca.[150] Interestingly, Augustine will later quote Epiphanius, yet without seeing in the naming of the city an expression of an eschatological expectation: "They hold it to be something divine and therefore call it Jerusalem." He passes on yet another reason for the designation: "It is called Jerusalem because Montanus and his prophetesses Prisca and Maximilla lived there."[151] But let us return to Tertullian.

The African follower of the New Prophecy does not mention the name *Pepuza*, but in his writing *Against Marcion* he takes a position on visions of the heavenly Jerusalem. There he insists on the spiritual character of this "city," which will become visible only at the end of the ages. Only the prophets are allowed to see it already in this world:

> Ezekiel knew it [Ezek. 48:30–35], and the apostle John saw it [Rev. 21:2]. It is also attested in our faith by the word of the New Prophecy: it is predicted that the image of this city will become visible as a sign before its final appearance. This promise was recently fulfilled during the expedition into the East.[152] Even pagan witnesses confirm that in Judea every morning for forty days a city was seen floating in the sky. At dawn the outlines of its walls dissolved; on closer look nothing more was to be seen. We maintain that this city was created by God to receive the saints after their resurrection.[153]

Here Tertullian is not speaking expressly about the center of the movement but only showing that a vision of the heavenly Jerusalem was nothing unusual. For him the phenomenon is connected with millenarian concepts, with the notion of a thousand-year dominion of Christ before the final Parousia, and thus with ideas that were widespread in the second century.[154]

Consequently, in the sources there is no support for the idea that the designation of Pepuza with the symbolic name *Jerusalem* was originally the expression of an apocalyptic near expectation; for the followers the center of the New Prophecy was a place in which the Spirit of God had been manifested in a special way and was supposed to be manifested further. At the time when Epiphanius was writing, Pepuza doubtless had great significance as a center of worship and place of pilgrimage for the movement, and it is well possible that in popular Montanism eschatological expectations were nourished, for conceptions of the end of the world were still alive in the fourth century within and outside of Christianity.[155] Yet in the overall polemic against the New Prophecy, Pepuza, called "Jerusalem," plays hardly any role.[156] The widespread idea that Montanism was an apocalyptically oriented movement has only one—nonetheless important—

point of support: according to Epiphanius, Maximilla is supposed to have said that the end would come after her. We will speak more of this in the next section.

Prophetic Ecstasy

We now come to the last point in the early dispute over the New Prophecy: ecstasy. "It is *the* controversial issue between us and the physicals," said Tertullian,[157] and we know from Jerome that the theologian from Carthage wrote a six-volume work on this important theme[158]—it is hardly a coincidence that this very book did not survive! Thus today we have only a short but clear comment by Tertullian on the standpoint of the New Prophecy (in his view):

> Are we simply taken in by an error or have we good reasons to assert in the matter of the New Prophecy that ecstasy, that is, the loss of consciousness, is a gift of grace?[159] If a person is seized by the Spirit, and especially if he sees the glory of God or if God speaks through him, he necessarily loses sensible perception, since he is overshadowed by divine power.[160]

In support of his argumentation Tertullian chose an awkward example, namely, Peter, who at the transfiguration wanted to erect three dwellings, "not knowing what he said" (Luke 9:33)—for the theologian, proof of his rapture. In his six-volume work he has probably cited more appropriate Bible quotations. As model example of prophetic ecstasy and Spirit-effected speech he names, in another context, Adam's deep sleep during the creation of Eve from his rib and the following act of naming.[161] This "scriptural proof," which may surprise us, is explained by the fact that the "deep sleep" that God causes to fall on Adam (Gen. 2:21) is rendered in the Greek translation, the Septuagint, as *ekstasis*. The text was apparently a favorite, for we find it again in the dispute led by Epiphanius. He held the opinion that with Adam it was not a question of an "ecstasy of the senses and the ability to perceive."[162]

In the same style the bishop of Salamis tries to weaken the New Testament Bible passage that Tertullian would certainly not have missed, since it talks expressly of the ecstasy of an apostle, in the middle of the day, after a prayer: Peter has his vision of unclean animals that he is supposed to eat—a symbolic encouragement to evangelize among non-Jews (Acts 10:9ff.). Again the heresiologist articulates a position counter to the Montanists' view: "As long as prophets were needed, the saints of the Lord spoke prophetically in the true Spirit with clear understanding and full consciousness."[163] Yet we must remember that Epiphanius is writing two hundred years later at a time in which real prophecy hardly ever still occurred in the churches: it "was no longer needed," as he put it.[164] For him the question is academic.

Thus we see that the opponents of the Phrygian church construct an antithesis between the ecstatic experiences that are attested for biblical prophecy and the ecstatic experiences in the New Prophecy. Yet the debate has become more precise than in Anonymus, who criticized ecstasy as such. Certainly the New Prophets themselves point to the ecstatic phenomena in their ranks in order to "prove" the working of the Spirit. Thus there was an effort to distinguish between ecstasy and ecstasy, although in antiquity various forms of rapture were regarded as a "normal" accompanying phenomenon of prophetic emotion[165] and were also highly favored in orthodox circles.[166] The vigorous defense of mainstream church authors may also be explained by the reverse polemic of New Prophets, who used the reference to trancelike conditions as propaganda.

Paul distinguished between ecstatic prayer and prophecy as interpretive speech. Yet ecstasy then becomes the "trademark," as it were, of charismatic proclamation. There is agreement that God speaks through prophetesses and prophets, but there are different theories about the function of the rapture. Did Tertullian's view that in prophecy consciousness *must* be turned off so that God can speak agree with the ideas of his models Prisca, Maximilla, and Montanus? The answer must be sought in analysis of the extant oracles, to which we now turn.

d. Inspired Proclamation:
The Extant Sayings

But did Montanus speak prophetically at all? The question may be surprising, yet Heinz Kraft points out that Montanus "was not considered a prophet by his first followers and became one only in later tradition."[167] He gives two reasons for this thesis: (1) Anonymus, the earliest witness, does not name him in the succession that leads from Old and New Testament prophets and prophetesses through Ammia and Quadratus to the New Prophecy, and (2) of the sayings handed down under Montanus's name only one makes "a real statement; it concerns the interpretation of a Daniel passage."[168]

What are we to make of Kraft's thesis? Against the first argument one can object that the "later tradition" he mentions begins already with Anonymus himself, who names Montanus before Prisca and Maximilla and presents him as a tool of the adversary who, "seized by the Spirit," falls into ecstasy and "speaks prophetically" against church tradition (5.16.7). Only then does he introduce, without naming them, "two women" whom the devil "has filled with the spirit of deception, so that they talk incomprehensibly, inopportunely, and strangely, like the aforementioned" (5.16.9). In the following sentence he reluctantly concedes that at times all three express reasonable and trustworthy admonitions—naturally, only to deceive their hearers!

And other early witnesses? In Tertullian, as we have seen, Montanus, Prisca, and Maximilla appear together as representatives of the New Prophecy: whoever rejects them rejects the Paraclete; the bishop of Rome was ready to recognize the prophecy of Montanus, Prisca, and Maximilla, but Praxeas prevented it. Yet the theologian from Carthage hands down no oracle of Montanus. Hippolytus of Rome (d. 235), who left behind not only the already often mentioned *Apostolic Tradition* but also a *Refutation of All Heresies*,[169] does not belong to the first generation of witnesses; he also calls Montanus a prophet. Yet he mentions him only in second position, and of the women he says only that they are revered more than the apostles by followers of the movement. Doubtless he accords them far greater significance than Montanus. Consequently he describes the "heretics of Phrygian origin" as follows:

> They were seduced by females[170] named Priscilla and Maximilla, whom they call prophetesses and upon whom they say the Spirit, the Paraclete, has come; and they also praise a certain Montanus before[171] them as a prophet. . . . They revere these women more than the apostles and every charisma, so that some of them even assert that in these women something more happened than in Christ.[172]

Then, is Kraft wrong? Yes and no. According to the early witnesses it is improbable that Montanus was not active at all prophetically. As we saw, in the Phrygian movement there were doubtless not just three but a multitude of charismatics.[173] In a slightly modified form, however, Kraft's thesis can be fully substantiated, as we shall demonstrate: *The real prophetic authority in the "Montanist" movement lay not with Montanus but with Prisca and Maximilla.*[174] This makes the old formula of the "paraclete Montanus" understandable: he was the "advocate" of the prophetesses, not their "inspirer," as was later held. This situation is still echoed in the common expression, "Montanus and 'his' prophetesses." This is confirmed by another fact: all the sayings ascribed to Montanus come from later sources. This raises the question: How were the oracles of the New Prophecy passed on?

From the early church witnesses we learn that collections of the sayings of Maximilla, Prisca, and Montanus (as well as, presumably, other prophets and prophetesses) were published under their names and that followers of the movement considered them "inspired writings." As we saw, Hippolytus reports that some of them even held the view that "in these [the prophetesses] something more happened than in Christ."[175] Eusebius faults the overzealous Cataphrygians for writing "new scriptures," which led to a discussion about the canon, and he mentions the confiscation of their books under Constantine.[176] Finally, the *Discussion of a Montanist and an Orthodox* polemicizes against the writings of Prisca and Maximilla.[177]

In spite of these testimonies, Pierre de Labriolle is oddly skeptical at this point. He concedes that there were ecstatics who wrote down their visions, yet in the case of the New Prophecy he says that such activity must be called into question: "One can hardly imagine that these 'spirituals' of an excited type wrote down their apocalypses [*sic*] quietly and with a clear head. It is easier to imagine that their short utterances—which have such a harsh and passionate tone, vibrating and at the same time breathless—were caught in flight in the middle of the prophetic crisis [*sic*] by attentive listeners and immediately fixed in writing."[178] To support his construction he cites a comparison from the eighteenth century! I see no grounds for following de Labriolle here, especially since the extant oracles do not sound at all like ecstatic stammering. Authorship by women was possibly an additional reason to demolish the writings of the New Prophecy, but there was no formal prohibition of women writing books.[179] In any case, the destruction was completely successful: only fifteen short sayings have survived in quotations—and even they must be tested to see if they are genuine.

That is what we shall now do for the extant oracles of the New Prophecy. The choice of a sequence here is neither accidental nor insignificant. Typically the presentation by de Labriolle, Schneemelcher, Aland, and Heine[180] of the logia regarded as genuine all begin with Montanus, who is usually followed by the anonymous oracles and then the sayings of Prisca and Maximilla. Given the current state of the research, one would have expected a listing that begins with the oldest historical testimonies, for example:

> second century: two sayings of Prisca, one of Maximilla, three
>   anonymous sayings;
> fourth century: one saying of Prisca, three of Maximilla, five of
>   Montanus.

If one proceeds according to the importance of each prophetic proclamation of the personalities, Prisca would have to be first. The order in my examination results from a combination of the aspects of chronology and content: I begin with Maximilla, since one of her oracles is the oldest, and then take the remaining ones ascribed to her. Because of their structural similarity I then examine the oracles of Montanus. The anonymous oracles and the sayings of Prisca come last because of the importance of their content and assertions.

Maximilla: A Persecuted Prophetess

The first logion of Maximilla is preserved in the writing of Anonymus, the oldest source on the New Prophecy:

> I am persecuted like a wolf among the sheep. I am not a wolf; I am word and
> spirit and power.[181]

The author probably places this saying correctly in its original context: it is the response of the prophetess to the attacks of the bishops—obviously less an "oracle" than a self-assertion in which Maximilla articulates both her painful experience and her sense of mission: she is a persecuted prophetess.

The three other logia are preserved by Epiphanius, the bishop of Salamis (Cyprus), who not only describes the New Prophecy in detail but also attempts a theological discussion.[182] Unfortunately, we are left in the dark in regard to both the historical and the literary context of the transmission of the sayings he quotes. The shortest logion reads:

> Do not listen to me; listen rather to Christ![183]

One could again presume that this sentence expresses prophetic authority: "Christ speaks out of me." Yet the heretic fighter Epiphanius understands it in a totally orthodox way as a pointing away from one's own person. Since even the most orthodox church father could hardly object to this imperative, the logion is interpreted on the one hand as a "lie," as a trick of the prophetess, but on the other as a victory of truth, which even speaks in false prophets: the demon condemns himself here.

Another saying of Maximilla offers the opponent more opportunity for attack:

> The Lord has sent me as follower, revealer, interpreter of this toil and covenant and promise, compelled, willing and unwilling, to learn knowledge of God.[184]

In the Greek text the participles for "compelled, willing and not willing" have masculine endings. The nouns are likewise masculine but have no variants with feminine endings—hence they can also be used for women. Thus one could ask: Is this oracle from Maximilla at all? Was Montanus perhaps originally the subject of the statement? Or is the Paraclete himself speaking here? Pierre de Labriolle, however, has already refuted such speculation, for the combining of a feminine subject with adjectives and participles in masculine form is not unusual in Greek.[185] Thus there is no reason to doubt the authenticity of this saying.

In "compelled" Epiphanius sees his previously voiced suspicion confirmed that the prophetic pernicious spirit, the demon of the false prophets, violates people and their freedom; this is profoundly foreign to God's Holy Spirit. Apparently, much is read into a text here that attests to being seized but not to lack of freedom—no more than Paul's exclamation: "An obligation is laid on me, and woe to me if I do not proclaim the gospel!" (1 Cor. 9:16). In both cases an awareness of apostolic-prophetic mission is expressed.

Surprising is *learn* where one would expect *proclaim*. And thus Epiphanius interprets the sentence contrary to the wording: Maximilla "teaches" in ecstasy without wanting to. In combination with *learn*, however, *compel* has a different sense: a painful learning process is described. The formulaic combination of *toil* (*ponos*), *covenant* (*synthēkē*), and *promise* (*epangelia*) has not yet been studied, since the commentary of the heresiologist directs attention toward the involuntary nature of prophetic speech, which he interprets as ecstasy. Yet there is nothing at all about this in the logion.

The words in this saying are little used otherwise. Behind the expression "toil and covenant and promise" one could presume the central contents of the Christian message: cross, resurrection, sending of the Spirit,[186] which were concretely lived by the women and men disciples in the tribulations of discipleship, possibly even connected with persecution and martyrdom, in the celebration of the Eucharist,[187] and in the hope of future glory, anticipated in the experience of the new life "in the Spirit": precisely here is the "knowledge of God" that has to be laboriously learned before it can be shared with others.

Maximilla's self-designations are: *follower* (*hairetistēs*), *revealer* (*mēnytēs*), and *interpreter* (*hermēneutēs*). Again we have in part seldom used terms, but they are unambiguous: the first designates belonging to a group defined by its special teaching and way of life; the other two describe the essential duty of prophetesses and prophets: to "reveal" (in the sense of "point to, announce") and to "interpret." Thus we find here no deviation from the biblical understanding of prophecy.

Finally, Epiphanius quotes another oracle of Maximilla, which for him discredits the entire prophetic movement:

After me there will be no more prophets; it will instead be the culmination.[188]

Since then 290 years have passed and the end has still not come, comments the heresiologist; the prophetess could not even correctly predict her own end, let alone the culmination! If this saying by Maximilla is authentic, it seems advisable to follow the church father in his judgment. Yet there are reasons to doubt its authenticity.

As we have already seen, neither the early polemic nor the testimony of sympathizers and followers indicates that the Phrygian movement was characterized by apocalyptic near expectation. Thus the saying has to be surprising. Yet in one statement this oracle agrees with the testimony of the opponents: after Maximilla's death there were no more prophets in the movement! Anonymus uses this very fact as an argument against the movement: this charisma must live on in the church until the end of the ages, yet in Phrygia it has been extinguished for fourteen years; hence the succession has been interrupted: this cannot have been genuine ecclesiastical prophecy.[189] Yet we must wonder: if Maximilla at that time was really called the last prophetess and the end of the ages had been predicted, would one not expect an indication of this in Anonymus? But he faults the prophetess only because the predicted wars and persecutions had not happened for more than thirteen years. There is obviously a contradiction here that leads to further questions.

Why is such a statement found later on Maximilla's lips? Was the oracle invented by opponents in order to discredit the prophetess? Not necessarily. The general extinction of prophecy was just as much a problem for the followers of the Phrygian church as for the mainstream church, which faced the reproach of having suffocated prophetic charisma, the great eschatological gift to the church.[190] How the problem was overcome in the Catholic church can be seen in an already-quoted formulation of the bishop of Salamis: God called prophets "as long as they were needed."[191] Yet Epiphanius seems not to rule out the idea that in the future God could again evoke charismatic gifts, but for him only those of the past were real.[192] In any case, with the concept of a "prophecy according to need" the idea of an ongoing "succession" and thus a constant presence of prophetesses and prophets in the church was basically relinquished.

For a movement that defined itself entirely on the basis of prophecy, the end of charismatic phenomena was doubtless more difficult to accept. Thus it is quite conceivable and indeed probable that also in the Phrygian church theories arose regarding the end of prophecy. Possibly there was an old oracle of Maximilla that simply read: "There will be no more prophets; it will instead be the culmination."[193] This assertion would be entirely in the spirit of Pauline theology. One needs to add only the words "after me" to change the function of the logion. For followers this was a help: Maximilla foresaw the end of prophecy! For opponents the minor retouching made it possible to make the

prophetess of the Phrygian church look ridiculous with an alleged false pre-
diction of the end of the world.[194] Nonetheless, it seems extremely daring to
assume "near expectation" in the early period of the movement merely on
the basis of this saying. In any case, nothing of the kind can be deduced for
Maximilla from the other three extant logia, but only the quite moderate claim
of being a Spirit-filled prophetic announcer and interpreter of the Christian
message.

Montanus: Spokesman of God

The claim of speaking in God's name is formulated entirely differently in
words that are attributed to Montanus:

> I am the Father and I am the Son and I am the Holy Spirit.[195]

For our ears this is a monstrous assertion! Yet we must ask two questions
here: (1) Is the oracle genuine? (2) How is it meant? It is found, at any rate, in
two traditions. The first is the *Discussion of a Montanist and an Orthodox.*
There it introduces a Trinitarian debate, which was certainly not held in the
early period of the Phrygian movement. The Montanist, however, does not reject the logion but responds to the orthodox: "And you say: 'A different one
is the Father, a different one is the Son, a different one is the Holy Spirit.'"
Thus the words are not understood by the adversaries as a self-assertion of
Montanus but as statement of Trinitarian doctrine. Didymus of Alexandria
quotes the same oracle[196] in a treatise on the Trinity as proof of the false teaching that Father, Son, and Spirit are only one person.[197] Thus we are presumably not dealing here with an authentic prophetic saying of Montanus but
with a later oracle that arose in the discussion of the doctrine of the Trinity
and was used as an argument.[198] The following two sayings of Montanus
sound somewhat less formulaic, yet they can be understood as a description of
the incarnation:

> I [am] the Lord, God the Almighty, come down in humankind.[199] Neither an
> angel nor an emissary, but I the Lord, God the Father, have come.[200]

The argumentation of Epiphanius, who quotes the sayings, is contradictory,
since he expressly certified Montanus's orthodoxy in questions of Trinitarian
doctrine but now accuses him, through identification with the Father, of failing
to glorify Christ.[201] It may be a question here of later christological interpretations of older oracles. Originally they could have been introductory formulas for
authentic revelatory speeches, which expressed the awareness of divine inspiration, similar to the biblical "Thus says the Lord." In any case, the sayings are
most certainly not to be regarded as self-assertions.[202]

Only one saying of Montanus clearly describes an experience of the Spirit; it
can be divided into word of God and commentary, and it is similar to an oracle
of Maximilla already quoted:

Look, the human being is like a lyre, and I fly to it like a drumstick. The human being sleeps, and I am awake. Look, it is the Lord who lifts[203] the hearts of human beings above himself and gives human beings [new] hearts.[204]

This logion with the beautiful imagery of the lyre on which God plays was quoted by Epiphanius as proof of the false nature of the New Prophecy: the Spirit that inspires it does away with human reason and does not respect human freedom. He saw this confirmed by Maximilla's saying, as we have already seen. The guardian of orthodoxy has obviously interpreted "compulsion" into both oracles. In Montanus's saying "ecstasy" is characterized in a good biblical way as sleep. In another context and in a very natural way, Sozomen uses the same image of the musical instrument for prophetic inspiration in order to support the idea that the oracles of the Greeks also could have announced the coming of Christ.[205]

Epiphanius passes on a final saying of Montanus as an example of his distortion of scripture. The meaning of the short text can hardly be clarified, yet the fact that it is a commentary on a Bible passage is an indication of the Sitz im Leben: Prophetic proclamation comments on and interprets Holy Scripture in the worship service.

Why do you call the superhuman one saved? For the righteous human being, he says, will shine a hundred times brighter than the sun, but the small ones among you, who are saved, will shine a hundred times brighter than the moon.[206]

Result. It is very striking that before the fourth century not a single oracle of Montanus was passed on. Thus there is great doubt that all these sayings really go back to the contemporary and "advocate" of Prisca and Maximilla. But they may, nonetheless, be authentic testimonies from the Phrygian tradition. The oracle that describes the experience of inspiration with the image of the lyre is completely free of traces of theological controversy; it may best reflect the spirituality of the New Prophecy in its beginnings. It is possible that old, anonymous oracles were later ascribed to Montanus. These questions must remain open.

As already said, it is surprising that none of the sayings handed down contain a message—this deficit noted by Kraft, moreover, is true of Maximilla's oracles in almost the same way. Yet there is an explanation: the opponents objected far less to the content of the prophecies than to the claim of the prophets and prophetesses, which called into question other church authorities. Separated from concrete sermons, such introductory formulas had a shocking effect in later times and were therefore especially suited to discrediting their originators. It remains only to point out that not a single saying fits the notion that it was uttered in excited ecstasy—more stammered than spoken. In no way do the oracles presuppose trancelike conditions.

Anonymous: Encouragement in Martyrdom

If the previously considered logia were only the expression of empowerment for prophetic speech, the sayings we will examine now have concrete assertions and a direct reference to ecclesiastical problems. We have already seen the three anonymous oracles passed on by Tertullian—they are recalled here once again. The first two speak of martyrdom:

> You are publicly exposed; that is good for you. For whoever is not publicly exposed before people will be publicly exposed before God. Do not be ashamed; righteousness leads you into the middle. Why are you ashamed? You will receive praise. Something powerful will occur while people look at you.
>
> Do not wish to die in bed, in miscarriage, or with debilitating fever, but in martyrdom, in order to glorify the one who suffered for you.[207]

These two oracles have an edifying-encouraging character: as we saw, they could well have been spoken in a prayer meeting of Christians with the persecuted brothers and sisters in prison before martyrdom. The concern is to master a difficult situation, not to "reveal" truths of a basic kind.

The third anonymous oracle, the short saying on penance, clearly has a different character from the other two:

> The church can forgive sins, but I do not want it to, so that they will not commit other sins.[208]

Clearly this logion is used to support a certain church regulation that the theologian wants to impose. It is true that Tertullian also used the other two oracles intentionally, but he did not find the rejection of flight that he advocated directly in the wording but had to read it in. Here the "I" of the Paraclete suspiciously resembles the "I" of the rigorist. As commentary on this prophetic saying, he says two things: (1) the certainty that the church can forgive sins is anchored more weakly in the mainstream church than in the New Prophecy, because the former was not ready to assume express confirmation through the supplementary revelation of the Paraclete; (2) the strictness demanded by the oracle is itself proof of the genuineness of the revelation, for a false prophet would ingratiate himself through moderation. Thus we clearly have here a tendentious oracle in a basic issue of ecclesiastical discipline: the obvious assumption is that it comes from Tertullian himself or was "ordered" by him.[209]

Prisca: Christ in Female Form

A very short first logion of Prisca is quoted by Tertullian in his writing *On the Resurrection of the Flesh;* it is directed against Christian Gnostics, who reject the idea of a bodily resurrection.[210] The oracle reads:

> They are flesh and [yet] hate the flesh![211]

Prisca's saying seems at first to belong in a dogmatic context. Yet in the context of the oracle the question of the resurrection of the flesh is by no means treated in a speculative, abstract way as a metaphysical problem. Rather, the polemicist reproaches the Gnostics for their way of life: "None live according to the flesh as much as those who deny the resurrection of the flesh! Because they deny the punishment, they also deny the discipline."[212] Thus the debate is concerned very concretely with the importance of asceticism. Prisca's saying, which sounds more like a clever bon mot than a divinely inspired oracle, is not aimed at an article of faith but at a certain way of living. Freely translated, Prisca's critique of the Gnostics might read: "They believe they do not need asceticism, because they do not take human corporeality seriously." Did Tertullian insert the quotation here in accordance with his original intention? Because of the brevity of the formula, one cannot say. In any case, the threatening reference to "punishment" is not to be found in the prophetess—thus one must again presume an intensification in the interpretation.

The second oracle of Prisca that the theologian from Carthage passes on is not dogmatically oriented either:

> Purification creates harmony; then they see visions, and if they bow their heads, they hear clear voices, wholesome and mysterious.[213]

The introduction of the logion in Tertullian has great importance. First he quotes the apostle Paul: "To set the mind on the flesh is death, but to set the mind on the Spirit is eternal life in Christ Jesus our Lord" (Rom. 8:6, modified). Then he continues: "Likewise it is proclaimed [*evangelizatur*] by the holy prophetess Prisca that a holy servant of the Holiness knows how to serve."

A holy prophetess Prisca who like Paul proclaims the gospel! For the pious copyists—who apparently did not take exception to the ascetic rigorism of this work, which clearly originated in the "Montanist" phase—that was, nonetheless, too much: they simply left the passage out![214]

Tertullian had incorporated this oracle of Prisca into his *Exhortation to Chastity,* which he had written in order to advise a widower strongly against a second marriage: he should instead take advantage of his newly won "freedom from the flesh." In the argumentation the resourceful theologian generalizes Paul's concession of a married couple's occasional sexual continence for the purpose of prayer:[215] People must always pray[216] and therefore should always live in continence. Concerning a second marriage he stresses: "If even one marriage separates one from the Holy Spirit, how much more then the second!" (10).

How much Tertullian's framework has colored the interpretation of the oracle is shown by the translations of *purificantia* as "continence." This word formation is, to be sure, unusual, but the root is clearly *purus,* "pure"; thus it has no immediate reference to sexual behavior. Pierre de Labriolle holds that the neutral translation-interpretation that "purity creates union (with God)" is absolutely acceptable: "La pureté crée l'union (mystique avec Dieu)." But in his commentary he decides for "above all sexual purity" ("pureté—surtout sexuelle") and speaks generally about "chasteté."[217] Finally, in his translation we find "continence."[218] Yet his main interest in the interpretation concerns the question whether the "harmony" refers to the inner peace of a person or to the relationship with God, and he decides for the former.[219]

Even crasser is the interpretation in Tertullian's spirit by Frederick Klawiter. Although he likewise clearly acknowledges the possibility of a neutral rendering, he translates directly with "sexual abstinence" and justifies it "because it fits well with Prisca's own religious experience and her later actions as a prophetess of the New Prophecy."[220] Here the sources are really treated a little too freely! Unfortunately, we know virtually nothing about Prisca's "own religious experience." And even if the assertion of Anonymus is correct that Prisca and Maximilla left their husbands because of their prophetic calling—which at least cannot be ruled out—one can hardly conclude from this that Prisca saw sexual continence as a precondition to having visions. In any case, there is nothing in the text that goes beyond a general connection between ascetic purity and spiritual experience.[221] Heinrich Weinel confirms this indirectly through his indication that this oracle of Prisca is the only passage in which sexual asceticism is connected with visions.[222] In fact, however, the connection is not made in the prophetess's logion but only in Tertullian's interpretation.

One could argue, to be sure, that the saying must have had this sense, because Tertullian used it in this way. Yet there are doubts here. Since we still have the letters of Paul, we can check the ascetic theologian's methods of interpretation: clearly he has boldly combined quite different statements from the apostle and (re)interpreted them in the sense of an extreme denial of sexuality. The writings of the prophetess are lost, yet the interpreter may have proceeded in the same way: a general formula is interpreted in a narrow and rigorist fashion. The aims of Prisca's oracle and Tertullian's writing are fundamentally different. The prophetess gives instructions on how one can have charismatic prayer experiences and in so doing emphasizes the importance of purity and inner harmony. Tertullian, by contrast, is basically fighting the custom of remarriage in the interest of a perfect spiritualization, which for him excludes any sexual activity.

As we have seen, in questions of asceticism the movement of the New Prophecy advocates no extreme positions. How rigorously it fought second marriage we cannot say, because we have no authentic statements from the early period. In any case, a radical demand for continence cannot be demonstrated from the extant testimonies. There is nothing to support the idea that Montanist influence led Tertullian to become increasingly a rigorist; rather, the New Prophecy may have advocated a middle position between the enthusiastically ascetic theologian and the mainstream church. The words of the prophetess voice the same position as that advocated in Catholic circles, whereas the theologian defends maximal demands. Yet later the mere mention of this woman "heretic" obviously evoked more fear than the real heresy: eradicating the name Prisca was sufficient to validate the writing as a work from the "Catholic" period![223]

We come now to the third oracle attributed to Prisca. The two previously examined sayings are early and are passed on by a follower—thus with them we may hope to hear the *ipsissima vox* of the prophetess. The third oracle, by contrast, is not attested until the fourth century by Epiphanius, who himself says that he does not know exactly whether it comes from Prisca or Quintilla.

> In the form of a woman in white garment, Christ came to me and placed wis-dom inside me; he revealed to me that this place is holy and that Jerusalem will come down from heaven here.[224]

The quotation of the vision is introduced by the writer of the *Panarion* with a disparaging remark: "These Cataphrygians or Priscillists assert that in Pepuza, Quintilla or Priscilla—I cannot say exactly which—that in Pepuza one of them, as I said, went to sleep and then Christ came to her and slept with her[225] in the fashion recounted by the [woman] overcome by deception."[226]

The framework of this oracle has given wings to the imagination of some in-terpreters. Schepelern sees here the anticipation of the "romantic meetings" with the "heavenly bridegroom" described by medieval women mystics.[227] Similarly Frederick Klawiter: "The sexual overtones of the experience seem at least im-plicit—'Christ came to me and *threw* [*enebalen*] wisdom in to me.'"[228] Appar-ently he imagines the transmission of wisdom in the form of an ejaculation. There is no reason, however, not to translate the Greek verb as "place inside."[229] The vision is absolutely free of "sexual overtones," since Christ appears in feminine form. For this reason alone one cannot see here a parallel to the *hieros gamos* of ancient cults that is supposed to represent the sexual union of a goddess with a god.[230] The expression "slept with her" used by Epiphanius occurs only in this passage;[231] thus it is certainly not a usual euphemism for sexual intercourse. Sex-ual love as a metaphor for the human relationship with God is, of course, by no means to be rejected, and it definitely occurs in other early Christian traditions; yet the comparison itself makes it clear that with Prisca such concepts are not present.[232] In all likelihood, Epiphanius did not intend to insinuate anything of the kind either.

Having anticipated the content of the vision, we must now clarify the ques-tion of authorship: does the logion go back to Prisca or Quintilla? Previous re-search has mostly left the question open.[233] Absolute certainty is hardly to be gained, but we will try to assemble arguments for the two hypotheses, beginning with Prisca.

The account of Christ's appearance contains several statements: (1) it is a dream vision; (2) in the form of a woman dressed in white Christ imparts wis-dom to the prophetess; (3) the place where this occurs is holy; (4) in this place Jerusalem is to come down from heaven. How do these statements relate to what we know about Prisca and the early period of the movement?

(1) We have not previously encountered a dream vision in the texts about Phrygian prophecy, though we have in other texts that speak of prophetic phe-nomena: let us recall Perpetua and Saturus.[234] Though these dream visions were recounted in prayer meetings, they did not originate there in a spontaneous

trance, in distinction to Tertullian's detailed description of the vision of an Anonyma in Carthage.[235] We have seen how the authors of anti-Montanist writings attempted to play ecstatic and nonecstatic prophecies off against each other, but they obviously created an antithesis that did not exist in that form. In the prophetic tradition of the Bible, as also in early church prophecy, the dream as a medium of revelation was regarded as a specific form of ecstasy. For the previously mentioned logia, the question of origin remains open; only one of the sayings speaks of sleep. Also, according to ancient understanding it was not important whether the experience consisted in perceiving a voice or a sight; in this sense there was no difference between an oracle and a vision.[236] The dream was the nightly form of ecstasy; during the day the Spirit was manifested through special circumstances of rapture. According to David Aune, these were especially important in the mystery cults.[237] Thus a dream vision fits well into the beginning period of the Phrygian movement when the various forms of charismatic manifestations were not yet played off against each other in the battle of the churches.

(2) The appearance of Christ, who imparts wisdom to the prophetess, has the character of a calling. It is quite possible that Prisca is recounting here the beginning of her own prophetic inspiration and activity. At the same time this would clarify her authority as a leader or one of the leaders of the movement. In this role she is characterized not as an ecstatic but as a teacher of wisdom. The vision of Christ in the form of a woman is unusual and bold: there is no direct parallel in early Christian literature! The Gnostic Sophia figure, the concept of the feminine nature of the Holy Spirit, and the personification of Jerusalem as a bride belong to other traditions—as de Labriolle has indicated.[238] Luise Abramowski has voiced the assumption that Christ appears here as the personified "lady wisdom"[239]—a suggestion that requires further study.[240]

(3 and 4) Here Pepuza is first called "holy." The already reported Christophany of the founding prophetess would be sufficient explanation for the holiness of the place in which the movement had its center. A further reason is found in the future destiny of Pepuza: it will be the place of descent of the heavenly Jerusalem. Determining the time of this descent is not involved here—thus we are not dealing with apocalyptic near expectation.

Conclusion. There is no reason not to regard this oracle of Prisca as authentic. The meaning of the vision corresponds to the role that the prophetess must have played in the early period of the movement. The unusual appearance of Christ would explain why the little town of Pepuza—insignificant in both the empire and the church—became the center of the New Prophecy, in which later "women and men were led into the mysteries[241] in the expectation of seeing Christ there," as Epiphanius attests.[242]

Are there, nevertheless, reasons for attributing this vision not to Prisca but to Quintilla? First we must ask: Who was Quintilla? This prophetess is mentioned only in the presentation of the Phrygian movement by the bishop of Salamis. This is also true of the group of *quintilloi,* a designation derived from her name.[243] Epiphanius describes these Quintillists (also called Priscillists or Pepuzists)[244] as a movement within the Cataphrygians; thus it is a question—according to him—of a subgroup of the New Prophecy. Whether it was a recognized or a splinter group remains open. Quintilla was probably not a contemporary of Prisca, Maximilla, and Montanus, as her name does not occur in the early sources. Since we have no reason to assume that Epiphanius simply invented her and the movement named after her, this group may have existed in his time but represented a minority within the charismatic church. The bishop mentions her only for the sake of completeness, as it were, in an appendix to his presentation of the Phrygian heresy, and he treats her very summarily; by contrast he dealt earlier with the arguments of the New Prophecy and especially of Montanus and Maximilla in detail and with intensity.[245]

What Epiphanius reports about this group is striking: women in it are admitted to the ministries of priest and bishop, and this is supported with arguments from the scripture:

> Women among them are named prophetesses, yet I do not know precisely whether [only] among them or [generally] among the Cataphrygians. For they are together and have the same ideas. They use the Old and New Testaments and also confess the resurrection of the dead. Quintilla is their leader [*archēgos*] and also Priscilla, the Cataphrygian. They present many meaningless [scriptural] witnesses: they give special significance to Eve because she was the first to eat from the tree of knowledge. They call Moses' sister a prophetess and claim thereby to justify the acceptance of women into the clergy. "Did Philip not have four daughters who were prophetesses?" they say.
>
> Often in their church seven virgins enter with torches in white clothes in order to speak prophetically to the people. They show a kind of enthusiasm with which they deceive the laity present and bring them to tears. They perform rites of penance, as it were, shed tears, and through their attitude lament the people's way of living. There are among them women who are bishops and women who are priests and so forth,[246] as if nature did not make them different. For in Christ [there is] neither male nor female [Gal. 3:28]. This much we have learned. They are also called Artotyrites, because they use bread and cheese with their mysteries.[247]

It is not surprising that the bishop of Salamis rejects female colleagues while appealing to the subordination of women taught by the church. Yet we are interested in the question of how to evaluate the movement that apparently arose in a later phase within the Phrygian church. Since it is hardly otherwise attested,[248] nor is its practice of opening its highest ecclesiastical offices to women,[249] we cannot say how long it was able to survive. Apparently this group around Quintilla continued most consistently the heritage of the early New Prophecy, while in the overall movement there was a gradual accommodation to the hierarchical structures of Catholicism.

To a certain degree the Quintillists themselves followed this development. The formerly spontaneous prophecy now appears ritualized and clericalized: seven virgins are given the role. The symbolic number seven[250] may have been consciously chosen. Female prophecy now seems to be relegated to the order of voluntarily unmarried women. The ministries of presbyter and bishop are also exercised, but with a big difference: they are also accessible to women. This apparently led to conflicts not only with the hierarchy of the mainstream church but presumably also within the Phrygian church that came out of the prophetic tradition, in which the Quintillists became a fringe group, if not a totally separate sect. In any sense, the cited "scriptural proofs" clearly attest to the disagreements about the role of women as prophetesses, elders, and bishops. Thus in this small group, which was apparently especially influential in Pepuza (as we can infer from their designation as Pepuzists), the consciousness of the equality of man and woman "in Christ" had remained alive in the fourth century and had led to real equality in the church.

Yet let us return to the question: Can the vision of Christ in female form be attributed to Quintilla, the leading prophetess of this movement? An argument for this could be the fact that on the basis of the conflicts in her time a more serious theoretical discussion of the women's question had already taken place. That women could be prophetesses was not disputed in the early church. But later the disagreement was over whether this empowerment by the Spirit—which in the mainstream church received visible expression as ordination in the rite of laying on hands and addressing this very Spirit—could in the case of women also be recognized beyond the prophetic charisma. It is conceivable that Quintilla received this vision under the psychic pressure of the disagreement. Women could have then appealed to her for the legitimation of their claim. And not only women: men in the Quintillist movement also recognized female ministers and may have defended them against their opponents from their own ranks as well as against the Catholics.

Nonetheless, two things speak against this hypothesis. (1) The appearance explains the cultic importance of Pepuza, which from the beginning was the center of the New Prophecy: therefore it is unlikely that the vision comes from a later phase of the movement. (2) The appearance of Christ in female form in the traditional logion has a certain unreflective naturalness. No purpose is connected with it. That makes it unlikely that the vision originated as a tendentious oracle against the background of the disagreement over the women's issue.

The later reflective conviction in the movement around Quintilla that "in Christ there is neither male nor female" has found its expression here in immediate spontaneity. In a bold inspiration it also encompasses the person of the Redeemer: the earthly Jesus was a man, but Christ is no longer to be grasped in the categories of male and female. So now he can appear to his disciples in male or female form. We have seen in the martyrdom visions how Perpetua in the moment of her highest identification with Christ, in the moment when she in symbolic battle defeated Satan, changed into a man. In the real martyrdom of Blandina the Christians were able to see in her the crucified One. With Prisca the identification of a woman with Christ reaches its high point, because now it is not she but he who changes and assumes the form of the opposite sex.

Summary. The oracle, which speaks of the calling of the prophetess and of the heavenly Jerusalem becoming visible, seems to belong at the beginning of the movement. In a time when women were suppressed even in the Phrygian church, a small group around Quintilla appealed to the person and message of Prisca in order to ward off this development. Yet those who defended the equality of women and men in the church ultimately were defeated there also. In Prisca's vision this consciousness of equality in early Christendom found its boldest and most beautiful expression.

Conclusion

Detailed examination has largely confirmed Kraft's thesis: Montanus was not a leading prophet in the "Montanist" movement. The oracles ascribed to him point rather to a later phase of the conflict. Maximilla's oracles are more moderate in language and at least one is attested early. As the last prophetess she was presumably subject to more persecution than the others. The sayings of both express the self-consciousness of a prophet or prophetess: in certain situations they are seized by the Spirit and can then impart inspired messages to individuals or the church in the name of God or Christ.

In the three sayings handed down from Prisca we can still perceive contents of her proclamation: the prophetess criticizes the Gnostic deprecation of human corporeality (in order to encourage asceticism, according to Tertullian); elsewhere she emphasizes internalization as the way to charismatic experience. On account of her vision of Christ, Pepuza became the spiritual center of the movement. All of this suggests—more cannot be said on the basis of the few surviving fragments—that Prisca was the real initiator and inspirer of the movement that was organized and structured by Montanus.

This impression is confirmed by Tertullian's testimony: he mentions Montanus only twice (once alone as the spokesman of the Paraclete, once together with Prisca and Maximilla); by contrast, he quotes Prisca and introduces her sayings with a certain solemnity: "The holy prophetess Prisca proclaims"; "The Paraclete speaks through the prophetess Prisca." Thus she also appears in his writings as the most significant figure of the New Prophecy.

e. The Opposition: Why?

If the New Prophecy in the second century neither advocated false doctrine nor was extremely ascetic or extremely apocalyptic, then why did it evoke strong opposition, even in its early period, which flared up again and again and finally led to its annihilation? Did this lie perhaps in the special role that women played first in this movement and later in this church? Before we address these questions, let us take a brief look at the last centuries of Montanist history.[251]

When Constantine, by means of imperial legislation, took action against all "heretics" in order to place a great, united church in service to his empire as state religion, he was not able to implement the prescribed measures (confiscation of churches and general prohibition of assembly even in private houses) "in Phrygia and the neighboring countries"; for "there they [the Phrygians] had become extremely numerous, as they still are today"—so reports Sozomen around 450.[252] From Eusebius, who passes on the emperor's decree, we learn a further detail: book raids were carried out in order to be able to convict heretics on the basis of their manuscripts[253]—a method that had been applied in the general persecution of Christians shortly before by the not yet converted emperors!

In the Theodosian legislation the measures became considerably more severe. In 398 the Montanist clergy in the cities of the empire are excluded from public life; if they hold gatherings in the country, they are banished and their property seized. Even those who rent a house for such assemblies are severely punished: if they do not chase away and denounce the heretics, the house is confiscated. A book burning is ordered before the eyes of the judges; those who hide writings are subject to the death penalty.[254]

Even more pointed is the law enacted in 407 by Honorius in Rome. It states specifically that the "Manichaeans and the Phrygians or Priscillianists"[255] are to be most severely punished. Their offense is declared a *crimen publicum,* for "the attack on the divine religion injures the rights of all." Montanists lose the right of disposition over their property: they may neither receive nor give gifts and legacies, they have no right to buy or sell, and contracts are prohibited. As with lèse-majesté, these sanctions may also be applied posthumously. Slaves can speak out against their masters without fear. Houses in which prayer meetings have taken place are confiscated; if the owner was unaware, then the manager is whipped and sentenced to a life of slave labor in the mines. Even provincial administrators are threatened with severe fines if they do not prosecute heretics according to the law.[256]

In the West this law seems to have actually meant the end of the Phrygian church. We read that the Roman bishop Innocent (401–417), who possibly had decisive influence on the imperial legislation of Honorius, "found many Cataphrygians, whom he banished into the exile of a monastery."[257] After this only once are actual existing Montanists mentioned, by Gregory the Great: he counts them among the heretics whose baptism is not valid.[258]

In the East, however, things were different. Here a law from the year 410 shows the New Prophecy's courage in martyrdom: "They scorn these punishments."[259] Now they are excluded from the higher official positions and expressly kept in the lower ones. This indicates a certain leniency in comparison with the total exclusion from public life decreed in the West, yet the offices left to them were positions of service without status.[260] In 415 the prohibition of assembly is renewed, and the installation of clergy forbidden. "Buildings"—that is, churches with their treasures—are turned over to the orthodox.[261] In 423 the measures against "the Manichaeans and the Phrygians, who are also called Pepuzists or Priscillianists or another still unknown name," are again affirmed.[262] The law of 428 again applies to the followers of the Phrygian church and many other heretics a strict prohibition of assembly "on Roman soil."[263]

Such a massive proceeding against Christian dissidents is astonishing and frightening. And yet not even all these laws were able to break the Montanist resistance. More than a hundred years later Justinian has to repeat the regulations, which now name heretics and "pagans" in the same breath.[264] He himself gives the reasons for this new enactment: "We have learned that the heretics dare, despite our laws, still to gather and install leaders of their mania, to call them exarchs, to perform baptisms, and try to claim privileges if they have work places within the holy district, which should be reserved for the orthodox."[265]

Thus the old penal measures are again intensified and turned especially against the Phrygian church: "They must all be chased [out of Constantinople]." Indeed, they are no longer permitted to stay in the holy district. Their love feasts are also prohibited because they try there "to win the simple souls." They are even forbidden to sell slaves, so that these cannot be used as secret missionaries. The poor among them may not receive public assistance, and anyone who helps these poor will be fined. The administrators must also pay a large fine if they prove to be negligent in the persecution in their provinces. The Jews and other heretics are permitted, nevertheless, to conduct trials among themselves if they do not speak out against the orthodox; the Phrygians, however, are denied every legal action.[266]

In this way the feared sect was slowly stamped out—but with such sacrifices! In 550 the Byzantine historian Procopius reported "that the Montanists in Phrygia locked themselves in their own churches, set them on fire, and burned themselves up."[267] In the same year the Asian bishop John is supposed to have found the bones of Montanus, Maximilla, and Prisca and consigned them to the flames, along with the Montanist churches, which burned to the ground.[268]

Pierre de Labriolle, at the end of his presentation of the resistance of the New Prophets, cannot withhold his admiration: "Where does one find (apart from the Manichaean sect) another example of such a stubborn will to live, of such persistent and incredible effort to stand firm in the face of extreme hostility by an oppressive coalition of religion and politics? The seed of highest spirituality that the Phrygian prophets planted in souls must have been of unique quality to be able to survive under such unfavorable conditions and produce such a long-lasting bloom!"[269] This raises all the more, however, the question of the motives for rejection on the part of the imperial church. Was the special role of women in the New Prophecy an important reason for fighting it?

The Question of Women

So it may seem when one reads later sources. For example, in sixth-century Gaul the practice of two priests, who let women take the cup and distribute the blood of Christ as "cohostesses" (*conhospitae*) in the celebration of the Eucharist, is criticized. Three bishops energetically forbid the participation of such *sociae*, for they indignantly believe that they are experiencing here the appearance of the "terrible sect" that the fathers of the East called the "Pepodian" sect and condemned. Here the prophetic movement is all but forgotten—the name "Pepodian," behind which one still divines "Pepuzian," is derived from the "founder Pepodius"! Only one thing remains: the specter of women at the altar![270] A comment of Ambrosiaster attests to similar ignorance: he holds the practice of ordaining deaconesses, which was highly orthodox in the East, to be the product of the Phrygian heresy.[271]

One thing is clear: the polemic against the Montanist church grows with increasing temporal distance from the founders. Their members—like the followers of other confessions in general—are increasingly equated with non-Christians ("Jews and pagans"):[272] converts are even required to be rebaptized![273] In the worst case they are indicted for all sorts of crimes: blasphemy, deception, child murder, adultery, idolatry.[274] Naturally, this polemic also concerned Montanus: priest of idols, circumcised one, half man, adulterer, criminal, a horror, an impure and godless one![275] Nevertheless, he advanced to become head of the sect: in Cyril of Jerusalem and in the *Discussion of a Montanist and an Orthodox* he has the title of "exarch," which corresponds to a bishop.[276] Yet in Cyril he is the "exarch of the evil ones"; the Council of Sardica even made him the "leader of all heretics."[277]

With Prisca and Maximilla, however, the polemic is far more stereotyped. In addition to the derogatory "females" (Ger. "Weiber"), which is found far more often in translations than in the Greek and Latin original texts,[278] one insult appears—at first only in the West!—again and again: "crazy women" (*insanae feminae*), "crazy seers" (*insanae vates*).[279] Certainly the biblical designation *prophetess* was consciously replaced by the "pagan" term *seer*. Epiphanius had connected Prisca and Maximilla with Pythia—naturally in a deprecatory way.[280] This corresponds to the characterization of Montanus as priest of Apollo in the *Discussion*.[281] Both witness indirectly to the importance of early Christian prophecy, which is compared with the famous Delphic oracle. In the East the anti-Montanist polemic grows—possibly under Western influence—only after the annihilation of the New Prophets: in the great historical work of the seventh century, the *Chronikon Paschale*, we again find the "crazy" women; an undatable Pseudo-Chrysostom makes them "adulteresses"; and Timothy of Constantinople (seventh century) even calls them "whores."[282] A fifth-century Western source had already treated them similarly: the "highly obscene followers" (*obscenissimae sequaces*)[283] of Montanus.

Yet these insults say nothing about the development of the Montanist church; they merely testify to a growing misogyny and even contempt for women in certain orthodox circles! Here it is no longer only a question of forbidding teaching and refusing church ministries, but of a denigration of the female sex in general. Prophetesses are not even granted the negative "honorary title" of "heresiarch," of "heretic leader": they are simply crazy or immoral or both!

In the early reactions to the Phrygian movement we do not hear such tones. Instead, opponents are on the defensive: "We recognize the [true] prophetesses," they hurry to emphasize, and they do not admonish the women that they have to be quiet in church. In the early period only one person did: Origen (d. 253), the famous theologian from the catechetical school in Alexandria. For him the "speaking in the church"[284] apparently practiced by Prisca and Maximilla is plainly proof that they must be "false prophetesses," for—so he argues—genuine prophetesses would not have spoken *in the church*. In a commentary on 1 Corinthians[285] he makes their (male) followers especially responsible for this "abuse": "All speak and can speak when they receive a revelation, but 'the women,' says the apostle, 'are to be silent in the church.' This command is not obeyed by the disciples of the women, those who let themselves be taught by Prisca and Maximilla." Yet "benevolently" Origen adopts the arguments of the New Prophets: they had apparently referred to the four daughters of Philip (Acts 21:9), Deborah (Judges 5), Miriam (Ex. 15:20–21), Huldah (2 Kings 22:14ff.), and Anna (Luke 2:36ff.) as biblical prophetesses. The Alexandrian does not argue with this, but the daughters of Philip, he says, did not speak in the church—at least, there is nothing about it in Acts. And Deborah? She made no speech to the people like Isaiah and Jeremiah. But Huldah? Yes, she spoke to the people, yet only in her own house. Anna did not speak "in the church" either. And finally Miriam? She spoke only to a group of women! It is obvious how differently Origen must interpret *ekklēsia* in these cases in order to "prove" that the genuine prophetesses observed the same rules as those later prescribed to the only women ministers in the church, the deaconesses!

Only once do we find similar debate on the role of women in the New Prophecy; it is in the fourth century in *Discussion of a Montanist and an Orthodox:* there it is no longer public speaking but public writing that offends. Again the "Montanist" cites Deborah and the daughters of Philip; the "orthodox" also concedes to him Miriam, as well as Mary, the mother of Jesus (as author of the Magnificat). The debate begins with a trick question:

> *MONTANIST:* Why do you reject the saints Maximilla and Priscilla and assert that women are not allowed to speak prophetically? Were the four daughters of Philip not prophetically gifted, and was Deborah not a prophetess? And why does the apostle speak of "any woman who prays or prophesies with her head unveiled" [1 Cor. 11:5] if women may not pray and speak prophetically?

> *ORTHODOX:* We have nothing against the prophecy of women. Holy Mary also spoke prophetically when she said: "From now on all generations will call me blessed" [Luke 1:48]. And as he[286] says, St. Philip had daughters who spoke prophetically; also Miriam, Aaron's sister, spoke prophetically. But we do not allow them to speak in the church and exercise authority over men [1 Tim. 2:12], or to write books in their own name. That, you see, is their "praying and speaking prophetically without head covering," and in this way they humiliate their head, the husband. Could not Mary, the holy mother of God, have written books in her name? But she did not do it, in order not to dishonor the head by exercising authority over men.

M.: Thus praying and speaking prophetically without head covering are the same as writing books?

O.: Exactly.

M.: When holy Mary says: "From now on all generations will call me blessed," she is speaking with frankness [*parrhēsia*] and without head covering, right?

O.: She has the evangelist as a veil. For the Gospel is not written in her name.

M.: Do not confuse allegories with dogmas!

[A lengthy debate follows on allegories.]

M.: So, you do not want to recognize Prisca and Maximilla because they wrote books?

O.: Not only that, but because they were false prophetesses, along with their exarch Montanus.

M.: How are they false prophetesses?

O.: Do they say the same thing as Montanus?

M.: Yes.

O.: Montanus was accused of saying things that contradict the scripture; consequently they are to be rejected like him.[287]

Thus ends the *Discussion.* Again, it is obvious that the "scriptural proof " against Prisca and Maximilla is far-fetched. Nonetheless, the "orthodox" stresses: "We have nothing against the prophecy of women"! Yet to hold to this testimony in the fourth century was no more than lip service: spontaneous public prophecy in worship was no longer practiced. It is surprising that the "orthodox" plainly postulates a male pseudonym for women writers—unfortunately he does not name a concrete case from his time. Women who write anonymously or under a pen name do so, nevertheless, for "political" reasons, not to express subordination and "feminine modesty," as is insinuated here. Finally, we must note that here the "saints" Prisca and Maximilla are played off against "holy" Mary: a further indication of the veneration of early Christian women, who increasingly fall into the shadow of the cult of Mary!

In the *Discussion* one misses the women bishops and presbyters attested by Epiphanius. Since in the older texts we never find an allusion to official liturgical actions by Prisca, Maximilla, or any other prophetess,[288] we must assume that they in fact did not perform such acts. Does this speak of a "modesty" of women, a consciousness of not being permitted to claim church ministries for themselves? On the contrary, we must presume that they ranked the free charisma of prophecy higher than the ministry of the elected servants of the church. As we have seen, this ranking is attested for the early period in the *Didache;* there the prophets are expressly allowed at the Sunday celebrations "to give thanks as much as they want."[289] How the worship services and the Eucharist were celebrated in Phrygia at the time of Prisca, Maximilla, and Montanus we do not know.

The high esteem for charismatic gifts that cannot in any way be institutionalized expresses a certain understanding of Christianity and church: inspired proclamation and convincing conduct are the guarantee of spiritual authority, whereas organizational and cultic functions play only a subordinate role. This spiritual attitude is also familiar from Paul, who boasts that he baptized almost no one in Corinth (1 Cor. 1:16–17). In the later period such an attitude made prophetesses appear arrogant, yet at the same time it protected them from the reproach from orthodox circles of having claimed priestly functions for themselves. Thus the women's question is not to be seen as the real bone of contention.

Authority in the Church

At the beginning of this chapter we raised the question whether Montanus was the "founder and head" of the Phrygian prophetic movement. In the meantime, we have seen that these "titles" were more appropriate for Prisca. Hence, for Pierre de Labriolle's somewhat puzzled assertion that "we are more poorly informed about Montanus than about most of the great heresiarchs of the second century,"[290] there is a very simple explanation: Montanus was not a "great heresiarch"! One may presume a feminist interest behind this logic, yet it is not a matter of belittling the services of the "advocate of the prophetesses" in the Phrygian movement. It was not his fault that because of his gender he moved more and more into the foreground in the course of the centuries, so that the "New Prophecy" finally became "Montanism."[291] With regard to the forgotten women, it is doubtless a justified concern to demonstrate how this happened.

Yet this is only one aspect of the phenomenon. Just as important is the fact that the New Prophecy did not define itself in terms of a "head." Through the fixation on Montanus, not only was a woman suppressed by a man, but also a certain ecclesiastical structure—the episcopal—was projected back on the prophetic movement and thus an important concern of the early resistance was blurred.

In the second century the decision in the conflict between charismatically legitimated authorities and elected ministers was still open. The vehement rejection of the New Prophecy articulated the reaction of certain Christian circles that were increasingly organized episcopally. This endeavor is especially clear in the letters of the well-known martyr-bishop Ignatius (d. 110), which he, while on the way from Antioch to his trial in Rome, directed to several churches in order to encourage them to support their bishop. Bauer points out that only certain churches in Asia Minor were addressed, and their selection was probably not accidental.[292] At the beginning of the second century the bishop of Antioch seems to have represented a minority position, yet Bauer concedes: "Naturally, it is certainly possible that in individual towns the Ignatius group actually represented the majority. But in view of Ignatius's trembling excitement, one cannot as a rule take this for granted in advance."[293] Thus his letters promoted the new episcopal structure to possible sympathizers and indirectly fought the churches who wanted to hold fast to the original prophetic-charismatic order. Still, the opposition between these two directions in this early phase must not be overdrawn.[294]

Even in the few circles oriented toward the mainstream church, the attempt to legitimize prophecy through succession shows a tendency to "officialize" free charisma; we have already heard about an attempted ordination of prophets! Conversely, bishops tried to gain a hearing for themselves as charismatics. Thus Ignatius acted completely in "Montanist" style: "I . . . cry with God's voice: Hold to the bishop and to the presbyteriate and to the deacons."[295] Thus episcopal church order is legitimated here prophetically! Otto Michel has correctly pointed out that in Ignatius one can already detect a slight weakening of the charisma so highly regarded originally: "Ignatius was a prophet, martyr, and bishop; not a prophet as bishop, but a prophet as martyr. His martyrdom turned him into a prophet. That is the sign of a later time."[296] The various ministries are gradually placed in a hierarchical relationship to each other, though the order is controversial.

In the middle of the third century Cyprian of Carthage, who was certainly no Montanist,[297] still appeals to "revelations" in the manner of a prophet, in order to justify the measures he has taken.[298] As a bishop he especially had to deal with the legitimation problem in his church, since he had hidden during the persecution under Decius and therefore could not appear with the authority of a martyr. Thus he cited instead his own or others' visions.[299] Indeed, he emphasized as proof of authenticity even the frequent ecstasy of two young prophets (*pueri*) staying with him, who were still at an "innocent age"![300]

Ambivalence and thus the danger of abuse are inherent in charismatic phenomena; whether this reproach can be made against Cyprian is not at issue here.[301] Nonetheless, his attempt to prevail with prophetic instead of episcopal authority shows the high regard that the witnesses of the Spirit still had in his time. Charismatic legitimation was recognized as *via extraordinaria* and indeed in some cases valued higher than the *via ordinaria,* that is, election by the church. Regarding a confessor that Cyprian wants to ordain presbyter, it is expressly stated that he became a member of the clergy "not through voting [*humana suffragatione*] but through divine empowerment [*divina dignatione*]."[302] It is true that the candidate Celerinus hesitated, but a nocturnal vision encouraged him to accept the ecclesiastical ministry. We have here again the concept of the "graceful empowerment," which can refer both to the "witness" and to the prophetic charisma.[303] Thus Cyprian recognized both the authority of the martyr and that of the prophet, but at least that of the confessor remains subordinated to that of the bishop, for the charismatically legitimated are additionally ordained. In regard to prophecy we learn from him that some Christian contemporaries remained skeptical about it: "Some find dreams ridiculous and appearances silly."[304] Were these rationalists true followers of the church hierarchy? Not at all: they were "above all those who would rather believe everything that goes against the bishops than to give credence to the bishop himself"—that is, obviously generally critical church members!

The opposition to the movement in Phrygia has its roots in these conflicts over authority in the church. Early churches, as the *Didache* describes them, built entirely on the "foundation of the apostles *and* prophets."[305] This old foundation began increasingly to shake, and out of the original unity of prophetic-apostolic charisma now came an opposition on which the spirits separated: apostles *or* prophets? We have already seen that in this dispute the question of succession was brought into play in order to legitimate one's own position.[306] Nevertheless, whereas at first the same conduct of predecessors and successors in faithfulness to the original message was regarded as the prerequisite for an authentic *diadochē*, in the controversy the concept increasingly gained a legal character: the chain of the laying on of hands. In Catholicism *diadochē* finally became the classical technical term for "apostolic succession";[307] by contrast, the idea of a "prophetic succession" fell into oblivion. Apostles are now only the twelve, and the elected and legally ordained bishops are their sole successors.

Irenaeus himself, who can be considered the "architect" of the apostolic succession of bishops, still advocated the middle position, for he continued to respect the special charismatic authority of prophetesses and prophets. Kraft has correctly pointed out that this theologian, who was shaped by the martyr church in Lyon, used the title *bishop* very sparingly and persistently addressed the Roman bishop Victor in particular as "presbyter."[308] Yet in Catholicism the day was finally carried by those who saw in the strong leadership position of the one bishop the best guarantee of church unity and who therefore strengthened his authority on all levels.

How did development proceed in the New Prophecy? In the beginning it apparently had no one individual—male or female—at its head. The spirituality of the movement was determined by prophetic personalities of both sexes, above all Prisca and Maximilla; others took care of the practical organization: here Montanus and Theodotus must have especially distinguished themselves. Did the original ethos of equality take root in the institutions of the Phrygian church? Given the few extant sources, the question is hard to answer, yet it seems rather as if mainstream church development "rubbed off." It seems not to have been only the work of the opponents, however, when the New Prophecy finally became Montanism: rather, the Phrygian church developed its own hierarchical structure, in which women hardly played a role.

Yet one point is to be noted: since in Catholicism, which was now the imperial church under the care of the emperor, the power of the bishops had considerably increased, there were still clear differences between the two church structures even in the fourth century. We learn this from Jerome, who voiced criticism about it in a letter to Marcella, a theologically well-educated Roman woman,[309] who had had a discussion with a Montanist:

With us the bishops have the place of the apostles; with them the bishop is in third place. In first place they have the patriarchs[310] of Pepuza in Phrygia; in second place, those they call *koinōnoi*;[311] in third place—and that means, so to speak, last place—they put the bishops, as if their religion is more demanding because they put in last place what we have in first place.[312]

The testimony about the deviating church structure of the Phrygians is confirmed by the *Codex Justinianus,* which lists the ministries of the Montanists: "Patriarchs, *koinonoi,* bishops, presbyters, deacons, and additional clergy."[313] What functions did these patriarchs and "sharers" (*koinōnoi*) have? Since we have no other sources about them, we can only make assumptions.[314] De Labriolle sees behind both titles "the charismatic element of the hierarchy, in memory, on the one hand, of Montanus and the prophetesses and, on the other, of zealous acolytes like Alcibiades and Themiso."[315]

Nonetheless, it is also possible that the Phrygian "patriarchs" had functions similar to the Catholic "bishops," whereas Phrygian "bishops" were presumably local church leaders outside the large urban centers.[316] Heinz Kraft: "In Montanism an earlier state in the structure of church law . . . still obtained. Here the bishop does not have the importance that he receives in Catholicism but occupies a relatively insignificant rank."[317] Between patriarchs and bishops we find the "sharers," the "order" of the charismatics, located where the "confessors" had their place in many early church structures, as we saw. A possible interpretation of *koinōnos* also points in the direction of martyresses and martyrs: it is supposed to express the "sharing" in the suffering of Christ. We find the connection several times in the New Testament,[318] and Polycarp of Smyrna, apparently the first executed bishop, is called a *koinōnos* of Christ.[319]

Behind the Phrygian hierarchy Kraft presumes an analogy to Jewish structure,[320] since the Greek equivalent of the rabbi title is used in a canon from the end of the fourth century for converted clergy of the Phrygian church: they are to be rebaptized even if they were *megistoi* ("the greatest").[321] Kraft identifies them with the *koinōnoi,* yet it could as well mean the patriarchs or both together. According to de Labriolle the title *patriarch* is perhaps also of Jewish origin. Thus it is possible that at the head of the Phrygian church was a collegial committee that consisted of patriarchs and *koinōnoi.* This may be indicated by the plural that Jerome uses when he speaks of "the patriarchs of Pepuza"; one would actually expect only one there. Were there women in this collegium? As we saw, that was probably the case only in the group around Quintilla, and we do not know how long she was able to maintain her position. The women who served in Gaul as *sociae* in worship certainly do not belong to the Phrygian church; a connection with the old title *koinōnos* is extremely unlikely.[322]

It is surprising to find prophets no longer in the description of the Phrygian hierarchy. Still, the practice of spontaneous prophecy died out everywhere around the end of the third century, so that the martyrs and martyresses alone remained the bearers of charismatic authority and now carried on the witness of the prophetesses and prophets in the churches. Perhaps the term *koinōnoi* also implied a special sharing of the Spirit, a special nearness to God, but that cannot be demonstrated. After the time of the persecutions the order of the confessors also disappeared; now the heirs and successors were the men and women ascetics, and later the nuns and monks. Yet none of these found a place in the church hierarchies.

The Phrygian churches also participated in this general development in Christianity. Thus the *koinōnoi* may have maintained a memory of the charismatic early period, which hardly corresponded to concrete reality.[323] In fact, an institutionalization process had also begun here, and since Montanus had laid the foundations for holding the prophetic movement together, he could with a certain justification be regarded as the "founder." In the fourth century two similarly structured churches faced each other: one knew itself committed to the prophetic heritage, while the other increasingly negated it.

On the basis of this development it would be a mistake to see in the "church of the prophets" a kind of incarnation of what is positive, antihierarchical, and "feminine," and to see in the "church of the bishops" the incarnation of what is negative, patriarchal, and "masculine." Yet it cannot be denied that the early New Prophecy was at first a community of women and men equals, whereas Catholicism, which was developing into the episcopal imperial church, increasingly represented a sexual hierarchy or, to put it better, carried the increasingly emphasized ideas of hierarchy over to the sexes. In this sense there is a causal relationship between the clericalization of the ministries and the exclusion of women from them.

Nonetheless, we cannot now turn around and glorify the long-bedeviled New Prophecy. Even if one ignores all the polemics of the anti-Montanists, justified points of criticism remain: in particular, the danger of all prophecy of sliding down into subjectivity, exclusivity, and arbitrariness. Catholicism wanted to defend itself against the dangers of pseudoprophecy, yet in the process it succumbed to the opposite danger. As Hans von Campenhausen writes: "The progress of ecclesiastical development everywhere ultimately leads to a strengthening and ever more emphatic predominance of the ministerial element and its one-sided authority, beside which the spiritual life of the church more and more shrivels up and is generally ignored."[324] One may ask whether ecclesiastical development would have taken this form if prophecy's principle of equality had been transformed into a brotherly-sisterly ministerial structure, so that women could have likewise exercised authority.

Inspiration and Revelation

In a comparison of charismatic awakenings in the course of church history from the feminine perspective, Elaine C. Huber has made "authority through inspiration" the key concept of her investigation.[325] Whether this is especially characteristic of women is a question we shall postpone for the time being.[326] Yet the concept aptly characterizes the central question that was at issue in the second century. In fact, in the controversy over prophetesses and prophets it was a question not only of whether they were ranked above or below the bishops; just as important

was the related question of whether their prophecies were to be considered inspired revelations. This in turn led to a fundamental problem: Was "revelation"
to be understood as a unique event that ended in the past or as a dynamic process
that continues forever?

How central this theme was in the disagreements over the New Prophecy is
shown by the fact that the *role of the Paraclete* is the point that in the various positions and presentations of the movement through the centuries is the most often named and discussed in the battle against the Phrygian church. A central
theme here is the New Testament statement: "When the Spirit of truth comes,
he will guide you into all the truth" (John 16:13). How was this saying to be interpreted: in the sense of a continued growth of revelation or only in the sense
of a better comprehension? In the discussion about this question, in addition to
the promises of the Gospel of John about the Paraclete,[327] the Pauline texts on
the charismata played an especially important role.[328]

The New Prophecy and other early Christian movements were apparently
convinced that their proclamation continued the revelation process that began
in the old people of God and found in Jesus, the quintessential prophet,[329] a high
point but not the end. How, then, did the advocates of the idea of a unique,
closed revelation deal with the fact that many of their sisters and brothers in the
faith appeared with the claim of speaking prophetically and imparting revelations? One answer was the attempt to limit prophecy to a certain time period.[330]
Yet this argumentation could not be used until spontaneous charismatic proclamation in the worship service was only seldom practiced. Here it was already a
matter of the *written* revelations of Prisca, Maximilla, and Montanus, that is, the
question whether these writings could be considered inspired by the Spirit in the
same way that was assumed for the books of the Bible.

Now, the *temporal boundary* is set quite differently. The most radical opponents of new revelations appealed to the scriptural saying, "The law and the
prophets were in effect until John came" (Luke 16:16), and derived from this
that after Christ there could be no more prophets at all. We find this quotation
as an anti-Montanist argument in an Anonymus of the fourth century: "Let us
also speak against this wretched Phrygian, who asserts that after the Lord came
Montanus and Priscilla. . . . How could another prophet appear after the coming of the Redeemer?"[331] The same position is reflected in the *Discussion* and in
Didymus[332] in the form of a Montanist reproach against the orthodox: "You assert that after Christ there are no prophets!" Yet the accusation is rejected; the
orthodox naturally also know that in the Gospel the Lord himself promised the
sending of prophets: "Therefore I send you prophets, sages, and scribes, some
of whom you will kill and crucify, and some you will flog in your synagogues and
pursue from town to town" (Matt. 23:34). The *Discussion* has a comment on
this scriptural saying: "Thus we confess that there were prophets after Christ and
that the apostles themselves likewise possessed the gift of prophecy." This argumentation is used only to reject the attempt to give the Christian prophetesses
and prophets who lived after the apostles a higher authority than those whose
proclamation is contained in the New Testament. Didymus, by contrast, inter-

prets the statement about prophets much more restrictively: "By this the Redeemer meant the apostles, who proclaimed a great deal about what is coming,
the end time, and the kingdom of heaven." With a "perhaps" he allows the idea
that the "martyr-bishops" could also have been meant. Then he names recognized prophetesses: the daughters of Philip, Miriam, and Mary, the mother of
Jesus—since these left no writings, they are not a problem for his theological concept! Thus this theologian links the prophetic charisma at first exclusively with
the apostles and then lets it be absorbed into the office of the bishop.

A link with the apostles is similarly found in Irenaeus: the "fullness of revelation" is transferred to them at Pentecost in all perfection without the possibility
of later expansions.[333] Yet the bishop of Lyon did not have the New Prophecy in
mind but Gnostic directions, which distinguished between a simple revelation for
ordinary believers and, for the "perfect," an additional esoteric revelation by the
resurrected One. Thus for Irenaeus it was mainly a question of being against the
division of Christians into two classes. He does not sharply distinguish himself
from the idea of a gradually developing revelation, for it corresponds to a basic
tenet of his theology—yet the idea of only an "imperfect" revelation in the New
Testament is unbearable for him.[334]

In addition, the time boundary of Pentecost obviously became problematic,
since if taken strictly, it would exclude the apostle Paul as a bearer of revelation.
We still find traces of this discussion in Augustine, yet in the fourth century the
debate had already shifted: an end to revelation is generally accepted. Yet since
the end is connected more and more with the coming of the Spirit, new theories
arise regarding the time of the descent of the Paraclete: he came not at Pentecost but, as some say, in Paul, or, as the Phrygians say, in Montanus and Priscilla,
or in Mani.[335]

A further "scriptural proof" that is supposed to quash the claim of the New
Prophecy with a still later time limit comes to us through Origen. In his Matthew
commentary he deals with the argument that the end of prophetic proclamation
came with the demise of Jerusalem—that is, in the year 70—for according to the
word of the Lord, no prophet can be killed outside Jerusalem (Luke 13:33).[336]
For the Alexandrian this is not valid, since Acts mentions the prophecies of
Agabus and the daughters of Philip. How does he solve this (pseudo)problem?
By spiritualizing the sense of the text: every righteous person is "in Jerusalem."[337] Yet Origen does not want this rejection to support the authority of
Christian prophets; on the contrary, for him they do not count as mediators of
revelation, for in his opinion this came to an end in Christ.[338] In what, then, does
the work of the Paraclete consist? "The Advocate, the Holy Spirit . . . will teach
you everything, and remind you of all that I have said to you" (John 14:26). The
theologian favors a restrictive reading of the Gospel of John, which later prevailed: the Paraclete teaches only what the Lord taught.[339] Revelation can happen only through the passing on of the words of the Lord. That means concretely
that Christian prophetesses and prophets do not receive the Spirit in order to impart new revelations but solely to interpret what is already present. Thus the *dispute over prophecy* gradually becomes a *dispute over the scripture*.

Yet in the early period the idea of a temporal limitation could not prevail at first: too deeply was the conviction anchored in many that the Spirit, who had spoken from Jesus, had descended upon Christians and now spoke from them. Thus those who wanted to reject the claim of the New Prophecy had to offer other valid reasons. We find three kinds: (1) The *contents* of prophecy are examined for their agreement with the "scripture"[340] or with the "doctrine of the church."[341] We have already seen that anti-Montanist criticism hardly found any real substance here. (2) The *form* of the prophecy is criticized: ecstatic phenomena are rejected as allegedly unbibilical. This opposition was apparently fabricated or at least exaggerated. (3) The *conduct* of the prophets and prophetesses is discredited: this made their proclamation also seem unbelievable. This tactic was extensively used against the New Prophets by Anonymus and Apollonius, as we have seen. Apparently this argument is the oldest in the disagreement over true and false prophecy; it comes from a time when many prophets and prophetesses were active in the churches: genuine charismatics were believable because the testimony of their lives guaranteed the authenticity of their message.

What claim to revelation did the prophetesses and prophets of the Phrygian movement make themselves? One thing is certain: in their prophecy they saw the "charisma" realized, the gracious gift of the Spirit that Paul discussed. The express reference to the "Paraclete" of John's Gospel, by contrast, is first found in Tertullian:[342] we are already familiar with his presentation of the work of the Spirit. Now, does the distinction he introduced between *doctrine* and *discipline* correspond to the ideas of the early New Prophecy? We do not have a single witness to this. The obvious conclusion seems to be, rather, that because the proclamation of the first generation did not refer to doctrinal questions but rather was entirely praxis oriented, it was possible for the theologian to use this distinction to limit the claim of revelation and thus assure the authority of scripture and church doctrine. Yet in this milder form revelation remained for Tertullian a dynamic process. His division of salvation according to revelation media—law and prophets, gospel of Christ, prophecies of the Paraclete—encompassed the time until the end of the world: the New Prophets do not appear at all as "the last prophets."

In the beginnings of the Phrygian movement there was no argument over the time at which revelation or a part of it was supposed to end, since from their viewpoint there could be absolutely no talk of such an end within historical time. When Hippolytus of Rome indignantly reports that the followers of the New Prophecy "venerate these women more than the apostles"—that many, indeed, hold the opinion that "in them something more happened than in Christ"[343]— he has hit upon something absolutely correct: the idea that revelation and salvation history have moved on since Jesus' death and that therefore today has something "more" than yesterday. In the century and a half between the Pentecost event and the manifestations of the Spirit in Phrygia, imperfect things had been left behind and more perfect ones had come, and this process would continue. Nothing indicates that the New Prophecy understood itself as the final revelation.

They are by no means alone in this opinion. In the next chapter we will meet ideas that were entertained in Gnosticism. Yet even in the traditions of the mainstream church the view was widespread that revelation is an open, dynamic process that always presupposes new revelations.[344] As we saw, the redactor who handed down the visions of Perpetua and Saturus together with his account of the brave deaths of two women and four men was firmly convinced that the proofs of the Spirit described by him were greater than those in the beginning. "In the last days it will be, God declares, that I will pour out my Spirit upon all flesh, and your sons and your daughters shall prophesy" (Acts 2:17)—like Irenaeus, the anonymous author from Carthage quotes the well-known promise and places it as a motto over the double "testimony." He continues, "Since we acknowledge and honor the new promised visions just like the [old] prophecies, and also count the other deeds of power of the Holy Spirit . . . among the instruments of the church,[345] we must therefore hold fast to [them] and celebrate [them] through reading to the glory of God." (1.5).[346] Thus the author naturally presumes that his report will be read publicly in the prayer meetings of the church.

Thus we come to the conclusion that in the second century the idea of an "end" of revelations was the opinion of a minority rather than a majority of Christians. Therefore the appeal to scripture as the "old" revelation was not at all plausible: instead, age spoke against it. For us it seems very understandable that ultimately, in the face of never-ending "private revelations," which were used for very different purposes, criteria of truth and binding force had to be developed. In the time of Prisca and Maximilla the problematic aspects were just becoming visible. Therefore the prophetesses could still in all spontaneity regard and impart their experiences and insights, emanating from the emotion of prayer, as "revelations." The distinction introduced by Tertullian between a once-and-for-all revealed "faith" and an evolving "discipline" represented an attempt to harmonize two fundamentally different concepts of revelation. His very attempt, however, also shows that it is not so much "scripture" and "New Prophecy" that are problematic, but rather their application in service to an ideology.

With regard to the historical development, we must first simply note that through the establishment of a "canon" of Holy Scripture the idea of a revelation process continuing to the end of time moved increasingly into the background, until finally only the "old" revelations were still regarded as normative. Yet this statement necessarily raises the question, Was the canon already ideology? This complex problem will not be discussed here, yet there is no question that by this means a selection in the tradition occurred that was certainly not objective and impartial with regard to the role of women. Already in moving from the early to the late writings in the New Testament one can demonstrate an increasing resistance to feminine claims through the techniques of silence and reinterpretation.[347] The later exclusive fixation on the twelve apostles as the mediators of revelation to the disadvantage of prophetesses and prophets led to women being completely eliminated as inspired recipients and bearers of revelations of the Christian message, although Mary Magdalene and presumably also other women disciples may have been no less qualified as apostles than many of "the twelve." When the testimony of women gained entrance to the New Testament, it happened, if at all, only in very indirect ways.

3. The Eucharist of a Prophetess

After our long investigation of Prisca and Maximilla, we will now end this chapter with a report on a prophetess who belonged to the mainstream church but was ultimately opposed there. Anonyma of Caesarea is the last concrete female personality about whose prophetic activity we can learn something from the extant sources, and she is also the only prophetess of the mainstream church about whom we know more than we do about Ammia.

In a letter Firmilian, the bishop of Caesarea in Cappadocia, reports on Anonyma's activity in his city.[348] The occasion for his writing was the controversy over baptism by heretics: the Roman bishop Stephen I recognized the validity of baptism by heretics—not least of all for reasons of church politics: the aim was to ease the transfer of schismatics into the mainstream church. Cyprian, the bishop of Carthage, fought bitterly against this practice and sought support from his colleague Firmilian, which he promptly received.[349] Was Anonyma, who is mentioned in this controversy over heretics, therefore a heretic herself? That is nowhere stated in the text of the letter. She is not connected with a specific false doctrine, either, but merely called a "false prophet." Yet in order to be able to use her in the controversial issue, Firmilian begins his report with the terse statement: "There is no distinction between a false prophet and a heretic."[350] Thus Anonyma was a "heretic" only as a "false prophet." To illustrate his assertion the bishop gives a detailed account of a scandalous incident, which he meticulously dates in the years after 235:

> 10.1   I should like now to recount to you an incident, relevant to this present matter, which happened in our area.
>
> About twenty-two years ago, in the period after the Emperor Severus Alexander [222–235], a great number of trials and tribulations befell in these parts both the whole community generally and the Christians in particular. There occurred a long succession of earthquakes, as a result of which many buildings throughout Cappadocia and Pontus collapsed, and even towns were swallowed up by crevasses opening out in the ground, sinking into the abyss.[351] In consequence, there arose against us a violent persecution for the Name; it broke out suddenly after there had been a lengthy period of peace, and its effect was all the more devastating in throwing our people into disarray because trouble of this kind was so unexpected and novel to them. Serenianus was governor of our province at the time, a bitter and relentless persecutor.
>
> 10.2   The faithful, finding themselves in the midst of this upheaval, took to flight in all directions in fear of persecution; they abandoned their home territories and moved to other parts of the country (they were free so to move, in

that this persecution was local and did not extend to the whole world). Suddenly, a certain woman started up in our midst: she presented herself as a prophetess, being in a state of ecstasy and acting as if she were filled with the Holy Spirit. But she was so deeply under the sway and control of the principal demons that she managed to disturb and deceive the brethren[352] for a long time by performing astonishing and preternatural feats, and she even promised that she would cause the earth to quake: not that her devil had such power that he was able to cause an earthquake or disturb the elements by his own efforts, but that, as an evil spirit, possessing the gift of foreknowledge and therefore perceiving that there was to be an earthquake, he sometimes pretended that he was going to do that which he saw was going to happen.

10.3   Thus, by means of these mendacious and boastful pretensions he so succeeded in subjecting the minds of certain devotees to his sway that they gave him their obedience and would follow him wherever he directed and led. And as for that woman, he would make her go in the very depths of winter through the bitter snow in bare feet, and not be in the least troubled or injured by her walk; he would say that he must be off to Judea and Jerusalem, giving the false impression that he had come from there.

10.4   And here, too, he so managed to trick one of the presbyters, a country fellow,[353] and another also, a deacon, that they lay with this woman. This was discovered shortly afterwards, for one of the exorcists suddenly appeared before him; this was a man of established integrity and of exemplary life in all matters of religious observance, having been urged and exhorted by a number of the brethren who were themselves praiseworthy and steadfast in the faith. And so he drew himself up against this evil spirit to overpower him—and by a subtle piece of trickery that spirit had even foretold shortly beforehand that there was about to come against him a certain hostile assailant, an unbeliever. Nevertheless, that exorcist, being inspired with the grace of God, stoutly withstood him and succeeded in revealing that the spirit which had previously been thought holy was in fact thoroughly evil.

10.5   And that woman, through the illusions and trickeries of the devil, had devised a number of ways for deceiving the faithful. Among other practices by which she deceived many, she frequently dared even to use this one: employing a by no means despicable form of invocation, she would pretend to sanctify the bread and celebrate the Eucharist, and she would offer the sacrifice to the Lord not[354] without the sacred recitation of the wonted ritual formula. And she would baptize many also, adopting the customary and legitimate wording of the baptismal interrogation.[355] And all this she did in such a way that she appeared to deviate in no particular from ecclesiastical discipline.

11.1   What, then, are we to say about such a baptism, where an evil demon is baptized through the agency of a woman? Can it be that Stephen and his adherents extend their approval even to this baptism, especially as it came complete with Trinitarian credal formula and the legitimate baptismal interrogation of the Church? (ACW 47:84–86)

What are we to make of this astonishing story? First we note that the author cleverly changes the subject in the course of the presentation: the woman is replaced by the demon. Apparently Anonyma is burdened with four deeds or "miracles" that are actually performed by the demon: (1) she/he "caused" an earthquake (presumably predicted an actual quake); (2) in the depths of winter she went barefoot in the ice-cold snow without injury; (3) he (the demon, not the woman!) seduced a presbyter and a deacon: both slept with the prophetess; and (4) the real monstrosity: with mainstream church ritual she dispensed baptism and celebrated the Eucharist.

The role of the exorcist remains curiously vague: he is not confronted directly by the real woman but only by the demon (the exorcist "appears" to the demon!); the nature of his victory is not described. Did he undertake a ritual exorcism of the woman? Probably not, since nothing of the kind is said.

What facts remain when we remove the demon miracles from the story? Apparently, during the time of persecution a woman recognized by the church as a prophetess held the Christians together with her preaching and over an extended period of time celebrated the Eucharist and baptized—with the rite of the mainstream church. Neither the confession of the Trinity nor the correct ecclesiastical interrogation was lacking! Moreover, she presumably predicted an earthquake that actually happened and perhaps also a persecution connected with the earthquake.[356] Apparently she impressed believers with her ascetic way of life: even in the snow she went barefoot. Her followers included a presbyter and a deacon: ministers of the mainstream church. An exorcist—that is, a minister of lower rank—protested against the woman's activity: presumably he eventually brought the majority of Christians over to his side. We do not learn how her activity came to an end. In any case, the prophetess advocated no foreign doctrine and held to the mainstream ritual: thus she did not belong to a sect. Nevertheless, the angry bishop condemns the event in his own way: "An evil demon baptized through the agency of a woman"! (11)

This judgment raises questions: What role does the sex of the prophetess play for Firmilian? How misogynistic was he? Does he equate every baptism by a woman with a baptism by the demon? That could be suggested by the sentence quoted above, but here it is not at all a question of an unambiguous rejection of baptism by women as we know it in Tertullian;[357] for the bishop says neither that women in general may not baptize nor that a baptism dispensed by them is invalid.[358] For such reticence there are two possible explanations: (1) in a milieu so friendly to women he did not dare to make such a decidedly misogynistic statement; (2) he actually did not hold this view. From the text we cannot decide which of the two explanations applies. In any case, the bishop's judgment of the prophetess is relatively mild: in his eyes she deceived the people, but she herself was the victim and instrument of the demon. Expected barbs against the female sex are lacking in this letter. Even the alleged sexual offense is not charged to Anonyma but to the presbyter and the deacon.

Is the incident historical at all? The question is important, for it concerns the only extant testimony that without doubt attests the celebration of the Eucharist by a woman in the mainstream church. Otherwise there is only one further indication of this: the eleventh canon of the Council of Laodicea at the end of the fourth century: "So-called women presbyters (*presbytidas*) or presidents (*prokathēmenas*) may not be appointed in the church."[359] It is reasonable to assume that anything that is prohibited has actually occurred. If the words had masculine endings, no one would doubt that priests and bishops were meant here. Even in the feminine form the canon really needs only an "interpretation" if one presupposes that there can in any case be no Eucharist-celebrating woman priest in the Catholic church, but at most in the Montanist church;[360] for in the latter, as we saw, in the same century and in the same Phrygia, the real existence of women presbyters and bishops is attested by Epiphanius[361] and perhaps also by a Phrygian inscription.[362]

Firmilian himself, in any case, reports the incident in Caesarea clearly as historical fact ("historia quae apud nos facta est"). Are there, nonetheless, reasons to doubt the historicity? Two points could raise doubts: (1) The incident took place after 235: by this time a leadership role for prophetesses and prophets in the mainstream church can no longer be demonstrated. (2) Firmilian is apparently attempting to carry to its absurd extreme the Roman opinion that heretic baptism is valid if it contains the right Trinitarian formulas. Thus one could assume that to this end he "staged" a baptism by *women* heretics according to all the rules of the church.

Yet the counterarguments are stronger. Regarding the first reason, the prophetess's activity is attested for a short period of persecution, a time of general confusion in which the authority of a charismatic woman leader could be relatively easily recognized. On the second, such an occurrence—the prophetic activity of a woman "for a long time" (*per longum tempus*), who "frequently" (*frequenter*) celebrated the Eucharist and dispensed baptism but was then opposed—would probably have attracted attention in Caesarea. It is therefore extremely unlikely that the story was simply invented by the bishop of this city for polemical purposes. The intentional use of a real, relatively well-known event is considerably more plausible, especially since the author goes to great pains to prove the facticity of his account. Also speaking against the invention of the prophetess for misogynist purposes is the fact that Firmilian at no point uses the account for a general polemic against feminine claims to authority. His whole argumentation is aimed not at women but at heretics, whose baptism he does not want to recognize: in his view they are the devil in person. He does not deal at all with the question of a possible baptism by women: his criticism concerns the "false" prophetess, because such a person is for him also the instrument of the devil. Thus we must maintain the historicity of what is reported. It is no longer crucial what Firmilian personally may have thought or intended, but rather that *here, at least for a time, a mainstream congregation recognized a prophetess who baptized and celebrated the Eucharist.*

Another, differently expressed hypothesis[363] must also be investigated: Could the nameless woman have belonged to the New Prophecy? Three elements in the text seem to support this idea: (1) ecstasy is emphasized; (2) going barefoot in the snow suggests ascetic strictness; (3) the demon claims to come from Jerusalem. *But* ecstasy and asceticism are also found outside Montanism, and the Jerusalem mentioned here is not identified with Pepuza. Thus the text has no specific points of contact with the New Prophecy.

Furthermore, there are additional counterarguments. In his writing Firmilian earlier mentions expressly the "sect of the Cataphrygians"—their baptism cannot be recognized because their confession is not correct: they believe in Christ, who sent the Spirit who spoke from Montanus and Prisca.[364] Why would the bishop of Caesarea not identify his anonymous prophetess as a Cataphrygian if she belonged to the Phrygian church? Yet in 235 it is hardly conceivable that a New Prophetess would be active in the mainstream church and find wide recognition there, since at this time the movement was already set apart as a "sect" and perhaps even used its own liturgical formulas. The hypothesis of a Montanist background for Anonyma is not tenable.

Thus the nameless prophetess in Caesarea belonged to the mainstream church. Unfortunately, Firmilian's account does not indicate how this episode ended. In any case, Anonyma was ultimately denied prophetic authority. Her sex may have been a secret reason, but officially she was rejected not as a prophetess but only as a false prophetess. But since no convincing reasons are given for this falsehood, it seems that here as earlier in the dispute over Prisca, Maximilla, and Montanus, opposition to uncontrollable prophecy in general was a primary reason. It had become suspect in mainstream Christianity.

4. Conclusion

1. The prophecy of women. If we look back on the prophetic tradition in early Christianity and ask about the participation of women, we learn that there were conflicts on this point very early. In Paul's time the conflict in Corinth was decided in favor of women, even if with certain conditions: they could speak prophetically just like men, except that they had to wear a veil. Yet the opposition quickly went further. In the postapostolic period two parties faced each other: one affirmed proclamation by women; the other rejected it. Both directions, which are attested literarily by the alleged "Pauline" letters to Timothy and Titus or by the so-called acts of Paul, attempted to legitimize their standpoints with the authority of the apostle to the Gentiles.[365] This time developments did not favor women: texts with the prohibition of teaching were admitted to the New Testament canon, but the traditions about proclaiming women were finally rejected as "apocryphal," although the acts of Paul still enjoyed quasicanonical status for centuries.

2. Prophecy and episcopacy. The conflict around women was not the only point of contention regarding prophecy. In the development from the Jesus movement to the Christian church, prophetic authority itself was increasingly called into question. If the charismatic men and women proclaimers of the gospel who moved from place to place at first had greater "apostolic" prestige than the organizers of Christian meetings in the local churches, the weight soon shifted and local church leaders were now regarded as the real successors of the apostles; that is, the bishop became the most important figure. Simple church presidency developed into monarchical episcopacy. The later division of the church into "clergy" and "laity" began to be clearly evident.

3. The decline of prophecy. This development gradually led to a devaluation of the charismatic. When there were in fact no longer any prophetesses and prophets in the churches, there was also a change in theology. The "normal" charisma of all baptized persons became the extremely rare privilege of a few individuals in special situations; in individual cases this special charisma could also be shared by women. Such prophets and prophetesses might criticize church ministers, but they were basically subordinated to them. The charisma of the end time became, as it were, the charisma of the beginning, which one recalled full of admiration but no longer knew from experience.

4. Substitute for prophets. The functions of prophetesses and prophets were increasingly performed by ordained ministers. At least on the lowest level of the hierarchy, women were still involved as deaconesses. One should certainly not condemn institutionalization in general: a growing church had to create organs to meet the new situation. As long as ministers were elected by the churches, the people's participation in decisions was guaranteed. In charismatic movements, by contrast, ambivalent phenomena could arise and had to be discouraged. In the accusations of antiheretical writings it was not always simply a question of malicious polemics: it would be naive to believe that personality cults, brainwashing, sexual orgies, material enrichment of sect leaders, and similar scandals are exclusively a product of the twentieth century.

5. No substitute for prophetesses. Thus the disappearance of prophecy from the everyday life of the church could be regarded as the fruit of a sound process of institutionalization. In addition there was a change in religious mentality and spirituality: interest in subjective and especially in ecstatic forms of expression in prayer and worship had declined; liturgies developed that were able to encompass religious experience in an artistically aesthetic symbol world of ritual objectivity. This change could also be accepted without particular regret. In the sweep of this change, however, women were left by the wayside or systematically eliminated from church positions. As long as there was still a need for practical reasons, deaconesses in the Eastern church were allowed to carry out catechetical and liturgical functions for women. Yet their ordination was devaluated: deaconesses were no longer considered members of the higher clergy. Eventually, they disappeared entirely from the churches.

6. The elimination of women. This fundamental exclusion of women from ministries in the transition to set ecclesiastical institutions cannot be brought into harmony with the message of Jesus or the practice of early Christendom. A previously latent misogyny was sanctioned here in church law and structure. Certainly the loss of a charismatic understanding of the church is not primarily a women's problem.[366] The one-sided emphasis on the institution and the increasing dominance of a priest caste also affected men outside the clergy, who were now demoted to "laymen." Yet for women this sex-specific structural demarcation ultimately led to the doctrine of the inferiority of the feminine nature, as expressed in the theology of the Middle Ages.[367] This view was first overcome in the free churches of the modern period. Quakers in particular deserve credit for having recognized women again as equal proclaimers in their churches.[368]

7. *Authority and inspiration.* In her comparison of the Phrygian movement of the second century with the early Quaker movement in America, Elaine C. Huber highlights the aspect of the "authority of inspiration,"[369] perhaps better understood as authority *through* inspiration. Her presentation gives the impression that this form of authority is primarily represented by women, but this can hardly be supported by the sources: even among the leading charismatics, there were more men than women. Yet in both historical conflicts this "authority of inspiration" was finally subordinated to the "authority of the hierarchy." In the Christian women's movement of the twentieth century Huber sees a kind of "New Prophecy"—less in the form of inspired individual personalities than in the sense of a collective design: this could become a corrective to overcome the mistakes of the past and develop new alternative church structures, which could give back to prophetic inspiration its rightful place. One can certainly agree with the author's basic concern, but not necessarily with the presumed affinity between prophecy and feminine charisma.

8. *Charisma and egalitarian ethos.* Historically the decline of the charismatic and the repression of women coincide temporally. Yet to see here a direct causal relationship seems problematic, even if today there is still a tendency to insist on the institutional as "masculine" and the charismatic as "feminine." These very clichés produce gender-specific roles. In view of the current predominance of the institutional element in our churches, it is without doubt important to make room once again for the prophetic and charismatic. Yet it is just as important to no longer deny women entrance into the institutional realm. The importance of access to institutions is often underestimated, even by many feminist theologians.

In sum, the New Prophecy was not a "women's movement," and its challenge did not lie in feminine prophecy. The challenge was rather twofold: (1) charisma was valued more highly than ministry; (2) women and men were treated as equal. On both levels this challenge remains valid.

IV. REDEMPTION THROUGH KNOWLEDGE

Bright Women Teachers

As we have seen, the church history of Eusebius is one of the few mainstream church sources in which real prophetesses and prophets of the postapostolic period are named: Ammia of Philadelphia and Quadratus appear as connecting links between the "old" prophecy of the New Testament and the New Prophecy of the second century.[1] In spite of repeatedly emphasized praise of the prophetic gift, Catholic theologians made no especial effort to keep alive the memory of charismatically gifted women and men preachers from their own ranks! By contrast, the memories of controversial personalities were written down much more zealously, so that today we know, paradoxically, more about "heretical" than "orthodox" prophets and prophetesses. The mainstream church quickly developed away from early Christian prophecy and soon forgot (or repressed?) the memory of its own beginnings. Other Christian movements, however, remained "conservative" with regard to the original prophecy: in theory *and* in practice these Christians made an effort to preserve the heritage of the primitive church. Indeed, as we saw, they plainly sought methods for promoting prophetic ability and keeping the old charisma alive.

It is notable that in the polemical denigration of these groups outside the mainstream church we encounter relatively often the names of women who together with men actively and publicly proclaimed and taught.[2] The strictly orthodox theologian Jerome sees in this feminine support the heretical movements' secret of success:

It was with the help of the harlot Helena that Simon Magus founded his sect. Bands of women accompanied Nicolas of Antioch, that deviser of all uncleanness. Marcion sent a woman [Anonyma] before him to Rome to prepare men's minds to fall into his snares. Apelles possessed in Philumena an associate in his false doctrines. Montanus, that mouthpiece of an unclean spirit, used two rich and high born ladies Prisca and Maximilla first to bribe and then to pervert many churches. Leaving ancient history I will pass to times nearer to our own. Arius intent on leading the world astray began by misleading the Emperor's sister [Constantia]. The resources of Lucilla helped Donatus to defile with his polluting baptism many unhappy persons throughout Africa. In Spain the blind woman Agape led the blind man Elpidius into the ditch. [She] was followed by Priscillian, an enthusiastic votary of Zoroaster and a magician before he became a bishop. A woman named Galla seconded his efforts and left a gadabout sister

[Anonyma] to perpetuate a second heresy of a kindred form. Now also the mystery of iniquity is working. Men and women in turn lay snares for each other.[3]

This was written by Jerome, who himself was known to have gathered around him a supportive circle of ascetic women and who maintained an intensive relationship especially with Paula![4] Despite the extremely polemical style, the letter attests impressively to the significant role that women played in the discussions about true church doctrine and proper Christian conduct. Yet the writer adopts a "patriarchal" perspective in the fight against heretics: it is notable that he never names women of the early period as sect leaders but always and only as helpers of attacked heresiarchs. The presumably generally known women of his own time, by contrast, appear as inspirers and leaders. It would be rewarding to investigate historically the cases named above, but the movements of the fourth century in Africa[5] and Spain[6] cannot be treated here. We already encountered the Nicolaitans in Eusebius.[7] Our interest will now be directed toward Gnostically oriented Christianity, which is conjured up by the names Simon and Helena, as well as Marcion, Philomena, and Apelles.

Religiosity in Late Antiquity

What was Gnosticism? Much puzzling and writing has been done about this great spiritual current in late antiquity, which cannot be attributed to any particular religion.[8] For a long time it could be examined only through the writings of the church fathers who fought it as heresy. The most important source was the first two books of the major work of Irenaeus: *Adversus haereses*, in which the bishop of Lyon presents the leading personalities and their schools from his perspective. Not until the eighteenth and nineteenth centuries were a few Gnostic manuscripts in Coptic from the fourth and fifth centuries discovered, edited, and translated.[9] Then in the middle of this century a spectacular find was made in the Egyptian desert: near Nag Hammadi a large collection of Coptic manuscripts from the fourth century was discovered; it was a whole library of writings that were previously unknown or believed lost, whose full significance is still being intensively explored.[10] Thus it is now possible to change perspective and look at the mainstream church through the critical eyes of the men (and women?) striving for knowledge.[11]

Gnosticism is neither an independent religion nor a unified conceptual model—the variety of systems is itself characteristic of Gnosticism. The background is formed by a dualistic worldview in various versions. Common to all is one fundamental religious expectation: *salvation through knowledge*. Gnosticism strives for a radical spiritualization, as well as liberation from all earthly fetters. Was this basic position not irreconcilably opposed to mainstream Christianity, which promised *salvation through faith* and with its incarnation and resurrection theology seemed to promise an embodiment of the spirit rather than a spiritualization of the body? Yet many Christians understood themselves as Gnostics— for them this contradiction obviously did not exist. In recent times the works of Elaine Pagels have created a stir, for she demonstrates that especially in the beginning the boundary between Gnosticism and the mainstream church was open and indeed that in most writings in the New Testament canon we can find traditions to which Gnostically oriented Christians could relate with full justification.[12] Before her Luise Schottroff had stated in reference to the Fourth Gospel: "John is the first system known to us in detail of a Gnosticism that adapted itself to Christian traditions. Through the Gospel of John the Gnostic doctrine of salvation entered the canon."[13]

Misogynistic or Philogynous?

Was Gnostic Christianity more philogynous, more amicable toward women, than the mainstream church? The question is the subject of strong disagreement.[14] Yet here we must distinguish between *factual* and *ideological* philogyny (and misogyny): at least in some Gnostic churches an *egalitarian praxis* that matched the early Christian equality ethos seems to have survived, while the Gnostic doctrine of creation and redemption sees in the "fall of Sophia"[15] a *metaphysical feminine principle as the cause of evil*—not just a single historical female figure or the female sex, as in certain Christian interpretations of the biblical account of the Fall, which we know today to be incorrect.[16] Thus on this point the theory in many Gnostic systems is by no means more philogynous than the theology of the mainstream church.

Another typical Gnostic concept, the teaching of paired partners (*syzygoi*), can take on both philogynous and misogynistic traits: as the *polar duality* of humankind and the divinity, the feminine and the masculine are of equal worth and equal rank; a *hierarchical dualism,* by contrast, leads via the associative chains masculine-spiritual-good and feminine-corporeal-evil to the devaluation and even rejection of the feminine. The interaction between ideology and social reality with regard to the women's issue still must be clarified. But one thing is certain: the real praxis of religious movements can in no way be simply derived from their particular mythos. For Gnosticism it has been mainly the "ideology" that has been investigated (that is, the function of feminine symbols and metaphors, etc.) rather than the concrete life of Gnostic women.[17] In what follows, however, the focus will be on real women. In view of the complex nature of the phenomenon, it is not possible with the present state of research to answer the question of the relationship between mythos and praxis: there is obviously not one single Gnosticism but only many Gnostically oriented movements, which vary considerably in terms of their philogyny or misogyny and have developed differently.

Which Gnostic women are still known to us today? Heresiologists place the legendary figures Simon and Helena[18] at the beginning. In accordance with the teaching of the *syzygoi* we see embodied in them the archetype of an originator-couple. In his *Apology* Justin reports in detail on the sorcerer Simon and refers to his companion Helena, whom he characterizes as a former prostitute.[19] The assertion that Simon was worshiped by his people as a god, which was put into circulation by this early apologist, has in the meantime been clearly refuted, for the inscription cited by Justin as proof, "Simoni Deo Sancto" ("To the Holy God

Simon"), was excavated in 1574. It reads, however, "Semoni Sanco Deo Fidio" and relates to an old Sabine god Semo Sancus with the sobriquet "Dius Fidius."[20] Thus the remaining disparaging statements about Simon and Helena are probably also not to be given any credence. Nevertheless, it is extremely difficult to establish anything that is historically certain, and it will not be attempted here. The mythicization of the couple began very early.[21]

In Gnosticism we also find a similar mythicization for Mary Magdalene—a tradition that likewise needs thorough investigation.[22] Here Mary, the favorite woman disciple, is the female counterpart of the favorite male disciple John; both stand out above all others. One could assume that they are to be seen so to speak as the earthly counterparts of the heavenly Christ and his paired partner Sophia.[23] These ideas cannot be treated here, but we will point to two important aspects: (1) The mythologized female figures are not invented; in each case the myth goes back to the *memory of historically real women*. (2) The interest is not so much in the heroization of individual persons as in the *mythicization of a couple:* thus both sexes are similarly anchored in the Divine.

The previously quoted listing of Jerome can be expanded: we know the name of Marcellina, through whose preaching the strongly ascetically oriented movement of the Egyptian Carpocrates was spread in Rome under Anicetus (d. ca. 166)[24] and who advocated an egalitarian ethos. According to the testimony of Celsus, the early opponent of Christians, the followers of this school were called "Marcellians"; he mentions earlier that some "Simonists" are also called "Helenians."[25]

Are these Gnostic women who taught openly to be regarded as prophetesses? We find the title in the discussions here much less often than in the polemic against the Phrygian movement, as the Gnostic currents in general are not known primarily for prophecy. Yet Leopold Zscharnack pointed out that Gnosticism contains Eastern-prophetic and Western-philosophical elements.[26] Philomena is clearly characterized in the sources as a prophetess, and we saw that it was a Gnostic teacher who undertook the attempt to awaken the prophetic charisma through a ritual.[27] If one looks at the actual function of women in the Gnostic churches, the title *prophetess* seems thoroughly appropriate. Yet for the "gnosis" movement there is a more widespread vocabulary in which the wisdom traditions of Judaism[28] and Hellenism (Philo-Sophia!) meet: *school, teacher, pupil,* and so on. Thus the term *didaskalos*[29] may reasonably expand the specific character of a Gnostic prophetess as a kind of teacher of wisdom.

In the early period, in any case, we cannot assume a sharp boundary between the charismata of male and female apostles, prophets, and teachers,[30] but only different accents: missionary preaching, proclamation in worship services, catechetical instruction. Only when the conflicts over publicly active women multiplied and intensified were prophecy and teaching pitted against each other. In the New Testament contradictory statements stand side by side: Paul attests that in Corinth prophetically active women apparently could speak in church; the pastoral letters, by contrast, generally want to obligate women to silence in church and in particular, they forbid them to teach.[31] Through a strict differentiation of charismata the opposite viewpoints could be harmonized: women could proph-

esy but not teach. In reality the contradictory New Testament statements resulted in controversy among Christians about women who both taught and
prophesied. In the one text the practice is affirmed; in the other, assailed.

For the second century, then, one should not overemphasize the difference
between women who prophesy and women who teach. The gift of prophecy had
the same high regard in all early Christian movements, whether their flavor was
Gnostic, charismatic, or mainstream Christian. There are even more commonalities between Gnosticism and the New Prophecy than one would initially assume.[32] Let us only recall that Prisca received from Christ the gift of wisdom,
and Maximilla said that she must "learn knowledge."[33]

Before we turn to Philomena, who is mentioned by Jerome, we will first present a nameless Gnostic woman, who caused a stir in the African metropolis.

1. Baptism without Water?

The Cainite Anonyma in Carthage

"The one from the sect of Cain," who according to Tertullian's polemic "did
away with baptism,"[34] apparently had the authority of a prophetess, although she
is not so named. Judging by the rage with which the theologian characterizes this
Anonyma as a "venom-filled adder," a "monster," and a "beast,"[35] she must have
been highly influential in Carthage, and probably not only in groups on the
fringe of the church; for she "seduced very many through her teaching"![36] With
what and to what end? She disputed the necessity of water baptism; that is, she
advocated an understanding of baptism that was "more spiritual" than the mainstream church's sacramental theology, which was strongly oriented toward external rites. In this she was not alone. For Gnostic circles Irenaeus attests four
different positions on the practice of baptism:

> [1] Some prepare a bridal chamber[37] and perfect the consecration of those to be
> perfected with certain discussions, and they call this process spiritual marriage af-
> ter the model of heavenly connections.
>
> [2] Others lead them to the water and say: . . . [various baptismal formulas are
> quoted] . . . Then they anoint the perfected with oil of balsam, because this salve
> is an imitation of the otherworldly fragrance.
>
> [3] Others assert that it is superfluous to lead the one to be perfected to wa-
> ter; with similar formulas of consecration they mix oil and water together and
> pour this on his head . . .
>
> [4] Still others reject all these customs and say that one must not try to pre-
> sent the secret of the unpronounceable and invisible Power through visible and
> transitory creatures, nor the inconceivable and incorporeal Being through tan-
> gible and material things. The mere knowledge of the inexpressible Entity is per-
> fect redemption.[38]

Anonyma and her followers could have advocated the first or fourth position.
Tertullian calls the group the "sect of Cain," which he in turn identifies in a

different passage with the "Nicolaitans," who are criticized in Rev. 2:20 because "you tolerate that woman Jezebel, who calls herself a prophet."[39] Were there connections between, on the one hand, the prophetic tradition attested in Revelation or the antiprophetic opposition that is coupled with misogyny in Thyatira and, on the other hand, the otherwise unknown "Cainite" tradition in Carthage? It is more probable that opponents threw various movements with equality for women into the same pot and applied the same discrediting judgment.

Did Anonyma herself practice a rite of initiation without water? Zscharnack seems to infer from Tertullian's account that the Cainite woman baptized,[40] yet that is not in the text and even contradicts the actual assertion. We must assume, rather, that she belonged to a movement that rejected all ritualization. Obviously there were vigorous discussions in Carthage about the practice of baptism, which required the mainstream theologian to defend the water rite energetically.[41] His treatise *On Baptism* begins with the mentioned polemic against the Cainites. In a later chapter the possible dispensation of the sacrament by women is also indignantly rejected, again against the background of topical discussions.[42] Yet the women who want to baptize—Tertullian castigates their "presumption"!—did not appeal to Gnostic women but to the example of the teaching and baptizing Thecla.[43] This story was invented, counters the polemicist: the apostle could not have allowed Thecla to baptize, since he did not even allow women to teach! For this indignant man, women who dare to claim such a right are "new beasts similar to the earlier ones," yet they have opposite aims: these want to "dispense" baptism; those wanted to "dispense with" it.[44] Unfortunately, that is all that we know about Anonyma's activity.

2. "Wiser than Marcion"

The Virgin Philomena, Prophetess in Rome

The contentious theologian from Carthage also disagreed intensively with another prophetess: the virgin Philomena in Rome, who was more persuasive to the Marcion student Apelles than was his old teacher, and who thus brought to life a new movement.[45] The two names, Philomena and Apelles, are hardly known to us today, although they were among the great figures of the early period. Tertullian repeatedly addresses the trio of Marcion, Apelles, and Valentinus[46] and wrote an individual treatise against each one; the writing against Apelles, however, has not survived. Leopold Zscharnack calls Philomena "the prophetess in Gnosticism who in the extant traditions stands far above all the other women teachers and prophetesses in the individual sects through her esteem and her significance as a founder."[47]

First, however, let us take a look at Marcion, the fascinating figure who occupied the great liberal theologian Adolf von Harnack all his life.[48] Coming from Pontus in Asia Minor to Rome, Marcion soon became the most influential theologian of the second century.[49] As a Gnostic he was atypical,[50] since he integrated no mythological systems into his teaching. Yet he advocated a strict theological dualism and rejected the Old Testament as a source of Christian revelation. After his excommunication in 144 the Marcionites developed into an independent church, which lasted into the sixth century.[51] In it women had the right to baptize.[52] The existence of teaching prophetesses is indirectly attested by Tertullian's polemic: he denies the women around Marcion any charisma, because they do not speak in ecstasy. The same criticism is also leveled at male teachers, as well as at Marcion himself.[53] As we saw, according to Jerome, Marcion sent a woman ahead to Rome in order to pave the way for his message,[54] yet since this late information is found in a both antifeminist and antiheretical context, it should be handled with care. By contrast, it is certain that the Marcion student Apelles, who later in his writings made crucial corrections to the teaching of the master, followed the prophetess Philomena. What do we know of her?

a. The Teacher of Apelles

The Polemic of Rhodo:
"A Possessed Virgin"

Our oldest testimony comes from the Tatian student Rhodo (end of second century),[55] who knew Apelles and carried on a public debate with him. He reports a split in the Marcionite camp; one side holds to the strict dualism of the master: the "two principles," that is, the two different origins of good and evil (in Marcion, the "evil God" of creation and the old covenant versus the "good God," the Father of Jesus Christ); others know even three "primal beings," while still others—like orthodox Christianity—accept only a single principle. The last group includes Apelles:

> This [man] from their group, who is esteemed because of his way of life and his age, confesses a single principle, but he asserts that the prophetic scriptures come from a contrary spirit, for he lets himself be persuaded by the utterances of a possessed virgin named Philomena.[56]

In other words, he (or she), like Marcion, criticizes the Old Testament ("the prophetic scriptures") but, like the mainstream church, advocates a monistic-monotheistic conception of God ("a single principle"). The teaching clearly goes back to Philomena. It is not surprising that her opponent calls the prophetess, who is held to be heretical, "possessed"; it is astonishing, rather, that he does not call into question her status as a virgin! Even in the later polemic she is not accused on this level.[57]

Is the alleged "possession" to be understood as prophetic ecstasy? At first the statement says only that Philomena appeared to be an authentic prophetess, for in the opinion of the church fathers the slyness of the devil includes producing the same phenomena as those evoked by the Holy Spirit.[58] Three points speak against conspicuous ecstatic phenomena:

1. Rhodo calls her utterances *apophthegmata* ("apothegms"). This word designates a literary genre known in antiquity,[59] which in Christianity is found again

in the ascetic tradition: the "utterances" of the desert fathers and mothers[60] are gathered as instructions for the spirit-filled life. Thus apothegms are anything but incomprehensible oracles uttered in a trance.

2. Nor do we find in the later testimonies about Philomena any indications of unusual forms of prophecy. With the term *phanerōseis* ("manifestations")[61] as the title of the collection of her utterances, a word was chosen that designates a supersensory but not really supernatural form of perception.[62]

3. Ecstatic forms of expression do not fit the instructional contents of her proclamation. The fact that she did not write down her utterances herself does not mean anything: even the sayings of Jesus, the prophet par excellence, are known to us only through followers who wrote them down! The same is also true of the philosopher Socrates.

Only very late, in an interpolation in Augustine's comments on Apelles, are strange visions and miracles described that have nothing to do with the historical Philomena,[63] but even there it is not a question of ecstasy. When modern authors call this prophetess an ecstatic,[64] it demonstrates a prejudgment: prophecy is easily connected with trancelike circumstances, especially when women are involved. Yet Philomena belongs in the tradition of Marcionite women teachers for whom Tertullian did not want to approve the title *prophetess*, precisely because they were not ecstatics.[65]

For Rhodo, Apelles made a weak figure in the discussion. If we read the report of his utterances, however, we have before us not a born fanatical sectarian but a man who advocated an impressive will toward peace and a great respect for individual conscience:[66]

> When the old man Apelles met with us, he was shown that he had presented many things badly, but he said: "One should not talk a conviction [*logos*] to death; everyone should abide by his faith. Those who put their hope in the crucified One will attain salvation if they contrive to do good works." He commented that the God question was for him the most difficult of all questions. In this he held fast to the one principle, which also corresponds to our conviction [*logos*].[67]

Thus in the central question of the understanding of God there was no dissension between Apelles and the representatives of the mainstream church. On what, then, does Rhodo base his protest? He had demanded that Apelles produce a "proof" for the correctness of the "one principle." This was refused by Apelles on two levels: (1) He did not know a "scriptural proof": the Christian doctrine of God could not be derived from the texts of the Old Testament. (2) On the God question he had no certain "knowledge": he followed his faith intuition.[68] Rhodo could not accept this position. In his view a genuine teacher must be able to "prove" his conviction! Hesitation and procrastination in questions of faith are not permissible. Thus the dissent here is not in the understanding of God but in the understanding of church dogmatics!

From this discussion, what information can we derive about Philomena and her proclamation? (1) She belonged to the ecclesiastical *order of virgins*. (2) Her *utterances (apophthegmata)* were regarded as *Spirit-effected.* For Philomena's prophecy *no ecstatic context* is to be assumed. (3) She *did not recognize* the *Old Testament* (yet this statement will have to be qualified in light of the other sources). (4) She advocated *no good-evil dualism* but held to the *unity of God.* (5) If the view of the Spirit attested for Apelles is also exemplary for her, she advocated an *undogmatic theology,* which was more oriented toward "orthopraxy" than orthodoxy.

The Polemic of Tertullian:
"An Angel of Seduction"

Our second source of information is again Tertullian, who treats this prophetess, however, with by no means the same sympathy that he showed toward the representatives of the New Prophecy. Nevertheless, he dealt with her intensively and read her apothegms in particular, which Apelles had recorded under the title *Phaneröseis* ("manifestations").[69] In his antiheretical writings the apologist fights both the teachings of Marcion and the views held by Philomena and Apelles. What questions are involved?

In his *On the Prescription against Heretics*[70] Tertullian advocates a strict "revelation positivism" compared to other Christians who want to engage in philosophical argumentation. Whereas the "heretics" hear in the promise, "Search, and you will find" (Matt. 7:7), the call to deal with new teachings, their opponent refuses to recognize anything at all beyond the faith handed down by the apostles. In particular he rejects any discussion of the scripture: it belongs to the church and can be correctly read only in the light of the *regula fidei* ("rules of faith"). The faith is "apostolic"—no one who lives after the apostles can add anything to it. In his *Against Marcion* he attempts to demonstrate the unity of the Old and New Testaments and fights the negation of the real corporeality of Christ and the denial of the bodily resurrection—topics that he treats again in the treatises *On the Flesh of Christ* and *On the Resurrection of the Flesh,* again in express rejection of the teachings held by Marcion, Philomena, and Apelles. He composed another writing, "Against the Apellians," which has not survived.[71]

Let us summarize what we have learned about Philomena from Tertullian's antiheretical polemic:

1. [Context: the antithesis in questions of faith between arbitrary selection by the heretics and obedient acceptance by the faithful] "If an angel from heaven proclaimed a different gospel, he would be accursed by us [cf. Gal. 1:8]. For the Holy Spirit already foresaw at that time that an angel of seduction would appear in a certain virgin Philomena, changed into an angel[72] of light; instigated by his signs and magic tricks, Apelles introduced a new heresy."[73]
2. [Context: polemic against Marcion, who was not a contemporary of the apostle] "If we research the genealogy of Apelles, he no more belonged to the ancient ones than did Marcion, his teacher and shaper; rather, he fell because of a woman, gave up Marcionite continence, and withdrew from the eyes of the holiest master to

Alexandria. Years later he returned home no longer a Marcionite but none the better; he joined another woman, that virgin Philomena whom we already mentioned above: she later became the insane whore and enmeshed him in her operations [*energēma*],[74] so that he wrote down the *phanerōseis*[75] that she conveyed to him. There are still [people] alive who knew her, including her students and followers; hence they cannot dispute that she was younger [than the apostles]."[76]

3. [Context: polemic against Marcion's docetism] "That virgin Philomena persuaded Apelles and the other opponents of Marcion of the faith that Christ assumed flesh, yet not through birth but through the union of the elements."[77]

4. [Same context] "Some students of the [man] from Pontus [= Marcion] are more intelligent than their teacher and admit that the corporeality of Christ was genuine but did not come from birth. They say: 'The Lord had flesh, but it was not born.' Thus we are jumping, as they say, from the pan into the fire when we move from Marcion to Apelles: after the latter gave up Marcion's discipline, he fell victim to a woman according to the flesh; then later to the virgin Philomena according to the spirit. From her he received [the commission] to proclaim that Christ had a concrete body, yet independent of a birth. But against this angel of Philomena the apostle directed those words with which he had already predicted him: 'But even if we or an angel from heaven should proclaim to you a gospel contrary to what we proclaimed to you, let that one be accursed!' [Gal. 1:8]."[78]

5. [Context: the quotation above] "In the same manner he [the Holy Spirit, who speaks in the prophets] refers to the operations [*energēma*] of the Apellian virgin Philomena."[79]

6. [Context: the question of the preexistence of souls] "Apelles . . . who has souls exist as male and female beings before the origin of the bodies, as he learned from Philomena, has the flesh, with its later origin, receive the sex from the soul."[80]

The last quotation leads to a completely new theme: the question of the preexistence of souls and their sex or sexlessness. Let us leave that problem aside for the moment and note at this point only that here Tertullian, the anti-Marcionite and anti-Apellian, has strongly emphasized five times that Philomena is the originator of the teaching advocated by Apelles! Inspired by the one who appears as an angel of light, he brings to life an independent school;[81] from her come the *phanerōseis* that he wrote down; she convinces the former Marcion student of the reality of Christ's body; she caused Apelles to preach this message; and from her he learned the theory of souls. In the question of authorship, Tertullian is refreshingly different from modern presenters of the "Apellian" system, who forget the teacher because of the student![82]

Apelles' dependence on Philomena's prophetic proclamation was already reported by Rhodo. When Tertullian now alludes to it, he is referring to the *phanerōseis,* which in his time were accessible to everyone. Apelles himself had apparently made known there his role as a recipient. When Tertullian emphasizes this dependence, it is not a polemical trick intended to discredit the teaching of his opponent as "female talk"; rather, he merely reproduces what he found in the authentic source.

Now, how is the polemic in the sexual realm to be evaluated (quotations 2 and 4)? It is noteworthy that it has only Apelles as its object. With polemics of this sort caution is generally advised, for it is a question of the usual moral accusation that pagans make against Christians and Christians against pagans, as well as Christians among themselves. In the present case, the voice of the reader from Carthage contradicts the eyewitness Rhodo, who credits Apelles with an admirable lifestyle. Furthermore, a similar story was spread later about Marcion: he was supposedly excommunicated because he seduced a virgin.[83] Thus this criticism is presumably groundless.[84]

What about the insulting of Philomena as an "insane whore" (quotation 2)? Since this epithet occurs only in Tertullian and in his writings only here, although he names the prophetess six times, expressly calls her a virgin four times, and mentions the association with an angel three times, the literal interpretation is probably not appropriate. The alleged "carnal" fall of Apelles was with another woman—Philomena's "whoring" is therefore to be understood as spiritual seduction, as it is described in quotation 4. The prophetess is apparently not vulnerable on the moral level (eyewitnesses who knew her are still alive!). Therefore Tertullian generalizes his attack: as a woman she is a seductive Eve on all levels, not only in the sexual realm.[85] Nevertheless, his criticism of Philomena remains astonishingly reserved and implicit. If the otherwise so sarcastic polemicist did not dare to give his pen free reign with regard to her, this testifies indirectly to the high regard the prophetess enjoyed: we must assume that she really appeared to her followers as an "angel of light." Nonetheless, she must also have impressed Tertullian very much, since he could see in Paul's emphatic statement about an angel who might appear from heaven (Gal. 1:8) a historically concrete prophecy concerning Philomena and her proclamation (quotations 1, 4, 5).

b. The Confession of Faith
of Her Followers

Can we still grasp the contours of Philomena's prophetic message? Since the apothegms of the prophetess are no longer available to us but she is emphatically called the founder of the Apellian school, it is both necessary and legitimate to draw into the investigation all the testimonies about the teaching ascribed to Apelles.[86] It is not possible in the overall system to distinguish the individual contributions of Philomena and Apelles. Only one thing can be discerned: the student stands out above all in the discussion of the "law and prophets," whereas the real corporeality of Jesus seems to have been especially important to the teacher. Since Philomena was in any case unquestionably the initiator, in what follows the conceptual system will, contrary to usual practice, not be credited to Apelles but to the actual originator or to the two together. For this system the *Panarion* of Epiphanius will be instructive, since it may well contain this movement's confession of faith.[87]

We know that in the early period there were many such confessions, or *symbola*,[88] that had their place in life in the great Easter baptismal celebrations and

the preceding catechesis. The larger church centers developed their own traditions. Only in the wake of the christological and Trinitarian controversies did
these liturgical texts gain dogmatic importance. Thus the creeds used at the
Councils of Nicaea (325) and Constantinople (381) acquired normative character; that is, all other confessions had to agree with them and be interpreted in the
sense of the council decrees. Finally it was forbidden to compose new confessional formulas.[89] Even today the so-called Nicaeno-Constantinopolitan creed—
originally the local confession of the church of Constantinople—is considered
the fundamental confession of faith of Christendom.[90]

Such a *symbolon* of Gnostic provenance seems to be quoted by the "denomi-
nations expert" Bishop Epiphanius of Salamis in his chapter on the Apellians,[91]
in which Philomena is not even mentioned! At the beginning of his comments
he refers to a text that he ascribes to Apelles. If we omit the objections of the
heretic-fighter, we have before us, in terms of language and structure, a confession of faith:

> [1.4] . . . There is one single, good God, a first Principle [*archē*], a Power that
> cannot be named. This one God or this one Principle has nothing to do
> [*memelētai*] with what happens in this world, [5] yet this holy and good God
> from above made [*poiēsen*] another God. And this other God built [*ektise*] every-
> thing: heaven and earth and everything in the world. Yet he was not good, and
> his creatures were not well made [*eirgasmena*], for they were built [*ektistae*] by
> him in accordance with his smaller intelligence [*phaulēn dianoian*] . . .[92]
>
> [2.1] Yet Christ came in the last time, the Son of the good God from above,
> as well as his Holy Spirit, for the salvation of those who attain his knowledge
> [*gnōsis*]. [2] He not only seemed to come but truly took on flesh, not from the
> Virgin Mary, and yet he had real flesh and a body, but not from the seed of a
> man or from a virginal woman. [3] Nevertheless, he had true flesh in the fol-
> lowing way: when he descended from heaven, he came to earth and gathered
> his body from the four elements. . . .[93] [5] [He took] the dry from the dry, the
> warm from the warm, the wet from the wet, the cold from the cold, and in this
> way he formed [*plasas*] himself a body, really appeared in the world, and taught
> us the knowledge from above. [6] [He taught us] to despise the demiurge[94] and
> renounce his works. He showed us where in the scripture to find the words re-
> ally spoken by him and where those of the demiurge are . . .[95]
>
> [7] Then Christ allowed his body to suffer, and he was really crucified and
> really buried, and he has really risen; and he showed his disciples this very flesh.
> [8] Then he dissolved this human shape again and gave each element its share
> back: warm to the warm, cold to the cold, dry to the dry, wet to the wet. And
> after he had thus again dissolved his fleshly body, he ascended into heaven, from
> which he had come. [He went forth to the good father and left in the world the
> seed of life for those who would believe in him through his disciples.][96]

There are *three peculiarities* about this *symbolon* with regard to its structure.
First, at the end it lacks an "article of faith" on the Holy Spirit. In the Epipha-

nius version the text breaks off with the ascension, but in Hippolytus we can reconstruct a closing sentence that describes the ongoing work of the resurrected One in the world, without mentioning the Holy Spirit. In another passage, however, he is named: like the Son he is also subordinated to the "good God from above" as his Spirit, and like the Son he comes down "for the salvation of those who attain his knowledge" (2.1). The formulations suggest that at least a part of the confession or its basic structure is old. An intratrinitarian pneumatology has not yet developed; Son and Spirit are seen in the perspective of salvation history. Even the council fathers at Nicaea (325) did not develop a theology of the *pneuma*. The confession presented there ends simply with the formula: "and [we believe] in the Holy Spirit."[97]

We find a quite similar view in Irenaeus, who in the disagreements of the second century developed a theology of the divine plan of salvation: for him also the descent of the Spirit, through whom the new church attains the perfection of knowledge, forms the aim and goal of the incarnation event. Yet in the writings of the bishop of Lyon the initially similar theology is at the same time oriented against Gnosticism: revelation is bound to the apostles and came to an end in the Pentecost event.[98]

Second, in the classical *symbola* the article on the incarnation is immediately followed by the article on death and resurrection, without mentioning Jesus' proclamation. This corresponds entirely to the general tendency of Greek theology to focus less on the human individual Jesus than on the divine person of the incarnate Word. In this perspective incarnation and redemption are identical: salvation is achieved in the assumption of human nature by the divine. The commentaries of the fathers in baptismal catecheses[99] explicate this theology already contained in the structure of the *symbola*.

Nevertheless, in the confession of Philomena and Apelles we find at this point—between the articles of faith on the incarnation and the passion—an insertion that speaks of Jesus' proclamation: Christ taught us three things: (a) "the knowledge from above": in the language of the Synoptic Gospels this corresponds to Jesus' announcement of the kingdom of God; (b) "to despise the demiurge and foreswear his works": this certainly recalls the scene of Jesus' temptation, which again has its echo in the rite of renouncing Satan in Christian baptism; (c) in which scriptures to find what he has spoken: this formulation recalls the scene of the Emmaus disciples to whom the resurrected One appears: "Were not our hearts burning within us . . . while he was opening the scriptures to us?" (Luke 24:32). The dialogues of the men and women disciples with the resurrected One are the typical revelation situation in the many Gnostic writings.[100]

Third, in the quoted *symbolon* "evil" is mentioned. Yet this interpretation presupposes that based on the clear parallel with the baptismal ritual, the "demiurge" in the passage is to be identified with Satan. In the usual confessions of faith the devil is never named, and for good reason: the dogmatically understood *symbolon* developed from the liturgical confession of God and Christ, which in solemn baptism has its place after the renunciation of Satan.[101] Thus the focus here was the concrete battle against evil, not an abstract theory about the origin of evil. Since the Gnostic *symbolon* never expressly says that the demiurge is evil or the originator of evil, the formulaic words could perhaps also be understood in the general sense of a renunciation of the world, yet the echo of the renunciation formula is very strong. In the following this interpretation will be presupposed.

Hidden behind this last part of the insertion—in the scriptures Christ and the demiurge speak—is above all the question of the interpretation of the Old Testament. We also find it in the Nicaeno-Constantinopolitan creed, yet in a much more inconspicuous place and not in connection with Christ: "[We believe in the Holy Spirit] . . . who spoke through the prophets." How the Apellian text is to be understood will soon be examined more precisely. The development of an early Christian theology of the Old Testament, which lies behind these two different formulas, cannot be sketched here.

We are occupied rather with the question, Does this confession authentically reproduce the teaching of the Philomenians? In order to answer it we can draw on other witnesses from the early period who had read the writings of Apelles: Hippolytus, Origen, and perhaps another Anonymus (Pseudo-Tertullian).[102] Now let us, on the basis of the articles of the *symbolon*, pursue the questions that were controversial between the Marcionites, the Philomenians, and the mainstream church. We will first look at the insertion that raises the question of the interpretation of scripture, then the question of the Creator-God and the origin of evil, and finally the question of the body of Christ and the resurrection of the flesh.[103]

i. The Interpretation of the Scripture

We customarily call the pre-Christian part of the Bible the Old Testament. Since this expression implies an interpretation, it will be avoided in the following, and we will speak instead of the "Jewish Bible."[104] The Jews themselves call their holy scripture by the abbreviation *Tanak,* which is composed of the initial letters of the three main parts: Law (*Torah*), Prophets (*nebiim*), and Writings (*ketubim*). In New Testament writers and the church fathers the almost identical formula, *the law and the prophets,* is frequently found. The fathers' corresponding term for the New Testament is *the gospel and the apostle.* For us "law" has a negative connotation, but it should be remembered that *Torah* would be better rendered as "guidance." In the following it is always a question of certain books of the Bible; *law* means the Pentateuch, the first five books of the Holy Scriptures, whose author traditionally is Moses.

Rejection of the Law and Prophets?

By a stroke of luck, we have the writing of a Gnostic from the Valentinian school who, like Apelles, is accused of blasphemy against God's law: *The Letter of Ptolemy to Flora.*[105] It allows us to determine what really lies behind the alleged blasphemies from a Gnostic pen and thus can also throw light on the debate around Philomena and her followers.

The author, about whom nothing else is known[106] (and the same is true of the addressee), gives a very clear answer to the Christian position on the Jewish law.[107] First, it comes by no means from evil (3.5). Not all the laws handed down in the Bible are to be judged in the same way: some come from God himself and are therefore good (for Ptolemy, the Ten Commandments); others are from Moses, and again others from the elders of the people—here good and bad are mixed (4.1–2; 5.3). The originally good laws were reestablished and perfected by Jesus, and the bad and mixed abolished (5.1). In addition there is another category of laws that have a "typological and symbolic function"—the cultic laws—which can be carried over from the external-visible into the spiritual (5.2). "The Law" as a whole, in which good and bad are mixed, goes back to the demiurge, who as "just" is somewhere in the middle between the good God and the originator of evil (7.2–5).

Only a single point makes this writing recognizable as Gnostic: the mention of the demiurge. Everything else could have been written just as well by an ardent defender of orthodoxy. In his judgment of the Jewish law Ptolemy names a criterion that is hard to contest: the criticism exercised by the historical Jesus himself. Concretely he refers to the Jewish divorce practice[108] and the gift to the temple as a substitute for caring for one's parents.[109]

The "blasphemies" of Apelles may have sounded similar, even if his criticism seems to have been more radical at some points. It is attested that in several of his own books (not in the *Phanerōseis* of Philomena recorded by him) he deals with the interpretation of the Jewish Bible. Thus Rhodo writes: "Apelles has sinned a thousand times against the law of Moses; in several writings he blasphemes the divine words and makes no small effort to reveal and refute them, as he says."[110] Hippolytus writes: "He deposes the law and the prophets: they record what is human and false."[111] At first Pseudo-Tertullian only notes summarily, "The law and the prophets he rejects," but then attests to the title of Apelles' main work: "[Besides the *Phanerōseis*] he has his books, which he calls *Syllogisms:* in them he claims to prove that everything that Moses wrote about God is not true but false."[112] Origen mentions Apelles more by accident, when he expresses himself in his disagreement with Celsus on the question whether before Jesus others (namely, angels) came down from heaven: "The Marcion student Apelles, the father of a heresy, holds the writings of the Jews to be legends [*mythos*]. He is of the opinion that only Jesus came from God to humankind. . . . Apelles does not believe in the books of the Jews that report miracles."[113] In another place he notes: "Even if [Apelles] did not fundamentally question that the law and the prophets come from God, he is still to be called a heretic . . . [because of his creation teaching]."[114]

These different testimonies show without doubt that Philomena and Apelles did not reject the Jewish Bible wholesale, yet they apparently advocated a rather critical form of reading—Harnack speaks of "impertinent rationalism."[115] Apelles criticizes the Law and the Prophets not only on theological grounds like Marcion but also on "scientific" ones: fragments that are extant in quotations by

Origen[116] almost all refer to the creation account and try to demonstrate that this could not be history but only myth. He reports similar criticism of the flood story: according to the measurements given in the Bible not even four elephants could have found room on the ark—"Thus it is certain that this is an invented story [*fabula*]; consequently this scripture cannot be from God."[117] Impertinent rationalism might be charged also, and even more, against the fundamentalists of the time who understood such stories in the sense of scientific-historical fact. Apelles' main concern was presumably to refute the "scriptural proofs" of his opponents when in their arguments on the question of God they appealed to Old Testament texts—we will return to this. In any case, the dispute between the Philomenians and the mainstream church was over *how* the Jewish Bible was to be understood.

Against this background let us read again—in a very literal translation—the crucial sentence from the confession: "[Christ] showed us in which scripture something was really [*physei*] spoken by him and what is from the demiurge." Epiphanius then adds a direct quotation from Apelles as commentary: "For thus, said he [Apelles], did he [Christ] speak in the gospel: 'Be clever money changers!' For, said he [Apelles],[118] I select from each writing what is useful and use it." This agraphon of the money changers was a favorite in the early church—thirty-seven quotations and twenty allusions have been demonstrated.[119]

In a superficial reading one could understand the sentence on scripture as follows: Christ speaks in the New Testament, not in the Old. Yet in reality the sentence presupposes that different scriptures contain words of Christ and words of the demiurge, which must be distinguished. Thus a *criterion* for judging is developed: *"what is useful."* This principle of critical selection corresponds to what Origen and Hippolytus indicated about Apelles' treatment of the scripture: the Alexandrian teacher attests his incredulity regarding miracle stories; the Roman theologian reproaches him for "deposing" the Jewish Bible and reading it as human words. In his critique the latter also refers to Apelles' relationship to the New Testament canon: "He selects from the Gospels and the apostle only what pleases him.[120] And he holds to the sayings of a certain Philomena as a prophetess in the so-called *Phaneröseis.*"[121] In other words, Apelles does not find the "word of Christ" everywhere in the Bible recognized by the church, and he can perceive it in writings that do not belong to the canon. Unfortunately, we do not know which texts were recognized by the Philomenians as "spoken from Christ."

Where Does Christ Speak?

Again, the dispute concerns not *whether* one is still to read the Law and the Prophets but *how* one is to read them. The results of a similar debate can be found in the *Didascalia:* there the author considered only the Ten Commandments obligatory as the "first law," while he polemicized most violently against the "second law" (the remainder of the Mosaic legislation). Yet that did not keep him from drawing on Old Testament books for edification and even recommending them in place of "pagan" reading matter.[122] For him 1 and 2 Kings are a substitute for historical accounts, the prophets for philosophers, the psalms for poetry, the creation account for the explanation of the world. The "second law," by contrast, should not even be read. Yet the Ten Commandments, the "first law," are the words of Christ. How can this be? The connection is made by means of a mysticism of letters: *ten* is written in Hebrew with the letter yod, which is also the initial letter of the name *Jesus*.[123] Thus here too a criterion is offered for discerning the voice of Christ in the Jewish Bible.

The author of the *Didascalia* represents the same antiphilosophical standpoint that we met in Tertullian—an attitude that will prevail more and more in later tradition. By contrast, we find a quite different view in the works of the first great Christian scholar, Clement of Alexandria (d. before 215). He sees law and prophets on the one hand and Greek philosophy on the other not as irreconcilable opposites but as differing yet converging ways of salvation, through which God prepared Jews and Greeks for the coming of Christ.[124] A similar open attitude was held by the philosopher and martyr Justin (d. ca. 165), in the teaching of the *logos spermatikos,* the seeded word: before his appearance on earth Christ sowed the seed of truth not only in the Jewish people but also in all of humankind, in order to prepare everyone for the fullness of revelation. These seeds of the word can be recognized in writings that wise individuals wrote before Christ.[125] Here too it is a question of making the right selection.

Thus Philomena and Apelles were not doing anything unusual when they read the Bible critically and selected only "what is useful," which they regarded as instruction spoken by Christ. Their task as Christians was precisely to perceive the divine Word, the heavenly Logos, in the words of human wisdom, as the image of the "money changer" suggests, for he must transfer money from one "currency" into another; that is, he has to change the good, which is found everywhere, into Christian coins.[126] The vocation of the money changer includes being able to distinguish the true from the false, the genuine from the bogus.

If this stance is consistently maintained, the sharp separation of "scripture" from "not scripture" is eliminated; revelation then occurs inside and outside of scripture. For Philomena and Apelles this was true not only for the past but equally for the future, for according to their belief Christ did not cease to reveal himself and speak through people after his exaltation. "Test everything; hold fast to what is good," proclaimed Paul as a motto in regard to prophecy in the church, as the preceding verses show: "Do not quench the Spirit. Do not despise the words of prophets" (1 Thess. 5:19–21). The Philomenians applied this principle to the testing and selection of all scripture—both to *the Law and the Prophets* and to *the Gospels and the letters of the apostle*—as well as to extracanonical documents of proclamation. And they found "useful" things both in the canon of church books and in the *Phanerōseis* of their prophetic teacher!

Allegorical Interpretation as Solution?

Yet what were their specific reservations with regard to the reading of the Bible practiced in the mainstream church? We know already that Marcion emphatically rejected an allegorical interpretation of the scripture, that is, an interpretation in which a deeper meaning is presumed behind the immediate statement. In his main work *Antitheses*[127] he expresses the principle: "The scripture must not be allegorized."[128] Philomena and Apelles also had no great interest in claiming the Jewish Bible for Christianity via reinterpretation.

Now, the allegorical interpretation of writings was by no means practiced only by Christians.[129] Greek thinkers had already had problems with the Homeric divine myths: radical critics rejected them entirely; others sought a "more conservative solution"[130] and interpreted them allegorically. The Jewish Alexandrian Philo (d. ca. 50) also applied this method in order to bring biblical stories into harmony with philosophical statements.[131] The Greek, Jewish, and Christian allegorists have in common that they distinguish between one literal sense and one or perhaps more hidden meanings. This method allows a moderate "critical" reading: the original assertion can be declared superseded without having to give up the text itself. For the mainstream church, Marcionites, and Philomenians were in complete agreement on one point: the holy scripture of the Jews could not, without further ado, also be the Bible of the Christians.

Even within Gnosticism there were "allegorical" interpretations.[132] In some movements extreme forms developed—one could ask whether it was still a question of allegory—in which the original meaning of the text is reversed: eating from the tree of knowledge (*gnōsis!*) was understood as an emancipatory act vis-à-vis the lesser God of creation and the world; Eve was venerated as a prophetess and the snake was seen as an angelic mediator figure opposed to the demiurge.[133] Irenaeus connects Marcion with this extreme exegesis, according to which the "rebels" of the Old Testament, for example, Cain, are redeemed and the "righteous" like Abel are not.[134] Such a reversal of text meaning is not attested for Philomena and Apelles. They place the Jewish Bible as *mythos*[135] on the same level with Homer's stories of the gods.

Allegorical interpretation in the mainstream church developed especially in Alexandria; one of its fathers was Origen, an opponent of Philomenian-Apellian rationalism. In Antioch, by contrast, a school developed in the third century that was more strongly oriented toward the literal meaning of the scripture and a historical understanding.[136] It was finally defeated, but not without having imposed a certain moderation on the allegory-addicted imagination. As earlier for the Greeks with Homer, for the Christians, too, a reading of the Jewish Bible prevailed that accepted a not immediately evident deeper meaning as the real revelation.[137] "At that time the Old Testament could not have maintained its acceptance otherwise," according to Woltmann.[138]

Central to the allegorical scripture interpretation of the fathers is a radical monopolization of the Bible from the Christian viewpoint: all the texts and events of Jewish history are read retroactively according to the schema of promise-fulfillment—not just the explicitly messianic and eschatological prophecies. The result is familiar to us: *the Law and the Prophets* became the *Old Testament*. Such a reading is emphatically rejected by Philomena and Apelles: for them it is Moses, not Jesus, who speaks in the Jewish Bible. The Law and the Prophets in their totality are not the anticipatory revelation of the incarnate and resurrected One. What is more, "What Moses taught about God is wrong!"[139] And what did Moses teach? God himself created the world. That in turn means that even evil in the world goes back to God—an unacceptable idea! With this we come to the crucial point of contention. Beforehand, however, we will attempt to summarize and evaluate critically the essential points of this understanding of scripture.

Result

1. Selection instead of interpretation. In the second and third centuries there was among Christians no unified theory about the Law and the Prophets as "Old Testament." For one side it was God's word; for the other a very human book of fables. Philomena and Apelles were among the educated people who had as much difficulty with the Jewish scripture as with the ancient myths of the Greek gods; their spiritual home was the philosophical culture of rational argumentation. They found it hard to perceive "revelation" in the colorful narrations of the Bible. Nonetheless, they did not simply reject the the Law and the Prophets that were read in the church but sought a key, which they found in the moral category of the "useful." The idea of Christ being able to speak in all writings, without therefore speaking everywhere in scripture, and also of revealing himself outside of scripture, represents an attempt to bring the new gospel into harmony with the old law and at the same time to remain open to other sources of revelation. Hence their *hermeneutical principle* is *critical selection,* not interpretation!

2. An open understanding of revelation. The idea of Christ speaking in different ways in different writings has a certain similarity with the teaching of the Paraclete in the New Prophecy. It is true that for the Gnostics the resurrected One himself was the mediator of revelation, whereas for the New Prophets it was the Holy Spirit; yet common to both Gnostics and New Prophets was the view that *revelation* is not a closed event but *an ongoing process.*[140] This open, inclusive understanding of scripture guards against any dogmatic misuse of the Bible.

3. Jesus' authority instead of apostolic authority. Philomena and Apelles believed they had found a key to the Christian reading of the Law and the Prophets (and also to the "gospel" and the "apostle"). Yet what does "useful" mean? Such a criterion points primarily to the realm of conduct. Since it is even more difficult here than in doctrine to find an answer valid for all times, the question may and must be raised and answered again and again. Thus such an understanding of revelation is *praxis-oriented* and avoids dogmatic determinations. In the position of the historical losers, the "heretics," one thing is especially to be emphasized as a critical corrective to the domineering opinion of the mainstream church: here was an attempt to develop by means of reason a *qualitative criterion* based on the content of Jesus' message, in order to judge "revelation"—not a *formal criterion*, such as apostolicity understood as temporal boundary. The "canon" ("guideline, norm") of the "Holy Scripture" was not a collection of certain books but a reliable standard for judging them.[141]

4. *Open questions.* Would this understanding of scripture not have to lead to *arbitrary and subjective interpretation?* This was without doubt a risk—yet it may have been the "lesser evil." The allegorical interpretation of scripture was, in fact, no less arbitrary—only it was implemented by a binding and seemingly objective doctrine of faith. After two thousand years of church history the danger of dogmatic ossification is more to be feared than the danger of subjective dissolution, for an open understanding of scripture at least contains within itself the possibility of self-correction. For Philomena and Apelles, however, it led to their being able to read *the Law and the Prophets* as a "useful" book—and even to hearing there in certain places the voice of Christ—and yet it also led to their rejecting so central an assertion as the creation of the world by God. We will now look at their reasons for this.

ii. The Creator-God and the Origin of Evil

When we examine the original teaching of Philomena and Apelles, we first discover that in this article of faith there is a clear contradiction between the formulations of the confession and the testimony of the early sources: the *symbolon* speaks of a "different God," but Rhodo, Hippolytus, and Pseudo-Tertullian expressly attest that there was no second God in Apelles' system. Nor do Tertullian and Origen mention a doctrine of two Gods.

According to the *symbolon* this "other God" established the world: Thus he is doubtless identical with the "demiurge," although that word is not used here. It is mentioned twice, however, in a different context: (1) in the scriptures there are "utterances from the demiurge"; that is, he is the originator of imperfect revelation; (2) "the demiurge is to be despised and his works foresworn": that is, he is "the evil one." This threefold identity of the one lesser "God"—builder of the world, inspirer of scripture, Satan—is in contradiction with the sources. How are these three secondary originator functions described there?

The Original Teaching

In the earliest testimonies, whose assertions cannot be easily harmonized, we encounter a complicated teaching on angels,[142] which corresponds to the conceptual world of Hellenism and Jewish Christianity in late antiquity (emphasis added):

> PSEUDO-TERTULLIAN: "[Apelles] introduced *one God* into the upper regions, who created *many powers and angels.* Therefore he calls the *other power* of which he speaks *'Lord'* but represents it as an *angel.* He is supposed to have established the world in imitation of the higher world. Yet this world

was tinged with regret[143] because he did not create it as perfect as the higher world."[144]

HIPPOLYTUS: "Apelles says the following: There is a *good God* (as Marcion also presupposed). The founder of the universe [or: all things] is *just*—he who produced [*edēmiourgēse*] what has come to be. A third one spoke to Moses— this one is *fiery*. There is still a further, fourth one: the *cause of evil*. This one he calls an angel."[145]

"Since Apelles, [Marcion's] student, did not agree with the statements of his teacher, as we said already, he proposed a different thesis: there are four Gods. The first he calls *good*: he was not known by [the law and] the prophets; Christ was his Son. The second is the *producer* [*dēmiourgos*] of the universe; this one is not supposed to be God [but a power of God]. The third is the *fiery* one, who appeared to [Moses]. The fourth is *evil* [*ponēron*]. These he calls angels. When he adds Christ, he finds a fifth."[146]

RHODO: "[Apelles] confesses a single principle but asserts that the prophetic scriptures come from an adversarial spirit."[147]

How are these various angels to be evaluated? Are the testimonies contradictory or complementary? If we compare the statements carefully, the following picture emerges:

Hippolytus and Pseudo-Tertullian essentially agree in their statements: over against God, the "one origin" (principle), stand on a lower level a number of other originators—namely, angels. To one of them is ascribed the "construc- tion" of the imperfect world (Pseudo-Tertullian says nothing about the remain- ing powers/angels). In the confession as well as in the named authors, the verb used for the "creation" of the angels by the good God is different from that used for the "production" of the world by one of these angels,[148] who is called "demi- urge, artisan"—that is, a word that for Greeks and Romans had a derogatory con- notation: manual labor was slave labor.

In addition Pseudo-Tertullian develops an unusual idea that he adopted from Tertullian:[149] on the basis of experiencing his own imperfection, the builder of the world brought regret into the world. Before the story of the Flood, the Bible says: "And the Lord was sorry that he had made humankind on the earth" (Gen. 6:6). For the Gnostics this sentence was doubtless a conclusive argument: a cre- ator who regretted his work could not be identical with the perfect God! It is in- teresting that the biblical motif of regret was adopted by the Philomenians not for God himself but for the creator-angel as a positive dimension of the world. Was the intention to relativize evil? Or to assert the possibility of leading the im- perfect to perfection? The meaning of this formulation needs to be examined more carefully.[150]

Hippolytus differentiates the "powers" even more exactly than Pseudo-Tertul- lian: opposite the "one good God" and on the level of angels he sets three origina- tor principles, which may stand in an inexactly defined hierarchical relationship.[151]

The sole Origin is followed by the demiurge as the first secondary originator: he is called "just."[152] The second originator "spoke to Moses" and is "fiery": a clear allusion to the burning bush (Ex. 3:1ff.) and the appearance of God in fiery form on Mount Sinai (Ex. 19:18). The third originator is called the "cause of evil." In parallel passages we find the same basic assertion with minor variations. Thus Hippolytus identifies the good God with the Father of Christ. "He was not known by the prophets": there are similar passages in the New Testament, which the Philomenians surely used as arguments in this controversy: "Many prophets and righteous people longed to see what you see, but did not see it, and to hear what you hear, but did not hear it."[153]

The quotation passed on by Rhodo does not talk of the creator of the world and the originator of evil, but only of the inspirer of the "prophetic scriptures" as an "adversarial spirit." This is a negative characterization; Rhodo spoke, as we have seen, only of a devaluation of the Jewish Bible as human words, not of a radical rejection based on the "evil nature" of its originator. Thus Rhodo's statement is not in contradiction with Hippolytus.

The "Fiery Angel"

The evaluation of the "fiery angel," the originator of the Law and Prophets, is especially difficult. Why is he distinguished from the creator-angel? In Apelles' systematization here, is he following the Bible, which assumes between the one God and his adversary the devil not only one but many angels? Apparently the former student of Marcion and now of Philomena wanted to see the demiurge neither as an antigod nor as a singular middle being between the good and the bad principle. Thus he divided the functions ascribed to the demiurge in Gnostic systems between two different angels.

Harnack[154] interprets the *fiery one* negatively but concedes that the relationship between this one and the world creator is unclear. According to Hippolytus, Apelles calls the world creator an angel and distinguishes him from the fiery and the evil angel and from Christ—pure errors for Harnack. Yet nowhere does it say that this "second angel fell away totally from the highest God."[155] The remark about Christ as the fifth one is surely intended ironically, for Hippolytus obviously wants to make Apelles look ridiculous with "four Gods." Why should he make a mistake here by conceding the angel designation, when this contradicts his polemical interests? Hence it seems more accurate to evaluate negatively only the one angel who in the Philomenian-Apellian system is expressly characterized as the "evil one" or "originator of evil." The "fiery one" would then be, like the world-builder, less than God and incomplete, but not "evil," as in Marcion. The *Letter to Flora* shows that the originator of the Law and the Prophets could be regarded quite positively in Gnostic circles; yet there he is not distinguished from the demiurge.[156]

This interpretation could be contested at most on the basis of Tertullian's polemical invectives against the Apellians, where the various angels are likewise brought into play. Nonetheless, the context is different there: Hippolytus and

Pseudo-Tertullian had presented Apelles' teaching on God and creation; Tertullian, in contrast, is mostly concerned with the corporeality of Christ and the resurrection of the flesh. In this connection the quotations below are cited:[157]

> The Apellians despise the flesh, which *that fiery chairperson of evil* is supposed to have bound with the souls lured down.[158]

> They call a certain *angel famous* who *established the world* and after the establishment is supposed to have allowed regret [*paenitentiam*] to come in.[159]

> Apelles reports that the souls were lured out of their heavenly places with earthly food by the *fiery angel, Israel's God* and ours,[160] who then shaped sinful flesh around them.[161]

> They call the body bad, although according to Apelles it was *created by a fiery being or angel.*[162]

> Apelles makes I know not which *glorious angel* of the higher God, whom he calls *fiery*, into the *creator* and *God of the law and Israel.*[163]

With little system, the anti-Apellian mixes the three originators: once he identifies the "fiery angel" with the "originator of evil" but three times with the judge of the world, whom he also calls a "famous" (*inclitum*) and "glorious" (*gloriosum*) angel, and twice with the "God of Israel." Thus here too the dominant impression is that both the creator-angel and the fiery angel have positive functions for Apelles, or at least cannot be simply equated with the "originator of evil," as their polemical opponent did (but only once!). Thus Hippolytus's more differentiated presentation is to be preferred to Tertullian's fuzzy one.

If the former accurately reproduces Philomena and Apelles' teaching, then we have here an important difference compared to the strict dualism of the good and evil God in Marcion: *neither the world nor the Jewish Bible have their origin in the principle of evil.* It is true that they do not participate in God's goodness, but they are not bad from the start, either.

The Article in the *Symbolon*

In the present article of faith in the *symbolon* on the question of God this differentiation has been lost linguistically but not in terms of content. Apparently, specific contents of the Philomenian-Apellian system have been connected here with general Marcionite or Gnostic means of expression. That means, concretely, that the idea of the originator-angels was linked with the talk of the demiurge as another God. Thus in its wording this part of the confession passed on by Epiphanius may be no longer directly traceable to Philomena and Apelles.[164]

Yet if we disregard this linguistic deviation, we find again the conceptual system worked out before as Philomenian-Apellian: on the one side stands *the one good God as sole origin*, the unnameable power that has nothing to do with the world. On the other side stand *three lesser originator-principles*: (1) the demiurge, the *builder of the world*, who is "not good"; his imperfection consists in a lower degree of spirituality; (2) the angel *who speaks in the scripture*—nothing more is said about him; (3) the *evil* angel, who should be despised and whose works should be renounced.

Thus in its content this article in the *symbolon* remains true to Philomenian-Apellian thought: the earthly world, humankind, and their history are within the sphere of influence of powers that are heavenly but do not participate in divine perfection. Above everything as origin and aim, however, stands the good God, who revealed his Son Christ in order to convey to humankind redeeming knowledge. Through the creation-mediation of an angel, who was "not good" and "not evil" either, but merely of "lower spirituality," the necessary distance is maintained between the wholly spiritual, wholly good, and perfect God and the imperfect world, in which material and spiritual, good and evil are mixed. The same is true of the Bible. Evil is ultimately attacked on the practical level of fighting and overcoming, as its inclusion in the baptismal formula shows. Did this not create a bridge to mainstream orthodoxy?

No to the Creator—Yes to the Creation?

Let us again call to mind Marcion's scheme: even in Rhodo's judgment "he made it easy for himself,"[165] when he simply attributed evil and good to two contending principles. Adolf von Harnack also ascertained at this very point a "logical weakness,"[166] which gave Apelles [or Philomena before him] a point of attack: two equally divine archprinciples, good and evil, cannot be in a hierarchical relationship to each other as the good and the evil God would be. Therefore Philomena and Apelles maintained the unity of the divine, placed evil as a principle on a lower level of spiritual power, and did not let it merge with the principle of creation. Between Marcion's gloomy *negativism* (the world is bad and thus not the work of the good God) and the *positivism* of the mainstream church (the world is God's work and thus it is good) they chose a rational theological *realism:* the world is too bad to be immediately affirmed as God's creation and yet too good to be simply identified with evil. It has the character of the provisional, the transitory, which the spiritual human being leaves behind. For us today it is certainly a problem that the prophetess and her followers required a spiritual, heavenly, intermediate world for this solution; it was not for her contemporaries.

Thus the critique of Epiphanius in his glosses on the *symbolon* also concerns not the introduction of the angels as such but the faulty logic of the system. And he was without doubt right when he noted that the mediation of an angel in the creation of the world does not solve the problem of God's responsibility for evil but only shifts it, for God created the angel who creates evil! In the second century, however, another problem had to be solved before the theodicy issue: two very different conceptions of God had to be brought into harmony with each other.

This was first of all a cultural problem, for the Jewish image of God was shaped by the graphic narrative language of the Bible; by contrast, the Hellenist image of god—more correctly, the Hellenistic concept of God—was articulated in the abstract language of speculative reflection. Marcion's scheme was an attempt to resolve the contradiction: "Marcion made a distinction between the two Gods because he could not reconcile the anthropomorphic traits of the Old Testament God with the philosophical concept of an essentially good God" (MM 145). The dilemma was real. The contradiction between the Jewish-biblical and the Greek-philosophical images of God in regard to creation can be expressed in a simple formula: in the *Bible* it is the *relationship with the world* that is constitutive for God; in *philosophy* it is the *antithesis to the world*. Hellenistically educated Christians of the second century could not escape the conflict between the two images of God: they encountered the first one in Christian liturgy and catechesis; the other was a component of their culturally shaped prior understanding. What did the individual attempts at a solution look like for Marcion, the mainstream theologians, and Philomena?

Attempts at a Solution

1. Marcion "made it easy for himself"—he turned the two conceptions of God into two Gods. The one who first appeared was the "God-in-relationship-with-the-world," the creator/demiurge, the God of the Law and the Prophets, the evil God. Not until in Christ was the previously "foreign," entirely spiritual God revealed, the "God-in-antithesis-to-the-world," the God of the gospel and the apostle, the good God. Without conscious intention, Marcion let the Christian God merge with the philosophical God and placed him over the Jewish God. The result: radical negation of the world! The material world is bad. In late antiquity many people held this view, especially many Gnostics. Yet Marcion went further: even the human spirit is bad. At this point neither Platonists nor Gnostics could follow him anymore. Here the theologian steeped in Greek dualism radicalized Paul: whereas the apostle spoke of the enslavement of *all* people, Jews and Greeks, to sin (Rom. 3:9), Marcion spoke of the enslavement of the *entire* person, body and spirit, to sin.[167] This connection of the Pauline antagonism of law and gospel with Gnostic dualism leads to a radicalism that, according to May, is singular in the second century[168]—and that may also be the source of the special fascination of this theological scheme. The Marcion system made Christians the sole "possessors" of the true God.

2. Theologians of the mainstream church. Vis-à-vis this extreme position, which emphasized the exclusivity and uniqueness of Christian divine revelation, it was without doubt a considerable accomplishment of the men and women theologians of the mainstream church to see two things: (1) the God of Jesus was none other than the God of the Jews, and (2) the Hebrew and the Hellenistic conceptions of God were fundamentally different but not irreconcilable. On this foundation the church fathers and mothers[169] created a synthesis of the two images of God that determined the entire later tradition of Christianity. The first great architect of this synthesis was Irenaeus of Lyon,[170] who maintained unity against all dual and dualistic schemes: the Creator is also the Redeemer; the God of Jesus spoke to the Jews through Moses and the prophets; there is only one single salvation history, which began with creation and will culminate in the kingdom of God.[171] And evil? This was not a central question for Irenaeus: from the beginning God wanted to lead humankind to himself in a slow growth process. Humanity fell away from him in a childish lack of understanding, but by means of the law God gradually led human beings to maturity and then sent his Son to make ultimate restoration and perfection possible.

3. *Philomena and Apelles'* position lay between Marcionite pessimism and Irenaean optimism. Their concern was twofold. (1) The radical distinction between God and the world, between spirit and matter should be maintained—here they advocated a Greek-Gnostic position. (2) The predicate "good" in the absolute sense is reserved for God alone. Yet for this reason matter, world, and above all human beings should not simply be regarded as "evil"—here they were close to the biblical message and the position of the mainstream church. Their affirmation of the world and humankind places them closer to Irenaeus than to Marcion, yet they could not conceive of God in immediate relationship with this world. They bridged the chasm by means of a multilevel teaching on angels—a mythologem that was natural to their contemporaries but to us today is almost completely lost. This idea of an intermediate world failed to gain entrance into the church's doctrine of creation but found a place instead in the doctrine of original sin developed later: in the theologoumenon of the "fall of the angels."[172] The concern that was hidden behind the Gnostic dualism of "another God" was the question of the origin of evil. It was not satisfactorily answered with a simple affirmation of the biblical faith in creation.

iii. Corporeality, Resurrection, and Christology

In the preceding section we discovered connections between creation faith and resurrection hope. The two theologoumena come together in Christology, when we raise the question of Jesus' corporeality, the nature of his bodily existence. Does the *symbolon* contain Philomena and Apelles' original teaching? Let us first recall the wording of the christological article, in order then to compare it with the statements of early witnesses:

> He *not only seemed to come* but *truly took on flesh,* not from the Virgin Mary, and yet he had real flesh and a body, but *not from the seed of a man or from a virginal woman.* Nevertheless, he had true flesh in the following way: when he descended from heaven, he came to earth and gathered his body from the four elements. . . . [He took] the dry from the dry, the warm from the warm, the wet from the wet, the cold from the cold, and in this way he formed himself a body, really appeared in the world, and taught us the knowledge from above. . . . Then Christ allowed his body to *suffer,* and he was really *crucified* and really *buried,* and he has really *risen;* and he *showed his disciples this very flesh.* Then he dissolved this human shape again and gave each element its share back: warm to the warm, cold to the cold, dry to the dry, wet to the wet. And after he had thus

again dissolved his fleshly body, he ascended into heaven, from which he had come.[173]

In Rhodo we find, surprisingly, no information on the dispute over incarnation and resurrection. That may be due to arbitrary selection by Eusebius, who, as Robert Grant has correctly remarked, was "writing a *Church History* in which the real difficulties posed by heretics were never faced."[174]

In Tertullian, by contrast, the question of the nature of Jesus' body played a central role in the dispute with his Gnostic opponents:

> That virgin Philomena persuaded Apelles and the other opponents of Marcion to believe that *Christ assumed flesh, yet not through birth but through the union of the elements.*[175]
>
> Some students of the [man] from Pontus [= Marcion] are more intelligent than their teacher and admit that the corporeality of Christ was genuine but did not come from birth. They say: *"The Lord had flesh, but it was not born."* Thus we are jumping, as they say, from the pan into the fire when we move from Marcion to Apelles: after the latter gave up Marcion's discipline, he fell victim to a woman according to the flesh; then later to the virgin Philomena according to the spirit. From her he received [the commission] to proclaim *that Christ had a concrete body, yet independent of a birth.*[176]

Pseudo-Tertullian precedes the information with a negative evaluation of the Philomenian-Apellian conception of the incarnation:

> About Christ [Apelles] says neither, like Marcion, that he had an apparent body [*phantasma*], nor, like the gospel, that he had the substance of a genuine body, but that when he descended from the higher regions, he took on, during this very descent, *an astral and airy kind of flesh.*[177] At his resurrection and ascension he gave this back to the individual elements, which he had transformed on his descent, and thus after the scattering of the components of his body he returned to heaven as only spirit.[178]

From Hippolytus we have a summary and a detailed presentation:

> [Apelles] said that *Christ did not assume flesh from the virgin but from the substance of the world [kosmos] already at hand.*[179]
>
> [Apelles] said that Christ came down from the higher power, that is, from the good God, whose Son he is. *He was neither born of the virgin nor without flesh when he appeared; rather, he took a part of the substance of the universe and created from it his body,* namely warm and cold, wet and dry. In this body, hidden from the cosmic powers, he lived during his lifetime in this world. Crucified by the Jews, he *died;* after three days he *arose* and *appeared* to the disciples. He showed them the nail marks and his side in order to convince them that he was no spirit but had flesh. *After he showed them the flesh, he gave it back to the earth, from which the substance came.* He did not acquire anything foreign, but after he had used it for a while, he gave back to each its own, as he *removed*

the fetters of the body: warm to the warm, cold to the cold, wet to the wet, dry to the dry. And so he went forth to the good father and left in the world the seed of life for those who would believe in him through his disciples.[180]

Conclusion: Pseudo-Tertullian's evaluation—"no genuine body"—is in contradiction to all other testimonies. By contrast, Hippolytus's comments in the christological part coincide exactly with the article of the *symbolon* and also with Tertullian's statements. Beyond this, the *symbolon* contains only expansions and refinements. Thus we can assume here at least an authentic reproduction of Philomena's original proclamation and perhaps even original formulations.

The Body of Jesus

Jesus was not only an apparent human being: he had a real body! From Tertullian's account we learn that this particular amendment to Marcion's teaching was especially important to the prophetess: thus we are dealing here with a central concern of her preaching. Yet in spite of her insistence on real corporeality, she rejected the idea of a virgin birth of Jesus. Did she have "scientific" reasons, as Apelles had in his critique of the creation account? Yes and no: the scientific objection (there can be no virgin birth) is secondary here to the theological argument (birth is not an adequate means for the incarnation of God).

Thus Philomena's criticism of the virgin birth does not lie on the same level as that of the Jewish Christians, who regarded Jesus as the son of Mary and Joseph.[181] The Roman prophetess advocated a "high" Christology no less than the Gnostics, Marcion, and the mainstream theologians: the theologoumenon of the Son of God who was preexistent as a spiritual being[182] is assumed as a matter of course. She holds a second premise in common with her opponents: the incarnation of the Son of God had to be accomplished outside the laws of a normal birth. Why does she, nonetheless, reject the idea of a virgin birth? Because for this radical advocate of the spiritual nature of human beings, a virgin birth would have been only a half-hearted solution. Why have this strange mythos that partially suspended the laws of biology but still did not bring liberation from the flesh? Not conceived like a human being, and yet born like a human being? Philomena had a more consistent conceptual model for the incarnation: when the Son of the good God descended to earth, he assumed from the earth what he needed for his existence in an earthly body; and he sovereignly gave these elements back when he left the earth again. What was he supposed to do with a body in God's spiritual world? With this conceptual model the reality of the incarnation, the presence of God in the world—even as the mainstream church understood it—could be affirmed without subjecting God himself to biological necessities and without giving up the sovereignty of the Spirit over matter.

Epiphanius is not entirely incorrect when he notes in his comments on the Apellians that here a "Greek" conception of the incarnation was adopted: that of the "old poets."[183] Yet as the testimonies clearly indicate, Philomena was not thinking of a transitory appearance on earth: Jesus was not to be compared with gods in human form like Hermes or Zeus. Not for a moment is the authenticity of his human nature called into doubt. In Hippolytus's presentation we find all the formulas of the mainstream church's confession of faith—reinforced in the *symbolon* three times by a "really" (*en alētheia*): suffered, was crucified, died, arose, ascended into heaven. Unlike other Gnostics, Philomena does not even call into question the real corporeality of the resurrected One appearing to the disciples:[184] not until the moment of the ascension is the earthly body dissolved. In this conception Christ himself always remains the sovereign subject:[185] he assumes the body, he decides to suffer in the body, he dissolves the body again. On all these issues the *symbolon* remains entirely within the framework of mainstream Christology.

Bodiless Resurrection

Thus the question of the *resurrection of the flesh* was the *real point of contention* on which the spirits differed[186]—not, be it noted, the resurrection of the dead! That Christ arose and that those who follow him would also arise were convictions common to both mainstream and Gnostic Christians, yet the mainstream church insisted on corporeality, while for the Gnostics resurrection could mean only a purely spiritual mode of existence. On this question Philomena combines scientific and theological critique: (1) the *scientific* argument: a human body cannot exist timelessly, eternally; (2) the *theological* argument: an eternal corporeal existence contradicts the grandeur of the spiritual nature of God and also the spiritual nature of the human soul.

Thus in anthropology we encounter *two different paradigms* and at the same time an antithesis similar to that in the doctrine of God. (1) In the *religious tradition of the Jews* the *unity of body and soul* was assumed. The "soul" here was understood less as "spirit" than as the vital force that gives life to the human body. (2) The *philosophical tradition of the Greeks*, by contrast, saw the soul primarily as spirit and stressed the *antagonism of body and soul*. This view corresponded to *two paradigms of postmortal existence*. (1) For Jewish conceptions it meant the *ongoing life of soul and body*, without much reflection on this other-worldly "corporeality." (2) The Greeks, however, believed in the *ongoing life of the soul without the body;* they had no interest at all in the resurrection of the body, for it was the "grave"[187] of the soul from which human beings wanted finally to be freed.

Now, for Hellenistic Christians these two paradigms had to be brought into harmony in the confession of faith. To this end, there were various models. (1) *Radical Gnostics* chose the "spiritual" solution; that is, they understood the appearances of Christ after his death as spiritual experiences that were possible for all believers and knew no temporal limitation. (2) The *mainstream church* insisted on the real corporeality of the resurrected One and declared the Lukan theology to be obligatory; that is, appearances to certain witnesses were limited to forty days, after which Christ was assumed into heaven with his body. (3) *Philomena* sought to solve the problem by holding to the real corporeality of the resurrected One for the forty days until the ascension. After that a body no longer made sense to her. Christ could return to heaven "only as spirit."[188]

"There is no resurrection of the body": this statement certainly conveys the conviction of Philomena and her followers correctly. Since we ourselves today are shaped by the tradition of the mainstream church, we find this interest in a total spiritualization of the resurrected One surprising. Yet Christians from the Gnostic tradition found the "docetic" solution more convincing: the Redeemer did not have a real material body during his lifetime, and still less afterward, for in Jesus Christ, God intervened salvifically in the world, at the same time maintaining his distance from the world. Thus for Christian Gnostics the opposite question arises: Why did Philomena, this radical defender of the spiritual nature of human beings, insist so emphatically on the real corporeality of the Redeemer in his earthly existence? Was the body not worthy of contempt?

Disdain for the Body?

Fundamentally, Marcion's docetism was logically consistent: body and matter were regarded as radically bad; consequently God and Christ could have nothing to do with them.[189] Did Philomena and Apelles also hold this negative view of human corporeality, even though they rejected the idea of only an apparent body for Jesus? It seems so when we read Tertullian's critique: "The Apellians despise the flesh,"[190] he asserts; "they call the body bad."[191] Did they really? Or does he declare only on the basis of polemical interests that the rejection of a resurrection of the body is equivalent to a general disdain for human corporeality?

The latter is indicated by a contradiction in which the theologian entangles himself with the curious mixture of angel figures. He tries, namely, to slay Philomena and Apelles with their own weapons: even if the human body were not created by God himself, but only by a "fiery being or angel," he argues, it would still be glorious enough to be worthy of resurrection.[192] This reference to the grandeur of the creator does not fit well with his assertion that according to Apelles' teaching the "fiery originator of evil" lured souls down in order then "to form sinful flesh around them."[193] Moreover, since we do not find similar assertions in the writings of other witnesses, we can presume a more positive teaching behind these negative distortions. It could have gone like this: the spiritual soul of human beings was created by the demiurge, the "glorious angel of the higher God";[194] the body, however, came from the "fiery angel" and was bound by him to the preexistent soul.[195] Thus in their souls as in their bodies human beings are created by angels, that is, by beings "of lower spirituality";[196] both body and soul participate in their imperfection. All the same, however, the earthly human body comes from a higher being and is therefore "not bad": *on earth* the bodily existence of human beings is absolutely to be affirmed![197]

Are there arguments that could support this hypothesis? I see at least one: there is no ascetic rigorism attested for Philomena. At one point Tertullian incidentally classifies Apelles with those heretics who forbid marriage,[198] yet he himself asserts in another context that Apelles abandoned the "continence of Marcion."[199] Since a Philomenian prohibition of marriage is nowhere attested, we can give the polemicist no credence here. Even if Philomena chose celibacy for herself, her striving toward spirituality does not seem to have been connected with a general hostility toward marriage and the body, which is so emphatically attested for Marcion. In Harnack's description: "No Christian community has prescribed a more other-worldly and difficult order and conduct of life than the Marcionite. For his believers [Marcion] totally forbade marriage and any sexual activity."[200] In the testimonies on Philomena and Apelles, however, we never find the reproach of excessive asceticism.

The Sex of Souls

This positive attitude toward life in the world is complemented by a final feature in Philomena's teaching: she affirms the sexual differentiation of human beings even beyond earthly existence. For this information we are again indebted to the polemic of Tertullian, who in his treatise *On the Soul* (*De anima*) notes the following:

> Apelles . . . who lets souls exist as male and female beings before the creation of their bodies, as he learned from Philomena, also has the flesh, as the later creation, receives its sex from the soul. (36.3)

In this writing the theologian from Carthage wanted to prove two things: (1) the soul has a beginning and is "corporeal"; (2) body and soul come into being simultaneously. In other words, he was fighting the idea of a preexistent spirit-soul, which was advocated by Platonic philosophers and Gnostic theologians, but also by church fathers considered orthodox—in particular, Origen. Yet the doctrine of the preexistence of souls was increasingly opposed in the mainstream church; in the context of the Origenist controversies in the sixth century it was finally condemned.[201]

Tertullian defended his radical rejection of this teaching with a mixture of scientific-medical and philosophical-theological arguments. His interest is in proving that body and soul originate at the same time in the moment of conception. From this simultaneity he concludes that the sex of a human being is derived neither from the soul for the body nor from the body for the soul: "The unseparated seed of both substances [that is, body and soul] and their united issue effect together the origination of the sex." Yet this is immediately followed by a limitation, in order to maintain a sexual hierarchy: "Certainly here too the original rule prevails according to which the male being is formed earlier (for Adam came first) and the female somewhat later (for Eve was created later)" (36.4).

Philomena's view stands in contrast to this: preexistent spirit-souls are male or female; the body receives its sex from the soul. Because of the meager information available we can no longer discern how the prophetess understood femaleness and maleness in the purely spiritual realm of the soul, but the fact alone is important, since in her time many theologians regarded the soul as sexless.[202] They defined maleness and femaleness by the body; by means of continence the state of angel-like *sexlessness* could be attained already on earth, which at the same time could mean the *abolition of the sexual hierarchy*. We have already encountered these ideas in the chapter on ascetic women.[203] For Philomena, however, sexlessness was not a desirable state: even in their purely spiritual existence people were women and men, both before and after their bodily existence. Spiritualization did not abolish the sexual difference. Such a *fundamental affirmation of the human division into two sexes* is doubtless an important feature in this thinker's theological scheme.

At this point other questions arise. Did Philomena support a *sexual hierarchy?* That is hardly to be assumed, since according to her theory both femaleness and maleness participate equally at the highest level of human spirituality. Does she assume *polar complementarity?* That is possible, for as we saw, various Gnostic systems encompass femaleness and maleness with the conceptual category of mutually complementary "paired partners."[204] Does she ascribe *different functions* to women and men in human society and in the Christian church? That seems very unlikely in view of the role that she herself played. We can state with certainty that she *affirmed sexual difference* as constitutive of concrete human existence. It is to be presumed that she presupposed *equality of rank,* which also meant concretely *equality of rights.*

c. Summary

In second-century Rome Marcion, one of the greatest theologians of his time and founder of an independent church, stood over against a no less great theologian: the virgin and prophetess Philomena. With her proclamation, ultimately supported by the writing activity of her student Apelles, she was able to win for herself a considerable number of the followers of Marcion and convince them of the necessity of undertaking crucial corrections of the doctrinal system of the master from Pontus. In an impressive and exemplary way she seems to have set out on a path of spiritualization, without falling into contempt for the world and hostility to life.

Yet before we emphasize her uniqueness, let us look first at what bound her to her era. Philomena was a typical representative of highly educated Hellenistic Christianity. Her concern was to exhibit the rationality of Christian convictions and at the same time to criticize theological opinions that seemed irrational. Like mainstream, Gnostic, and Marcionite men and women teachers, she sought ways to bring the message of Jesus, as formulated in the language of the Bible, into harmony with the religious-cultural heritage of Hellenism, in which theological conceptual models had been developed whose level of sophistication many wanted to retain.

We have seen where Philomena, as well as the other intellectuals of her time, had difficulties:

> What significance did the religious tradition of Judaism have for philo-
> sophically educated Greeks who wanted to accept the message of the
> gospel?
> How was a God thought to be totally spiritual and totally good to be re-
> lated to a world that was imperfect and in which there was evil?
> How were resurrection and eternal life with God to be understood when
> the end of human corporeality remained an indisputable fact?

On none of these questions did Philomena hold an extreme position: she did
not postulate a rejection of the "Old Testament" in principle, nor did she promote a radical renunciation of the world, nor did she teach a devaluation of human corporeality and sexuality. Yet her starting point was the primacy of the spiritual. Only the spirit was capable of the perfect and the eternal. Everything
corporeal and material was transitory and could have meaning only in the context of temporality.

Yet this orientation toward the spiritual did not lead Philomena to abandon
reality. Thus she could reject the incarnation of the Son of God through a real
birth—even in the form of a not quite so real virgin birth!—and yet hold unhesitatingly to the real corporeality of the historical Jesus. Her speculative theory did not lead to reinterpreting earthly states of affairs contrary to appearance. She knew how to distinguish between history and myth: the Jesus
reported in the Gospels was a real human being. The account of the virgin
birth, however, was a myth that was supposed to explain the "how" of the incarnation; she did not feel bound to it and replaced it with a "more scientific"
explanatory model.

Realism and *rationality*—these are the two crucial characteristics of
Philomenian theology. Christianity is lived in the world, and concrete human existence in a body; there was no reason to negate or denigrate this factual situation. Real existence in this world was the natural destination of every path of spiritualization. Just as natural, however, was the fact that with death one leaves
behind the earthly, bodily mode of existence.

What distinguishes Philomena from Marcion is the *acceptance of the imperfect*.
For her, evil is not a metaphysical but a moral problem. At this point she is not
essentially different from positively minded theologians like Irenaeus. Is it accidental that he includes Marcion in his long list of Gnostic "heretics" but neither
Philomena nor Apelles? Did the bishop of Lyon perhaps still see no unbridge-
able gulf between their teaching and that of the mainstream church, whose advocate he had made himself?

Where Philomena distanced herself from official doctrine and from Marcion,
she did so in the name of rationality and philosophy. Had she thus entered a
"fateful confederacy" with the "educated Greeks whom Christianity opposed,"
for which Harnack reproaches Apelles?[205] Or did she in exemplary fashion endeavor to grasp and impart the Christian message in the language of her time?
Success was hers for only a short time. When Christian teaching was to be

conveyed to broader classes, the conceptual structure she and Apelles developed proved too complicated and demanding. Did it simply die out, or are elements of her concerns to be found again in later traditions?

d. History of Influence?

Against the radical good-evil dualism of Marcion and the strict spirit-matter dualism of Philomena, the message of Irenaeus, who unreservedly affirmed human beings in their corporeality and their history, seemed at first to prevail; among the schemes of his time, his theology was one of the most life-friendly and liberating. At the same time it was minimally speculative and hence easier to pass on. Yet the optimistic view of the bishop of Lyon had little permanent influence on Christian tradition—especially in the West. The questions raised by Marcion and the Gnostics about evil in the world were raised anew in later centuries and found an answer, which we know today under the name *original sin*.

The West

With Irenaeus a shift in accent occurred. The Gnostics had sought the one responsible for evil in the world in a divine or at least other-worldly spiritual realm. Now the bishop of Lyon pointed to a different subject as the originator when he recalled a statement from Paul: "Sin came into the world *through one man,* and death came through sin" (Rom. 5:12). Yet whereas Irenaeus understood this "sin" entirely as "imitation of Adam" and death as the resulting weakening of human nature, a later great theologian, Augustine, with his teaching of radically bad human beings, let Marcion back in through the back door, as it were.

Augustine did not directly refer to the master from Pontus, the latter's teaching was absorbed into Manichaeanism,[206] which left a lasting imprint on the bishop of Hippo.[207] Like no other, he refined the problem of the contradiction between the justice and the goodness of God—and ultimately resolved the theodicy question by burdening human beings: they and they alone, through the abuse of their freedom, are responsible for the world's troubles and hence must be punished with eternal damnation. In the meantime, it has become known that this Augustinian view does not correspond to Paul's intentions and indeed is ultimately based on a translation error.[208] Nevertheless, it made theological history. It was intensified by the medieval satisfaction theory of Anselm of Canterbury and finally by Luther's doctrine of justification and Calvin's doctrine of predestination. The affinity between Marcion and Reformation theology in its negative judgment of humankind, as well as the strong emphasis on the *extra nos* of redemption, is to be felt even in Harnack's sympathy with the "gospel of the foreign God": it is not for nothing that he names Marcion a "real reformer" and the "first Protestant."[209] Thus for the West the answer to the question of the "two principles," the question of the origin of evil, can be grasped in the formula: God is good; evil comes from human beings.

The East

Against the background of this "neo-Marcionite" development of Western theology, one can ask whether in the East there could have been a "neo-Philomenianism." Philomena lived in Rome and thus in the "West," yet in her time Roman theology was still entirely "Eastern," that is, shaped by speakers of Greek. A specifically "Western," Latin—theology does not begin until the African Tertullian. Within the context of this study the question of traces of Philomenian thinking in the Eastern church cannot be examined comprehensively; we will only spotlight a few commonalities with later Greek Orthodox theology.

1. *Human beings as the victims of evil.* First, it is notable that the Eastern *doctrine of original sin,* which differs considerably from the *doctrine of inherited sin* in the West, gives great significance to the "fall of the angels." It took place before the "fall of Adam"; only in this way could evil come to human beings at all: in this perspective human beings are first victims and only then doers.[210] The mythological theologoumenon of the fall of the angels[211] may seem of little help to us today, but let us not overlook the important function it had. In the Western doctrine of inherited sin the theodicy question is decided at the expense of human beings: they bear the responsibility for evil in the world and therefore deserve punishment. In the theology of the Eastern church, by contrast, they are relieved of that burden: they are victims and deserve mercy. Naturally, one cannot speak of a direct influence of the Philomenian school and its angel teaching, yet much of its concern is preserved here, for it also wanted to see goodness above all in God, without at the same time taking all goodness away from human beings.

2. *Divine-human cooperation.* Another tradition of Eastern theology belongs in the area of the doctrine of original sin. Marcion related the saying about humankind being created in God's "image" and "likeness" (Gen. 1:28) to the body and the soul: since both were created by the evil God, the demiurge, both were evil. In other words, on their own, body and soul could not attain redemption; of themselves they were not "capable of redemption."[212] This radically negative view of humankind was rejected by Philomena and many Hellenist Christians. Now, in the tradition of Eastern patristics we find a different interpretation: the terms *image* and *likeness*[213] are related to the whole person: being in the "image of God" is an enduring spiritual dignity of humankind that cannot be lost even through sin; only the "likeness" is destroyed. Through redemption in Christ it is initially reestablished and perfected through lifelong asceticism ("practice") under the impetus of the Spirit.[214] Both elements of this Easter doctrine of divine-human *synergeia,*[215] which is the counterpart of the Western doctrine of justification, are found in the short confession of Apelles that is passed on to us by Rhodo: "Those who put their hope in the crucified One will attain salvation if they contrive to do good works."[216]

3. *Distance from the world.* This concern of the Philomenian school is also preserved in the later orthodox theology of the East: Gnosticism sought to assure God's distance from the world through the distinction between a completely

spiritual God far from the world and a less spiritual creator devoted to the world. In Eastern theology this distinction was integrated into the doctrine of the one God: according to his essence (*ousia*) God remains unknowable by human beings, yet he communicates himself by means of his active power (*energeia*) in the world.[217] Thus he remains inaccessible to humankind and yet at the same time evident.

4. *The friendliness of the good God.* The concern of the "good God," to whom wrath, retribution, and thus punitive intervention in the world are foreign, has also found its place in the Orthodox doctrine of God. Whereas in the West God's omnipotence and role as judge are emphasized, in the East his loving mercy is especially praised.[218] In this theology God's most important attribute is his goodness, and the liturgy praises him as "the friend of humankind." Thus a modern Orthodox theologian remarks: "Luther's anxious question, 'How do I get a gracious God?' cannot be appreciated in the East, for the dominant idea there is love for humankind."[219]

5. *The inclusion of the universe.* When Philomena has the incarnation of God happen not through birth but through the uniting of elements, the theologoumenon of the "cosmic Christ" stands out very clearly. Certainly today's orthodoxy would reject this notion of the incarnation. Yet in Eastern theology the inclusion of the whole universe in the salvation event is a central idea, whereas in the West redemption is regarded anthropocentrically as reconciliation between God and humankind, while nature is ignored. Today the debate over the origin of Jesus' body has become obsolete, since in our conceptual world the idea of an incarnation of God tends to include rather than exclude normal biological procreation. This very process accomplishes the "uniting of elements" that Philomena and Apelles wanted to postulate apart from birth. Yet with this uniting they in their own way expressed the participation of humankind in the cosmos and thus the inclusion of the world in the salvation event. Today this aspect of a theology of God's incarnation has again become an important concern for us in view of the global destruction of nature.

This is not meant to assert that in all the foregoing points there was a direct influence by Philomena. Rather, her concerns were shared not only by Gnostic but also by many mainstream Christians who were indebted to their philosophical heritage. These women and men were all precursors and pioneers of the Greek Orthodox tradition. Yet what May writes about Apelles must apply all the more to his inspirer Philomena; "He [she] belongs to the series of second century theologians who—whether Gnostics or catholics—through their intellectual endeavors created the foundations for a comprehensive speculative development of Christian doctrine."[220]

Perhaps the time has come when we not only can accept without reservation the much-abused "hellenization of Christianity" as a fact but also can see how much Christianity has been enriched by the integration of the religious heritage of "pagan" antiquity. Without doubt, much more of this ancient legacy has been preserved in Eastern Christianity than in the West, and today the synthesis created by the fathers is consciously preserved in the East. In the historical constellation in which Christianity developed, contemporary Eastern theologians see a *providentia Dei* and conclude that Christianity's Hellenistic garment is indispensable.[221] Yet this seems to me a false conclusion: with foreign cultures new syntheses of what is Christian must be created again and again.

Philomena's theology was such an attempt. Much of it has become foreign to us today. But is this distance from the Christian ideas familiar to us due to its "heresy" or to the different nature of its time? From today's perspective we are accustomed to interpreting the insistence of the church fathers on the creation and resurrection faith positively as affirmation of the world. Yet was that the intention? When we compare Gnosticism with the mainstream church in terms of their concrete, practical attitudes toward the world, the differences are not as great as it might seem on the theoretical level. Asceticism and celibacy are praised by both. And the mainstream church's defense of creation and resurrection faith has in no way protected Christianity from traditions that turn away from the world and are hostile to life. The result of the theological development is completely ambivalent. On the one hand, the Christian teaching of the creation of the world by God and the resurrection of the flesh have doubtless rescued a bit of world-affirming this-worldliness from the Jewish Bible. On the other hand, the anti-Gnostic emphasis on the "material nature" of the resurrection body has burdened the Christian resurrection message with a hypothesis that to this day presents a difficulty for many: at this point we could perhaps let ourselves be inspired again by the spiritual traditions of early Christianity.

Yet the solutions of *our* intellectual problems do not lie in the past; without doubt we need different conceptual models for today. The positive element in the mainstream church's insistence on the bodily resurrection lies in the holistic view of being human: people, women and men, are not to be thought of apart from their bodies; only in a corporeal mode of existence can they experience themselves as persons. But that is a psychological assertion of modern anthropology. In order to harmonize it with the Christian hope of resurrection that was articulated two thousand years ago, we will indeed require "clever money changers"!

EPILOGUE

Women's liberation in the Christianity of late antiquity? This question was raised at the beginning of our investigation. Is a provisional answer now possible? Let us recall two dimensions of the inquiry:

1. Did early Christianity, which ultimately suppressed the other religions of late antiquity, help or hinder the emancipation of women?

2. Were Christian women in late antiquity able to live autonomously? Which initiatives came from them? What did they contribute to "history in general"?

Summary

Our intention here was to look not at ideally typical and normative ideas of femininity but at women who really existed in the first centuries of Christianity. Where possible we avoided the usual, but often a posteriori division into "heretics" and "orthodox," since from the beginning we faced a pluralistic Christendom that was shaped by rather different movements and regional traditions. Later these became separate, independent confessions and churches, which there was an effort to unite after the Constantinian transformation.

The first chapter of this study dealt with four works whose authors expressly wanted to write church histories. The examination showed that women increasingly disappeared from view. In the time of persecution, about which Eusebius reports, many are among the victims, and in the sources some outstanding women figures are described. Socrates, Sozomen, and Theodoret, who tell us about the century after the Constantinian transformation, mention women seldom and mostly anonymously—with two exceptions: we often encounter the ecclesiastically recognized group of women who voluntarily renounced marriage and family, and we find ordained ministers: the deaconesses. Where there are several accounts of an event involving a woman, we can ascertain especially in Theodoret a clear tendency to modify the traditional story in the direction of certain normative ideas of femaleness.

Now, the question arises: Do the accounts in the church histories correspond to reality? Examination of the acts of the martyrs confirms the impression that is conveyed by Eusebius: in terms of numbers the men are predominant, but when women are mentioned, they seem to share equality with the men. The "clergy" of martyresses and martyrs enjoyed the highest regard in the churches, even if there were also clear efforts to subordinate their authority to that of the bishops. Yet this "confessing church" was only partially representative of the totality of Christians.

We then turned to the prophetic traditions and became witnesses to a great early church conflict. Later times often made so-called Montanism and its (alleged) ecstatic women responsible for prophecy falling into disrepute and women's teaching activity coming to an end. A close examination of the sources, however, shows that the problems resulted from the ambivalence of prophecy itself. In general, charismatic proclamation by women was also recognized in the mainstream church. There was controversy, nonetheless, over whether the authority of prophetesses and prophets was to be set higher than that of bishops and the other ordained ministers.

In the early period of the New Prophecy, charismatic women and men apparently had preeminence, and at the same time "monepiscopal" church leadership was rejected. The result was a church split that, despite all mediation efforts, could not be overcome. In this prophetically oriented current of Christianity in the second century, Prisca was doubtless the most outstanding personality.

We also encountered teaching women among Christian men and women who sought redemption in Gnosticism. Philomena, the most important theologian among them, gathered a considerable number of former Marcionites around her. She may have belonged to Gnostically oriented circles of the mainstream church, who were opposed but not excommunicated. Still in the third century we meet in Anonyma a prophetess who by all appearances preached, baptized, and even celebrated the Eucharist in the mainstream church in Caesarea during a period of Christian persecution. Yet in the same period we increasingly meet testimonies that reveal efforts to restrict the influence of women.

Theory and Practice

Were these efforts successful? It seems so if we look at the statistical evidence that results from the investigation of the three later church histories. If, however, we draw on other source material, we can determine that the participation of women in church life in the fourth century was greater than it seems in the presentation by ancient historiography.

Let us demonstrate the comparison with some outstanding personalities. In the *early period,* the martyrs Perpetua and Felicity were married women with children; Blandina was a slave; as a virgin, the theologian Philomena was a member of the clergy in the broader sense, as were also perhaps the prophetesses Prisca and Maximilla. These women were not individual fighters, isolated "feminists" of the second century; rather, they stood beside men who recognized their equality: beside Perpetua we find her catechete Saturus; the old bishop Pothinus dies in the shadow, as it were, of the slave Blandina; Philomena's proclamation is taken up by her student Apelles; Montanus places his organizational talents at

the service of a movement that owes its character to two women, Prisca and Maximilla.

How do things look *two centuries later?* Jerome sees himself called upon in
Rome to polemicize against men who let themselves be taught by women. Proba,
who is doubtless only one among many, an "incomparable wife" and mother of
several sons, created, a large theological work. Her critic Jerome himself cultivated contacts with numerous educated and influential Roman women, such as
Paula and Marcella. Equally well known is the intellectual exchange between
Rufinus and Melanie. Basil of Caesarea and Gregory of Nyssa, the two most important Greek theologians, received crucial inspiration from their sister Macrina
in regard to both an ascetic ordering of life and questions of Christian dogmatics. In anchorite as well as cenobite asceticism there were numerous "Spiritual
mothers" like Synkletike, whose advice was sought and whose wisdom about life
was passed on in apothegms. Eustolium was the Spiritual partner of the presbyter
and later bishop Leontius; Anonyma and Ammon gained fame as an ascetic married couple. In Constantinople we find the physician Nicarete living alone; she
joined no community and turned down an ecclesiastical office. She is only one
of numerous women we know who entered the conflict with the imperial court
on the side of the ultimately exiled bishop John Chrysostom and were friends of
his. They included more than a few influential deaconesses like Olympias. The
situation was similar outside the imperial church: let us recall the Macedonians
Matrona and Eusebia.

Thus in view of the facts we may assume that the "relapse into developmental
stages already almost overcome by pre-Christian life and thought,"[1] which was
correctly attested for early Christianity, at first took place mainly on paper. In fact,
the situation for women in the church remains more or less the same as in Roman
society in general: they play an important role even where they remain officially
deprived of political power through the denial of offices. In practice, restrictive
measures against female activity reached into the churches only very slowly.

This was true, however, only for women from the upper class; slaves are no
longer found in positions of leadership. Only in ascetic circles is genuine equality still practiced. The crucial stimuli for the urbane cloister, which was further
developed by Basil for men in the East, no doubt goes back to his sister Macrina,
who in her own family persuaded both her mother and her brothers of the
"philosophical" ideal of life. Under her guidance the house community gradually changed into an ascetic community in which there was no longer any difference between lordship and servanthood.[2]

The Egalitarian Ethos

Thus, in spite of many misogynistic utterances and restrictions, we can state
that in the Christianity of late antiquity the great conflicts at first did not arise—
or in any case did not only arise—because of women; rather, the central focus
was the dispute between a hierarchical and an egalitarian ethos.[3] If we want to
present women's liberation in antiquity, we must not forget that it was possible

only in a society divided into masters and mistresses, and male and female slaves. And growing Christendom indeed increasingly adapted itself to this environment—whether it "had to" is another question. Thus at first the line of demarcation of the conflict ran between the men and women representatives of a radical church of the elite, and those of a less radical direction, who wanted to pave the way to the people's church and later to the imperial church.

We must not overlook the fact that aristocratic women, who profited from legal equality in marriage and family, could—just like men—forgo the challenges of an egalitarian ethos in the social hierarchy. It is true that in antiquity the relationship of masters and slaves, mistresses and slave women, became increasingly humanized, but the power structure was not basically called into question. Within the upper class, however, an increasingly egalitarian ethos prevailed with regard to the sexes, even if we cannot talk of equality in today's sense.

The Hellenistic Roman women who chose the new religion were thus "emancipated" women in the literal sense—they no longer were under the *manus* of their husband. In the sources we have no indication that by converting to Christianity they hoped for an improvement in their *condition féminine*. It is true that ascetic propaganda used the "autonomy" of virgins for recruitment and painted the "slavery" of marriage in a highly drastic way; the pain of childbirth and the concern over the multiplication of offspring were stressed. Here it was probably a thoroughly realistic perception of the negative side of female reality—yet from the perspective of ascetically oriented men! When they recruited with the "freedom" of the unmarried, they implicitly presupposed the old-fashioned model of subordination in marriage. Yet the recognition of such a norm is not attested by any early Christian woman author, and it did not correspond to reality: for women of the upper class self-determinism was also possible within marriage. The problems with pregnancy were real, but the concern over the low birth rate in the Roman Empire shows that these were kept within limits.

Liberation and Sex Roles

Since in spite of all ascetic propaganda, even in the first centuries most followers of Jesus' message continued to get married and have children, we may assume that the early Christian praise for continence was primarily a theological and literary tendency and was only in small part a reflection of actual practice. Yet there were many single women who decided as Christians against a traditional family life. This phenomenon requires an explanation. Was it a question here of some kind of feminist revolt?

Speaking against this is, first, the fact that in late antiquity preference for continence was a general phenomenon that was neither specific to women nor limited to Christians. Epictetus speaks disparagingly of marriage in a way similar to John Chrysostom, and the Neoplatonist Hypatia is, as it were, a sister of Macrina, who devoted herself to the Christian-ascetic "philosophy." Yet the voluntarily celibate women created for themselves organizations within the churches, which in Hellenism are unique in their extent. Outside of Christianity it was almost always only isolated individuals who rejected the traditional role of wife and mother. In Christianity a large group of women had the possibility of various lifestyles that were not defined by biological determination. Through the institution the meeting of material needs was guaranteed, as was a high degree of social recognition. The link between women and a certain social role was thereby broken and transcended. Without doubt it was the Christian women themselves who laid the foundation for these new female lifestyles, and even today the alternatives to marriage in cloisters, communities, and organizations of the most varied sort are chosen by considerably more women than men. This new definition of feminine self-understanding in contradiction to biological determination was certainly an important contribution to the history of emancipation.

Sexual Hostility and Sexual Hierarchy

Yet this relativization of the old sex role had its own problems. (1) Biological determination could be escaped only through radical sexual renunciation. (2) The nonwife and nonmother found social recognition in Christianity only when this sexual renunciation had a religious-ascetic basis. At this very point conflicts developed, for the motivation of women who decided against the usual family life was obviously of different kinds. For some sexual renunciation also meant radical rejection of a secular life, and it was then accepted by the church and ultimately praised. But if sexual renunciation was chosen in order to be free of biological forces and take up other tasks, it was regarded by many as reaching for the "masculine" role and its accompanying claim to leadership. In exceptional cases this could be tolerated, but as a mass phenomenon it was apparently felt to be a threatening development.

The result was *ambivalent reactions*. The "positive" solution was the theological construct of the "sexless" *parthenos* ("virgin"), that is, the radical transcending of gender, which in theory was supposed to lead to the perfect equality of women and men, and in practice to unself-conscious, siblinglike interaction. In this model a hierarchy of the sexes was inconceivable. The desired overcoming of the sexual is not to be simply equated with sexual hostility, but it could easily come to that.

The "negative" solution is found in a part of the ascetic movement, in which a specific form of misogyny soon dominates: anxiety in the face of a possibly no longer controllable sex drive evokes the hostile image of the seductress. This tendency increasingly prevailed and led to the principle of the separation of the sexes. Now a fateful reciprocal effect developed: in the imperial church hierarchical thinking more and more suppressed the old egalitarian ethos and rubbed off on asceticism; conversely, the growing sexual pessimism also had its effect outside the cloisters. Finally, concrete walls were erected to protect the sexes from each other—in fact, it was the convents that were thus surrounded!

Within the communities, even with increasing restrictions, a certain measure of female autonomy was preserved, and the early Christian ideal of *adelphotēs* ("brotherhood") was still cultivated; yet since the brothers and sisters were now separated, this led only to equality within each sex. Unmarried women who wanted to participate actively in the life of the church were even more strongly opposed, as we have seen; they were finally eliminated from the clergy. Gradually a doctrine prevailed that basically categorized women as second-class beings. In the definition of the relationship of the sexes hierarchical thinking finally triumphed—not until the free church movements of the modern period did the egalitarian ethos gain ground again within Christianity.

In view of this later development, which not only led to the hierarchy of the sexes but also established a hierarchy between married and single, between clergy and lay, it is hard to see in the sexual renunciation of early Christian women a revolutionary break with the old sex role and the beginning of new spheres of action. It is rather questionable whether we do justice to their attempted abstraction from sex when we give this endeavor the modern label *women's liberation* in the sense of feminine self-realization. They themselves saw therein—as did many celibate men—above all an anticipation of the eschaton as a purely spiritual mode of existence. Yet the measures that were instituted against the ecclesiastical order of virgins and then also against married women attest to a very secular battle of the sexes, in which the feminine side lost. Is "Christianity" to be made responsible for this development?

Religion and Misogyny

Two things must be clearly distinguished here: the question of *historical facticity* and the question of *causal connections*. Therefore in the following we will differentiate between the concrete category *Christendom* and the abstract concept *Christianity*. The answer to the historical question is clear: in the real Christendom of late antiquity there was a change of direction in the matter of women's liberation. Up to this point, however, there is still not a clear answer to the question of causal connections: we must still clarify the extent to which the growing opposition to emancipatory strivings may, can, or even must be explained by Christianity as such, that is, as a religion with a specific message. It is generally true that demonstrable misogyny *in* a religion is by no means always explained *out* of that religion; rather, one must examine whether there is an ideological misuse of religion in order to legitimate suppression already being practiced. Since discrimination on the basis of sex is a universal phenomenon, the latter may usually be the more likely hypothesis.

The present historical investigation focused first on *facts*, which made it clear that in regard to the old apologetical thesis that early Christendom was relatively philogynous but then had to accommodate itself to its "patriarchal" environment, the first half is correct, but the second false. The Hellenist, "pagan" Roman women were already emancipated women before they became Christians. Their suppression did not occur in large numbers until a time when there could be no more question of "necessary accommodation." Also proven false are two theses that basically represent only the apologetic-feminist or conservative-antifeminist variations of a similar fallacy: (1) the heresies were more philogynous than the mainstream church; (2) because of the heretics' success with women, the church had to forbid women to teach. It showed rather that even in the embattled "heretical" churches a consistent egalitarian ethos could not long be maintained. Thus the demarcation line between misogyny and philogyny in late antiquity was identical with neither religious nor confessional boundaries.

The Question of Christianity

Within the framework of this study we can discuss neither the exegetical question of the original *message of the historical Jesus* nor the dogmatic question of the *nature of Christianity*. Yet one thing is indisputable: the catch phrase *egalitarian ethos* is an appropriate name for a central concern of Jesus' proclamation and praxis, which was understood programmatically by his male and female followers: "You are all brothers" (Matt. 23:8, literal). It is almost paradoxical that at this very point a way of speaking that excludes women is used to express the radical ("going to the root") dimension of the ethos of the equality of all. If it said, "You are all brothers and sisters," it would emphasize belonging to one "family" without necessarily calling into question a familial hierarchy between the sexes. Instead, the familial brother-sister relationship is universalized with the terminology of *brotherhood,* which feels sexist to us.

As we have already seen, in the egalitarian ethos the Hellenistic idea of humanity and the Christian message meet. For Jesus the social-ethical dimension stood in the foreground: his preaching was directed above all against the oppression of slaves and the exploitation of the poor. The ancient world, by contrast, stressed the same human dignity of all, women and men, slaves and masters, poor and rich. Actually, one would have expected an alliance between the Christian and the ancient egalitarian ethos. Since the historical development ran differently, other factors must have been at work. Thus the radical feminist accusation can already be rejected: the increasing discrimination against the female sex in the history of Western Christendom cannot be explained by the spread of Christianity *alone.* Therefore, rather than immediately looking for the "guilty," it seems more pertinent to ask first in a neutral way: What hindered women's liberation? Here we can display a whole palette of factors. Three seem to me especially important: (1) the implementation of hierarchical structures, (2) sexual hostility, (3) the devaluation of education.

Now, let us ask further: What relationship do these factors have to the proclamation of Jesus? (1) In the first case the answer is clear: the vertical exercise of power stands in contradiction to the brotherhood and the authority of the servant ethos preached by Jesus. (2) The answer to the second question is less clear: one cannot derive from Jesus' preaching a general devaluation of sexuality, but we do find a rather strong relativization of marriage and family. (3) The answer on the third point is the most difficult: education as a positive value hardly comes into the picture in Jesus' preaching. It appears, if at all, as a privilege of the upper class and is called into question in its function as an instrument of power. It already appears negatively in the New Testament as a "prohibition of teaching" for women, yet this proves at first to be unenforceable.

Let us go a step further: In what constellation do the three factors appear in Hellenistic Christendom? (1) In the churches as in the Roman Empire, there is a rivalry between egalitarian ethos and political power interests; the principle of equality predominates mainly in the private realm. (2) Sexual hostility does not come from Christianity but is a general phenomenon of late antiquity that received its special form in Christendom. (3) Education was a Hellenistic ideal that in Christendom was neglected and in part disparaged. This contributed considerably to perceiving a woman exclusively as a "body."

In traditional Christian apologetics the reproach of sexual hostility is often passed on to the Greeks, while appealing to the biblical legacy. Yet here we are being too easy on ourselves. In actual fact early Christendom did not simply adopt from Hellenism the tendency to turn away from the world but also considerably intensified it with its original imminent expectation of the judgment of the world. This becomes especially clear in the ideal of continence: whereas in non-Christian late antiquity the decision for an ascetic life could remain ultimately a question of individual preference, in the teaching of the church celibacy received with time prominence based on salvation history. This led directly to a devaluation of the sexual and indirectly to a devaluation of women, who, if they did not live continently, were increasingly defined in a one-sided biological way as sexual beings.

Thus we must *finally conclude with regard to Christianity* that progress in women's liberation in late antiquity was opposed by an agglomeration of developments in theology and church politics, which did not necessarily result from Jesus' proclamation but cannot be easily separated from it either. The synthesis with Greek thinking integrated both positive and negative elements. With regard to misogyny, therefore, "Christianity" as a real religion cannot be absolved of a certain "complicity"[4] any more than the women themselves, who let an already achieved emancipation be taken away from them. Nevertheless, the actual "perpetrators" remain certain "Christian" men who were oriented more toward political power interests than toward the preaching of Jesus.

Yet another question should be asked, though it would go beyond the scope and temporal boundaries of this study. Is it possible that nontheological factors changed the development of the relationship between the sexes? Here we only point to two historical upheavals that need to be thoroughly studied and could be instructive for the history of women and emancipation. (1) One is the cultural and political *fall of the western half of the Roman Empire* in the confusion of tribal migrations; in the Christian empire of the East women seem to have maintained the achieved level of emancipation far longer. It is also notable that in the West the early Christian egalitarian ethos emerged again in the missionary movement of Irish-Scottish asceticism. (2) Economic conditions seem to have effected the *gradual dissolution of the ancient institution of slavery*. This resulted in a total reorganization of the social structure and a radically new division of labor. Here the suspicion arises that the loss of privileges in the upper class could have affected women in particular.

Women as Subjects

The real aim of the present study was to look at women as subjects of their emancipation, their Christian identity, and the history common to us all. Here we will recall in brief form the answers already given—sometimes in great detail—to the three questions posed at the beginning of this epilogue.

1. Were Christian women in late antiquity able to live autonomously? In the public realm married and single women of the upper class were largely barred from political office, but otherwise they were free in their decisions and independent economically.

For slave women autonomy was possible only if their owners were ready to grant it to them; among Christians this occurred more and more rarely in the late period.

2. Which initiatives came from them? Regardless of their family status, many women were highly educated and were therefore able to participate intensively in the development of church theology. Much research on the details is still needed here.

In the early period married and unmarried participated at all levels of church life. Later this was possible only for single women by means of clerical office, but indirect influence remained important.

Many women chose sexual continence; they then chose between a radical autonomy in asceticism, a Spiritual partnership, and life in a community of women; celibacy could also be chosen in regard to activity as a church minister.

They proved themselves the "better Christians" voluntarily or involuntarily in the realm of social involvement, which was more and more decisively turned over to them by Christian men.

When they were placed in monastic seclusion, they developed their own spiritual culture of community life.

3. What did they contribute to "history in general"? A thorough study of the available source material leads us to the conclusion that women were far more intensively involved in the spread of Christianity and in its internal development than the widespread image of women suggests.

If Christianity could finally be perceived from outside as a religion of love of neighbor, that was due in large part to the initiative of women.

The decision of numerous Christian women to live alone was an important contribution to the differentiation of feminine self-understanding apart from a biologically determined sex role.

In this way they transformed motherhood into the spiritual or they abandoned it completely in favor of spiritual, intellectual, and charity activities.

They regarded a partnership relationship with men not as part of their biological destiny but as an object of their free choice.

They also cultivated friendships and relationships outside of marriage.

4. One final question remains: Was there a special early Christian women's culture? Since there are too few extant works created by Christian women themselves, this question may still be hard to answer even after all the extant material has been researched. Yet despite the meager sources, the contrast between the fathers' literary image of women and the testimonies of early Christian mothers is striking: of the four women authors[5] only one seems to have been single; the other three were married and had children. And something else is notable about these three: they were in special measure bridge builders between the old Hellenistic, religiously shaped culture and the message of the gospel. Were they representative of their sex or of a specifically feminine contribution to the development of Christianity? They are, in any case, the few witnesses to a time in which many women—alone, married, or in free partnership with men—made decisive contributions to passing on, in discipleship to Jesus, both the Jewish heritage and the legacy of antiquity as a world religion open to all. They deserve better thanks than oblivion!

Appendix I
Texts

A. Cyprian, Letter 4

1.1. Our dearest brother, we have read your letter which you sent by our brother Paconius: in it you urgently request that we write back to you stating our views on the question of these virgins, who, it has been discovered, despite the fact that they once made the firm resolve to preserve with unwavering steadfastness their chaste state, have subsequently shared the same bed with men (one of these, you note, being a deacon). They admit to having slept with men, but it is also true that they insist on their virginity.

1.2. . . .

2.1. . . . we should not allow virgins to dwell with men—I do not mean sleep together, but they should not even live together. Not only is there the weakness of their sex, but they are at a still vulnerable age and ought to be guided completely by our direction and control. Otherwise the devil may be given an opportunity to do them harm as he lies in ambush, on the watch to wreak havoc amongst us. As the Apostle also says: *Give no opportunity to the devil.*

2.2. . . . In cases like this we must intervene with promptness, so that they may be separated while they can still be separated unharmed; it will not be possible to part them subsequently, even if we do intervene, once they have been united by a common sense of guilt.

2.3. Accordingly, we see how many men are thus coming to dreadful ruin, whilst it causes us extreme distress to observe that very many virgins are being corrupted by unlawful and perilous associations of this kind. If they were fully sincere in dedicating themselves to Christ, then they ought to persevere in their modesty and chastity without giving rise to any sort of gossip, and thus with constancy and steadfastness await the reward of their virginity. If, on the other hand, they are unwilling or unable to persevere, then it is better that they should marry than fall into the fire by their sins. Clearly they must avoid causing any scandal for their brothers and sisters, since it is written: *If the food scandalizes my brother, I will not eat of meat while this world lasts, for fear I may cause him scandal.*

3.1. No one should imagine that she can defend herself with the plea that it can be proven by examination whether she is a virgin, since the hand and the eye of midwives may frequently be mistaken and, besides, even if she is found to be an unsullied virgin in her private parts, she could have sinned all the same in some other part of her person which can be sullied and yet cannot be examined. There can be no doubt that a great deal of shameful and sinful conduct is admitted by the mere fact of going to bed together, of embracing, of talking together, of kissing, and—disgraceful and disgusting conduct—of two people lying and sleeping together.

3.2. If a husband should come along and see his own wife lying with another man, is he not outraged, is he not incensed, in grief and jealousy perhaps even seizing a sword in his hand? Christ is our Lord and our Judge: when He observes His own virgin who has been vowed to Him and dedicated to His holy estate lying with another man, imagine His rage and His fury and the punishments He threatens to exact for such unchaste associations.

3.3. It is our duty to take pains to ensure by every possible means that every one of our brothers can escape His spiritual sword and the approaching day of His judgment. All are obliged to uphold the discipline without fail: all the more is this duty incumbent upon church leaders and deacons in that they should provide others with teaching and example by the way in which they live and behave. How can they be overseers of innocence and chastity if they are indeed the very source and origin of corruption and instruction in vice?

4.1. Accordingly, my dearest brother, you have shown wisdom and firmness in excommunicating the deacon who has stayed with a virgin on a number of occasions, as well as the other men who were in the habit of sleeping with the virgins. If these virgins have done penance for their unlawful intimacy and have broken off their relationships, they should be, first of all, submitted to a careful examination by midwives, and if they are found to be virgin, they should be received into the Church and admitted to communion—with this warning, however, that if at a later date they return to these same men or if they dwell with them in the same house and under the same roof, they will be censured more severely and will be cast out, and will not be readily readmitted to the Church for any such misconduct in the future.

If, on the other hand, it is discovered that any of them has been corrupted, she should do full penance. The crime she has committed is not against a husband; she has committed adultery against Christ, and, therefore, only when there has elapsed what is judged an appropriate period and she has publicly confessed, may she return to the Church.

4.2. But if they continue to be obstinate and refuse to be separated from each other, they can rest assured that such persistence in impurity on their part entails that we can never admit them into the Church: our fear is that by their sins they may point the way to ruination for others.

And they should not think that there is still hope of life and salvation for them if they have refused to obey their bishops and priests. . . .

4.3. . . . .

5.1. . . . . They who have once *castrated themselves for the sake of the kingdom of heaven* must endeavour to please God in all things; they must not fail to pay heed to the bishops of God, they must not make of themselves a cause for scandal to their brethren throughout the Church.

5.2. . . .

(Translated by Graeme W. Clark, ACW 43:57–61)

B. The Martyrdom of Blandina

Ἡ δὲ Βλανδίνα ἐπὶ ξύλου κρεμασθεῖσα προύκειτο βορὰ τῶν εἰσβαλλομένων θηρίων· ἢ καὶ διὰ τοῦ βλέπεσθαι σταυροῦ σχήματι κρεμαμένη διὰ τῆς εὐτόνου προσευχῆς πολλὴν προθυμίαν τοῖς ἀωνιζομένοις ἐνεποίει, βλεπόντων αὐτῶν ἐν τῷ ἀγῶνι καὶ τοῖς ἔξωθεν ὀφθαλμοῖς διὰ τῆς ἀδελφῆς τὸν ὑπὲρ αὐτῶν ἐσταυρωμένον, ἵνα πείσῃ τοὺς πιστεύοντας εἰς αὐτὸν ὅτι πᾶς ὁ ὑπὲρ τῆς Χριστοῦ δόξης παθὼν τὴν κοινωνίαν ἀεὶ ἔχει μετὰ τοῦ ζῶντος θεοῦ. καὶ μηδενὸς ἁψαμένου τότε τῶν θηρίων αὐτῆς, καθαιρεθεῖσα ἀπὸ τοῦ ξύλου ἀνελήφθη πάλιν εἰς τὴν εἰρκτήν, εἰς ἄλλον ἀγῶνα τηρουμένη, ἵνα διὰ πλειόνων γυμνασμάτων νικήσασα, τῷ μὲν σκολιῷ ὄφει ἀπαραίτητον ποιήσῃ τὴν καταδίκην, προτρέψηται δὲ τοὺς ἀδελφούς, ἡ μικρὰ καὶ ἀσθενὴς καὶ εὐκαταφρόνητος μέγαν καὶ ἀκαταγώνιστον ἀθλητὴν Χριστὸν ἐνδεδυμένη, διὰ πολλῶν κλήρων ἐκβιάσασα τὸν ἀντικείμενον καὶ δι᾿ ἀγῶνος τὸν τῆς ἀφθαρσίας στεψαμένη στέφανον.

(Euseb. Ch.Hist. 5.1.41–42, SC 41:17)

C. Logia from the New Prophecy

1. Prisca

a. (Paraclitus per prophetidem Priscam:) *Carnes sunt, et carnem oderunt.*

(Tertullian, On the Resurrection of the Flesh 11.2, CCSL 2:933)

b. (Per sanctam prophetidem Priscam ita evangelizatur:) *Purificantia enim concordat, ait, et visiones vident, et ponentes faciem deorsum etiam voces audiunt manifestas, tam salutares quam et occultas.*

(Tertullian, Exhortation to Chastity 10.5, SC 319:106)

c. (. . . ἢ Κυΐντιλλα ἢ Πρίσκιλλα . . . ἔλεγεν:) Ἐν ἰδέᾳ, φησί, γυναικός, ἐσχηματισμένος ἐν στολῇ λαμπρᾷ ἦλθε πρός με Χριστὸς καὶ ἐνέβαλεν ἐν ἐμοὶ τὴν σοφίαν καὶ ἀπεκάλυψέ μοι τουτονὶ τὸν τόπον εἶναι ἅγιον καὶ ὧδε τὴν Ἰερουσαλὴμ ἐκ τοῦ οὐρανοῦ κατιέναι.

(Epiph. Pan. 49.1.3, GCS 31:242)

2. Maximilla

a. (Καὶ μὴ λεγέτω . . . τὸ διὰ Μαξιμίλλης πνεῦμα:) Διώκομαι ὡς λύκος ἐκ προβάτων· οὐκ εἰμὶ λύκος, ῥῆμά εἰμι καὶ πνεῦμα καὶ δύναμις.

(Anon. in Euseb. Ch.Hist. 5.16.17)

b. (Φάσκει γὰρ ἡ λεγομένη παρ᾿ αὐτοῖς Μαξίμιλλα ἡ προφῆτις ὅτι, φησί:) Μετ᾿ ἐμὲ προφήτης (variant: προφῆτις) οὐκέτι ἔσται, ἀλλὰ συντέλεια.

(Epiph. Pan. 48.2.4, GCS 31:222)

c. (Μαξίμιλλα . . . λέγει:) Ἐμοῦ μὴ ἀκούσητε, ἀλλὰ Χριστοῦ ἀκούσατε.

(Epiph. Pan. 48.12.4, GCS 31:235

d. (Φάσκει δὲ πάλιν ἡ αὐτὴ Μαξίμιλλα … :) Ἀπέστειλέ με κύριος τούτου τοῦ πόνου καὶ τῆς συνθήκης καὶ τῆς ἐπαγγελίας αἱρετιστὴν μηνυτὴν ἑρμηνεύτην, ἠναγκασμένον, θέλοντα καὶ μὴ θέλοντα, γνωθεῖν γνῶσιν θεοῦ.

(Epiph. Pan. 48.13.1, GCS 31:237)

3. Montanus

a. (Ὁ Μοντανός φησιν:) Ἰδού, ὁ ἄνθρωπος ὡσεὶ λύρα κἀγὼ ἐφίπταμαι ὡσεὶ πλῆκτρον· ὁ ἄνθρωπος κοιμᾶται κἀγὼ γρηγορῶ. ἰδού, κύριός ἐστιν ὁ ἐξιστάνων καρδίας ἀνθρώπων καὶ διδοὺς καρδίαν ἀνθρώποις.

(Epiph. Pan. 48.4.1, GCS 31:224–25)

b. (Λέγει γὰρ [Μοντανὸς] ἐν τῇ ἑαυτοῦ λεγομένῃ προφητείᾳ:) Τί λέγεις τὸν ὑπὲρ ἄνθρωπον σῳζόμενον; λάμψει γὰρ (φησίν) ὁ δίκαιος ὑπὲρ τὸν ἥλιον ἑκατονταπλασίονα, οἱ δὲ μικροὶ ἐν ὑμῖν σῳζόμενοι λάμψουσιν ἑκατονταπλασίονα ὑπὲρ τὴν σελήνην.

(Epiph. Pan. 48.10.3, GCS 31:232–33)

c. (Ὁ Μοντανὸς οὕτως λέγων:) Ἐγὼ κύριος ὁ θεὸς ὁ παντοκράτωρ καταγινόμενος ἐν ἀνθρώπῳ.

(Epiph. Pan. 48.11.1, GCS 31:233)

c. (… φησὶ … Μοντανὸς ὅτι:) Οὔτε ἄγγελος οὔτε πρέσβυς, ἀλλ᾽ ἐγὼ κύριος ὁ θεὸς πατὴρ ἦλθον.

(Epiph. Pan. 48.11.9, GCS 31:235)

Doubtful:

e. (Λέγει [Μοντανός]:) Ἐγώ εἰμι ὁ πατὴρ καὶ ἐγώ εἰμι ὁ υἱὸς καὶ ἐγὼ ὁ παράκλητος.

(*Discussion of a Montanist and an Orthodox,* ed. Ficker, 452)

f. (Μοντανὸς … εἶπεν :) Ἐγώ εἰμι ὁ πατὴρ καὶ ὁ υἱὸς καὶ ὁ παράκλητος.

(Didymus, On the Trinity 3.41.1, PG 39:984)

4. Anonymous (prophetess or prophet)

a. (… ipsum paracletum in prophetis novis dicentem:) *Potest ecclesia donare delictum, sed non faciam, ne et alia delinquant.*

(Tertullian, On Worthiness 21.7, CCSL 2:1326)

b. (… sermone illo Spiritus probat:) *Publicaris, inquit, bonum tibi est; qui enim non publicatur in hominibus, publicatur in Domino. Ne confundaris, iustitia te producit in medium. Quid confunderis laudem ferens? Potestat fit, cum conspiceris ab hominibus.*

(Tertullian, On Flight 9.4, CCSL 2:1147)

c. (Sic et alibi): *Nolite in lectulis nec in aborsibus et febribus mollibus optare exire, sed in martyriis, uti glorificetur qui est passus pro vobis* (ibid.). Cf. *On the Soul* 55.5: *… ut paracletus monet, non in mollibus febribus et in lectulis, sed in martyriis …* (CCSL 2:863).

APPENDIX II
OVERVIEW

Abbreviations

Ar	Arian
C	child
D	deaconess
E	educated
H	heterodox
M	martyress
Mac.	Macedonian
Man.	Manichaean
N	negatively described
P	prophetess
S	slave
V	virgin
V/W	virgin or widow
V+Wf	continent wife or partner
W	widow
Wf	wife
X	not characterized
< >	secondary listing
[ ]	name or designation completed from another source
★	non-Christian
/	parallel report available
+	and; wife of

EUSEBIUS	SOCRATES	SOZOMEN	THEODORET

0. Women from Ruling Houses

EUSEBIUS	SOCRATES	SOZOMEN	THEODORET
Salome Wf ★	Helena Wf /	Constantia WF /	Helena Wf /
Anonyma X ★	Constantia Wf /	Helena Wf /	Anonyma Wf /
Herodias Wf ★	Anonyma Wf+C	Anonyma Wf /	Constantia Wf /
Helena X ★	Anonyma WF /	Anonyma Wf ★	[Helena] Wf /
Mammea Wf ★	Eusebia Wf /	Eusebia Wf /	[Domnica] Wf H /
Severa Wf ★	Helena Wf	Domnica Wf /	<Mavia Wf>
[Constantia] Wf [H]	Anastasia C	<Mavia W>	Justina Wf H /
	Carosa C	Flacilla E /	Flacilla Wf /
	Severa Wf	Justina Wf H	Sisters V /
	Justina Wf H	Eudoxia Wf /	
	Galla Wf	Pulcheria V [Wf] /	
	Justa V	Arcadia V /	
	Grata V	Marina V /	
	(Galla) Placidia Wf /	(Galla) Placidia Wf /	
	Flacilla Wf /	Honoria C	
	<Mavia W> /		
	Anonyma Wf		
	Eudoxia Wf /		
	Eudocia Wf		
	Eudoxia Wf		

1. Apostle

	SOCRATES	SOZOMEN	THEODORET
	Anonyma V? /	Anonyma V? /	Anonyma V? /
	Mavia W /	Mavia W /	Mavia W /

2. Prophetess

4 **Anonymae** P V
Philomena H P V
Prisca H V/W?
Maximilla H P V/W?
Ammia P X

EUSEBIUS	SOCRATES	SOZOMEN	THEODORET

3. Martyress

EUSEBIUS	SOCRATES	SOZOMEN	THEODORET
Flavia Domitilla X	**Anonyma** Wf+C /	**Anonyma** V	Virgins /
Anonyma Wf	Virgins	**Tarbula** V	Widows and orphans
Agathonike	Widows and orphans	**Anonyma** S V	Virgins and priests
[Wf+C] /			
Blandina S X	Women X	**Anonyma** W	**Anonyma** Wf+C /
Anonyma X	<Hypatia E * [V]>	Women	Virgins
Biblis X		Virgins	
Potamiaina V [S]		**Anonyma** Wf+C /	
Marcella Wf+C		Women+C H	
Heraïs X		**Nonnichia** Wf	
Quinta X			
Apollonia V			
Ammonarion V			
Mercuria X			
Dionysia Wf+C			
Anonyma X			
Anonyma Wf			
Anonyma H X			
Anonyma Wf+C			
2 **Anonymae** V			
2 **Anonymae** V			
Anonyma Wf			
Anonyma E X			
Thecla X			
Theodosia V			
Anonyma V			
Valentina V			
Ennathas V			
8X: Women X			

4. Ascetic

EUSEBIUS	SOCRATES	SOZOMEN	THEODORET
"Therapeutae" V *	Women V/W /	Women V/W /	
([Jewish] mixed	Women/convents	Women	
community)	V/W H	V/W/V+Wf? /	
	Women	Women V/W	
	V/W/[V+Wf]		

EUSEBIUS	SOCRATES	SOZOMEN	THEODORET

5. Spiritual Partner (*Syneisakta*)

EUSEBIUS	SOCRATES	SOZOMEN	THEODORET
Many V/W	Eustolium [V] / **Anonyma** V+C / *Syneisaktai* V/W	**Anonyma** V+Wf /	**Eustolium** [V] / **Anonyma** V+Wf

6. Widow

EUSEBIUS	SOCRATES	SOZOMEN	THEODORET
1,500 widows (+ poor)		<Anonyma M W> Widows Widows	Widows

7. Virgin

EUSEBIUS	SOCRATES	SOZOMEN	THEODORET
Mary 2? **Anonymae** <4 Anonymae P> <Philomena> <Juliana E [V]> <11 Martyresses> <Ascetics> <*Syneisaktai*>	**Irene** / Virgins <Virgins M> <Ascetics> <*Syneisaktai*>	**Irene** / Virgins <Tarbula M> <Anonyma M S> Virgins **Anonyma** <Virgins M> Virgins Virgins <Matrona D H> <Ascetics> <Deaconesses>	Virgins Virgins <Virgins M> <Virgins M> <Virgins M>

8. Deaconess

EUSEBIUS	SOCRATES	SOZOMEN	THEODORET
		Nectaria N V/W? **Matrona** D? H V **Pentadia** [D] W **Olympias** W **Nicarete** D? V **Eusebia** H V/W?	**Anonyma** V/W? **Publia** D?

EUSEBIUS	SOCRATES	SOZOMEN	THEODORET

9. Educated

Chrysophora X	<Anonyma E H X>	<Deaconesses>	<Deaconesses>
Anonyma E X	**Hypatia** E M [V] ★		
Juliana E [V]			
Girl E?			

10. Slave

<Blandina M X>		<Anonyma M V>	
<Potamiaina M [S] V>		**Anonyma** H? X	

11. Heterodox

Helena N	**Anonyma** E Man. X	Women X	Prominent Ar. X
<Philomena P V>	<Convent> Mac.	<Matrona D Mac. V>	Young Ar. N
<Prisca P V/W?>	V/W	**Anonyma** Mac. Wf	<Wife>
<Maximilla P V/W?>	**Anonyma** X /	<her slave Mac.?>	**Anonyma** Ar. X
<Anonyma M X>		**Anonyma** Man. X /	
		<Eusebia D Mac. V/W?>	

12. Other

Maria Wf+C	**Anonyma** X /	**Anonyma** N	**Anonyma** X /
Anonyma Wf	**Anonyma** Wf ★	**Anonyma** X /	**Anonyma** N
Anonyma Wf	**Anonyma** X /	**Anonyma** Wf+C /	**Anonyma** Wf+C /
Mary Wf	**Anonyma** N	**Anonyma** N /	**Anonyma** N
Anonyma X	**Anonyma** X /	**Anonyma** N	Women Wf
Alke X		**Anonyma** X	**Anonyma** Wf+C
Anonyma Wf		**Anonyma** X /	**Anonyma** X
Anonyma Wf		**Anonyma** C /	**Anonyma** C /
Anonyma X		**Anonyma** X	
Women V X		**Anonyma** Wf	
Anonyma Wf		Ignorant women N	
2 **Anonymae** V/W		**Anonyma** X /	
Women Wf		Crying women X	
Women N ★		**Anonyma** Wf	
Women Wf C		**Anonyma** Wf	

Appendix III
Tables

Women in the Church Histories
(Elaboration of the overview)

Women in Eusebius

0. From Ruling Houses

Salome Wf ★ (+ Alexander; sister of Herod the Great): 1.8.13 (cites Josephus)
Anonyma X ★ (queen of Ethiopia): 2.1.13
Herodias Wf ★ (+ Herod Antipas; exiled): 2.4.1
Helena X ★ (queen of Adiabene): 2.12
Mammea Wf ★ (mother of Emperor Severus Alexander; has Origen summoned): 6.21.3–4
Severa Wf ★ (+ Philippus Arabs; Origen writes a letter to her): 6.36.3
[Anonyma] Wf ("sister of Constantine" [Constantia] is married to Licinius): 10.8.4

1. Apostle

Prisca Wf (NT, as persecution victim, not as apostle): 2.18.9

2. Prophetess

4 **Anonymae** P V [1 = Wf?] (daughters of Phillip): 3.30, 31, 37, 39; 5.17.3, 5.24.2
Philomena H P V (Gnostic, Rome): 5.13.2 (cites Rhodo)
Prisca H V/W? (New Prophecy): 5.14, 18, 19
Maximilla H P V/W? (New Prophecy): 5.14, 16, 18
Ammia P X (Philadelphia): 5.17.2ff.

3. Martyress

Flavia Domitilla X (relative of a Roman consul, exiled): 3.18.4
Anonyma Wf (+ the apostle Peter): 3.30.2 (cites Clement)
Agathonike [Wf+C] (Pergamon): 4.15.48 /MA/
Blandina S X (battles with beasts, Lyon): 5.1.17ff., 37, 41–42, 53ff.
Anonyma X (Blandina's mistress, battle with beasts, Lyon): 5.1.18
Biblis X (battle with beasts, Lyon): 5.1.25–26
Potamiaina V [S] (threatened with rape, burned in boiling tar, Alexandria): 6.5 [Pall. *Hist.Laus.* 3]
Marcella Wf+C (Potamiaina's mother, burned, Alexandria): 6.5.1
Heraïs X (catechumen, burned, Alexandria): 6.4.3
Quinta X (dragged through the city, stoned, Alexandria): 6.41.4 (cites Dionysius)
Apollonia V (prominent, old, burned, Alexandria): 6.41.7 (cites Dionysius)

Ammonarion V (tortured, beheaded, Alexandria): 6.41.18 (cites Dionysius)
Mercuria X (old, beheaded, Alexandria): ibid.
Dionysia Wf+C (mother, beheaded, Alexandria): ibid.
Anonyma X (beheaded with Ammonarion, Mercuria, and Dionysia; Alexandria): ibid.
Anonyma Wf (wife of Chairemons, bishop of Nilus; died in flight): 6.42.3 (cites Dionysius)
Women X (Egypt; "of every race and every age," martyrdom by fire or sword): 7.11.20 (cites Dionysius)
Anonyma H X (Marcionite, battle with beasts, Caesarea [Palestine]): 7.12
Women X (families beheaded and burned; men and women are said to have thrown themselves into the flames, Nicomedia): 7.6.6
Women X (burned, drowned, or beheaded with men and children after torture, Egypt): 8.8
Women X (Thebais; sadistic methods of persecution, families executed): 8.9.1ff.
Women X (towns in Phrygia burned with women and children): 8.11.1
Anonyma Wf+C (mother with 2 daughters, rich, noble, well-known; threw themselves into the river to escape violation; Antioch): 8.12.3–4
2 **Anonymae** V: ibid.
2 **Anonymae** V (sisters, prominent, beautiful, thrown into the sea, Antioch): 8.12.3–4
Women X (some by suicide to escape violation): 8.14.14
Anonyma Wf (prominent, escapes Emperor Maxentius through suicide, Rome): 8.14.16–17
Anonyma E X (prominent, rich, resisted the plots of Emperor Maximinus, burned and dispossessed; Alexandria): 8.15.15
Thecla X ("our Thecla," i.e., not the Thecla of the *Acts of Paul;* battle with beasts, Caesarea): *MP* 3.1; 6.3
Women V Wf (delivered to pimps): *MP* 5.3
Theodosia V (not yet 18 years old, from Tyre; drowns in the sea after torture): *MP* 7.1–2
Women X (Alexandria; maimed and blinded in the left eye together with men and children): *MP* 8.1
Anonyma V (from Gaza, "a woman in body but male in attitude," threatened with prostitution; spoke against Maximinus, tortured, burned): *MP* 8.5, 8
Valentina V (from Caesarea, joined "as a sister" in the martyrdom of Anonyma of Gaza): *MP* 8.6–8
Ennathas V (from Skythopolis, displayed naked, beaten, burned): *MP* 9.6–8

4. Ascetic

"Therapeutae" V ★ ([Jewish] mixed community near Alexandria): 2.17 (cites Philo)

5. Spiritual Partner (Syneisakta)

Numerous *syneisakta* V/W (in the clergy of Antioch): 7.30.12–15

6. Widow

1500 widows (+ poor of the Roman church): 6.43.11 (cites Cornelius)

7. Virgin

Mary, Mother of Jesus (genealogy; virgin birth): 1.7.17; 2.1.2; 3.27.2; 6.17
2? **Anonymae** (daughters of Nicolaus, without number): 3.29.3 (cites Clement)
<4 Anonymae P (daughters of Philip): 3.30, 31, 37, 39; 5.17.3, 5.24.2>

<Philomena P H: 5.13.2>
<Juliana E [V]: 6.17 /[Pall. *Hist.Laus.* 64]/>
<11 Martyresses>
<Ascetics>
<*Syneisaktai*>

8. Deaconess

9. Educated

Chrysophora X (writing of Bishop Dionysius of Corinth dedicated to her): 4.23.13
Anonyma E X (foster mother of Origen): 6.2.13
Juliana E [V] (contacts with Symmachus and Origen): 6.17 /[Pall. *Hist.Laus.* 64]/
Girl E? (calligrapher, secretary to Origen): 6.23.2

10. Slave

<Blandina M X: 5.1.17ff., 41ff., 53ff.>
<Potamiaina M [S] V: 6.5>

11. Heterodox

Helena N (companion of Simon Magus): 2.13.4 (cites Justin), 6
<Philomena P V (Gnostic): 5.13.2>
<Prisca P V/W? (New Prophecy): 5.14, 18, 19>
<Maximilla P V/W? (New Prophecy): 5.14, 16, 18>
<Anonyma M X (Marcionite): 7.12>
<Women with Paul of Samosata, not characterized as heretics: 7.30.9–16>
<Unbridled sexual activity among the Nicolaitans (women not mentioned): 3.29.1ff.>

12. Other

Estha, wife of Matthan (NT, genealogy of Jesus): 1.7.8
Ruth (OT): 1.7.13
Maria Wf+C (mother, daughter of Eleazar): 3.6.21ff. (cites Josephus)
Anonyma Wf (Nicolaus offered his jealously loved, pretty wife to others for marriage): 3.29.2ff. (cites Clement)
Anonyma Wf (wife of the apostle Paul [*sic*]): 3.30.1 (cites Clement)
Mary Wf (wife of Clopas): 3.32.4
Anonyma X (sinner): 3.39.17
Alke X (sister of Nikete): 4.15.41 (cites *Martyrdom of Polycarp*)
Anonyma Wf (applies for divorce): 4.17.2ff. (cites Justin)
Anonyma Wf (mother of Origen): 6.2.4–5, 12
Susanna (OT; story genuine?): 6.31.1
Anonyma X (hemorrhagic, Caesarea Philippi): 7.18 [Matt. 9.20ff.] /Soz/
Women V X (includes women's choir, followers of Paul of Samosata): 7.30.9–10 (cites synodal letter)
Anonyma Wf (released by Paul of Samosata): 7.30.14 (cites synodal letter)
2 **Anonymae** V/W (constant companions of Paul of Samosata): 7.30.14 (cites synodal letter)

Women X (were released with old men and children from the embattled part of Alexandria and rescued): 7.32.9–10

Women Wf (before the persecution rulers allowed court people to belong to Christianity with wives, children, and slaves, and preferred them): 8.1.3

Women X (accusations against Emperor Maximinus: violation and torture, murder of women): 8.14.2ff.

Women N * (were forced to make false statements about Christians, Damascus): 9.5.2

Women Wf and C (accusations against Emperor Licinius: violation of women and girls): 10.8.13

Women in Socrates

0. From Ruling Houses

Helena Wf (mother of Constantine): 1.17, 18 /Ruf/Soz/The/
Constantia Wf (+ Licinius, sister of Constantine): 1.2, 18, 25 /Ruf/Soz/The/
Anonyma Wf+C (queen of "India" [Ethiopia]): 1.19 Ruf
Anonyma Wf (queen of "Iberia" [Georgia]): 1.20 /Ruf/Soz/The/
Eusebia Wf (+ Constantius II): 3.1 /Soz/
Helena Wf (+ Julian; sister of Constantius II): 3.1
Anastasia C (daughter of Valens): 4.9
Carosa C (daughter of Valens): 4.9
Severa Wf (+ Valentinian I): 4.31
Justina H Wf (+ Valentinian I, who married both women by special law!): 4.31; 5.11 /Soz/The/
Galla Wf (+ Theodosius I, second marriage, daughter of Justina): 4.31
Justa V (daughter of Justina): 4.31
Grata V (daughter of Justina): 4.31
(Galla) **Placidia** Wf (+ Constantius III; daughter of Galla): 4.31; 7.24 /Soz/
Flacilla Wf (+ Theodosius I, first marriage): 4.31; 5.12 /Soz/The/
<Mavia W>: 4.36 (*see below:* Apostle)
Anonyma Wf (daughter of Mavia): 4.36
Eudoxia Wf (+ Arcadius): 6.8, 11, 15, 18 /Soz/
Eudocia/Athenaïs Wf (+ Theodosius II): 7.21, 44, 47
Eudoxia Wf (daughter of Eudocia): 7.44

1. Apostle

Anonyma V? (prisoner of war who converted "Iberia" [Georgia] by example and preaching): 1.20 /Ruf/Soz/The/
Mavia W (queen of the Saracens who wages war against the Romans, Christianizes her people, and gets her choice of bishop): 4.36 /Ruf/Soz/The/

2. Prophetess

Maximilla (without reference to the prophecy): 2.37

3. Martyress

Anonyma Wf+C (prevented a massacre of Christians in Edessa): 4.18 /Ruf/Soz/The/
Virgins in Alexandria (undressed and whipped—some to death—during persecution of orthodox Christians by Arians): 2.28 (cites Athanasius) /The/

Widows and orphans (are not spared): ibid.
Women X (suffer brutalities under the Arian Macedonius): 2.38
<Hypatia E ★ [V]> (*see below:* Educated)

4. Ascetic

Women V/W (Synod of Gangra condemned ascetics with Eustathius): 2.43 (cites synodal letter) /Soz/
Women V/W H (Macedonian bishop established cloister for men and women): 2.38
Women V/W/[V+Wf] (among the ascetics in the desert are women): 4.23 (cites Palladius)

5. Spiritual Partner (Syneisakta)

Eustolium V (lived with the presbyter Leontius, who had himself castrated but still became the
bishop of Antioch): 2.26 /The/ [Soz has only Leontius without the story]
Anonyma V+Wf (on her wedding night her husband Ammon talks her into the ideal of continence): 4.23 /Soz/[Pall. *Hist.Laus.* 8]/
Women V/W (writing of John Chrysostom against the so-called *syneisaktai*): 6.3

6. Widow

[Widows, orphans M (are not spared during persecution by the Arians): 2.27]

7. Virgin

Irene: 1.12 /Ruf/Soz/
Virgins in Jerusalem (the virgins entered in the church register were invited to a banquet by Empress Helena and served by her): 1.17 /Ruf/Soz/The/
<Virgins in Alexandria M: 2.27>
<Ascetics>
<*Syneisaktai*>

8. Deaconess

9. Educated

<Anonyma E H X (educator of Mani): 1.22>
Hypatia E M [V] ★(Neoplatonic philosopher, murdered by Christians): 7.15

10. Slave

11. Heterodox

Anonyma E Man. X (educator of Mani, gave him books): 1.22
—Discussion of Arian doctrine with women at court: 2.2
<Macedonian convent V/W: 2.38>
Anonyma X (crossover of a Manichaean; legality was doubted): 6.9 /Soz/

12. Other

—Clergy may engage in sexual activity after ordination: 1.11 /Soz/
Anonyma X (healed in Jerusalem): 1.17 /Ruf 1.7/Soz/The/
—Chastity laws in Heliopolis: 1.18 /Soz 1.8/

Anonyma Wf * (prehistory of Manichaeism): 1.22
Anonyma X (nurse, let sick child be healed by prisoner of war): 1.20 /Ruf/Soz/The/
Anonyma N (thoughts of an ascetic upon meeting an actress): 4.23
Anonyma X (compromises a clergyman through public confession): 5.19 /Soz/
—Sexual activity after ordination; second marriage: 5.22
—Sermon against women (John Chrysostom): 6.15

Women in Sozomen

0. From Ruling Houses

Constantia Wf (+ Licinius; sister of Constantine): 1.7; 2.27 /Ruf/Soc/The/
Helena Wf (mother of Constantine): 2.1.2 /Ruf/Sox/The/
Anonyma Wf (queen of "Iberia" [Georgia]): 2.7 /Ruf/Soc/Soz/
Anonyma Wf * (queen of Persia): 2.12
Eusebia Wf (+ Constantius II): 5.2 /Soc/
Domnica Wf (+ Valens): 6.16 ("wife of Valens"); 7.1 /The/
<Mavia Wf>: 6.38 (*see below:* Apostle)
Flacilla E (+ Theodosius I, first marriage): 7.6 /Soc/The/
Justina Wf H (+ Valentinian I): 7.13 /Soc/The/
Eudoxia Wf (+ Arcadius; in the dispute with John Chrysostom): 8.8, 10, 13, 15, 16, 18, 20, 27 ("wife of the emperor, empress") /Soc/
Pulcheria V [Wf] (+ Marcian, regent as sister of Theodosius II): 9.1, 2, 3 /The/
Arcadia V (sister of Pulcheria): 9.1, 3 /The/
Marina V (sister of Pulcheria): 9.1, 3 /The/
(Galla) **Placidia** Wf (daughter of Galla): 9.16 /Soc/
Honoria C (daughter of Constantius III and Galla Placidia): 9.16

1. Apostle

Anonyma V? (prisoner of war who converted "Iberia" [Georgia] by example and preaching): 2.7 /Ruf/Soc/The/
Mavia W (queen of the Saracens who wages war against the Romans, Christianizes her people, and gets her choice of bishop): 6.38; 7.1 /Ruf/Soc/The/

2. Prophetess

Daughters of Philip (as miracle workers, not as prophetesses): 7.27

3. Martyress

Anonyma V (daughter of the presbyter Ananias, executed, Persia): 2.11
Tarbula V (sister of Bishop Simeon, wrongfully accused of sorcery, sawed to pieces, Persia): 2.12
Anonyma S V (slave of Tarbula, "shared her way of life"): ibid.
Anonyma W (sister of Tarbula, with whom she lived after the death of her husband): ibid.
Women (great persecution in Persia): 2.14
Virgins in Heliopolis (brought out naked, tortured, finally thrown to the swine): 5.10
Anonyma Wf+C (prevented a massacre of Christians in Edessa): 6.18 /Ruf/Soc/The/
Women+C H (persecution of Arian Christians beyond the Danube): 6.37

Nonnichia Wf (has her husband kill her in order not to be raped by soldiers): 9.13

4. Ascetic

Women V/W (Therapeutae/Philo): 1.12 /Eus/
Women V/W/V+Wf? (Eustathius/Gangra): 3.14 /Soc/
Women V/W (convents/Julian): 5.16
—Law of Theodosius: women who cut their hair short will be excommunicated: 7.16

5. Spiritual Partner (Syneisakta)

Anonyma V+Wf (on her wedding night her husband Ammon talks her into the ideal of continence): 1.14 /Soc/Pall./

6. Widow

<Anonyma M (sister of Tarbula): 2.12>
Widows (Emperor Julian ended the feeding of virgins and widows): 5.5
Widows (Emperor Jovian suspends Julian's measures against virgins and widows): 6.3

7. Virgin

Irene: 1.11 /Ruf/Soc/
Virgins in Jerusalem (the virgins entered in the church register were invited to a banquet by Empress Helena and served by her): 2.2 /Ruf/Soc/The/
<Tarbula M: 2.12>
<Anonyma M S (slave of Tarbula): 2.12>
Virgins (Emperor Julian ended the feeding of virgins and widows): 5.5
Anonyma (hides Athanasius): 5.6 /Ruf/[Pall.]/
<Virgins in Heliopolis M: 5.10>
Virgins (Emperor Jovian suspends Julian's measures against virgins and widows): 6.3
Virgins (under Julian many tried to marry virgins; now such marriages are punishable by death): ibid.
<Matrona D H: 7.21>
<Ascetics
<Deaconesses>

8. Deaconess

Nectaria N V/W? (accused of perjury; ordination doubted): 4.24
—Law of Theodosius: only widows over 60 who have had children are to be admitted to the diaconate: 7.16
Matrona D? H V (Macedonian, guarded relics of John the Baptist, resisted the emperor, famous abbess): 7.21
Pentadia [D] W (denied asylum; diaconate not mentioned but known from other sources; Constantinople): 7.7
Olympias W (supported John Chrysostom; tried for arson; Constantinople): 8.9, 24, 27
Nicarete D? V (offered diaconate but supposedly rejected ordination; known for healing successes; reputation for great holiness; Constantinople): 8.23
Eusebia H V/W? (Macedonian, friend of the empress; hid the bones of the 40 martyrs of Sebaste; these are discovered through Pulcheria's miracle): 9.2

9. Educated

<Deaconesses>

10. Slave

<Anonyma M V (slave of Tarbula): 2.12>
Anonyma H? X: 8.5

11. Heterodox

Women X (men and women sing songs of Apollinaris while working): 6.25
<Matrona D Mac. V: 7.21>
Anonyma Wf (Macedonian who tried to deceive husband with a host maneuver; miracles): 8.5
<her slave, Mac.? X>
Anonyma X (crossover of a Manichaean; legality was doubted): 8.12 /Soc/
<Eusebia D Mac. V/W?: 9.2>

12. Other

—Chastity laws in Heliopolis: 1.8
—Laws favorable to celibacy: 1.9
Anonyma N (left husband in spite of adultery, became ascetic): 1.13
—Clergy may engage in sexual activity after ordination: 1.23 /Soc/
Anonyma X (healed in Jerusalem): 2.1 /Ruf/Soc/The/
Anonyma Wf+C (let sick child be healed by prisoner of war): 2.7 Ruf/Soc/The/
Anonyma N (slandered Athanasius: alleged rape): 2.25 /Ruf/The/
Anonyma N (provoked Ephraim, who never looked at women): 3.16
Anonyma X (saved the bones of martyrs): 5.9
Anonyma X (healed hemorrhagic): 5.21 /Eus/
Anonyma C (healing of one possessed): 6.20 /The/
Anonyma X (sister of a monk; he visited her on order of the bishop but closed his eyes in or-
der not to see her): 6.29
Anonyma Wf (a pregnant woman awakened from the dead): 7.5
Ignorant women N ("especially women and the masses" hold the church of a martyr to be the
grave of the apostle Paul): 7.10
Anonyma X (compromises a clergyman through public confession): 7.16 /Soc/
—Vision of a raging woman with whip before an insurrection as symbol of the demonic: 7.23
<Pentadia D W (denied asylum): 8.7>
Crying women X (exile of John Chrysostom): 8.21
Anonyma Wf (friend of deaconess Eusebia): 9.2
Anonyma Wf (prominant Roman defended her chastity): 9.10

Women in Theodoret

0. From Ruling Houses

Helena Wf (mother of Constantine): 1.18 /Ruf/Soc/Soz/
Anonyma Wf (queen of "Iberia" [Georgia]): 1.24 /Ruf/Soc/Soz/
Constantia Wf (sister of Constantine): 2.3 /Ruf/Soc/Soz/

Wife of Julian [Helena] Wf: 3.13 /Soc/
Wife of Valens [Domnica] Wf H: 4.12 /Soz/
<Mavia Wf>: 4.23 (*see below:* Apostle)
Justina Wf H (+ Valentinian I): 5.13 /Soc/Soz/
Flacilla Wf (+ Theodosius I, first marriage): 5.19, 20 /Soc/Soz/
Sisters of Theodosius II [Pulcheria, Arcadia, Marina]: 5.39 /Soz/

1. Apostle

Anonyma V? (prisoner of war who converted "Iberia" [Georgia] by example and preaching): 1.24 /Ruf/Soc/Soz/
Mavia W (queen of the Sarazens who wages war against the Romans, Christianizes her people, and gets her choice of bishop): 4.23 /Ruf/Soc/Soz/

2. Prophetess

3. Martyress

Virgins in Alexandria (undressed and whipped—some to death—during persecution of orthodox Christians by Arians): 2.14 (cites Athanasius) /Soc/
Widows and orphans (are not spared): ibid.
Virgins and priests in Ascalon and Gaza (thrown to the swine): 3.7
Anonyma Wf+C (prevented a massacre of Christians in Edessa): 4.17 /Ruf/Soc/Soz/
Virgins in Alexandria (violation, murder): 4.22

4. Ascetic

5. Spiritual Partner (Syneisakta)

Eustolium V (lived with the presbyter Leontius, who had himself castrated but still became the bishop of Antioch): 2.24 /Soc/
—Allusion? (the Audian sect accuses orthodox clergy of extramarital contacts with women): 4.10
Anonyma V+Wf (Pelagius, bishop of Laodicea, on his wedding night talks his bride into continence): 4.13

6. Widow

—Grain for virgins and widows: 1.11

7. Virgin

—Grain for virgins and widows: 1.11
Virgins in Jerusalem (the virgins entered in the church register were invited to a banquet by Empress Helena and served by her): 1.18 /Ruf/Soc/Soz/
<Virgins in Alexandria M (Arian author): 2.14>
<Virgins in Ascalon and Gaza M: 3.7>
<Virgins in Alexandria M: 4.22>

8. Deaconess

Anonyma V/W? (converted the son of a pagan priest): 3.14
Publia D? (provoked Emperor Julian by singing certain psalm verses): 3.19

9. Educated

<Deaconesses>

10. Slave

11. Heterodox

Prominent Arian women X (in trials against the orthodox): 1.4
Unbridled young Arian women N (discredited Christianity): ibid.
<Wife of Valens (like Adam, the emperor let himself be misled by his Arian wife): 4.12>
Anonyma X (Arian who murdered an orthodox bishop with bricks): 5.4

12. Other

Anonyma X (healed in Jerusalem): 1.18 /Ruf/Soc/Soz/
Anonyma N (committed perjury for money against the bishop of Antioch, the alleged father
    of her child): 1.21–22
Anonyma Wf+C (let sick child be healed by prisoner of war): 1.24 Ruf/Soc/Soz/
—Slandering of Athanasius: alleged rape: 1.30 /Ruf/Soz/
Anonyma N (prostitute ordered to the room of a bishop): 2.9
Women in Rome Wf (achieve through the emperor the return of Bishop Liberius): 2.17
Anonyma Wf+C (wife of a pagan priest; Christian?): 3.14
Anonyma X (woman murdered by Julian; foretold from her liver [?]): 3.26
Anonyma C (demon spoke through a pagan girl): 4.21 /Soz/

Women in Rufinus

(Includes only women also mentioned by Socrates, Sozomen, or Theodoret)
Irene V (daughter of Bishop Spyridon [*vir unus ex ordine prophetarum*]; worked miracles after her
    death): 1.5 /Soc/Soz/
Helena Wf (mother of Constantine): 1.7–8 /Soc/Soz/The/
Virgins in Jerusalem (the virgins entered in the church register were invited to a banquet by Em-
    press Helena and served by her—"famula famularum Dei"): ibid. /Soc/Soz/The/
Anonyma X (healed in Jerusalem): ibid. /Soc/Soz/The 1.18/
Anonyma Wf+C (queen of "India" [Ethiopia]): 1.9
Anonyma V? (prisoner of war who converted "Iberia" [Georgia] by example and preaching):
    1.10 /Soc/Soz/The 1.24/
Anonyma Wf (queen of "Iberia"): ibid.
Anonyma Wf+C (let sick child be healed by prisoner of war): ibid.
Constantia Wf (sister of Constantine who protected an Arian presbyter): 1.12 /Soc/Soz/
Anonyma N (slandered Athanasius: alleged rape): 1.17 /Soz/The/
Anonyma M Wf+C (prevented a massacre of Christians in Edessa): 2.5 /Soc/Soz/The/

Mavia W (queen of the Saracens who wages war against the Romans, Christianizes her people, and gets her choice of bishop): 2.6 /Soc/Soz/The/
Justina H Wf (supported Arians): 2.15 /Soc/Soz/The/

Women from the Ruling House

Salome Wf ★ (+ Alexander; sister of Herod the Great): Eus 1.8.13
Anonyma X ★ (queen of Ethiopia): Eus 2.1.13
Herodias Wf ★ (+ Herod Antipas; exiled): Eus 2.4.1
Helena X ★ (queen of Adiabene): Eus 2.12.3
Mammea Wf ★ (mother of Emperor Severus Alexander): Eus 6.21.3–4
Severa Wf ★ (+ Philippus Arabs): Eus 6.36.3
Constantia Wf (+ Licinius; sister of Constantine): Eus 10.8.4; Soc 1.2, 25; Soz 1.7
Helena Wf (mother of Constantine): Soc 1.17, 18; Soz 2.1, 2; The 1.18
Anonyma Wf+C (queen of "India" [Ethiopia]): Soc 1.19; Ruf 1.9
Anonyma Wf (queen of "Iberia" [Georgia]): Soc 1.20; Soz 2.7; The 1.24; Ruf 1.10
Eusebia Wf (+ Constantius II): Soc 3.1; Soz 5.7
Helena Wf (+ Julian; sister of Constantius II): Soc 3.1
Anastasia C (daughter of Valens): Soc 4.9
Carosa C (daughter of Valens): Soc 4.9
Severa Wf (+ Valentinian I): Soc 4.31
Justina H Wf (+ Valentinian I, who married both women by special law!): Soc 4.31; 5.11; Soz 7.13; The 5.13
Galla Wf (+ Theodosius I, second marriage, daughter of Justina): Soc 4.31
Justa V (daughter of Justina): Soc 4.31
Grata V (daughter of Justina): Soc 4.31
(Galla) **Placidia** Wf (+ Constantius III; daughter of Galla): Soc 4.31; 7.24; Soz 9.16
Flacilla Wf (+ Theodosius I, first marriage): Soc 4.31; 5.12; Soz 7.6; The 5.19, 23
Mavia W (queen of the Saracens): Soc 4.36
Anonyma Wf (daughter of Mavia): Soc 4.36
Eudoxia Wf (+ Arcadius): Soc 6.8, 11, 15, 18; Soz 8.8, 10, 13, 15, 16, 18, 20, 27
Eudokia/Athenaïs Wf (+ Theodosius II): Soc 7.21, 44, 47
Eudoxia Wf (daughter of Eudokia): Soc 7.44
Anonyma Wf ★ (queen of Persia): Soz 2.12
Domnica Wf (+ Valens): Soz 6.16 ("wife of Valens"); 7.1; The 4.12 ("consort")
Pulcheria V (later wife of Markian; regent as sister of Theodosius II): Soz 9.1, 2, 3; The 5.39 ("sister of Theodosius")
Arcadia V (sister of Pulcheria): Soz 9.1, 3; The 5.39 ("sister of Theodosius")
Marina V (sister of Pulcheria): Soz 9.1, 3; The 5.39 ("sister of Theodosius")
Honoria C (daughter of Constantius III and Galla Placidia): Soz 9.16

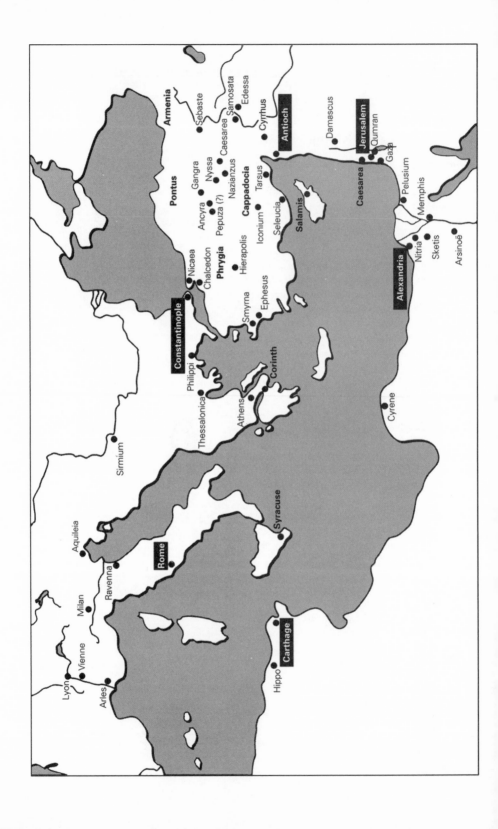

WEST | **EAST**

Gaul	Rome	Africa (Carthage)	Asia Minor	Egypt (Alexandria)	Syria (Antioch)	Palestine (Jerusalem)	Persia
Blandina *Irenaeus*	*Hermas* Marcellina *Marcion* Philomena *Apelles* *Justin* *Hippolytus*	Anonyma Perpetua Felicity *Tertullian* *Cyprian*	*Polycarp* Thecla Ammia Prisca Maximilla *Montanus*	*Clement* *Origen*	*Ignatius*		

ca. 300 —

Gaul	Rome	Africa	Asia Minor (Constantinople)	Egypt	Syria	Palestine	Persia
Ambrose (Milan) *Rufinus* Egeria	Proba Paula Eustochium Marcella Melanie the Elder *Jerome* Melanie the Younger	*Augustine*	*John Chrysostom* Olympias Nicarete *Socrates* *Sozomen* Eudocia (Athenaïs)	Synkletike *Arius* *Athanasius* Hypatia *Cyril*	*Eusebius* *Epiphanius* (Cyprus) *Theodoret*	Paula Eustochium *Jerome*	Anonyma (Georgia) Tarbula

Macrina
Basil
Gregory of Nyssa
Gregory of Nazianzus

NOTES

Preface

1. The research project "Woman and Christianity" was divided into two subprojects: I. "Sexuality, Marriage, and Alternatives to Marriage in the First Four Centuries"; II. "Being a Christian Woman in the Twentieth Century." In 1982 Bernadette Brooten undertook subproject I; in 1985 I took over the project after her departure and combined it with my *Habilitation* plans. Subproject II was carried out between 1983 and 1986 by Doris Kaufmann. Hans Küng was the responsible director and Elisabeth Moltmann-Wendel the advisor of the overall project.

2. This is the basic thesis of Mary Daly in her evaluation of Christianity. First a Catholic theologian, Mary Daly then developed her own religious philosophy for women. Cf. Mary Daly, *The Church and the Second Sex;* idem, *Beyond God the Father: Toward a Philosophy of Women's Liberation;* idem, *Gyn/ecology: The Metaethics of Radical Feminism;* idem, *Pure Lust: Elemental Feminist Philosophy.*

3. Cf. Bernadette J. Brooten, "Early Christian Women and Their Cultural Context."

4. Cf. Karin Hausen, "Women's History in den Vereinigten Staaten"; Gisela Bock, "Historische Frauenforschung: Fragestellungen und Perspektiven"; idem, "Geschichte, Frauengeschichte, Geschlechtergeschichte"; Ute Frevert, "Bewegung und Disziplin in der Frauengeschichte."

5. Gisela Bock, "Geschichte," 367.

6. Joan Kelly-Gadol, "The Social Relation of the Sexes"; cf. Bock, "Geschichte."

7. Within the scope of the project Bernadette J. Brooten published the following articles on Jewish women's right of divorce and on the cultural context of Rom. 1:26 (homosexuality of women): "Konnten Frauen im alten Judentum die Scheidung betreiben? Überlegungen zu Mk 10,11–12 und 1 Kor 7,10–11"; "Zur Debatte über das Scheidungsrecht der jüdischen Frau"; "Patristic Interpretations of Romans 1:26"; "Paul's Views on the Nature of Women and Female Homoeroticism."

8. I have adopted this new formation (instead of *gynecocentric*) because its usage is beginning to be common.

9. Cf. Hausen, "Women's History," 363.

10. Here I have consciously replaced the term *patriarchal,* common in the women's movement, with the new coinage *virist* (from *vir,* "man," in analogy to *feminist* from *femina,* "woman"), meaning focused on the interests of men. I avoid the outworn and misleading catchword *patriarchy;* cf. Karin Hausen, "Patriarchat: Vom Nutzen und Nachteil eines Konzepts für Frauengeschichte und Frauenpolitik."

11. Doris Kaufmann, *Frauen zwischen Aufbruch und Reaktion: Protestantische Frauenbewegung in der ersten Hälfte des 20. Jahrhunderts.*

12. N.B.: In feminist linguistics the term *inclusive* has special usage. *Inclusive language* means a manner of speaking in which women are always explicitly named. Cf. Hildburg Wegener,

"Sprache/Sprachveränderung," in *Wörterbuch der Feministischen Theologie* (Gütersloh, 1991), 378–80.

13. Elisabeth Schüssler Fiorenza, *In Memory of Her*, 45 (on this important work see below: Introduction).

14. For the holy scriptures of Jews and Christians I use the usual terms in Christian theology, *Old* and *New Testament*, because finding other adequate terminology would be very complicated. The problems with these terms are discussed in IV.2b.

Introduction

1. On Franz Josef Dölger cf. *ANRW* II.23.1 (1979), 4ff.

2. Cf. Eric Dodds, *Pagan and Christian in an Age of Anxiety;* Robert M. Grant, *Early Christianity and Society;* Peter Brown, *The Making of Late Antiquity; Existence païenne au début du christianisme* (text anthology); Robert L. Wilken, *The Christians: As the Romans Saw Them;* Stephen Benko, *Pagan Rome and Early Christians;* Antonio Quacquarelli, *Reazione pagana e trasformazione della cultura;* Wolfgang Speyer, *Frühes Christentum im antiken Strahlungsfeld* (essays); *Das frühe Christentum im römischen Staat; ANRW* II.23.1–2, (1979–80); *Pietas,* FS Bernhard Kötting; *Antiquité païenne et chrétienne,* Mémorial André-Jean Festugière; *Histoire de la vie privée,* ed. Philippe Ariès and Georges Duby, vol. 1, *De l'Empire romain à l'an mil; Christentum und antike Gesellschaft,* ed. Jochen Martin and Barbara Quint.

3. Cf. Brooten, "Early Christian Women," 69ff.

4. Günter Stemberger, "Die Juden im Römischen Reich: Unterdrückung und Privilegierung einer Minderheit."

5. Cf. *ANRW* II.17.1–4 (1981–84).

6. Walter F. Otto, *Die Götter Griechenlands,* 10.

7. Heb. *goyim;* Gk. *ethnikoi;* Lat. *gentiles.*

8. Used disparagingly are *ethnikoi/gentiles* (originally the foreign "tribes" as opposed to the Romans) and *pagani* (originally the uneducated people in the country).

9. In the United States, Jewish and Christian feminist theologians often work together in approaches that encompass more than one religion; cf., e.g., Ross S. Kraemer, *Ecstatics and Ascetics: Studies in the Function of Religious Activities for Women in the Greco-Roman World; Images of Women in Antiquity,* ed. Averil Cameron and Amélie Kuhrt; *Maenads, Martyrs, Matrons, Monastics* (text anthology), ed. Ross S. Kraemer. On Jewish women in antiquity cf. Bernadette J. Brooten, *Women Leaders in the Ancient Synagogue;* Guenther Mayer, *Die jüdische Frau in der hellenistisch-römischen Antike;* on Greek and Roman women cf. Sarah B. Pomeroy, *Goddesses, Whores, Wives, and Slaves: Women in the Classical Antiquity;* Dacre Balsdon, *Roman Women;* Mary R. Lefkowitz and Maureen B. Fant, *Women's Life in Greece and Rome* (text anthology); Edith Specht, *Schön zu sein und gut zu sein: Mädchenbildung und Frauensozialisation im antiken Griechenland.*

10. On the problem of anti-Judaism in Christian feminist theology cf. Judith Plaskow, "Christian Feminism and Anti-Judaism"; idem, "Blaming Jews for Inventing Patriarchy"; idem, "Feministischer Antijudaismus und der christliche Gott"; also the collection *Verdrängte Vergangenheit, die uns bedrängt,* ed. Leonore Siegele-Wenschkewitz; on the feminist rereading of the Jewish religion, cf. *On Being a Jewish Feminist: A Reader,* ed. Susannah Heschel; Judith Plaskow, *Standing Again at Sinai: Judaism from a Feminist Perspective.*

11. On Thecla see below: I.5b and the beginning of II.

12. Cf. Walter Bauer, *Rechtgläubigkeit und Ketzerei im ältesten Christentum;* Alain Le Boulluec, *La notion d'hérésie dans la littérature grecque: IIe–IIIe siècles,* vol. 1, *De Justin à Irénée;* vol. 2, *Clément*

d'Alexandrie et Origène (cf. rev. by Norbert Brox, *TRev* 83 [1987]: 199–204); Norbert Brox, s.v. "Häresie," *RAC* 13:248–97.

13. On the Syrian women's traditions outside the imperial church cf. the annotated anthology of sources: *Holy Women of the Syrian Orient,* ed. Sebastian P. Brock and Susan Ashbrook Harvey.

14. Cf. Brooten, "Early Christian Women," 67.

15. *Methoden in der Frauenforschung,* 86 (Claudia Opitz).

16. On the "confusion of prescriptive and descriptive literature" cf. Brooten, "Early Christian Women," 73.

17. Cf. Archiv für philosophie- und theologiegeschichtliche Frauenforschung (series), ed. Elisabeth Gössmann.

18. Harnack, *Die Mission und Ausbreitung des Christentums,* 589–611.

19. "Egalitarian ethos" refers to the brotherly-sisterly equality of all people in the sense of the gospel.

20. Cf. the examples in Brooten, "Early Christian Women," 72ff.

21. Klaus Thraede, s.v. "Frau," *RAC* 8; cf. also idem, "Ärger mit der Freiheit: Die Bedeutung von Frauen in Theorie und Praxis der alten Kirche," 31–182.

22. Ida Raming, *Der Ausschluss der Frau vom priesterlichen Amt.* Cf. also Haye van der Meer, *Priestertum der Frau? Eine theologiegeschichtliche Untersuchung.*

23. *Inter Insigniores* 5, *AAS* 69 (1977): 98–116; Ger.: *Erklärung der Kongregation für die Glaubenslehre zur Frage der Zulassung der Frauen zum Priesteramt,* Verlautbarungen des Apostolischen Stuhls 3, ed. Deutsche Bischofskonferenz (1976). On the binding nature of this document cf. Peter Hünermann, "Roma locuta—causa finita?"; Hervé Legrand, "Die Frage der Frauenordination aus der Sicht katholischer Theologie," in *Warum keine Ordination der Frau?* 89–111.

24. Thomas Hopko, "On the Male Character of Christian Priesthood," and Deborah Belonick, "The Spirit of the Female Priesthood," both in *Women and the Priesthood,* 97–190.

25. See II.6 below. Meanwhile, even Eastern church theologians have recognized that this argument is not anchored in the patristic tradition; cf. Elisabeth Behr-Sigel, *Le ministère de la femme dans l'Eglise;* idem, "Ordination von Frauen?" in *Warum keine Ordination der Frau?* 50–72; John Erickson, "La prêtrise dans l'enseignement patristique."

26. *Image of God and Gender Models in Judaeo-Christian Tradition,* ed. Kari Elisabeth Børresen (1991). (I was not able to examine it before the completion of this study.) The *imago dei* debate is also found in the "querelle des femmes," which was examined by Elisabeth Gössmann. Several of her studies are on the theology of women in the Middle Ages.

27. Kari Elisabeth Børresen, "Women's Studies of the Christian Tradition."

28. Cf., e.g., Otto Bangerter, *Frauen im Aufbruch: Die Geschichte einer Frauenbewegung in der Alten Kirche;* Cettina Militello, *Donna e Chiesa: La Testimonianza di Giovanni Crisostomo;* Clementina Mazzucco, *"E fui fatta maschio": La donna nel Cristianesimo primitivo;* Suzanne Tunc, *Brève histoire des femmes chrétiennes* (the largest part of the book concerns the early church); Joëlle Beaucamp, *Le statut de la femme à Byzance;* Martin Ibarra Benlloch, *Mulier fortis: La mujer en las fuentes cristianas (280–313);* J. J. Thierry (male author), *Vrouwen in de vroegchristelijke kerk.*

29. Cf. Rosemary (Radford) Ruether, "Misogynism and Virginal Feminism in the Fathers of the Church" (1974); idem, "Mothers of the Church: Ascetic Women in the Late Patristic Age" (1979); Jo Ann McNamara, "Sexual Equality and the Cult of Virginity in Early Christian Thought" (1976); idem, *A New Song: Celibate Women in the First Three Christian Centuries* (1985); Ross S. Kraemer, "The Conversion of Women to Ascetic Forms of Christianity" (1980); Elizabeth A. Clark, "Ascetic Renunciation and Feminine Advancement: A Paradox of Late Ancient Christianity" (1981); Elizabeth Castelli, "Virginity and Its Meaning for Women's Sexuality in Early Christianity" (1986).

30. Cf., e.g., the following anthologies: Elizabeth A. Clark, *Jerome, Chrysostom, and Friends;* idem, *Ascetic Piety and Women's Faith.*

31. Davies holds that all apocryphal *Acts of the Apostles* were written by women and also advocates bold hypotheses that are hardly supported by the sources; cf. the critique of Dennis R. MacDonald, "The Role of Women in the Production of the Apocryphal Acts of Apostles," *The Iliff Review* 40/4 (1984): 21–38.

32. Cf. also the short version: Virginia Burrus, "Chastity as Autonomy: Women in the Stories of Apocryphal Acts" (with response by Jean-Daniel Kaestli); as well as Jean-Daniel Kaestli, "Fiction littéraire et réalité sociale."

33. After finishing my work I learned of a dissertation by Eva Maria Synek, "Heilige Frauen der frühen Christenheit."

34. Cf., however, the paper by Klaus Thraede, "Zwischen Eva und Maria," in which the advantages and disadvantages of the married and single states *(matrona/virgo)* are compared.

35. Cf. Elaine H. Pagels, *The Gnostic Gospels,* esp. chap. 3: "God the Father/God the Mother." For more on women in Gnosticism see chap. IV below.

36. Cf. Susanne Heine, *Frauen der frühen Christenheit,* 117–35.

37. Cf. Elisabeth Moltmann-Wendel, *Ein eigener Mensch werden: Frauen um Jesus;* idem, ed., *Frauenbefreiung: Biblische und theologische Argumente;* idem, *Das Land, wo Milch und Honig fliesst: Perspektiven feministischer Theologie.*

38. On the martyrdom of Perpetua and Felicity see below: II.4.

39. On Proba see I.4e below.

40. The writing of Egeria is not examined here; see Bibl. I for sources.

41. On Eudocia see I.4e below.

42. In 1971 the first version of this work in a modern language appeared in the Italian translation, without commentary, of Caterina Carridi.

43. Elisabeth Schüssler Fiorenza published her hermeneutical principles again in *Bread Not Stone: The Challenge of Feminist Biblical Interpretation.*

44. Cf. the review by Susanne Heine, "Brille der Parteilichkeit: Zu einer feministischen Hermeneutik," in EvK 23 (1990): 354–57.

45. In regard to writings handed down anonymously, it may be in part a question of works by women, and it is at least not improbable that there were also publications under masculine pseudonyms. Feminine influence on the works of men is often attested; all this needs to be thoroughly investigated.

46. Cf. Bibl. I under "Life."

47. In addition to the literature already mentioned cf. Elena Giannarelli, *La tipologia femminile nella biografia e nell'autobiografia cristiana del IV° secolo;* Anne Ewing Hickey, *Women of the Roman Aristocracy as Christian Monastics;* as well as the translation, with detailed commentary, of the life of Melanie by Elizabeth A. Clark (see Bibl. I under "Life").

I. Women in the Church Histories
Development into the Church of Men

1. The epigraph quotation is from Socrates *Ch.Hist.* 5, Introd., NPNF, 2nd series, 2:118.

2. Cf. Glenn F. Chesnut, *The First Christian Histories: Eusebius, Socrates, Sozomen, Theodoret, and Evagrius;* Robert M. Grant, *Eusebius as Church Historian;* Monika Gödecke, *Geschichte als Mythos: Eusebs "Kirchengeschichte";* cf. also the introductions of the editions cited in Bibl. I.

3. The *Church History* of Eusebius has been edited in its entirety by Gustave Bardy in the SC; the old German translation of the BKV by Philipp Haeuser has been newly revised by Hans Arnim Gärtner (2nd ed., 1981); cited here is the authorized edition of the Wissenschaftlichen

Buchgesellschaft (Darmstadt, 1984). Also drawn into the study is the *Palestinian Martyrs* (SC 55; BKV 9), which probably followed book 8 of the *Church History* (cf. Bardy, SC 55:121).

4. For editions and translations see below and Bibl. I. With Theodoret the chapter introduction is not consistent: I have adopted the numbering of the BKV, which deviates only a little from the Greek edition of the text (GCS).

5. For the *Church History* of Socrates there are currently only the edition of Jacques-Paul Migne (*PG* 67) and an old English translation by A. C. Zenos (NPNF, 2nd series, 2); a German translation has been announced by Anton Hiersemann Verlag Stuttgart.

6. Sozomen's *Church History* was completely edited by Joseph Bidez (GCS 50) and has been revised by Guy Sabbah (introd. by Bernard Grillet); appearing thus far are books 1 and 2 (SC 306); there is an old English translation by Chester D. Hartranft (NPNF, 2nd series, 2).

7. Theodoret's *Church History,* ed. Léon Parmentier (GCS 19); German: Andreas Seider (BKV 51). The old English translation of Blomfield Jackson (NPNF, 2nd series, 3) has a different chapter numbering.

8. Rufinus, *Church History,* ed. Theodor Mommsen (GCS 9/2); Ital. trans. (Lorenzo Dattrino), see Bibl. I; cf. Françoise Thélamon, *Païens et chrétiens au IVe siècle: L'apport de l' "Histoire ecclésiastique" de Rufin d'Aquilée.* The two chapters of Rufinus may go back to the lost church history of Gelasius of Caesarea (d. 395).

9. The writing of Clement may refer to so-called *1 Clement* (letter to the church in Corinth) or to the Pseudo-Clementines (cf. SC 306:116, n. 1). The historical works of Hegesippus and Julius Africanus, as well as Sozomen's summarizing work, have been lost.

10. "Peut-on voir en lui le continuateur d'Eusèbe? En aucune façon: Sozomène est un laïc et il observe l'histoire de l'Eglise de l'extérieur, en profane" (SC 306:35).

11. This new situation, mentioned by Grillet with a mere "incidentally," is quite correctly described by him: ". . . avec le triomphe de l'Eglise, celle-ci et l'Etat tendent à se confondre" (ibid.).

12. Cf. Carl Andresen, " 'Siegreiche Kirche' im Aufstieg des Christentums"; Anne Jensen, *Die Zukunft der Orthodoxie: Konzilspläne und Kirchenstrukturen,* 47ff. (A.II.1: "Das Ideal der 'Symphonia' im byzantinischen Reich"); Michael J. Hollerich, "Religion and Politics in the Writings of Eusebius."

13. Cf. here above all the introduction by Günther Christian Hansen in the Sozomen edition by Joseph Bidez, GCS 50, pp. XLIV-XLVII, and by Guy Sabbah, SC 306:59–87.

14. Cf. Socrates 2.1.

15. ". . . *l'Histoire ecclésiastique* de Sozomène réalisa la coexistence du présent chrétien et de la tradition hellénique d'une manière plus harmonieuse et plus complète que ne l'avait fait l'oeuvre de Socrate, ressentie, après seulement quelques années, comme irrémédiablement *anachronique*" (SC 306:87; emphasis by Sabbah).

16. "That Socrates was the finer mind, that he had larger sympathies, that he was concerned to produce documents in an ampler degree, that he follows the development of the Church with a sharper and brighter criticism, no one can doubt; he is conspicuously superior in almost every quality of a historian . . . but that does not set aside the distinct and supplemental value of Sozomen and his fullness in lines, however zigzag, which had been neglected by others" (Hartranft, NPNF, 2nd series, 2:221).

17. Chesnut, *First Christian Histories,* 167.

18. Zenos, NPNF, 2nd series, 2:xv.

19. Cf. the opening quotation at the beginning of this chapter (and elsewhere).

20. Sabbah, SC 306:80.

21. Hartranft, NPNF, 2nd series, 2:203.

22. Cf. Aloys Grillmeier, *Christ in Christian Tradition,* vol. 1, 2nd ed. (Atlanta, 1975), 463.

23. Parmentier, GCS 19, p. XCVIII.

24. Regarding these women cf. Wolfgang Schuller, *Frauen in der römischen Geschichte,* chap. 7.

25. Cf. Acts 18:2; Euseb. *Ch.Hist.* 2.18.9.

26. The German *Einheitsübersetzung der Katholischen Bibelanstalt des NT* (1972) still has "Junias," yet von Harnack (*Mission,* 592) was extremely doubtful about the male gender; without comment, Zscharnack (*Dienst der Frau,* 102) includes Junia among the women; in his commentary on Romans, Marie-Joseph Lagrange points out that Junia is a feminine given name and that it is therefore to be presumed that Andronicus and Junia were a married couple (*L'Epître aux Romains* [Paris, 1950], 365–66). Detailed investigations include: Bernadette J. Brooten, " 'Junia—hervorragend unter den Aposteln' (Röm 16,7)"; Valentin Fàbrega, "War Junia(s), der hervorragende Apostel (Röm 16,7), eine Frau?"; and Peter Lampe, "Iunia/Iunias: Sklavenherkunft im Kreise der vorpaulinischen Apostel (Röm 16,7)."

27. *Menologion,* 17 May; yet in the hymns Andronicus is central and Junia appears only as his companion.

28. "Junias": RSV, NEB, JB, NIV; "Junia": KJN, NRSV.

29. On the effects of an androcentric perception in the presentation of "facts" cf. the hermeneutical comments in Schüssler Fiorenza, *In Memory of Her* (part I, chap. 2).

30. Or 10 if one includes the "sisters of Theodosius" mentioned without name or number.

31. The number included is not uniform in the various editions.

32. Naturally, the lengths of the various church histories must also be considered here. Eusebius, Socrates, and Sozomen are of approximately equal length (each about 800 columns in the *PG*); Eusebius, to be sure, has a small surplus, since included here are the "Palestinian martyrs" (about 60 columns in the *PG*). Theodoret, by contrast, is clearly shorter (about 400 columns in the *PG*).

33. These traditions will be treated later in more detail.

34. For the two centers of early Christianity, Rome and Carthage, social-historical studies are available: Georg Schöllgen, *Ecclesia Sordida? Zur Frage der sozialen Schichtung frühchristlicher Gemeinden;* Peter Lampe, *Die stadtrömischen Christen in den ersten beiden Jahrhunderten.* Cf. also Georg Schöllgen, "Probleme der frühchristlichen Sozialgeschichte."

35. Cf. below: II.6.

36. Cf. below: II.3.

37. Cf. Pall. *Hist.Laus.* 3.

38. Cf. Bauer, *Rechtgläubigkeit und Ketzerei.*

39. On Simon and Helena see the beginning of chap. IV below.

40. In some sources she is called Priscilla.

41. The prophetic movement around Prisca, Maximilla, and Montanus is treated under III.2.

42. Philomena and her school are examined below under IV.2.

43. This has been a frequent commentary on the pastoral letters and one that continues today. Thus, for example, Norbert Brox writes in the 5th ed. of the *Regensburger Neues Testament* of 1989: ". . . the ecclesiastical defenders against heretics could report that for reasons of moral susceptibility, gullibility, etc., the heretics preferred to turn to women or had greater successes among women. In any case, behind these reproaches that discredit the heretics [but not perchance the women!—A.J.], it is still evident that women required greater protection or more intensive instruction in order to withstand the temptation of heresy" (132).

44. Such utterances are attested by Celsus, Julian, and Porphyry; cf. below: I.2e.

45. Norbert Brox has pointed out that the bitter conflict between orthodoxy and heresy in antiquity is a specifically "Christian" phenomenon ("Häresie," 248ff.).

46. From the Hebrew *'ebyon,* "poor"; the designation goes back to a spiritual movement in Judaism.

47. Pall. *Hist.Laus.* 64 (ACW 34:145–46); on Palladios see below: I.4d.

48. Bauer, *Rechtgläubigkeit und Ketzerei,* 62–63. Gustave Bardy holds that the orthodox attitude insinuated here is improbable (SC 41:86, n. 12), paradoxically by referring to the cited text of Bauer.

49. On the Nicolaitans cf. below: IV.1.

50. The same accusation was also made against early Christianity; cf. Theophilus of Antioch (2nd cent.), *Ad Autolycum* 3.4.

51. Earlier Eusebius had mentioned the heresy complaint summarily in a dependent clause: the bishop sees in Christ only a human being (7.27.2).

52. Cf. Bertold Altaner and Alfred Stuiber, *Patrologie,* 214.

53. On early Christian developments and discussions of congregational singing, choral singing, and male and female choirs, cf. Johannes Quasten, *Musik und Gesang in den Kulten der heidnischen Antike und der christlichen Frühzeit.*

54. Gustave Bardy, *Paul de Samosate,* 185 with n. 4; Pierre de Labriolle, "Mulieres in ecclesia taceant."

55. BKV II.1 (1932) (thus also in the 1981 revision by Hans Arnim Gärtner).

56. On Philo and his adoption by Eusebius see below: I.2d.

57. More on this in chaps. III and IV.

58. Chaps. III and IV of this study are devoted to Prisca, Maximilla, Philomena, and some other bearers of the prophetic charisma.

59. Cf. Erich Fascher, *Prophētēs: Eine sprach- und religionsgeschichtliche Untersuchung.*

60. Seneca the Elder *Controversiae* 1.9; cf. *LC,* 34–35.

61. For further literature on prophecy see the beginning of chap. III.

62. Cf. *Sogni, Visioni et Profezie;* John S. Hanson, "Dreams and Visions in the Graeco-Roman World and Early Christianity."

63. Cf. esp. 1 Corinthians 11 and 14. In addition to the usual commentaries cf. esp. the feminist exegetical discussion: Elaine H. Pagels, "Paul and Women"; Luise Schottroff, "Wie berechtigt ist die feministische Kritik an Paulus?"; Schüssler Fiorenza, *In Memory of Her,* 226–33; Dominique Stein, "Lecture des textes de Paul concernant les femmes."

64. Cf. 1 Cor. 12:28ff.

65. Cf. here Peter Corssen, "Die Töchter des Philippus." Corssen holds that the traditions about the daughters of the apostle Philip are an apocryphal exaggeration of the canonically attested daughters of the evangelist Philip, since miracle stories are reported about them. In my view this argument is not sufficient to exclude the possibility of historical reminiscences.

66. Eusebius cites Clement of Alexandria (3.30.1), Polycrates (3.31.2–3; 5.24.2), Proclus/Gaius (3.31.4), Luke (3.31.5), Papias (3.39.9), and one anonymous writer who refers to Miltiades (5.17.3) . In the sources Philip the apostle and Philip the "deacon" are confused.

67. Literally: "prophesied"; in the following the Greek verb will be rendered variously according to context: "be a prophet(ess)," "speak prophetically," "have the prophetic gift," and so on.

68. Jerome, letter 130.4 (to Demetrias).

69. Clement *Stromata* 3.52.5.

70. Also mentioned in Soz. *Ch.Hist.* 7.27; on the significance of the tradition cf. Corssen, "Töchter des Philippus," 292–93.

71. Cf. Acts 6:5; 8; 21:8 versus John 1:43–48; Acts 1:13; etc.

72. Cf., e.g., the treatises on virginity and against remarriage of Tertullian, John Chrysostom, Gregory of Nyssa, Augustine, and Ambrose, which I analyzed briefly in "Auf dem Weg zur Heiligen Jungfrau," 48–54.

73. Clement *Stromata* 2.137–47 and 3 (entire book). On the Encratite movements cf. s.v. "Enkrateia," *RAC* 5:343–65; Giulia Sfameni Gasparro, *Enkrateia e antropologia* (cf. rev. by Kari Elisabeth Børresen in *RTL* 17 [1986]: 215–18); *La Tradizione dell'Enkrateia;* from the perspective of the history of medicine: Aline Rousselle, *Porneia;* on the ascetic traditions: Peter Nagel, *Die Motivierung der Askese in der alten Kirche und der Ursprung des Mönchtums;* Arthur Vööbus, *Celibacy, a Requirement for Admission to Baptism in the Early Syrian Church;* idem, *History of Ascetism in the Syrian Orient;* Peter Brown, *The Body and Society: Men, Women, and Sexual Renunciation in Early Christianity.*

74. Clement *Stromata* 3.52.5–53.1; Clement is referring to Phil. 4:3, where a *syzygos* ("companion") is addressed; it could also be a proper name. In modern translations *syzygos* is naturally assumed to be a male. The female reading and tradition of Paul's marriage is also attested by Origen, who does not reject it but presupposes that the wife released the apostle; in this way he was free from the slavery (*sic*) of marriage (*Commentary on Romans* 1.1).

75. Clement, *Paidagogos* 2.83.1ff.

76. On the mother of Jesus cf. Euseb. *Ch.Hist.* 2.1.2; 3.27.2; 6.17 (in 1.7.17 in the context of the genealogy of Joseph).

77. See below: I.3f.

78. On the concept of apostle, "the twelve," and apostolicity cf. Wolfgang A. Bienert, "Das Apostelbild in der altchristlichen Überlieferung" (*NA* 2:6–28), and the literature given there.

79. Cf. Eugen Fehrle, *Die kultische Keuschheit im Altertum.*

80. Tertullian, *To His Wife* 1.6.3; in the following verses he polemicizes further against "pagan cults of Satan" with traditions of abstinence; likewise in *Exhortation to Chastity* 13.1ff.

81. For some preliminary reflections cf. Jensen, "Auf dem Weg" 58ff. For the Thecla cult in Seleucia, which was in competition with an Athena shrine, an interdisciplinary study is being prepared jointly with the historian of the ancient period Edith Specht.

82. Euseb. *Ch.Hist.* 5.17.3. Quadratus is otherwise unknown.

83. Ibid., 5.17.4.

84. Ibid., 5.17.2; it is not a question of differentiating between Old and New Testament prophecy but between biblical and nonbiblical.

85. Euseb. *Ch.Hist.* 5.17.4.

86. Cf. Rev. 3:7–13.

87. Philo of Alexandria *On the Contemplative Life or Suppliants* (*De vita contemplativa*).

88. The origin and exact meaning of the terms *therapeutae* and *therapeutrides* are not clear; cf. Philo *Werke* 7:44, n. 1. On the women in the community cf. Ross S. Kraemer, "Monastic Jewish Women in Greco-Roman Egypt"; also Dorothy Sly, *Philo's Perception of Women,* 209–11. This book became available to me only after the completion of my investigation; the author develops Philo's picture of women; especially interesting is the way he reads "virginity" into the biblical texts.

89. Eusebius quotes Philo here literally, yet omitting part of the last sentence: "since the Father lets intelligible rays enter it [the soul] as seed through which it can consider the dogmas of wisdom" (68).

90. Cf. Philo, §§ 2.32–33, 68–69, 80, 83–88.

91. Philo, § 65. On the feast of Pentecost cf. the comments and bibliography in the edition of François Daumas.

92. Cf. Rosemary Rader, *Breaking Boundaries.* Rader, however, has hardly expounded the problems of the "ascetic restriction" and rather apologetically claimed the development of "heterosexual friendship" for Christianity (cf. the critical rev. by Ross Kraemer, *JES* 23 [1986]).

93. Cf. Hans Achelis, *Virgines subintroductae.* Originally the last part of this book was supposed to be devoted to (women) "Spiritual partners," but the treatment of the very extensive

material already gathered would have gone beyond the scope of this study. Later publication is planned.

94. From the Greek *pneuma,* "[Holy] Spirit."

95. Cf. the treatise of John Chrysostom, which will be discussed below (I.4d).

96. See above; *subintroducta* is the literal translation of *syneisakta* ("brought in together").

97. Gustave Bardy did not want to accept Achelis's conclusions on spiritual marriage: "Dans la réalité, cette bienveillance n'a jamais existé, car l'Eglise a toujours reconnu la faiblesse de la chair" (*Paul de Samosate,* 189). But Adolf Jülicher, "Die geistliche Ehe in der alten Kirche," agreed with Achelis. Scorn was heaped on Achelis and Jülicher by Pierre de Labriolle in "Le 'Mariage spirituel' dans l'antiquité chrétienne."

98. Cf. Ambrose *Letters to Syagrios;* the numbering varies: 32/33 in FaCh 26; V/VI in *PL* 16; announced as 56/57 in CSEL.

99. First Tim. 5:3–16; cf. also 2:9–13 (prohibition of teaching, subordination, and the general necessity for women to bear children). This incredible denigration of a certain group of Christian women is hardly given a second thought in the latest commentaries; cf. Helmut Merkel, NTD (1991); Norbert Brox, RNT, 5th ed. (1989). There are still attempts to explain the polemics through "bad experiences" and alleged "deplorable situations" (Merkel, 43; Brox, 134, 194–95). Jürgen Roloff, EKKNT (1988), has critical reservations, but here too the dominant tendency is to justify the writer of the pastoral epistles.

In my comments I draw especially on the manuscript of a lecture by Jean-Daniel Kaestli ("Die Witwen in den Pastoralbriefen und in den apokryphen Apostelgeschichten"), who plans to issue a commentary on the pastoral letters (Commentaire du Nouveau Testament, 2nd series [Neuchâtel-Paris]). On misogynist precepts in the New Testament and their background in ancient Judaism, cf. also Max Küchler, *Schweigen, Schmuck und Schleier.* It should be noted that the misogynistic exegesis examined by Küchler—especially of the creation report—is not to be found in the canon of the Jewish Bible; it is "canonized" in the New Testament.

100. The conflict over celibacy and the right to teach was investigated by my research assistent Gerlinde Keppler in "Das Bild der Frau in den Pastoralbriefen und in der Thekla-Tradition." On the contrast between the picture of Paul in the pastoral letters and the acts of Paul in general cf. Dennis R. MacDonald, *The Legend and the Apostle.*

101. Cf. s.v. *"chēra," TWNT.*

102. Cf. s.v. *"digamus," RAC* 3. In early Christianity the Roman woman's ideal of *univira* as strict monogamy even after the death of her partner also became the norm for men; any second marriage was considered a weakness and prompted ecclesiastical penance.

103. Tertullian *On the Veiling of Virgins* 9.4. Tertullian is disturbed because she sits among the widows but as a virgin wears no veil (for him the symbol of female subordination).

104. Research on virgins and widows is found in all the works on women in early Christianity. Cf. the useful but incomplete and sometimes incorrect collection of sources (Gk. and Lat. only) of Josephine Mayer, *Monumenta.* Among the older studies are Leopold Zscharnack, *Der Dienst der Frau,* 44–156, and Hugo Koch, "Virgines Christi"; more recent is Otto Bangerter, *Frauen im Aufbruch.* The most comprehensive, source-based investigation at this time is Roger Gryson, *The Ministry of Women in the Early Church;* especially on widows: Bonnie Bowman Thurston, *The Widows.*

105. The presence of "virgins and widows" in the house of Marcellus, described in the novel-like *Acts of Peter,* may actually reflect historical reality (8, 19, 22, 29, and elsewhere).

106. Virginia Burrus; see above: Introduction.

107. In Justinian we even find priesthood (*hierosynē*) for the clergy in the broad sense (*Novellae* 6.6).

108. On the development of ecclesiastical orders cf. Edward Schillebeeckx, *Das kirchliche*

Amt. Peter Lampe does not even notice the clerical character of widows; cf. *Stadtrömische Christen,* 103–4.

109. The term *order* (Gk. *taxis;* Lat. *ordo*) has many levels: it means first "place in the worship service," then "rank in the ecclesiastical hierarchy," and at the same time designates a certain "group of persons." In later Latin theology *ordo* can refer to both the ordination and the ordained.

110. On the *Didascalia* see below: II.5e and 6a (conclusion).

111. Cf. *Didascalia* 14 and 15.

112. Presumably also to the deaconesses, who in the *Didascalia* (9 and 16) are seen as the female counterpart of the deacons; in the division of gifts to the clergy they are not expressly named. On the deaconess in the *Didascalia* cf. below: I.5a and II.5e.

113. *Didascalia,* chap. 9.

114. On the text see Bibl. I; here I am citing according to Bernard Botte, *La Tradition apostolique de Saint Hippolyte,* 5th rev. ed. Cf. also the Duensing edition and that of Till and Leipoldt (the numbering in these editions is not identical). The bilingual edition of Geerlings appeared after the conclusion of my work.

115. This oldest extant Roman eucharistic prayer has been in use again as one of the canons of the mass since the reform of the liturgy by the Second Vatican Council.

116. The Greek text of the original can be only partially reconstructed; Lat.: *sacerdotium* (Gk. presumably *hierosynē*) and *ministerium* (*hypēresia*).

117. On male confessors (and female, who do not appear in Hippolytus) see below: II.6.

118. That is, a formula of blessing without the laying on of hands.

119. On the central concepts of the text: "appoint": *kathistanai;* "ordain": *cheirotonein* (literally, "lay on hands")—in the Latin: *ordinare* or *imponere manum* (I translate uniformly as *ordain*)—"liturgical office, liturgy": *liturgia*—this broad term can mean, among other things, the celebration of the Eucharist, a worship activity in general, and more commonly, a public function.

120. Cf. below: II.6.

121. Cf. Botte, *Tradition apostolique,* 31, n. 1.

122. In later theology the diaconate is regarded as the lowest level of the priesthood.

123. For more details see below: II.5e.

124. Tertullian *On the Veiling of Virgins;* cf. the translation and instructive commentary by Christoph Stücklin (Bibl. I).

125. Cf. Jochen Martin, "Das Patriarchat in Rom."

126. Cf. Max Kaser, *Römisches Privatrecht,* 14: "Handlungsfähigkeit"; § 58: "Ehe und Ehegewalt" (*manus*); § 60: "Die väterliche Gewalt" (*patria potestas*); § 63: "Die Vormundschaft über Frauen" (*tutela mulierum*).

127. On the beginnings of female monasticism cf. Ruth Albrecht, *Das Leben der heiligen Makrina;* Benedicta Ward, *Harlots of the Desert.*

128. See Bibl. I for Eng. trans.

129. Cf. Albrecht, *Das Leben der heiligen Makrina,* 138ff.; Benedicta Ward, "Apophthegmata Matrum."

130. On the life of Synkletike there is only a French translation (see Bibl. I under "Life").

131. Thus in the critical edition of Cuthbert Butler and the translation of St. Krottenthaler (BKV); it is correct, however, in A. Lucot (TeD), Robert T. Meyer (ACW), and Jacques Laager. On Palladius see below: I.3e.

132. On education in antiquity specifically for women cf. Edith Specht, *Schön zu sein und gut zu sein.*

133. See above: I.2b.

134. Pall. *Hist.Laus.* 64.

135. Tatian *Oration to the Greeks,* 33.6.

136. Ibid., 33.14.

137. The term was coined by Elisabeth Schüssler Fiorenza for the early Jesus movement; cf. *In Memory of Her* (part 2).

138. In the following I refer to my manuscript "Hellenen—Sklaven—Frauen: Drei Verheissungen—drei Konflikte"; especially to be noted in the extensive literature is the old, very critical study of Franz Overbeck, "Über das Verhältnis der alten Kirche zur Sklaverei im römischen Reiche," *Studien zur Geschichte der alten Kirche* 1 (1875): 158–230, and the more moderate one of Franz Laub, *Die Begegnung des frühen Christentums mit der antiken Sklaverei,* Stuttgarter Bibelstudien 107 (Stuttgart, 1982); both come to similar conclusions. Cf. also Siegfried Schulz, *Gott ist kein Sklavenhalter.*

139. See n. 138 above.

140. See Pomeroy, *Goddesses,* 190–204.

141. Colossians 3:8–4:1; Eph. 5:21–6:9; 1 Peter 2:13–3:7; Titus 2:1–10; 1 Tim. (2:1–15) 6:1–2. Yet the passages in the pastoral letters are not "household rules" in the strict sense but church regulations, inspired by household rules, which are also found in the writings of the apostolic fathers; cf. the collection of passages in Schulz, *Gott ist kein Sklavenhalter,* 198. Cf. also Klaus Thraede, "Zum historischen 'Hintergrund' der 'Haustafeln' des NT"; Schüssler Fiorenza, *In Memory of Her,* 251–79.

142. Ignatius *Letter to Polycarp* 4.3.

143. Cf. Philemon; Seneca *47th Letter to Lucilius.*

144. Cf. s.v. "Genossenschaft," *RAC* 10:83–155; Schüssler Fiorenza, *In Memory of Her,* 175–84.

145. Ignatius also names there two further female heads of house churches: "I greet the house of Tavia, for whom I wish that she may remain in faith and love, fleshly as well as spiritual. I greet Alke, the name dear to me" (*To the Smyrnians* 13.2). "I greet all individually, also the widow of Epitropos with the whole household of her and the children. . . . I greet Alke, the name dear to me" (*To Polycarp* 8.2–3).

146. Euseb. *Ch.Hist.* 4.15.41; *Martyrdom of Polycarp* 17.

147. Cf. Pliny *Letters* 10.96.8. Often we find "deaconesses" as the translation of *ministrae,* but at the beginning of the second century the ministries of the church were not yet precisely defined.

148. Euseb. *Ch.Hist.* 2.17.1–24; he even claims to recognize there the "liturgical preeminence of deacons" and "the highest rank of the bishops" (23).

149. In the gnostically oriented *Acts of Thomas* the equality of slave and free is stressed (83); *NA* 2:336.

150. Justinian *Novellae* 5.9.

151. Cf. Anne Jensen, s.v. "Orden," *Wörterbuch der feministischen Theologie,* 310–15.

152. On Justin's report cf. the discussion in Lampe, *Stadtrömischen Christen,* 200ff.

153. Cf. below: III.2e; on the "laity" cf. Alexandre Faivre, *Les laïcs aux origines de l'Eglise;* idem, "Théologiens 'laïcs' et laïcs théologiens."

154. Identification of this woman with the adulteress of John 8:2–11 is rather unlikely; cf. SC 31:157, n. 12.

155. Cf. SC 41:192, n. 11.

156. In biblical metaphor "redemption" is more strongly associated with battles victoriously survived and deliverance from enemies.

157. On Julian see below: I.4e.

158. Cf. here the comments of Guy Sabbah (SC 306:267ff.); *Holy Women of the Syrian Orient,* 63–99; also the collection *Ausgewählte Akten persischer Märtyrer* (BKV 22).

159. Ulfilas made the first Germanic (i.e., Gothic) translation of the New Testament, fragments of which are extant.

160. In the *Akten persischer Märtyrer* she has the name Tarbo.

161. This according to Sozomen; in the *Akten persischer Märtyrer* Tarbula was offered marriage. On death by bisection cf. Wolfgang Speyer, "Eine rituelle Hinrichtung des Gottesfeindes: Die Zweiteilung," in idem, *Frühes Christentum,* 305–21.

162. Literally, "virgins" (meant here in the biological sense).

163. Suicide for the preservation of chastity is more a Roman than a Christian motive for martyrdom. Among Christians it was controversial; cf. below: II.2b.

164. Cf. below: II.1b.

165. Socrates 2.28; Theodoret 2.14; both quote Athanasius, *Apologia de fuga sua* 6.

166. Cf. below: II.2b.

167. Socrates 4.18; Sozomen 6.18; Theodoret 4.17.

168. Cf. above: I.3b (quotation in n. 43).

169. Theodoret 2.17.

170. Cf. Socrates 1.25; Sozomen 2.27; Theodoret 2.3; Rufinus 1.12.

171. Cf. Socrates 2.2.

172. On Domnica, wife of Valens, cf. Sozomen 6.16; 7.1; Theodoret 4.12; on Justina, wife of Valentinian I and opponent of Bishop Ambrose in Milan, cf. Socrates 5.11; Sozomen 7.13; Theodoret 5.13; Rufinus 2.15.

173. On Mani and Manichaeanism cf. Henri-Charles Puech, *Le manichéisme;* Geo. Widengren, *Mani und der Manichäismus.*

174. For example, the *Acta Archelai,* which according to Widengren is a "Christian novel of lies" about Mani (*Mani,* 77).

175. The text does not reveal whether the Anonyma from Thebes was herself educated.

176. The English version (NPNF, 2nd series, 2:391) has "servant" here. The text is not entirely clear: "Matrona, who was a holy virgin and for him [John the Baptist] *diakonos* and guardian." For the overall position that Matrona had at this shrine, the ministerial title *deaconess* seems to me likely, especially since the heads of convents often had this function; cf. below: I.5a.

177. Literally, "holy" (*hiera*): it is a question of the characterization of a sacral function, not of the moral evaluation of the person.

178. Gk. *hēgoumenē*—still the usual designation for an abbess of a convent in the Eastern church.

179. According to extant fragments, it was a matter of the nature of the soul of Christ; cf. Grillmeier, *Christ in Christian Tradition* 1:337ff.

180. Cf. as a vivid example the story of the dispute over the cult of one Christian martyr near the Apollo temple of Daphne (Rufinus 1.35; Sozomen 5.19); see below: I.4c.

181. Cf. below: I.5a.

182. See below: I.4e.

183. Rufinus 1.5: "vir unus ex ordine prophetarum."

184. The topic there is the claim of an Arian synod that it proclaims the catholic faith.

185. This story already told by Rufinus (1.35) is reproduced by Sozomen in a greatly elaborated form (5.19); cf. also John Chrysostom, *Speech on Babylas and Against the Greeks* (SC 362 [1990]). Julian himself also mentions the incident; cf. Julian, "Misopogon," in *Works* 2:485–86 (Bibl. I).

186. Cf. Acts 16:16ff.

187. The Roman poet Virgil was also considered a prophet by many Christians, an idea expressed especially by Proba in her *Cento;* on Proba see below: I.4e.

188. On the Sibyl see David Aune, *Prophecy in Early Christianity and the Ancient Meditteranean*

World, 36ff.; on the Jewish and Christian reworkings of the *Sibylline Oracles* see Bertold Altaner and Alfred Stuiber, *Patrologie,* 119ff., as well as editions by Johannes Geffcken (GCS 8) and Alfons Kurfess (*Sibyllinische Weissagungen* [Munich, 1951]). On the Sibylline writings cf. Guy Sabbah, SC 306:112, n. 1.

189. *Sibylline Oracles* 6.26.

190. Euseb. *Ch.Hist.* 4.18.8 and 5.7.3–6; cf. below: III.1.

191. Cf. esp. III.2e.

192. Gk. *prophētikos bios;* emphasis added.

193. Cf. Veronica Krienen, "Prophetische Züge in den Apophthegmata Patrum." In the Eastern church the monks and nuns are still considered heirs of the prophetic charisma; cf. Irénée Hausherr, *Direction spirituelle en orient autrefois.*

194. Cf. Sozomen 1.1. He devotes the following chapters to the description of monasticism: 1.12–14; 3.14; 6.28–34.

195. See above: I.2d.

196. Sozomen 3.14 and 7.16 (see below).

197. On Palladius see below.

198. In 1.13 Socrates reports on a Novatian monk Eutyches; in 1.21 he refers to the *Life of St. Anthony* of Athanasius. In 4.23 he describes the life of monks in Egypt.

199. On Palladius, *Historia Lausiaca,* see Bibl. I. Cf. esp. the introductions of Cuthbert Butler on his critical edition of 1898 and Robert T. Meyer on the Eng. translation, ACW 34, which contains information going beyond Butler on the status (at that time) of textual criticism.

200. Cf., e.g., Peter Nagel, *Die Motivierung der Askese;* Ruether, *Misogynism and Virginal Feminism,* 153ff.; Jensen, "Auf dem Weg," 48ff.

201. Gk. *philotheos historia ē askētikē politeia. Politeia* is often translated "way of life"; at the same time, in distinction to *bios* the word brings to mind a concrete group that practices this way of life. The traditional Latin title is *Historia religiosa*—thus the old designations are again less "sexist" than the modern titles; cf. the Gk./Fr. edition, *L'Histoire des moines de Syrie,* and the Ger. trans. *Mönchsgeschichte.*

202. The work actually has three prefaces: (1) the prologue (which may not have come from Palladius himself); (2) the dedication to Lausus; (3) the (untitled) introduction to the book proper, which is then divided into 71 individual stories. The translation of Jacques Laager begins immediately with the introduction (confusingly called the prologue).

203. See below: II.5. On the monk as the successor of the martyr cf. Edward E. Malone, *The Monk and the Martyr.*

204. Thus "courage" is given as "zeal," "battle" as "effort," and so on.

205. Cf. Jerome's letters to Paula and Eustochium; on prominent Roman women ascetics, whose best-known representative was Melanie, cf. Anne Ewing Hickey, *Women of the Roman Aristocracy;* cf. also the various editions of *The Life of Melanie the Younger* (Bibl. I).

206. Gk. *andreias* (from the root word for "man"); another possible translation: "brave." On the "manly women" see below.

207. This could also refer to the noble background of the women, but it is more likely the evaluation of personal achievement, as the use of the adjective *asteios* in the following section shows.

208. Augustine *On Continence* 23.

209. Cf. below: "Spiritual Partners."

210. The word *philotheos* ("friend of God") is also used in the text as a term for ascetics.

211. The BKV translation means: "She . . . cleanses her sex of the inherited shame of the first mother." Perhaps with *to genos* Theodoret means the female sex, but it could just as well be simply the human race that is freed from the shame of primeval sin. The Greek equivalent of

the Western *original sin* is *propatorikon hamartēma* "sin of the forefathers"; here we have *progonikē aischynē,* literally "ancestral shame." Thus in the text neither Eve nor the female sex is expressly mentioned.

212. The synodal letter of the Synod of Gangra with its twenty canons is part of a collection of canons that represents the foundation of orthodox church law. For the text and Fr. trans. see Péricleès-Pierre Joannou, *Les canons des synodes particuliers* (Bibl. I: "Canons"); on the date of the synod see p. 81.

213. The verb *keirein* literally means "to cut"; so it is a question of a kind of tonsure.

214. Cf. Jean Gribomont, "Eustathe de Sébaste," in *Dictionnaire de Spiritualité;* idem, "Eustathe le Philosophe et les voyages du jeune Basile de Césarée"; idem, "Le monachisme au IVe siècle en Asie Mineure: De Gangres au messialisme"; cf. also Albrecht, *Das Leben der heiligen Makrina,* 174–87.

215. On Eustathian influence in Basil's ascetic writings cf. Gribomont, "Le monachisme."

216. Cf. Gribomont, "Eustathe de Sébaste," 1709.

217. Joannou's Fr. trans. with "ils" at this point is unfortunately incorrect: although the subject earlier was women and men, in the Gk. and Lat. texts the participles are feminine.

218. *Acts of Thecla* 25 and 40; Ger. in *NA* 2. On Thecla see below: I.5b (end) and II (beginning).

219. Sozomen 7.16.11; cf. *Codex Theodosianus* 16.2.27.

220. Cf. Kari Vogt, "Devenir mâle"; Gail Paterson Corrington, "The 'Divine Woman'?"; Kerstin Aspegren, *The Male Woman* (the book was not available during my research; the author examines the concepts of male and female from Plato to Methodius of Olympus).

221. *Apophthegmata:* Sarrha, 5.

222. On the conceptions of "the sex of the soul" in late antiquity and Christianity see below: IV.2b.

223. Cf. John Anson, "The Female Transvestite in Early Monasticism"; Evelyne Patlagean, *L'histoire de la femme deguisée;* this is possibly also the historical basis of the medieval legend of "Pope Joan," a woman who in a monastery managed to acquire an education reserved for men; cf. Elisabeth Gössmann, "Die 'Päpstin Johanna'" and idem, "Zur Rezeptionsgeschichte."

224. In the *Historia Monachorum,* which survives through the translation of Rufinus, after the separation Ammon's wife lives in a convent. On the complicated dependency of this monastic history on Palladius and others, cf. the introduction to the edition by Eva Schulz-Flügel (PTS 34, 1990).

225. Cf. esp. the ascetic treatises of John Chrysostom (Bibl. I).

226. Yet in Gal. 3:28 the formulation is androcentric: *heis* (masc.) instead of *hen* (neut.), as "one" is expressed here; the Latin translation of Jerome, the Vulgate, also has the neuter (*unum*).

227. Cf. Peter Browe, *Zur Geschichte der Entmannung.*

228. On the requirements for the clergy cf. *Apostolic Canons* 21–23 (Joannou, *Les canons* 1/2:17–18).

229. Cf. the accusations of the ascetic sect of the Audiani against the mainstream church: their clergy would live unmarried with women (Theodoret 4.10.4).

230. Cf. Rufinus 1.17; Sozomen 2.25; Theodoret 1.30.

231. Cf. Theodoret 1.21–22; 2.9; 4.10.

232. Cf. Palladius 63; Sozomen 5.6.

233. There were possibly also couples of the same sex, but this cannot be demonstrated from ancient sources. John Boswell points to a benedictory formula from the ninth or tenth century in *Rediscovering Gay History,* 18f; a monograph on lesbian love in early Christianity by Bernadette J. Brooten is forthcoming.

234. Rufinus 1.5; Socrates 1.12; Sozomen 1.11.

235. "Vir unus ex ordine prophetarum."
236. Rufinus 1.8; Socrates 1.17; Sozomen 2.2; Theodoret 1.18.
237. This goes back to Gregory the Great (d. 604); cf. Hans Küng, *Die Kirche*, 551–52.
238. Cf. Socrates 2.27; Theodoret 2.14; 4.22.
239. Cf. Theodoret 3.7.1.
240. Theodoret 3.19.2; on Publia see below: I.5a.
241. In 18 B.C. Augustus promulgated the *lex Julia de maritandis ordinibus* and in A.D. 9 the *lex papia Poppea*, which prescribed matrimony for the man from age 25 to 60 and the woman from 20 to 50 and sought to promote the wealth of children through inheritance laws; cf. s.v. "Ehegesetze," *RAC* 4:677–80.
242. On the vestals cf. Hildegard Cancik-Lindemaier, "Kultische Privilegierung und gesellschaftliche Realität."
243. On the laws of celibacy for clergy cf. also Socrates 1.11 and 5.22; on the celibacy of clergywomen—that is, specifically, of deaconesses—see below: I.5a.
244. It was written by her brother: Gregory of Nyssa, *The Life of St. Macrina;* cf. Albrecht, *Das Leben der heiligen Makrina*, 87ff.
245. On Olympias see below: I.5a. Cf. also Anne-Marie Malingrey and Elizabeth A. Clark in their introductions to the life of the deaconess Olympias (Bibl. I).
246. On Nicarete see below: I.5a.
247. On Publia see below: I.5a.
248. Cf. Sozomen 5.5; 6.3; Theodoret 1.11.
249. Sozomen 6.3.5–6; cf. *Codex Theodosianus* 9.25.2, which speaks of "consecrated virgins and widows." Sozomen mentions only virgins.
250. See below: 1.4e.
251. On Julian cf. *Julian Apostata,* ed. Richard Klein, esp. B. Carmon Hardy, "Kaiser Julian und sein Schulgesetz," 387–408.
252. Julian, letter 55.
253. Hardy, "Kaiser Julian," 388; cf. there the references to the Christian protest.
254. Cf. Socrates 3.1, 3, 12, 19, 23; Sozomen 5.3–5, 16–22; 6.1, 2; Theodoret 3.26.
255. Cf. Hans Raeder, "Kaiser Julian als Philosoph und religiöser Reformator," in *Julian Apostata,* 206–21.
256. For the text see Bibl. I. under Proba, esp. *The Golden Bough,* ed. Elizabeth A. Clark and Diane F. Hatch. On the genre of the cento, "patchwork poem" (from Gk. *kentōn*), cf. the studies of Filippo Ermini, Ilona Opelt, Maria R. Cacioli, Reinhart Herzog, Vinzenz Buchheit, Wolfgang Kirsch (see Bibl. II).
257. A similar attempt was undertaken by her contemporary, the poet Prudentius; cf. Marianne Kah, *"Die Welt der Römer . . ."* On *pietas* ("piety, godliness"), this key concept of Roman ethics and religion, cf. Josef Liegle, "Pietas."
258. Cf. the preface of the cento, 3–4 (the copyist's dedication to the emperor).
259. Jerome, letter 53.7.
260. "Sola femina inter ecclesiasticos viros posita," Isidore, *De viris illustribus* 18.22 (*PL* 83:1093).
261. Isidor, *Etymologies* 1.38.25–26 (*PL* 82:121). Isidore is amazed that the "Virgilian cento" is on the list of apocryphal books, the so-called *Decretum Gelasianum* (6th cent.; cf. *NA* 1:30ff.); but even there Proba is not mentioned by name.
262. Cf. the commentaries in the editions, as well as: Elizabeth A. Clark, "Faltonia Betitia Proba and Her Virgilian Poem: The Christian Matron as Artist," in idem, *Ascetic Piety and Women's Faith,* 124–52; idem and Diane F. Hatch, "Jesus as Hero in the Virgilian Cento of Faltonia Betitia Proba," ibid., 153–71; cf. also Vinzenz Buchheit, "Vergildeutung im Cento

Probae"; Anne Jensen, "Die ersten Christinnen der Spätantike"; idem, "Faltonia Betitia Proba"; and Ilona Opelt, "Der zürnende Christus im Cento der Proba," who examines the literary achievement of Proba and in my opinion did not understand her theology.

263. This is what she calls herself: "Proba vates" (*Cento* 12); she understands her work as proclamation of the Christian message, not simply as poetry.

264. *Uxor inconparabilis*—thus the grave inscription, which came from her husband; cf. *The Golden Bough*, 98.

265. See Bibl. I.

266. Sozomen 2.12; cf. above: I.4d.

267. Sozomen 8.5; cf. above: I.4c.

268. On the deaconesses see below: I.5a.

269. See below: I.5b.

270. The most important extant ancient source was written a century after her death: Damascius *The Life of Isidore;* yet it is far less reliable than the report of Socrates. Cf. Wolfgang Alexander Meyer, *Hypatia von Alexandria;* John M. Rist, "Hypatia," *Phoenix* 19 (1965): 214–25. I am grateful to Alan Scott for a paper he gave in 1988 in Chicago at the annual meeting of the American Academy of Religion: "Damascius' account of the Death of Hypatia." I am not aware of a more recent monograph from the feminist perspective, but there is an excellent book for youth, Arnulf Zitelmann, *Hypatia,* which also contains translated sources in the appendix.

271. On the conflicts between Jews and Christians in Alexandria cf. Socrates 7.13–16.

272. Cf., e.g., *Handbuch der Kirchengeschichte* 2/1:109ff.

273. We are indebted to Synesius for information about Hypatia. Seven of his letters to her have survived (10, 15, 16, 33, 81, 124, 154), and she is mentioned in two others (133, 137).

274. From an ancient poem to her praise (Palladas, *Anthologia graeca* 9:400; quotation according to Rist, "Hypatia," 225).

275. Socrates says nothing about her relative youth (she died at age forty-five), her beauty, and her virginity, but they are known from other sources (cf. Meyer, *Hypatia,* 1ff., 11, 17ff.; Rist, "Hypatia," 220–21).

276. Cf. above: I.4d (in Rufinus the empress "serves" the virgins).

277. Also *Placilla* (thus in Theodoret).

278. In 450 after the death of Theodosius II Pulcheria married Marcian—after the writing of our three church histories.

279. Cf. the summary parallel report in Theodoret 5.39.

280. Not until the 17th cent. did women in orders succeed in becoming active outside the convent walls in areas of charity and education; cf. Jensen, s.v. "Orden."

281. Cf. on this the overview in Appendix II under "Other."

282. Cf. Socrates 5.19; Sozomen 7.16.

283. Cf. below: II.6.

284. Naturally, this measure has a long prior history; cf. s.v. "Bussdisziplin," *LTK* 2:811; Herbert Vorgrimler, "Busse und Krankensalbung," in *Handbuch der Dogmengeschichte* (Freiburg, 1978), 4/3:72–73.

285. Canon 9 of St. Basil (Joannou, *Les canons* 2:108–9).

286. Cf. s.v. "Ehescheidung," *RAC* 4:707–19.

287. Cf. ibid.

288. On the debate about the prohibition of divorce in the New Testament from a feminist perspective cf. Bernadette Brooten, "Konnten Frauen"; idem, "Zur Debatte"; also Monika Fander, *Die Stellung der Frau,* 85–110.

289. Cf. s.v. "digamus," *RAC* 3:1016–24; Hermann Funke, "Univira"; Majorie Lightman and William Zeisel, "Univira."

290. For examples see below: II.2b.

291. The *Canons of the Holy Apostles* (in Theodor Schermann, *Die allgemeine Kirchenordnung* 1:12–34) were presumably written in Egypt at the beginning of the 4th cent.; cf. Gryson, *Ministry of Women*, 44. (They are also called the *Ecclesiastical Canons of the Apostles* and are not to be confused with the *Apostolic Canons;* cf. Joannou, *Les canons* 1/2.)

292. The Gk. *didaskalos* is the translation of the NT *rabbi;* the usual translation as "master" shifts the meaning (see below).

293. *Canons of the Holy Apostles,* 24–28; cf. Gryson, *Ministry of Women,* 46–47.

294. Cf. the literature mentioned above on widows and virgins, as well as Adolf Kalsbach, *Die altkirchliche Einrichtung der Diakonissen;* idem, s.v. "Diakonisse," *RAC* 3:917–28; Cipriano Vagaggini, "L'ordinazione delle diaconesse"; Aimé Georges Martimort, *Les diaconesses;* Christian Oeyen, "Frauenordination"; Anne Jensen, s.v. "Diakonin."

An important study by Evangelos Theodorou is available only in New Greek (see Bibl. II), but there is a working translation by Anne Jensen at the Institut für ökumenische Forschung of the University of Tübingen. Cf. Theodorou, "Die Tradition der orthodoxen Kirche in bezug auf die Frauenordination."

295. Cf. Gerhard Lohfink, "Weibliche Diakone im Neuen Testament"; Luise Schottroff, "DienerInnen der Heiligen."

296. Cf. *Didascalia* 16. The statements about deaconesses are analyzed below in the context of the theologies of martyrdom and baptism: cf. II.5.

297. Cf. Gryson, *Ministry of Women,* 35–43; on the editions see Bibl. I.

298. Cf. Gryson, *Ministry of Women,* 42.

299. First in the 19th canon of the Council of Nicaea (325), then especially in the *Apostolic Constitutions.*

300. Cf. canon 15 of the Council of Chalcedon (451) cited below, as well as the *Novellae* of Justinian 3.1–2; 6.6; 123.30 (and elsewhere).

301. Cf. Elisabeth Schüssler Fiorenza, "Der Dienst an den Tischen."

302. Cf. Theodorou, "Die Tradition," 33ff.

303. Some aspects of the problem will be mentioned in connection with the ecclesiastical position of women martyrs and prophets; see below: II.6, III.2e, III.3, and IV.1.

304. The term here is *anathema,* that is, exclusion from the church, not ecclesiastical penance through exclusion from Communion.

305. Cf. Theodorou, "Die Tradition," 34.

306. Theodorou, "Ordination," 447; for discussion of the 19th canon cf. Gryson, *Ministry of Women,* 48–49.

307. On later Western imitations cf., e.g., Gryson, *Ministry of Women,* 92ff.; most were abbesses, who were given the title *diaconissa* in a kind of ordination.

308. Cf. canon 28 of the Council of Chalcedon; the bishop of the old Rome, Leo I, refused to ratify it.

309. Justinian *Novellae* 3.1.

310. *Codex Theodosianus* 16.2.27 (adopted in the *Codex Justinianus* 1.3.9; in the *Novellae* 123.13, however, forty years); cf. Soz. *Ch.Hist.* 7.16.11.

311. John Chrysostom, letters 94, 104, 185.

312. Idem, *Letter to Olympias* 9.4.49.

313. Cf. ibid.; see also Bibl. I under *The Life of Olympias.*

314. On this honorary title for (surviving) martyrs see below: II.6.

315. For details see Malingrey and Clark (Bibl. I under *The Life of Olympias*).

316. Theodorou assumes that she was ultimately ordained deaconess ("Famous Deaconesses," 157).

317. Literally, "was deemed worthy of the charisma of the diaconate."

318. Astonishingly, the gnostic term *demiourgos* is used here for the Creator; cf. below: IV.5b.

319. This may indicate an affinity with Gnostic Christian circles, which would also fit in with the emphasis on teaching activity; cf. below, chap. IV (beginning).

320. Cf. Julian, letter 39, reported in Sozomen 5.16.

321. Lat. *doctores;* the Gk. version is not extant, but *didaskaloi* can be presumed. Hippolytus is not specific about the gender of the teachers; in both languages the word can be used for men and women.

322. Gk. *parrēsia kata theon; parrēsia* is frankness in speaking; it is used in Acts to describe the appearance of the apostles before the court and the boldness of their preaching (2:29; 4:13, 29, 31; 9:27–28; 13:46; 14:3; 18:26; 19:8; 26:26; 28:31).

323. Literally, "insensitivity"; the reference is to Psalm 115 with its polemic against the dumb, blind, deaf, and thus "dead" idols of the Gentiles in contrast to the "living" God of Israel.

324. The word *choros* occurs three times in this translation as (1) "company"; (2) a paraphrase: she "put still greater energy into their chaunt"; (3) "choir."

325. See below: II.5; cf. also I.4d (*athlete* as a designation for ascetics).

326. Theodoret, letter 17.

327. Theodoret, letter 101.

328. Cf. Gryson, *Ministry of Women,* 90–91, and the index in the French original.

329. It is treated briefly by Albrecht, *Das Leben der heiligen Makrina,* 221–29. On male teachers cf. Ulrich Neymeyr, *Die christlichen Lehrer im zweiten Jahrhundert* (the author does not even raise the question of the teaching activity of women!); Faivre, "Théologiens 'laïcs' et laïcs théologiens" (briefly mentions Proba and the women around Jerome).

330. I am indebted to the Jewish theologian Evelyn Goodman-Thau for pointing out a still usual linguistic usage: the verb *learn* without an object is a technical term for theological discussion of the scripture. This explains a formulation in the pastoral epistles (1 Tim. 5:13) that is the source of numerous misinterpretations to the effect that women "learn to be idle, gadding about from house to house" (NRSV), whereas the Greek actually means that the women must not "gad about from house to house in order to learn"; Jean-Daniel Kaestli, in his planned commentary (see n. 99 above), has come to the same conclusion.

331. Yet theology was in fact often monopolized by the clergy. Here we cannot go into the problem of the tension between the charisma of the theologian and the teaching ministry of the bishop.

332. Into the Middle Ages it was discussed whether "female gender" is a "natural" or only a "canonical" obstacle to ordination; cf. Elisabeth Gössmann, "Äusserungen zum Frauenpriestertum."

333. On the text see Bibl. I; cf. Gryson, *Ministry of Women,* 64–69. The Greek original was lost. The numbers given refer to the translation from the Syriac of François Nau and Pio Ciprotti, and the Ethiopic of Robert Beylot.

334. Today they are called Old Eastern (*altorientalische*) churches; cf. *Handbuch der Ostkirchenkunde* 1:34ff.

335. So called because they emphasized the one divine nature in the human person of the Redeemer against the two-natures doctrine of Chalcedon.

336. In the Syrian tradition an especially high value was placed on the ascetic and charismatic; cf. *Holy Women of the Syrian Orient* (introd.); also Vööbus, *Celibacy,* and idem, *History of Ascetism.*

337. In the Ethiopic version the bishop comes first with the presbyters, then behind them the widows on the left and the deacons on the right; on the third row are subdeacons, lectors, deaconesses, and others who "have received a gift" (16).

338. Cf. the precise examination of the concept in Gryson, *Ministry of Women*, 66, esp. n. 198.

339. This is how the attempt has been made to explain away the disturbing "women presbyters"; cf. Gryson, *Ministry of Women*, 66.

340. The Syriac version has no parallel.

341. On eucharistic celebration by a prophetess cf. below: III.3.

342. Cf. Dorothea Wendebourg, "Die alttestamentlichen Reinheitsgesetze."

343. On sacerdotalization cf. Schillebeeckx, *Das kirchliche Amt*, 83ff.

344. On the juxtaposition of charismatic and presbyterial church discipline cf. Küng, *Die Kirche*, 477ff.

345. Cf., e.g., Edward Schillebeeckx, *Der Amtszölibat;* Martin Boelens, *Die Klerikerehe;* Roger Gryson, *Les origines du célibat ecclésiastique;* Kurt Hagemann, *Der Zölibat der römisch-katholischen Kirche.*

346. Also conceivable, however, is a prohibition of marriage after ordination, which developed in the East for higher clergy (see below).

347. On the relationship of the *Didascalia* to the *Apostolic Constitutions* see chap. II. 5e.

348. Theodorou, "Ordination," 457–58 (on the tradition about the fiancée of Patriarch Sergius of Ravenna cf. Kalsbach, *Die altkirchliche Einrichtung der Diakonissen,* 79). On the marriage of Gregory of Nyssa cf. Michel Aubineau's introduction to *Traité de la Virginité* (SC 119), 65–76.

349. In the Eastern tradition the law still states that while married men may be ordained, the unmarried may not marry after ordination. Moreover, it became customary to recruit bishops from the monasteries when possible.

350. Rufinus 2.6; Socrates 4.36; Sozomen 6.38; Theodoret 4.23. On the Christianization of the Arabian peoples cf. *Handbuch der Kirchengeschichte* 2/1:194–95; Thélamon, *Païens et chrétiens,* 123–47.

351. Cf. *Geschichte der Kirche* 1:293.

352. Although we have three testimonies that speak a quite different language, it is nevertheless Theodoret's picture of the convert Mavia—who in feminine modesty "begs" for the anchorite Moses as bishop—that is found in today's *Handbuch der Kirchengeschichte* (2/1:194), although in the author's footnote he gives as his source not the bishop of Cyrrhus but Sozomen!

353. Rufinus 1.10; Socrates 1.20; Sozomen 2.7; Theodoret 1.24.

354. The church histories have *Iberia,* which Klaus Thraede mistakenly identified with Spain (*Freunde in Christus,* 146); cf. also Heinz Heinen, "Sollte das Christentum in Spanien . . ." There is, however, an early apocryphal tradition (3rd cent.) that connects women with the evangelization of Spain: on the lives of Xanthippe, Polyxena, and Rebecca, see Bibl. I; cf. Eric Junod, "Vie et conduite des saintes femmes."

355. Cf. *The Life of Nino* in Bibl. I.

356. Cf. *Handbuch der Kirchengeschichte* 2/1:198–99; *Geschichte der Kirche* 1:293; Thélamon, *Païens et chrétiens,* 85–122, who demonstrates the influence of a Georgian mythos on the formation of the narrative in Rufinus.

357. It is hard to see why her sex would not allow a visit with the queen. In Socrates and Theodoret this refusal is interpreted as a gesture of humility; Sozomen merely summarizes the scene: "She was healed in the same way."

358. Literally, "not yet introduced to the holy [things/sacraments]"; the formulation presupposes the old unity of baptism, confirmation, and Eucharist as initiation.

359. In a standard modern work we read about this missionary: "She was a slave who made an impression on the Georgian royal family through the radiance of her piety and through the healings effected by her prayers" (*Geschichte der Kirche* 1:293).

360. Susanne Heine, *Frauen*, 167.

361. Cf. Willy Rordorf, "Tradition et composition dans les Actes de Thècle: Etat de la question," in idem, *Liturgie*, 457–68; Eng. trans. (without notes): "Tradition and Composition in the Acts of Thecla: The State of the Question," *Semeia* 38 (1986): 43–52. The most comprehensive investigation at present is Albrecht's, *Das Leben der heiligen Makrina*, 239–326 (chap. 5: "Die Wandlung Theklas von der predigenden und taufenden Apostelschülerin zum Vorbild der Asketinnen und der Frauenklöster"). Cf. also my short essay "Thekla: Vergessene Verkündigerin"; and my translation of the *Acts of Thecla* with detailed commentary: *Thekla die Apostolin: Ein apokrypher Text neu entdeckt* (Freiburg, 1992).

362. The *Acts of Paul* includes the *Acts of Thecla*. See Bibl. I under *The Acts of Christ's Holy Apostle and Martyr Thecla*.

363. There are in all five edifying "apostle novels," named for Peter, Paul, John, Andrew, and Thomas; for the German text see *NA* 2. For recent research see *Les actes apocryphes des apôtres*; "The Apocryphal Acts of the Apostles," *Semeia* 38 (1986). On the continence stories see the studies of Stevan L. Davies and Virginia Burrus in Bibl. II.

364. It is described by Egeria in the report of her pilgrimage (23); cf. Albrecht, *Das Leben der heiligen Makrina*, 286ff.

365. Cf. *Vie et miracles de Sainte Thècle* (in Bibl. I under *Acts of Thecla*).

366. *Das Leben der heiligen Makrina*, 286ff.

367. A reference to the gospel as a dangerous memory ("gefährliche Erinnerung"), a phrase coined by Johann Baptist Metz.

II. Women in Martyrdom
Courageous Confessors

1. Cf. *Acta apostolorum apocrypha*, ed. Lipsius and Bonnet, 1:235.

2. Euseb. *Ch.Hist.* 3.25.4.

3. Euseb. *MP* 3.1; 6.3.

4. Tertullian *On Baptism* 17; cf. below: IV.1.

5. William M. Ramsay, *The Church in the Roman Empire*, chap. 16: "The Acta of Paul and Thekla," 375–428.

6. Henri Leclercq, *Les Martyrs*, vol. 1.

7. Ibid., "Préface," xxvii.

8. Jean-Daniel Kaestli, "Les principales orientations de la recherche sur les actes apocryphes des apôtres," in *Les actes apocryphes des apôtres*, 57.

9. Cf. Bibl. I under "Martyrs." There is no standard collection. The most comprehensive is *La geste du sang*, but it has no scholarly apparatus, and the translation is often extremely imaginative. If not otherwise noted, references are to *The Acts of the Christian Martyrs* (ed. Herbert Musurillo, abbreviated *ACM*). The Persian acts of martyrs are not included in the investigation. The new edition by A.A.R. Bastiaensen et al. first came to my attention after the completion of my study; cf. the discussion by Jan de Boeft and Jan Bremmer, "Notiunculae Martyrologicae IV," *Vigiliae Christianae* 45 (1991): 105–22. On the literary genre cf. Karl Holl, "Die Vorstellung vom Märtyrer"; for further literature see below.

10. On the following cf. Friedrich Augar, *Die Frau im römischen Christenprozess*; Hippolyte Delehaye, *Les origines du culte des martyrs*; idem, *Les passions des martyrs*; Albert Ehrhard, *Die Kirche der Märtyrer*; Hans von Campenhausen, *Die Idee des Martyriums*; Hans-Werner Surkau, *Martyrien in jüdischer und frühchristlicher Zeit* (Göttingen, 1938); Josef Vogt and Hugh Last, s.v. "Christenverfolgung"; William Frend, *Martyrdom and Persecution in the Early Church*; William Carl Weinrich, *Spirit and Martyrdom*; Judith Perkins, "The Apocryphal Acts of the Apostles"; Dorothea

Wendebourg, "Das Martyrium in der Alten Kirche"; Gary Bisbee, *Pre-Decian Acts of Martyrs;* as well as the detailed bibliography in *Ausgewählte Märtyrerakten* (see Bibl. I under "Martyrs"). Cf. also the corresponding articles in *Das frühe Christentum im römischen Staat, ANRW* 2.23.1 (1979); Willy Rordorf, *Liturgie, foi et vie* For further literature on martyrdom theology cf. below: II.6a. There is no comprehensive study of martyr traditions from the *perspective of feminist theology*, but cf. Adriana Valerio, "Le figure femminile"; Franca Ela Consolino, "Modelli di santità femminile"; Francine Cardman, "Acts of Women Martyrs."

11. Wendebourg, "Das Martyrium," 306. She cites the martyrdom of Apollonius: "I like living" (30), and that of Pionius: "Living is beautiful" (5.4). On the differing attitudes of Christians toward martyrdom cf. also Corssen, "Töchter des Philippus," 499; on the Gnostic criticism of martyrdom cf. Klaus Koschorke, *Die Polemik der Gnostiker,* 127–37; Pagels, *Gnostic Gospels,* chap. 4. Cf. also Clemens Scholten, *Martyrium und Sophiamythos.*

12. Cf. *Didascalia:* "Receive those who for the sake of faith are persecuted and move from town to town *in accordance with the command of the Lord.*" (19). Chapters 19 and 20 are a typical presentation of the moderate attitude toward martyrdom. For further comments on flight see Wendebourg, "Das Martyrium."

13. In addition to the already mentioned literature cf. Rudolf Freudenberger, *Das Verhalten der römischen Behörden;* Joachim Molthagen, *Der römische Staat und die Christen.*

14. Willy Rordorf, "Die neronische Christenverfolgung," 367.

15. Tacitus *Annals* 15.44 (Grant, 365–66).

16. The majority of scholars agree with the identification of Tacitus's "Chrestians" with Christians; also conceivable, however, is a confusion with the Jewish followers of the agitator Chrestos (cf. nn. 63 and 65 in Heller's edition of the *Annals* [see Bibl. I]).

17. On *odium humani generis,* also used against the Jews, cf. Frend, *Martyrdom and Persecution,* 162.

18. Cf. Rordorf, "Die neronische Christenverfolgung." On the unpopularity of Christians with their contemporaries cf. also Eric R. Dodds, *Pagan and Christian;* Robert Wilken, *The Christians.*

19. *ACM* 86–87. In this martyrdom five women and seven men were beheaded.

20. Cf. Augar, *Die Frau,* 72–73. Yet it is disputed whether confession to Christianity was condemned as a religious or political offense; cf. Molthagen, *Der römische Staat und die Christen,* 33ff.

21. Leclercq, *Les Martyrs,* xlvi: "C'est la marque probable de la plus haute antiquité." Cf. *ATh* 14 (Paul is brought to court as a Christian) and 1 Peter 4:12–16 (Christians punished as Christians).

22. Cf. the famous correspondence between Pliny and Trajan in Pliny *Letters* 10.96, 97.

23. Cf. Molthagen, *Der römische Staat und die Christen,* 38ff.

24. The Roman state tolerated private religious associations (*collegia*), even for non-Roman religions, as long as the state cult remained unaffected. In many of these associations equality of men and women, as well as of slaves, was practiced. Cf. s.v. "Genossenschaft" in *RAC* 10; Schüssler Fiorenza, *In Memory of Her,* 179ff.

25. *ACM* 146–47.

26. "La destination de ce recueil m'engage en outre à omettre toute explication sur un supplice infâme qui demeure la honte du pouvoir qui en fit un moyen de châtiment" (cxvi–cxvii).

27. Yet this tendency is prevalent in the later literature.

28. Cf. also Anton Linsenmayer, "Die Behandlung der Frauen im römischen Christenprozess." Linsenmayer, who takes a position on Augar, gives more emphasis to the discretion of the judge but offers no new information.

29. Augar, *Die Frau,* 7.

30. See examples below; on the Romans' basically positive attitude toward suicide see Wendebourg, "Das Martyrium," 297–98.

31. Augar, *Die Frau,* 8.

32. Euseb. *MP* 7.4. Perhaps male authors find it easier to speak about the rape of women than about the humiliation of their own sex through castration.

33. Tacitus *Annals* 5.9 (Grant, 199). Parallel accounts are in Dio Cassius 8.11.5 and Suetonius *Tib.* 61.5 (according to Augar, *Die Frau,* 77).

34. *Institutiones* 1.12.3: "servi poenae efficiuntur, qui in metallum damnantur et qui bestiis subiciuntur." In general, slave women could be prostituted by their owners if this was not specifically excluded by a contrary provision in their sale.

35. Unpublished quotation. I am grateful to Hildegard Cancik-Lindemaier for material made available to me and for many suggestions.

36. Tertullian, *Apologeticum* 50. For a more exact examination of this passage as well as more ambiguous testimonies of Tertullian on this practice, see Augar, *Die Frau,* 5ff.

37. Hippolytus, *Commentary on Daniel* 4.51. Cf. Augar, *Die Frau,* 10ff.

38. Cyprian, *On Mortality* 15: "corruptelae et lupanaria"; cf. Augar, *Die Frau,* 15–16.

39. *ACM* 136–67.

40. On the role of confessors see below: II.6.

41. The Greek text contains a gender-neutral genitive plural; among the five arrested, a Macedonia is mentioned (2; 11), but we learn nothing further about her.

42. The title of *confessor* may have already been bestowed on Sabina because of this previously suffered persecution.

43. Cardman, "Acts of Women Martyrs," 146.

44. *ACM* 149.

45. *ACM* 147.

46. For the martyrdom of Agape, Irene, and Chione in Thessalonica, see *ACM* 280–93.

47. Ibid., 290–91.

48. Ibid.

49. Euseb. *Ch.Hist.* 6.5. Eusebius's text is adopted by Musurillo (*ACM* 132–35). A variation of the account is found in Pall. *Hist.Laus.* 3; it is considered less reliable historically.

50. Cf. Bardy, *Histoire Ecclésiastique* (SC 41), 91–92, n. 5. Musurillo makes no reference to these text variants.

51. Euseb. *MP* 8.5–8.

52. Euseb. *Ch.Hist.* 8.9; Williamson, 337.

53. Ibid., 8.12. Later these women were venerated as saints under the names Bernice, Prosdoke, and Domnina. A sermon of John Chrysostom on their feast day has been handed down (*PG* 50:629–40; Bareille 4:362–80); the following homily on the raising of Lazarus also refers to these women.

54. Cf. Augar, *Die Frau,* 81: "We should add that even a husband who is present cannot intervene for his wife, for the loss of freedom abolishes any existing marriage."

55. Euseb. *Ch.Hist.* 8.14.

56. Soz. *Ch.Hist.* 9.13.

57. John Chrysostom, *In Praise of St. Pelagia* (*PG* 50:579–84; Bareille 4:285–94); Ambrose *Concerning Virgins* 3.32–34.

58. Here Ambrose has presumably joined the tradition about Pelagia with the report of the voluntary death of the mother and her virginal daughters, since both cases involve events in Antioch.

59. Augustine reported fundamental reservations regarding such actions, yet he rejected passing judgment on martyresses, who were perhaps following a special inspiration from God (*De civitate Dei* 1.22–27).

60. The acts of Didymus and Theodora are contained only in the old collection of Ruinart. Cf. Augar, *Die Frau,* 34ff.

61. Pall. *Hist.Laus.* 65. Palladius names a work of Hippolytus as his source. Cf. Augar, *Die Frau,* 12ff. (he has a different chapter numbering for Palladius).

62. Ambrose *Concerning Virgins* 2.22ff.

63. Cf. also Augustine *City of God* 1.16: rape during persecution does not defile the soul.

64. Soc. *Ch.Hist.* 2.38; NPNF, 2nd series, 2:66.

65. Ibid.

66. Soc. *Ch.Hist.* 7.15; cf. above: I.4e.

67. See above: I.3a. and I.4a. For a comprehensive list of known martyresses see Zscharnack, *Der Dienst der Frau,* 27–37; cf. Harnack, *Mission,* 606–7.

68. *ACM* 26ff.; cf. Valerio, "Le figure femminile," 30–33.

69. *ACM* 56–57.

70. *ACM* 86–87.

71. *ACM* 133 (Euseb. *Ch.Hist.* 6.5).

72. *ACM* 302–9. Augustine reports on her as a wife and mother (*De Sancta Virginitate* 45); nothing of the kind can be found in the acts.

73. *ACM* 220–21 (*Martyrdom of Montanus and Lucius* 8).

74. Cf. *Les martyrs de Lyon;* Charles Saumagne and Michel Meslin, "De la légalité du procès de Lyon"; Heinrich Kraft, "Die Lyoner Märtyrer und der Montanismus"; Winrich A. Löhr, "Der Brief der Gemeinden von Lyon und Vienne." The traditional dating in 177 is not absolutely certain; cf. Löhr, "Der Brief," 141–42.

75. On the division of the letter cf. Löhr, "Der Brief," 136–37. The actual report of the martyrdom is found in Euseb. *Ch.Hist.* 5.1 (Williamson, 193–203); the following references are to this chapter (quotations are from Williamson's translation); in the much shorter chaps. 5.2–4 there are further excerpts from the letter. Musurillo incorporated only 5.1–2 into *ACM.* Cf. also the fully annotated translation of Oda Hagemeyer, *Ich bin Christ* (Bibl. I).

76. For more on this list see Bardy, *Histoire Ecclésiastique* (SC 41), 21, n. 69.

77. Cf. Garth Thomas, "La condition sociale de l'Eglise de Lyon en 177," in *Les Martyrs de Lyon,* 93–106.

78. Tradition has also applied the term *paraclete* to Montanus. On the connections of martyrs with the New Prophecy see below: III.2a.

79. Naturally, *clergy* does not yet have the ecclesiastical, "clerical" meaning that distinguishes ministers from laity. I let the term stand here because it has an official connotation and also evokes a particular group, and this is lost in a free translation.

80. On the theological relevance of this concept of martyrdom cf. below: 2.6a.

81. *Athlete* is a typical concept in the terminology of both martyrdom and baptism (see below: II.5); on the *agōn* metaphor in this account cf. Löhr, "Der Brief," 138.

82. Literally, "her mistress according to the flesh."

83. The statement is made in regard to his eloquence. In Greek it is formulated negatively: "He was not uninvolved with the apostolic charisma." On the disagreements about handling the Roman citizen Attalus cf. Löhr, "Der Brief," 142–43.

84. In the Greek text Blandina is the subject of the sentence; that is, she convinces those who believe. The statement about the one who is crucified is inserted as a genitive absolute. Musurillo and Bardy (among others) relate the dependent clause to Christ. For a precise analysis of the passage see below: II.6a.

85. For a precise analysis of this passage see below: II.6c.

86. An allusion to 2 Maccabees 7, where before their mother's eyes seven sons are tortured to death, and finally she follows them into martyrdom.

87. On Carthage—after Rome the most important center of the Western church in the second and third centuries—cf. Georg Schöllgen, *Ecclesia sordida?* Cf. also Margaret R. Miles, *Patriarchy as Political Theology* (treats conflicts over women among Tertullian, Cyprian, and Augustine).

88. In the following references, R = redactor's account (1–2, 14–21), P = Perpetua's account (3–10), and S = Saturus's account (11–13). The English translations are from *ACM*. In order not to disturb the flow of the narrative, issues of interpretation are largely treated in the notes.

89. Ehrhard, *Die Kirche der Märtyrer,* 49.

90. In addition to already cited works and commentaries in the various collections of the acts of martyrs, cf. esp. the critical edition of Cornelius van Beek, *Passio Sanctarum Perpetuae et Felicitatis* (which contains a collection of quotations from church fathers); Marie-Louise von Franz, "Die Passio Perpetuae"; Åke Fridh, *Le problème de la passion des saintes Perpétue et Félicité;* Mary Lefkowitz, "The Motivations for St. Perpetua's Martyrdom"; William H. C. Frend, "Blandina and Perpetua: Two Early Christian Heroines," in *Les martyrs de Lyon,* 167–77 (repr. in idem, *Town and Country in the Early Christian Centuries* [London, 1980]); Rosemary Rader, "The Martyrdom of Perpetua: A Protest Account of Third-Century Christianity," in *A Lost Tradition,* 1–32; Louis Robert, "Une vision de Perpétue martyre" (contains interesting symbolic material); Peter Dronke, *Women Writers of the Middle Ages,* 1–35 ("From Perpetua to the Eighth Century"); Mary Ann Rossi, "The Passion of Perpetua"; Alvyn Pettersen, "Perpetua—Prisoner of Conscience"; Jacqueline Amat, "L'authenticité des songes de la passion de Perpétue et de Félicité."

91. So renowned a historian as Frend declares both Blandina and Perpetua to be adherents of the same "sectarian christianity" ("Blandina and Perpetua," 174); we can only call it anti-feminist cynicism when martyrdom is equated with self-realization and one says of the martyr: "Perpetua was obviously an adored only daughter who grew up into a spoilt and wilful young woman, but in her case, her frustrations drove her into fanatical adherence to an apocalyptic form of Christianity and hostility to the society in which she had been reared" (175).

92. *ACM* xxvi. On the introduction to the document, often regarded as "Montanist," cf. below: III.2e (end).

93. Since many other conceptions about Montanism are likewise false, I would like to spare myself a complicated discussion of the arguments. As the following examination will show, the high estimation of Spirit-effected prophecy as an eschatological gift is one common element of theology in the second and third centuries (cf. Weinrich, *Spirit and Martyrdom,* 225–36: "Passion of Perpetua and Montanism"). Yet typical features of the New Prophecy (the names Prisca, Maximilla, Montanus, the teaching of the Paraclete, reference to Pepuza, emphasis on ecstatic prophecy) are missing (see below: III.2).

94. Cf. Timothy D. Barnes, "Pre-Decian Acta Martyrum"; Weinrich, *Spirit and Martyrdom,* 223ff.; and above all Åke Fridh, *Le problème,* who very carefully examines the question of translation and original, as well as authorship, on the basis of linguistic rhythms. Walter Shewring had come to similar conclusions in "Prose Rhythm in the Passio S. Perpetuae" and "En marge de la Passion des Saintes Perpétue et Félicité."

95. On dating cf. Barnes, "Pre-Decian Acta Martyrum," 522.

96. Cf. the conclusions in Fridh, *Le problème,* 82–83. Robert, "Une vision de Perpétue martyre," holds that Perpetua wrote in Greek; he does not seem to have taken Fridh's work into consideration.

97. Lefkowitz, "Motivations." The extremely feminist reading leads interestingly to points of contact with Frend's antifeminist interpretation.

98. Valerio, "Le figure femminile." On the Jewish martyrs cf. Surkau, *Martyrien in jüdischer*

und frühchristlicher Zeit, who, contrary to Campenhausen, stresses the literary and theological similarities between Jewish and Christian acts of martyrs. For Frend also, the development of a Jewish theology of martyrdom is a crucial prerequisite for a Christian one (65). In the acts of the martyrs themselves, the mother with her seven sons (2 Maccabees 7) and Daniel in the lion's den, as well as the young men in the fiery furnace appear as models for the Christian martyrs.

99. Rader, "Martyrdom of Perpetua"; cf. also Rossi, "Passion of Perpetua"; and Clementina Mazzucco, "Perpetua e Saturo"; both became available to me only after the completion of my study. Birgit Schlegel, to whom I am thankful for several references, is writing a dissertation on the reception history of the martyrdom account.

100. Von Franz, "Passio Perpetuae." In this very knowledgeable study, however, there are some errors in the details of church history. For example, Tertullian appears as the bishop of Carthage. The author also adopts from her sources (above all Bonwetsch and de Labriolle) the tendency to connect all prophetic phenomena with the "Montanist heresy." In terms of comparative religious history cf. also the detailed studies of Franz Josef Dölger (Bibl. II); they will be cited as appropriate.

101. Amat, "L'authenticité des songes de la passion."

102. *Matronaliter nupta,* that is, Perpetua's marriage was performed in the most solemn way, which was possible only among patricians. An echo of this statement is found at the end of the martyrdom when Perpetua is called *matrona Dei* (18). Incomprehensibly, Musurillo renders this as "newly married."

103. *ACM*'s "I was baptized" (instead of "we were") for *baptizati sumus* is probably an error of oversight.

104. Actually, the coemperor Geta (cf. 7.9: "natale tunc Getae Caesaris").

105. Schöllgen, *Ecclesia sordida?* 248–49.

106. Cf. Lefkowitz, "Motivations." In American feminist theology there is a tendency to see emancipatory autonomy especially in the ascetic's denial of marriage, but not all early church "liberated" women fit into this schema. Even with Hagemeyer, whose orientation is not toward feminism but toward spiritual edification, there is an interest in seeing Perpetua as a "consecrated woman" who is absolved of all family ties. Valerio puts more stress on the relativizing of traditional family order through the equal treatment of the slave Felicity; this is entirely correct with regard to the behavior of the group—if Felicity really was a slave. Valerio, however, falsely connects the designation *conserva* with the relationship between Perpetua and Felicity.

107. To see behind this account a conflict with father and authority and even "unconscious incest" (Lefkowitz, "Motivations," 420) seems to me erroneous, even if the strong bond between father and daughter is apparent. One of Ross Kraemer's students even went so far as to make Perpetua's father the father of the child, which Kraemer found "interesting" ("Monastic Jewish Women," 351, n. 35). Von Franz interprets the conflict not in an individual, biographical way, but paradigmatically in terms of the history of religion: the father embodies the spirit of the old religion—in a positive as well as negative sense.

108. Thus Lefkowitz; Valerio is more moderate. The attempt to forestall martyrdom through an appeal to motherly pity is also found in the account of Agathonike, who replies: "God will have pity on him [her son], for he cares for all" (44). Eutychia, the companion of Irene in Thessalonica, is also pregnant. Eusebius reports on the martyress Dionysia, "the mother of a large family but just as devoted to her Lord" (*Ch.Hist.* 6.41). The Anonyma of Edessa, whose exemplary courage ultimately prevented a massacre, had a child in arms when she volunteered herself (Soc. 4.18; Soz. 6.18; The. 4.17); cf. above: I.4a.

109. Cf. Revelation 12; *ACM* xxvi.

110. Cf. 1 Cor. 14:39; on the prophecy in Corinth cf. below: III.1.

111. On martyrdom as witness see below: II.6a.

112. On the visions cf. also: Cecil M. Robeck, *The Role and Function of the Prophetic Gifts* (investigates Perpetua's and Saturus's dreams as well as accounts of visions in Tertullian and Cyprian).

113. The same word was already used in the introduction in speaking of "grace" through martyrs and revelations. On *divina dignatio* as a term of legitimation in Cyprian cf. below: II.6a and III.2e.

114. Lat. *laborare/labor*, rendered here as "suffering" and "trouble," are also used for the torments of the martyrs (see below).

115. Lat. *poena*, which can also be translated "punishment." On the interpretation of this passage cf. Franz Josef Dölger, "Antike Parallelen zum leidenden Dinocrates."

116. Ibid.

117. Augustine *De anima ad Renatum* 1.10ff.; cf. here van Beek, *Passio,* 154*; von Franz, "Passio Perpetuae," 444; Dölger, "Antike Parallelen" (4. "Die eschatologische Bewertung der 'Dinocratesvision' durch Vincentius Victor und Augustinus"), 20–28. The argument is over the necessity of baptism for salvation, which is called into question here.

118. Dölger mentions that the newly baptized were also given a similar power, but he adduces no support for this ("Antike Parallelen," 17, n. 32). Thecla, in her role as a martyr, likewise prays before her baptism for the dead Falconilla (*ATh* 28–29). Cf. also Ernst Dassmann, *Sündenvergebung durch Taufe.*

119. Lat. *conlaboro tecum;* here the same expression is used for the battle of the martyrs as was used earlier for the "suffering" of the dead Dinocrates.

120. *Porta Sanavivaria:* the gate of the amphitheater through which the victorious gladiators departed, in contrast to the *Porta Libitinensis,* the gate through which the dead were carried away.

121. In Greek, the liturgical language of the time.

122. Cf. Jean Daniélou, *Bible et liturgie;* Alois Stenzel, *Die Taufe* (an anthology of catechetical homilies of the church fathers); Victor Saxer, *Les rites de l'initiation chrétienne.*

123. A warding off of evil that even today is a component of the baptismal rite; post-Vatican II liturgical reform, however, abandoned the old symbolic language (cf. *Die Feier der Eingliederung Erwachsener in die Kirche nach dem neuen Rituale Romanum* [Einsiedeln-Cologne-Freiburg-Vienna, 1975], 72ff.). On the origin cf. Franz Josef Dölger, "Der Exorzismus im altchristlichen Taufritual."

124. Exodus 3:8; Num. 13:27.

125. Cited here according to *La Tradition apostolique,* ed. Bernard Botte, 5th ed. (see Bibl. I; cf. also the Ethiopic and Coptic texts—the numbering in these editions is not identical).

126. On the controversy over baptism in Carthage see below: IV.1.

127. Tertullian *On Baptism* 9.

128. Tertullian *From the Wreath of the Soldiers* 3. Cf. also Saxer, *Les rites,* 121–38 (VIII. "Tertullian et la 'Passion de Perpétue'").

129. Tertullian *On Baptism* 16.

130. A common bath wish in antiquity; cf. Franz Josef Dölger, "Gladiatorenblut und Martyrerblut."

131. Cf. von Franz, "Passio Perpetuae," 445ff.

132. Cf. ibid., 454.

133. Ibid., 492 (with n. 118).

134. Ibid., 485. Tertullian also attests this in his own way: "The devil . . . imitates the divine sacraments in his mysteries of idols" (*On the Prescription against Heretics* 40).

135. Jung uses Heraclites' concept of the running together of all things into their opposites

to characterize the relationship between the conscious and the unconscious; for references see von Franz, "Passio Perpetuae," 495.

136. Ibid., 495–96.

137. The catechist is the opposite of the catechumen: from the active or passive participle of the verb *katechizein,* "let [the word] resound"; this refers especially to explaining the scripture. We also find *didaskalos,* "teacher."

138. Since a passive form is used here, it is not entirely clear whether these exorcisms are undertaken by catechists, but based on the context, this is probable.

139. Lat. *sustineo te;* one could also translate: "I am sustaining you." In this case the formula would have its parallel not in Pomponius's greeting (*expectamus te,* "we are waiting for you") but in his promise: *conlaboro tecum,* "I am struggling with you" (see below).

140. The Greek word in a Latin text is an indication of liturgical language.

141. In the Coptic version the water bowl is missing (Till and Leipoldt, 46).

142. Tertullian *From the Wreath of the Soldiers* 3.3.

143. *ACM* 220 (*Martyrdom of Montanus* 8). On the parallels in non-Christian cults cf. von Franz, "Passio Perpetuae," 439ff.

144. Lat. "experrecta sum . . . et intelleximus" (4); "experrecta sum et cognivi" (7); "experrecta sum, tunc intellexi" (8); "experrecta sum et intellexi . . . sed sciebam" (10). In the account of Saturus's vision we find only "gaudens experrectus sum," ("joyful, I awoke"; 13) without an interpretation of the vision.

145. Cf. Lefkowitz, "Motivations," 421.

146. Herbert Musurillo, *The Acts of the Pagan Martyrs* (Bibl. I).

147. Cf. the writings of early Christian apologists.

148. Euseb. *Ch.Hist.* 10.4.

149. Ibid., 5.1.4, 14, 16, 23, 25, 27, 38, 42.

150. On the interpretation of the Egyptian cf. von Franz, "Passio Perpetuae," 462ff., and Franz Joseph Dölger, "Der Kampf mit dem Ägypter."

151. The baptismal candidate is anointed with this afterward.

152. Baptism as the restoration of the paradisiacal state is one of the classical topoi of baptismal theology. On victory symbols cf. Robert, "Une vision," 266ff., and Amat, "L'authenticité des songes de la passion," 181–82.

153. Robert, "Une vision," 257ff.; according to Robert, in Carthage Perpetua experienced battles following the model of the Pythian games of Delphi.

154. Von Franz, "Passio Perpetuae," 490, seems to see ecstatic elements here—wrongly, I think, especially since she mixes the texts: " 'lifted into the air' . . . she sings hymns"; in the dream it is not Perpetua but her assistants who sing, and then only after her victory. In her real martyrdom, by contrast, Perpetua sings a psalm upon entering the arena. The lack of understanding is probably to be seen more as a numbing condition, which is also reported of Blandina.

155. On the wedding motif and the designation *matrona Christi* see below: II.6d.

156. Cf. Valerio, "Le figure femminile," 43.

157. Genesis 3:15; in the Hebrew text, as well as the Greek, the same verb is used for striking the head and the heel. In the Vulgate, Jerome's Latin Bible translation, this is no longer recognizable: "ipsa [the correct form would be *ipse*] conteret caput tuum, et tu insidiaberis calcaneo eius"—"she [he] will tread on your head and you will chase his heel."

158. Cf. Augustine *Sermones,* 280–82, *PL* 38:1280–86.

159. This is true for Blandina (Euseb. *Ch.Hist.* 5.1.42), as well as for Papylus (*ACM* 26) and Celerinus (Cyprian *Letters* 21 and 39).

160. On the following cf. Rader, "The Martyrdom of Perpetua," 9ff. Valerio does not go

into this aspect at all, and Amat only tangentially ("L'authenticité des songes de la passion," 186–87). Lefkowitz sees in the dream a "concern with destroying threatening male figures" but does not explain why Perpetua changes herself into a man for this purpose. Treading on the opponent is directed toward her father, according to Lefkowitz ("Motivations," 419). Cf., by contrast, the careful analysis of the father-daughter relationship in von Franz, "Passio Perpetuae," 468ff.

161. Such an idea is expressed, for example, in logion 114 of the *Gospel of Thomas:* "Every woman who makes herself a man will enter the kingdom of heaven."

162. This is not the place to analyze the Jungian concept of androgyny and the underlying categories of "the" feminine and "the" masculine, which von Franz adopts uncritically. Cf. here Verena Kast, "Eine Auseinandersetzung"; Ursula Baumgardt, *König Drosselbart und C. G. Jungs Frauenbild;* Judith Christoffel, "Animus und Anima" (I am grateful to Maria Kassel for this reference). Cf. also Doris Brockmann, *Ganze Menschen—Ganze Götter.*

163. Von Franz, "Passio Perpetuae," 471.

164. Ibid., 474–75. The assertions about the doctrine of the Trinity and patriarchal social order need to be carefully investigated; I am concerned with the *aspect of psychic endangerment* that is developed here.

165. *Herm. Vis.* I.

166. On Prisca's vision see below: III.2d.

167. Von Franz, "Passio Perpetuae," 476 (with n. 61).

168. Tertullian *On Baptism* 17; cf. below: IV.1.

169. Tertullian *On the Prescription against Heretics* 41. Cf. Gryson, *Ministry of Women,* 17.

170. Tertullian *On Baptism* 17.

171. For the editions see Bibl. I; Funk presents a synoptic edition with the Greek text of the *Constitutions* and the Latin version of the *Didascalia,* in which the additions to the *Constitutions* are marked; Connolly has an English translation of the Syriac text in synopsis with the Latin fragments; Achelis and Flemming present the Syriac text in German translation, which is followed by, in addition to notes, four extensive treatments. Vööbus offers the Syriac text with English translation.

172. *Didascalia,* chap. 9 (*AC* 2.26). In the translation I am following the Latin text, which has *typus* five times; for the bishop/God and for the deacon/Christ, the Greek version has a simple *hōs* (as), otherwise *typos.* In the Syriac text are two different words with similar meaning (Connolly and Vööbus translate "place" or "likeness"); the Greek word rendered "likeness" could be *typos, morphē,* or *homoiōma* (I am grateful to Luise Abramowski for this information). The German text in Achelis and Flemming is less exact.

173. On the idea of representation see below.

174. Chapter 15, which deals exclusively and often polemically with the widow. Chapter 14 is devoted to the "Appointment of the Widow": a minimum age of fifty years is set, and a second marriage discouraged.

175. Cf. here Carolyn Osiek, "The Widow as Altar."

176. Pliny *Letters* 10.96; cf. above: I.3e.

177. But cf. the participation of (nonordained!) women in the baptismal rite in the fanciful *Acts of Thomas* 121 and 157 (*NA* 2:350, 363).

178. Cf. *Gospel of Philip* 17a (*NA* 1:157).

179. This is how the *Didascalia* understands the New Testament phrase, "the Mary of James" (Mark 15:40, literal), usually rendered "Mary the mother of James."

180. Chapter 16.

181. Chapter 15 (*AC* 3.9). In addition to "unallowed" and "dangerous" the *Apostolic*

Constitutions add "godless" (*asebes*) and a long commentary on the subordination of women. The commissioning of the deaconess for the catechetical instruction of women after baptism is omitted. Lay men were also forbidden all "holy activity" (3.10).

182. Later Catholic church law granted women the right to "emergency baptism," yet the crucial point was not greater philogyny but a very narrow conception of the absolute necessity of baptism for salvation: it should immediately follow birth if possible, in order to minimize the risk of the newborn dying unbaptized. For this reason even non-Christians were given the right to baptize.

183. Cf. the already cited comments of Frend on Perpetua's alleged fanaticism, as well as Lefkowitz: "In *seeking* martyrdom she was as much concerned with solving problems in this life as with attaining perfection in the next" ("Motivations," 421, emphasis added). According to the self-testimony she *sought* neither martyrdom nor perfection; only after her first dream in prison did she stop hoping for life "in this world" (4/P).

184. Von Franz, "Passio Perpetuae," 443, 461; so also Pettersen, "Perpetua—Prisoner of Conscience," 147. Cf. Amat, "L'authenticité des songes de la passion," who presents Perpetua's personality more positively than that of her teacher Saturus.

185. Cf. Pettersen, "Perpetua—Prisoner of Conscience," 149: "Perpetua, the martyr, became an *alter Christus*."

186. Cf. Zeph Stewart, "Greek Crowns and Christian Martyrs"; the author describes the shifting of the metaphor from competitor to soldier without expounding the problems involved. Cardman, by contrast, judges the battle metaphor critically ("Acts of Women Martyrs," 147–48).

187. Maria Kassel, "Tod und Auferstehung," raises this question not in regard to baptism but in regard to the interpretation of Jesus' death.

188. *Didascalia* 19 (*AC* 5.1).

189. *Apostolic Tradition* 9 (Till and Leipoldt, 34). The Ethiopic version already has detailed rules (Duensing, 24).

190. Cf. here the special bibliographies in the *Ausgewählte Märtyrerakten* (ed. Krüger and Ruhbach), pp. x, 133–34. Especially considered in the following section are Johann Ernst, "Der Begriff vom Martyrium bei Cyprian"; Peter Corssen, "Begriff und Wesen des Märtyrers"; Otto Michel, *Prophet und Märtyrer;* Marc Lods, *Confesseurs et martyrs;* Norbert Brox, *Zeuge und Märtyrer;* Bernhard Kötting, "Die Stellung des Konfessors in der alten Kirche." Theofried Baumeister, *Genese und Entfaltung der altkirchlichen Theologie des Martyriums,* Traditio Christiana 8 (Bern, 1991), appeared after the completion of my study.

191. Corssen, "Begriff und Wesen des Märtyrers," 484.

192. Cf. letters 15–17 (on the confessors' practice of forgiveness in general) and 26–27 (to Lucianus).

193. In the conflict over the apostates Cyprian basically supports moderation, whereas later in Rome, Novatian took a rigorist standpoint, which led to schism (cf. letter 68) that also spread beyond Rome (cf. above: I.4b).

194. Appointed were: Optatus as subdeacon (29), Aurelius, because of his youth, first only as lector (38), Celerinus also only as lector, for which Cyprian excuses himself, as it were (39), Numidicus as presbyter (40); the function of—at least some—lectors included the instruction of catechumens (29).

195. "Many certificates have been issued in the name of Aurelius, also, a young man who has endured tortures; they have been written out in the hand of the same Lucianus, on the grounds that Aurelius is illiterate" (27.1; ACW 43:112).

196. Letters 21 and 22; on the content see below.

197. Ernst, "Der Begriff vom Martyrium bei Cyprian," 341–42.

198. In the NT *martyrein, martyria, martyrion,* and *martys* occur very frequently, *homologein* and *homologia* more seldom, and *homologētēs* not at all.

199. Corssen, "Begriff und Wesen des Märtyrers," 490–91.

200. Cf., however, the transference of this title to Olympias (Pall. *Hist.Laus.* 56).

201. *ACM* 136; cf. also Krüger and Ruhbach, 46. Both are based on the text edition of Oscar von Gebhardt, "Das Martyrium des heiligen Pionius," *Archiv für slawische Philologie* 18/1–2 (1896): 156–71. It was also used by Rauschen (BKV), but he translates according to the Latin version (ed. Ruinart).

202. *La geste,* 89.

203. Rauschen, BKV 14:345 with n. 1.

204. Shortly beforehand the Roman bishop Fabian had suffered martyrdom.

205. The numbers refer to Euseb. *Ch.Hist.* 5 (Williamson, 192ff.). Cf. n. 79 regarding the term *clergy.*

206. Cf. Acts 15:20, 29; 21:25.

207. A reference to Judas (John 17:12), whom Jesus was unable to save.

208. Here the whole church is addressed. Cf. Matt. 16:19 where the same sentence in the singular is related to Peter.

209. Tertullian *To the Martyrs* 1.

210. Later he rejects any ecclesiastical forgiveness mediated by human beings; cf. below: III.2c.

211. From chap. 4 on, the topic is almost always the bishop or the church in its relationship to him. Chapter 19 is dedicated to the confessors, and chap. 20, "On the Resurrection of the Dead," actually deals with the martyrs as well.

212. *Didascalia* 19 (*AC* 5.1).

213. Chapter 9 (*AC* 2.26–27). This is followed by the Trinitarian association of the bishop with the Father, the deacon with Christ, and the deaconess with the Holy Spirit.

214. Cf. chap. 5 (2.11): power to bind and loose; chap. 7 (2.19–20): relationship of bishop to laity; chap. 8 (2.25): accumulation of OT offices in the person of the bishop: priest, prophet, king, mediator between God and people, and so forth; chap. 9 (2.28–29): the deacon as mediator between laity and bishop, as Christ is mediator between believers and God; chap. 11 (2.44): unity between bishop and deacon like that between God and Christ.

215. Chapter 7. Chaps. 5–7 deal with the question of penance.

216. In the passage in *AC* (5.1) that is parallel to chap. 19, the words "as an angel of God or God on earth" are omitted; in 2.11, however, the power "to rule over all people" is added to the bishop's power to bind and loose.

217. Euseb. *Ch.Hist.* 5.1.17–19; 41–42; 53–56; for the full texts see above.

218. Valerio, "Le figure femminile," 35. Cf., for example, Hamman's edition, in which Blandina is called "jeune fille" ("girl"; p. 49), "vierge" ("virgin"; p. 54), and "jeune femme" ("young woman"; p. 57)—a totally arbitrary addition: the Gk. text has only her name. Stewart calls her "slave-girl," although in the same breath he makes a comparison with the sevenfold mother of Maccabaean martyrs ("Greek Crowns," 120).

219. Gk. *exodos,* an echo of the exodus from Egypt.

220. Cf. Matt. 22:1–14; 25:1–13 (cf., Matt. 9:15; John 3:29; Rev. 21:2, 9; 22:17; 2 Cor. 11:2; Eph. 5:23–32; and elsewhere).

221. The application of the bride metaphor to virgins contributes to no longer thinking of them as autonomous. The metaphor implicitly presupposes a hierarchical, sacralized model of marriage, which developed only gradually; cf. on this Urs Baumann, *Die Ehe—ein Sakrament?*

222. Gk. *dia,* "through, by means of."

223. On *Inter Insigniores* cf. above: Introduction.

III. Women in Proclamation
Charismatic Prophetesses

1. On the relationship of the two charismata cf. Michel, *Prophet und Märtyrer;* Marc Lods, *Confesseurs et martyrs.* The most detailed information on prophetesses is found in Zscharnack, *Dienst der Frau* (parts II.1 and III). On early church prophecy in general cf. Heinrich Weinel, *Die Wirkungen des Geistes;* Fascher, *Prophētēs.* Hans von Campenhausen, *Kirchliches Amt und geistliche Vollmacht;* James L. Ash, "The Decline of Ecstatic Prophecy in the Early Church"; Aune, *Prophecy in Early Christianity;* Cecil M. Robeck, *The Role and Function of the Prophetic Gifts for the Church of Carthage 202–258;* Gerald F. Hawthorne, "The Role of the Christian Prophets in the Gospel Tradition"; and "Sogni, visioni e profezie." For literature on the New Prophecy (Montanism) see below: III.2.

2. Cf. Gerhard Dautzenberg, *Urchristliche Prophetie;* Michael Theobald, "Prophetenworte verachtet nicht!" (this issue of *TQ* [171 (1991)] also includes articles by Gregor Siefer, Walter Gross, and Norbert Greinacher).

3. From the Greek words used here: *glōssē* ("tongue, language") and *lalein* ("talk").

4. In the view of many exegetes 1 Cor. 14:33b–36 is a later interpolation; cf. Max Küchler, *Schweigen, Schmuck und Schleier,* 54–55. In addition to the usual commentaries cf. esp. the feminist exegetical discussion: Pagels, "Paul and Women"; Schottroff, "Wie berechtigt ist die feministische Kritik an Paulus?"; Schüssler Fiorenza, *In Memory of Her,* 226–33; Stein, "Lecture des textes de Paul."

5. Cf. Küchler, *Schweigen,* 73–112.

6. The Greek has *kephalē* ("head") twice, but the second occurrence refers to the husband as the "head of his wife" (cf. 11:3).

7. Cf. 1 Cor. 12:3 (connection of the Spirit and the confession of Christ); 2 Cor. 3:6 (the new covenant as Spirit versus the "letter" of the old).

8. Justin *Dialogue with the Jew Trypho* 82.1.

9. Euseb. *Ch.Hist.* 4.18.8 (Williamson, 180).

10. As often happens, the translation "young men" here intensifies the androcentricism: the masculine plural form—literally, "the young"—does not explicitly exclude women, but "young men" does. The point here is the opposition between young and old.

11. Iren. *AH* 3.11.9; for text and examination see below: 3.2a.

12. Euseb. *Ch.Hist.* 5.7.6 (Williamson, 210); Iren. *AH* 5.6.1.

13. Cf. Euseb. *Ch.Hist.* 5.7.1ff.; Iren. *AH* 3.31.2, 32.4.

14. For *Hermas* this question has been explicitly investigated by Martin Leutzsch (see below).

15. On the *Didache* cf. the comprehensive commentaries of Willy Rordorf and André Tuilier, Klaus Wengst, and Kurt Niederwimmer (see Bibl. I). The bilingual edition of Georg Schöllgen (FCh 1) appeared after the completion of this work.

16. On the ethos of itinerant proclaimers cf. Gerd Theissen, "Wanderradikalismus: Literatursoziologische Aspekte der Überlieferung von Worten Jesu im Urchristentum," in idem, *Studien zur Soziologie des Urchristentums;* Kurt Niederwimmer, "Zur Entwicklungsgeschichte des Wanderradikalismus." Appearing after the completion of this work: Luise Schottroff, "Wanderprophetinnen."

17. Literally, "ordain" (*cheirotonēsate*).

18. On its significance cf. Küng, *Die Kirche* (C.II.3. "Die bleibende charismatische Struktur"; E.II.2. "Die diakonische Struktur").

19. Cf. also 11.1–2 (introduction to the instructions for apostles and prophets).

20. Wengst sees in the Eucharist here only a "slightly Christianized Jewish-Hellenistic

meal"—for him "something completely different from the Lord's Supper in Paul and the Last Supper in the Synoptics" (*Didache*, 53, 56). This view is not shared by the majority of scholars; cf. Niederwimmer, *Die Didache*, 173–80 (Bibl. I under *Didache*).

21. Cf. *Didache* 10.7, 13, 15 with *AC* 7.26.6, 29, 31.

22. On *Hermas* cf. Jannes Reiling, *Hermas and the Christian Prophecy;* Martin Leutzsch, *Die Wahrnehmung sozialer Wirklichkeit im "Hirten des Hermas"* (esp. chap. VII: "Imagination des Weiblichen und Situation der Frau"); Carolyn Osiek, "The Second Century through the Eyes of Hermas." On the person of Hermas cf. also Lampe, *Die Stadtrömischen Christen,* 182–88. After the completion of this work a new annotated translation by Norbert Brox appeared (see Bibl. I).

23. Cf. Osiek, "Second Century," 118–19. Michel: "One sees . . . how the prophet is receding in importance" (*Prophet und Märtyrer,* 63).

24. *Hermas, Visions,* 2.4.1. On Sibyl cf. above: I.4c.

25. "Clement" may refer to the Roman bishop or the author of the so-called *First Letter of Clement,* but all of this is very uncertain.

26. *Hermas, Visions* 2.4.3.

27. Ibid.

28. Iren. *AH* 1.13. We must forgo a close examination of this interesting passage.

29. Irenaeus also accuses him and his followers of the worst sexual offenses.

30. Cf. the shift in the translation or interpretation of the verb *prophēteuein* from "prophetic gift" to "prophetic office."

31. Irenaeus demonstrates this apostolic succession representatively for all churches through the example of Rome: *AH* 3.3; cf. Euseb. *Ch.Hist.* 5.6. But Irenaeus has another, more comprehensive understanding of apostolic succession; cf. Hermann Josef Vogt, "Zum Bischofsamt."

32. Cf. above: I.4c.

33. Cf. the comments of Schüssler Fiorenza: "We must learn to read [the] 'silences' [of androcentic texts]" (*In Memory of Her,* 41; cf. 41ff).

34. On the *Acts of Paul* cf. above: I.5b (end).

35. Cf. Schneemelcher, *NA* 2:208.

36. *Acts of Paul* (letter to the Corinthians 1.8), quoted according to *NA* 2:231. Among the controversial issues is the appeal "to the prophets," which, however, could mean the Old Testament.

37. Schneemelcher: "That is, he will stand above all the believers"; *NA* 2:235, n. 11.

38. *Acts of Paul,* quoted according to *NA* 2:235–36.

39. Cf. Justin *Dialogue with the Jew Trypho* 82.1.

40. *Hermas, Mandates* 11; cf. Reiling, *Hermas and the Christian Prophecy.*

41. Cf. Ash, "Decline of Ecstatic Prophecy," 231ff., and Heinz Kraft, "Vom Ende der urchristlichen Prophetie," esp. 180–81: "Die vergebliche Suche nach einem Kriterium für die Prophetie."

42. *Hermas, Mandates* 11. (title).

43. No opposition is intended here: Greek "philosophy" as a way of life and Jewish prophecy are very close in their ethical orientation.

44. Nearness to the Bible and the concrete existential dimension appear also in Cecil M. Robeck (see above) as characteristics of early Christian prophecy in the Carthage of Perpetua, Tertullian, and Cyprian.

45. For *Prisca* many texts have *Priscilla* (the same phenomenon as in the NT Prisca/Priscilla, the wife of Aquila).

46. On the following cf. Nathanael Bonwetsch, *Die Geschichte des Montanismus;* de Labriolle, *La crise montaniste* (= *LC*); idem, *Les sources de l'histoire du montanisme* (= *LS*); Wilhelm

Schepelern, *Der Montanismus und die phrygischen Kulte;* Bauer, *Rechtgläubigkeit und Ketzerei* (esp. chap. VII); Frederick Klawiter, "The New Prophecy in Early Christianity" (this dissertation begins with a survey of the literature from 1841 to 1967); August Strobel, *Das heilige Land der Montanisten;* Elaine C. Huber, *Women and the Authority of Inspiration* (Huber compares the Montanist movement with the Quakers). On the current state of research cf. William H. C. Frend, "Montanism: Research and Problems" (he does not even mention Prisca and Maximilla!), and other articles below.

47. There is now a corresponding, somewhat abbreviated and differently arranged collection of original texts with Eng. trans., without commentary: *The Montanist Oracles and Testimonia* (= *MOT*).

48. *LC* 26.

49. Cf. Frederick Klawiter, "The Role of Martyrdom and Persecution in Developing the Priestly Authority of Women"; concealed behind this "case study in Montanism" is the martyrdom of Perpetua and Felicity.

50. *LC* 3.

51. Strobel, *Das heilige Land,* 228.

52. Ibid., 230.

53. Ibid., 235–36.

54. Ibid., 274.

55. Cf. above: I.3c.

56. Zscharnack, *Dienst der Frau,* 179–90 (III.2: "Frauen im Montanismus"); Bauer, *Rechtgläubigkeit und Ketzerei,* 134–49; W. M. Calder, "Philadelphia and Montanism"; idem, "Leaves from an Anatolian Notebook"; idem, "Early Christian Epitaphs from Phrygia." Heinz Kraft, "Die altkirchliche Prophetie und die Entstehung des Montanismus"; idem, "Die Lyoner Märtyrer und der Montanismus"; Kurt Aland, "Bemerkungen zum Montanismus und zur frühchristlichen Eschatologie"; J. Massingberde Ford (female author), "Was Montanism a Jewish-Christian Heresy?"; Karlfried Froehlich, "Montanism and Gnosis"; Joseph A. Fischer, "Die antimontanistischen Synoden"; François Blanchetière, "Le Montanisme originel"; Ronald E. Heine, "The Role of the Gospel of John in the Montanist Controversy."

57. The *montanoi* are found parallel to the "Phrygians" for the first time in Cyril of Jerusalem (*Catecheses* 16.8; *LS* 89), who was also the first to spread the rumor of ritual child murder.

58. The *kata phrygas hairesis;* in Latin and other translations *kata phrygas* commonly became the *Cataphrygians.*

59. Cf. *LS* 275–76: "Note sur l'onomastique montaniste."

60. The characterization as "new" may go back originally to opponents, but it was also used by the follower Tertullian; cf. Kraft, "Altkirchliche Prophetie," 249.

61. The Anonymus in Eusebius (see below).

62. According to Euseb. *Ch.Hist.* 4.27; 5.3.4 (*LS* 67–68) ca. 170; according to Epiph. *Pan.* 48.1.2 (*LS* 115) in 157. Timothy D. Barnes ("Chronology of Montanism") believes Eusebius's information to be more reliable. Attempts to discern a "pre-Montanism" more or less influenced by Judaism have produced little convincing result; cf. Calder and esp. Ford (also Frend, "Montanism," 530, 533); more recent is Christine Trevett, "Apocalypse, Ignatius, Montanism."

63. Anonymus's criticism included the fact that thirteen years after Maximilla's death her predictions of war and persecution had not come true (5.16.19). These thirteen years of peace are generally identified with the reign of Commodus (180–93).

64. In the 4th cent. Epiphanius attests to its great influence, especially in Constantinople (48.14.2; *LS* 137). On the 5th cent. cf. above: I.4b.

65. On the ancient definition of *oracle* cf. above: I.3c.

66. Later, in the ascetic tradition, the so-called *apophthegmata* of the Spiritual fathers and

mothers will replace the inspired words of the prophets; cf. Veronica Krienen, "Prophetische Züge in den Apophthegmata Patrum."

67. In addition to scattered information, the presentation of the New Prophecy is found in chaps. 14–19 of book 5, to which the following numbers refer; the translation is Williamson's. Almost all the quoted texts are contained in the original with Fr. trans. in de Labriolle's collection (LS). Cf. also the Eng. trans. in MOT.

68. Vettius Epagathus (see II.3 above and III.2a below).

69. Epiphanius: "On the Father, Son, and Holy Spirit they think like the catholic church" (Pan. 48.1.4; LS 115); Theodoret: "[Montanus] does not destroy the doctrine of the holy Trinity" (AH 3.2; LS 212—erroneously given there as 3.1). For Eusebius the question does not even arise.

70. Quoted according to LS 195; cf. also LC 472.

71. Cf. Kraft, "Lyoner Märtyrer," 250.

72. Euseb. Ch.Hist. 5.16.14. A legend developed about his death, which underlines the importance of Theodotus in the movement.

73. Euseb. Ch.Hist. 5.16.3.

74. Not identical with the aforementioned adherent of the New Prophecy in Phrygia.

75. Euseb. Ch.Hist. 5.4.1–2. Kraft presumes that Irenaeus was sent to Rome by the confessors at the beginning of the time of persecution in order to save him; cf. "Lyoner Martyrer," 257–58).

76. Cf. Hans-Jochen Jaschke, Der Heilige Geist im Bekenntnis der Kirche.

77. Cf. the initially cited scriptural quotation: Acts 2:14ff. (Joel 2:28–32 [3:1–5 in Heb.]).

78. In the mss. we find "pseudoprophetae . . . esse volunt ("they want to be false prophets")," which makes no sense. I follow de Labriolle's emendation of the text: "pseudoprophetas . . . esse nolunt ("they did not want there to be false prophets")" (LS 7); thus also MOT. Cf. SC 211:172–73: "pseudoprophetas . . . esse volunt (qui . . . soutiennent qu'il y a des faux prophètes et qui en prennent prétexte pour repousser de l'Eglise la grâce prophétique)." Klawiter discusses various interpretations but then supports the traditional text, which he wants to understand ironically ("New Prophecy," 199ff.).

79. Irenaeus 3.11.9 (LS 7–8); cf. LC 230–42.

80. Cf. above: III.1.

81. According to Bardy it is impossible to say more about Anonymus than is found in the quoted text itself: fourteen years after Maximilla's death he wrote a three-volume work against the New Prophets. Bardy calls him a bishop, without giving any reason (SC 41:46, n. 3). Wilhelm Kühnert, who takes all of Anonymus's statements at face value, identifies him with Polycrates of Ephesus ("Der antimontanistische Anonymus des Eusebius").

82. According to Eusebius, Miltiades also composed writings against the Greeks and the Jews, as well as an apology (5.17.5); they have not survived.

83. Apollonius is known only through Eusebius; cf. Bardy, SC 41:55, n. 3.

84. On the ecclesiastical politics cf. Joseph A. Fischer, "Antimontanistischen Synoden," esp. 249ff.

85. Text variant: "the whole brotherhood in Christ throughout the world" (cf. Bardy, SC 41:59, n. 3).

86. Bauer, Rechtgläubigkeit und Ketzerei, 147. In chap. 7, "Art und Weise der Auseinandersetzung zwischen Rechtgläubigkeit und Ketzerei" (135–49), Bauer examines the two sources used by Eusebius.

87. Ibid., 147, n. 1.

88. Discussion (Bibl. I; see n. 97), ed. Ficker, 463 (LS 108).

89. Germanus of Constantinople (after 726); quoted according to LS 247.

90. Libellus Synodicus (late 9th cent.), quoted according to *LS* 252.

91. In Euseb. *Ch.Hist.* 5.16.3–17.5 (*LS* 69ff.).

92. Bauer, *Rechtgläubigkeit und Ketzerei*, 138.

93. Yet it is possible that this is the echo of the eschatological place Ardab in 4 Ezra 9:26, which de Labriolle, however, holds to be improbable (*LC* 12); cf. also Kraft, "Lyoner Martyrer," 260.

94. *Discussion*, ed. Ficker, 455 (*LS* 103); Didymus of Alexandria *On the Trinity* 3.41.3 (*LS* 160).

95. Jerome *Letters* 41.4 (*LS* 170).

96. Cf. *LC* 20.

97. The *Discussion of a Montanist and an Orthodox* was edited in 1905 by Gerhard Ficker under the curiously abbreviated title of "Widerlegung eines Montanisten" (Refutation of a Montanist), *ZKG* 26 (1905): 449–63. Didymus is dependent on it, not vice versa; cf. Ficker, *Discussion*, 461.

98. Ficker, *Discussion*, 455 (*LS* 103). It is, of course, possible that Jerome knew Didymus's tract, but he uses the derogation "castrated one" without mentioning anything about the earlier pagan priesthood. De Labriolle wanted, nonetheless, to hold to the hypothesis of the former priest of Cybele; cf. *LC* 20 and *LS* xcvii; also Strobel, *Das heilige Land,* 35; Frend, "Montanism," 531, holds to "pagan priest" without further substantiation.

99. In the martyrdom of Pionius a confessor of the Phrygian sect is mentioned, Eutychian, whom the group around Pionius finds in prison (11); no qualms about contact are mentioned there.

100. Apollonius, Euseb. *Ch.Hist.* 5.18.1–14 (*LS* 78ff.).

101. Bauer, *Rechtgläubigkeit und Ketzerei*, 141.

102. Today the location of these towns is no longer certain; cf. Strobel, *Das heilige Land,* 29ff.

103. On the designation *Jerusalem* and the question of the near expectation see below: III.2c.

104. Only Jerome speaks once of "opulentes feminas" ("opulent women"); *Letters* 133.4 (*LS* 180).

105. Bauer, *Rechtgläubigkeit und Ketzerei*, 144.

106. Cf. *LC* 24.

107. Nothing is known about the content; cf. Andrew F. Walls, "The Montanist 'Catholic Epistle.'"

108. Bauer, *Rechtgläubigkeit und Ketzerei*, 145.

109. That is, theologians who write in Latin.

110. Jerome *On Illustrious Men* 53 (*LS* 174). On Tertullian cf. Timothy David Barnes, *Tertullian.* His turning to the New Prophecy is dated around 207.

111. Jerome *On Illustrious Men* 53. Twice in his writings Tertullian clearly includes himself among the laity: *On the Exhortation of Chastity* 7.3; *On Monogamy* 12.2; cf. Barnes, *Tertullian,* 10ff.

112. Presumably it was Zephyrinus (199–217); cf. *LC* 267–75; Klawiter, "New Prophecy," 196ff.

113. That is, the Roman bishops who did not want to recognize the New Prophecy.

114. Tertullian *Adversus Praxean* 1 (*LS* 43–44).

115. Cf. John 14:16–17, 26; 16:7–11, 13–14.

116. On the various positions cf. below: III.2e.

117. I quote according to the very well annotated edition/translation of Christoph Stücklin; cf. the excerpt in *LS* 12–15.

118. Cf. Jensen, "Auf dem Weg," 51.

119. Isidore of Seville *Etymologiae* 8.5.27 (*LS* 242).

120. See below: III.2e.

121. Rigorous opponents of the prophets were of the opinion that the time of the prophets ended with John the Baptist, and they supported this with Matt. 11:13; cf. below: III.2e.

122. Tertullian *On the Soul* 9.3–4, cited here according to the German edition of Jan H. Waszink, which also contains more detail on Tertullian's teaching on the soul. Cf. also below: IV.2b (end).

123. Tertullian *On the Veiling of Virgins* 16.4.

124. Tertullian *On Monogamy* 1 (*LS* 28–29).

125. Tertullian does not shy away from adopting here Gnostic vocabulary that goes back to the Pauline characterization of the old and new Adam: the first human being was "natural, animal-like" (*psychikos*), the "last" human being, Christ, is "spiritual" (*pneumatikos*); cf. 1 Cor. 15:45ff. This statement, which is to be understood in terms of salvation history, is used, nonetheless, to divide Christians into two classes. Tertullian speaks of *psychici* and *spiritales*.

126. As opposed to the "ungodly" continence of the heretics and pagans.

127. Tertullian *On Monogamy* 1 (*LS* 28–29).

128. Cf. above: I:4f.

129. On the so-called Easter feast controversy in Asia Minor cf. the accounts in Euseb. *Ch.Hist.* 5:22–25.

130. Irenaeus in Euseb. *Ch.Hist.* 5:24.12.

131. On the date of Easter and on the practice of fasting in Phrygia cf. *LC* 512ff.; Strobel, *Das heilige Land,* 250–57. Even today the question of the date of Easter and the fasting rules plays a decisive role in the theological tradition of the Easter Orthodox churches, as the preparatory documents for the panorthodox council show; cf. Jensen, *Zukunft der Orthodoxie.*

132. On the changing attitude toward fasting cf. Kraft, "Altkirchliche Prophetie," 257ff.

133. Tertullian *On Fasting* 1 (*LS* 37–38).

134. Ibid., 12 (*LS* 40).

135. Kraft, "Altkirchliche Prophetie," 270; yet in the attitude toward martyrdom Kraft sees only a secondary reason for fighting the movement. We have already referred to Klawiter's exaggerations; one example: "Montanus, Priscilla, Maximilla and Theodotos reflect the characteristics of ecstatic prophets (or prophetesses) zealous for martyrdom" ("New Prophecy," 157–58; cf. 189ff). The theory of enthusiasm for martyrdom has, in the meantime, been refuted by William Tabbernee, "Early Montanism and Voluntary Martyrdom."

136. An additional writing, *To the Martyrs,* has an edifying character.

137. Tertullian *From the Wreath of the Soldiers* 1 (cf. *LS* 23–24, which has only the commentary, not the account of the incident itself).

138. Tertullian *On Flight* 14 (*LS* 26).

139. Ibid., 9 (*LS* 25).

140. *Martyrdom of Polycarp* 4.

141. This is presumed by Hans von Campenhausen: *Bearbeitungen und Interpretationen des Polycarpmartyriums,* 20. For further discussion of the passage cf. Klawiter, "New Prophecy," 101ff.; *MOT* xii; Tabbernee, "Early Montanism," 41.

142. Tertullian *On Flight* 9 (*LS* 25).

143. Tertullian *On Honesty* 21 (*LS* 49).

144. Cf. Barnes, *Tertullian,* 247; Klawiter, "New Prophecy," 291.

145. Tertullian *On Honesty* 21 (*LS* 49).

146. On the Novatians cf. above: I.4b; only in a few later heresiologies are the Montanists called rigorists on the repentance question; cf. *LS* 146 (Pacian); 168, 176 (Jerome); 247 (Germanus).

147. Euseb. *Ch.Hist.* 5.18.6 (*LS* 80). For discussion of the passage cf. Klawiter, "New Prophecy," 120. He, along with de Labriolle, von Campenhausen, and Schepelern, holds the view that in the New Prophecy martyrs and prophets were granted the right to forgive.

148. The Tertullianists were mentioned by Augustine, *Against Heresies* 86 (*LC* 469, n. 4); de Labriolle holds this testimony to be believable (*LC* 469ff.), Barnes doubts it (*Tertullian,* 258–59).

149. Apollonius in Euseb. *Ch.Hist.* 5.18.2.

150. Epiph. *Pan.* 48.14.1 and 49.1.3 (*LS* 137, 139); on Epiphanius see above: I.4b; on Prisca's vision see below: III.2d.

151. Augustine *Against Heresies* 27 (*LS* 189–90. This information is found again in similar form in *Praedestinatus* and John of Damascus (*LS* 215, 248).

152. Probably the campaign into the East under Septimius Severus; cf. Klawiter, "New Prophecy," 270.

153. Tertullian *Adversus Marcionem* 3.24 (*LS* 19).

154. Cf. Revelation 20. On the concept of the millennium see s.v. "Chiliasmus" in *TRE* 7; cf. also Kurt Aland, "Bemerkungen zum Montanismus," 129ff. He demonstrates that there is no essential difference between the eschatology of the New Testament and that of the Montanists.

155. Cf. Henry Chadwick, "Oracles of the End in the Conflict of Paganism and Christianity in the Fourth Century."

156. Pepuza/Jerusalem is mentioned by Philaster of Brescia, Theodoret of Cyrrhus, and Timothy of Constantinople (*LS* 150, 211, 241).

157. Tertullian *Adversus Marcionem* 4.22 (*LS* 20).

158. Jerome *On Illustrious Men* 40, 53 (*LS* 173–74). The book *On Ecstasy* contained as volume seven a writing against Apollonius.

159. Lat.: ". . . defendimus in causa novae prophetiae gratiae ecstasin, id est amentiam, convenire." Unfortunately, in both *LS* and CCSL typographical errors have crept in: *LS* has "prophetae" instead of "prophetiae" and (somewhat further down) "amentiam Patri" instead of "amentiam Petri"; CCSL has "amantiam instead of "amentiam." Tertullian's idea is clear: ecstasy and its related loss of consciousness (*amentia*) go well with the gift of grace (*gratia*).

160. Tertullian *Adversus Marcionem* 4.22 (*LS* 20).

161. Tertullian *On the Soul* 11.

162. Epiph. *Pan.* 48.6.4 (*LS* 124).

163. Epiph. *Pan.* 48.3.1 (*LS* 118).

164. On this new view of prophecy see below: III.2e.

165. Cf. Wolfgang Speyer, "Realität und Formen der Ekstase im griechisch-römischen Altertum," in idem, *Frühes Christentum,* 353–68.

166. Cf. *LC* 555ff.

167. Kraft, "Altkirchliche Prophetie," 263.

168. Ibid., 264.

169. Hippolytus *Refutation of All Heresies,* also called *Philosophumena* (see Bibl. I).

170. *Ta gynaia:* this derogatory word is found extremely rarely in polemical writings and only here in the early period.

171. *Pro autōn:* "before or above them." Siouville has "before them"; de Labriolle: "above them"; Konrad Preysing: "their predecessor"; Ronald E. Heine: "before them." Do we already have here in Hippolytus an awkward attempt to place Montanus above the women?

172. *Pleion ti Christō* (*LS/MOT: Christou*): this means the continuation of revelation and the salvation event; cf. below: 3.2e (end). The quotation is from Hippolytus *Refutation of All Heresies* 8.19.1–2 (*LS* 57); cf. also 10.25.1 (*LS* 58).

173. We may recall Alcibiades, Theodotus (Euseb. *Ch.Hist.* 5.4.3, 5.16.14), the martyr

Themiso (5.16.17, 5.18.5), and Alexander (5.18.6ff.), as well as the three anonymous oracles in Tertullian.

174. Kraft raises the question whether the sources possibly talk about four different prophet-esses: Prisca, Priscilla, Maximilla, and Quintilla. I see no reason to abandon the traditional equa-tion of Prisca and Priscilla; the name Quintilla is mentioned only by Epiphanius (see p. 163).

175. Hippolytus *Refutation of All Heresies* 8.19.2 (*LS* 57).

176. Euseb. *Ch.Hist.* 5.20.3 (*LS* 83–84); idem, *The Life of Constantine* 3.56 (*LS* 87).

177. *Discussion of a Montanist and an Orthodox,* ed. Gerhard Ficker, 456–57 (*LS* 105–6); cf. below: III.2e.

178. *LC* 36.

179. On the polemic against female authorship cf. below: III.2e.

180. Here I follow Wilhelm Schneemelcher, who collected the sayings in *NA,* 4th ed. (1971), 486–87 under the title "Apokalyptische Prophetie"; in the commentary of this edition he had already called into question the apocalyptic character of the movement. Probably for this reason *NA,* 5th ed. (1989), no longer contains the sayings but has only a short note on Mon-tanism (p. 581). Pierre de Labriolle presents nineteen Montanist oracles (four are marked as un-certain), which he examines in turn (*LC* 34–105). Cf. also the collection of genuine and false oracles in Kurt Aland, "Bemerkungen zum Montanismus," 143–48 (only Gk./Lat.) and in Ronald E. Heine, *MOT* 2–9. The original texts cited by de Labriolle, as well as previous ones, have in each case been checked with the latest editions (cf. Heine, *MOT*) and are printed in the appendix; the following references refer to the annotated passages in *La crise montaniste* (*LC*), not *LS.*

181. Euseb. *Ch.Hist.* 5.16.17 (*LC* 9).

182. On Epiphanius see above: I.4b.

183. Epiph. *Pan.* 48.12.4 (*LC* 71).

184. Ibid., 48.13.1 (*LC* 73). In the Gk. text (GCS/*MOT*) is the unusual term *gnōthein,* "know" (*LS/LC: mathein,* "learn").

185. Cf. *LC* 74ff.

186. Cf. Luke 24:49: "I am sending upon you my Father's *promise* [*epangelia*]" (literal trans-lation).

187. Cf. Matt. 26:28: "This is my blood of the *covenant* [*diathēkē*]."

188. Epiph. *Pan.* 48.2.4 (*LC* 68). Text variant: prophetess.

189. Euseb. *Ch.Hist.* 5.17.4 (*LS* 77–78).

190. More on this below: III.2e.

191. Epiph. *Pan.* 48.3.1 (*LS* 118).

192. Cf. ibid., 48.2.1ff. (*LS* 116ff.).

193. This is similarly interpreted by Froehlich, who understands "culmination" as "perfec-tion of knowledge" ("Montanism and Gnosis," 105).

194. This corresponds to general conceptions; cf. Kurt Aland, "Bemerkungen zum Mon-tanismus."

195. *Discussion,* ed. Ficker, 452 (par. Didymus of Alexandria *On the Trinity* 3.41.1) (*LC* 38).

196. Didymus seems to have known and used the *Discussion;* cf. Ficker, 459ff.

197. The conceptuality of the doctrine of the Trinity was still open at this time: the later equated terms *hypostasis* and *prosōpon* for person appear in the Montanist formula (according to Didymus) as opposing terms for difference and unity: three divine hypostases in one *prosōpon;* cf. *LS* 153 and 155–56.

198. Karl Holl calls this oracle a "cruder version" of the following saying handed down by Epiphanius (48.11.1); cf. footnote 18 in his edition (GCS 25, 233). Ronald E. Heine lists it un-der "Questionable Oracles" (*MOT* 6).

199. Epiph. *Pan.* 48.11.1 (*LC* 37).

200. Epiph. *Pan.* 48.11.9 (*LC* 38).

201. Cf. Epiph. *Pan.* 48.1.4, 48.11.1ff. (*LS* 115, 131ff.). The oracle is understood as incarnation doctrine: in Christ the Father became human; later orthodox teaching differed: not the Father (God in general) but the Son of God.

202. On this polemical interpretation of some church fathers as well as modern theologians cf. *LC* 39ff. and *NA* 2, 4th ed. (1971), 487.

203. The Gk. verb has the same root as the noun *ekstasis*.

204. Epiph. *Pan.* 48.4.1 (*LC* 45–46).

205. Soz. *Ch.Hist.* 1.1.8.

206. Epiph. *Pan.* 48.10.3 (*LC* 43). Cf. Dan. 12:3 and Matt. 13:43; Epiphanius stops with only "a hundred times" brighter, since Matthew says only "like the sun." De Labriolle sees here conceivably a reference to two categories of the elect; *LC* 43ff.

207. Tertullian *On Flight* 9.4.

208. Tertullian *On Honesty* 21.7.

209. On the attempt to legitimize church disciplines "prophetically" cf. below: III.2e.

210. On Gnostic concepts of the resurrection cf. below: IV.2b.

211. Tertullian *On the Resurrection of the Dead* 9.4 (*LC* 85): "Carnes sunt et carnem oderunt."

212. Ibid.

213. Tertullian *On the Exhortation of Chastity* 10.5 (*LC* 77): "Purificantia enim concordat, ait, et visiones vident, et ponentes faciem deorsum etiam voces audiunt manifestas, tam salutares quam et occultas." One would spontaneously expect rather an antithesis between "manifestas" and "occultas" (manifest/hidden); thus Schneemelcher translates: ". . . they hear salvation-bringing voices, as clear as they are hidden" (*NA* 2 [1971], 486). On the interpretation of the passage cf. the commentary of Claudio Moreschini (SC 319:177ff.); he expresses the assumption that Tertullian translated a saying of Prisca from Greek. The sometimes recommended correction, "cum cor dat" for "concordat," is no longer found in the new editions. Hans-Veit Friedrich, in his edition (1990), emends the Latin text: "purificantia [cum spiritu sancto] concordat" and translates very freely: "the pure harmonize with the Holy Spirit."

214. Rigault, a Tertullian editor of the 17th cent., referred with shame to this passage in a footnote; nevertheless, it is missing in the *Patrologia Graeca* of Migne, although the latter used Rigault; cf. also *LC* 77ff.

215. Cf. 1 Cor. 7:5: "Do not deprive one another except perhaps . . ."!

216. Cf. 1 Thess. 5:17: "Pray without ceasing."

217. *LC* 83–84; Schepelern also interprets in Tertullian's sense (*Montanismus*, 59, 143).

218. *LC* 77.

219. Ibid. At the same time he seeks to avoid the misunderstanding that the previously mentioned "minister" is a clergyperson—in Tertullian the statement is general. Moreschini essentially affirms de Labriolle's interpretation, yet the translation (by Jean-Claude Frédouille) does not adopt the focus on the sexual realm: "La pureté apporte l'harmonie . . ." (*Exhortation à la chasteté*, 107).

220. Klawiter, "New Prophecy," 92, n. 4. Moreover, Klawiter has a circular argument here. First he asserts: "The need for sexual purity was undoubtedly part of the parousia hope," which he then supports with Prisca's oracle interpreted by him in this sense (as further "proofs" [!] he merely refers to Luke 20:34–35 and 1 Corinthians 7).

221. Cf. de Labriolle: ". . . une pensée qui n'est pas spécifiquement chrétienne . . ., mais elle cadre bien avec l'esprit du christianisme, et rien de l'esprit 'sectaire' ne s'y trahit" (*LC* 84).

222. Heinrich Weinel, *Die Wirkungen des Geistes und der Geister*, 226. Here too is the already noted translation or interpretation phenomenon: Weinel translates *purificantia* as "Reinheit"

("purity," 163) but understands it as "sexual continence" (226). In the 4th cent., as we saw, Jerome made a connection between prophetic visions and continence; cf. above: I.3c ("The daughters of Philip").

223. Cf. the example quoted by de Labriolle (Trumel): ". . . nous n'avons pas de motif de placer ce traité dans la période montaniste" (*LC* 77–78, n. 3).

224. Epiph. *Pan.* 49.1.2 (*LC* 87).

225. Not in the sexual sense.

226. Epiph. *Pan.* 49.1.2 (*LC* 86–87).

227. Schepelern, *Montanismus*, 145. According to Elisabeth Gössmann (personal communication) Schepelern's characterization of medieval women mystics is erroneous.

228. Klawiter, "New Prophecy," 90–91 (emphasis added).

229. Thus Schneemelcher in *NA* 2 (1971), 486. De Labriolle: "Il m'inocula la sagesse" (*LC* 87); Ronald E. Heine: "put wisdom into me" (*MOT* 5).

230. Thus Schepelern, *Montanismus*, 143–44; Kraft rejected this idea as "completely mistaken"; cf. "Altkirchliche Prophetie," 262, n. 43.

231. According to G.W.H. Lampe, *A Greek Patristic Lexicon* (Oxford, 1961), the verb *synhypnoō* occurs only in this passage; in Henry George Liddel and Robert Scott, *A Greek-English Lexicon* (Oxford, 1968), it is not attested.

232. In a fragment from *Questions of Mary* Jesus brings a woman forth from his side in order to unite with her; cf. Epiph. *Pan.* 26.8.1; *NA* 2:311–12. This was presumably supposed to characterize Gnostic rites as obscene practices.

233. Cf., however, Kurt Aland, "Bemerkungen zum Montanismus," 119: he decides for Prisca; on the argumentation see below. On the basis of the late tradition, Heine ascribes it to Quintilla without further substantiation.

234. In most cases only "visions" or "revelations" are mentioned, without specifying how and when they were received.

235. Tertullian *On the Soul* 9.3–4; for the text see above: III.2c.

236. Cf. *LC* 87.

237. Aune, *Prophecy in Early Christianity*, 47–48.

238. Cf. *LC* 87ff.

239. In the discussion following my paper of 23 August 1991 at the 11th International Oxford Conference on Patristic Studies: "Prisca—Maximilla—Montanus: Who was the Founder of 'Montanism'?" Elisabeth Gössmann has also expressed this opinion in a private communication.

240. *Auf den Spuren der Weisheit: Sophia—Wegweiserin für ein weibliches Gottesbild,* ed. Verena Wodtke (Freiburg, 1991), appeared after the completion of my work.

241. That is, were baptized.

242. Epiph. *Pan.* 49.1.4 (*LS* 140). Kurt Aland also sees in the vision the reason for making Pepuza a cultic place and therefore ascribes it to Prisca ("Bemerkungen zum Montanismus," 122).

243. The names are also found in Augustine and John of Damascus but were adopted there from Epiphanius; cf. *LS* 189, 248–49.

244. Epiph. *Pan.* 48.14–49.2 (*LS* 137–41). Other designation: *Taskodrygites* (because of the custom of keeping a finger on the nostrils during prayer) and *Artotyrites* (because of the custom of using bread and cheese in the Eucharist; see below). On the customs cf. Strobel, *Das heilige Land,* 257–63.

245. Interestingly, the ratio is reversed in the *anakephalaiōsis* ("summary"): the theological discussion is greatly abbreviated, but the description of the Quintillists is retained.

246. This means the other church ministries.

247. The term comes from *artos* ("bread") and *tyros* ("cheese"). Presumably this is a remnant of the old practice of having milk at the Eucharist or the custom of blessing food for the meal accompanying the Eucharist; cf. Strobel, *Das heilige Land*, 257–61.

248. The sources that mention it seem to go back to Epiphanius.

249. In distorted form it appears in two later Western sources; see below: III.2e.

250. Kraft ("Altkirchliche Prophetie," 257) presumes a connection with the "parable of the seven [*sic*] foolish and seven wise virgins" (Matt. 25:1–13). This is probably a slip, since the NT speaks of five virgins in each case.

251. In this section on the late period of the Phrygian church I am following the source collection of de Labriolle (*LS*); most quotations and references are taken from there.

252. Soz. *Ch.Hist.* 2.32 (*LS* 207–8). Theodoret, however, stresses the successful "purging" (*AH* 3.6 [*LS* 213]).

253. Eusebius, *Life of Constantine* 3.63ff. (*LS* 84ff.). The decree was presumably issued between 337 and 340. The following "heresies" were listed: Novatians, Valentinians, Marcionites, Paulianists, and Cataphrygians.

254. *Codex Theodosianus* 16.5.34 (*LS* 196–97). In addition to the Montanists, the followers of Eunomius are named.

255. "Priscillianists" here clearly means the Phrygian church; in the minds of the legislators, however, the followers of Priscilla were possibly equated with the followers of Priscillian of Avila; cf. *LC* 477. The latter was executed in 386, apparently without sufficient grounds, as inspirer of an ascetic movement (cf. Henry Chadwick, *Priscillian of Avila*). Also in this movement women played an important role.

256. *Codex Theodosianus* 16.5.40 (*LS* 197ff.).

257. *LS* 183 (*Liber pontificalis*); cf. also *LC* 477. This information is historically uncertain; cf. Kurt Aland, "Augustin und der Montanismus," 151.

258. *LS* 239–40 (Gregory the Great, letter 11.67). On recognition of Montanist baptism cf. *LC* 523–24.

259. *Codex Theodosianus* 16.5.48 (*LS* 200).

260. Ibid. (cf. also *LC* 531).

261. Ibid., 16.5.57 (*LS* 201–2).

262. Ibid., 16.5.59 (*LS* 202). The variety of names suggests that the Montanists sought to escape persecution through various designations. The imperial legislation tries to encompass them as fully as possible (cf. *LC* 530–31).

263. Ibid., 16.5.65 (*LS* 203).

264. "The laws against pagans, Manichaeans, Borborians, Samaritans, Montanists, Tascodrogites, Ophites, and the other heretics . . .," *Codex Justinianus* 1.5.18 (*LS* 230–31). The cited laws were enacted in the years 529–531 in Constantinople.

265. Ibid., 1.5.20 (*LS* 231).

266. Ibid., 1.5.20 and 21 (*LS* 231ff.).

267. *LS* 236–37 (Procopius *Historia arcana*). Yet the council of 691 (called the quinisext or Trullan) in canon 95 still mentions the Montanists and equates them with pagans in regard to baptism (*Les canons,* ed. Joannou, 230ff. [*LS* 243]). A self-immolation is again reported in 722— after a compulsory baptism of Jews and Montanists by Leo III Flavius (Isaurus): cf. *LS* 250–51 and *LC* 536.

268. Cf. *LS* 238 and *LC* 535.

269. *LC* 536.

270. Cf. *LS* 226ff.

271. Cf. *LS* 109.

272. Cf. *LS* 183 (*Liber pontificalis*); *Codex Justinianus* 1.5.19 (*LS* 231; cf. also *LS* 220, 236, 250).

273. *LS* 90 (Synod of Laodicea); *LS* 224 (Gennadius of Marseille); *LS* 240 (Gregory the Great); *LS* 241 (Timothy of Constantinople).

274. *LS* 221 (Isidore of Pelusium).

275. Cf. *LS* 103, 160, 170, 221, 240, 245.

276. *LS* 89, 107.

277. *LS* 88.

278. Cf., for example, the 1981 revision of Euseb. *Ch.Hist.* by Hans Arnim Gärtner (following the translation of Philipp Haeuser, BKV, 1932). In the early sources "females" is found only in Hippolytus of Rome.

279. The "insanae feminae" or "vates" is found in Hilarius of Poitiers, Jerome (five times!), Augustine, Victor of Lérins, and Prosper of Aquitaine (*LS* 108, 165, 172, 173, 176, 179, 191, 205).

280. Epiph. *Pan.* 48.12.7 (*LS* 134).

281. Cf. *Discussion,* ed. Ficker, 455 (*LS* 103).

282. *LS* 243 (*Chronikon Paschale*); *LS* 245 (Pseudo-Chrysostom); *LS* 241 (Timothy of Constantinople).

283. *LS* 226 (Pseudo-Gelasius).

284. The Gk. *ekklēsia* can mean "church," "congregation," or "assembly." In 1 Cor. 14:34 it clearly means the worship gathering. In 1 Tim. 2:12 a general prophibition of teaching is expressed, without mentioning *ekklēsia.* Origen apparently interpreted "speaking in the church" as "public speech."

285. It has survived only in fragments through the so-called catenas, that is, collections of individual sentences from the church fathers on certain scriptures or scriptural passages; *LS* 55–56.

286. This apparently means the already quoted evangelist Luke, who is also considered the author of Acts.

287. *Discussion,* ed. Ficker, 456ff. (*LS* 105ff.).

288. On the prophetess Anonyma from Caesarea, who is often—incorrectly—called a Montanist in the literature, see below: III.3.

289. *Didache* 10.7; on the *Didache* cf. above: III.1.

290. *LC* 21.

291. In the *LTK,* for example, Prisca is not entered under her own name, but Montanus is, with the reference, "s. Montanismus."

292. On the following cf. Bauer, *Rechtgläubigkeit und Ketzerei,* 65ff.

293. Ibid., 67.

294. Klawiter probably correctly stresses here the commonalities between Ignatius and the later New Prophecy (155ff.); cf. also Hermann Josef Vogt, "Ignatius von Antiochien über den Bischof und seine Gemeinde," 17ff.

295. Ignatius *Phil.* 7.1.

296. Michel, *Prophet und Märtyrer,* 59.

297. On Cyprian as bishop and martyr cf. above: II.6a.

298. Cf. also Adolf von Harnack, "Cyprian als Enthusiast"; on Cyprian as visionary cf. also Robeck, *Role and Function of the Prophetic Gifts.*

299. Cf. Cyprian, letters 11.3–6; 16.4; 39.1; 40.1; and elsewhere.

300. Cf. letter 16.4.

301. In the cumulation of the episcopal office and prophetic authority in Cyprian, von Harnack sees a kind of anticipation of the doctrine of infallibility ("Cyprian," 186); there is a kernel of truth here, yet we must also consider the problems of the bishop of Carthage, who had to hold together a divided and persecuted church.

302. Cyprian, letter 39.1.

303. Here the two charismata are coupled; cf. the use of the concept in the martyrdom of Perpetua (1.5; 4.1; 7.2); see above: II.4b. Harnack does not seem to have seen this double meaning, for he equates "divina dignatio" in one passage with "revelation" where martyrdom is obviously meant; "Cyprian," 184, n. 1.

304. Cyprian, letter 66.10.

305. Eph. 2:20; cf. also 3:4.

306. Cf. Anonymus in Euseb. *Ch.Hist.* 5.17.1–5 (*LS* 76ff.); cf. above: III.1.

307. Cf. Irenaeus *AH* 1.27.1 and esp. 3.3; cf. also Euseb. *Ch.Hist.* 3.11.

308. Cf. Kraft, *Lyoner Märtyrer,* 259ff.; "Altkirchliche Prophetie," 268.

309. After the conclusion of my study I received the following reference from Elisabeth Gössmann: Karin Sugano, "Marcella in Rom: Ein Lebensbild" (see Bibl. II).

310. Later *patriarch* will designate, esp. in the East, the "first" bishop, who is the *primas* in a regional church association; yet this usage does not come until the 5th cent.

311. The Lat. mss. have *cenoni* and other formations based on the ambiguous Gk. term *koinōnoi* ("companions, comrades, partners, sharers," etc.), which is attested as a Montanist title by the *Codex Justinianus* 1.5.20.3 (*LS* 232), as well as by an inscription; cf. Henri Gregoire, "Du nouveau sur la hiérarchie de la secte Montaniste d'après une inscription grecque trouvée près de Philadelphie en Lydie," in *Byzantion* 2 (1925): 329–35; Henri Leclerq, s.v. "Montaniste (Epigraphie)," *DACL* 11:2529–44; Kurt Aland, "Augustin und der Montanismus," 158–59.

312. Jerome, letter 41.3 (*LS* 168).

313. *Codex Justinianus* 1.5.20.3 (*LS* 232).

314. Cf. *LC* 496ff.; Kraft, "Altkirchliche Prophetie," 268; Klawiter, "New Prophecy," 127; Strobel claims to see "financial officials" here: the ingenious cumulation of capital and spirit— no doubt a mistaken assumption (*Das heilige Land,* 270–74).

315. *LC* 506.

316. Soz. *Ch.Hist.* 7.19.2 (*LS* 210): "The Phrygians ordain bishops in villages."

317. Kraft, "Altkirchliche Prophetie," 268.

318. Cf. Phil. 3:10; 2 Cor. 1:7; Heb. 10:33; 1 Peter 5:1.

319. *Martyrdom of Polycarp* 6.2; cf. also 17.3.

320. Kraft, "Altkirchliche Prophetie," 268–69.

321. Synod of Laodicea, canon 8.

322. Cf. *LC* 498ff.

323. Phrygian grave inscriptions also speak of this consciousness of belonging to a charismatically oriented church: "Lupikinos in memory of his *Christian spiritual life companion Muntane";* "Here lies the *Christian and spiritual doctor Alexander"* (*DACL* 11:2539, 2541). Yet whether inscriptions such as "From Christians for Christians" are to be regarded as Montanist is controversial; on the state of the discussion cf. Frend, "Montanism," 528–30, 534.

324. Von Campenhausen, *Kirchliches Amt,* 328.

325. Huber, *Women and the Authority of Inspiration.* On women in the New Prophecy, there is hardly any new historical work; moreover, Huber attributes Perpetua's visions to Montanism.

326. On Huber's position see below: III.4 (7).

327. Cf. John 14:16–17, 26; 16:7–11, 13–14.

328. Cf. Rom.12:3–8; 1 Cor. 12–14; Eph. 4:1–13.

329. The messianic expectations in Judaism included the appearance of a prophet "like Moses" (cf. Deut. 18:15); for Christians he came in Jesus (cf. Acts 3:22–26; John 6:14; 7:40).

330. The dispute over the end of prophecy is also found later in the disagreements between Judaism, Christianity, and young Islam; cf. Carsten Colpe, *Das Siegel der Propheten.*

331. *LS* 92. This Anonymus, alias Pseudo-Athanasius, was presumably a contemporary of the real Athanasius (the statement is also found in a second Pseudo-Athanasius, whose date, however, is uncertain; cf. *LS* 182).

332. *LS* 96–97, 159.

333. Cf. Irenaeus, *AH* 3.1.

334. On the understanding of revelation in Gnosticism and in Irenaeus see below: IV.2b.

335. Augustine *On the Christian Fight* 27 (*LS* 183ff.); cf. also *Contra Faustum* 32.17 (*LS* 185–86); letter 237 (*LS* 191).

336. The "prophet murders" asserted in the New Testament are not attested in the canonical tradition of Judaism; it is a question of legends eagerly adopted by Christian anti-Jewish polemic: cf. Hans-Joachim Schoeps, "Die jüdischen Prophetenmorde."

337. Origen *On Matthew* (fragments) 28 (*LS* 54). James L. Ash asserts that Origen knows no prophets after Christ. In the cited passage, however, he confuses Origen's position with that of the opinion rejected by him ("The Decline of Ecstatic Prophecy," 247–48).

338. Cf. also Gunnar af Hällström, *Charismatic Succession*.

339. Origen *On Matthew* 15.30 (*LS* 53).

340. Cf. Jerome, letter 41.2 (*LS* 167): "They do not agree with the authority of the Old and New Scripture [that is, OT and NT]."

341. Cf. Firmilian of Caesarea in Cyprian, letter 45.7 (*LS* 61): Grace is only "in the church that the presbyters head."

342. Cf. Ronald E. Heine, "The Role of the Gospel of John in the Montanist Controversy." Heine (in contrast to Kurt Aland) comes to the conclusion: "There is no solid evidence for assuming that the earliest Montanists in Phrygia made any use of the Paraclete passages in John. These passages became significant in the controversy at a later period when each side of the debate found itself in a theological situation which was considerably different from that of Montanus, Priscilla, and Maximilla, and the early Asian theologians who first opposed them" (19).

343. Hippolytus *Heresies* 8.19 (*LS* 57); cf. also Theodoret, *AH* 3.2 (*LS* 211–12—incorrectly given here as 3.1): Montanus called the works of Prisca and Maximilla prophetic books; these were more venerated by the Phrygians than the divine gospel.

344. Cf. Hans Reinhard Seeliger, "Fortgesetzte Offenbarung."

345. The term *instrumentum ecclesiae* is hardly translatable. De Labriolle's "appareil (scripturaire)" interprets narrowly in regard to the scripture (*LS* 10); Musurillo does not translate but paraphrases the entire passage with more general expressions.

346. Musurillo clearly translates incorrectly: "So too we hold in honour and acknowledge *not only new prophecies but new visions as well,* according to the promise" (107); he has inserted a "new" in the text where the meaning requires "old" ("nos qui sicut prophetias ita et visiones novas pariter repromissas et agnoscimus et honoramus").

347. Cf. here Schüssler Fiorenza, *In Memory of Her,* 48–53. She speaks elsewhere of the necessity of developing a new paradigm for understanding biblical revelation; cf., e.g., p. 33.

348. Cyprian, letter 75.10–11. The Eng. trans. of Cyprian's correspondence by Graeme W. Clarke (ACW 43/44 and 46/47) contains a detailed commentary (see letter 75 in ACW 47).

349. On the heretic controversy cf. letters 67–75; on Cyprian's role cf. Hermann Josef Vogt, "Cyprian—Hindernis für die Ökumene?"

350. Letter 75.9.2 (ACW 47:84).

351. On the historical background (earthquake, persecutions in Cappadocia) cf. Clarke, ACW 47:263–65, nn. 44–48 (with further bibl.).

352. *Brotherhood* (*fraternitas*) was an early designation for the community of Christians, which expresses a certain understanding of the church; cf. 1 Peter 5:9. Tertullian counts the *apellatio fraternitatis* among the criteria of ecclesiastical apostolicity (*On the Prescription against Heretics* 20.8).

353. *Rustikus* could also be a name.

354. The negative is missing in the text but must be added; otherwise the argumention would make no sense. Another recommended correction would be to replace "without" (*sine*) with "or" (*sive*) (cf. Hartel, GCS 3/2:816). This would mean that the prophetess celebrated the Eucharist either with a free giving of thanks (*invocatione non contemptibili*) or with the usual rite (*sacramento solitae praedicationis*), but this is less likely (cf. Clarke, ACW 47:267, n. 56).

355. This means the two confessional questions that have come down in many variations: "Do you reject the evil one? Do you believe in God?"

356. Cf. the reproach against Maximilla: the wars and persecutions she foretold have not occurred (Anonymus in Eusebius V.16.19).

357. See below: IV.1.

358. Cf. the similarly careful formulation in the *Didascalia:* baptism by a woman is "dangerous" (chap. 15).

359. Canon 11 of Laodicea (Joannou 1/2:135); cf. Gryson, *Ministry of Women,* 53–54.

360. Cf., e.g., the interpretation of a patristics scholar of the Eastern church, Nicolas Afanasiev, "Presbytides or Female Presidents." Mary Ann Rossi, "Priesthood, Precedent, and Prejudice," appeared after completion of my work.

361. Epiph. *Pan.* 49.2.5 and 3.2.

362. In the grave inscription, "Bishop Diogas to the memory of the presbyteress Ammion," the people are not explicitly characterized as Montanists or even as Christians; cf. Elsa Gibson, *The "Christians for Christians" Inscriptions of Phrygia,* 136–37.

363. Cf. Clarke, ACW 47:265–66, n. 50; Kurt Aland even believes that identification with Quintilla is possible ("Bemerkungen zum Montanisumus," 117). De Labriolle had already rejected the linking of Anonyma with Montanism; cf. *LC* 487.

364. Letter 75.7.3.

365. Cf. Dennis R. MacDonald, *The Legend and the Apostle.*

366. The issue was discussed in Catholic theology in connection with Vatican II without reference to feminist concerns; cf., e.g., Küng, *Die Kirche* (esp. C.II.3: "Die bleibende charismatische Struktur").

367. In the Middle Ages the question whether the female sex was a natural hindrance to ordination or only a canonical one was still in dispute, but Thomas Aquinas adopted the Aristotelian view of the inferiority of women; cf. Gössmann, "Äusserungen zum Frauenpriestertum."

368. In 1661 the polemical writing of the cofounder of the "Society of Friends" (wife of founder George Fox) appeared: Margaret Fell, *Womens Speaking Justified;* cf. Jensen, "Im Kampf um Freiheit."

369. Cf. Huber, *Women and the Authority of Inspiration,* esp. chaps. 1, 4, and 5.

IV. Redemption through Knowledge
Bright Women Teachers

1. Euseb. *Ch.Hist.* 5.17.2 and 4.
2. Cf. Zscharnack, *Dienst der Frau,* 156–90.
3. Jerome, letter 133.4 (to Ktesiphon; this letter is a kind of compact antiheretical writing).
4. Cf. Elizabeth A. Clark, "Friendship between the Sexes: Classical Theory and Christian Practice," in idem, *Jerome, Chrysostom, and Friends;* idem, "Theory and Practice in Late Ancient Asceticism"; Rosemary Rader, *Breaking Boundaries,* 86–110.
5. The group around Donatus in Carthage did not want to recognize ministers who apos-

tatized during persecution; hence in 314 a schism developed. The movement had in part traits of a social revolution. On the role of women there cf. Rose Lockwood, "Potens et Factiosa Femina."

6. Elpidius was excommunicated in 380; Priscillian was executed in 386, apparently without sufficient grounds, although important bishops like Martin of Tours and Ambrose of Milan had intervened on his behalf. Cf. Henry Chadwick, *Priscillian of Avila*.

7. Cf. above: I.2b, as well as below: IV.1.

8. Hans Jonas, *Gnosis und spätantiker Geist*; Norbert Brox, *Offenbarung, Gnosis und gnostischer Mythos bei Irenäus von Lyon*; idem, *Erleuchtung und Wiedergeburt*; Luise Schottroff, *Der Glaubende und die feindliche Welt*; Elaine H. Pagels, *The Johannine Gospel in Gnostic Exegesis*; idem, *The Gnostic Paul*; idem, *The Gnostic Gospels*; Kurt Rudolph, *Die Gnosis* (idem, research reports in *TRev*, ending with "Die Gnosis: Texte und Übersetzungen," in *TRev* 55 [1990]: 113–52); *Gnosis*, FS Hans Jonas; Klaus Koschorke, *Die Polemik der Gnostiker*; Erik Peterson, *Frühe Kirche, Judentum und Gnosis; Gnosis und Politik*, ed. Jacob Taubes; Henry A. Green, *The Economic and Social Origins of Gnosticism* (this study offers nothing on the women's issue and seems hardly convincing; cf. the review by Walter Schmithals in *TLZ* 112 [1987]: 332–33); Jorunn Jacobsen Buckley, *Female Fault and Fulfilment in Gnosticism; Images of the Feminine in Gnosticism*, ed. Karen L. King; Alexander Böhlig, *Gnosis und Synkretismus*.

9. Above all the *Pistis Sophia* and the two *Books of the Jeû* (ed. Carl Schmidt, GCS 13, 1905); cf. Rudolph, *Die Gnosis*, 31ff. and *NA* 1:290–300.

10. Cf. the Nag Hammadi editions in Bibl. I; John Dart, *The Jesus of Heresy and History*.

11. Cf. here Koschorke's instructive study *Polemik der Gnostiker*; the question of the position of women does not appear there as a point of contention. The author demonstrates that the polemic of the Gnostics against the church was not as harsh as vice versa; cf. 233ff. and 240–41.

12. Pagels, *Johannine Gospel; Gnostic Paul; Gnostic Gospels*.

13. Schottroff, *Der Glaubende*, 295. Today the author would modify her view of Johannine dualism (personal communication).

14. Cf. Pagels, *Gnostic Gospels*, chap. 3, which is strongly criticized by Susanne Heine, *Frauen der frühen Christenheit*, 117–35.

15. Cf. here Schottroff, *Der Glaubende*, 42–86 (chap. 2: "Probleme des Sophiamythos in gnostischer Literatur"). This negative aspect is neglected by Pagels.

16. Cf. Helen Schüngel-Straumann, *Die Frau am Anfang*.

17. Cf. Buckley, *Female Fault*.

18. Jarl Fossum and Gilles Quispel, s.v. "Helena," *RAC* 14:338–55.

19. Justin *Apologies* 1.26; quoted in Euseb. *Ch.Hist.* 2.13.3–4.

20. Cf. Rauschen on Justin in BKV 12:38, n. 2; Bardy on the Justin quotation in Eusebius, SC 31:67, n. 3.

21. Cf. Iren. *AH* 1.23. Eusebius refers to him (2.13.5).

22. Cf. the brief study by Renate Schmid, *Maria Magdalena in gnostischen Schriften*; Jensen, "Auf dem Weg," 41ff.

23. Cf. *Pistis Sophia* 96 (*NA* 1:295); on Sophia as a paired partner cf. *NA* 1:291.

24. Iren. *AH* 1.25.6; Epiph. *Pan.* 27.6.1; cf. Lampe, *Stadtrömischen Christen*, 269–70.

25. Origen *Against Celsus* 5.62. Yet Celsus wrongly distinguished two groups: "the Marcellians [coming] from Marcella and the Harpocratians of Salome." The Gnostic Christians in Egypt derive their legitimacy from Salome (cf. Zscharnack, *Dienst der Frau*, 169; he holds the form *Harpocrates* to be original and Carpocrates the grecization); on the "gospel of the Egyptians" and the Salome tradition cf. *NA* 1:174–79.

26. Zscharnack, *Dienst der Frau*, 158.

27. Cf. above: III.1.

28. Cf. the so-called wisdom literature in the Bible: the books of Proverbs, Wisdom of Solomon, Ecclesiastes, Ecclesiasticus.

29. On the ministry of the *didaskalos* cf. above: I.5a.

30. Cf. the list of charismata: apostles, prophets, teachers, etc. in 1 Cor. 12:28 with the list of apostolically active women and men in Rom. 16:1–16 and Acts 13:1: Paul and Barnabas are among the prophets and teachers in Antioch.

31. Cf. 1 Cor. 11:2–16 and 1 Tim. 2:11–15.

32. Cf. Froehlich, "Montanism and Gnosis."

33. Cf. above: III.2d (Epiph. *Pan.* 49.1.2 and 48.13.1).

34. Tertullian *On Baptism* 1.2: "quaedam de Caina haeresi." This otherwise unknown group is not to be confused with the sect named after the biblical Cain (cf. Iren. *AH* 1.31.1–2; Ps.-Tertullian *Her.* 2.5–6; Epiph. *Pan.* 38).

35. Tertullian *On Baptism* 1 and 17.

36. Ibid., 1.

37. The motif of the anticipation of a heavenly wedding plays a central role in Gnostic initiation rites. The idea is a heavenly reunion of the masculine and the feminine, which went different ways after the "separation" of Eve from Adam at creation; cf. *Images of the Feminine in Gnosticism,* 223–27, 235–38; Wayne A. Meeks, *The Image of Androgyne.*

38. Iren. *AH* 1.21.3ff.

39. Tertullian *On the Prescription against Heretics* 33.10–11; he connects Rev. 2:6 (where the Nicolaitans are named for Ephesus without further description) with Rev. 2:20 (polemic against the prophetess Jezebel in Thyatira because of fornication and eating meat sacrificed to idols). The Nicolaitans are otherwise presented as a libertine sect; cf. Epiph. *Pan.* 25.

40. Cf. Zscharnack, *Dienst der Frau,* 167.

41. Cf. Tertullian *From the Wreath of the Soldiers* 3: he polemicizes there against the Roman custom of bestowing a wreath; he is also trying to show that not everything can or must be substantiated only by scripture: the traditional church rite of baptism, which is considered obligatory, goes beyond what is attested in scripture.

42. Cf. Tertullian *On Baptism* 17.

43. On Thecla see above: I.5b (end). In the acts of Thecla only her self-baptism is reported (34 and 40); in the life of Thecla written very much later (see *Acts of . . . Thecla* in Bibl. I) she also baptizes others (24).

44. A play on words in the Latin: *conferre/auferre.*

45. On Philomena cf. Zscharnack, *Dienst der Frau,* 175ff., and Jensen, "Philumene" (a brief version of the present discussion), as well as the following literature on Marcion and Apelles, esp. Adolf von Harnack, *Marcion* (abbreviated HM). On the current state of research cf. Gerhard May, "Marcion in Contemporary Views" (abbreviated MM); idem, "Apelles und die Entwicklung der markionitischen Theologie" (abbreviated MA here). Cf. also Jörg Woltmann, "Der geschichtliche Hintergrund der Lehre Markions"; Barbara Aland, "Marcion"; Robert M. Grant, "Marcion and the Critical Method"; R. Joseph Hoffmann, *Marcion* (not available to me; May's verdict: "a failure" [MM 131]—cf. his review in *TRev* 51 [1986]: 404–13); idem, "How Then Know This Troublous Teacher?"

46. Cf. Tertullian *On the Prescription against Heretics* 33; 34; 37; this trio is also found in Origen; cf. HM 332★. Irenaeus especially attacks the school of Valentinus.

47. Zscharnack, *Dienst der Frau,* 175–76.

48. On the present state of research see MM; May's summary: ". . . everything seems more complicated than in the past, and the new syntheses are lacking" (131).

49. On the situation in Rome cf. Hubert Cancik, "Gnostiker in Rom," as well as the corresponding chapter in Lampe, *Die stadtrömischen Christen*.

50. Harnack set Marcion apart from Gnosticism; recent research gives more emphasis to his Gnostic credentials. Thus Rudolph (*Die Gnosis*, 334–35) writes: "[Marcion] adopts . . . a special position in that he stands, so to speak, with only one foot in Gnostic tradition and the other in an idiosyncratically understood Pauline-Christian system. . . . But he is not to be understood without [Gnosticism] and therefore belongs to its history"; cf. also Barbara Aland, "Marcion," 423–24; MM 130; Koschorke, *Polemik der Gnostiker*, 239.

51. Cf. HM 153–60.

52. Epiph. *Pan.* 42.4.5.

53. Tertullian *Adversus Marcionem* 5.8. Zscharnack infers from this passage a prophetic self-understanding for Marcion and his followers (*Dienst der Frau*, 174).

54. Jerome, letter 133.4; see above.

55. Rhodo in Euseb. *Ch.Hist.* 5.13; on Rhodo cf. Lampe, *Stadtrömischen Christen*, 245ff.

56. Ibid., 5.13.2.

57. Cf. Hippolytus *The Refutation of All Heresies* 5.38 and 10.16; Pseudo-Tertullian *AH* 6.6; Jerome, letter 133.4; addendum to Augustine *Against Heresies* 24. Epiphanius mentions only Apelles (44). On Tertullian, who once calls her a "whore," see below.

58. So argues, e.g., Firmilian about the anonymous prophetess in Caesarea; see above (Cyprian, letter 75).

59. Cf. s.v. "Apophthegma," *RAC* 1:545–50.

60. Cf. *The Sayings of the Desert Fathers* (see Bibl. I under *Apophthegmata*).

61. Cf. Tertullian *On the Prescription against Heresies* 30.6; the work has not survived.

62. Cf. s.v. "*apokalyptō*," *TWNT* 3:595. I have intentionally not used the usual, but misleading, "revelations" for this term. In Paul each individual charisma is called the "manifestation of the Spirit for the common good" ("phanerōsis tou pneumatos pros to sympheron," 1 Cor. 12:7).

63. Augustine *Against Heresies* 24: "This [Apelles] said, moreover, that a certain girl Philomena was inspired by God to foretell the future. He presented everything [CCSL: *omnia*; Harnack: *somnia*, "dreams"] to her and especially heatings of his Spirit, and he was used to receiving secret revelations through her prophecies and predictions, for the same Spirit (*phantasma*) always appeared to this Philomena in the form of a boy, who sometimes claimed to be Christ and sometimes Paul. She questioned this Spirit and customarily shared the answers with her followers. She is also supposed to have worked some miracles: the most noteworthy was that she introduced a large loaf of bread into a glass bottle with a very small neck and would retrieve it unchanged with the tips of her fingers: this was the food given to her by God, as it were, and she was satisfied with it."

Curiously, Harnack ascribed this abstruse miracle story to Tertullian on stylistic grounds (*Geschichte*, 200), although the latter reports nothing of the kind about Philomena (see below: "The polemic of Tertullian"). The interpolation is found in the Augustine work at the wrong place, namely, after section 24; Apelles is the topic in section 23.

64. Harnack calls Philomena "an ecstatic virgin" (HM 213); Gustave Bardy comments on the utterance cited by Rhodo: ". . . qui exposent les idées développées par Philomène, au cours de ses extases" (SC 41:44, n. 9). May also presumes ecstasy and therefore places Philomena close to Montanism (MA 8–9).

65. Tertullian *Adversus Marcionem* 5.8.

66. In Harnack's view we have here the resignation of age, in which Apelles "again threw off Gnosticism" (HM 195)—this interpretation hardly reflects Rhodo's opinion! On Harnack's

reading of this passage cf. also MA 20–21. Koschorke speaks generally of a typically Gnostic *humilitas* ("humility") vis-à-vis ecclesiastical contentiousness (*Polemik der Gnostiker,* 166–73).

67. Rhodo in Euseb. *Ch.Hist.* 5.13.5.

68. On the concept of "being moved" used here cf. MA 23–24.

69. Tertullian *On the Prescription against Heresies* 30.6; on the title see above.

70. The *praescriptio* is a technical legal term: its purpose is the dismissal of trials in advance.

71. Tertullian mentions it himself in *On the Flesh of Christ* 8.2–3.

72. From these allusions it has been inferred that Philomena received her revelations through an angel (cf. Zscharnack, *Dienst der Frau,* 177); it is more likely that she herself appeared to her followers as an "angel of light."

73. Tertullian *On the Prescription against Heresies* 6.5–6. Here we recall the concrete dimension of the word *heresy:* a heretical party, sect, etc. The last sentence contains a Latin pun: *inductus/induxit.*

74. BKV: "Zauberkünste"; SC (de Labriolle): "énergie diabolique." The Gk. foreign word used here is neutral, but is certainly meant by Tertullian to be derogatory.

75. The Gk. word is in the text.

76. Tertullian *On the Prescription against Heresies* 30.5–7.

77. Tertullian *Adversus Marcionem* 3.11.2.

78. Tertullian *On the Flesh of Christ* 6.1–2.

79. Ibid., 24.2.

80. Tertullian *On the Soul* 36.3.

81. It is not very likely that the "heresy" has its own churches; it is rather to be assumed that Christian Gnostics remained in the churches; cf. Koschorke, *Polemik der Gnostiker,* 89–90, 140–41, 228ff. "Gnostic insight and church faith are not opposites but only stages" (ibid., 183).

82. Rudolph mentions Philomena only tangentially as "a prophetess familiar to him" (*Die Gnosis,* 339); similarly, MM 150; MA 8–9; and Lampe, *Die stadtrömischen Christen,* 350; Cancik does not mention her at all, and even Barbara Aland names only Apelles as Marcion's opponent ("Marcion," 443); Harnack acknowledges her function as inspirer, but of the "woman who understood how to fetter such a highly educated man as Apelles" (H*M* 177–78), he knows nothing better to report than the silly miracle story from the already mentioned Augustine interpolation (see above for the text).

83. Cf. Ps.-Tertullian, *Her.* 6.2; Epiph. *Pan.* 42.1.3ff. (here Marcion is even excommunicated by his own father).

84. May holds the break reported only by Tertullian and the stay in Alexandria to be historically uncertain (MA 5ff.).

85. Cf. his invective against the woman Eve, who caused the man Adam to fall: "You are the devil's door! . . . With ease you have shattered the image of God, the man [or human being: *homo*]." (Tertullian *On the Attire of Women* 1.1–2).

86. The sources are assembled and briefly commented on in Harnack, *Geschichte,* 1.1, reprinted in the original text in H*M* 404★–420★ (suppl. 8); cf. also the overall presentation "Apelles und seine Sekte" (8.3), 177–96.

87. Harnack even held that this *symbolon* was an excerpt, passed on by Hippolytus, of Tertullian's lost treatise against the Apellians (*Geschichte,* 198), yet that seems highly unlikely since the confession is at some points contradictory to the earlier sources, especially to Hippolytus himself (see below).

88. Cf. the collection of early church confessions in DS, nos. 1–76.

89. Council of Ephesus (431), canon 7. (Joannou 1.1, 61–62; COD, 65–66).

90. Today the acknowledgment of this creed is the prerequisite for membership in the World Council of Churches.

91. Epiph. *Pan.* 44.
92. Insertion by Epiphanius: the institution of a created creator only shifts the problem, since God must have foreseen the work of the demiurge.
93. Insertion by Epiphanius: this idea of incarnation follows the "ancient Greek writers"!
94. The demiurge (literally, "artisan") in the Gnostic systems is the lower (in Marcion and others, the "evil") God of creation and the Old Testament. See below: "The Creator-God and the origin of evil."
95. An Apelles quotation is inserted here: "For thus, he says, has he spoken in the gospel: 'Be honest money changers!' For, he says, I choose from all scriptures what is useful." On this see below: "The interpretation of the scripture."
96. The last sentence is completed according to Hippolytus *Refutation of All Heresies* 7.38.5.
97. DS 125.
98. Cf. Iren. *AH* 3.1.
99. Cf., e.g., Cyril of Jerusalem *Catechetical Lectures;* Ambrose *On the Mysteries;* idem *On the Sacraments;* Theodore of Mopsuestia *Catechetical Homilies;* interestingly, Theodore, the great exegete of the Antioch school, reflects on this missing reference to the historical Jesus and inserts a passage on his activity and proclamation (6).
100. Cf. "Dialoge des Erlösers," *NA* 1:189–284; Schneemelcher points here to the literary relationship with the ancient dialogues.
101. Cf. Hippolytus *Apostolic Tradition* 21.
102. The writer of the *Against Heresies* falsely attributed to Tertullian was active around the same time or a little later. Possibly he used only Tertullian's lost writing *Against the Apellians;* cf. Harnack, *Geschichte,* 198–99.
103. Those for whom the long way through early church dogmatic history is too arduous may satisfy themselves with the summaries. The central concerns of Philomenian theology are treated in the last four sections: "The body of Jesus" etc.
104. Since the "Jewish Bible" in Hellenism naturally meant the Greek version, the Septuagint, it would not make sense to speak of the "Hebrew" Bible; the intra-Jewish controversy over the Hebrew and the Greek canons will not be considered here.
105. Epiph. *Pan.* 33.3–7. This section was separately edited and annotated by Gilles Quispel: *Ptolémée, Lettre à Flora,* SC 24bis (Paris, 1966).
106. Irenaeus merely presents the "Teaching of the Ptolemies" (*AH* 1.12); the numbers below refer to Iren. *AH.*
107. Ptolemy refers to the Torah in the narrower sense, i.e., the Pentateuch. Similar directives are also found in Iren. *AH* 4.8ff.
108. *AH* 4.4 with reference to Matt. 19:3–9.
109. *AH* 4.11–12 with reference to Matt. 15:4–9.
110. Rhodo in Euseb. *Ch.Hist.* 5.13.9.
111. Hippolytus *Refutation of All Heresies* 7.38.2.
112. Pseudo-Tertullian *Her.* 6.4 and 6.
113. Origen *Against Celsus* 5.54.
114. Origen *Commentary on Titus* (fragments in the *Apologia pro Origene,* PG 17:554); cf. HM 227/1 and 336★.
115. HM 179.
116. The Origen passages in turn survived only through Ambrose (*On Paradise*); cf. the collection in HM 412★–418★.
117. Origen, *Second Homily on Genesis* in HM 413★.
118. In the Eng. trans. Frank Williams left one *phēsi* ("he says") untranslated, so that the impression is given that Christ is not only the one who speaks but also the one who selects. Yet in

the entire confessional formula a *phēsi* always introduces the teaching of Apelles: thus he (and with him every Bible reader) is the one who must make the selection.

119. Cf. Joachim Jeremias, *Unbekannte Jesusworte*, 95–98 (includes detailed information of sources and literature). An *agraphon* is an "unwritten" saying of Jesus, that is, one handed down outside the scripture.

120. Apelles' "selection" may have been identical with Marcion's canon; cf. MA 6.

121. Hippolytus *Refutation of All Heresies* 7.38.2.

122. *Didascalia* 2 and 3.

123. *Didascalia* 26 (beginning).

124. Clement of Alexandria *Stromata* 1.28ff.; 1.99.

125. Cf. Justin *First and Second Apologies*.

126. In this sense the agraphon of the money changer is also quoted in the church history of Socrates (3.16). The reverse possibility, changing Christian coins into pagan, did not occur to these fathers, since revelation was thought to be a straight, forward-moving process.

127. Its contents are known mainly through Tertullian's polemical *Adversus Marcionem*.

128. Cf. *HM* 66–67; Woltmann, "Der geschichtliche Hintergrund," 34; Grant, "Marcion and the Critical Method," 211.

129. Cf. Heinrich Dörrie, "Zur Methodik antiker Exegese."

130. Woltmann, "Der geschichtliche Hintergrund," 34; cf. Grant, "Marcion," 211–12, and Dörrie, "Zur Methodik".

131. Cf. *ANRW* 2.21.1 (1984; all the contributions of this volume relate to Philo): Jacques Cazeaux, "Philon d'Alexandrie, exégète," 156–226, and Burton L. Mack, "Philo Judaeus and Exegetical Traditions in Alexandria," 227–71.

132. Cf. Jonas, *Gnosis* 1:116ff.; Brox, *Offenbarung*, 46ff.; Barbara Aland, "Marcion," 432.

133. Cf. Jonas, *Gnosis* 1:221ff. A Gnostic gospel is attested under Eve's name (Epiph. *Pan.* 26.2.6; 3.1); cf. *NA* 1:288ff.

134. Iren. *AH* 1.27.3.

135. Cf. the already mentioned saying of Origen: "Apelles . . . holds the writings of the Jews to be legends [*mythos*]" (*Against Celsus* 5.54).

136. Cf. Altaner and Stuiber, *Patrologie*, 188–216.

137. Cf. Dörrie, "Zur Methodik," 122.

138. Woltmann, "Der geschichtliche Hintergrund," 34.

139. Pseudo-Tertullian *Her.* 6.6.

140. Cf. Koschorke: the Gnostics criticize the "static faith of the church" vis-à-vis their own "dynamic of seeking" (*Polemik der Gnostiker*, 200); cf. also Patricia Cox Miller, "Words with an Alien Voice."

141. Cf. here the modern debate on the canon issue: Inge Lonning, *Kanon im Kanon*.

142. Cf. the very comprehensive article "Engel" in *RAC* 5:53–322. Those for whom the discussion of the conceptions of angels is too tedious may turn ahead to "No to the Creator—Yes to the Creation?"

143. A similar statement is found in Tertullian himself: "They call a certain angel famous who established the world and afterwards is supposed to have admitted regret (*paenitentiam*)" (*On the Flesh of Christ* 8.2).

144. Pseudo-Tertullian *Her.* 6.4.

145. Hippolytus *Refutation of All Heresies* 7.38.1–2.

146. Ibid., 10.20.

147. Rhodo in Euseb. *Ch.Hist.* 5.13.2.

148. Beside *poiein/facere*, "create," stands *ktisein*, "establish"; beside *ergazesthai, dēmiourgein*, "make," and *instituere*, "set up."

149. Tertullian *On the Flesh of Christ* 8.2 (for text see above).

150. Harnack interprets the regret as a sign of distance from God and therefore infers an apostsy of the angel, because according to Tertullian (*On the Flesh of Christ* 8.3) the Apellians compared the creator of the world with the lost sheep (HM 190–91).

151. A gradual apostasy from God by the angels, as suggested by Harnack (HM 191), is not apparent to me.

152. Marcion also characterized the demiurge as just but at the same time malicious; cf. HM 271*ff. (with numerous examples).

153. Matt. 13:17; cf. also Rom. 16:25ff.; 1 Peter 1:10–12.

154. On the following cf. HM 191–92, esp. n. 2.

155. Ibid., 191.

156. Ptolemy *Letter to Flora* (in Epiph. *Pan.* 33), 3.1ff. and 7.2ff.

157. Emphasis added.

158. Tertullian *On the Flesh of Christ* 8.2.

159. Ibid.

160. That is, Christians who do not distinguish the good God from the Creator-God.

161. Tertullian *On the Soul* 23.3.

162. Tertullian *On the Resurrection of the Flesh* 5.2.

163. Tertullian *On the Prescription against Heresies* 34.4.

164. May presumes an immediate student of Apelles as the author but does not exclude Apelles himself as possible author (MA 18).

165. Rhodo in Euseb. *Ch.Hist.* 5.13.4.

166. HM 188. Yet he did not therefore absolutely concede "superiority of content" to Apelles. Cf. also Barbara Aland, "Marcion," 443.

167. On the Gnostics' or Marcion's anthropology and understanding of redemption cf. also Barbara Aland, "Marcion," 433ff.

168. Cf. MM 147–48.

169. At least three women theologians and church mothers can be named who sought to hand down the Christian message in the framework of the tradition of classical education: Macrina, Proba, and Eudocia (see above: "Introduction").

170. Barbara Aland, "Marcion," 446, also points to Irenaeus.

171. Iren. *AH* 3–5. On unity as the theological key to the work of Irenaeus cf. André Benoit, *Saint Irénée* (chap. 6).

172. Mentioned briefly below under "History of Influence?"

173. Epiph. *Pan.* 44.2.2ff. (emphasis added); see above for the complete text of the symbolon.

174. Grant, "Marcion," 207.

175. Tertullian *Adversus Marcionem* 3.11.2.

176. Tertullian *On the Flesh of Christ* 6.1.

177. According to May we have here two opposing conceptions of the cosmic material of the body of Christ: it comes either from the planets (Pseudo-Tertullian; Hippolytus) or the four elements of the earth (*symbolon*). At the same time the early Christian conception (the Son of God conceals his nature from the demons) is demythologized in order to explain the "substance" of the body of Christ "scientifically" (MA, 15ff.).

178. Pseudo-Tertullian, *Her.* 6.5.

179. Hippolytus *Refutation of All Heresies* 10.20.

180. Ibid., 7.38.2–5.

181. The fact that Jewish Christians rejected the idea of the virgin birth is broadly attested; cf. von Campenhausen, *Die Jungfrauengeburt.*

182. Cf. Karl-Josef Kuschel, *Geboren vor aller Zeit?*

183. Epiph. *Pan.* 44.2.4.

184. For comments on this as well as textual evidence see Pagels, *Gnostic Gospels*, chap. 1; idem, *Visions, Appearances, and Apostolic Authority*, 415–430. The insistence on the bodily character is connected with the legitimation of power; cf. also John G. Gager, "Body-Symbols and Social Reality."

185. In the New Testament, by contrast, it is God the Father who sent Jesus and resurrects and exalts him after his suffering.

186. The contention was conditioned in part by a misunderstanding: *flesh* was equated by the Greeks with *body* in contrast to *spirit*, whereas in Hebrew it designated transitory creatures in contrast to the eternal God.

187. Cf. the word play on body (*sōma*) as the grave (*sēma*) of the soul (Plato *Gorgias* 493a, *Cratylus* 400c).

188. Pseudo-Tertullian, *Her.* 6.5.

189. Cf. Barbara Aland, "Marcion," 437–38. She stresses that despite this docetism Marcion's Christology was in no way "heretical" in its intention; his understanding of redemption corresponded completely to that of the mainstream church.

190. Tertullian *On the Flesh of Christ* 8.2.

191. Tertullian, *On the Resurrection of the Flesh* 5.2.

192. Ibid.

193. Tertullian, *On the Flesh of Christ* 8.2; *On the Soul* 23.3.

194. Tertullian, *On the Prescription against Heresies* 34.4.

195. On the preexistence of souls see below: "The Sex of Souls."

196. Thus is the demiurge characterized in the *symbolon* (Epiph. *Pan.* 44.1.5).

197. May maintains the "evil" characterization for the "fiery angel" (MA 10) but in terms of content comes to a similar conclusion for Apellian theology: "All this means a weakening of Marcion's relentless dualism and a differentiated evaluation of the world" (14).

198. Tertullian *On the Prescription against Heresies* 33.6.

199. Ibid., 30.5.

200. H*M* 148; cf. the documents, 277*–278*.

201. Cf. DS 403.

202. Cf. on this the documents in the commentary on Tertullian *On the Soul* (ed. Waszink), 420.

203. Cf. above: I.4d.

204. Yet we must remember that neither Marcion nor Philomena nor Apelles hark back to a preworld mythos.

205. H*M* 195–96.

206. Cf. H*M* 158ff.; Rudolph, *Die Gnosis*, 339, 349.

207. Cf. here Hermann Häring, *Die Macht des Bösen*.

208. Cf. Rom. 5:12: "Sin came into the world *through one man*, and death came through sin, and so death spread to all because all have sinned." Augustine understood this "because" (Gk. *eph' hō*/Lat. *in quo*) as a relative clause: "in quo omnes peccaverunt"—"in him [i.e., in Adam] all have sinned." Cf. Häring, *Macht des Bösen*, 221ff.

209. H*M* 198 (with reference to Neander).

210. Cf. Dumitru Staniloae, *Orthodoxe Dogmatik* 1:379–416.

211. The theologoumenon of the fall of the angels also existed in Western theology but did not play the same role in the doctrine of original (inherited) sin. In the modern Western discussion the topic is no longer treated; cf., e.g., Urs Baumann, *Erbsünde?*

212. The conviction of the "natural incapability of redemption" was generally Gnostic; cf. Barbara Aland, "Marcion," 434ff., and Schottroff, "Animae naturaliter salvandae."

213. Gk. *eikōn* and *homoiōsis*.

214. Cf. Paul Evdokimov, *L'Orthodoxie*, 77–85; Vladimir Lossky, *A l'image et à la ressemblance de Dieu* (ET: 1974).

215. The cooperative work of God and humankind; in Evdokimov and others designated by the (unfortunately sexist) term *theandrism* (from *theos*, "God," and *anēr*, "man"): occasionally one also finds *theanthropism;* in German, *Gottmenschentum*. Cf. Evdokimov, *L'Orthodoxie*, 13ff.; Vladimir Solovjev, *Vorlesungen über das Gottmenschentum;* Sergei Bulgakov, *Die christliche Anthropologie;* Dimitru Staniloae, *Orthodoxe Dogmatik* 2:232–88.

216. Rhodo in Euseb. *Ch.Hist.* 5.13.5. Harnack always refers only to the first half of the sentence, the "saying on the cross"; cf. H*M* 182ff.; similarly, MA 22, and Barbara Aland, "Marcion," 443 (but she mentions the last clause in a footnote).

217. This conceptuality, which has its roots in the apophatic tradition of the Eastern church, was developed in the 14th cent. in the so-called Palamite crisis; cf. John Meyendorff, *Introduction à l'étude de Grégoire Palamas* (Eng. trans.: New York, 1974); Staniloae, *Orthodoxe Dogmatik*, 137–255 (*energeiai* is inaccurately rendered as "Werke"); Dorothea Wendebourg, *Geist oder Energie*.

218. Cf. Jensen, "Wie patriarchalisch ist die Ostkirche?" esp. 141ff.

219. Anastasios Kallis, *Orthodoxie*, 54.

220. MA 24.

221. Cf. Jensen, *Die Zukunft der Orthodoxie*, 168.

Epilogue

1. Klaus Thraede, s.v. "Frau," *RAC* 8:265.

2. Cf. Gregory of Nyssa *The Life of St. Macrina,* as well as the often cited monograph by Ruth Albrecht, *Das Leben der heiligen Makrina.*

3. Let it be remembered that I understand "equality" here not in the sense of an "egalitarianism" but, as already noted in the Introduction, as the "brotherly-sisterly equality of all people in the sense of the gospel." Thus equality stands opposed not to legitimate authority but to the authoritarian exercise of power.

4. An allusion to the discussion that was stimulated by an article by Christina Thürmer-Rohr: "Aus der Täuschung in die Ent-Täuschung."

5. Cf. Introduction.

BIBLIOGRAPHY

Explanatory Notes

1. Under each source the first listing is a critical edition of the original (with a German, English, or French translation); then further important editions or translations are given. The names of editors, commentators, and translators are given as a rule only when they are cited in the work.

2. Collections of sources are given in part II under their titles and marked with an asterisk (★).

3. Monographs are listed by author; collected works by title.

4. Double family names are listed by the *second* name (thus Elisabeth *Schüssler Fiorenza* appears under "F").

5. Given names are indicated whenever possible, because it is relevant whether a book is written by a man or a woman. Moreover, the use of initials contributes to making women invisible as authors.

I. Sources

The Acts of Christ's Holy Apostle and Martyr Thecla and Her Miracles.
Gk./Fr.: *Vie et miracles de Sainte Thècle,* ed. Gilbert Dagron, with the collaboration of Marie Dupre la tour. Subsidia Hagiographica 62. Brussels, 1978.

Ambrose. *Concerning Virginity (De virginitate).*
Lat.: ed. Egnatius Cazzaniga. Corpus Scriptorum Latinorum Paravianum 47. Turin, 1954.
Fr.: "De la Virginité." In *Ecrits sur la virginité,* ed. Marie-Gabriel Tissot. Solesmes, 1980.
———. *Concerning Virgins (De virginibus).*
Lat.: ed. Egnatius Cazzaniga. Corpus Scriptorum Latinorum Paravianum 1. Turin, 1948.
Fr.: "Des Vierges." In *Ecrits* (see above).
Eng.: "Concerning Virgins." NPNF 2nd series, 10.
Ger.: BKV 32, 1917.
———. *Concerning Widows (De viduis).*
Lat.: *PL* 16:247–78.
Fr.: "Exhortation aux Veuves" In *Ecrits* (see above).
Eng.: "Concerning Widows." NPNF 2nd series, 10.
———. *On the Instruction of a Virgin (De institutitone virginis et S. Mariae virginitate perpetua).*
Lat.: *PL* 16:319–48.
Fr.: "De l'instruction d'une viergè." In *Ecrits* (see above).
———. *Exhortation of Virginity (De exhortatione virginitatis).*
Lat.: *PL* 16:347–80.
Fr.: "Exhortation à la virginité." *Ecrits* (see above).

———. *Letters.*
Lat.: CSEL 82/1, 3 (2 has not yet appeared). 1968, 1983.
Eng.: FaCh 26.

Apocrypha.
Gk.: *Acta Apostolorum Apocrypha,* ed. Ricardus Adelbertus Lipsius and Maximilianus Bonnet, 3 vols. 1891/1898/1903, repr. 1959. Cf. also: Richard Adelbert Lipsius, *Die apokryphen Apostelgeschichten und Apostellegenden: Ein Beitrag zur altchristlichen Literaturgeschichte* (I, II/1 + 2, supl. vols.), 1883/1887/1884/1890.
Gk.: *Apocrypha anecdota: A Collection of thirteen apocryphal Books and Fragments,* ed. Montague Rhodes James. 2 vols. Cambridge, 1893, repr. 1967.
Gk./Lat./Fr.: *Les Apocryphes du Nouveau Testament,* ed. Joseph Bousquet and Emile Amann. Vol. 1, *Le protévangile de Jacques,* ed. Emile Amann. Vol. 2, *Les actes de Paul et ses lettres apocryphes,* ed. Léon Vouaux. Vol. 3, *Les actes de Pierre,* ed. Léon Vouaux. Paris, 1910/1913/1922.
Syr./Eng.: *The Apocryphal Acts of the Apostles: Edited from Syriac Manuscripts in the British Museum and other Libraries with English Translation and Notes,* ed. William Wright. 2 vols. London, 1871, repr. 1968.
Fr.: *Evangiles Apocryphes,* ed. Paul Peeters. Paris, 1914.
Eng.: *The Apocryphal New Testament: Apocryphal Gospels, Acts, Epistles, and Apocalypses with other Narratives and Fragments Newly Translated,* ed. Montague Rhodes James. Oxford, 1924, repr. 1953 (corrected).
Eng.: *New Testament Apocrypha,* ed. Wilhelm Schneemelcher. Vol. 1, *Gospels and Related Writings.* Rev. ed., Cambridge-Louisville, Ky., 1991. Vol. 2, *Writings Relating to the Apostles; Apocalypses and Related Subjects.* Rev. ed., Cambridge-Louisville, Ky., 1992.
Ger.: *Neutestamentliche Apokryphen,* ed. Wilhelm Schneemelcher. Vol. 1, *Evangelien.* 5th ed. Tübingen, 1987. Vol. 2, *Apostolisches, Apokalypsen und Verwandtes.* Tübingen, 1989.

Apophthegmata.
Gk.: *PG* 65:71–440.
Eng.: *The Sayings of the Desert Fathers: The Alphabetical Collection,* ed. Benedicta Ward. London-Oxford, 1975.
Ger.: *Weisung der Väter: Apophthegmata Patrum, auch Gerontikon oder Alphabeticum genannt,* introduced and translated by Bonifaz Miller. Sophia 6. Freiburg, 1965.

Apostolic Constitutions.
Gk./Fr.: *Les Constitutions Apostoliques,* ed. Marcel Metzger. Vols. 1–2, SC 320, 1985. Vols. 3–6, SC 329, 1986. Vols. 7–8, SC 336, 1987.
Gk./Lat.: *Didascalia et Constitutiones Apostolorum,* ed. Franz Xaver Funk, 2 vols. 1905. Cf. also Franz Xaver Funk. *Die Apostolischen Konstitutionen: Eine litterarisch-historische Untersuchung.* Rottenburg, 1891.
Ger.: BKV. 1874.

Apostolic Tradition. *See* **Hippolytus.**

Athanasius. *Apology for Those Who Reproach Him for His Flight from Persecution (Apologia de fuga sua)*
Gk.: "Apologien." In *Werke* 2/1, ed. Hans-Georg Opitz. Berlin-Leipzig, 1935–41.
Gk./Fr.: *Deux apologies (A l'empereur Constance; Pour sa fuite).* SC 56 bis. 1987.
———. *History of the Arians.*
Gk.: "Historia Arianorum." *Werke* 2/1, ed. Hans-Georg Opitz. Berlin-Leipzig, 1935–41.

314 Bibliography

Augustine. *Works.*

Lat./Fr.: *Edition complète des oeuvres de Saint Augustin en 85 volumes environ, réparties en dix séries* (not yet complete).

―――. The following ascetic treatises in *Oeuvres* (see above), first series: *Opuscules, II. Problèmes Moraux,* ed. Gustave Combes. Paris, 1948. *III. L'Ascétisme Chrétien,* ed. J. Saint-Martin. Paris, 1949.

―――. *Against Heresies.*

Lat.: *De haeresibus.* CCSL 46. 1969.

―――. *City of God.*

Lat.: *De civitate Dei.* CCSL 47/48. 1955.

Ger.: BKV. 1911.

―――. *Easter Sermons.*

Lat./Fr.: *Sermons pour la Pâque,* ed. Suzanne Poque. SC 116. 1966.

―――. *On Adulterous Unions.*

Lat.: *De adulterinis coniugiis* 1–2. CSEL 41. 1900.

Ger.: *Die ehebrecherischen Verbindungen.* Würzburg, 1949.

―――. *On Continence.*

Lat.: *De continentia.* CSEL 41. 1900.

Ger.: *Die Enthaltsamkeit.* Würzburg, 1949.

―――. *On the Good of Marriage.*

Lat.: *De bono coniugali.* CSEL 41. 1900.

Ger.: *Das Gut der Ehe.* Würzburg, 1949.

―――. *On the Good of Widowhood.*

Lat.: *De bono viduitatis.* CSEL 41. 1900.

Ger.: *Das Gut der Witwenschaft.* Würzburg, 1952.

―――. *On Holy Virginity.*

Lat.: *De sancta virginitate.* CSEL 41. 1900.

Ger.: *Heilige Jungfräulichkeit.* Würzburg, 1952.

―――. *Treatise on the Gospel of John.*

Lat.: *Tractatus in Joannis evangelium.* CCSL 36, 1954.

Ger.: BKV 19. 1914.

Books of Jeu. See *Pistis Sophia.*

Canons, Apostolic.

Gk./Lat./Fr.: *Les canons des conciles oecuméniques; Les canons des synodes particuliers; Les canons des Pères grecs,* ed. Périclès-Pierre Joannou. Fonti IX, t. I,1/2 and II. Grottaferrata (Rome), 1962/1963.

[Ecclesiastical] Canons of the Holy Apostles

Gk. in Theodor Schermann. *Die allgemeine Kirchenordnung* 1:12–34 (see Bibl. II).

John Chrysostom. *Works.*

Fr.: *Oeuvres Complètes,* ed. Jean Bareille. Paris, 1864–78.

―――. *Instruction and Reproach of Those Cohabiting with Virgins on How to Preserve Virginity.*

Gk./Fr.: *Les cohabitations suspectes/Comment observer la virginité,* ed. Jean Dumortier. Paris, 1955.

Eng.: "Instruction and Refutation Directed against Those Men Cohabiting with Virgins/On the Necessity of Guarding Virginity." In Clark, *Jerome* (see Bibl. II).

Ger.: "Gegen jene (Mönche), welche Jungfrauen in's Haus aufnehmen und als Schwestern bei sich wohnen lassen/Dass gottgeweihte Jungfrauen nicht mit Männern zusammenleben sollen." In *Ascetische Schriften,* ed. Jakob Fluck. Freiburg, 1866.

————. *Letters to Olympias.*

Gk./Fr.: *Lettres à Olympias/Vie anonyme d'Olympias,* ed. Anne-Marie Malingrey. SC 13 bis. 1968.

————. *On Virginity.*

Gk./Fr.: *La Virginité,* ed. Herbert Musurillo and Bernard Grillet. SC 125. 1966.

Eng.: *On Virginity,* ed. Sally Rieger Shore and Elizabeth A. Clark. Studies in Women and Religion 9. Lewiston, N.Y., 1983.

Ger.: "Von dem jungfräulichen Stande." In *Ascetische Schriften* (see above).

————. *To a Young Widow.*

Gk./Fr.: *A une jeune veuve,* ed. Bernard Grillet and Gérard H. Ettlinger. SC 138. 1968.

Eng.: "Against Remarriage." In *On Virginity* (see above).

Ger.: "An eine junge Witwe." In *Ascetische Schriften* (see above).

————. *Speech on Babylas and Against the Greeks.*

Gk./Fr.: *Discours sur Babylas/Homélie sur Babylas.* SC 362. 1990.

Clement of Alexandria. *Works.*

Gk.: BEP 7/8. 1956.

————. *Paidagogos.*

Gk./Fr.: *Le Pédagogue* 1–3, SC 70/108/158. 1960/1965/1970.

Ger.: BKV II, 7/8. 1934.

————. *Stromateis.*

Gk.: *Stromata* 1–6, GCS (no volume indication), 4th ed., 1985.; 7–8, GCS 17, 2nd ed., 1970.

Gk./Fr.: *Les Stromates* 1, SC 30, 1951; 2, SC 38, 1958; 5, SC 278/279, 1981.

Ger.: BKV II, 17/19/20. 1936/1937/1938.

Codex Justinianus. See *Corpus Juris Civilis.*

Codex Theodosianus.

Lat.: ed. Theodor Mommsen and Paul Krüger. Berlin, 1905.

Corpus Juris Civilis.

Gk./Lat.: I, *Institutiones/Pandectae,* ed. Paul Krüger and Theodor Mommsen. Berlin, 1905. II, *Codex Justinianus,* ed. Paul Krüger. Berlin, 1900. III, *Novellae,* ed. Rudolf Schoell and Wilhelm Kroll. Berlin, 1904.

Ger.: ed. Carl Eduard Otto, Bruno Schilling, and Carl Friedrich Ferdinand Sintenis, 9 vols. Leipzig, 1830–39.

Cyprian of Carthage. *Works.*

Lat.: *Opera omnia,* ed. Wilhelm Hartel. CSEL 3/1–3.

Ger.: *Sämtliche Schriften.* BKV 34, 1918, and 60, 1928.

————. *Letters.*

Eng.: ed. Graeme W. Clarke. ACW 43/44/46/47. 1984–89.

Lat. and Ger.: see above.

————. *On Mortality.*

Eng.: *On the Mortality.* ANF 5.

Lat. and Ger.: see above.

Cyril of Jerusalem. *Catecheses.*

Gk./Fr.: SC 126. Paris, 1966.

Eng.: *Catechetical Lectures.* NPNF 2nd series, 7.

Ger.: BKV 41. 1922.

Damascius. *The Life of Isidore.*
Gk.: *Damascii vitae Isidori reliquiae,* ed. Clemens Zintzen. Hildesheim, 1967.
Ger.: *Das Leben des Philosophen Isidoros,* ed. Rudolf Asmus. Philosophische Bibliothek, n.s., 125. Leipzig, 1911.

Didache.
Gk./Ger.: in *Didache, Barnabasbrief, Zweiter Klemensbrief, Schrift an Diognet,* ed. Klaus Wengst. Schriften des Urchristentums 2. Darmstadt, 1984.
Gk./Ger.: *Zwölf-Apostel-Lehre,* ed. Georg Schöllgen. FaCh 1. 1991.
Ger. (with comments by section): Kurt Niederwimmer. *Die Didache.* Kommentar zu den Apostolischen Vätern 1. Göttingen, 1989.
Gk./Fr.: ed. Willy Rordorf and André Tuilier. SC 248. Paris, 1978.

Didascalia.
Gk./Lat.: *Didascalia et Constitutiones Apostolorum* 1/2, ed. Franz Xaver Funk. 1905.
Eng.: *Didascalia Apostolorum: The Syriac Version translated and accompanied by the Verona Latin Fragments,* ed. R. Hugh Connolly. Oxford, 1929.
Syr./Eng.: *The Didascalia Apostolorum in Syriac,* ed. Arthur Vööbus. CSCO, 1979, vols. 401/2, 407/8, tom. 175/6, 178/9.
Ger.: *Die syrische Didaskalia,* ed. Hans Achelis and Johannes Flemming. TU 25, n.s., 10. 1904.

Didymus of Alexandria. *On the Trinity.*
Gk.: *PG* 39:269–992 (complete).
Gk./Ger.: *De trinitate* I, ed. Jürgen Hönscheid. BKP 44. *De trinitate* II, 1–7, ed. Ingrid Seiler. BKP 52. 1975 (incomplete).

Discussion of a Montanist and an Orthodox.
Gk.: ed. Gerhard Ficker. *ZKG* 26 (1905): 449–63.
Gk./Fr.: *LS* 93–108.

Egeria. *Pilgrim Journey.*
Gk./Fr.: *Egérie, Journal de voyage,* ed. Pierre Maraval. SC 296. Paris, 1982.
Eng.: ed. Patricia Wilson-Kastner. In *A Lost Tradition* (see Bibl. II), 71–134.
Ger.: *Die Pilgerreise der Aetheria,* ed. Hélène Pétré, trans. Karl Vretska. Vienna, 1958.

Epiphanius of Salamis. *Ancoratus (Ankyrotos).*
Gk.: GCS 25. 1915.
Ger.: *Der Festgeankerte.* BKV 38. 1919.
―――. *Panarion.*
Gk.: ed. Karl Holl. GCS 25/31/37. 1915/1922/1933. 2nd expanded ed., ed. Jürgen Dummer. 1980/1985.
Eng.: ed. Frank Williams. *The Panarion,* Book I (sections 1–46). Leiden, 1987.
Eng.: ed. Philip R. Amidon. *The Panarion of St. Epiphanius, Bishop of Salamis: Selected Passages.* Oxford-New York, 1990.
―――. *Summary (Anakephalaiosis/Recapitulatio).*
Gk.: *PG* 42:833–86.
Ger.: BKV 38. 1919.

Eudocia. *The Acts of St. Cyprian and St. Justina.*
Gk. in Theodor Zahn. *Cyprian von Antiochien und die deutsche Faustsage,* 139–53 (only book 1). Erlangen, 1882.

Eng.: in *A Lost Tradition* (see Bibl. II), 135–71.
Ger. in Theodor Zahn (see above), 21–72.

Eusebius of Caesarea. *Church History.*
Gk./Fr.: *Histoire Ecclésiastique,* ed. Gustave Bardy. 1–4, SC 31, 1978. 5–7, SC 41, 1955. 8–10
 and "Les martyrs en Paléstine," SC 55, 1984. "Introduction" (Gustave Bardy) and "Index"
 (Pierre Perichon), SC 73 bis, 1971.
Eng.: *The History of the Church from Christ to Constantine.* Trans. G. A. Williamson. Baltimore:
 Penguin, 1965.
Ger.: *Des Eusebius Pamphili Bischofs von Cäsarea Kirchengeschichte.* BKV 2/1. 1932 (revision by
 Hans Arnim Gärtner, Munich, 1981).
———. *The Life of Constantine.*
Gk.: *PG* 20:909–1232.
Eng.: NPNF 2nd series, 1.
Ger.: BKV 9. 1913.
———. *Martyrs in Palestine.*
Gk./Fr.: *Les martyrs en Paléstine,* ed. Gustave Bardy. SC 55. 1984.
Ger.: BKV 9. 1913.

4 Ezra *(Liber Ezrae quartus).*
Lat.: *Der lateinische Text der Apokalypse des Esra,* ed. A. Frederik J. Klijn. TU 131. 1983.
Ger.: *Der Prophet Esra,* ed. Hermann Gunkel. Tübingen, 1900.

Gregory of Nyssa. *The Life of St. Macrina.*
Gk./Fr.: *Vie de Sainte Macrine,* ed. Pierre Maraval. SC 178. 1971.
Ger.: BKV 56. 1927.
———. *On Virginity.*
Gk./Fr.: *Traité de la Virginité,* ed. Michel Aubineau. SC 119. 1966.
Ger.: ed. Wilhelm Blum. Bibliothek der griechischen Literatur 7. Stuttgart, 1977.

Hermas. *The Shepherd.*
Gk./Fr.: *Le Pasteur,* ed. Robert Joly. SC 53 bis. 1986.
Ger.: *Der Hirt des Hermas.* BKV 35. 1918.
Ger.: *Der Hirt des Hermas,* ed. Norbert Brox. Kommentar zu den Apostolischen Vätern 7. 1991.

Hippolytus of Rome. *Works.*
Gk.: BEP 5/6. 1955/1956.
———. *Apostolic Tradition.*
Lat./Gk./Ger.: *Apostolische Überlieferung,* ed. Wilhelm Geerlings. FaCh 1. 1991.
Gk./Fr.: *La Tradition Apostolique,* ed. Bernard Botte. SC 11 bis. 1984. 5th ed., corrected and
 edited by Albert Gerhards in collaboration with Sabine Felbecker: Bernard Botte, *La Tra-
 dition apostolique de Saint Hippolyte: Essai de reconstitution.* Liturgiewissenschaftliche Quellen
 und Forschungen 39. Münster, 1989.
Copt./Ger.: Der koptische Text der Kirchenordnung Hippolyts, ed. Walter Till and Johannes
 Leipoldt, TU 58. 1954.
Eth./Ger.: *Der aethiopische Text der Kirchenordnung des Hippolyt,* ed. Hugo Duensing. Abhandlungen der Akademie der Wissenschaften in Göttingen, Philologisch-Historische Klasse 3,
 32. Göttingen, 1946.
———. *Commentary on Daniel.*
Gk.: GCS (1), without volume indication. 1897.

Fr.: *Commentaire sur Daniel.* SC 14. 1947 (new Gk./Fr. edition in preparation).
————. *Commentary on Song of Songs.*
Ger.: ed. Nathanael Bonwetsch. TU, n.s., 8. 1903.
————. *Refutation of All Heresies (Philosophumena).*
Gk.: *Refutatio omnium haeresium,* ed. Miroslav Markovich. PTS 25. 1986.
Eng.: *The Refutation of All Heresies.* ANF 5.
Fr.: *Philosophumena ou Réfutation de toutes les hérésies,* ed. A. Siouville. Milan, 1988.
Ger.: BKV 40. 1922.

Ignatius of Antioch. *Letters.*
Gk./Ger.: in *Die Apostolischen Väter,* ed. Joseph A. Fischer. Schriften des Urchristentums 1.
    Darmstadt, 1981.

Irenaeus of Lyon. *Against Heresies (Adversus omnes haereses).*
Gk./Fr.: *Contre les Hérésies.* 1, SC 263/264, 1979. 2, SC 293/294, 1982. 3, SC 210/211, 1974.
    4, SC 100, 1965. 5, SC 152/153, 1969.
Ger.: *Gegen die Häresien,* BKV 3/4. 1912.

Isidore of Seville. *Etymologies (Origines).*
Lat.: *Etymologiarum libri XX.* PL 82.
————. *On Illustrious Men.*
Lat.: *De viris illustribus,* ed. Carmen Codoñer Merino. Salamanca, 1964.

Jerome. *Letters.*
Lat.: ed. Isidorus Hilberg. CSEL 54/56. 1910/1918.
Eng.: NPNF 2nd series, 6; ACW 33 (letters 1–22), 1963.
Ger.: *Ausgewählte Briefe.* BKV II, 16/18. 1936/1937.
————. *On Illustrious Men.*
Lat.: *De viris illustribus.* PL 23:631–766.
Eng.: *Lives of Illustrious Men.* NPNF 2nd series, 3.
————. *On the Perpetual Virginity of Mary: Against Helvidius.*
Lat.: *De perpetua virginitate beatae Mariae adversus Helvidium.* PL 23:193–216.
Ger.: BKV 15. 1914.

Josephus, Flavius. *Antiquities of the Jews.*
Gk.: *Antiquitates Judaicae,* ed. Benedictus Niese. Marburg, 1887–96.
Ger.: ed. Heinrich Clementz. 5th ed. 1983.

Julian. *Works.*
Gk./Eng.: *The Works of the Emperor Julian,* ed. Wilmer Cave Wright. 3 vols. London, 1913/23.
————. *Letters.*
Gk./Ger.: *Briefe,* ed. Bertold K. Weis. Munich, 1973.

Justin. *Works.*
Gk.: BEP 3/4. 1955.
————. *Apologies.*
Gk: *PG* 6:327–470; BEP 3. 1955.
Ger.: ed. Gerhard Rauschen. BKV 12. 1913.
————. *Dialogue with Trypho.*
Gk.: *PG* 6:471–800; BEP 3. 1955.
Eng.: ANF 1.
Ger.: BKV 33. 1917.

Justinian. See *Corpus Juris Civilis.*

The Life of Macrina. See **Gregory of Nyssa.**

The Life of Melanie the Younger
Gk./Lat.: *Vitae Melaniae Junioris: Santa Melania Giuniore, senatrice romana: documente contemporei e note,* ed. Mariano del Tindaro Rampolla. Rome, 1905.
Gk./Fr.: *Vie de Sainte Mélanie.* SC 90. 1962.
Eng.: *The Life of Melanie the Younger,* ed. Elizabeth Clark. Studies in Women and Religion 14. New York-Toronto, 1984.
Ger.: BKV 5. 1912.

The Life of Nino.
Eng.: "St. Nino and the Conversion of Georgia." In *Lives and Legends of the Georgian Saints,* ed. David Marshall Lang, 13–39. London, 1956.
Ger.: "Die Bekehrung Georgiens, Mokcevay Kartlisay," ed. Gertrud Pätsch. In *Bedi Kartlisa, revue de Kartvélologie* 33:288–337. Paris, 1975.

The Life of the Deaconess Olympias.
Gk./Fr.: *Vie anonyme d'Olympias,* ed. Anne-Marie Malangrey. SC 13 bis. 1968.
Eng.: "The Life of Olympias." In Clark, *Jerome* (see Bibl. II).

The Life of the Holy and Blessed Teacher Synkletike.
Gk.: *PG* 28:1485–1558.
Fr.: *Vie de Sainte Synclétique,* ed. Odile B. Bermard. Spiritualité Orientale 9. Abbaye de Bellefontaine, 1972.

The Life of Thecla. See *The Acts.*

The Lives of Xanthippe, Polyxena, and Rebecca.
Gk.: *Acta Xanthippae et Polyxenae,* ed. Montague Rhodes James. In *Apocrypha anecdota* 1. Text and Studies II, 3. Cambridge, 1893.
Eng.: "The Acts of Xanthippe and Polyxena." In ANF 10. 1980.
(For the early church lives of other women cf. Ruth Albrecht, *Das Leben des Heiligen Makrina,* 426–27 [see Bibl. II].)

Macrina. *See* **Gregory of Nyssa.**

The Martyrdom of Perpetua and Felicity.
Gk./Lat.: *Passio Sanctarum Perpetuae et Felicitatis,* ed. Cornelius van Beek. Nijmegen, 1936 (Latin version with Greek translation and a collection of quotations from the church fathers); ed. Cornelius van Beek. Florilegium Patristicum 43. Bonn, 1938. (For further editions and translations see the collections of acts of martyrs [except Hugo Rahner] mentioned below.)

Martyrs, Acts of.
Lat.: *Acta primorum martyrum sincera et selecta,* ed. Theodoricus Ruinart. Paris, 1689: repr. Regensburg, 1859.
Gk./Lat./Eng.: *The Acts of the Christian Martyrs,* ed. Herbert Musurillo. Oxford, 1972.
Gk./Eng.: *The Acts of the Pagan Martyrs: Acta Alexandrinorum,* ed. Herbert Musurillo. Oxford, 1954.
Gk./Lat.: Guiseppe Lazzati. *Gli sviluppi.* See Bibl. II.
Gk./Lat./Ital.: *Atti e passioni dei martiri,* ed. Antonius Adrianus Robertus Bastiensen et al. Arnoldo Mondadori editore. 1987.

Fr.: Henri Leclerq. *Les Martyrs* I. See Bibl. II.

Ger.: *Echte alte Märtyrerakten,* ed. Gerhard Rauschen. BKV 14, 1913. *Ausgewählte Akten persischer Märtyrer,* ed. Oskar Braun. BKV 22. 1915.

Fr.: *La geste du sang,* ed. Henry Daniel-Rops and Adalbert Hamman. Paris, 1953. Ger.: *Das Heldentum der frühen Martyrer.* Aschaffenburg, 1958.

Gk./Lat.: *Ausgewählte Märtyrerakten,* ed. Gustav Krüger and Gerhard Ruhbach (revision of the Knopf edition). 4th ed. Tübingen, 1965.

Ger.: *Ich bin Christ: Frühchristliche Märtyrerakten,* ed. Oda Hagemeyer. Düsseldorf, 1961.

Ger.: *Die Märtyrerakten des 2. Jahrhunderts,* ed. Hugo Rahner. Zeugen des Wortes 18. Freiburg, 1953.

Melanie. See **Life of.**

Nag Hammadi Codices.

Copt.: *The Facsimile Edition of the Nag Hammadi Codices.* Leiden, 1972ff.

Eng.: *The Nag Hammadi Library in English,* ed. James M. Robinson. 3rd ed. Leiden/Cologne, 1988.

Nino. See **Life of.**

Olympias. See **Life of.**

Origen. *Against Celsus.*

Gk./Fr.: *Contre Celse,* ed. Marcel Borret, 1–2, SC 132, 1967; 3–4, SC 136, 1968; 5–6, SC 147, 1969; 7–8, SC 150, 1969; Introduction, Index, SC 227, 1976.

Eng.: ed. Henry Chadwick. Cambridge, 1953.

Ger.: *Gegen Celsus* 1–4, BKV 52, 1926; 5–8, BKV 53, 1927.

―――. *Commentary on Romans.*

Lat./Ger.: ed. Theresia Heither (books 1 and 2). FCh 2/1. 1990.

―――. *On Matthew.*

Gk.: GCS 38 (Comm. ser.), 1933; GCS 40 (10–17), 1935; BEP 13/14, 1957/1958.

Gk./Fr.: *Commentaire sur l'évangile selon Matthieu,* 10 + 11. SC 162. 1970.

Ger.: *Der Kommentar zum Evangelium nach Matthäus,* ed. Hermann-Josef Vogt, 10–13, BGL 18, 1983; 14–17, BGL 30, 1990.

Palladius. *Dialogue on the Life of St. John Chrysostom.*

Gk.: ed. P. R. Coleman-Norton. Cambridge, 1928.

Gk./Fr.: *Dialogue sur la vie de Jean Chrysostome.* SC 341, 342. 1988.

―――. *Paradise (Historia Lausiaca).*

Gk.: *The Lausiac History of Palladius* I/II, ed. Cuthbert Butler. 1898 (repr. Hildesheim, 1967).

Gk./Fr.: *Histoire Lausiaque (Vies d'ascètes et de Pères du désert),* ed. A. Lucot. TeD 15. Paris, 1912.

Eng.: *The Lausiac History,* ed. Robert T. Meyer. ACW 34. 1965.

Ger.: *Des Palladius Leben der Heiligen Väter.* BKV 5. 1912; *Historia Lausiaca: Die frühen Heiligen in der Wüste,* ed. Jacques Laager. Zurich, 1987.

Philo. *On the Contemplative Life.*

Gk./Fr.: *De vita contemplativa,* ed. François Daumas and Pierre Miquel. Les oeuvres de Philon d'Alexandrie 29. Paris, 1963.

Gk./Eng.: "On the contemplative life or suppliants." In *Philo* 10, ed. F. H. Colson. London, 1941 (repr. 1960).

Ger.: "Über das betrachtende Leben oder die Schutzflehenden." In *Die Werke in deutscher Übersetzung,* ed. Leopold Cohn, Isaak Heinemann, Maximilian Adler, and Willy Theiler, 7:44–70. Berlin, 1964.

Pistis Sophia (and *Books of Jeu*).
Gk.: ed. Carl Schmidt. GCS 13. 1905.
Ger.: *NA* 1:290–300 (excerpts).

Pliny. *Letters.*
Lat./Ger.: ed. Helmut Kasten. Schriften und Quellen der Alten Welt 35. Munich, 1982.

Polyxena. See *The Lives of Xanthippe, Polyxena, and Rebecca.*

Proba (Faltonia Betitia). *Cento.*
Lat.: *Probae Cento,* ed. Carolus Schenkl. CSEL 16 (Poetae Christiani Minores I), 511–609. Vienna, 1888.
Lat./Ital.: *Il centone di Proba Petronia,* ed. Caterina Carridi. Naples, 1971.
Lat./Eng.: *The Golden Bough, the Oaken Cross: The Virgilian Cento of Faltonia Betitia Proba,* ed. Elizabeth A. Clark and Diane F. Hatch. American Academy of Religion, Texts and Translations Series 5. Chico, Calif., 1981.
Eng.: in *A Lost Traditon* (see Bibl. II).

Ptolemy. *Letter to Flora* (= Epiphanius, *Panarion* 33:3–7).
Gk./Fr.: *Lettre à Flora,* ed. Gilles Quispel. SC 24 bis. 1966.
Eng.: Epiphanius, *Panarion* (see above)

Rebecca. See *The Lives of Xanthippe, Polyxena, and Rebecca.*

Rufinus. *Church History.*
Lat.: *Historia Ecclesiastica.* GCS 9/1–2. 1903/1909.
Ital.: *Storia della Chiesa,* ed. Lorenzo Dattrino. Rome, 1986.
————. *The History of Monks.*
Lat.: *Historia Monachorum,* ed. Eva Schulz-Flügel. PTS 34. 1990.

Sibylline Oracles.
Gk.: ed. Johannes Geffcken. GCS 8. 1902, repr. 1967.
Gk./Ger.: ed. Alfons Kurfess. Munich, 1951.

Socrates. *Church History.*
Gk.: *PG* 67:33–842.
Eng.: *Church History,* ed. A. C. Zenos. NPNF 2nd series, 2.

Sozomen. *Church History.*
Gk.: Joseph Bidez. GCS 50. 1960.
Gk./Fr.: *Histoire Ecclésiastique,* ed. André-Jean Festugière; Introduction: Bernard Grillet and Guy Sabbah, books I–II. SC 306. 1983.
Eng.: *Church History,* ed. Chester D. Hartranft. NPNF 2nd series, 2.

Synesius of Cyrene. *Letters.*
Gk.: *Epistolae,* ed. Antonius Garzya. Rome, 1979.
Eng.: *The Letters of Synesius of Cyrene,* ed. Augustine Fitzgerald. Oxford, 1926.

Synkletike. See *The Life of . . . Synkletike.*

Synod of Gangra.
Gk./Fr.: Joannou (see **Canons**), t. 1.2, 83–99.

Tacitus. *Annals.*
Lat./Ger.: *Annalen,* ed. Erich Heller. Munich-Zurich, 1982.
Eng.: *The Annals of Imperial Rome.* Trans. Michael Grant. Harmondsworth, England, 1973.

Tatian. *Oration to the Greeks.*
Gk.: BEP 4. 1955.
Gk./Eng.: *Oratio ad Graecos,* ed. Molly Whittaker. Oxford, 1982.
Ger.: *Rede an die Bekenner des Griechentums.* BKV 12. 1913.

Tertullian. *Works.*
Lat.: CCSL 1/2. 1954.
Ger.: *Sämtliche Schriften,* trans. Karl Ad. H. Kellner. 2 vols. Cologne, 1882. Also BKV 7, 1912,
and 24, 1915.

In the following only writings in other editions are given:
————. *Adversus Marcionem.*
Eng.: *Against Marcion.* ANF 3.
————. *Adversus Praxean.*
Eng.: *Against Praxeas.* ANF 3.
————. *Apology (Apologeticum).*
Lat./Ger.: ed. C. Becker. In *Mnemosyne.* Bibliotheca philologica Batavorum. 2nd ed. Leipzig-
Leiden, 1961.
————. *On Baptism (De baptismo).*
Lat./Fr.: *Traité du baptême,* ed. François Refoule. SC 35. 1952 (new edition in preparation).
————. *On Flight (De fuga in persecutione).*
Eng.: ANF 4.
————. *On Monogamy (De monogamia).*
Lat./Fr.: *Le mariage unique,* ed. Paul Mattei. SC 343. 1988.
————. *On Penitence (De paenitentia).*
Lat./Fr.: *La pénitence,* ed. Charles Munier. SC 316. 1984.
————. *On the Attire of Women (De cultu feminarum).*
Lat./Fr.: *La toilette de femmes,* ed. Marie Turcan. SC 173. 1971.
————. *On the Exhortation of Chastity (De exhortatione castitatis).*
Lat./Ger.: *Ermahnung zur Keuschheit,* ed. Hans-Veit Friedrich. Beiträge zur Altertumskunde 2.
Stuttgart, 1990.
Lat./Fr.: *Exhortation à la chasteté,* ed. Claude Moreschini. SC 319. 1985.
————. *On the Prescription against Heretics (De praescriptione haereticorum).*
Lat./Fr.: *De la prescription contre les hérétiques,* ed. François Refoule and Pierre de Labriolle. SC
46. 1957.
————. *On the Resurrection of the Dead (De resurectione mortuorum).*
Eng.: *On the Resurrection of the Flesh.* ANF 3.
————. *On the Soul (De anima).*
Lat.: ed. Jan H. Waszink. Amsterdam, 1947.
Ger.: ed. Jan H. Waszink. Zurich-Munich, 1980.
————. *On the Veiling of Virgins (De virginibus velandis).*
Lat./Ger.: *De virginibus velandis,* ed. Christoph Stücklin. Frankfurt/Main, 1974.
————. *To His Wife (Ad uxorem)*
Lat./Fr.: *A son épouse,* ed. Charles Munier. SC 273. 1980.

The Testament of Our Lord Jesus Christ.
Syr./Lat.: *Testamentum Domini nostri Iesu Christi,* ed. Ignatius Ephraem Rahmani. Mainz, 1899.
Fr.: *La version syriaque de l'Octateuque de Clément,* translated by François Nau, reedited by Pio
Ciprotti. Paris, 1967.
Eng.: *The Testament of Our Lord,* ed. James Cooper and Arthur John Maclean. Edinburgh, 1902.
Copt./Fr.: *Testamentum Domini éthiopien,* ed. Robert Beylot. Louvain, 1984.

Thecla. See **The** *Acts* **of Christ's Holy Apostle** . . .

Theodore of Mopsuestia. *Catechetical Homilies.*
Copt./Fr.: *Les Homélies Catéchétiques,* ed. Raymond Tonneau and Robert Devreesse. Studi e Testi 145. Rome, 1949.

Theodoret. *Against Heresies.*
Gk.: *PG* 83:335–556 (Airetikēs kakomythias epitomē).
———. *Church History.*
Gk.: ed. Léon Parmentier. GCS 19. 1911; 2nd ed. revised by Felix Scheidweiler. GCS 44. 1954.
Eng.: *Church History,* ed. Blomfield Jackson. NPNF 2nd series, 3.
Ger.: *Des Bischofs Theodoret von Cyrus Kirchengeschichte,* ed. Andreas Seider. BKV 51. 1926.
———. *Letters.*
Gk.: *PG* 83:1171–1494.
Gk./Fr.: SC 40, 1955; SC 98, 1964; SC 111, 1965.
Eng.: *Theodoret, Jerome, Gennadius, Rufinus: Historical Writings.* NPNF 2nd series, 3.
———. *Religious History (Historia Religiosa).*
Gk./Fr.: *Histoire des Moines de Syrie,* ed. Pierre Canivet and Alice Leroy Molinghen. SC 234, 1977 and SC 257, 1979.
Ger.: *Des Bischofs Theodoret von Cyrus Mönchsgeschichte,* ed. Konstantin Gutberlet. BKV 50. 1926.

Theophilus of Antioch. *To Autolycus.*
Gk./Eng.: *Ad Autolycum,* ed. Robert M. Grant. Oxford, 1970.
Gk./Fr.: *Trois livres à Autolykus.* SC 20. 1948.
Ger.: BKV 14. 1913.

Xanthippe. See **The Lives of.**

II. Secondary Literature

Achelis, Hans. *Virgines subintroductae: Ein Beitrag zum 7. Kapitel des 1. Korintherbriefs.* Leipzig, 1902.
Les actes apocryphes des apôtres: Christianisme et monde païen, ed. François Bovon. Publications de la Faculté de Théologie de l'Université de Genève 4. Geneva, 1981.
Afanasiev, Nicolas. "Presbytides or Female Presidents." In *Women and the Priesthood,* ed. Thomas Hopko, 61–74. Crestwood, N.Y., 1983.
Aland, Barbara. "Marcion: Versuch einer neuen Interpretation." *ZTK* 70 (1973): 420–47.
Aland, Kurt. "Augustin und der Montanismus." In idem, *Kirchengeschichtliche Entwürfe,* 149–64. Gütersloh, 1960.
———. "Bemerkungen zum Montanismus und zur frühchristlichen Eschatologie." Ibid., 105–48.
Albrecht, Ruth. *Das Leben der heiligen Makrina auf dem Hintergrund der Thekla-Traditionen: Studien zu den Ursprüngen des weiblichen Mönchtums im 4. Jahrhundert in Kleinasien.* Forschungen zur Kirchen- und Dogmengeschichte 38. Göttingen, 1986.
Altaner, Bertold, and Alfred Stuiber. *Patrologie: Leben, Schriften und Lehre der Kirchenväter.* 8th ed. Freiburg, 1978.
Amat, Jacqueline. "L'authenticité des songes de la passion de Perpétue et de Félicité." In "Sogni, Visioni et Profezie," 177–91.
Andresen, Carl. "'Siegreiche Kirche' im Aufstieg des Christentums: Untersuchungen zu Eusebius von Caesarea und Dionys von Alexandrien." *ANRW* II.23.1, pp. 387–459.
Anson, John. "The Female Transvestite in Early Monasticism: The Origin and Development of a Motif." In *Viator,* 1–32. Medieval and Renaissance Studies 5. Berkeley-Los Angeles-London, 1974.

Antiquité Païenne et Chrétienne. Mémorial André-Jean Festugiere, ed. Enzo Lucchesi and Henry Dominique Saffrey. Cahiers d'Orientalisme 10. Geneva, 1984.

The Apocryphal Acts of the Apostles. Semeia 38. 1986.

Archiv für philosophie- und theologiegeschichtliche Frauenforschung [series], ed. Elisabeth Gössmann. Munich, 1984ff.

Ash, James L. "The Decline of Ecstatic Prophecy in the Early Church." *TS* 37 (1976): 227–52.

Atkinson, Clarissa W. "'Your Servant, My Mother': The Figure of Saint Monica in the Ideology of Christian Motherhood." In *Immaculate and Powerful,* 139–72.

Auf den Spuren der Weisheit: Sophia—Wegweiserin für ein weibliches Gottesbild, ed. Verena Wodtke. Freiburg-Basel-Vienna, 1991.

Augar, Friedrich. *Die Frau im römischen Christenprozess: Ein Beitrag zur Verfolgungsgeschichte der christlichen Kirche im römischen Reich.* TU 28. Leipzig, 1905.

Aune, David E. *Prophecy in Early Christianity and the Ancient Mediterranean World.* Grand Rapids, 1983.

Balsdon, Dacre. *Roman Women.* 5th ed. London, 1977.

Bangerter, Otto. *Frauen im Aufbruch: Die Geschichte einer Frauenbewegung in der Alten Kirche.* Neukirchen-Vluyn, 1971.

Bardy, Gustave. *Paul de Samosate.* Louvain-Paris, 1923.

Barnes, Timothy D. "Pre-Decian Acta Martyrum." *JTS,* n.s., 19 (1968): 509–31.

———. "The Chronology of Montanism." *JTS,* n.s., 21 (1970): 403–8.

———. *Tertullian: A Historical and Literary Study.* Oxford, 1971.

Bauer, Walter. *Rechtgläubigkeit und Ketzerei im ältesten Christentum.* Beiträge zur historischen Theologie 10. Tübingen, 1934 (2nd ed., revised by Georg Strecker, 1964).

Baumann, Urs. *Erbsünde? Ihr traditionelles Verständnis in der Krise heutiger Theologie.* Freiburg, 1970.

———. *Die Ehe—ein Sakrament?* Zurich, 1988.

Baumgardt, Ursula. *König Drosselbart und C. G. Jungs Frauenbild: Kritische Gedanken zu Anima und Animus.* Olten, 1987.

Beaucamp, Joëlle. *Le statut de la femme à Byzance (4e–7e siècle),* 1. "Le droit impérial." Travaux et mémoires du centre de recherche d'histoire et civilisation de Byzance, Collège de France, monographies 5. Paris, 1990.

Behr-Sigel, Elisabeth. *Le ministère de la femme dans l'Eglise.* Paris, 1987.

———. "Ordination von Frauen? Ein Versuch des Bedenkens einer aktuellen Frage im Lichte der lebendigen Tradition der orthodoxen Kirche." In *Warum keine Ordination der Frau?* 50–72.

Benko, Stephen. *Pagan Rome and the Early Christians.* Bloomington, Ind., 1986.

Benoit, André. *Saint Irénée: Introduction à l'étude de sa théologie.* Paris, 1960.

Bisbee, Gary A. *Pre-Decian Acts of Martyrs and Commentarii.* Harvard Dissertations in Religion 22. Philadelphia, 1988.

Blanchetiere, François. "Le Montanisme originel." *Revue des Sciences Religieuses* 52 (1978): 118–34, and 53 (1979): 1–22.

Bock, Gisela. "Historische Frauenforschung: Fragestellungen und Perspektiven." In *Frauen suchen ihre Geschichte: Historische Studien zum 19. und 20. Jahrhundert,* ed. Karin Hausen, 24–62. 2nd ed. Munich, 1987.

———. "Geschichte, Frauengeschichte, Geschlechtergeschichte." *Geschichte und Gesellschaft* 14 (1988): 364–91.

Boelens, Martin. *Die Klerikerehe in der Gesetzgebung der Kirche unter besonderer Berücksichtigung der Strafe: Eine rechtsgeschichtliche Untersuchung von den Anfängen der Kirche bis zum Jahre 1139.* Paderborn, 1968.

Böhlig, Alexander. *Gnosis und Synkretismus: Gesammelte Aufsätze zur spätantiken Religionsgeschichte,* part 1. Tübingen, 1989.

Bonwetsch, Nathanael. *Die Geschichte des Montanismus*. Erlangen, 1881.

Børresen, Kari Elisabeth. *Subordination and Equivalence: The Nature and Role of Women in Augustine and Thomas Aquinas*. Washington, D.C., 1981.

————. "Male/Female Typology in Church." *TD* 31 (1984): 23–26.

————. "Imago Dei, privilège masculin? Interprétation augustinienne et pseudo-augustinienne de Gen 1,27 et 1 Cor 11,7." *Aug* 25 (1985): 213–34.

————. "Women's Studies of the Christian Tradition" (survey of the literature). In *Contemporary Philosophy: A New Survey*, vol. 6, ed. Guttorm Floistad and Raymond Klibansky. Dordrecht-Boston-London, 1990.

See also *Image of God*.

Boswell, John. *Christianity, Social Tolerance, and Homosexuality*. Chicago, 1980.

————. *Rediscovering Gay History: Archetypes of Gay Love in Christian History* (Gay Christian Movement: The Fifth Michael Harding Memorial Address). London, 1982.

Brockmann, Doris. *Ganze Menschen—Ganze Götter: Kritik der Jung-Rezeption im Kontext feministisch-theologischer Theoriebildung*. Paderborn-Munich-Vienna-Zurich, 1991.

Brooten, Bernadette J. " 'Junia—hervorragend unter den Aposteln' (Röm 16,7)." In *Frauenbefreiung,* 148–51.

————. "Jüdinnen zur Zeit Jesu." In *Frauen in der Männerkirche*, ed. Bernadette J. Brooten and Norbert Greinacher, 141–48. Mainz, 1982.

————. *Women Leaders in the Ancient Synagogue: Inscriptional Evidence and Background Issues*. Chico, Calif., 1982.

————. "Konnten Frauen im alten Judentum die Scheidung betreiben? Überlegungen zu Mk 10,11–12 und 1 Kor 7,10–11." *EvT* 42 (1982): 65–80.

————. "Zur Debatte über das Scheidungsrecht der jüdischen Frau." *EvT* 43 (1983): 466–78.

————. "Early Christian Women and Their Cultural Context: Issues of Method in Historical Reconstruction." In *Feminist Perspectives on Biblical Scholarship*, ed. Adela Yarbro Collins, 65–91. Chico, Calif., 1985.

————. "Patristic Interpretations of Romans 1:26." In *Studia Patristica 18* (Papers of the 1983 Oxford Patristic Conference). Vol. 1 (1985), 287–90.

————. "Paul's Views on the Nature of Women and Female Homoeroticism." In *Immaculate and Powerful*, 61–87.

Browe, Peter. *Zur Geschichte der Entmannung: Eine religions- und rechtsgeschichtliche Studie*. Breslauer Studien zur historischen Theologie, n.s., 1. Breslau, 1936.

Brown, Gabrielle. *The New Celibacy: Why More Men and Women Are Abstaining from Sex—and Enjoying It*. New York, 1980.

Brown, Peter. *The Making of Late Antiquity*. Cambridge, Mass.-London, 1978.

————. *The Body and Society: Men, Women, and Sexual Renunciation in Early Christianity*. Lectures on the History of Religions, n.s., 13. New York, 1988.

Brox, Norbert. *Zeuge und Märtyrer: Untersuchungen zur frühchristlichen Zeugnis-Terminologie*. Studien zum Alten und Neuen Testament 5. Munich, 1961.

————. *Offenbarung, Gnosis und gnostischer Mythos bei Irenäus von Lyon*. Salzburg-Munich, 1966.

————. S.v. "Häresie." *RAC* 13:248–97.

————. *Erleuchtung und Wiedergeburt: Aktualität der Gnosis*. Munich, 1989.

Buchheit, Vinzenz. "Vergildeutung im Cento Probae." *Grazer Beiträge* 15 (1988): 161–67.

Buckley, Jorunn Jacobsen. *Female Fault and Fulfilment in Gnosticism*. Chapel Hill, N.C.-London, 1986.

Bulgakov, Sergei. "Die christliche Anthropologie." In *Kirche, Staat, Mensch: Russisch-orthodoxe Studien*, 209–55. Geneva, 1937.

Burris, Virginia. "Chastity as Autonomy: Women in the Stories of Apocryphal Acts" (response by Jean-Daniel Kaestli). *Semeia* 38 (1986): 101–35.

————. *Chastity as Autonomy: Women in the Stories of Apocryphal Acts.* Studies in Women and Religion 23. Lewiston, N.Y.-Queenston, Ont., 1987.

Cacioli, Maria R. "Adattamenti semantici e sintattici nel Centone virgiliano di Proba." *SIFC* 41 (1969): 188–246.

Calder, William Moir. "Philadelphia and Montanism." *Bulletin of the John Rylands Library* 7 (1923): 309–54.

————. "Leaves from an Anatolian Notebook." *Bulletin of the John Rylands Library* 13 (1929): 254–71.

————. "Early Christian Epitaphs from Phrygia." *Anatolian Studies* 5 (1955): 25–38.

Campenhausen, Hans von. *Die Idee des Martyriums in der alten Kirche.* Göttingen, 1936.

————. *Bearbeitungen und Interpretationen des Polycarpmartyriums.* Heidelberg, 1957.

————. *Die Jungfrauengeburt in der Theologie der alten Kirchen.* Sitzungsberichte der Heidelberger Akademie der Wissenschaften, Philosophische-historische Klasse 46/3. Heidelberg, 1962.

————. *Kirchliches Amt und geistliche Vollmacht in den ersten drei Jahrhunderten.* Beiträge zur historischen Theologie 14. 2nd ed. Tübingen, 1963.

Cancik, Hubert. "Zur Entstehung der christlichen Sexualmoral" (first published in 1976). In *Sexualität und Erotik in der Antike,* ed. Andreas Karsten Siems, 347–74. WdF 605. Darmstadt, 1988.

————. "Gnostiker in Rom: Zur Religionsgeschichte der Stadt Rom im 2. Jahrhundert nach Christus" In *Gnosis und Politik,* 163–84.

Cancik-Lindemaier, Hildegard. "Kultische Privilegierung und gesellschaftliche Realität: Ein Beitrag zur Sozialgeschichte der virgines Vestae." In *Saeculum* 41 (Freiburg-Munich, 1990), 1–16.

Cardman, Francine. "Acts of Women Martyrs," *ATR* 70 (1988): 144–50.

Castelli, Elizabeth. "Virginity and Its Meaning for Women's Sexuality in Early Christianity." *JFSR* 2 (1986): 61–88.

Cazeaux, Jacques. Philon d'Alexandrie, exégète." *ANRW* II.21.1, pp. 156–226.

Chadwick, Henry. *Priscillian of Avila: The Occult and the Charismatic in the Early Church.* Oxford, 1976.

————. "Oracles of the End in the Conflict of Paganism and Christianity in the Fourth Century." In *Antiquité Païenne et Chrétienne,* 125–29.

Chesnut, Glenn F. *The First Christian Histories: Eusebius, Socrates, Sozomen, Theodoret, and Evagrius.* Paris, 1977.

Christentum und antike Gesellschaft, ed. Jochen Martin and Barbara Quint. WdF 649. Darmstadt, 1990.

Christoffel, Judith. "Animus und Anima—das Konzept C. G. Jungs in der Sichtweise moderner Jungianerinnen." In idem, *Neue Strömungen in der Psychologie von Freud und Jung: Impulse von Frauen,* 35–63. Olten, 1989.

★Clark, Elizabeth A. *Jerome, Chrysostom, and Friends: Essays and Translations.* New York-Toronto, 1979.

————. "Ascetic Renunciation and Feminine Advancement: A Paradox of Late Ancient Christianity." *ATR* 63 (1981): 240–57; also in idem, *Ascetic Piety,* 175–208.

————. *Ascetic Piety and Women's Faith: Essays on Late Ancient Christianity.* Studies in Women and Religion 20. Lewiston, N.Y.-Queenston, Ont., 1986.

★————. *Women in the Early Church.* 2nd ed. Wilmington, Delaware, 1987.

————. "Foucault, the Fathers, and Sex." *JAAR* 56 (1989): 619–41.

————. "Theory and Practice in Late Ancient Asceticism: Jerome, Chrysostom, and Augustin." *JFSR* 5 (1989): 25–46.

Colpe, Carsten. *Das Siegel der Propheten: Historische Beziehungen zwischen Judentum, Judenchristen-*

tum, Heidentum und frühem Islam. Arbeiten zur neutestamentlichen Theologie und Zeitgeschichte 3. Berlin, 1989.

Consolino, Franca Ela. "Modelli di santità femminile nelle più antiche Passioni romane." *Aug* 24 (1984): 83–113.

Corrington, Gail Paterson. "The 'Divine Woman'? Propaganda and the Power of Celibacy in the New Testament Apocrypha: A Reconsideration." *ATR* 70 (1988): 207–20.

Corssen, Peter. "Die Töchter des Philippus." *ZNW* 2 (1901): 289–99.

———. "Begriff und Wesen des Märtyrers in der Alten Kirche." *Neue Jahrbücher für das Klassische Altertum* 35/1 (1915): 481–501.

Daly, Mary. *Beyond God the Father: Toward a Philosophy of Women's Liberation.* Boston, 1973.

———. *The Church and the Second Sex, with a New Feminist Postchristian Introduction by the Author.* 2nd ed. New York, 1975.

———. *Gyn/ecology: The Metaethics of Radical Feminism.* Boston, 1978.

———. *Pure Lust: Elemental Feminist Philosophy.* London, 1984.

D'Angelo, Mary Rose. "Women Partners in the New Testament." *JFSR* 6 (1990): 65–86.

Daniélou, Jean. *Bible et liturgie: La théologie biblique des sacrements et des fêtes d'après les Pères de l'Eglise.* 2nd ed. Paris, 1958.

Dart, John. *The Jesus of Heresy and History: The Discovery and Meaning of the Nag Hammadi Gnostic Library.* San Francisco, 1988.

Dassmann, Ernst. *Sündenvergebung durch Taufe, Busse und Märtyrerfürbitte in den Zeugnissen frühchristlicher Frömmigkeit und Kunst.* Münsterische Beiträge zur Theologie 36. Münster, 1973.

Dautzenberg, Gerhard. *Urchristliche Prophetie: Ihre Erforschung, ihre Voraussetzungen im Judentum und ihre Struktur im ersten Korintherbrief.* Stuttgart-Berlin-Cologne-Mainz, 1975.

Davies, Stevan L. *The Revolt of the Widows: The Social World of the Apocryphal Acts.* Carbondale-Edwardsville, Ill., 1980.

Delehaye, Hippolyte. *Les origines du culte des Martyrs.* Brussels, 1912.

———. *Les passions des Martyrs et les genres littéraires.* Brussels, 1921.

Demarolle, Jeanne-Marie. "Les femmes chrétiennes vues par Porphyre." JAC 13 (1970): 42–47.

Denzler, Georg. *Die verbotene Lust: 2000 Jahre christliche Sexualmoral.* Munich, 1988.

Dodds, Eric R. *Pagan and Christian in an Age of Anxiety.* Cambridge, 1965.

Dölger, Franz Joseph. "Der Exorzismus im altchristlichen Taufritual: Eine religionsgeschichtliche Studie." In *Studien zur Geschichte und Kultur des Altertums* 3:1–175. Paderborn, 1909.

———. "Gladiatorenblut und Martyrerblut. Eine Szene der Passio Perpetuae in kultur- und religionsgeschichtlicher Beleuchtung." In *Vorträge der Bibliothek Warburg 1923–1924,* ed. Fritz Saxl, 196–214. Leipzig-Berlin, 1926.

———. "Antike Parallelen zum leidenden Dinocrates in der Passio Perpetuae." *AuC* 2 (1930): 1–40.

———. "Der Kampf mit dem Ägypter in der Perpetua-Vision: Das Martyrium als Kampf mit dem Teufel." *AuC* 3 (1932): 177–88.

Dörrie, Heinrich. "Zur Methodik antiker Exegese." *ZNW* 64 (1974): 121–38.

Dronke, Peter. *Women Writers of the Middle Ages: A Critical Study of Texts from Perpetua (203) to Marguerite Porete (1310).* Cambridge-New York-Melbourne, 1984.

E Dio li creò . . . : Coppie straordinarie nei primi 13 secoli di cristianesimo da Perpetua e Saturo a Eloisa e Abelardo, ed. Clementina Mazzucco, Cettina Militello, and Adriana Valerio. Milan, 1990.

Ehrhard, Albert. *Die Kirche der Märtyrer: Ihre Aufgaben und ihre Leistungen.* Munich, 1932.

Die Entstehung der jüdischen Martyrologie, ed. Willem van Henten. Studia Post-Biblica 38. Leiden-New York-Cologne, 1989.

Erickson, John. "La prêtrise dans l'enseignement patristique." *Contacts* 41 (1989, No. 146): 109–23.

Ermini, Filippo. *Il centone de Proba e la poesia centonaria latina.* Rome, 1909.

Ernst, Johann. "Der Begriff vom Martyrium bei Cyprian." *Historisches Jahrbuch* 34 (1913): 328–53.

Eva—Verführerin oder Gottes Meisterwerk? Philosophie- und theologiegeschichtliche Frauenforschung, ed. Dieter R. Bauer and Elisabeth Gössmann. Hohenheimer Protokolle 21. Stuttgart, 1987.

Evdokimov, Paul. *L'Orthodoxie.* Paris, 1965; repr., 1979.

★*Existence païenne au début du christianisme: Présentation de textes grecs et romains,* ed. René Kieffer and Lars Rydbeck. Paris, 1983.

Fabrega, Valentin. "War Junia(s), der hervorragende Apostel (Röm 16,7), eine Frau?" In JAC 27/28 (1984/1985), 47–64.

Faivre, Alexandre. *Les laïcs aux origines de l'Eglise.* Paris, 1984.

———. "Théologiens 'laïcs' et laïcs théologiens: Position des problèmes à l'époque paléochré-tienne." *Irénikon* 60 (1987): 193–217, 350–77.

Fander, Monika. *Die Stellung der Frau im Markusevangelium unter besonderer Berücksichtigung kultur- und religionsgeschichtlicher Hintergründe.* Münsteraner Theologische Abhandlungen 8. 2nd ed. Altenberge, 1990.

Fascher, Erich. *Prophētēs: Eine sprach- und religionsgeschichtliche Untersuchung.* Giessen, 1927.

Fehrle, Eugen. *Die kultische Keuschheit im Altertum.* Religionsgeschichtliche Versuche und Vorarbeiten 6. Giessen, 1910.

Fell, Margaret. *Womens Speaking Justified, Proved and Allowed of by the Scriptures.* London, 1661; repr., Los Angeles, 1979.

★*La Femme: Les grands textes des Pères de l'Eglise,* ed. France Quere-Jaulmes. Paris, 1968.

Ficker, Gerhard. See Bibl. I: *Discussion.*

Fiorenza, Elisabeth Schüssler. *In Memory of Her: A Feminist Theological Reconstruction of Christian Origins.* New York, 1983.

———. *Bread Not Stone: The Challenge of Feminist Biblical Interpretation.* Boston, 1984.

———. "'Der Dienst an den Tischen': Eine kritische feministisch-theologische Überlegung zum Thema Diakonie." *Concilium* 24 (1988): 306–13.

Fischer, Balthasar. "Jesus, unsere Mutter" (review of the literature). *Geist und Leben* 14 (1985).

Fischer, Joseph A. "Die antimontanistischen Synoden des 2./3. Jahrhunderts." *Annuarium Historiae Conciliorum* 6 (1974): 241–73.

Ford, J. Massingberde. "Was Montanism a Jewish-Christian Heresy?" *JEH* 17 (1966): 145–58 (female author).

Fossum, Jarl, and Gilles Quispel. S.v. "Helena." *RAC* 14:338–55.

Franz, Marie-Louise von. "Die Passio Perpetuae: Versuch einer psychologischen Deutung." In *Aion: Untersuchungen zur Symbolgeschichte,* ed. Carl G. Jung, 387–496. Psychologische Abhandlungen 8. Zurich, 1951.

Frauenbefreiung: Biblische und theologische Argumente, ed. Elisabeth Moltmann-Wendel. 2nd ed. Munich-Mainz, 1978.

Die Frau im Urchristentum, ed. Gerhard Dautzenberg, Helmut Merklein, and Karlheinz Müller. QD 95. 1983 (special edition 1989).

Frauen in Spätantike und Frühmittelalter: Lebensbedingungen-Lebensnormen-Lebensformen (Beiträge zu einer internationalen Tagung am Fachbereich Geschichtswissenschaften der Freien Universität Berlin 18.-21. Februar 1987), ed. Werner Affeldt. Sigmaringen, 1990.

Frend, William H. C. *Martyrdom and Persecution in the Early Church: A Study of a Conflict from the Maccabees to Donatus.* Oxford, 1965.

———. "Montanism: Research and Problems." In idem, *Archaeology and History in the Study of Early Christianity,* vol. 7. London, 1988.

Freudenberger, Rudolf. *Das verhalten der römischen Behörden gegen die Christen im 2. Jahrhundert, dargestellt am Brief des Plinius an Trajan und den Reskripten Trajans und Hadrians.* Münchener Beiträge zur Papyrusforschung und antiken Rechtsgeschichte 52. Munich, 1965.

Frevert, Ute. "Bewegung und Disziplin in der Frauengeschichte: Ein Forschungsbericht." *Geschichte und Gesellschaft* 14 (1988): 240–62.

Fridh, Åke. *Le Problème de la Passion des Saintes Perpétue et Félicité.* Studia graeca et Latina Gothoburgensia 26. Göteburg, 1968.

Froehlich, Karlfried. "Montanism and Gnosis." OCA 195 (1973): 91–111.

Das frühe Christentum im römischen Staat, ed. Richard Klein. WdF 267. Darmstadt, 1971.

Funke, Hermann. "Univira: Ein Beispiel heidnischer Geschichtsapologetik." JAC 8/9 (1965/1966): 183–88.

Gager, John G. "Body-Symbols and Social Reality: Resurrection, Incarnation, and Asceticism in Early Christianity." *Religion* 12 (1982): 345–63.

Gasparro, Giulia Sfameni. *Enkrateia e antropologia: Le motivazioni protologiche della continenza e della verginità nel cristianesimo dei primi secoli e nello gnosticismo.* Coll. Studia Ephemeridis "Augustinianum" 20. Rome, 1984.

Giannarelli, Elena. *La tipologia femminile nella biografia e nell'autobiografia cristiana del IVº secolo.* Studi Storici 127. Rome, 1980.

Gibson, Elsa. *The "Christians for Christians" Inscriptions of Phrygia.* Harvard Theological Studies 32. Missoula, Mont., 1978.

Geschichte der Kirche, ed. Ludovicus Jacobus Rogier, Roger Aubert, and Michael David Knowles. Einsiedeln-Zurich-Cologne, 1963.

Gnosis. FS Hans Jonas. Göttingen, 1978.

Gnosis und Politik, ed. Jacob Taubes. Paderborn, 1984.

Gödecke, Monika. *Geschichte als Mythos: Eusebs "Kirchengeschichte."* Frankfurt/Main, 1987.

Gössmann, Elisabeth. "Äusserungen zum Frauenpriestertum in der christlichen Tradition." In *Warum keine Ordination der Frau?* 9–25.

———. "Die 'Päpstin Johanna.' Zur vor- und nachreformatorischen Rezeption ihrer Gestalt." In *Eva,* 143–66.

———. "Zur Rezeptionsgeschichte der Gestalt der Päpstin Johanna." In *Weiblichkeit,* 93–111. *See* Archiv.

Grant, Robert M. *Early Christianity and Society.* San Francisco, 1977.

———. *Eusebius as Church Historian.* Oxford, 1980.

———. "Marcion and the Critical Method." In *From Jesus to Paul,* 207–15. Waterloo, Ont., 1984.

Green, Henry A. *The Economic and Social Origins of Gnosticism.* Society of Biblical Literature Dissertation Series 77. Atlanta, 1985.

Gribomont, Jean. "Le monachisme au IVe siècle en Asie Mineure: De Gangres au messialisme." *Studia Patristica* 2 (TU 64) (1957): 400–415.

———. "Eustathe le Philosophe et les voyages du jeune Basile de Césarée." *RHE* 54 (1959): 115–24.

———. "Eustathe de Sébaste." *Dictionnaire de Spiritualité* 4/2 (1961), 1708–12.

Grillmeier, Aloys. *Christ in Christian Tradition.* Vol. 1, *From the Apostolic Age to Chalcedon (451).* 2nd ed. Atlanta, 1975.

Gryson, Roger. *Les origines du célibat ecclésiastique du premier au septième siècle.* Recherches et Synthèses, Section d'Histoire 2. Gembloux, 1970.

———. *The Ministry of Women in the Early Church.* Collegeville, Minn., 1976.

Hagemann, Kurt. *Der Zölibat der römisch-katholischen Kirche.* Mannheimer Sozialwissenschaftliche Studien 5. Meisenheim, 1971.

Hagemeyer, Oda. See Bibl. I: *Martyrs*.

Hällström, Gunnar af. *Charismatic Succession: A Study on Origen's Concept of Prophecy*. Publications of the Finnish Exegetical Society 42. Helsinki, 1985.

Hamman, Adalbert. See *L'initiation chretienne* and Bibl. I: *Martyrs*.

Handbuch der Kirchengeschichte, ed. Hubert Jedin. Freiburg-Basel-Vienna, 1962ff. (special edition, 1985).

Handbuch der Ostkirchenkunde, ed. Wilhelm Nyssen, Hans-Joachim Schulz, and Paul Wiertz. 2 vols. Düsseldorf, 1984–1989.

Hanson, John S. "Dreams and Visions in the Graeco-Roman World and Early Christianity." *ANRW* II.23.2, pp. 1395–1427.

Hardy, B. Carmon. "The Emperor Julian and His School Law." *CH* 37 (1968): 131–43.

Häring, Hermann. *Die Macht des Bösen: Das Erbe Augustins*. Ökumenische Theologie 3. Zurich-Cologne-Gütersloh, 1979.

Harnack, Adolf von. *Geschichte der altchristlichen Literatur bis Eusebius*, 2 vols. Leipzig, 1893–1904 (2nd ed., revised by Kurt Aland, 1958).

———. "Cyprian als Enthusiast." *ZNW* 3 (1902): 177–91.

———. *Die Mission und Ausbreitung des Christentums in den ersten drei Jahrhunderten*. Leipzig, 1902 (4th ed., 1924).

———. *Marcion: Das Evangelium vom fremden Gott: Eine Monographie zur Geschichte der Grundlegung der katholischen Kirche*. 2nd ed. TU 45. Leipzig, 1924 (repr. Darmstadt, 1960, with "Neue Studien zu Marcion," TU 44/4, 1923).

Harvey, Susan Ashbrook. *Ascetism and Society in Crisis: John of Ephesus and the Lives of the Eastern Saints*. Berkeley-London, 1990.

———. "Women in Early Syrian Christianity." In *Images of Women*, 288–98.

Hausen, Karin. "Women's History in den Vereinigten Staaten. *Geschichte und Gesellschaft* 7 (1981): 347–63.

———. "Patriarchat: Vom Nutzen und Nachteil eines Konzepts für Frauengeschichte und Frauenpolitik." *Journal für Geschichte* 5 (1986): 12–21, 58.

Hausherr, Irénée. *Direction spirituelle en orient autrefois*. OCA 144. Rome, 1955.

Hawthorne, Gerald F. "The Role of the Christian Prophets in the Gospel Tradition." In *Tradition and Interpretation in the New Testament*, FS E. Earle Ellis, ed. Gerald F. Hawthorne and Otto Betz, 119–33. Grand Rapids-Tübingen, 1987.

Heiler, Friedrich. *Die Frau in den Religionen der Menschheit*. Berlin-New York, 1976.

★*Heilige Frauen des Altertums*, ed. Wilhelm Schamoni. Düsseldorf, 1963.

Heine, Ronald E. "The Role of the Gospel of John in the Montanist Controversy." *The Second Century: A Journal of Early Christian Studies* 6 (1987/1988[1]): 1–19. See also *The Montanist Oracles*.

Heine, Susanne. *Frauen der frühen Christenheit: Zur historischen Kritik einer feministischen Theologie*. Göttingen, 1986.

———. "Selig durch Kindergebären? Die verschwundenen Frauen der frühen Christenheit." In *Theologie feministisch: Disziplinen, Schwerpunkte, Richtungen*, ed. Marie-Theres Wacker, 59–79. Düsseldorf, 1988.

Heinen, Heinz. "Sollte das Christentum in Spanien tatsächlich von Frauen eingeführt worden sein?" *Trierer Theologische Zeitschrift* 98 (1989): 227–29.

Herzog, Reinhart. *Die Bibelepik der Lateinischen Spätantike: Formgeschichte einer erbaulichen Gattung* 1 (esp. "Proba," xlix–li, and "Der Cento Probae: Maro mutatus in melius," 3–51). Munich, 1975.

Hickey, Anne Ewing. *Women of the Roman Aristocracy as Christian Monastics*. Studies in Religion 1. Ann Arbor, Mich., 1987.

Histoire de la vie privée, ed. Philippe Aries and Georges Duby. Vol. 1, *De l'Empire romain à l'an mil,* ed. Paul Veyne. Paris, 1985.

Hoffmann, R. Joseph. *Marcion: On the Restitution of Christianity, An Essay on the Development of Radical Paulinist Theology in the Second Century.* Chico, Calif., 1984.

————. "How Then Know This Troublous Teacher? Further Reflections on Marcion and His Church." *The Second Century: A Journal of Early Christian Studies* 6 (1987/1988): 173–91.

Holl, Karl. "Die Vorstellung vom Märtyrer und die Märtyrerakte in ihrer geschichtlichen Entwicklung." *Neue Jahrbücher für das Klassische Altertum* 33 (1914): 521–56.

Hollerich, Michael J. "Religion and Politics in the Writings of Eusebius: Reassessing the First 'Court Theologian.'" *CH* 59 (1990): 309–25.

★Holy Women of the Syrian Orient, ed. Sebastian P. Brock and Susan Ashbrook Harvey. Berkeley-Los Angeles-London, 1987.

Huber, Elaine C. *Women and the Authority of Inspiration: The Reexamination of Two Prophetic Movements from a Contemporary Feminist Perspective.* Lanham, Md., 1985.

Hünermann, Peter. "Roma locuta—causa finita? Zur Argumentation der vatikanischen Erklärung über die Frauenordination." *Herder Korrespondenz* 31 (1977): 206–9.

Ibarra Benlloch, Martin. *Mulier fortis: La mujer en las fuentes cristianas (280–313).* Monografias de historia antigua 6. Saragossa, 1990.

Image of God and Gender Models in Judaeo-Christian Tradition, ed. Kari Elisabeth Børresen. Oslo, 1991.

Images of the Feminine in Gnosticism, ed. Karen L. King. Studies in Antiquity and Christianity. Philadelphia, 1988.

Images of Women in Antiquity, ed. Averil Cameron and Amélie Kuhrt. London-Sydney, 1983.

Immaculate and Powerful: The Female in Sacred Image and Reality, ed. Clarissa W. Atkinson, Constance H. Buchanan, and Margaret R. Miles. Boston, 1985.

★Im Reiche des Eros, Sämtliche Liebes- und Abenteuerromane der Antike, ed. Bernhard Kytzler. Munich, 1983.

★L'initiation chrétienne. Textes recueillis et présentés par Adalbert Hamman. Paris, 1980.

Inter Insigniores: Erklärung der Kongregation für die Glaubenslehre zur Frage der Zulassung der Frauen zum Priesteramt, ed. Deutsche Bischofskonferenz. Verlautbarungen des Apostolischen Stuhls 3. 1976. Lat.: *AAS* 69 (1977): 98–116.

Jaschke, Hans-Jochen. *Der Heilige Geist im Bekenntnis der Kirche: Eine Studie zur Pneumatologie des Irenäus von Lyon im Ausgang vom altchristlichen Glaubensbekenntnis.* Münsterische Beiträge zur Theologie 40. Münster, 1976.

Jensen, Anne. "Wie patriarchalisch ist die Ostkirche? Frauenfragen in der orthodoxen Theologie." *US* 40 (1985): 130–45.

————. *Die Zukunft der Orthodoxie: Konzilspläne und Kirchenstrukturen.* Ökumenische Theologie 14. Zurich-Cologne, 1986.

————. "Im Kampf um Freiheit in Kirche und Staat: Die 'Mutter des Quäkertums,' Margaret Fell." In *Gegenentwürfe: 24 Lebensläufe für eine andere Theologie,* ed. Hermann Häring and Karl-Joseph Kuschel (to Hans Küng on his sixtieth birthday), 169–80. Munich, 1988.

————. "Thekla: Vergessene Verkünderin." In *Zwischen Ohnmacht und Befreiung: Biblische Frauengestalten,* ed. Karin Walter, 173–79. Freiburg, 1988.

————. "Auf dem Weg zur Heiligen Jungfrau: Vorformen des Marienkultes in der frühen Kirche." In *Maria—für alle Frauen oder über allen Frauen?* ed. Elisabeth Gössmann and Dieter R. Bauer, 36–62. Freiburg, 1989.

————. "Maria von Magdala: Traditionen der frühen Christenheit." In *Maria Magdalena—Zu einem Bild der Frau in der christlichen Verkündigung,* ed. Dietmar Bader, 33–50. Schriftenreihe der Katholische Akademie Freiburg. Munich-Zurich, 1990.

————. "Philumene—oder das Streben nach Vergeistigung" In *Sanft und rebellisch: Mütter der Christenheit*, ed. Karin Walter, 221–32. Freiburg, 1990.

————. "Die ersten Christinnen der Spätantike." In *Auch wir sind die Kirche: Frauen in der Kirche zwischen Tradition und Aufbruch*, ed. Veronika Straub, 35–58. Munich, 1991.

————. "Faltonia Betitia Proba—eine Kirchenlehrerin der Spätantike." In *Mit allen Sinnen Glauben: Feministische Theologie unterwegs* (to Elisabeth Moltmann-Wendel on her 65th birthday), 84–93. Gütersloh, 1991.

————. S.v. "Diakonin" and "Orden." *Wörterbuch der Feministischen Theologie*, 58–60 and 310–15. Gütersloh, 1991.

————. "Prisca—Maximilla—Montanus: Who Was the Founder of 'Montanism'?" *Studia Patristica* 26 (1993): 147–50.

Jeremias, Joachim. *Unbekannte Jesusworte*. 4th ed. Gütersloh, 1965.

Joannou, Périclès-Pierre. See Bibl. I: *Canons*.

Jonas, Hans. *Gnosis und spätantiker Geist*, part 1: *Die mythologische Gnosis*. 3rd ed. Göttingen, 1964; part 2/1: *Von der Mythologie zur mystischen Philosophie*. 2nd ed. Göttingen, 1966.

Julian Apostata, ed. Richard Klein. WdF 509. Darmstadt, 1978.

Jülicher, Adolf. "Die geistlichen Ehe in der alten Kirche." *Archiv für Religionswissenschaft* 7 (1904): 373–86.

Junod, Eric. "Vie et conduite des saintes femmes Xanthippe, Polyxène et Rébecca (BHG 1877)." *Oecumenica et Patristica*, FS Wilhelm Schneemelcher, 83–106. Stuttgart, 1989.

Kaestli, Jean-Daniel. "Fiction littéraire et réalite sociale: Que peut-on savoir de la place des femmes dans le milieu de production des actes apocryphes des apôtres?" In *La fable apocryphe* 1:279–302. Apocrypha: Le champ des apocryphes 1. Turnhout, 1990.

————. "Die Witwen in den Pastoralbriefen und in den apokryphen Apostelgeschichten." Paper presented to the working group of the Institute for Ecumenical Research of the University of Tübingen, 1990.

Kah, Marianne, *"Die Welt der Römer mit der Seele suchend . . .": Die Religiosität des Prudentius im Spannungsfeld zwischen 'pietas christiana' und 'pietas Romana.'* Hereditas 3, Studien zur Alten Kirchengeschichte. Bonn, 1990.

Kallis, Anastasios. *Orthodoxie—was ist das?* Mainz, 1979.

Kalsbach, Adolf. *Die altkirchliche Einrichtung der Diakonissen bis zu ihrem Erlöschen*. Freiburg, 1926.

————. S.v. "Diakonisse." *RAC* 3:917–28.

Kaser, Max. *Römisches Privatrecht*. 15th ed. Munich, 1989.

Kassel, Maria. "Tod und Aurerstehung." In *Feministische Theologie: Perspektiven zur Orientierung*, 191–226. 2nd ed. Stuttgart, 1988.

Kast, Verena. "Eine Auseinandersetzung mit dem Animus- und Animabegriff C. G. Jungs." In idem, *Paare: Beziehungsphantasien oder wie Götter sich in Menschen spiegeln*, 157–77. Stuttgart, 1984.

Kaufmann, Doris. *Frauen zwischen Aufbruch und Reaktion: Protestantische Frauenbewegung in der ersten Hälfte des 20. Jahrhunderts*. Munich-Zurich, 1988.

Kelly-Gadol, Joan. "The Social Relation of the Sexes: Methodological Implications of Women's History." *Signs* 1 (1976): 809–24. Repr. in idem, *Women, History, and Theory*. Chicago, 1984.

Keppler, Gerlinde. "Das Bild der Frau in den Pastoralbriefen und in der Thekla-Tradition." Examination paper in the Evangelisch-Theologische Fakultät. Tübingen, 1988.

Kirsch, Wolfgang. *Die lateinische Versepik des 4. Jahrhunderts*. Schriften zur Geschichte und Kultur der Antike 28. Berlin, 1989.

Klawiter, Frederick Ch. "The New Prophecy in Early Christianity: The Origin, Nature, and Development of Montanism." Diss., Chicago, 1975. Microfiche.

————. "The Role of Martyrdom and Persecution in Developing the Priestly Authority of Women in Early Christianity: A Case Study of Montanism." *CH* 49 (1980): 251–61.

Koch, Hugo. "Virgines Christi: Die Gelübde der gottgeweihten Jungfrauen in den ersten drei Jahrhunderten." TU 31 (1907): 59–112.

Koschorke, Klaus. *Die Polemik der Gnostiker gegen das kirchliche Christentum: Unter besonderer Berücksichtigung der Nag-Hammadi-Traktate "Apokalypse des Petrus" (NHC VII,3) und "Testimonium Veritatis" (NHC IX,3)*. Nag Hammadi Studies 12. Leiden, 1978.

Kötting, Bernhard. "Die Stellung des Konfessors in der alten Kirche." JAC 19 (1976): 7–23.

Kraemer, Ross S. *Ecstatics and Ascetics: Studies in the Function of Religious Activities for Women in the Greco-Roman World*. Princeton, N.J., 1976.

————. "The Conversion of Women to Ascetic Forms of Christianity." *Signs* 6 (1980): 298–307.

————. "Monastic Jewish Women in Greco-Roman Egypt: Philo Judaeus on the Therapeutrides." *Signs* 14 (1989): 342–70. See also *Maenads*.

Kraft, Heinrich (Heinz). "Die altkirchliche Prophetie und die Entstehung des Montanismus." *TZ* 11 (1955): 249–71.

————. "Vom Ende der urchristlichen Prophetie." In *Prophetic Vocation*, 162–85.

————. "Die Lyoner Märtyrer und der Montanismus." In *Pietas*, FS Bernhard Kötting, 250–66. JAC suppl. 8 (1980).

Krienen, Veronica. "Prophetische Züge in den Apophthegmata Patrum." *OS* 39 (1990): 181–92.

Küchler, Max. *Schweigen, Schmuck und Schleier: Drei neutestamentliche Vorschriften zur Verdrängung der Frauen auf dem Hintergrund einer frauenfeindlichen Exegese des Alten Testamentes im antiken Judentum*. Novum Testamentum et Orbis Antiquus 1. Fribourg-Göttingen, 1986.

Kühnert, Wilhelm. "Der antimontanistische Anonymus des Eusebius." *TZ* 5 (1949): 436–46.

Küng, Hans. *Die Kirche*. 2nd ed. Freiburg, 1967.

Kuschel, Karl-Josef. *Geboren vor aller Zeit? Der Streit um Christi Ursprung*. Munich, 1990.

Labriolle, Pierre de. "'Mulieres in ecclesia taceant': Un aspect de la lutte antimontaniste." *Bulletin d'ancienne littérature et d'archéologie chrétiennes* 1 (1911): 3–24, 103–22, 292–98.

————. *La crise montaniste*. Paris, 1913.

————. ★*Les sources de l'histoire du montanisme (textes grecs, latins, syriaques publiés avec une introduction critique, une traduction française, des notes et des "indices")*. Paris, 1913.

————. "Le 'mariage spirituel' dans l'antiquité chrétienne." *Revue historique* 46 (1921 [tome 137]): 204–25.

Lampe, Peter. "Iunia/Iunias: Sklavenherkunft im Kreise der vorpaulinischen Apostel (Röm 16,7)." *ZNW* 76 (1985): 132–34.

————. *Die stadtrömischen Christen in den ersten beiden Jahrhunderten. Untersuchungen zur Sozialgeschichte*. 2nd ed. Wissenschaftliche Untersuchungen zum Neuen Testament, 2nd series, 18. Tübingen, 1989.

Laporte, Jean. *The Role of Women in Early Christianity*. Studies in Women and Religion 7. Lewiston, N.Y., 1982.

Last, Hugh. *See* Joseph Vogt.

Lazzati, Guiseppe. *Gli sviluppi della letteratura sui martiri nei primi quattro secoli,* con appendice di testi. Studi Superiori 7. 1956.

Le Boullec, Alain. *La notion d'hérésie dans la littérature grecque. IIe–IIIe siècles*. Vol. 1, *De Justin à Irénéé*. Vol. 2, *Clément d'Alexandrie et Origène*. Etudes Augustiniennes. Paris, 1985.

Leclerq, Henri. *Les Martyrs*. Vol. 1, *Les Temps Néroniens et le Deuxième Siècle*. Paris, 1903.

Lefkowitz, Mary R. "The Motivations for St. Perpetua's Martyrdom." *JAAR* 44/3 (1976): 417–21.

★Lefkowitz, Mary R., and Maureen B. Fant. *Women's Life in Greece and Rome*. London, 1982.

Leipoldt, Johannes. *Die Frau in der antiken Welt und im Urchristentum*. Gütersloh, 1962.

Lerner, Gerda. *The Creation of Patriarchy*. Women and History 1. New York, 1986.

Leutzsch, Martin. *Die Wahrnehmung sozialer Wirklichkeit im "Hirten des Hermas."* FRLANT 150. Göttingen, 1989.

Liegle, Josef. "Pietas." In *Römische Wertbegriffe*, ed. Hans Oppermann, 229–73. WdF 34. Darmstadt, 1967.

Lightman, Marjorie, and William Zeisel. "Univira: An Example of Continuity and Change in Roman Society." *CH* 46 (1977): 19–32.

Linsenmayer, Anton. "Die Behandlung der Frauen im römischen Christenprozess." *Historisch-politische Blätter für das katholische Deutschland* 141 (1908): 886–94.

Lockwood, Rose. "Potens et Factiosa Femina: Women, Martyrs, and Schism in Roman North Africa." *Augustinian Studies* 20 (1989): 165–82.

Lods, Marc. *Confesseurs et martyrs: Successeurs des prophètes dans l'Eglise des trois premiers siècles*. Neuchâtel-Paris, 1958.

Lohfink, Gerhard. "Weibliche Diakone im Neuen Testament." In *Die Frau im Urchristentum*.

Löhr, Winrich A. "Der Brief der Gemeinden von Lyon und Vienne." In *Oecumenica et Patristica*, FS Wilhelm Schneemelcher, 135–49. Stuttgart, 1989.

Lønning, Inge. *"Kanon im Kanon": Zum dogmatischen Grundlagenproblem des neutestamentlichen Kanons*. Forschungen zur Geschichte und Lehre des Protestantismus 10/43. Oslo-Munich, 1972.

Lossky, Vladimir. *A l'image et à la ressemblance de Dieu*. Paris, 1967 (Eng.: *In the Image and Likeness of God*. Crestwood, N.Y., 1974).

★*A Lost Tradition: Women Writers of the Early Church*, ed. Patricia Wilson-Kastner et al. Washington, D.C., 1981.

MacDonald, Dennis R. *The Legend and the Apostle: The Battle for Paul in Story and Canon*. Philadelphia, 1983.

———. *There Is No Male and Female: The Fate of a Dominical Saying in Paul and Gnosticism*. Harvard Dissertations in Religion 20. Philadelphia, 1987.

Mack, Burton L. "Philo Judaeus and Exegetical Traditions in Alexandria." *ANRW* II.21.1, pp. 227–71.

Macmullen, Ramsey. "Women in Public in the Roman Empire." *Hist* 29 (1980): 208–18.

★*Maenads, Martyrs, Matrons, Monastics: A Sourcebook on Women's Religions in the Greco-Roman World*, ed. Ross S. Kraemer. Philadelphia, 1988.

Maier, Johann. *Grundzüge der Geschichte des Judentums im Altertum*. Grundzüge 40. Darmstadt, 1981.

The Making of Orthodoxy: Essays in Honour of Henry Chadwick, ed. Rowan Williams. Cambridge, 1989.

Malone, Edward E. *The Monk and the Martyr: The Monk as the Successor of the Martyr*. Washington, D.C., 1950.

Martimort, Aimé Georges. *Les diaconesses. Essai historique*. Bibliotheca "Ephemerides Liturgicae," Subsidia 24. Rome, 1982.

Martin, Jochen. "Das Patriarchat in Rom: Die hausväterliche Gewalt." *Journal für Geschichte* 5 (1986): 30–35.

Les Martyrs de Lyon. Lyon, 20–23 September 1977. Colloques internationaux du CNRS no. 571. Paris, 1978.

May, Gerhard. "Marcion in Contemporary Views: Results and Open Questions." The Second Century. A Journal of Early Christian Studies 6, 1987/1988: 129–172.

———. "Apelles und die Entwicklung der markionitischen Theologie" (to appear in *ANRW*; the author has graciously made the manuscript available to me).

Mayer, Guenther. *Die jüdische Frau in der hellenistisch-römischen Antike*. Stuttgart, 1987.

*Mayer, Josephine. *Monumenta de viduis diaconissis virginibusque tractantia* (a collection of sources on widows, deaconesses, and virgins). Bonn, 1938.

Mazzucco, Clementina. *"E fui fatta maschio": La donna nel Cristianesimo primitivo.* Florence, 1989.

———. "Perpetua e Saturo." In *E Dio li creò . . .* , 27–46.

McNamara, Jo Ann. "Sexual Equality and the Cult of Virginity in Early Christian Thought." *FSt* 3 (1976): 145–58.

———. "Wives and Widows in Early Christian Thought." *IJWSt* 2 (1979): 575–92.

———. *A New Song: Celibate Women in the First Three Christian Centuries.* New York, 1985.

Meeks, Wayne A. "The Image of Androgyne: Some Uses of a Symbol in Earliest Christianity." *HR* 13 (1973/1974): 165–208.

Van der Meer, Haye. *Priestertum der Frau? Eine theologiegeschichtliche Untersuchung.* QD 42. Freiburg-Basel-Vienna, 1969.

Methoden in der Frauenforschung (symposium at the Free University of Berlin, 30 Nov. 1982–2 Feb. 1983). Frankfurt, 1984.

Meyendorff, John. *Introduction à l'étude de Grégoire Palamas.* Paris, 1959 (Eng. trans.: *A Study of Gregory Palamas.* New York, 1974).

Meyer, Wolfgang Alexander. *Hypatia von Alexandria: Ein Beitrag zur Geschichte des Neuplatonismus.* Heidelberg, 1886.

Michel, Otto. *Prophet und Märtyrer.* Beiträge zur Förderung christlicher Theologie 37/2. Gütersloh, 1932.

Miles, Margaret R. "Patriarchy as Political Theology: The Establishment of North African Christianity." In *Civil Religion and Political Theology,* ed. Leroy S. Rouner. Boston University Studies in Philosophy and Religion, vol. 8. Notre Dame, Ind., 1986.

———. *Carnal Knowing: Female Nakedness and Religious Meaning in the Christian West.* Boston, 1989.

Militello, Cettina. *Donna e Chieza: La Testimonianza di Giovanni Crisostomo.* Facolta teologia di Sicilia, studi 3. Palermo, 1987.

Miller, Patricia Cox. "'Words with an Alien Voice': Gnostics, Scripture, and Canon." *JAAR* 57 (1989): 459–83.

Molthagen, Joachim. *Der römische Staat und die Christen im zweiten und dritten Jahrhundert.* Hypomnemata 28. Göttingen, 1970.

Moltmann-Wendel, Elisabeth. *Ein eigener Mensch werden: Frauen um Jesus* (1980). 5th ed. Gütersloh, 1985.

———. *Das Land, wo Milch und Honig fliesst: Perspektiven einer feministischen Theologie.* Gütersloh, 1985.

The Montanist Oracles and Testimonia, ed. Ronald E. Heine. Patristic Monograph Series 14. Macon, Ga., 1989.

Munier, Charles. "Propagande gnostique et discipline ecclésiale d'après Tertullien." *Revue des Sciences Religieuses* 63 (1989): 195–205.

Musurillo, Herbert. See Bibl. I: *Martyrs.*

Nagel, Peter. *Die Motivierung der Askese in der alten Kirche und der Ursprung des Mönchtums.* Berlin, 1966.

Neymeyr, Ulrich. *Die christlichen Lehrer im zweiten Jahrhundert: Ihre Lehrtätigkeit, ihr Selbstverständnis und ihre Geschichte.* Leiden-Cologne, 1989.

Niederwimmer, Kurt. "Zur Entwicklungsgeschichte des Wanderradikalismus im Traditionsbereich der Didache." *Wiener Studien* 90 (1977): 145–67.

See Bibl. I: *Didache.*

Nugent, Rosamund M. *Portrait of the Consecrated Woman in the Greek Christian Literature of the First Four Centuries.* Washington, D.C., 1941.

Nürnberg, Rosemarie. *Askese als sozialer Impuls: Monastrisch-asketische Spiritualität als Wurzel und Triebfeder sozialer Ideen und Aktivitäten der Kirche in Südgallien im 5. Jahrhundert.* Hereditas: Studien zur Alten Kirchengeschichte 2. Bonn, 1988.

————. "'Non decet neque necessarium est, ut mulieres doceant': Überlegungen zum altkirchlichen Lehrverbot für Frauen." *JAC* 31 (1988): 57–73.

Oeyen, Christian. "Frauenordination: Was sagt die Tradition wirklich?" *IKZ* 75 (1985): 97–118.

On Being a Jewish Feminist: A Reader, ed. Susannah Heschel. New York, 1983.

Opelt, Ilona. "Der zürnende Christus im Cento der Proba." *JAC* 7 (1964): 106–16

Osiek, Carolyn. "The Widow as Altar: The Rise and Fall of a Symbol." *The Second Century* 3 (1983): 159–69.

————. "The Second Century through the Eyes of Hermas: Continuity and Change." *Biblical Theology Bulletin* 20 (1990): 116–22.

Otto, Walter F. *Die Götter Griechenlands: Das Bild des Göttlichen im Spiegel des griechischen Geistes.* 3rd ed. Frankfurt, 1947.

Pagels, Elaine H. *The Johannine Gospel in Gnostic Exegesis: Heracleon's Commentary on John.* Society of Biblical Literature Monograph 17. Nashville-New York, 1973.

————. "Paul and Women: A Response to Recent Discussion." *JAAR* 42 (1974): 538–49.

————. *The Gnostic Paul: Gnostic Exegesis of the Pauline Letters.* Philadelphia, 1975.

————. "What Became of God the Mother? Conflicting Images of God in Early Christianity." *Signs* 2 (1976): 293–303.

————. "Visions, Appearances, and Apostolic Authority: Gnostic and Orthodox Traditions." In *Gnosis,* 415–30.

————. *The Gnostic Gospels.* New York, 1979.

————. *Adam, Eve, and the Serpent.* New York, 1988.

Patlagean, Evelyne. "L'histoire de la femme deguisée en moine et l'évolution de la sainteté féminine à Byzance." *StMed,* Seria Terza 17/2 (1976): 547–623.

Perkins, Judith. "The Apocryphal Acts of the Apostles and the Early Christian Martyrdom." *Arethusa* 18 (1985): 211–30.

Peterson, Erik. *Frühe Kirche, Judentum und Gnosis: Studien und Untersuchungen.* Darmstadt, 1982.

Pettersen, Alvyn. "Perpetua—Prisoner of Conscience." *Vigiliae Christianae* 41 (1987): 139–53.

Pietas. FS Bernhard Kötting. JAC suppl. 8 (1980).

Plaskow, Judith. "Christian Feminism and Anti-Judaism." *CrossCur* 28 (1978/1979): 306–9.

————. "Blaming Jews for Inventing Patriarchy." *Lilith* 7 (1980): 11–13.

————. "Feministischer Antijudaismus und der christliche Gott." *Kirche und Israel* 5 (1990): 9–25.

————. *Standing Again at Sinai: Judaism from a Feminist Perspective.* San Francisco, 1990.

Pomeroy, Sarah B. *Goddesses, Whores, Wives, and Slaves: Women in Classical Antiquity.* New York, 1975.

Portefaix, Lilian. *Sisters Rejoice: Paul's Letter to the Philippians and Luke-Acts as Received by First-Century Philippian Women.* Coniectanea Biblica—New Testament Series 20. Uppsala, 1988.

Pourkier, Aline. *L'hérésiologie chez Epiphane de Salamine.* Christianisme Antique 4. Paris, 1992.

Powell, Douglas. "Tertullianists and Cataphrygians." *Vigiliae Christianae* 29 (1975): 33–54.

Prophetic Vocation in the New Testament and Today, ed. Johannes Panagopoulos. Leiden, 1977.

Puech, Henri-Charles. *Le Manichéisme: Son fondateur—sa doctrine.* Paris, 1949.

Quacquarelli, Antonio. *Reazione pagana e trasformazione della cultura (fine IV secolo d. C.).* Quaderni di "Vetera christianorum" 19. Bari, 1986.

Quasten, Johannes. *Musik und Gesang in den Kulten der heidnischen Antike und der christlichen Frühzeit.* Liturgiegeschichtliche Quellen und Forschungen 25. Münster, 1930.

Quispel, Gilles. *See* Fossum, Jarl.

Rader, Rosemary. *Breaking Boundaries: Male/Female Friendship in Early Christian Communities.* New York-Ramsay, N.J.-Toronto, 1983.

Raeder, Hans. "Kaiser Julian als Philosoph und religiöser Reformator" (first published 1944). In *Julian Apostata*, ed. Richard Klein, 206–21. WdF 509. Darmstadt, 1978.

Raming, Ida. *Der Ausschluss der Frau vom priesterlichen Amt: Gottgewollte Tradition oder Diskriminierung? Eine rechtshistorisch-dogmatische Untersuchung der Grundlagen von Kanon 968 § 1 des Codex Iuris Canonici.* Cologne-Vienna, 1973.

Ramsay, William M. *The Church in the Roman Empire before AD 170.* London, 1893.

Reiling, Jannes. *Hermas and the Christian Prophecy: A Study of the Eleventh Mandate.* Leiden, 1973.

Robeck, Cecil M. *The Role and Function of the Prophetic Gifts for the Church of Carthage, 202–258.* Ann Arbor, Mich., 1985. Microfiche.

Robert, Louis. "Une vision de Perpétue martyre à Carthage en 203." In *Comptes rendus de l'Académie des Inscriptions et Belles-Lettres 1982,* 228–76.

Rordorf, Willy. *Liturgie, Foi et Vie des Premiers Chrétiens: Etudes Patristiques.* Théologie Historique 75. Paris, 1986.

———. "Die neronische Christenverfolgung im Spiegel der apokryphen Paulusakten." *NTS* 28 (1982): 365–74.

Rossi, Mary Ann. "The Passion of Perpetua, Everywoman of Late Antiquity." In *Pagan and Christian Anxiety: A Response to E. R. Dodds,* ed. Robert C. Smith and John Lounibos, 53–86. Lanham, Md.-New York-London, 1984.

———. "Priesthood, Precedent, and Prejudice: On Recovering the Women Priests of Early Christianity" (containing a translation from the Italian of "Notes on the Female Priesthood in Antiquity," by Giorgio Otranto). *JFSR* 7 (1991): 73–93.

Rousselle, Aline. *Porneia: De la maîtrise du corps à la privation sexuelle, 2e-4e siècles de l'ère chrétienne.* Paris, 1983. Ger.: *Vom Ursprung der Keuschheit.* Stuttgart, 1983.

Rudolph, Kurt. *Die Gnosis: Wesen und Geschichte einer spätantiken Religion.* Leipzig, 1977.

Ruether, Rosemary (Radford). "Misogynism and Virginal Feminism in the Fathers of the Church." In *Religion and Sexism: Images of Women in the Jewish and Christian Traditions,* ed. idem, 150–83. New York, 1974.

———. "Mothers of the Church: Ascetic Women in the Late Patristic Age." In *Women of Spirit: Female Leadership in the Jewish and Christian Traditions,* ed. idem and Eleanor McLaughlin, 71–98. New York, 1979.

Saumagne, Charles, and Michel Meslin. "De la légalité du procès de Lyon de l'année 177." *ANRW* II.23.1.

Saxer, Victor. *Les rites de l'initiation chrétienne du IIᵉ au VIᵉ siècle: Esquisse historique et signification d'après leurs principaux témoins.* Spoleto, 1988.

Schepelern, Wilhelm. *Der Montanismus und die phrygischen Kulte: Eine religionsgeschichtliche Untersuchung.* Tübingen, 1929.

Schermann, Theodor. *Die allgemeine Kirchenordnung, frühchristliche Liturgien und kirchliche Überlieferung.* 3 vols. Studien zur Geschichte und Kultur des Altertums suppl. 3. Paderborn, 1914–1916.

Schillebeeckx, Edward. *Das kirchliche Amt.* Düsseldorf, 1981.

———. *Der Amtszölibat: Eine kritische Besinnung.* Düsseldorf, 1967.

Schmid, Renate. *Maria Magdalena in gnostischen Schriften.* Arbeitsgemeinschaft für Religions- und Weltanschauungsfragen, Material-Edition 29. Munich, 1990.

Schmithals, Walter. *Das kirchliche Apostelamt: Eine historische Untersuchung.* Göttingen, 1961.

Schoeps, Hans-Joachim. "Die jüdischen Prophetenmorde." Symbolae Biblicae Upsalienses 2 (1943).

Schöllgen, Georg. *Ecclesia Sordida? Zur Frage der sozialen Schichtung frühchristlicher Gemeinden am Beispiel Karthagos zur Zeit Tertullians.* JAC suppl. 12 (1984).

———. "Probleme der frühchristlichen Sozialgeschichte: Einwände gegen Peter Lampes Buch über 'Die stadtrömischen Christen in den ersten beiden Jahrhunderten.'" JAC 32 (1989): 23–40.

Scholten, Clemens. *Martyrium und Sophiamythos im Gnostizismus nach den Texten von Nag Hammadi.* JAC suppl. 14 (1987).

Schottroff, Luise. "Animae naturaliter salvandae, zum Problem der himmlischen Herkunft des Gnostikers." In *Christentum und Gnosis,* ed. Walter Eltester, 65–97. Berlin, 1969.

———. *Der Glaubende und die feindliche Welt: Beobachtungen zum gnostischen Dualismus und seiner Bedeutung für Paulus und das Johannesevangelium.* Neukirchen-Vluyn, 1970.

———. "Wie berechtigt ist die feministische Kritik an Paulus? Paulus und die Frauen in den ersten christlichen Gemeinden im Römischen Reich." *Einwürfe* 2 (1985): 94–111.

———. "'Anführerinnen der Gläubigkeit' oder 'einige andächtige Weiber': Frauengruppen als Trägerinnen jüdischer und christlicher Religion im ersten Jahrhundert n. Chr." In *Weil wir nicht vergessen wollen . . . : Zu einer Feministischen Theologie im deutschen Kontext,* ed. Christine Schaumberger, 73–88. An Fragen 1. Diskussionen Feministischer Theologie. 1987.

———. "Maria Magdalena und die Frauen am Grabe Jesu." *EvT* 42 (1982): 3–25.

———. "DienerInnen der Heiligen: Der Diakonat der Frauen im Neuen Testament." In *Diakonie—biblische Grundlagen und Orientierungen,* ed. Gerhard K. Schäfer and Theodor Strohm, 222–42. Heidelberg, 1990.

———. "Wanderprophetinnen: Eine feministische Analyse der Logienquelle." *EvT* 51 (1991): 332–44.

Schuller, Wolfgang. *Frauen in der griechischen Geschichte.* Konstanzer Bibliothek 3. Constance, 1985.

———. *Frauen in der römischen Geschichte.* Konstanzer Bibliothek 4. Constance, 1987.

Schulz, Siegfried. *Gott ist kein Sklavenhalter: Die Geschichte einer verspäteten Revolution.* Zurich-Flamberg-Hamburg, 1972.

Schüngel-Straumann, Helen. *Die Frau am Anfang: Eva und die Folgen.* Freiburg, 1989.

———. "Maria von Magdala—Apostolin und erste Verkündigerin der Osterbotschaft." In *Maria Magdalena—Zu einem Bild der Frau in der christlichen Verkündigung,* ed. Dietmar Bader, 8–32. Katholische Akademie Freiburg, 1990.

Seeliger, Hans Reinhard. "Fortgesetzte Offenbarung: Kirchengeschichtliche Beobachtungen." In *Offenbarungsanspruch und fundamentalistische Versuchung,* ed. Jürgen Werbick, 141–60. QD 129. Freiburg-Basel-Vienna, 1991.

Sexualität und Erotik in der Antike, ed. Andreas Karsten Siems. WdF 605. Darmstadt, 1988.

Shewring, Walter. "Prose Rhythm in the Passio S. Perpetuae." *JTS* 30 (1929): 56–57.

———. "En marge de la Passion des Saintes Perpétue et Félicité." *RBén* 43 (1931): 15–22.

Sly, Dorothy. *Philo's Perception of Women.* Brown Judaic Studies 209. Atlanta, 1990.

"Sogni, Visioni e Profezie nell' Antico Cristianesimo" (XVII incontro di studiosi dell'antichità cristiana, Rome, 5–7 May 1988). *Aug* 29/1–3 (1989).

Solowjew, Wladimir. "Vorlesungen über das Gottmenschentum (1877–81)." In *Werke* 1:537–750. Munich, 1978.

Specht, Edith. *Schön zu sein und gut zu sein: Mädchenbildung und Frauensozialisation im antiken Griechenland.* Reihe Frauenforschung 9. Vienna, 1989.

Speyer, Wolfgang. *Frühes Christentum im antiken Strahlungsfeld: Ausgewählte Aufsätze.* Tübingen, 1989.

Stagg, Evelyn, and Frank Stagg. *Woman in the World of Jesus.* Philadelphia, 1978.

Staniloae, Dumitru. *Orthodoxe Dogmatik*. Ökumenische Theologie 12 and 15. Zurich–Cologne–Gütersloh, 1985, 1990.

Stein, Dominique. "Lecture des textes de Paul concernant les femmes." In idem, *Lectures psychanalytiques de la Bible*, 89–113. Paris, 1985.

Stemberger, Günter. "Die Juden im Römischen Reich: Unterdrückung und Privilegierung einer Minderheit." In *Christlicher Antijudaismus und jüdischer Antipaganismus: Ihre Motive und Hintergründe in den ersten drei Jahrhunderten*, ed. Herbert Frohnhofen, 6–28. Hamburger theologische Studien. Hamburg, 1990.

Stenzel, Alois. *Die Taufe: Eine genetische Erklärung der Taufliturgie*. Innsbruck, 1958.

Stewart, Zeph. "Greek Crowns and Christian Martyrs." In *Antiquité Païenne et Chrétienne*, 119–24.

Stöcker, Lydia. *Die Frau in der alten Kirche*. Sammlungen gemeinverständlicher Vorträge und Schriften aus dem Gebiet der Theologie und der Religionsgeschichte 47. Tübingen, 1907.

Strobel, August. *Das heilige Land der Montanisten: Eine religionsgeographische Untersuchung*. Religionsgeschichtliche Versuche und Vorarbeiten 37. Berlin–New York, 1980.

Stücklin, Christoph. See Bibl. I: Tertullian, *On the Veiling*.

Sugano, Karin. "Marcella in Rom: Ein Lebensbild." In *Roma Renascens: Beiträge zur Spätantike und Rezeptionsgeschichte*, FS Ilona Opelt, ed. Michael Wissemann. Frankfurt, 1988.

Synek, Eva Maria. "Heilige Frauen der Frühen Kirche: Ein Beitrag über Frauenbilder hagiographischer Texte der Kirchen des Ostens." *US* 48 (1988): 289–98.

———. "Heilige Frauen der frühen Christenheit: Zu den Frauenbildern in hagiographischen Texten des christlichen Ostens." Diss., Vienna, 1990 (to be published in the series Das östliche Christentum).

Tabbernee, William. "Early Montanism and Voluntary Martyrdom." *Colloquium* 17/2 (1985): 33–44.

Tavard, George H. *Woman in Christian Tradition*. Notre Dame, Ind., 1973.

Theissen, Gerd. *Studien zur Soziologie des Urchristentums*. 3rd ed. Tübingen, 1989.

Thélamon, Françoise. *Païens et chrétiens au IVe siècle: L'apport de l' "Histoire ecclésiastique" de Rufin d'Aquilée*. Paris, 1981.

Theobald, Michael. "'Prophetenworte verachtet nicht!' (1 Thess 5,20): Paulinische Perspektiven gegen eine institutionelle Versuchung." *TQ* 171 (1991): 30–47.

Theodorou, Evangelos. "I 'cheirotonia', i 'cheirothesia' tōn diakonissōn" (The ordination, the blessing of deaconesses). (Diss., Athens, 1954.) *Theologia* 25 (1954): 430–69, 576–601; 26 (1955): 57–76. Repr. in *Istoria kai theoria tis ekklisiastikis koinōnikis diakonias* (History and theory of church social service), 61–164 (Athens, 1985), as part 4 with the title: "I taxis tōn diakonissōn en ti ekklissia ap' archis mechri tou id' aiōnos" (The position of deaconesses in the church from the beginning to the fourteenth century), expanded by chap. 1: "I Thesis kai drasis tōn gynaikōn en ti Ekklessia" (The position and the work of the woman in the church) and chap. 5: "Epiphaneis diakonissai tōn Byzantinōn chronōn" (Famous deaconesses of the Byzantine period). These are cited by English title.

———. "Die Tradition der orthodoxen Kirche in bezug auf die Frauenordination." In *Warum keine Ordination der Frau?* 26–49 (including a list of numerous articles by Theodorou on the diaconate of women and similar topics).

Theologie feministisch: Disziplinen, Schwerpunkte, Richtungen, ed. Marie-Theres Wacker. Düsseldorf, 1988.

Thierry, J. J. *Vrouwen in de vroegchristelijke kerk*. 'S Gravenhage, 1990 (male author).

Thoams, Garth. "La condition sociale de l'Eglise de Lyon en 177." In *Les Martyrs de Lyon*, 93–106.

Thraede, Klaus. S.v. "Frau." *RAC* 8:197–269.

———. "Ärger mit der Freiheit: Die Bedeutung von Frauen in Theorie und Praxis der alten Kirche." In *Freunde in Christus werden . . . ,*" ed. Gerda Scharfenorth and Klaus Thraede, 31–182. Kennzeichen 1. Gelnhausen-Berlin, 1977.

———. "Zum historischen Hintergrund der 'Haustafeln' des NT." In *Pietas,* 359–68.

———. "Zwischen Eva und Maria: das Bild der Frau bei Ambrosius und Augustin auf dem Hintergrund der Zeit." In *Frauen in Spätantike und Frühmittelalter,* 129–39.

Thürmer-Rohr, Christina. "Aus der Täuschung in die Ent-Täuschung: Zur Mittäterschaft von Frauen" (revised version). In idem, *Vagabundinnen: feministische Essays,* 38–56. Berlin, 1987.

Thurston, Bonnie Bowman. *The Widows: A Women's Ministry in the Early Church.* Minneapolis, 1989.

La Tradizione dell'Enkrateia: Motivazioni ontologiche e protologiche (Atti del Colloquio Internationale Milano, 20–23 April 1982), ed. Ugo Bianchi. Rome, 1985.

Trevett, Christine. "Apocalypse, Ignatius, Montanism: Seeking the Seeds." *Vigiliae Christianae* 43 (1989): 313–38.

Tunc, Suzanne. *Brève histoire des "femmes" chrétiennes.* Paris, 1989 ("femmes" only on the cover).

Vagaggini, Cipriano. "L'ordinazione delle diaconisse nella tradizione greca e bizantina." *OCP* 40 (1974): 145–89.

Valerio, Adriana. "Le figure femminile negli Atti dei martiri del II secolo." *Rassteol* (1981): 28–44.

———. *Cristianismo al femminile: Donne protagoniste nella storia delle chiese.* Naples, 1990 (announced).

Verdrängte Vergangenheit, die uns bedrängt: Feministische Theologie in der Verantwortung für die Geschichte, ed. Leonore Siefele-Wenschkewitz. Munich, 1988.

Vogt, Hermann Josef. *Coetus Sanctorum: Der Kirchenbegriff des Novatians und die Geschichte seiner Sonderkirche.* Theophaneia: Beiträge zur Religions- und Kirchengeschichte des Altertums 20. Bonn, 1967.

———. "Ignatius von Antiochien über den Bischof und seine Gemeinde." *TQ* 158 (1978): 15–27.

———. "Zum Bischofsamt in der frühen Kirche." *TQ* 162 (1982): 221–36.

———. "Cyprian—Hindernis für die Ökumene?" *TQ* 164 (1984): 1–15.

Vogt, Joseph. "Von der Gleichwertigkeit der Geschlechter in der bürgerlichen Gesellschaft der Griechen." In *Akademie der Wissenschaften und der Literatur, Abhandlungen der geistes- und sozialwissenschaftlichen Klasse* (1960): 213–55; also in *Sexualität und Erotik.*

Vogt, Joseph, and Hugh Last. S.v. "Christenverfolgung" (1. historisch, 2. juristisch). *RAC* 2:1159–1228.

Vogt, Kari. "'Devenir mâle': Aspect d'une anthropologie chrétienne primitive." *Conc* 202 (1985): 95–108. Ger.: "'Männlichwerden': Aspekte einer urchristlichen Anthropologie." *Conc* 21 (1985): 414–42.

Vööbus, Arthur. *Celibacy, a Requirement for Admission to Baptism in the Early Syrian Church.* Stockholm, 1951.

———. *History of Asceticism in the Syrian Orient: A Contribution to the History of Culture in the Near East.* Vols. 1–3. *CSCO* Subsidia 14, 17, 81. 1958–1988.

Walls, A. F. "The Montanist 'Catholic Epistle' and Its New Testament Prototype." TU 88 (1964): 437–46.

Ward, Benedicta. *Harlots of the Desert: A Study of Repentance in Early Monastic Sources.* London-Oxford, 1987.

———. "Apophthegmata Matrum." TU 129 (1985 [*Studia Patristica* 16, papers presented to the Seventh International Conference on Patristic Studies held in Oxford, 1975]: 63–66.

Warum keine Ordination der Frau? Unterschiedliche Einstellungen in den christlichen Kirchen, ed. Elisabeth Gössmann and Dietmar Bader. Schriftenreihe der Katholischen Akademie Freiburg. Munich-Zurich, 1987.

Waszink, Jan H. See Bibl. I: Tertullian, *On the Soul.*

Weiblichkeit in der Theologie: Verdrängung und Wiederkehr, ed. Elisabeth Moltmann-Wendel. Gütersloh, 1988.

Weinel, Heinrich. *Die Wirkungen des Geistes und der Geister im nachapostolischen Zeitalter bis Irenäus.* Freiburg-Leipzig-Tübingen, 1899.

Weinrich, William Carl. *Spirit and Martyrdom: A Study of the Work of the Holy Spirit in the Contexts of Persecution and Martyrdom in the New Testament and Early Christian Literature.* Washington, D.C., 1981.

Wendebourg, Dorothea. *Geist oder Energie: Zur Frage der innergöttlichen Verankerung des christlichen Lebens in der byzantinischen Theologie.* Munich, 1980.

————. "Die alttestamentlichen Reinheitsgesetze in der frühen Kirche." *ZKG* 95 (1984): 149–70.

————. "Das Martyrium in der Alten Kirche als ethisches Problem." *ZKG* 98 (1987): 295–320.

Widengren, Geo. *Mani und der Manichäismus.* Stuttgart, 1961.

Wilken, Robert L. *The Christians: As the Romans Saw Them.* New Haven, Conn.-London, 1984.

Woltmann, Jörg. "Der geschichtliche Hintergrund der Lehre Markions vom 'fremden Gott.'" In *Wegzeichen,* 15–42. Würzburg, 1971.

Womanspirit Rising: A Feminist Reader in Religion, ed. Carol P. Christ and Judith Plaskow. New York-London, 1979.

Women and the Priesthood, ed. Thomas Hopko. New York, 1983.

Women of Spirit: Female Leadership in the Jewish and Christian Traditions, ed. Rosemary Ruether and Eleanor McLaughlin. New York, 1979.

Yarbrough, Anne. "Christianization in the Fourth Century: The Example of Roman Women." *CH* 45 (1976): 149–65.

Zeisel. *See* Lightman.

Zimmermann, Alfred F. *Die urchristlichen Lehrer: Studien zum Tradentenkreis der didaskaloi im frühen Urchristentum.* Wissenschaftliche Untersuchungen zum Neuen Testament, 2nd series, 12. Tübingen, 1984.

Zitelmann, Arnulf. *Hypatia.* Weinheim-Basel, 1988 (book for youth).

Zscharnack, Leopold. *Der Dienst der Frau in den ersten Jahrhunderten der christlichen Kirche.* Göttingen, 1902.

INDEX

Men

(Since this study is devoted to women,
only the most important men are listed here.)